Lecture Notes in Computer Science 8209

Commenced Publication in 1973
Founding and Former Series Editors:
Gerhard Goos, Juris Hartmanis, and Jan van Leeuwen

Willy Susilo   Reza Reyhanitabar (Eds.)

Provable Security

7th International Conference, ProvSec 2013
Melaka, Malaysia, October 23-25, 2013
Proceedings

 Springer

Volume Editors

Willy Susilo
University of Wollongong
Centre for Computer and Information Security Research
School of Computer Science and Software Engineering
Northfields Ave
Wollongong, NSW 2522, Australia
E-mail: wsusilo@uow.edu.au

Reza Reyhanitabar
École Polytechnique Fédérale de Lausanne, IC LASEC
Bâtiment INF, Station 14
1015 Lausanne, Switzerland
E-mail: reza.reyhanitabar@epfl.ch

ISSN 0302-9743   e-ISSN 1611-3349
ISBN 978-3-642-41226-4   e-ISBN 978-3-642-41227-1
DOI 10.1007/978-3-642-41227-1
Springer Heidelberg New York Dordrecht London

Library of Congress Control Number: 2013948620

CR Subject Classification (1998): E.3, K.6.5, K.4.4, D.4.6, C.2.0, J.1

LNCS Sublibrary: SL 4 – Security and Cryptology

Typesetting: Camera-ready by author, data conversion by Scientific Publishing Services, Chennai, India

Printed on acid-free paper

Springer is part of Springer Science+Business Media (www.springer.com)

Preface

The 7th International Conference on Provable Security (ProvSec 2013) was held in Melaka, Malaysia, October 23–25, 2013. The conference was organized by Universiti Teknikal Malaysia Melaka.

ProvSec 2013 received 44 submissions from 15 different countries all over the world. The review process was a challenging task. Almost all submissions were carefully evaluated by three reviewers, and then discussed among the Program Committee. Moreover, 30 external subreviewers gave review comments on their area of expertise. The Program Committee selected 18 papers for the program out of 44 submissions. Further, the program featured an excellent invited talk given by Serge Vaudenay (EPFL, Lausanne, Switzerland) titled "On Modeling Terrorist Frauds".

Many people contributed to the success of ProvSec 2013. First, we would like to thank all of the authors for submitting their works to ProvSec 2013. We deeply thank the 25 Program Committee members as well as the external reviewers for their volunteer work of reading and discussing the submissions. Their names may be found overleaf. We thank the General Co-chairs, Shekh Faisal Abdul Latip and Jennifer Seberry, for their excellent management and dedication in organizing and running the conference. We would also like to thank the Steering Committee and Local Organizing Committee. We also want to express our gratitude to our generous sponsors: PRESTARIANG and SKMM/MCMC. Finally, we would like to express our thanks to Springer for continuing to support the ProvSec conference and for help in the conference proceedings production.

October 2013

Willy Susilo
Reza Reyhanitabar

Organization

General Co-chairs

Shekh Faisal Abdul Latip   Universiti Teknikal Malaysia Melaka, Malaysia
Jennifer Seberry   University of Wollongong, Australia

Program Co-chairs

Willy Susilo   University of Wollongong, Australia
Reza Reyhanitabar   EPFL, Switzerland

Program Committee

Elena Andreeva	KU Leuven, Belgium
Man Ho Au	University of Wollongong, Australia
Joonsang Baek	Khalifa University of Science, Technology and Research, UAE
Feng Bao	Huawei, China
Ioana Boureanu	EPFL, Switzerland
Xiaofeng Chen	Xidian University, China
Sherman S.M. Chow	Chinese University of Hong Kong, China
Shoichi Hirose	University of Fukui, Japan
Qiong Huang	South China Agricultural University, China
Kauro Kurosawa	Ibaraki University, Japan
Fabien Laguillaumie	UCBL, France
Dong Hoon Lee	Korea University, South Korea
Jin Li	Guangzhou University, China
Joseph K. Liu	Institute for Infocomm Research, Singapore
Masahiro Mambo	Kanazawa University, Japan
Kazuhiko Minematsu	NEC Corporation, Japan
Miyako Ohkubo	NICT, Japan
Tatsuaki Okamoto	NTT, Japan
Josef Pieprzyk	Macquarie University, Australia
Reihaneh Safavi-Naini	University of Calgary, Canada
Tsuyoshi Takagi	Kyushu University, Japan
Duncan S. Wong	City University of Hong Kong, China
Guomin Yang	University of Wollongong, Australia
Kan Yasuda	NTT, Japan
Tsz Hon Yuen	University of Hong Kong, China

Steering Committee

Feng Bao	Huawei, China
Xavier Boyen	Queensland University of Technology, Australia
Yi Mu	University of Wollongong, Australia
Josef Pieprzyk	Macquarie University, Australia
Willy Susilo	University of Wollongong, Australia

External Reviewers

Ji-Eun Eom	Bart Mennink
Minhye Seo	Lihua Wang
Sebastian Faust	Nele Mentens
Jun Shao	Yanjiang Yang
Hyoseung Kim	Kirill Morozov
Petr Susil	Kazuki Yoneyama
Kitak Kim	Mridul Nandi
Koutarou Suzuki	Bingsheng Zhang
Hidenori Kuwakado	Ryo Nojima
Haibo Tian	Cong Zhang
Liang Liu	Seunghwan Park
Kerem Varici	Yinghui Zhang
Jhawar Mahavir	Le Trieu Phong
Serge Vaudenay	Youwen Zhu
Takahiro Matsuda	
Cong Wang	

Local Organizing Committee (UTeM, Malaysia)

Mohd Faizal bin Abdollah	Zakiah bt. Ayop
Khuzaipah binti Khamis	Sharifah Intan binti Osman
Mohd Khanapi bin Abd. Ghani	Nur Ain Zakirah binti Bahari
Sharudin bin Majid	Mohd Kamal Tarmizi bin Razak
Ahmad F. Nizam bin Abdul Rahman	Muhamad Sopian bin Baharom
Zulisman Maksom	Mohd Fahrulrazi bin Saji
Shahrizan bin Abdullah	Norasiken binti Bakar
Mohd Zaki Masud	Muhamad Syahrul Azhar bin Sani
Nor Azman bin Abu	Nor Hafizah Hamyadi
Othman bin Mohd	Siti Rahayu binti Selamat
Affindi bin Abu Bakar	Burairah bin Hussin
Burhanuddin bin Mohd Aboobaider	Robiah binti Yusof
Rabiah binti Ahmad	Emaliana binti Kasmuri
Norhidayah binti Mohd Zainudin	Muhammad Shazuan bin Zainal
Syarulnaziah bt. Anawar	Abidin
Mohammad Radzi bin Motsidi	

Table of Contents

Authenticated Encryption

Theory

Public Key Encryption

On Modeling Terrorist Frauds
Addressing Collusion in Distance Bounding Protocols

Serge Vaudenay

EPFL, Lausanne, Switzerland
http://lasec.epfl.ch

Abstract. Quite recently, distance-bounding protocols received a lot of attention as they offer a good solution to thwart relay attacks. Their security models at still unstable, especially when considering terrorist fraud. This considers the case where a malicious prover would try to bypass the protocol by colluding with an adversary without leaking his credentials. Two formal models appeared recently: one due to Fischlin and Onete and another one by Boureanu, Mitrokotsa, and Vaudenay. Both were proposed with a provably secure distance-bounding protocols (FO and SKI, respectively) providing security against all state-of-the-art threat models. So far, these two protocols are the only such ones.

In this paper we compare both notions and protocols. We identify some errors in the Fischlin-Onete results. We also show that the design of the FO protocol lowers security against mafia frauds while the SKI protocol makes non-standard PRF assumptions and has lower security due to not using post-authentication. None of these protocols provide reasonable parameters to be used in practice with a good security. The next open challenge consists in providing a protocol combining both approaches and good practical parameters.

Finally, we provide a new security definition against terrorist frauds which naturally inspires from the soundness notion for proof-of-knowledge protocols.

1 Introduction

Relay attacks and distance-bounding. Many access control protocols are vulnerable to relay attacks. This is the case of most of RFID-based protocols. To defeat this, distance-bounding protocols offer a practical solution. These protocols, originally proposed by Brands and Chaum [6], consist of proving that a *prover* is within a close distance to a *verifier* by using an interactive protocol. The protocol is based on the physical limits of communication. Namely, transmission cannot go faster than the speed of light. So, these protocols use a rapid-bit exchange phase in which the prover must respond extremely fast and messages are very short (typically: single bits), in order to prove that he is close enough.

Threat models. Clearly, distance-bounding shall resist to *distance fraud*, where a malicious prover tries to defeat the protocol by passing even though he is far

W. Susilo and R. Reyhanitabar (Eds.): ProvSec 2013, LNCS 8209, pp. 1–20, 2013.

away. They shall also defeat relay attacks and more general notions of man-in-the-middle attacks where an adversary abuse of a far-away prover to pass the protocol. This is what makes practitioners like distance-bounding protocols. These types of attacks are often refer to as *mafia frauds*, following a (quite unfortunate) terminology due to Desmedt [9]. A more subtle notion from [9] consists of the *terrorist fraud*. There, the prover is also malicious, but still far away. He is colluding with an adversary (who can be close to the verifier) to pass the protocol, but without leaking his credentials to him. As discussed below, this type of attack is very tricky, not always considered, and quite often incorrectly addressed.

Many protocols and (informal) security notions have been proposed. Some protocols have been semi-formally proven secure but most of results were shown to be incorrect. For instance, some protocols based on a pseudorandom function (PRF) were incorrectly proven secure, as shown in [2]. Consequently, and as far as we know, none existing protocols (except the two which are discussed in this paper) are proven to provide security against all the above threat models. We refer the reader to [5] for a selective survey on the evolution of protocols which has led to the current models and schemes.

There also exist some "more exotic" threat models such as distance hijacking [8] where a far away malicious prover abuses other provers to pass the protocol with the verifier.

The Problem of Terrorist Fraud. Originally, "terrorist fraud" [9] consisted in having a malicious prover helping an adversary to impersonate him but without leaking his credentials. To safeguard against this type of attack means that a malicious prover cannot help an adversary to impersonate him without making this help reusable. Namely, there must be no other way than transferring the credentials to a close participant in order to make the protocol succeed.

The Hancke-Kuhn protocol: a Case Study. To illustrate this notion, we first give the example of a prominent distance-bounding protocol: the Hancke-Kuhn protocol [14]. The prover and the verifier share a long-term secret x. (See Fig. 1.) They first exchange some nonces. Then, a PRF f keyed with x is used to derive some one-time n-bit keys a_1 and a_2. Then, they go through n rounds of rapid bit-exchange: the verifier sends a random challenge $c_i \in \{1, 2\}$ and the prover responds by the ith bit of a_{c_i}. A terrorist fraud is easy: the malicious prover helps the adversary to exchange the nonces then computes a_1 and a_2 and gives them to the adversary. So, the adversary can successfully go through the rapid bit-exchanges. Additionally, disclosing a_1 and a_2 does not expose x since we use a secure PRF.

One difficulty with resistance to terrorist fraud is that it is non-falsifiable. Indeed, we cannot falsify security just by exhibiting an attack. The attack must be such that we could prove that the credentials do not leak, which is not always easy to prove. (In the above example, this is based on the PRF assumption.)

A common technique to strengthen the Hancke-Kuhn protocol consists of using $a_2 = a_1 \oplus x$. This way, the prover cannot disclose a_1 and a_2 without exposing

Verifier
secret: x

Prover
secret: x

initialization phase

pick N_V $\xrightarrow{\quad N_V \quad}$

$\xleftarrow{\quad N_P \quad}$ pick N_P

$a_1 \| a_2 = f_x(N_P, N_V)$ $\qquad\qquad\qquad$ $a_1 \| a_2 = f_x(N_P, N_V)$

distance bounding phase
for $i = 1$ to n

pick $c_i \in \{1, 2\}$

start timer$_i$ $\xrightarrow{\quad c_i \quad}$

stop timer$_i$ $\xleftarrow{\quad r_i \quad}$ $r_i = \begin{cases} a_{1,i} & \text{if } c_i = 1 \\ a_{2,i} & \text{if } c_i = 2 \end{cases}$

$\#\{i : r_i \text{ and timer}_i \text{ correct}\} \geq \tau$ $\xrightarrow{\quad \text{Out}_V \quad}$

Fig. 1. The Hancke-Kuhn Distance-Bounding protocol [14]

x. Unfortunately, it becomes vulnerable to a man-in-the-middle attack [15] in which the man-in-the-middle flips one challenge c_i and sends $\bar{c}_i$ to the prover. So, he can learn the ith bit from $a_{\bar{c}_i}$ from the prover and deduce from the protocol outcome the ith bit of a_{c_i}. To avoid this attack, Kim *et al.* [15] proposed the Swiss-Knife protocol, in which the protocol transcript is authenticated before the protocol outcome is revealed. (See Fig. 2.)

Terrorist Fraud using resilience to noise. Unfortunately, this does not protect against terrorist fraud as soon as noisy channels are considered. Indeed, the rapid bit-exchange must be done under heavy constraints and it is likely that noise will corrupt a few rounds in honest executions. So, protocols must tolerate a constant number of incorrect rounds. In the protocols, we assume that authentication succeeds when the number of successful rounds is at least τ out of n. In practice, $\frac{\tau}{n}$ must be a constant ratio depending on physical constraints.

It was observed by Hancke [13] that a malicious prover could still provide some noisy versions of a_1 and a_2 so that the number of succeeding rounds is likely to be at least τ (due to noise resilience) but $a_1 \oplus a_2$ would only leak a noisy version of x. Concretely, we can imagine a function g mapping x to a small (but constant-sized) set of indices $g(x)$ and that a_1 and a_2 would be random at all positions specified in $g(x)$. So, the number of possible x is exponential and x does not leak. Without the noiseless version of x, we cannot evaluate the PRF. So, the credential does not leak.

Related work. Avoine *et al.* [1] give a complete but very informal security model for distance-bounding. A more promising model is the one due to Dürholz *et al.* [10]. It separates the use of rapid-bit exchange and regular communication and is based on communication traces in the rapid exchange phase. They propose the

Verifier   **Prover**

secret: x secret: x

initialization phase

pick N_V $\xrightarrow{\quad N_V \quad}$

$\xleftarrow{\quad N_P \quad}$ pick N_P

$a_1 = f_x(N_P, N_V)$ $a_1 = f_x(N_P, N_V)$

$a_2 = a_1 \oplus x$ $a_2 = a_1 \oplus x$

distance bounding phase

for $i = 1$ to n

pick $c_i \in \{1, 2\}$

start timer$_i$ $\xrightarrow{\quad c_i \quad}$

stop timer$_i$ $\xleftarrow{\quad r_i \quad}$ $r_i = \begin{cases} a_{1,i} & \text{if } c_i = 1 \\ a_{2,i} & \text{if } c_i = 2 \end{cases}$

verification phase

$\#\{i : r_i \text{ and timer}_i \text{ correct}\} \geq \tau \xleftarrow{\quad t \quad} t = f_x(\text{transcript})$

check t $\xrightarrow{\quad \text{Out}_V \quad}$

Fig. 2. The Swiss-Knife Distance-Bounding protocol [15]

notion of SimTF security to model resistance to terrorist frauds. Unfortunately, they show that essentially no existing protocol satisfies this notion and suspect in [11] that this notion may be too demanding. In [12], they finally provide a protocol (called the FO protocol in this paper) providing this security notion and all the above ones. In parallel, Boureanu *et al.* [3,4,5] propose another model which introduces the notion of location and communication time. They also propose to model resistance to terrorist frauds, but with a notion called *collusion fraud*. Additionally, they construct a family of protocols (the SKI protocols) which offer provable security against all the above security notions.

Our results. In this paper, we identify some errors from [12]. Namely, the modified SwissKnife (MSK) protocol does not satisfy the security which is proven in [12] and some probability parameters in the FO protocol are too low.

Then, we compare the FO and SKI protocols. We show that FO has a non-uniform security against distance frauds. We show that the SimTF notion that the FO protocol must satisfy degrades resistance to mafia frauds. Consequently, the number of rounds must be very high to obtain a good security. E.g., 163 rounds are needed for a security level equivalent to a 20-bit symmetric key. With SKI, this is the same for distance fraud (but with a uniform security), this is worse for collusion fraud (with 531 rounds), but the security against man-in-the-middle (what we like distance-bounding for) only requires 76 rounds. All this holds for $\tau/n = 90\%$.

Finally, we compare the security notions to protect against terrorist frauds. We also propose a new one which is naturally inspired from the notion of soundness in proofs-of-knowledge: a distance-bounding protocol is sound if there is an extractor who can extract the secret from the view of close participants by having the protocol successfully executed. We prove that SKI satisfies this notion and prove again strSimTF security for the FO protocol with corrected parameters.

Notations. In what follows, we will use B defined by

$$B(n, \tau, q) = \sum_{i=\tau}^{n} \binom{n}{i} q^i (1-q)^{n-i} \tag{1}$$

It is known [7] that for $\tau = nt$, t and q constant such that $t > q$, and $n \to +\infty$, we have

$$B(n, \tau, q) \sim \frac{1}{\sqrt{2\pi}} \int_{(t-q)\sqrt{\frac{n}{q(1-q)}}}^{+\infty} e^{-\frac{x^2}{2}} \, dx \sim \frac{1}{\sqrt{2\pi}} \sqrt{\frac{q(1-q)}{n(t-q)^2}} e^{-\frac{n(t-q)^2}{2q(1-q)}}$$

So, we have the following result.

Lemma 1. *For t and q constant such that $t > q$, we have*

$$\lim_{n \to +\infty} -\frac{1}{n} \ln B(n, nt, q) = \frac{(t-q)^2}{2q(1-q)}$$

2 The Fischlin-Onete Approach

2.1 SimTF Security

In [10], Dürholz *et al.* propose a way to formalize the security against terrorist fraud. It is referred to as the SimTF security in [12]. This model tells apart communications through a *lazy* (regular) channel from the ones through a time-critical channel. There is a special notion of *tainted* session which depends on the security notion.

Definition 2 (SimTF security). *We consider two experiments. In the first one, the malicious prover P^* and the adversary A interact with the verifier V. A rapid exchange between V and A is tainted if we can make a sequence of messages $m_{VA}, m_{AP^*}, m_{P^*A}, m_{AV}$ in chronological order such that m_{UV} is sent from U then received by V. We denote by p_A the probability that the verifier accepts in this first experiment. In the second experiment, we first run the previous experiment, then provide a simulator S with the final view of A. S then interacts alone with V in a new session. We denote by p_S the probability that the verifier accepts in this last session.*

We say that a terrorist fraud (A, P^*) is successful if for all S we have $p_S \leq p_A$.

So, P^* and A are not allowed to interact during the rapid exchange between V and A. In [11], it was shown that essentially none of the existing protocols offers SimTF security, but it was suggested that this could be due to the notion being too strong.

This notion was strengthened even more in [12] by changing the notion of tainted session. In this strengthened notion, P^* and A can interact during the distance bounding phase, but they are not allowed to have any single round (instead of the session) of rapid bit-exchange which goes through the V-A-P^*-A-V loop. This is the strSimTF notion.

2.2 GameTF Security

In [12], Fischlin and Onete proposed a weaker notion.

Definition 3 (GameTF security). *Let* $\mathsf{Adv}^{\mathsf{MF}}$ *be the best probability that a verifier accepts in a mafia-fraud attack. (The maximum is taken over all adversaries with limited complexity and number of queries to P and V.)*

A terrorist fraud (P^*, A) *is* helpful *to an adversary* A' *if running an experiment with* V, A, *and* P^* *and no tainted session, then running a second experiment with* V, A', *and* P, *with* A' *initialized with the final view of* A *and no tainted session, makes* V *accept with a probability* $P_{A'}$ *which is larger than* $\mathsf{Adv}^{\mathsf{MF}}$. *(The complexity bounds of* $\mathsf{Adv}^{\mathsf{MF}}$ *must be satisfied by* A'.) *We use the notion of tainted session from* strSimTF.

We have ε-GameTF *security if all terrorist fraud* (P^*, A) *succeeding with* $p_A \geq \varepsilon$ *are helpful for at least one adversary* A'.

Remark 4. The probability $\mathsf{Adv}^{\mathsf{MF}}$ of the best mafia-fraud attack is not a well-defined quantity if we do not impose an *exact* limitation on the adversary (e.g. in terms of complexity and number of queries). Indeed, if we consider all polynomially bounded adversaries, for each value of the security parameter, there is always a polynomially bounded attack (namely, the one making an exhaustive search up to this value of the security parameter and doing nothing beyond) succeeding with probability close to 1.

Remark 5. For every mafia-fraud adversary A, it is always possible to design another adversary A' with a small complexity overhead and doing a bit better: we assume that A makes enough observations. We define A' by first making a guess for the secret. Then, A' simulates A. If, during the observations, A' realizes that the guess for the secret is consistent with the information collected by A, then it stops simulating A and uses the guess to impersonate the prover. Otherwise, the simulation continues normally. By tuning the number of observations so that the probability that an incorrect guess is consistent is negligible against the probability to guess the secret correctly, this new adversary A' performs better and A.

In [12], Fischlin and Onete modify the Swiss-Knife protocol to make it GameTF-secure. The protocol is on Fig. 3.[1] We call it the MSK protocol (as for *Modified Swiss-Knife*). Essentially, they introduce a new shared secret y: x is only used for the PRF computation while y is used in $a_2 = a_1 \oplus y$. This protocol is GameTF-secure for $\varepsilon = \mathsf{Adv}^{\mathsf{MF}}$ [12, Prop.1]. It is further claimed that $\mathsf{Adv}^{\mathsf{MF}} = B(n, \tau, \frac{1}{2}) + \mathsf{negl}$ for a targeted reader session[2] where B is defined by Eq.(1).

Verifier
secret: x, y

Prover
secret: x, y

initialization phase

pick $N_V \xrightarrow{\quad N_V \quad}$

$\xleftarrow{\quad N_P \quad}$ pick N_P

$a_1 = f_x(N_P, N_V)$ $a_1 = f_x(N_P, N_V)$
$a_2 = a_1 \oplus y$ $a_2 = a_1 \oplus y$

distance bounding phase
for $i = 1$ to n

pick $c_i \in \{1, 2\}$
start timer$_i$ $\xrightarrow{\quad c_i \quad}$

stop timer$_i$ $\xleftarrow{\quad r_i \quad}$ $r_i = \begin{cases} a_{1,i} \text{ if } c_i = 1 \\ a_{2,i} \text{ if } c_i = 2 \end{cases}$

verification phase
$\#\{i : r_i \text{ and timer}_i \text{ correct}\} \geq \tau \xleftarrow{\quad t \quad} t = f_x(\text{transcript})$
check $t \xrightarrow{\quad \mathsf{Out}_V \quad}$

Fig. 3. The Modified Swiss-Knife (MSK) Distance-Bounding protocol [11]

Introducing a new secret y besides the one x used in PRF is a clever choice to avoid the problems based on PRF programming [2] making security results incorrect. We still need to have y honestly selected (as specified in [12]) for distance fraud. Otherwise, registering $y = 0$ leads to a trivial distance fraud.

---

[1] For the sake of clarity in this paper, our description slightly differs from the one in [12]. The main difference resides in that [12] uses two separate counters to count the number of rounds for which the timer expires, and for which the timer is acceptable but the response is incorrect. Our analysis remains valid for the original version in [12].

[2] We can infer this bound from [12, Prop.3] which applies to the original protocol. In this result, the first term of $\mathsf{Adv}^{\mathsf{MF}}$ is $q_R 2^{-\tau}$ where q_R is the number of (untargeted) adversary-reader sessions, other terms being negligible as they express that nonces may repeat or that the PRF property may be defeated.

Terrorist fraud against the MSK protocol. We now show a *practical* terrorist fraud contradicting the security proof for GameTF-security from [12]. We consider a malicious prover helping the adversary in the nonce exchange and the final transcript authentication, and just disclosing a_1 and y to the adversary. Clearly, the adversary using a_1 and $a_2 = a_1 \oplus y$ succeeds with probability 1. We have now to show that this adversary is not helpful *in practice*. He only discloses y. The (a_1, a_2) pairs can be learnt by running the protocol with the honest prover. So, we just have to consider a mafia fraud adversary getting y as an auxiliary input. We can show (see the Lemma below) that such an adversary is incapable of succeeding, except with negligible probability. So, it is clear that we do have a terrorist fraud succeeding with probability 1 and leaking no useful information to mount a mafia fraud attack.

Lemma 6. *In the MSK protocol, we consider an experiment with a far-away prover P, an adversary A receiving y as an auxiliary input, and a verifier V. The probability that a target session of V accepts is limited by $B(n, \tau, \frac{1}{2}) + \mathsf{negl}$.*

Proof. We first reduce to cases where nonces do not repeat and the PRF is replaced by a random function. Then, using hybrids, we reduce to a single session on P and V using the same nonces. Finally, we assume that if P and V see different transcripts, the protocol fails due to an incorrect t. All this induces a negligible term in the probability of success.

Due to the large distance between P and V, A can either send a random c_i' to P before he receives c_i from V (the Go-Early strategy), or answers to c_i without any clue and ask for some c_i' to P later (the Go-Late strategy).

Since A knows y, in the Go-Early strategy, A deduces the answer to all possible challenge c_i at round i. However, the correct tag t can only be obtained from P if $c_i = c_i'$, which happens with probability $\frac{1}{2}$.

In the Go-Late strategy, A has no clue about the response, so the probability to be correct is $\frac{1}{2}$.

Hence, in any case, the probability that one round is correct is $\frac{1}{2}$. Since we need τ correct rounds, the probability to win is $B(n, \tau, \frac{1}{2})$. □

It was proven in [12, Prop.1] that the MSK protocol is GameTF-secure. However, the proof makes no reference to the authenticating t in the protocol, which makes us believe that the result is incorrect. The above attack shows that either this is the case, or the GameTF security does not capture well the resistance to terrorist fraud. Indeed, it could be the case that a helpful attack is still relevant in practice, although ruled out by this notion, because the help provided is negligible.

2.3   FO: A SimTF-Secure Protocol

In [12], Fischlin and Onete propose another protocol which is SimTF and str-SimTF-secure. The protocol is on Fig. 4.[3] We call it the *FO protocol*. In a normal

---

[3] Like for the MSK protocol, the original FO protocol uses two separate counters. Our analysis for the original protocol will be discussed in Remark 7.

execution, we always have $b = 0$ and the protocol works like the one on Fig. 3. For $b = 1$, a special procedure is run: the accepted response r_i is different, and the verification for I is a bit special. Namely, the verifier now accepts $r_i = c_i$ as the correct answer.[4] For $b = 0$, the verifier checks that $I' = I$. Additionally, for $b = 1$, I is accepted with a probability $p_{d_H(I,y)}$ which depends on the Hamming distance between I and y. The value of p_d is adjusted to have SimTF security. So, the mafia fraud resistance corresponds to the terrorist fraud resistance. The idea is that the $b = 0$ case protects against distance frauds and mafia frauds, and that terrorist frauds leak some information y' close to y, and the $b = 1$ case protects against distance frauds only but requires such information y'.

Verifier
secret: x, y

Prover
secret: x, y

initialization phase

pick N_V $\xrightarrow{\quad N_V \quad}$ set $b = 0$

$\xleftarrow{\quad b, I, N_P \quad}$ pick N_P

$I'\|a_1 = f_x(N_P, N_V)$ $I\|a_1 = f_x(N_P, N_V)$
$a_2 = a_1 \oplus y$ $a_2 = a_1 \oplus y$

distance bounding phase
for $i = 1$ to n

pick $c_i \in \{1, 2\}$
start timer$_i$ $\xrightarrow{\quad c_i \quad}$
stop timer$_i$ $\xleftarrow{\quad r_i \quad}$ $r_i = \begin{cases} a_{1,i} & \text{if } c_i = 1 \\ a_{2,i} & \text{if } c_i = 2 \end{cases}$

verification phase

check $b, I, t,$ $\xleftarrow{\quad t \quad}$ $t = f_x(\text{transcript})$
$\#\{i : r_i \text{ and timer}_i \text{ correct}\} \geq \tau$ $\xrightarrow{\quad \text{Out}_V \quad}$

correctness conditions for $b = 0$	correctness conditions for $b = 1$
$I' = I$	correct with probability $p_{d_H(I,y)}$
$t = f_x(\text{transcript})$	
$r_i = a_{c_i,i}$	$r_i = c_i$
timer$_i \leq \mathbf{B}$	timer$_i \leq \mathbf{B}$

Fig. 4. The Fischlin-Onete Distance-Bounding protocol [12]

---

[4] In [12], it is written that the verifier *also* accepts $r_i = c_i$ which seems to mean that both $r_i = (a_{c_i})_i$ and $r_i = c_i$ are accepted. However, having two different possible responses could lead to an easy distance fraud: if for some value of c_i both answers are correct, we just prepare the answer for the other value $\bar{c}_i$. So, *only* the $r_i = c_i$ answer should be accepted.

We first note that it is pretty weird to have a piece of code (namely, the $b = 1$ case) which shall never be used for $b = 1$, and which provides an escape way to pass the protocol without knowing x. It may also introduce some strange attack models similar to distance hijacking [8], where far-away malicious provers take advantage of the proximity of honest participants to feed responses for them. Here, a far-away prover only needs someone to echo the challenges. We could also have a malicious participant $P_1^*(x)$ carrying the initialization and verification phases himself, and hijacking some $(P_2^*(x), A(x))$ pair running a terrorist fraud with $b = 1$. So, this protocol modification may induce some new "exotic" kinds of frauds in the family of distance fraud and distance hijacking.

Distance fraud. A malicious far-away prover could anticipate responses corresponding to $y_i = 0$ since they are independent of the challenge. Others are correct with probability $\frac{1}{2}$. *On average* over the distribution of y, one round succeeds with probability $\frac{3}{4}$. With y fixed, the probability of success of the distance fraud is $B(w, \tau - n + w, \frac{1}{2})$ with B defined by Eq.(1), where $w = d_H(0, y)$ is the Hamming weight of y. So, user receiving a key y with a low weight have a better incentive to cheat in a distance fraud! It could also induce some weird behaviors of malicious users asking for new credentials until they have a better Hamming weight. Another bad property is that the probability of $B(w, \tau - n + w, \frac{1}{2})$ is fixed once for all: a user succeeding to get a low w offline has always better chances to defeat distance fraud online. Clearly the security is non-uniform about the selection of y. On average, it is of $B(n, \tau, \frac{3}{4})$.

Mafia fraud. Due to the design of the FO protocol, terrorist frauds induce mafia frauds. Let us consider the following terrorist fraud (A, P^*) depending on a parameter e: let $g(x)$ be a set of indices of cardinality e. Then, we consider a malicious prover P^* disclosing y' such that $g(x) = \{i; y_i \neq y_i'\}$ and $\#g(x) = e$. Additionally, he helps the adversary A in the nonce exchange and provides a_1' matching a_1 on each position which is not in $g(x)$ and set to random bits in positions in $g(x)$. The adversary using a_1' and $a_2' = a_1' \oplus y'$ instead of a_1 and a_2 wins if the number of errors is below $n - \tau$. We know that errors happen randomly in a set of e. So, the probability to pass is $\rho_e = B(e, e - n + \tau, \frac{1}{2})$. Now, for an adversary S trying to pass the protocol by only knowing y', since he cannot forge t in the verification phase, the best strategy is to use the escape strategy with $b = 1$. Since he has no information about $g(x)$, y' remains the best approximation of y to him. By using $I = y'$, he passes with probability p_e. For instance, for $e = 2(n - \tau)$, we have $\rho_e = \frac{1}{2}$: it shall be enough to provide a y with twice more errors than allowed. Due to the SimTF definition, this attacks requires that we have $p_e \geq \rho_e$ for all e. In Th. 8, we will show that this condition is also sufficient.

However, the $p_e \geq \rho_e$ bounds creates a new mafia fraud attack: Now, we consider a mafia-fraud adversary who just tries to guess y' within a small distance to y and who uses the escape $b = 1$ in the protocol with this guess. Trying to guess vector at a distance e works with probability of success $\binom{n}{e} 2^{-n}$. Finally, the attack using $b = 1$ and a random I works with probability

$$p = \sum_{e=0}^{n} \binom{n}{e} 2^{-n} p_e$$

$$\geq \sum_{e=0}^{n} \binom{n}{e} 2^{-n} \rho_e$$

$$= \sum_{e=0}^{n} \binom{n}{e} 2^{-n} B\left(e, e-n+\tau, \frac{1}{2}\right)$$

$$= \sum_{e=0}^{n} \sum_{i=e-n+\tau}^{e} \binom{n}{e} \binom{e}{i} 2^{-n-e}$$

$$= \sum_{e=0}^{n} \sum_{i=0}^{n-\tau} \binom{n}{e} \binom{e}{i} 2^{-n-e}$$

$$= \sum_{i=0}^{n-\tau} \sum_{e=0}^{n} \binom{n}{e} \binom{e}{i} 2^{-n-e}$$

$$= \sum_{i=0}^{n-\tau} \sum_{e=0}^{n} \binom{n}{i} \binom{n-i}{n-e} 2^{-n-e}$$

$$= \sum_{i=0}^{n-\tau} \sum_{e=i}^{n} \binom{n}{i} \binom{n-i}{n-e} 2^{-n-e}$$

$$= \sum_{i=0}^{n-\tau} \binom{n}{i} 2^{-2n} 3^{n-i}$$

$$= \sum_{j=\tau}^{n} \binom{n}{j} \left(\frac{3}{4}\right)^{j} \left(\frac{1}{4}\right)^{n-j}$$

$$= B\left(n, \tau, \frac{3}{4}\right)$$

with B defined by Eq.(1). In contrast, the probability of success of the regular (i.e. with $b = 0$) mafia fraud is $B(n, \tau, \frac{1}{2})$ which is much lower. So, this modification of the Swiss-Knife protocol induces a significant security loss for mafia-fraud resistance.

As an application, we take $n - \tau = \frac{n}{10}$ (that is, we want 90% of the rounds to be correct to tolerate a noise level below 10%). For $n = 144$ rounds, we obtain $B(n, \tau, \frac{1}{2}) \approx 2^{-80}$, but $B\left(n, \tau, \frac{3}{4}\right) \approx 2^{-18}$. To reach $B\left(n, \tau, \frac{3}{4}\right) \approx 2^{-80}$, we need $n \geq 724$ to secure the FO protocol against the mafia fraud. On Fig. 5, we plot $-\log_2 B(n, \tau, p)$ for $\tau = \lceil n * 0.9 \rceil$ and $p \in \{\frac{1}{2}, \frac{3}{4}\}$. (Note that discontinuities are due to rounding τ.) Due to Lem. 1, it is clear that these curves are close to a line with slope $\frac{(\frac{\tau}{n}-p)^2}{2p(1-p)\ln 2}$. So, for the number of rounds n, we are loosing a factor $\frac{3}{4}\left(\frac{\frac{\tau}{n}-\frac{1}{2}}{\frac{\tau}{n}-\frac{3}{4}}\right)^2$ which is $\frac{16}{3}$ in this case.

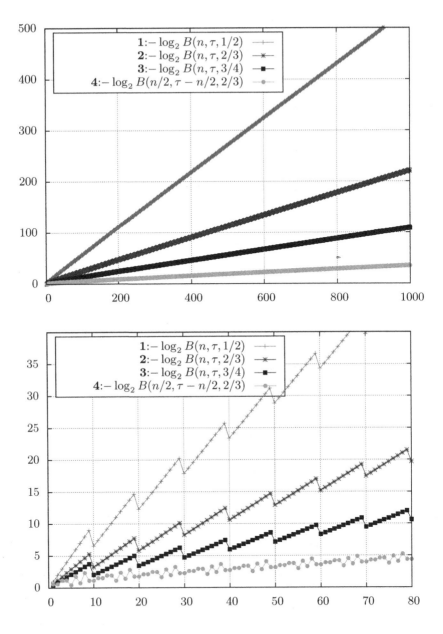

The security of FO follows the curve **3** for distance fraud, mafia fraud, and terrorist fraud while the security of MSK follows the curve **1** for mafia fraud. The security of SKI follows the curves **3**, **2**, and **4** for distance fraud, man-in-the-middle, and collusion fraud, respectively.

Fig. 5. Security (Equivalent Bitlength) in Terms of the Number of Rounds n for $\tau = \lceil n * 0.9 \rceil$

Note that this attack can self-improve: assuming that an adversary has got a good y', his probability of success in a mafia fraud will always be at least ρ_e. Furthermore, if this probability is low enough, by doing some statistics and using a hill climbing approach, the adversary can find a better y' and eventually obtain one within a distance $n-\tau$, which makes the attack work with probability 1. Fortunately, except in a terrorist fraud case, there is no better way to find a good y' than a random guess.

Another interesting observation is that we need $n-\tau \ll \frac{n}{4}$ for security. Indeed, for $n-\tau \approx \frac{n}{4}$, we have $p \approx \frac{1}{2}$ which makes the protocol insecure.

Remark 7. In [12], there are specific counters for the response errors and the timer errors. Namely, there should be no more than $E_{\max}$ errors and no more than $T_{\max}$ timeouts. Furthermore, it is specified that $p_d = \min(1, 2^{-d+T_{\max}+E_{\max}})$. We can adapt our strategy above by having the malicious prover to use two disjoin sets $g(x)$ and $g'(x)$ and disclosing y' with errors in $g(x)$ and holes in $g'(x)$. The adversary would run for a time out for every hole and work as above otherwise. For $e = 2E_{\max}$, the probability of success is $\frac{1}{2}$. Now, to approximate y, we have to fill the holes with random bits. So, we have a probability of success

$$\sum_{i=0}^{T_{\max}} \binom{T_{\max}}{i} 2^{-T_{\max}} p_{e+i} = \sum_{i=0}^{T_{\max}} \binom{T_{\max}}{i} 2^{-T_{\max}} \min(1, 2^{-e-i+T_{\max}+E_{\max}})$$

$$= \sum_{i=0}^{T_{\max}} \binom{T_{\max}}{i} 2^{-T_{\max}} \min(1, 2^{-E_{\max}-i+T_{\max}})$$

$$= \sum_{i=0}^{T_{\max}} \binom{T_{\max}}{i} 2^{-E_{\max}-i}$$

$$= \left(\frac{1}{2}\right)^{E_{\max}} \left(\frac{3}{2}\right)^{T_{\max}}$$

when $E_{\max} \geq T_{\max}$. This is smaller than $\left(\frac{3}{4}\right)^{T_{\max}}$. Clearly, this is not larger than $\frac{1}{2}$, when $E_{\max} \geq T_{\max} \geq 2$. So, the probabilities p_d provided in [12] are incorrect in this case.

Security proof for the FO protocol. With similar techniques as in [4], we can prove the strSimTF security with a p_e value matching the necessary condition which was identified above.

Theorem 8 (TF-Resistance of the FO protocol). *For $p_e = B(e, e-n+\tau, \frac{1}{2})$ for every e, the FO scheme is strSimTF-secure.*

Proof. In the experiment, we let A denote all participants close to V (by definition, they are all malicious) and P^* denote all far-away participants. We let View_i be the view of A just before receiving the challenge c_i and View be the final view. If View includes $b = 1$, it is clear that it leaks some I which is enough for a simulator S to pass the protocol with *exactly* the same probability. So, we only have to focus on the $b = 0$ case in the terrorist fraud.

We let w_i be the extra information (obtained from P^*), not contained in View_i, which is received by A before it is critical to answer r_i, and we denote $r_i = A(\text{View}_i, c_i, w_i)$. If A takes too long time, the answer r_i is unimportant and we denote $r_i = \perp$. Note that w_i is still defined as the information before it is critical to answer in this case. I.e., there is no time to have a round trip between A and P^* from the time A receives c_i to the time we set w_i. Due to the assumptions on tainted sessions and that c_i is randomly selected by V, we note that (View_i, w_i) is independent from c_i. We define a vector y' by

$$y'_i = A(\text{View}_i, 1, w_i^*) \oplus A(\text{View}_i, 2, w_i)$$

We consider a simulator S computing y' and using it with $b = 1$ to pass the protocol. We want to show that $p_S \geq p_A$. Let $e = d_H(y, y')$. Clearly, what we have to prove is that $E(p_e) \geq p_A$.

We let C_i be the set of all c's such that $A(\text{View}_i, c, w_i) = a_{c,i}$ with a computed from V. I.e., C_i is the set of challenges to which A answers correctly in round i. We let S be the set of all i such that $c_i \in C_i$. I.e., A answers correctly in round i. Clearly, $p_A = \Pr[\#S \geq \tau]$.

We let R be the set of all i's such that C_i has cardinality 2, i.e., A always answers correctly. Clearly, for $i \in R$, we have

$$y'_i = A(\text{View}_i, 1, w_i) \oplus A(\text{View}_i, 2, w_i) = a_{1,i} \oplus a_{2,i} = y_i$$

Since p_e is decreasing, we have $p_e \geq p_{n-\#R}$. Now, we want to prove that $E(p_{n-\#R}) \geq p_A$.

For every possible set R, we have $\Pr[\#S \geq \tau | R] \leq B(n - \#R, \tau - \#R, \frac{1}{2}) = p_{n-\#R}$. By averaging over R, we obtain $E(p_{n-\#R}) \geq p_A$.   □

3   The Boureanu-Mitrokotsa-Vaudenay Approach

3.1   A Two-Dimensional Notion

In [3], Boureanu *et al.* proposed another definition of terrorist fraud security which is sketched as follows:

Definition 9 ((γ, γ')-resistance to TF [3]). *We say that a DB protocol is (γ, γ')-resistant to terrorist-fraud if for any far-away, coerced prover P^*, it is the case that, below, (1) implies (2)*
— (1). an adversary A interfering up to his powers with an interaction between P^* and verifier V on their shared secret, where this interaction is successful with probability at least γ (over the random choices of V and A),
— (2). A can later succeed on his own to make the verifier accept in a new protocol run with a probability greater than γ' (taken over the new random choices made by V and A).

It is further said that this easily extends in a multiparty setting.

Interestingly, this definition separates the probability of success γ of the terrorist fraud and the one γ' of the further impersonation. This avoids having to consider a hard-to-define notion of optimal probability of success of an attack which cannot be asymptotic (see remark 4) but makes security be based on two dimensions (γ and γ') instead of one.

3.2   Collusion Fraud

In [5], Boureanu *et al.* proposed to replace this definition by the notion of *collusion fraud*:

> "A far-away prover holding x helps an adversary to make the verifier accept the proof. This might be in the presence of many other honest participants. However, there should be no man-in-the-middle attack constructed based on this malicious prover. I.e., the adversary should not extract from him any advantage to run (later) a man-in-the-middle attack."

which is further formulated in Vaudenay's FSE 2013 invited talk[5] as

> "$P(x)$ far from all $V(x)$'s interacts with $\mathcal{A}$ and makes one $V(x)$ accept, but View($\mathcal{A}$) does not give any advantage to mount a man-in-the-middle attack"

This resembles the GameTF notion where the final view of the adversary is provided in a further mafia fraud adversary. This notion is further made more precise in [4]:

Definition 10 ((γ, γ')-resistance to collusion-fraud [4]).
$(\forall s)(\forall P^*)$ $(\forall \mathsf{loc}_{V_0}$ *such that* $d(\mathsf{loc}_{V_0}, \mathsf{loc}_{P^*}) > \mathbf{B})$ $(\forall \mathcal{A}^{\mathsf{CF}}$ *ppt.) such that*

$$\Pr\left[\mathsf{Out}_{V_0} = 1 : \begin{array}{l} (x,y) \leftarrow Gen(1^s) \\ P^*(x) \longleftrightarrow \mathcal{A}^{\mathsf{CF}} \longleftrightarrow V_0(y) \end{array}\right] \geq \gamma$$

over all random coins, there exists a (kind of) MiM attack $m, \ell, z, \mathcal{A}_1, \mathcal{A}_2, P_i, P_j, V_{i'}$ *using P and P^* in the learning phase, such that*

$$\Pr\left[\mathsf{Out}_V = 1 : \begin{array}{l} (x,y) \leftarrow Gen(1^s) \\ P_1^{(*)}(x), \ldots, P_m^{(*)}(x) \longleftrightarrow \mathcal{A}_1 \longleftrightarrow V_1(y), \ldots, V_z(y) \\ P_{m+1}(x), \ldots, P_\ell(x) \longleftrightarrow \mathcal{A}_2(View_{\mathcal{A}_1}) \longleftrightarrow V(y) \end{array}\right] \geq \gamma'$$

where P^* is any (unbounded) dishonest prover and $P^{(*)}$ runs either P or P^*. Following the MiM requirements, $d(\mathsf{loc}_{P_j}, \mathsf{loc}_V) > \mathbf{B}$, for all $j \in \{m+1, \ell\}$. In a concurrent setting, we implicitly allow a polynomially bounded number of $P(x')$, $P^*(x')$, and $V(y')$ with independent (x', y'), but no honest participant close to V_0.[6]

---

[5] http://fse2013.spms.ntu.edu.sg/slides/Slides02.pdf
[6] "ppt." means "probabilistic polynomial-time algorithm".

Essentially, it allows the collusion fraud to be run several times until the adversary can extract enough information to mount an attack. In the definition, we assume that every running algorithms M are given a location which is denoted by loc_M. The value $\mathbf{B}$ is the maximal distance until which the prover is considered too far from the verifier. The man-in-the-middle (MiM) attack separates a *learning phase* with m provers and z verifiers, from an *attack phase* with $\ell - m$ far-away provers and one verifier. The learning phase can run with either the honest prover or the malicious one P^* which is being considered in the collusion fraud. The above theorem refers to a *kind of* MiM since it is assumed that the man-in-the-middle plays also with P^*, which is not the case in regular MiM attacks.

Clearly, this captures the scenario used in GameTF security.

3.3 SKI: A Collusion-Fraud Resistant Protocol

Boureanu *et al.* [3,4,5] further proposed the SKI distance-bounding protocols which provide security against collusion fraud. Compared to the protocols in the Swiss-Knife family, these protocols do not have a post-authentication phase, but require a larger set of challenges (namely, 3 instead of 2). (See Fig. 6.) The second secret y is further derived from the first one x by using a *leakage scheme* L_μ. Essentially, running a collusion fraud is bound to leak y which, based being run several times, allows to fully reconstruct x.

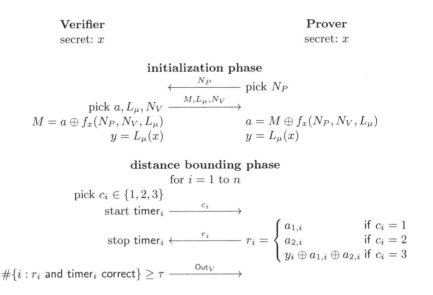

Fig. 6. The SKI Distance-Bounding Protocol [3,4]

The SKI security requires $n - \tau \ll \frac{n}{6}$, which imposes some restriction on the noise probability. Another disadvantage is that we need a stronger notion of PRF: a *circular-keying secure PRF*. The security of SKI is stated as follows.

Theorem 11 (Boureanu-Mitrokotsa-Vaudenay [4]). *If f is a (ε, T)-circular-keying secure PRF and the verifier requires at least τ correct rounds,*

- *all distance frauds (with complexity bounded by T) have a success probability bounded by* $\Pr[\mathsf{success}] \geq B(n, \tau, \frac{3}{4}) + \varepsilon$;
- *all man-in-the-middle attacks (with complexity bounded by T) have a success probability bounded by* $\Pr[\mathsf{success}] \geq B(n, \tau, \frac{2}{3}) + \frac{r^2}{2}2^{-k} + \varepsilon$, *where k is the nonce length and r is the number of participants in the experiment;*
- *for all collusion frauds such that $p = \Pr[\mathsf{CF\ succeeds}] \geq B(\frac{n}{2}, \tau - \frac{n}{2}, \frac{2}{3})^{1-c}$ and p^{-1} polynomially bounded, there is an associated man-in-the-middle attack with P^* such that* $\Pr[\mathsf{MiM\ succeeds}] \geq \left(1 - B(\frac{n}{2}, \tau - \frac{n}{2}, \frac{2}{3})^c\right)^s$, *for any c.*

B is defined by Eq.(1). On Fig. 5 we plot $-\log_2 B(n, \tau, p)$ for $p \in \{\frac{2}{3}, \frac{3}{4}\}$ and $-\log_2 B(\frac{n}{2}, \tau - \frac{n}{2}, \frac{2}{3})$ for $\tau = \lceil n * 0.9 \rceil$. Due to Lem. 1, it is clear that the first two curves are close to a line with slope $\frac{(\frac{\tau}{n}-p)^2}{2p(1-p)}$. By applying Lem. 1 with n and t replaced by $\frac{n}{2}$ and $2t - 1$, we obtain that the slope of the third one is $\frac{(2\frac{\tau}{n}-1-p)^2}{2p(1-p)}$ with $p = \frac{2}{3}$. To reach a security of 2^{-80} for distance fraud, we need a pretty high $n = 724$. For man-in-the-middle, $n = 353$ is enough. For collusion fraud, we still need a very high $n = 2\,388$, but this has no influence on the security against man-in-the-middle. If a security of 2^{-20} is considered as enough, we need $n = 76$ for man-in-the-middle, $n = 163$ for distance fraud, or $n = 531$ for collusion fraud. (Of course, figures become better with a larger τ/n ratio.)

Compared to the FO protocol, every distance fraud attacks is limited to a success probability of $B(n, \tau, \frac{3}{4})$. Furthermore, there is no auxiliary input such as some y' vector to ease a mafia fraud. All man-in-the-middle attacks are limited to a success probability of $B(n, \tau, \frac{2}{3})$.

3.4   Soundness

The idea behind SKI is that the secret is extractable from the collusion. Extractability may not always be necessary to protect against terrorist fraud but it looks like a convenient and easy-to-deal-with notion. As a matter of fact, Boureanu *et al.* [5] mentions that collusion resistance looks like some notion of *soundness* in interactive proofs.

Indeed, a distance-bounding protocol is an interactive proof for holding a secret (this is the authentication part) and of close distance. An associated notion of soundness for this proof could be formalized by means of an extractor. We propose the following definition:

Definition 12 (γ-m-soundness). *We say that a distance-bounding protocol is γ-sound if for all experiment* $\exp(\mathcal{V}, \mathsf{ID})$ *such that*

- *all provers and verifiers work for the same identity* ID,
- *there is no close prover,*
- *there is no close verifier,*
- $\mathcal{V}$ *accepts with probability at least* γ,

there exists a ppt algorithm $\mathcal{E}$ *called* extractor, *such that by running m times* $\exp(\mathcal{V}, \text{ID})$ *in some executions* $\exp_i(\mathcal{V}, \text{ID})$, $i = 1, \ldots, m$, *if* View_i *denotes the view of all close participants in* $\exp_i(\mathcal{V}, \text{ID})$ *and* Succ_i *is the event that* $\mathcal{V}$ *accepts in this experiment, we have*

$$\Pr\left[\mathcal{E}(\text{View}_1, \ldots, \text{View}_m) = x_{\text{ID}} \,\middle|\, \text{Succ}_1, \ldots, \text{Succ}_m\right] = 1 - \text{negl}(n)$$

Lemma 13 (Link between soundness and collusion frauds). *For any* $p \geq \gamma$ *such that* p^{-1} *is polynomially bounded, if the protocol is* γ-m-*sound, then it* $(p, 1 - \text{negl}(n))$-*resists to collusion fraud (in the sense of Def.10).*

Proof. Given a collusion fraud with a malicious prover $P^*(x_{\text{ID}})$ succeeding with probability $p \geq \gamma$, we have an experiment Exp satisfying the properties of the definition of γ-m-soundness. Thus, there must exist some extractor $\mathcal{E}$. This defines a learning phase of a man-in-the-middle attack involving $P^*(x_{\text{ID}})$, which just simulates, for $\Omega(mp^{-1})$ times the experiment so that at least m simulations succeed with probability $1 - \text{negl}(n)$. At the end of this learning phase, $\mathcal{A}$ computes x_{ID} by using $\mathcal{E}$. Then, we define an attack phase with an adversary alone with $V(y_{\text{ID}})$, receiving the x computed by $\mathcal{A}$. This attack succeeds with probability $1 - \text{negl}(n)$. So, the protocol $(p, 1 - \text{negl}(n))$-resists to collusion fraud. $\square$

With the new soundness definition, we can prove the following result.

Theorem 14 (Soundness of the SKI protocol). *For any* $\frac{\tau}{n} > \frac{5}{6}$ *and* γ *such that* $\gamma^{-1}B(\frac{n}{2}, \tau - \frac{n}{2}, \frac{2}{3}) = \text{negl}(n)$, *the SKI scheme is* γ-s-*sound.*

We cannot prove the soundness of the FO protocol (since the x part of the secret never leaks).

Proof. Again, we use techniques from [5]. The proof is similar to the one of Th. 8. With the same notations, R now denotes the set of i's such that the cardinality of C_i is 3, and we define

$$y_i' = A(\text{View}_i, 1, w_i) \oplus A(\text{View}_i, 2, w_i) \oplus A(\text{View}_i, 3, w_i)$$

For $i \in R$, we have $y_i' = \mu \cdot x$. So, we are interested in the majority of the y_i''s. Again, we have $\Pr[\#S \geq \tau | R] \leq B(n - \#R, \tau - \#R, \frac{2}{3})$. For $\#R \leq \frac{n}{2}$, we have $\Pr[\#S \geq \tau | R] \leq B(\frac{n}{2}, \tau - \frac{n}{2}, \frac{2}{3}) \leq B(\frac{n}{2}, \tau - \frac{n}{2}, \frac{2}{3})$. By averaging over all R's such that $\#R \leq \frac{n}{2}$, we obtain $\Pr[\#S \geq \tau, \#R \leq \frac{n}{2}] \leq B(\frac{n}{2}, \tau - \frac{n}{2}, \frac{2}{3})$ from which we deduce $\Pr[\#R \leq \frac{n}{2} | \#S \geq \tau] \leq \gamma^{-1}B(\frac{n}{2}, \tau - \frac{n}{2}, \frac{2}{3})$. So, with probability larger than $1 - \gamma^{-1}B(\frac{n}{2}, \tau - \frac{n}{2}, \frac{2}{3})$, the majority of the y_i''s equals $\mu \cdot x$. After s such attempts, we recover s linear bits of x, so we extract x. $\square$

4   Conclusion

We have identified some mistakes in [12]: The security result about the MSK protocol is incorrect, as well as the original probabilities specified in the FO protocol.

We have compared two notions of terrorist fraud resistance: SimTF and collusion fraud resistance. We have also compared the two protocols offering these resistance: FO and SKI, respectively. The advantages of FO are that

- it uses binary challenges;
- it is resilient to noise at a higher level $\frac{1}{4}$;
- it relies on standard PRF security.

The drawbacks are that

- it includes a weird code, not supposed to be used;
- its resistance to mafia fraud is lowered to $B(n, \tau, \frac{3}{4})$ due to the (too) strong requirements of SimTF security;
- it has a non uniform security $B(w, \tau - n + w, \frac{1}{2})$ for distance fraud.

About the prominent proposal for the SKI protocol, the advantages are that

- it has a uniform security of $B(n, \tau, \frac{3}{4})$ for distance fraud;
- it has a better security $B(n, \tau, \frac{2}{3})$ against man-in-the-middle;
- all elements of the protocol are used.

The drawbacks are that

- it uses non-binary challenges;
- it is only resilient to noise at a level of $\frac{1}{6}$;
- it relies on non-standard PRF security.

Clearly, designing a protocol offering all these types of resistance, still with reasonable parameters in practice, remains an important challenge.

Finally, we extended the collusion fraud resistance by the notion of soundness. This notion justifies itself by comparison to interactive proofs of knowledge based on an extractor.

We believe that an ideal protocol could combine both approaches of the FO and SKI protocols: to provide better security parameters, we should adopt the leakage scheme approach of SKI (at the cost of a non-standard PRF assumption) instead of the escape protocol with $b = 1$ (which lowers security) and adopt, like FO, the Swiss-Knife frame with only two possible challenges instead of three. It would provide uniform security for distance fraud and be resilient to noise up to a $\frac{1}{4}$ ratio. The only remaining drawback would be the non-standard PRF assumption. Designing such a provably secure protocol remains an open problem.

Acknowledgements. The author thanks Marc Fischlin and Cristina Onete for their feedbacks. Also: many thanks to Ioana Boureanu for some memorable discussions about terrorism in distance bounding.

References

1. Avoine, G., Bingöl, M., Kardas, S., Lauradoux, C., Martin, B.: A Framework for Analyzing RFID Distance Bounding Protocols. Journal of Computer Security 19(2), 289–317 (2011)
2. Boureanu, I., Mitrokotsa, A., Vaudenay, S.: On the Pseudorandom Function Assumption in (Secure) Distance-Bounding Protocols - PRF-ness alone Does Not Stop the Frauds! In: Hevia, A., Neven, G. (eds.) LatinCrypt 2012. LNCS, vol. 7533, pp. 100–120. Springer, Heidelberg (2012)
3. Boureanu, I., Mitrokotsa, A., Vaudenay, S.: Secure & Lightweight Distance-Bounding. In: Avoine, G., Kara, O. (eds.) LightSec 2013. LNCS, vol. 8162, pp. 97–113. Springer, Heidelberg (2013)
4. Boureanu, I., Mitrokotsa, A., Vaudenay, S.: Practical & Provably Secure Distance-Bounding. IACR Cryptology ePrint Archive 2013/465. IACR (2013), http://eprint.iacr.org/2013/465.pdf
5. Boureanu, I., Mitrokotsa, A., Vaudenay, S.: Towards Secure Distance Bounding. In: The Proceedings of FSE 2013 (to appear, 2013)
6. Brands, S., Chaum, D.: Distance-Bounding Protocols (Extended Abstract). In: Helleseth, T. (ed.) EUROCRYPT 1993. LNCS, vol. 765, pp. 344–359. Springer, Heidelberg (1994)
7. Bryc, W.: A Uniform Approximation to the Right Normal Tail Integral. Applied Mathematics and Computation 127, 365–374 (2002)
8. Cremers, C.J.F., Rasmussen, K.B., Schmidt, B., Čapkun, S.: Distance Hijacking Attacks on Distance Bounding Protocols. In: IEEE Symposium on Security and Privacy S&P 2012, San Francisco CA, USA, pp. 113–127. IEEE Computer Society (2012)
9. Desmedt, Y.: Major Security Problems with the "Unforgeable" (Feige-)Fiat-Shamir Proofs of Identity and How to Overcome Them. In: Congress on Computer and Communication Security and Protection Securicom 1988, pp. 147–159. SEDEP, Paris (1988)
10. Dürholz, U., Fischlin, M., Kasper, M., Onete, C.: A Formal Approach to Distance-Bounding RFID Protocols. In: Lai, X., Zhou, J., Li, H. (eds.) ISC 2011. LNCS, vol. 7001, pp. 47–62. Springer, Heidelberg (2011)
11. Fischlin, M., Onete, C.: Subtle Kinks in Distance-Bounding: an Analysis of Prominent Protocols. In: ACM Conference on Security and Privacy in Wireless and Mobile Networks WISEC 2013, Budapest, Hungary, pp. 195–206. ACM (2013)
12. Fischlin, M., Onete, C.: Terrorism in Distance Bounding: Modelling Terrorist-Fraud Resistance. In: Jacobson, M., Locasto, M., Mohassel, P., Safavi-Naini, R. (eds.) ACNS 2013. LNCS, vol. 7954, pp. 414–431. Springer, Heidelberg (2013)
13. Hancke, G.P.: Distance Bounding for RFID: Effectiveness of Terrorist Fraud. In: Conference on RFID-Technologies and Applications RFID-TA 2012, Nice, France, pp. 91–96. IEEE (2012)
14. Hancke, G.P., Kuhn, M.G.: An RFID Distance Bounding Protocol. In: Conference on Security and Privacy for Emerging Areas in Communications Networks SecureComm 2005, Athens, Greece, pp. 67–73. IEEE (2005)
15. Kim, C.H., Avoine, G., Koeune, F., Standaert, F.-X., Pereira, O.: The Swiss-Knife RFID Distance Bounding Protocol. In: Lee, P.J., Cheon, J.H. (eds.) ICISC 2008. LNCS, vol. 5461, pp. 98–115. Springer, Heidelberg (2009)

Authenticated Key Exchange Protocols Based on Factoring Assumption

Hai Huang

Department of Computer Science and Engineering,
Zhejiang Sci-Tech University, Hangzhou, 310018, China
haihuang1005@gmail.com

Abstract. This paper investigates authenticated key exchange protocols over signed quadratic residues group $\mathbb{QR}_N^+$, which is originally used for encryption schemes. The key technical tool developed by Hofheinz et al. is that in group $\mathbb{QR}_N^+$ the strong Diffie-Hellman (SDH) problem is implied by the factoring assumption.

To apply group $\mathbb{QR}_N^+$ to authenticated key exchange protocols in the enhanced Canetti-Krawczyk (eCK) model, we extend Hofheinz et al.'s technique and introduce a new proof approach called k-th power.

The k-th power proof approach is almost generic, i.e., applying it to many, if not all, existing authenticated Diffie-Hellman key exchange protocols in eCK model under gap assumption immediately produces protocols in eCK model under factoring assumption if they work over $\mathbb{QR}_N^+$.

As one application of k-th power approach, we show that FS protocol, in which k is a constant, is provably secure in eCK model under factoring assumption if it works over $\mathbb{QR}_N^+$.

Our technique also applies to other protocols, e.g., UP,HMQV and its variants, in which k is a non-constant, but at the cost of degrading a factor in the reduction.

Keywords: Authenticated key exchange, Factoring assumption, $\mathbb{QR}_N^+$, eCK model.

1 Introduction

Key exchange protocols enable two parties, Alice (A) and Bob (B), to establish a shared session key via an unsecured channel. The classic Diffie-Hellman (DH) key exchange protocol is as follows: Let $\mathbb{G} = \langle g \rangle$ be a cyclic group of prime order q. The exchange messages are $X = g^x, Y = g^y$ and the final session key is usually of the form $H(g^{xy})$. It is well known that DH protocol is only secure against a passive attacker and vulnerable to the active man-in-the-middle attacker. Subsequently, a lot of work has been dedicated to the design of *authenticated* key exchange protocols which are secure against the active attacker.

1.1 Signed Quadratic Residues

Hofheinz et al. introduced a group called signed quadratic residues ($\mathbb{QR}_N^+$). The group is useful for cryptography because it is a "gap group", in which the

W. Susilo and R. Reyhanitabar (Eds.): ProvSec 2013, LNCS 8209, pp. 21–37, 2013.

membership in the group can be publicly verified while the computational problem, i.e., computing square roots, is equivalent to factoring N. Then, they showed that in the $\mathbb{QR}_N^+$ group, the strong Diffie-Hellman (SDH) problem [1] is implied by the factoring assumption.

As one application of $\mathbb{QR}_N^+$ group, Hofheinz et al. re-analyzed the Hybrid ElGamal encryption scheme which was originally over prime order subgroups of $\mathbb{Z}_p^*$, and showed that the Hybrid ElGamal over $\mathbb{QR}_N^+$ is CCA secure in random oracle model under factoring assumption. Since the security proof of Hybrid ElGamal does not use knowledge about the order of underlying group, the scheme itself remains unchanged.

1.2   Problems with Authenticated Key Exchange Protocols over $\mathbb{QR}_N^+$ Group

It is natural to ask whether $\mathbb{QR}_N^+$ group can be used to design authenticated key exchange protocols under factoring assumption, espécially in a strong security model, e.g., eCK model. A natural example is as follows. The key derivation function is

$$k = H(Z_1, Z_2, Z_3, Z_4, X, Y, \hat{A}, \hat{B}), \quad \text{where } Z_1 = B^a, Z_2 = Y^a, Z_3 = B^x, Z_4 = Y^x \tag{1}$$

The protocol is clearly provably secure in eCK model under SDH assumption if the underlying group is a cyclic group of prime order q. On the other hand, the scheme is secure under factoring assumption if it works over $\mathbb{QR}_N^+$ group as the security proof does not use knowledge about the order of underlying group. However, the protocol requires 5 exponentiations which is unsatisfactory.

In the following, we provide some more efficient examples and their proof strategies in eCK model, and discuss the possibility of basing them on $\mathbb{QR}_N^+$ group. Assume that the owner of Test session is $\hat{A}$ and its peer is $\hat{B}$. Assume that the adversary can reveal the static private key of party $\hat{A}$ and no reveal query against the ephemeral private key of Test session is allowed, i.e, in the proofs the simulator sets the outgoing message of Test session to be $X = U$ and the static private key of the peer $B = V$, where (U, V) is a computational Diffie-Hellman (CDH) problem instance.

Example 1: HMQV protocol. The first example is HMQV protocol [10]. The key derivation function is

$$k = H(Z, X, Y, \hat{A}, \hat{B}), \quad \text{where } Z = (YB^e)^{x+ad}, e = h(Y, \hat{A}), d = h(X, \hat{B}) \tag{2}$$

In the security proof, with value Z, which is provided by the adversary, the simulator runs the adversary once again (forking lemma) and gets another Z'. Then, SIM computes

$$\left(\bar{Z} = \frac{Z/(YB^e)^{ad}}{Z'/(YB^{e'})^{ad}} \right)^{\frac{1}{(e-e')}} = \left(\frac{(YB^e)^x}{(YB^{e'})^x} \right)^{\frac{1}{(e-e')}} = \left(B^{x(e-e')} \right)^{\frac{1}{(e-e')}} = B^x = V^u \tag{3}$$

Example 2: FS protocol. The second example is FS protocol [4], which is most efficient one among FS protocol family (example 2, [4]). The key derivation function is

$$k = H(Z_1, Z_2, X, Y, \hat{A}, \hat{B}), \quad \text{where} \quad Z_1 = (YB)^{x+a}, Z_2 = (YB^c)^{x+ac} \quad (4)$$

where c is a constant, e.g., $c = 2$. In the security proof, with Z_1, Z_2, which is provided by the adversary, SIM computes

$$\left(\bar{Z} = \frac{Z_2/(YB^c)^{ac}}{Z_1/(YB)^a} \right)^{\frac{1}{(c-1)}} = \left(\frac{(YB^c)^x}{(YB)^x} \right)^{\frac{1}{(c-1)}} = \left(B^{x(c-1)} \right)^{\frac{1}{(c-1)}} = B^x = V^u$$

$$(5)$$

Example 3: UP protocol. The third example is UP protocol [15]. The key derivation function is

$$k = H(Z_1, Z_2, X, Y, \hat{A}, \hat{B}),$$
$$\text{where} \quad Z_1 = (YB^e)^{x+a}, Z_2 = (YB)^{x+ad}, e = h(Y), d = h(X) \quad (6)$$

In the security proof, with Z_1, Z_2, which is provided by the adversary, SIM computes

$$\left(\bar{Z} = \frac{Z_1/(YB^e)^a}{Z_2/(YB)^{ad}} \right)^{\frac{1}{(e-1)}} = \left(\frac{(YB^e)^x}{(YB)^x} \right)^{\frac{1}{(e-1)}} = \left(B^{x(e-1)} \right)^{\frac{1}{(e-1)}} = B^x = V^u \quad (7)$$

Note that the proofs of all the examples above are involved in the computation of the inverses of the exponents $\frac{1}{(e'-e)}, \frac{1}{(c-1)}$ and $\frac{1}{(e-1)}$ respectively, which requires the knowledge about the order of the group. However, since the order of $\mathbb{QR}_N^+$ group is unknown these protocols can not be trivially moved to $\mathbb{QR}_N^+$ group.

1.3   Our Contributions

The crux of the problem is that the inversion computation in the exponent is difficult in $\mathbb{QR}_N^+$ group with unknown order. To tackle this problem, we introduce a new proof approach called k-th power, which does not require the inversion computations in exponents. The k-th power approach extends the key technical tool developed by Hofheinz et al. which reduces the factoring problem to SDH problem in $\mathbb{QR}_N^+$ (Theorem 2,[6]).

The k-th power proof approach is almost generic, i.e., applying k-th power technique to many, if not all, existing authenticated Diffie-Hellman key exchange protocols under gap assumption immediately produces protocols under factoring assumption if they work over $\mathbb{QR}_N^+$.

As one application of k-th power approach, we show that FS protocol [4], in which k is a constant, is provably secure in eCK model under factoring assumption if it works over $\mathbb{QR}_N^+$.

Our technique also applies to other protocols, e.g., UP[15],KFU$_1$[9],HMQV[10] and its variants FHMQV,SMQV [13, 14], in which k is a non-constant, but at the cost of degrading a factor in the reduction.

1.4 Related Work

Cash et al. [3] introduced the "Twin Diffie-Hellman (TDH)" technique and showed that SDH assumption is implied by the standard CDH assumption. However, to apply TDH technique [12, 7–9], they have to modify the protocol at a cost of doubling computational overhead. In comparison, our technique directly yield a security proof under factoring assumption without modifying the protocol.

Boyd et al. [2] and Fujioka et al. [5] proposed authenticated key exchange protocols which can be instantiated under factoring assumption. However, their protocols are based on the generic CCA encryption scheme and thus clearly less efficient.

2 Preliminaries

Let the value κ be the security parameter. We write $[N] = \{1, ..., N\}$. For group elements g, X, we denote by $\log_g X$ the discrete logarithm of X to the base g.

2.1 Factoring Assumption

A prime number P is called safe prime, if $P = 2p + 1$ for some prime number p. We assume that $N = PQ$ where P, Q are safe prime numbers, and thus N is a blum integer number. Let $\text{RSAgen}(1^\kappa)$ be an algorithm that generates such elements (N, P, Q). For any probabilistic polynomial time (PPT) algorithm $\mathcal{A}$,

$$Pr[\mathcal{A}(N) = \{P, Q\}] \leq \epsilon(\kappa)$$

where $(N, P, Q) \leftarrow_R \text{RSAgen}(1^\kappa)$, and $\epsilon(\kappa)$ is negligible.

2.2 Signed Quadratic Residues

The set $\mathbb{QR}_N$ of quadratic residues modulo N is defined as $\mathbb{QR}_N := \{x \in \mathbb{Z}_N^* : \exists y \text{ and } x = y^2\}$. Since $\mathbb{Z}_N^* \cong \mathbb{Z}_2 \times \mathbb{Z}_2 \times \mathbb{Z}_{pq}$, $\mathbb{QR}_N \in \mathbb{Z}_N^*$ is cyclic group of order pq. By $\mathbb{J}_N$, we denote the subgroup of $\mathbb{Z}_N^*$ with Jacobi symbol 1.

For $x \in \mathbb{Z}_N$ we define $|x|$ as the absolute of x, where x is represented as a signed integer in the set $\{-(N-1)/2, ..., (N-1)/2\}$. We define the group of signed quadratic residues as $\mathbb{QR}_N^+ = \{|x| : x \in \mathbb{QR}_N\}$, where the group operation is defined by $g \circ h = |gh \bmod N|$. As all the computations will take place in $\mathbb{QR}_N^+$, we will omit the absolute values and simply write xy or $x \cdot y$ for $x \circ y$. The following facts have been noted in [6].

1. $(\mathbb{QR}_N^+, \circ)$ is a group of order $\phi(n)/4$, where $\phi(n)$ is Euler's totient function.
2. $\mathbb{QR}_N^+ = \mathbb{J}_N^+$ where $\mathbb{J}_N^+ = \mathbb{J}_N \bigcap [(N-1)/2]$. Thus, given only N the membership in $\mathbb{QR}_N^+$ is efficiently recognizable.
3. If $\mathbb{QR}_N$ is cyclic, so is $\mathbb{QR}_N^+$.

2.3   Strong Diffie-Hellman (SDH) Assumption

Let $\mathbb{G} = \langle g \rangle$ be the cyclic group whose order is not necessarily known. Define $\mathrm{CDH}(X,Y) := g^{(\log_g X)(\log_g Y)}$ where $X, Y \in \mathbb{G}$. For our purpose, we consider group $\mathbb{QR}_N^+$. For any probabilistic polynomial time algorithm $\mathcal{A}$,

$$Pr[\mathcal{A}^{\mathrm{DDH}_{g,X}(\cdot,\cdot)}(N,g,X,Y) = \mathrm{CDH}(X,Y)] \leq \epsilon(\kappa)$$

where $X, Y \leftarrow \mathbb{QR}_N^+$, and $\epsilon(\kappa)$ is negligible. $\mathrm{DDH}_{g,X}(\cdot,\cdot)$ denotes that $\mathcal{A}$ has oracle access to DDH, which given a two-tuples $(\hat{Y}, \hat{Z})$ in $\mathbb{QR}_N^+$, outputs 1 if $\hat{Y}^{\log_g X} = \hat{Z}$ and 0 otherwise.

The following theorem (Theorem 2,[6]) shows that in the $\mathbb{QR}_N^+$ group, the SDH problem is implied by the factoring assumption.

Theorem 1 ([6]). *If the factoring assumption holds then the strong DH assumption holds. In particular, for every SDH problem adversary $\mathcal{A}$, there exists a factoring adversary $\mathcal{B}$ with roughly the same complexity as $\mathcal{A}$.*

3   Our New Techniques and Applications

Before introducing our new idea, we recall the key technical tool developed by Hofheinz et al., which proved that in $\mathbb{QR}_N^+$ group SDH problem is implied by the factoring assumption (Theorem 2,[6]). We sketch the main idea as follows. For our convenience, the notations are slightly changed.

Factoring$\longrightarrow$SDH. A factoring algorithm $\mathcal{B}$, which uses a SDH adversary $\mathcal{A}$, is constructed as follows. $\mathcal{B}$ chooses uniformly $u \leftarrow_R (\mathbb{Z}_N^*)^+ \backslash \mathbb{QR}_N^+$ and sets $h = u^2$. Then, $\mathcal{B}$ chooses $x, b \in [N/4]$ and sets

$$g = h^2 \qquad X = hg^x \qquad B = hg^b$$

This implicitly defines $\log_g X = x + \frac{1}{2} \bmod \mathrm{ord}(\mathbb{QR}_N^+)$, and $\log_g B = b + \frac{1}{2} \bmod \mathrm{ord}(\mathbb{QR}_N^+)$.

$\mathcal{B}$ can implement the SDH oracle, i.e., answers $\mathcal{A}$'s oracle queries $\hat{X}, \hat{Z} \in \mathbb{QR}_N^+$ (the membership is efficiently recognizable) by checking $\hat{X}^{2b+1} \overset{?}{=} \hat{Z}^2$, which is equivalent to $\hat{X}^{\log_g B} \overset{?}{=} \hat{Z}$.

Finally, $\mathcal{A}$ output $Z = g^{(\log_g X)(\log_g B)} = g^{(x+1/2)(b+1/2)} = h^{2xb+x+b+1/2}$, from which $\mathcal{B}$ can extract $v = h^{1/2}$ with the knowledge about x, b. Now, with two non-trivial different square roots u, v of h, $\mathcal{B}$ can factor N by $\gcd(u - v, N)$ (or $\gcd(u + v, N)$).

Our New Technique. However, the situation for authenticated key exchange protocols is different. Since the secret values $Z_i (i = 1, 2, ..m)$ of key derivation function $\mathrm{H}(\cdot)$, where m is the number of the secret values, are usually a combination of the static/ephemeral public keys of two parties, and thus are not usually of the form $CDH(X, B)$ from which $v = h^{1/2}$ is extracted. In particular, it is hard to compute $CDH(X, B)$ from $Z_i(i = 1, 2, ..m)$ if the inversion computations in exponent are required because the order of $\mathbb{QR}_N^+$ group is unknown. For example, in order to compute $CDH(X, B)$ from Z_1, Z_2 the simulator of FS protocol requires the computation of the inverses $\frac{1}{(c-1)}$ in the exponent.

To tackle this problem, we extend Hofheinz et al.'s technique and introduce a new proof approach called k-th power. We sketch the main idea in the terminology of authenticated key exchange protocol. Assume that the Test session is $\Pi_{\hat{A},\hat{B}}^{s^*}$. Assume that the adversary queries the static private key of $\hat{A}$ and does not query the ephemeral private key of Test session.

$\mathcal{B}$ chooses uniformly $u \leftarrow_R (\mathbb{Z}_N^*)^+ \backslash \mathbb{QR}_N^+$ and sets $h = u^2$. Then, $\mathcal{B}$ chooses $x, b \in [N/4]$, and an additional value $\boxed{k}$, which is related to the protocol (e.g. $k = c - 1$ for FS protocol), and sets

$$g = h^{2k} \qquad X = hg^x \qquad B = hg^b$$

This implicitly defines $\log_g X = x + \frac{1}{2k} \bmod \text{ord}(\mathbb{QR}_N^+)$, and $\log_g B = b + \frac{1}{2k} \bmod \text{ord}(\mathbb{QR}_N^+)$. $\mathcal{B}$ sets the outgoing message of Test session and the static public key of $\hat{B}$ to be X, B respectively.

Now, $\mathcal{B}$ can keep the consistency of the oracle queries against session $\Pi_{\hat{B},\hat{D}}^s$. Take FS protocol as an example: upon receipt of queries $(\hat{X}, \hat{Z}_i(i = 1, 2))$, $\mathcal{B}$ computes $\bar{Z}_1 = \hat{Z}_1/(\hat{X}D)^Y$, $\bar{Z}_2 = \hat{Z}_2/(\hat{X}D^c)^Y$ where $Y = g^y$ is maintained by $\mathcal{B}$, and hence

$$(\hat{X}D)^{\log_g B} = \bar{Z}_1 \iff (\hat{X}D)^{2k \cdot \log_g B} = \bar{Z}_1^{2k} \iff (\hat{X}D)^{(2kb+1)} = \bar{Z}_1^{2k}$$

$$(\hat{X}D^c)^{c \cdot \log_g B} = \bar{Z}_2 \iff (\hat{X}D^c)^{2k \cdot c \cdot \log_g B} = \bar{Z}_2^{2k} \iff (\hat{X}D^c)^{c \cdot (2kb+1)} = \bar{Z}_2^{2k}$$

Thus, $\mathcal{B}$ can check the correctness of the value $\hat{Z}_i(i = 1, 2)$ by checking whether $(\hat{X}D)^{(2kb+1)} \stackrel{?}{=} \bar{Z}_1^{2k}$ and $(\hat{X}D^c)^{c \cdot (2kb+1)} \stackrel{?}{=} \bar{Z}_2^{2k}$.

Finally, $\mathcal{A}$ output $Z_i(i = 1, 2, ..m)$ from which $\mathcal{B}$ can extract the value of the form $\bar{Z} = CDH(X, B)^k$, e.g., for FS protocol $\bar{Z} = CDH(X, B)^k = CDH(X, B)^{(c-1)}$. While it is difficult to the compute inversion operation $\frac{1}{k}$ in exponent, since

$$\bar{Z} = CDH(X, B)^k = g^{(\log_g X)(\log_g B)k} = g^{(x+1/2k)(b+1/2k)k} = h^{(2k \cdot xb + x + b + 1/2k)k}$$

$\mathcal{B}$ can extract $v = h^{(1/2k)k} = h^{1/2}$ with the knowledge about x, b. Thus, with two non-trivial different square roots u, v of h, $\mathcal{B}$ can factor N by $\gcd(u - v, N)$ (or $\gcd(u + v, N)$). No inversion computations in exponents are required throughout the proof.

Applications. The k-th power proof approach is almost generic, i.e., applying k-th power technique to many, if not all, existing authenticated Diffie-Hellman key exchange protocols under gap assumption immediately produces protocols under factoring assumption if they work over $\mathbb{QR}_N^+$.

Note that the value k varies with the protocols and should be set to be some value σ whose inversion operation $\frac{1}{\sigma}$ in exponent is required.

Applying k-th power technique to protocols with constant σ, e.g., in FS protocol $\sigma = (c-1)$, immediately produces protocols provably secure in eCK model under factoring assumption if they work over $\mathbb{QR}_N^+$.

For protocols with non-constant σ, e.g., UP[15] in which $\sigma = e - 1$, our technique also works but at the cost of degrading a factor in the reduction.

4 Authenticated Key Exchange Protocols Based on Factoring Assumption

In this section, we discuss the protocol with constant k and defer the discussion on the protocols with non-constant k to Section 5.

4.1 The Scheme with Constant k

FS protocol over $\mathbb{QR}_N^+$. A typical example with constant k is FS protocol, which is most efficient one (example 2, [4]) among FS protocol family. Setting $c = 2$ results in an efficient protocol with 3 exponentiations. FS protocol was originally described in a cyclic group of known prime order q and provably secure in eCK model under gap assumption. Here we present the protocol over $\mathbb{QR}_N^+$ in Fig. 1 which is provably secure in eCK model under the factoring assumption. Our proof technique also applies to other protocols of FS protocol family with the different choices of the value k.

Let the value κ be the security parameter. Let $N = PQ$ be a RSA modulus generated by RSAgen(1^κ). Let $\mathbb{QR}_N^+ = \langle g \rangle$ be a cyclic group of order pq. Let $H : \{0,1\}^* \to \{0,1\}^{l(\kappa)}$ be a hash function.

The party Alice($\hat{A}$)'s static private key is $a \in [N/4]$ and its static public key is $A = g^a \in \mathbb{QR}_N^+$. Similarly, the party Bob($\hat{B}$)'s static private key is $b \in [N/4]$ and its static public key is $B = g^a \in \mathbb{QR}_N^+$. We omit writing explicitly " mod N" for calculations modulo N.

4.2 Security

Theorem 2. *Suppose that the factoring assumption holds for RSAgen, H is a hash function modeled as random oracle, then the proposed protocol in Fig. 1 is a secure authenticated key exchange protocol in the eCK model described in Appendix A.*

Proof. The first condition of Definition 3 follows immediately from the correctness of our protocol. That is, if two parties complete matching sessions, then they compute the same key. The proof for second condition of Definition 3 consists of showing that the probability that the adversary distinguishes a real session key from a random string is not more than $\frac{1}{2}$ plus a negligible fraction. Since all exchanged information and identities are included in $\mathbf{H}(\cdot)$ which is modeled as a random oracle, the probability that a non-matching session has the same session key with the Test session is negligible. Thus, the only way that the adversary

$\hat{A}$
$(A = g^a)$

$\hat{B}$
$(B = g^b)$

$x \in [N/4], X = g^x$

$y \in [N/4], Y = g^y$

$$\xrightarrow{\quad X \quad}$$
$$\xleftarrow{\quad Y \quad}$$

$Z_1 = (YB)^{x+a}$
$Z_2 = (YB^c)^{x+ac}$
$sk = H(Z_1, Z_2, X, Y, \hat{A}, \hat{B})$

$Z_1 = (XA)^{y+b}$
$Z_2 = (XA^c)^{y+bc}$
$sk = H(Z_1, Z_2, X, Y, \hat{A}, \hat{B})$

Fig. 1. FS protocol over $\mathbb{QR}_N^+$

M succeeds is *Forging attack*, in which the adversary M computes the values Z_1, Z_2 itself and then queries $\mathbf{H}$ with $(Z_1, Z_2, X, Y, \hat{A}, \hat{B})$.

To show that the success probability of Forging attack is negligible, we will construct a factoring problem solver SIM that uses an adversary M who succeeds with non-negligible probability in the attack. Assume that there are n honest parties $\hat{U}_1, \hat{U}_2, ..., \hat{U}_n$, and at most m sessions are activated.

- **Input to SIM.** The input to SIM is a factoring problem instance $N = PQ$. The goal of SIM is to compute P or Q.

According to freshness definition, there are two complementary cases that the adversary chooses the Test session: Test session without a matching session and Test session with a matching session.

4.2.1   Test Session Has No Matching Session
It suffices to discuss the following two subcases that: the adversary issues *either* CASE 1: a StaticKeyReveal query on party $\hat{A}$ *or* CASE 2: EphemeralKeyReveal query on the Test session.

CASE 1: SIM chooses $i, j \in \{k | \hat{U}_k\}$, and $s^* \in [m]$. We denote $\hat{U}_i, \hat{U}_j$ by $\hat{A}, \hat{B}$ respectively. With these choices, SIM guesses that the adversary M will select the session $\Pi_{\hat{A}, \hat{B}}^{s^*}$ as the Test session.

SIM chooses uniformly $u \leftarrow_R (\mathbb{Z}_N^*)^+ \backslash \mathbb{QR}_N^+$ and sets $h = u^2$. Then, SIM chooses $b \in [N/4]$ and computes $g = h^{2k}, B = hg^b$, where $\boxed{k=c-1}$. This implicitly defines $\log_g B = b + \frac{1}{2k} \bmod \mathrm{ord}(\mathbb{QR}_N^+)$. SIM sets the static public key B for $\hat{B}$, and random static key pairs for the remaining parties (including $\hat{A}$). SIM interacts with the adversary M as follows. Without loss of generality, we assume that $\hat{B}$ is the responder.

- $\mathbf{H}(Z_1, Z_2, X, Y, \hat{U}_i, \hat{U}_j)$: SIM maintains an initially empty list H^{list} with entry of the form $(Z_1, Z_2, X, Y, \hat{U}_i, \hat{U}_j, h)$. SIM simulates the oracle in usual way except for queries of the form $(Z_1, Z_2, X, Y, \hat{U}_i, \hat{U}_j)$ with $\hat{U}_i = \hat{D}, \hat{U}_j = \hat{B}$, i.e., we assume that $\hat{B}$ is the responder communicating with a peer $\hat{D}$. SIM responds to these queries in the following way:

- If $(Z_1, Z_2, X, Y, \hat{D}, \hat{B})$ is already there, then SIM responds with stored value h.
- Otherwise, if there are the entries of the form $(X, Y, \hat{D}, \hat{B}, *)$ in L^{list} (maintained in the Send query), SIM computes $\bar{Z}_1 = Z_1/(XD)^y, \bar{Z}_2 = Z_2/(XD^c)^y$, and hence

$$(XD)^{\log_g B} = \bar{Z}_1 \iff (XD)^{2k \cdot \log_g B} = \bar{Z}_1^{2k} \iff (XD)^{(2kb+1)} = \bar{Z}_1^{2k} \quad (8)$$

$$(XD^c)^{c \cdot \log_g B} = \bar{Z}_2 \iff (XD^c)^{2k \cdot c \cdot \log_g B} = \bar{Z}_2^{2k} \iff (XD^c)^{c \cdot (2kb+1)} = \bar{Z}_2^{2k} \quad (9)$$

Thus, SIM can check the correctness of the value $Z_i (i = 1, 2)$ by checking whether $(XD)^{(2kb+1)} \overset{?}{=} \bar{Z}_1^{2k}$ and $(XD^c)^{c \cdot (2kb+1)} \overset{?}{=} \bar{Z}_2^{2k}$. If the equalities hold, it returns from L^{list} the stored value SK to the adversary M, stores the new tuple $(Z_1, Z_2, X, Y, \hat{D}, \hat{B}, SK)$ in H^{list}.

- Otherwise, SIM chooses h at random, sends it to the adversary M and stores the new tuple $(Z_1, Z_2, X, Y, \hat{D}, \hat{B}, h)$ in H^{list}.

- **StaticKeyReveal(U_i):**
  - If $U_i = \hat{B}$, then SIM aborts.
  - Otherwise, SIM returns the corresponding static private key to the adversary M.

- **EstablishParty($\hat{U}_i$):** The adversary can arbitrarily register a user on behalf of the party $\hat{U}_i$. This way, the adversary totally controls the party $\hat{U}_i$.

- **EphemeralKeyReveal($\Pi_{\hat{U}_i, U_j}^s$):**
  - If $\Pi_{\hat{U}_i, U_j}^s$ is the Test session $\Pi_{\hat{A}, \hat{B}}^{s^*}$, then simulator fails.
  - Otherwise, SIM returns the stored ephemeral private key to the adversary M.

- **Send($\Pi_{\hat{U}_i, \hat{U}_j}^s, m$):** SIM maintains an initially empty list L^{list} with entries of the form $(X, Y, \hat{U}_i, \hat{U}_j, SK)$. SIM simulates the oracle in usual way except for Test session and the sessions of party $\hat{B}$. SIM responds to these queries in the following way:
  - If $\Pi_{\hat{U}_i, \hat{U}_j}^s$ is the Test session $\Pi_{\hat{A}, \hat{B}}^{s^*}$, SIM chooses $x \in [N/4]$, returns $X^* = hg^x$ to the adversary M.
  - If $\hat{U}_i = \hat{B}$, SIM chooses $y \in [N/4]$ and returns $Y = g^y$ to the adversary M. (For convenience, we assume that $\hat{B}$ is the responder, and denote $\hat{U}_j$ by $\hat{D}$ and m by X.)
    * SIM looks in H^{list} for the entry of the form $(*, *, X, Y, \hat{D}, \hat{B}, *)$. If finds it, SIM computes $\bar{Z}_1 = Z_1/(XD)^y, \bar{Z}_2 = Z_2/(XD^c)^y$. Then, SIM can check the correctness of the value $Z_i (i = 1, 2)$ by checking whether $(XD)^{(2kb+1)} \overset{?}{=} \bar{Z}_1^{2k}$ and $(XD^c)^{c \cdot (2kb+1)} \overset{?}{=} \bar{Z}_2^{2k}$.
      · If the equality does not hold, SIM chooses SK randomly and stores the new tuple $(X, Y, \hat{D}, \hat{B}, SK)$ in L^{list}.

· Otherwise, SIM stores the new tuple $(X, Y, \hat{D}, \hat{B}, h)$ in L^{list} where the value h is the last element from H^{list}.

* Otherwise (no such entries exist), SIM chooses SK at random and stores the new tuple $(X, Y, \hat{D}, \hat{B}, SK)$ in L^{list}.

– **SessionKeyReveal**($\Pi^s_{\hat{U}_i, \hat{U}_j}$):
  • If $\Pi^s_{\hat{U}_i, \hat{U}_j}$ is the Test session $\Pi^{s^*}_{\hat{A}, \hat{B}}$, then simulator fails.
  • Otherwise, SIM returns the stored value SK in L^{list} to the adversary M.

– **Test**($\Pi^s_{\hat{U}_i, \hat{U}_j}$):
  • If $\Pi^s_{\hat{U}_i, \hat{U}_j}$ is not the Test session $\Pi^{s^*}_{\hat{A}, \hat{B}}$, SIM aborts.
  • Otherwise, SIM randomly chooses ζ and returns it to the adversary M.

Finally, if the adversary M provides a correct guess at $Z_1 = (Y^* B)^{\log_g X^* + \log_g A}$, $Z_2 = (Y^* B^c)^{\log_g X^* + c \log_g A}$ where X^* is the outgoing message of Test session, and Y^* is the incoming message from the adversary, SIM proceeds with following steps:

$$\bar{Z}_1 = Z_1/(Y^* B)^{\log_g A} \tag{10}$$

$$\bar{Z}_2 = Z_2/(Y^* B^c)^{c \log_g A} \tag{11}$$

$$Z = \frac{\bar{Z}_2}{\bar{Z}_1} = \frac{(Y^* B^c)^{\log_g X^*}}{(Y^* B)^{\log_g X^*}} = B^{(c-1) \log_g X^*} = B^{k \log_g X^*} \tag{12}$$

Hence,

$$Z = B^{k \log_g X^*} = g^{k(\log_g B)(\log_g X^*)} = g^{k(b + \frac{1}{2k})(x + \frac{1}{2k})} = h^{k(2kbx + b + x + \frac{1}{2k})} \tag{13}$$

From (13), SIM can extract $v = h^{(k/2k)} = h^{1/2}$ with the knowledge about x, b. Thus, with two non-trivial different square roots u, v of h, SIM can factor N by $\gcd(u - v, N)$ (or $\gcd(u + v, N)$).

CASE 2: The setup of SIM is identical to that of CASE 1 except that SIM chooses $a, b \in [N/4]$ and computes $g = h^{2k}, A = hg^a, B = hg^b$, where $\boxed{k = c(c-1)}$. SIM sets the static public key A, B for $\hat{A}$ and $\hat{B}$ respectively, and random static key pairs for the remaining $n - 2$ parties.

– **H**($Z, X, Y, \hat{U}_i, \hat{U}_j$): SIM simulates the oracle in usual way except for queries with $\hat{U}_i = \hat{A}$ or $\hat{B}$, or $\hat{U}_j = \hat{A}$ or $\hat{B}$. For these queries the action of SIM is similar to that of CASE 1 for queries of the form $(Z, X, Y, \hat{U}_i, \hat{U}_j)$ with $\hat{U}_i = \hat{D}, \hat{U}_j = \hat{B}$.

– **StaticKeyReveal**(U_i):
  • If $U_i = \hat{B}$ (or $\hat{A}$), then SIM aborts.
  • Otherwise, SIM returns the corresponding static private key to the adversary M.

- **EstablishParty**(U_i): The action of SIM is identical to that of CASE 1.
- **EphemeralKeyReveal**(Π_{U_i,U_j}^s): SIM returns the stored ephemeral private key to the adversary M (including that of the Test session).
- **SessionKeyReveal**(Π_{U_i,U_j}^s): The action of SIM is identical to that of CASE 1.
- **Send**(Π_{U_i,U_j}^s, m):
  - If Π_{U_i,U_j}^s is the Test session $\Pi_{\hat{A},\hat{B}}^{s^*}$, SIM chooses $x \in [N/4]$, returns $X^* = g^x$ instead of $X^* = hg^x$. Otherwise,
    * If $U_i = \hat{B}$ (or $\hat{A}$), the simulation is similar to that of CASE 1 for party $\hat{B}$.
    * Otherwise, $(U_i \neq \hat{B}$ and $U_i \neq \hat{A})$, since SIM knows the static private key it follows the protocol specification.
- **Test**(Π_{U_i,U_j}^s): The action of SIM is identical to that of CASE 1.

Finally, if the adversary M provides a correct guess at $Z_1 = (Y^*B)^{\log_g X^* + \log_g A}$, $Z_2 = (Y^*B^c)^{\log_g X^* + c\log_g A}$ where X^* is the outgoing message of Test session, Y^* is the incoming message from the adversary, SIM proceeds with following steps:

$$\bar{Z}_1 = Z_1/(Y^*B)^{\log_g X^*} \tag{14}$$

$$\bar{Z}_2 = Z_2/(Y^*B^c)^{\log_g X^*} \tag{15}$$

$$Z = \frac{\bar{Z}_2}{\bar{Z}_1^{\ c}} = \frac{(Y^*B^c)^{c\log_g A}}{(Y^*B)^{c\log_g A}} = B^{c(c-1)\log_g A} = B^{k\log_g A} \tag{16}$$

Hence,

$$Z = B^{k\log_g A} = g^{k(\log_g A)(\log_g B)} = g^{k(a+\frac{1}{2k})(b+\frac{1}{2k})} = h^{k(2kab+a+b+\frac{1}{2k})} \tag{17}$$

From (17), SIM can extract $v = h^{(k/2k)} = h^{1/2}$ with the knowledge about a, b. Thus, with two non-trivial different square roots u, v of h, SIM can factor N by $\gcd(u - v, N)$ (or $\gcd(u + v, N)$).

4.2.2   Test Session Has a Matching Session

It suffices to consider the following four subcases.

CASE 3: The adversary issues the EphemeralKeyReveal queries on both the Test session and its matching session.

- The action of SIM is identical to that of CASE 2. However, as the value Y^* is from the matching session maintained by the simulator SIM, a more concise proof strategy is as following.
- SIM chooses uniformly $u \leftarrow_R (\mathbb{Z}_N^*)^+ \backslash \mathbb{QR}_N^+$ and sets $h = u^2$. Then, SIM chooses $a, b \in [N/4]$ and computes $g = h^{2k}, A = hg^a, B = hg^b$, where $\boxed{k=1}$. Then, SIM sets the static public keys of party $\hat{A}$ and $\hat{B}$ to be A, B respectively.

- The simulation is identical to CASE 2. However, the reduction is more direct as SIM knows $\log_g Y^*$. From value $Z_1 = (Y^*B)^{\log_g X^* + \log_g A}$, with the knowledge about $\log_g X^*$ and $\log_g Y^*$, SIM directly derives $Z = CDH(A, B) = g^{(\log_g A)(\log_g B)} = g^{(a + \frac{1}{2k})(b + \frac{1}{2k})} = h^{2k(ab + \frac{1}{2k}a + \frac{1}{2k}b + \frac{1}{4k^2})} = h^{(2ab + a + b + \frac{1}{2})}$. Then, SIM can extract $v = h^{1/2}$ with the knowledge about a, b. Thus, with two non-trivial different square roots u, v of h, SIM can factor N by $\gcd(u - v, N)$ (or $\gcd(u + v, N)$).

CASE 4: The adversary issues the StaticKeyReveal queries on both the party $\hat{A}$ and its peer $\hat{B}$.

- SIM chooses uniformly $u \leftarrow_R (\mathbb{Z}_N^*)^+ \backslash \mathbb{QR}_N^+$ and sets $h = u^2$. Then, SIM chooses $x, y \in [N/4]$ and computes $g = h^{2k}, X^* = hg^x, Y^* = hg^y$, where $\boxed{k=1}$. Then, SIM sets the ephemeral public keys of Test session and matching session to be X^*, Y^* respectively.
- The simulation is simple as SIM knows all the static private keys. The reduction is as follows. From value $Z_1 = (Y^*B)^{\log_g X^* + \log_g A}$, with the knowledge about $\log_g A$ and $\log_g B$, SIM directly derives $Z = CDH(X^*, Y^*) = g^{(\log_g X^*)(\log_g Y^*)} = g^{(x + \frac{1}{2k})(y + \frac{1}{2k})} = h^{2k(xy + \frac{1}{2k}x + \frac{1}{2k}y + \frac{1}{4k^2})} = h^{(2xy + x + y + \frac{1}{2})}$. Then, SIM can extract $v = h^{1/2}$ with the knowledge about x, y. Thus, with two non-trivial different square roots u, v of h, SIM can factor N by $\gcd(u - v, N)$ (or $\gcd(u + v, N)$).

CASE 5: The adversary issues the StaticKeyReveal query on the party $\hat{A}$ and the EphemeralKeyReveal query on the matching session.

- The action of SIM is identical to that of CASE 1. The more concise proof strategy is as following.
- SIM chooses uniformly $u \leftarrow_R (\mathbb{Z}_N^*)^+ \backslash \mathbb{QR}_N^+$ and sets $h = u^2$. Then, SIM chooses $a, b \in [N/4]$ and computes $g = h^{2k}, X^* = hg^x, B = hg^b$, where $\boxed{k=1}$. Then, SIM sets the ephemeral public key of Test session and the static public keys of $\hat{B}$ to be X^* and B respectively.
- The simulation is identical to CASE 1. However, the reduction is more direct as SIM knows $\log_g Y^*$. From value $Z_1 = (Y^*B)^{\log_g X^* + \log_g A}$, with the knowledge about $\log_g A$ and $\log_g Y^*$, SIM directly derives $Z = CDH(X^*, B) = g^{(\log_g X^*)(\log_g B)} = g^{(x + \frac{1}{2k})(b + \frac{1}{2k})} = h^{2k(xb + \frac{1}{2k}x + \frac{1}{2k}b + \frac{1}{4k^2})} = h^{(2xb + x + b + \frac{1}{2})}$. Then, SIM can extract $v = h^{1/2}$ with the knowledge about x, b. Thus, with two non-trivial different square roots u, v of h, SIM can factor N by $\gcd(u - v, N)$ (or $\gcd(u + v, N)$).

CASE 6: The adversary issues the EphemeralKeyReveal query on the Test session and the StaticKeyReveal query on the party $\hat{B}$.

- This case is symmetric to CASE 5, and omitted.

Together with all the subcases CASE 1-CASE 6, the success probability of SIM is

$$Pr[SIM] \geq \max\{\max_{i=1,2,3,5,6}\{\frac{1}{mn^2}p_i\}, \frac{1}{m^2}p_4\} \qquad (18)$$

where p_i is the probability of the event that the cases occurs and the adversary M succeeds in this case. If there is an adversary M who succeeds with non-negligible probability in any cases above, we can solve the factoring problem. This completes the proof of Theorem 2.

5   The Schemes with Non-constant k

UP Protocol over $\mathbb{QR}_N^+$. An example with non-constant k is UP protocol [16] which was originally described in a cyclic group of known prime order q and provably secure under gap assumption. Here we show that UP protocol is provably secure under the factoring assumption if it works over $\mathbb{QR}_N^+$.

$\hat{A}$ $\hat{B}$

$(A = g^a)$ $(B = g^b)$

$x \in [N/4], X = g^x$ $y \in [N/4], Y = g^y$

$$\xrightarrow{\quad X \quad}$$
$$\xleftarrow{\quad Y \quad}$$

$Z_1 = (YB^e)^{x+a}$ $Z_1 = (XA)^{y+be}$
$Z_2 = (YB)^{x+ad}$ $Z_2 = (XA^d)^{y+b}$
where $e = h(Y), d = h(X)$ where $e = h(Y), d = h(X)$
$sk = H(Z_1, Z_2, X, Y, \hat{A}, \hat{B})$ $sk = H(Z_1, Z_2, X, Y, \hat{A}, \hat{B})$

Fig. 2. UP protocol over $\mathbb{QR}_N^+$

Theorem 3. *Suppose that the factoring assumption holds for RSAgen, h, H are hash functions modeled as random oracles, then UP protocol over $\mathbb{QR}_N^+$ (Fig. 2) is a secure authenticated key exchange protocol in the eCK model described in Appendix A.*

Sketch of proof. The proof is similar to that of section 4.1 with a difference that in the setup SIM has to guess the value k as it is not a constant, which results in a loss of a factor. In the following, we provide a rough discussion on the setting of value k, and the more details will be given in the full version. Assume that Test session is $\Pi_{\hat{A},\hat{B}}^{s^*}$. We take into account the following two cases in which the setting of the value k is different.

CASE 1: SIM chooses uniformly $u \leftarrow_R (\mathbb{Z}_N^*)^+ \backslash \mathbb{QR}_N^+$ and sets $h = u^2$. Then, SIM chooses $k, b \in [N/4]$ and computes $g = h^{2k}, X^* = hg^x, B = hg^b$. SIM sets the ephemeral public key of Test session and the static public key of $\hat{B}$ to be X^* and B respectively.

In the interaction with the adversary M, SIM answers the query h(Y^*) with value $k + 1$ where Y^* is the incoming message of Test session. This implicitly sets $k = e - 1$ where $e =$ h(Y^*).

CASE 2: SIM chooses uniformly $u \leftarrow_R (\mathbb{Z}_N^*)^+ \backslash \mathbb{QR}_N^+$ and sets $h = u^2$. Then, SIM chooses $k_1, k_2, b \in [N/4]$ and computes $k = k_1 k_2, g = h^{2k}, A = hg^a, B = hg^b$. SIM sets the static public keys of $\hat{A}$ and $\hat{B}$ to be A and B respectively.

In the interaction with the adversary M, SIM sets h$(X^*) = k_1$ and h$(Y^*) = k_2 + 1$ where X^* is the outgoing message of Test session, and Y^* is the incoming message of Test session. This implicitly sets $k = (e - 1)d$ where $e =$ h(Y^*) and $d = h(X^*)$.

HMQV Protocol over $\mathbb{QR}_N^+$. HMQV protocol [10] is another typical example with a non-constant k which was originally described in a cyclic group of known prime order q and provably secure under gap assumption. Here we show that HMQV protocol is provably secure under the factoring assumption if it works over $\mathbb{QR}_N^+$.

$\hat{A}$

$(A = g^a)$

$x \in [N/4], X = g^x$

$\hat{B}$

$(B = g^b)$

$y \in [N/4], Y = g^y$

$$\xrightarrow{\quad X \quad}$$
$$\xleftarrow{\quad Y \quad}$$

$Z = (YB^e)^{x+ad}$

where $e = h(Y, \hat{A})$, $d = h(X, \hat{B})$

$sk = H(Z, X, Y, \hat{A}, \hat{B})$

$Z = (XA^d)^{y+be}$

where $e = h(Y, \hat{A})$, $d = h(X, \hat{B})$

$sk = H(Z, X, Y, \hat{A}, \hat{B})$

Fig. 3. HMQV protocol over $\mathbb{QR}_N^+$

Theorem 4. *Suppose that the factoring assumption holds for RSAgen, h, H are hash functions modeled as random oracles, then HMQV protocol over $\mathbb{QR}_N^+$ (Fig. 3) is a secure authenticated key exchange protocol in the eCK model described in Appendix A.*

Sketch of proof. We provide a rough discussion on the setting of value k, and the more details will be given in the full version. The proof strategy also applies to the variants of HMQV, e.g., CMQV,FMQV and SMQV. Assume that Test session is $\Pi_{\hat{A},\hat{B}}^{s^*}$. We take into account the following two cases in which the setting of the value k is different.

CASE 1: SIM chooses uniformly $u \leftarrow_R (\mathbb{Z}_N^*)^+ \backslash \mathbb{QR}_N^+$ and sets $h = u^2$. Then, SIM chooses $k_1, k_2, x, b \in [N/4]$ and computes $k = k_1 - k_2, g = h^{2k}, X^* = hg^x, B = hg^b$. SIM sets the ephemeral public key of Test session and the static public key of $\hat{B}$ to be X^* and B respectively.

In the interaction with the adversary M, SIM answers the query $h(Y^*, \hat{A})$ with value k_1 where Y^* is the incoming message of Test session. In the repeat experiment, SIM sets $h(Y^*, \hat{A})$ to be k_2. This implicitly sets $k = e - e'$ where e, e' are two different response values of $h(Y^*, \hat{A})$ in Forking lemma.

CASE 2: SIM chooses uniformly $u \leftarrow_R (\mathbb{Z}_N^*)^+ \backslash \mathbb{QR}_N^+$ and sets $h = u^2$. Then, SIM chooses $k_1, k_{21}, k_{22}, b \in [N/4]$ and computes $k = (k_{21} - k_{22})k_1, g = h^{2k}, A = hg^a, B = hg^b$. SIM sets the static public keys of $\hat{A}$ and $\hat{B}$ to be A and B respectively.

In the interaction with the adversary M, SIM sets $h(X^*, \hat{B}) = k_1$ and $h(Y^*, \hat{A}) = k_{21}$ where X^* is the outgoing message of Test session, and Y^* is the incoming message of Test session. In the repeat experiment, SIM sets $h(Y^*, \hat{A})$ to be k_{22}. This implicitly sets $k = (e - e')d$ where $d = h(X^*, \hat{B})$ and e, e' are two different response values of $h(Y^*, \hat{A})$ in Forking lemma.

Acknowledgments. The author would like to thank the anonymous reviewers for their valuable comments. This work was supported in part by Zhejiang Provincial Natural Science Foundation of China under Grant No. Y1110157, and Science Foundation of Zhejiang Sci-Tech University under Grant No. 1007827-Y.

References

1. Abdalla, M., Bellare, M., Rogaway, P.: The oracle Diffie-Hellman assumptions and an analysis of DHIES. In: Naccache, D. (ed.) CT-RSA 2001. LNCS, vol. 2020, pp. 143–158. Springer, Heidelberg (2001)
2. Boyd, C., Cliff, Y., Gonzalez Nieto, J., Paterson, K.G.: Efficient one-round key exchange in the standard model. In: Mu, Y., Susilo, W., Seberry, J. (eds.) ACISP 2008. LNCS, vol. 5107, pp. 69–83. Springer, Heidelberg (2008)
3. Cash, D., Kiltz, E., Shoup, V.: The twin Diffie-Hellman problem and applications. In: Smart, N.P. (ed.) EUROCRYPT 2008. LNCS, vol. 4965, pp. 127–145. Springer, Heidelberg (2008)
4. Fujioka, A., Suzuki, K.: Designing efficient authenticated key exchange resilient to leakage of ephemeral secret keys. In: Kiayias, A. (ed.) CT-RSA 2011. LNCS, vol. 6558, pp. 121–141. Springer, Heidelberg (2011)
5. Fujioka, A., Suzuki, K., Xagawa, K., Yoneyama, K.: Strongly secure authenticated key exchange from factoring, codes, and lattices. In: Fischlin, M., Buchmann, J., Manulis, M. (eds.) PKC 2012. LNCS, vol. 7293, pp. 467–484. Springer, Heidelberg (2012)
6. Hofheinz, D., Kiltz, E.: The group of signed quadratic residues and applications. In: Halevi, S. (ed.) CRYPTO 2009. LNCS, vol. 5677, pp. 637–653. Springer, Heidelberg (2009)
7. Huang, H., Cao, Z.: Strongly secure authenticated key exchange protocol based on computational Diffie-Hellman problem. In: Proceedings of Inscrypt 2008, pp. 65–77. Science Press of China (2009), http://eprint.iacr.org/2008/500

8. Huang, H., Cao, Z.: An ID-based authenticated key exchange protocol based on bilinear Diffie-Hellman problem. In: Li, W., Susilo, W., Tupakula, U.K., Safavi-Naini, R., Varadharajan, V. (eds.) ASIACCS, pp. 333–342. ACM (2009)

9. Kim, M., Fujioka, A., Ustaoğlu, B.: Strongly secure authenticated key exchange without NAXOS' approach. In: Takagi, T., Mambo, M. (eds.) IWSEC 2009. LNCS, vol. 5824, pp. 174–191. Springer, Heidelberg (2009)

10. Krawczyk, H.: HMQV: A high-performance secure Diffie-Hellman protocol. In: Shoup, V. (ed.) CRYPTO 2005. LNCS, vol. 3621, pp. 546–566. Springer, Heidelberg (2005)

11. LaMacchia, B.A., Lauter, K., Mityagin, A.: Stronger security of authenticated key exchange. In: Susilo, W., Liu, J.K., Mu, Y. (eds.) ProvSec 2007. LNCS, vol. 4784, pp. 1–16. Springer, Heidelberg (2007)

12. Lee, J., Park, J.H.: Authenticated key exchange secure under the computational Diffie-Hellman assumption. Cryptology ePrint Archive, Report 2008/344 (2008), http://eprint.iacr.org/

13. Sarr, A.P., Elbaz-Vincent, P., Bajard, J.-C.: A secure and efficient authenticated diffie–hellman protocol. In: Martinelli, F., Preneel, B. (eds.) EuroPKI 2009. LNCS, vol. 6391, pp. 83–98. Springer, Heidelberg (2010)

14. Sarr, A.P., Elbaz-Vincent, P., Bajard, J.-C.: A new security model for authenticated key agreement. In: Garay, J.A., De Prisco, R. (eds.) SCN 2010. LNCS, vol. 6280, pp. 219–234. Springer, Heidelberg (2010)

15. Ustaoglu, B.: Obtaining a secure and efficient key agreement protocol from (H)MQV and NAXOS. Des. Codes Cryptography 46(3), 329–342 (2008)

16. Ustaoglu, B.: Comparing sessionstatereveal and ephemeralkeyreveal for Diffie-Hellman protocols. In: Pieprzyk, J., Zhang, F. (eds.) ProvSec 2009. LNCS, vol. 5848, pp. 183–197. Springer, Heidelberg (2009)

A. Security Model

In this section, we review the eCK security model for authenticated key exchange protocols. For the details of the original eCK model, see [11, 15].

Participants. We model the protocol participants as a finite set $\mathcal{U}$ with each $U_i \in \mathcal{U}$ being a probabilistic polynomial time (PPT) Turing machine, which may execute a polynomial number of protocol instances in parallel. $\Pi^s_{U_i,U_j}(i,j \in N)$ denotes s-th instance of participant U_i with peer U_j.

Adversary Model. The adversary M is modeled as a PPT Turing machine and has full control of the communication network and may eavesdrop, delay, replay, alter and insert messages at will. We model the adversary's capability by providing it with oracle queries.

- **EphemeralKeyReveal($\Pi^s_{U_i,U_j}$)** The adversary obtains the ephemeral private key of $\Pi^s_{U_i,U_j}$.
- **SessionKeyReveal($\Pi^s_{U_i,U_j}$)** The adversary obtains the session key for a session s of U_i, provided that the session holds a session key.
- **StaticKeyReveal(U_i)** The adversary obtains the static private key of U_i.

- **EstablishParty**(U_i) The adversary can arbitrarily register a user on behalf of the party U_i. This way, the adversary totally controls the party U_i. If a party is registered by the adversary, then it is called *dishonest* (or *malicious*). Otherwise, it is called *honest*.
- **Send**(Π_{U_i,U_j}^s, m) The adversary sends the message m to the session Π_{U_i,U_j}^s and gets a response.
- **Test**(Π_{U_i,U_j}^s) Only one query of this form is allowed for the adversary. A random bit $\hat{b}$ is chosen, if $\hat{b} = 0$ then the real session key is returned; otherwise, an uniformly chosen random value ζ is returned.

Definition 1 (Matching Session). *Let Π_{U_i,U_j}^s be a completed session with identifier $(U_i, U_j, out, in, role)$, where U_i is the owner of the session, U_j is the peer, and out is U_i's outgoing message, in is U_j's outgoing message, and role is the U_i's role in the session (initiator or responder). The session Π_{U_j,U_i}^t is called the* matching session *of Π_{U_i,U_j}^s, if the identifier of Π_{U_j,U_i}^t is $(U_j, U_i, \overline{out}, \overline{in}, \overline{role})$, where $out = \overline{in}, in = \overline{out}, role \neq \overline{role}$.*

Definition 2 (Freshness of eCK model). *Let instance Π_{U_i,U_j}^s be a completed session, which was executed by an honest party U_i with another honest party U_j. We define Π_{U_i,U_j}^s to be* fresh *if none of the following three conditions hold:*

- *The adversary M reveals the session key of Π_{U_i,U_j}^s or of its matching session (if latter exists).*
- *U_j is engaged in session Π_{U_j,U_i}^t matching to Π_{U_i,U_j}^s and M issues either:*
  - *both* **StaticKeyReveal**(U_i) *and* **EphemeralKeyReveal**(Π_{U_i,U_j}^s) *queries; or*
  - *both* **StaticKeyReveal**(U_j) *and* **EphemeralKeyReveal**(Π_{U_j,U_i}^t) *queries.*
- *No sessions matching to Π_{U_i,U_j}^s exist and M issues either:*
  - *both* **StaticKeyReveal**(U_i) *and* **EphemeralKeyReveal**(Π_{U_i,U_j}^s) *queries; or*
  - **StaticKeyReveal**(U_j) *query.*

As a function of the security parameter κ, the advantage of the PPT adversary M in attacking protocol Σ is defined as $Adv_{M,\Sigma}^{AKE}(\kappa) \stackrel{def}{=} |Pr[b = \hat{b}] - \frac{1}{2}|$, where $Pr[b = \hat{b}]$ is the probability that the adversary queries **Test** oracle to a *fresh* session, outputs a bit b which is equal to the bit $\hat{b}$ of **Test** oracle.

Definition 3 (AKE Security). *An authenticated key exchange protocol Σ is said to be AKE-secure if following two conditions hold*

1. *If two parties complete the matching sessions, they compute the same session key.*
2. *For any PPT adversary M, the probability $Adv_{M,\Sigma}^{AKE}(\kappa)$ is negligible.*

Efficient, Pairing-Free, Authenticated Identity Based Key Agreement in a Single Round

S. Sree Vivek[1], S. Sharmila Deva Selvi[1],
Layamrudhaa Renganathan Venkatesan[1], and C. Pandu Rangan[1]

[1] Theoretical Computer Science Lab,
Department of Computer Science and Engineering,
Indian Institute of Technology Madras,
Chennai, India
[2] National Institute of Technology Tiruchi,
Tiruchirapalli, India

Abstract. Ever since Shamir introduced identity based cryptography in 1984, there has been a tremendous interest in designing efficient key agreement protocols in this paradigm. Since pairing is a costly operation and the composite order groups must be very large to ensure security, we focus on pairing free protocols in prime order groups. We propose a new protocol that is pairing free, working in prime order group and having tight reduction to Strong Diffie Hellman (SDH) problem under the CK model. Thus, the first major advantage is that smaller key sizes are sufficient to achieve comparable security. Our scheme has several other advantages. The major one being the capability to handle active adversaries. All the previous protocols can offer security only under passive adversaries. Our protocol recognizes the corruption by an active adversary and aborts the process. Achieving this in single round is significantly challenging. Ours is the first scheme achieving this property. In addition to this significant property, our scheme satisfies other security properties that are not covered by CK model such as forward secrecy, resistance to reflection, key compromise impersonation attacks and ephemeral key compromise impersonation attacks.

Keywords: Identity Based Key agreement, Provable Security, General forking lemma, Tight reduction, Random Oracle Model, Forward Secrecy, Reflection attacks, Key Compromise Impersonation attacks.

1 Introduction

Symmetric key cryptography is a system in which both encryption and decryption is performed using the same key unlike asymmetric system in which each user maintains a public key and a private key. Symmetric key cryptography is much easier to implement and demands less processing than asymmetric. But the main disadvantage with symmetric key cryptography is the establishment of the shared secret between the entities that want to communicate. A secure way of setting up the shared secret key is mandatory. The first key-agreement

W. Susilo and R. Reyhanitabar (Eds.): ProvSec 2013, LNCS 8209, pp. 38–58, 2013.

protocol was defined by Whitfield Diffie and Martin Hellman in 1976. This was based on the public key setting. Under this model, each user has to get his public key certified by a Certification Authority (CA), which is a trusted third party that issues certificates validating each user's public key. The idea was to use public key cryptography for key establishment and symmetric key cryptography for further communication using the shared secret key. But in this paradigm, the overhead associated with the CA will be high.

Identity Based Cryptography was introduced by Shamir [15] in 1984. In this infrastructure, each user's public key is his identity. A trusted party known as the Private Key Generator (PKG) maintains a master public key, master secret key pair. The master public key is known to everyone and the master secret key is known only to the PKG. It generates the private key of each user with the user's identity and master secret key. After the introduction of identity based cryptography, many schemes were proposed based on this model. In identity based key agreement protocol each user first obtains his private key from the PKG and engages in an interactive protocol with another user to establish a shared secret key. There is no need to transfer the public key certificates during the process. This is the main advantage of identity based system. Moreover there is a flexibility to use any string as the identity. It can be the user's email id, social security number, location and other attributes. The identity can also have a temporal value linked to it and hence the private key derived from it is invalid after a period of time. Hence identity based key agreement(IDKA) protocols are preferred rather than their public key based counterparts. An important factor to be considered with respect to key agreement is bandwidth requirement and number of rounds. Since IDKA eliminate the need to transfer public key verification certificates, they tend to reduce the bandwidth requirement. These are useful in situations where there is a constraint on the available bandwidth. Other properties like forward secrecy, resistance to man-in-the-middle attacks, reflection attacks and key compromise impersonation attacks should also be satisfied.

2   Previous Work and Our Contribution

After the discovery of identity based cryptography by Shamir [15], a number of key agreement protocols were developed in the identity based paradigm. But most of them involved pairing and hence their practical implementation was not efficient. Hence, we do not consider pairing based schemes for our comparison. The protocols which did not involve pairing were those of Gunther [7] and Saeednia [14]. Fiore [5] proposed a key agreement protocol without pairing which was an improvement over the protocols of Gunther [7] and Saeednia [14]. Cao [3] proposed a pairing free key agreement protocol but this was vulnerable to key-offset attack and known session specific secret information attack as presented in [8] by Islam. The protocol presented in [8] and [3] involves an initial agreement on who initiates the key agreement protocol. Therefore we do not consider [8] and [3] in the comparison. We will consider the works of Gunther [7], Saeednia [14] and Fiore [5] for comparison purpose.

The previous works on identity based key agreement do not consider an active adversary. An active adversary is one which can extract the messages that are exchanged during key agreement and modify them arbitrarily during transit. In the scheme presented in [5], the adversary can extract the ephemeral component g^{t_i} sent by user i to user j and modify it to g^{t_x} and send it to j. Similarly it can capture g^{t_j} sent from j to i and modify it to g^{t_x} and send to i. The component Z_2 calculated by i will be $(g^{t_x})^{t_i}$ and the one computed by j will be $(g^{t_x})^{t_j}$. Thus the final shared secret key of i and j will not be in agreement. Similar attacks are possible in Gunther [7] and Saeednia [14]. Our protocol avoids this kind of an attack by a signature on the ephemeral components. We compare computational power based on the number of exponentiation operations. We assume that the ephemeral components are chosen from a pre-computed list and hence we do not consider the cost of computing the ephemeral components. In our scheme, we use a Schnorr group and hence the exponentiation operations are cheaper than [5], [7], [14] even though it involves more exponentiation operations. This is because in a Schnorr group the exponent is from a group $Z_p{}^*$ where size of p is 224 bits according to *http://www.keylength.com/en/4/*. The additional security features like forward secrecy, resistance to reflection attacks, key compromise impersonation and ephemeral key compromise impersonation with respect to [5], [7], [14] are presented in Table 1.1 and Table 1.2.

Tightness of Security Reduction: We develop the security proof of the scheme as a game between a challenger and an adversary. If the adversary is able to break the scheme in polynomial time, then the adversary is said to succeed. Using the adversary's success, the challenger develops a solution to the underlying hard problem instance. Since there exists no solution to the hard problem that can be computed in polynomial time, the scheme cannot be broken and is considered secure.

The security parameter is set such that the adversary is not able to break the scheme in polynomial time through brute-force methods or sub-exponential algorithms. The relative hardness of breaking the scheme to that of breaking the computational assumption can be loose or tight. The use of forking lemma in security proofs makes the reduction inefficient by imposing an increase in the size of the modulus q. Hence, if we eliminate the use of forking lemma, the same level of security can be achieved with a smaller size modulus q. This contributes to the reduction in the number of bits required to realize the cryptographic primitive. Based on the work of Goh [6], in any discrete log based system, if the adversary can break the scheme in 2^n steps then forking lemma implies that the underlying discrete log problem can be solved in 2^{2n} steps. Here n is the security parameter. Therefore the scheme should be implemented in a group where the discrete log problem is believed secure with a security parameter of $2n$. In any discrete log system of a prime field Z_q, a factor α increase in the security parameter implies a factor α^3 increase in the size of the modulus q. Therefore if forking lemma is used in the security reduction, the security parameter increase by a factor of 2. Thus the size of the modulus increases by a factor of 8.

Our Contribution: In this paper, we present an identity based key agreement protocol which can be proved secure under the Strong-Diffie Hellman (SDH) assumption without using forking lemma. Thus we are able to achieve a tight reduction to the Strong Diffie Hellman problem based on the random oracle model. This tight reduction feature enables a reduction in the communication overhead thus making it efficient when compared to existing schemes. Moreover, our scheme is resistant to a dynamic active adversary which is allowed to modify the components exchanged during the key agreement. The scheme performs a check which will detect any tampering done on the components. In this way, a fully authenticated key agreement protocol is achieved. The protocol also satisfies additional security properties like forward secrecy, resistance to reflection attacks and key compromise impersonation attacks. But this level of security can be achieved with a smaller group size since our security proof does not involve the use of forking lemma and a tight reduction to SDH is possible. Table 1.1 and Table 1.2 compares our scheme for key lengths with the existing schemes that use forking lemma for the proof. Let $||\mathbb{G}||$ denote the number of bits needed to represent a group element. We have to set $||\mathbb{G}|| = 224$ for elliptic curve groups and $||\mathbb{G}|| = 1024$ for multiplicative groups as per $http://www.keylength.com/en/4/$.

Table 1. Comparison Table - Efficiency

Scheme	No of Rounds	Tightness	Exp	Communication Cost-Elliptic Curve Group	Communication Cost Multiplicative Group
Gunther [7]	2	Not tight	4	$2*(8*||\mathbb{G}||)=$ $2*(8*224)=3584$	$2*(8*||\mathbb{G}||)=$ $2*(8*2048)=32768$
Saeednia [14]	1	Not tight	3	$1*(8*||\mathbb{G}||)=$ $1*(8*224)=1792$	$1*(8*||\mathbb{G}||)=$ $1*(8*2048)=16384$
Fiore [5]	1	Not tight	2	$1*(8*||\mathbb{G}||)=$ $1*(8*224)=1792$	$1*(8*||\mathbb{G}||)=$ $1*(8*2048)=16384$
Ours	1	Tight	4	$2*(||\mathbb{G}||)+1*(224)=$ $2*224+1*224=672$	$2*(||\mathbb{G}||)+1*(224)=$ $2*2048+1*224=4320$

Remark 1 : Table 1 depict the resistance to the specified attacks. $\sqrt{}$ represents resistance and $\times$ represents vulnerability.

Remark 2 : The communication overhead and exponentiations are calculated for a single user.

Remark 3 : The key length is chosen based on the standard definition in $http://www.keylength.com/en/4/$. It states that to ensure security till the year 2030, the size of the elliptic curve group modulus should be 224 bits and 2048 bits for multiplicative groups. The size of the hash value is to be 224 bits for both elliptic curve and multiplicative groups.

Remark 4 : Generally the ephemeral components like t_i, w_i and g^{t_i}, g^{w_i} used during the protocol execution (see Table 2) are chosen from a pre-computed list. Hence they are not considered in the number of exponentiations.

Remark 5 : In our scheme, the computations of u_{j2}, v_{j2} by user i and u_{i2}, v_{i2} by user j in Step 2 of Table 2 are specific to a pair of users. So these computations are done only once for a pair of users and do not involve any session specific parameters. Hence these exponentiations are not included in computing the complexity of the protocol.

Remark 6 : Exponentiations of the form $g_0{}^{e_0}.g_1{}^{e_1}...g_{k-1}{}^{e_{k-1}}$ can be counted as a single exponentiation as in [12].

Remark 7 : When realized in elliptic curve groups, the first three schemes [7], [14] and [5] in Table 1.1 involve the specified number of exponentiation operations with exponent and base in a group with modulus size $8 * 224 \approx 2^{11}$ bits. Our scheme involves exponentiation operations where the exponent is from a group with modulus of 224 bits and base is from an elliptic curve group with modulus size $= 224$ bits. The complexity of an exponentiation x^y is given by $O\left(log_2{}^2 x.log_2 y\right)$. So the cost of one exponentiation in [5], [7], [14] will be $2^{2*11+8} = 2^{30}$. Cost of exponentiation in our scheme will be $2^{2*8+8} = 2^{24}$.

Remark 8 : When realized in multiplicative groups, the first three schemes [7], [14] and [5] involve the specified number of exponentiation operations with exponent and base in a group with modulus size $8*2048=2^{14}$ bits. Our scheme involves exponentiation operations where the exponent is from a Schnorr group with modulus of 224 bits and base is from a group with modulus size $= 2048$ bits. The complexity of an exponentiation x^y is given by $O\left(log_2{}^2 x.log_2 y\right)$. So cost of one exponentiation in [5], [7], [14] will be $2^{2*14+14} = 2^{42}$. Cost of exponentiation in our scheme will be $2^{2*11+8} = 2^{30}$.

Table 2. Comparison with the existing schemes - Security

Scheme	Forward Secrecy	Reflection Attacks	KCI	Ephemeral KCI	Dynamic adversary
Gunther [7]	√	×	√	×	×
Saeednia [14]	√	√	√	×	×
Fiore [5]	√	√	√	×	×
Ours	√	√	√	√	√

The PKI-based MQV [10] protocol involves sending 2 group elements and 1.5 exponentiation operations to compute the shared secret key. But certificates need to be sent in this system. We do not consider RSA signatures for certificates because RSA uses composite modulus. If we take into account Schnorr signature for certification purpose, we will have 1 more group element and a Schnorr group element to be sent and the signing and verification process will involve 3 more exponentiation operations. But these exponentiations will have exponent in a Schnorr group which is realized on elliptic curves. Hence the total number of exponentiation operations will be 1.5 with exponent size 8*224 and 3 with exponent size 224. Moreover this scheme does not achieve tight reduction unlike our protocol. Thus our scheme is better than the PKI based scheme with certificates.

3 Identity Based Key Agreement

In this section, we will give the definition of an identity based key agreement protocol and the description of the security model.

3.1 Definition of Identity Based Key Agreement Protocol

In Identity Based Key Agreement protocol, each entity i is defined by a unique identity, ID_i. The PKG maintains master public key and master secret key and generates the private key S_i for each user. The protocol is defined as follows:

Setup: The PKG chooses the public parameters and the master secret key. The public parameters are open to all users and the master secret key is known only to the PKG.

Key Generation: The user i submits its identity ID_i to the PKG and the PKG constructs the private key S_i for the user with identity ID_i.

Key Agreement: In order to establish the shared secret key between two users A and B with identities ID_A and ID_B and secret keys S_A and S_B, the users engage in a session by exchanging components and eventually set up the shared secret key. Either user A or B could initiate the protocol.

3.2 Definition of the Security Model

The security of our identity based key agreement protocol is analyzed based on the Canetti-Krawczyk (CK) model for key agreement [2]. CK model does not cover forward secrecy, resistance to reflection and key compromise impersonation attacks. We provide these additional security features. Now we define certain terms associated with identity based key agreement and formally define the security model.

An instance of the protocol defined in Section 3.1 is called a *session*. The user or entity that initiates a session is called the *owner* and the other user is called the *peer*. The components exchanged between the owner and the peer constitute the *session state*. The shared secret key obtained is called the *session key*. On successful completion of a session, each entity outputs the *session key* and deletes the *session state*. Otherwise, the session is said to be in *abort* state and no *session key* is generated in this case. Each entity participating in a session assigns a unique identifier to that session. For example, A sets the unique identifier as (A, B, out, in) where B is its peer and *out* and *in* are respectively the components sent to B and received by A. If B holds a session (B, A, in, out), then both the sessions are said to be *matching sessions*. There are three types of adversary:

- Type I : The adversary of this type does not belong to the system and hence has access only to the PKG's parameters. It is not given access to the private keys of users and does not impersonate anyone. This is the weakest adversary.
- Type II : The adversary belongs to the identity based system and can query for the private keys of polynomial number of users. It is not allowed to impersonate as any user.
- Type III : The adversary of this type belongs to the identity based system and it is given access to the private keys of polynomial number of users. It can also impersonate as any other user. This is the strongest adversary and we prove our scheme secure against this type of adversary.

Since we prove our scheme secure against the Type III adversary, it is also secure against Type I and Type II because they are weaker adversaries compared to Type III. We allow the adversary to access some of the parties secret information, via the following attacks: party corruption, state-reveal queries and session-key queries. In party corruption phase, the adversary learns the private keys of the users. In a state-reveal query to a party running a session, the adversary learns the session state for that session. In shared secret key query phase, the adversary learns the shared secret key of a complete session. A session is called *exposed* if it or its *matching session* (if existing) is compromised by one of the attacks described above. The security model of the identity based key agreement is modeled as a following game between the challenger and the adversary:

Setup: The challenger sets up the public parameters and the master secret key. The public parameters are made known to the adversary whereas the master secret key is kept private with the challenger.

Party corruption: In this phase, the adversary can query the challenger for the private key of any user with identity ID_i. The challenger has to compute the private key S_i corresponding to ID_i and return the response to the adversary.

Session Simulation: In this phase, the adversary is allowed to ask the shared secret key queries. The adversary queries for a shared secret belonging to a session established between two users A and B. The adversary can also emulate as one of the users, either A or B and present the challenger with the session state corresponding to that user. The challenger has to generate the session state for the other user of the session and obtain the shared secret key corresponding to that session. The adversary can also query for the session secret key between the two parties A and B from the challenger, where the adversary does not impersonate any of the user. In this case the challenger has to generate the session state for both the users and obtain the shared secret key corresponding to that session and provide it to the adversary.

Test Session: The adversary chooses a test session among all the completed and unexposed sessions. The challenger will toss a random bit $b \in_R \{0, 1\}$. If

$b = 0$ the challenger will give the adversary the session key K_0 of the test session. Otherwise the challenger will take a random shared secret key K_1 and provide the adversary with K_1.

Guess: The adversary makes a guess δ as to which key K_0 or K_1 was given by the challenger. The adversary wins if $\delta = b$.

The identity based key agreement protocol is said to be secure if no polynomial-time adversary has non-negligible advantage in winning the above game, i.e., distinguishing K_0 from K_1.

Note: The Send query present in [9] is not required here since our protocol is single round and it is a 2-party protocol. The adversary has access to the components exchanged and can modify them as per its wish.

4 Preliminaries

In this section, we present a brief overview of the hard problem assumptions.

Definition 1. *Computation Diffie-Hellman Problem (CDHP)* - *Given $(g, g^a, g^b) \in \mathbb{G}^3$ for unknown $a, b \in \mathbb{Z}_q^*$, where $\mathbb{G}$ is a cyclic prime order multiplicative group with g as a generator and q the order of the group, the CDH problem in $\mathbb{G}$ is to compute g^{ab}.*

The advantage of any probabilistic polynomial time algorithm $\mathcal{A}$ in solving the CDH problem in $\mathbb{G}$ is defined as

$$Adv_{\mathcal{A}}^{CDH} = Pr\left[\mathcal{A}(g, g^a, g^b) = g^{ab} \mid a, b \in \mathbb{Z}_q^*\right]$$

The CDH Assumption is that, for any probabilistic polynomial time algorithm $\mathcal{A}$, the advantage $Adv_{\mathcal{A}}^{CDH}$ is negligibly small.

Definition 2. *Decisional Diffie-Hellman Problem (DDHP)* - *Given $(g, g^a, g^b, h) \in \mathbb{G}^4$ for unknown $a, b \in \mathbb{Z}_q^*$, where $\mathbb{G}$ is a cyclic prime order multiplicative group with g as a generator and q the order of the group, the DDH problem in $\mathbb{G}$ is to check whether $h \stackrel{?}{=} g^{ab}$.*

The advantage of any probabilistic polynomial time algorithm $\mathcal{A}$ in solving the DDH problem in $\mathbb{G}$ is defined as

$$Adv_{\mathcal{A}}^{DDH} = |Pr\left[\mathcal{A}(g, g^a, g^b, g^{ab}) = 1\right] - Pr\left[\mathcal{A}(g, g^a, g^b, h) = 1\right]| \mid a, b \in \mathbb{Z}_q^*$$

The CDH Assumption is that, for any probabilistic polynomial time algorithm $\mathcal{A}$, the advantage $Adv_{\mathcal{A}}^{CDH}$ is negligibly small.

**Definition 3. *(Strong Diffie Hellman Problem (SDHP) [1]):* *Let κ be the security parameter and $\mathbb{G}$ be a multiplicative group of order q, where $|q| = \kappa$. Given $(g, g^a, g^b) \in_R \mathbb{G}^3$ and access to a Decision Diffie Hellman (DDH) oracle $\mathcal{DDH}_{g,a}(.,.)$ which on input g^b and g^c outputs True if and only if $g^{ab} = g^c$, the strong Diffie Hellman problem is to compute $g^{ab} \in \mathbb{G}$.*

The advantage of an adversary $\mathcal{A}$ in solving the strong Diffie Hellman problem is defined as the probability with which $\mathcal{A}$ solves the above strong Diffie Hellman problem.

$$Adv_{\mathcal{A}}^{SDHP} = Pr[\mathcal{A}(g, g^a, g^b) = g^{ab} | \mathcal{DDH}_{g,a}(.,.)]$$

The strong Diffie Hellman assumption holds in $\mathbb{G}$ if for all polynomial time adversaries $\mathcal{A}$, the advantage $Adv_{\mathcal{A}}^{SDHP}$ is negligible.

Note: In pairing groups (also known as gap groups), the DDH oracle can be efficiently instantiated and hence the strong Diffie Hellman problem is equivalent to the Gap Diffie Hellman problem [13].

5   The Proposed Identity Based Key Agreement Protocol

We now give the description of the identity based key agreement protocol and formally prove its security in the next section.

Setup: The PKG chooses a group $\mathbb{G}$ of prime order q. Let g be the generator of group $\mathbb{G}$. The PKG picks $s_1, s_2 \in_R Z_p^*$, where p divides $q - 1$, sets $y_1 = g^{s_1}$ and $y_2 = g^{s_2}$. The master secret key is $\langle s_1, s_2 \rangle$ and the master public key is $\langle y_1, y_2 \rangle$. It also defines the following hash functions: $H_1 : \{0,1\}^* \to \mathbb{G}$, $H_2 : \{0,1\}^* \times \mathbb{G} \to Z_p^*$, $H_3 : \{0,1\}^* \times \mathbb{G} \times \mathbb{G} \times \mathbb{G} \times \mathbb{G} \to Z_p^*$, $H_4 : \{0,1\}^* \times \mathbb{G} \times \mathbb{G} \times \mathbb{G} \times \mathbb{G} \to Z_p^*$, $H_5 : \mathbb{G} \times \mathbb{G} \to Z_p^*$ and $H_6 : \mathbb{G} \times \mathbb{G} \times \mathbb{G} \to Z_p^*$. The PKG makes *params* public and keeps *msk* to itself, where *params* and *msk* are defined as follows:

$$params = \langle \mathbb{G}, g, q, p, y_1, y_2, H_1, H_2, H_3, H_4, H_5, H_6 \rangle \text{ and } msk = \langle s_1, s_2 \rangle.$$

Key Extract: An user i with identity ID_i submits its identity to the PKG. The PKG does the following to generate the private key of the user i.

– The PKG chooses $x_i \in_R Z_p^*$.
– It computes $u_{i1} = g^{x_i}$ and sets $h_i = H_1(ID_i)$.
– It computes $v_{i1} = h_i^{x_i}$.
– It chooses $r_i \in_R Z_p^*$, computes $u_{i2} = g^{r_i}$ and $v_{i2} = h_i^{r_i}$.
– It sets $c_i = H_2(ID_i, u_{i1})$, $b_i = H_3(ID_i, u_{i1}, v_{i1}, u_{i2}, v_{i2})$ and $e_i = H_4(ID_i, u_{i1}, v_{i1}, u_{i2}, v_{i2})$.
– It computes $d_{i1} = x_i + s_1 c_i$ where s_1 is the master secret key. It also calculates $d_{i2} = x_i + r_i b_i + s_2 e_i$.
– Finally it sends $\langle u_{i1}, v_{i1}, u_{i2}, v_{i2}, d_{i1}, d_{i2}, h_i^{s_2} \rangle$ to the user i.

The user after receiving the private key components from the PKG performs the checks described in the appendix (Key Sanity Check) to ensure the correctness of the components.

Key Agreement: The two users i and j with identities ID_i and ID_j get their respective private keys from the PKG and choose ephemeral secret components $t_i, w_i \in_R Z_p^*$ and $t_j, w_j \in_R Z_p^*$ respectively and engage in a session as described in Table 2.

Table 3. Description of the Key Agreement protocol

User i	User j
1. Send $F_i = \langle u_{i1}, v_{i1}, d_{i2}, b_i, e_i, h_i{}^{s2}, ID_i \rangle$, $V_i = \langle w_i + d_{i1}.H_5\left(g^{t_i}, g^{w_i}\right), g^{t_i}, g^{w_i} \rangle$ to j.	1. Send $F_j = \langle u_{j1}, v_{j1}, d_{j2}, b_j, e_j, h_j{}^{s2}, ID_j \rangle$, $V_j = \langle w_j + d_{j1}.H_5\left(g^{t_j}, g^{w_j}\right), g^{t_j}, g^{w_j} \rangle$ to i.
2. (a) ***Check for correctness of F_j:*** Compute $u_{j2} = \left(\frac{g^{d_{j2}}}{u_{j1}.y_2{}^{e_j}}\right)^{b_j{}^{-1}}$ Compute $v_{j2} = \left(\frac{h_j{}^{d_{j2}}}{v_{j1}.\left(h_j{}^{s2}\right)^{e_j}}\right)^{b_j{}^{-1}}$ ***Check 1 :*** Check if $b_j \overset{?}{=} H_3(ID_j, u_{j1}, v_{j1}, u_{j2}, v_{j2})$ $e_j \overset{?}{=} H_4(ID_j, u_{j1}, v_{j1}, u_{j2}, v_{j2})$ If not equal abort, else proceed. (b) ***Check for correctness of V_j:*** ***Check 2 :*** Check if $\left[\frac{g^{\left(w_j + d_{j1}.H_5\left(g^{t_j}, g^{w_j}\right)\right)}}{\left(g^{x_j}\right)^{H_5\left(g^{t_j}, g^{w_j}\right)}\left(y_1\right)^{c_j.H_5\left(g^{t_j}, g^{w_j}\right)}}\right] \overset{?}{=} g^{w_j}$ where $c_j = H_2\left(ID_j, u_{j1}\right)$. If equal proceed to step 3, else abort.	2. (a) ***Check for correctness of F_i:*** Compute $u_{i2} = \left(\frac{g^{d_{i2}}}{u_{i1}.y_2{}^{e_i}}\right)^{b_i{}^{-1}}$ Compute $v_{i2} = \left(\frac{h_i{}^{d_{i2}}}{v_{i1}.\left(h_i{}^{s2}\right)^{e_i}}\right)^{b_i{}^{-1}}$ ***Check 1 :*** Check if $b_i \overset{?}{=} H_3\left(ID_i, u_{i1}, v_{i1}, u_{i2}, v_{i2}\right)$ $e_i \overset{?}{=} H_4\left(ID_i, u_{i1}, v_{i1}, u_{i2}, v_{i2}\right)$ If not equal abort, else proceed. (b) ***Check for correctness of V_i:*** ***Check 2 :*** Check if $\left[\frac{g^{\left(w_i + d_{i1}.H_5\left(g^{t_i}, g^{w_i}\right)\right)}}{\left(g^{x_i}\right)^{H_5\left(g^{t_i}, g^{w_i}\right)}\left(y_1\right)^{c_i.H_5\left(g^{t_i}, g^{w_i}\right)}}\right] \overset{?}{=} g^{w_i}$ where $c_i = H_2\left(ID_i, u_{i1}\right)$. If equal proceed to step 3, else abort.
3. ***Shared secret key generation:*** Compute $Z_1 = \left(u_{j1}y_1{}^{c_j}g^{t_j}\right)^{d_{i1}+t_i}$ $Z_2 = v_{i1}v_{j1}$ $Z_3 = \left(g^{t_j}\right)^{t_i}$. $Z = H_6\left(Z_1, Z_2, Z_3\right)$.	3. ***Shared secret key generation:*** Compute $Z_1 = \left(u_{i1}y_1{}^{c_i}g^{t_i}\right)^{d_{j1}+t_j}$ $Z_2 = v_{j1}v_{i1}$ $Z_3 = \left(g^{t_i}\right)^{t_j}$. $Z = H_6\left(Z_1, Z_2, Z_3\right)$.

Z is the shared secret key that is established between User i and User j.

Remark 9 : The protocol is asynchronous and consists of only one send per user per session. Hence the data transfer can occur in any order.

Remark 10 : The values in F_i are same for all sessions between a pair of users and is independent of the session.

Remark 11 : The values in V_i are freshly generated for every session in the following manner. In a preprocessing or a setup stage, the user i generates a large number of (β, g^β) pairs and stores them in a table T_i. For each session, user i extracts two fresh pairs from the table T_i and uses them to generate components of V_i. For security reasons, we assume that

(a) immediately after generating the components of V_i, w_i is erased from the system.

(b) $w_i + d_{i1}.H_5\left(g^{t_i}, g^{w_i}\right)$ is computed in a secured way so that w_i and d_{i1} are not leaked to the adversary and only $w_i + d_{i1}.H_5\left(g^{t_i}, g^{w_i}\right)$ is available to the adversary.

Remark 12 : The components in F_i, V_i and F_j, V_j is required to be sent only for the first time key establishment between users i and j. For subsequent key establishments between i and j, only V_i and V_j need to be exchanged. So we have considered only the components of V_i in communication overhead in Table 1.1. The exponentiations done in Check for correctness of components of F_i is one time and hence it is not included in computation cost. We include only the exponentiations in check for correctness of components in V_i and shared secret key generation in Table 1.1. We have to discuss the size of F_i and V_i in the cases of multiplicative groups and elliptic curve groups. The sizes in multiplicative group of order p which has a subgroup of order q, $|p|$ denoting the number of bits in p, $|q|$ referring to the number of bits in q and $|ID_i|$ denoting the length of the identity of user i are $F_i = 3.|q| + 3.|p| + |ID_i|$ and $V_i = 1.|q| + 2.|p|$. In the case of elliptic curve of order p, the sizes are $F_i = 6.|p| + |ID_i|$ and $V_i = 3.|p|$

Remark 13 : The intuition behind using the component Z_3 is to eliminate $g^{t_i.t_j}$ from Z_1 in the security proof to obtain the solution to the hard problem.

Remark 14 : *Check 1* is done to ensure that g and h_i are raised to the same exponent x_i. This is a crucial security requirement.

For valid components this check holds good. We prove it here.

$$\left(\frac{g^{d_{i2}}}{u_{i1}.y_2^{e_i}}\right)^{b_i^{-1}} = \left(\frac{g^{x_i+r_i.b_i+s_2.e_i}}{g^{x_i}.g^{s_2.e_i}}\right)^{b_i^{-1}} = \left(g^{r_i.b_i}\right)^{b_i^{-1}} = g^{r_i} = u_{i2}.$$

$$\left(\frac{h_i^{d_{i2}}}{v_{i1}.(h_i^{s_2})^{e_i}}\right)^{b_i^{-1}} = \left(\frac{h_i^{x_i+r_i.b_i+s_2.e_i}}{h_i^{x_i}.(h_i^{s_2})^{e_i}}\right)^{b_i^{-1}} = \left(h_i^{r_i.b_i}\right)^{b_i^{-1}} = h_i^{r_i} = v_{i2}.$$

The components that are recomputed are valid and hence the computation of $b_i = H_3(ID_i, u_{i1}, v_{i1}, u_{i2}, v_{i2})$ will match the one obtained if not for any tampering during transfer.

Remark 15 : *Check 2* is done to ensure that a dynamic adversary cannot tamper the components exchanged and affect the shared secret key generation. It verifies the signature $w_i + d_{i1}.H_5(g^{t_i}, g^{w_i})$ on g^{t_i}.

$$\frac{g^{\left(w_i+d_{i1}.H_5\left(g^{t_i},g^{w_i}\right)\right)}}{(g^{x_i})^{H_5\left(g^{t_i},g^{w_i}\right)}.(y_1)^{c_i.H_5\left(g^{t_i},g^{w_i}\right)}} = \frac{g^{\left(w_i+(x_i+s_1.c_i).H_5\left(g^{t_i},g^{w_i}\right)\right)}}{(g^{x_i})^{H_5\left(g^{t_i},g^{w_i}\right)}.(g)^{s_1.c_i.H_5\left(g^{t_i},g^{w_i}\right)}} = g^{w_i}$$

Lemma 1: The shared secret key computed by both the parties are identical.

Proof: User i computes :
$Z_1 = (u_{j1}y_1^{c_j}g^{t_j})^{d_{i1}+t_i} = \left(g^{(x_j+s_1c_j+t_j)}\right)^{(d_{i1}+t_i)} = g^{(d_{j1}+t_j)(d_{i1}+t_i)}$, since $u_{j1} = g^{x_j}$ and $x_j + s_1c_j = d_{j1}$.
User j computes:
$Z_1 = (u_{i1}y_1^{c_i}g^{t_i})^{d_{j1}+t_j} = \left(g^{(x_i+s_1c_i+t_i)}\right)^{(d_{j1}+t_j)} = g^{(d_{i1}+t_i)(d_{j1}+t_j)}$, since $u_{i1} = g^{x_i}$ and $x_i + s_1c_i = d_{i1}$.

Thus Z_1 computed by both the parties are identical. Z_2 and Z_3 are also consistent. Thus the final shared secret key computed by both the parties are consistent. □

6   Security Proof

In this section, we give the security proof of the scheme presented in the previous section. The proof is modeled based on the CK-model. The scheme is proved secure in the random oracle model. The scheme is reduced to the Strong Diffie-Hellman (SDH) problem. Since the proof technique eliminates the use of forking lemma, we are able to achieve a tight reduction to the underlying hard problem. The security proof is modeled as a game between the challenger and the adversary.

Setup: The challenger is given the SDH problem instance $\langle \mathbb{G}, g, q, p, C = g^a, D = g^b \rangle$ and access to the Diffie Hellman Oracle $DH(y_1, ., .)$. The challenger sets the master public key $y_1 = C$ and hence the master secret key s_1 is implicitly set as a. The challenger chooses $s_2 \in_R Z_p^*$ and sets $y_2 = g^{s_2}$. The challenger gives the tuple $\langle \mathbb{G}, g, q, p, y_1, y_2 \rangle$ to the adversary. The challenger simulates the hash oracles in the following way:

$H_1 Oracle$: The challenger is queried by the adversary for the hash value of the identity ID_i. If the H_1 $Oracle$ was already queried with ID_i as input, the challenger returns the value computed before which is stored in the hash list L_{h1} described below. Otherwise the challenger tosses a *coin* τ_i where the $Pr(\tau_i = 0) = \alpha$. The output of this oracle is defined as:

$$h_i = \begin{cases} g^{k_i}, & if\ \tau_i = 0 \\ (g^b)^{k_i}, & if\ \tau_i = 1 \end{cases}$$

where $k_i \in_R Z_p^*$. The challenger makes an entry in the hash list $L_{h1} = \langle h_i, ID_i, \tau_i, k_i \rangle$ for future use and returns h_i.

H_2 $Oracle$: The adversary queries the challenger with inputs (ID_i, u_{i1}). If the H_2 $Oracle$ was already queried with (ID_i, u_{i1}) as input, the challenger extracts the value c_i from the hash list L_{h2} described below and returns the value. Otherwise, the challenger chooses a random value $c_i \in_R Z_p^*$. It makes an entry in the hash list $L_{h2} = \langle c_i, u_{i1}, ID_i \rangle$ and returns c_i.

H_3 $Oracle$: The adversary queries the challenger with inputs $(ID_i, u_{i1}, v_{i1}, u_{i2}, v_{i2})$. If the H_3 $Oracle$ was already queried with $(ID_i, u_{i1}, v_{i1}, u_{i2}, v_{i2})$ as input, the challenger extracts the value b_i from the hash list L_{h3} described below and returns the value. Otherwise, the challenger chooses a random value $b_i \in_R Z_p^*$. It makes an entry in the hash list $L_{h3} = \langle b_i, ID_i, u_{i1}, v_{i1}, u_{i2}, v_{i2} \rangle$ and returns b_i.

H_4 $Oracle$: The adversary queries the challenger with inputs $(ID_i, u_{i1}, v_{i1}, u_{i2}, v_{i2})$. If the H_4 $Oracle$ was already queried with $(ID_i, u_{i1}, v_{i1}, u_{i2}, v_{i2})$ as input, the challenger extracts the value e_i from the hash list L_{h4} described below and returns the value. Otherwise, the challenger chooses a random value $e_i \in_R Z_p^*$. It makes an entry in the hash list $L_{h4} = \langle e_i, ID_i, u_{i1}, v_{i1}, u_{i2}, v_{i2} \rangle$ and returns e_i.

H_5 $Oracle$: The adversary queries the challenger with inputs (g^{t_i}, g^{w_i}). If the H_5 $Oracle$ was already queried with (g^{t_i}, g^{w_i}) as input, the challenger extracts the value f_i from the hash list L_{h5} described below and returns the value. Otherwise, the challenger chooses a random value $f_i \in_R Z_p^*$. It makes an entry in the hash list $L_{h5} = \langle f_i, g^{t_i}, g^{w_i} \rangle$ and returns f_i.

H_6 *Oracle* : The adversary queries the challenger with inputs (Z_1, Z_2, Z_3). If the H_4 *Oracle* was already queried with (Z_1, Z_2, Z_3) as input, the challenger extracts the value l_i from the hash list L_{h6} described below and returns the value. Otherwise, the challenger chooses a random value $l_i \in_R Z_p{}^*$. It makes an entry in the hash list $L_{h6} = \langle l_i, Z_1, Z_2, Z_3 \rangle$ and returns l_i.

Party corruption: The adversary presents the challenger with an identity ID_i and the challenger should return the private key of that entity. The challenger proceeds in the following way:

The challenger checks if the H_1 *Oracle* was already queried for ID_i. If yes and the corresponding $\tau_i = 1$, it *aborts*. Otherwise it extracts k_i, h_i from the list L_{h1} and proceeds to the next step. If ID_i was not queried before, the challenger runs the H_1 *Oracle* with ID_i as input. If $\tau_i = 1$, it *aborts*. Else the challenger chooses $k_i \in_R Z_p^*$, computes $h_i = g^{k_i}$, adds the tuple $\langle h_i, ID_i, \tau_i, k_i \rangle$ to the L_{h1} list.

The challenger does not know the master secret key s_1 as master public key $y_1 = g^a$ setting $s_1 = a$. Therefore in order to generate the private key of users, the challenger makes use of the random oracles and generates the private key as described below:

- The challenger chooses $c_i, b_i, e_i, x_i', r_i' \in_R Z_p{}^*$.
- It sets $u_{i1} = g^{x_i'}.y_1^{-c_i}$.
- It sets $H_2(ID_i, u_{i1}) = c_i$ and adds the tuple $\langle c_i, u_{i1}, ID_i \rangle$ the L_{h2} list.
- It sets $d_{i1} = x_i'$, $d_{i2} = x_i' + r_i'b_i + s_2e_i$ and $u_{i2} = g^{r_i'}.y_1^{c_i.b_i^{-1}}$.
- It computes $v_{i1} = g^{k_i.x_i'}.y_1^{-k_i.c_i}$ and $v_{i2} = g^{k_i.r_i'}.y_1^{k_i.c_i.b_i^{-1}}$.
- It also sets $H_3(ID_i, u_{i1}, v_{i1}, u_{i2}, v_{i2}) = b_i$, $H_4(ID_i, u_{i1}, v_{i1}, u_{i2}, v_{i2}) = e_i$ and adds the tuples $\langle b_i, ID_i, u_{i1}, v_{i1}, u_{i2}, v_{i2} \rangle$, $\langle e_i, ID_i, u_{i1}, v_{i1}, u_{i2}, v_{i2} \rangle$ to the lists L_{h3} and L_{h4} respectively.
- It computes $h_i{}^{s_2}$.
- It returns the tuple $\langle u_{i1}, v_{i1}, u_{i2}, v_{i2}, d_{i1}, d_{i2}, h_i{}^{s_2} \rangle$ as the private key of the user with identity ID_i and makes an entry in the list $L_E = \langle u_{i1}, v_{i1}, u_{i2}, v_{i2}, d_{i1}, d_{i2}, ID_i \rangle$.

Lemma 2: The private key returned by the challenger during the party corruption query are consistent with the system.

Proof: We now prove that the components returned by the challenger are consistent with that of the system. The components returned by the challenger should satisfy the 3 checks given in Key Sanity Check.

- ***Test 1*** : Check if $\dfrac{g^{d_{i1}}}{y_1^{H_2(ID_i, u_{i1})}} \overset{?}{=} u_{i1}$.

This can be verified as $\dfrac{g^{x_i'}}{g^{a.H_2(ID_i, u_{i1})}}$ where $c_i = H_2(ID_i, u_{i1})$. This is equal to $g^{x_i' - a.c_i} = g^{x_i'}.y_1^{-c_i} = u_{i1}$.

- **Test 2 :** Check if $\dfrac{g^{d_{i2}}}{u_{i2}{}^{H_3\left(ID_i,u_{i1},v_{i1},u_{i2},v_{i2}\right)}.y_2{}^{H_4\left(ID_i,u_{i1},v_{i1},u_{i2},v_{i2}\right)}} \stackrel{?}{=} u_{i1}$.

This can be verified as $\dfrac{g^{x'_i+r'_i b_i+s_2 e_i}}{\left(g^{r'_i}.y_1{}^{c_i.b_i}{}^{-1}\right)^{b_i}.g^{s_2.e_i}} = g^{x'_i-a.c_i} = g^{x'_i}.y_1{}^{-c_i} = u_{i1}$, as

$b_i = H_3\left(ID_i, u_{i1}, v_{i1}, u_{i2}, v_{i2}\right)$ and $e_i = H_4\left(ID_i, u_{i1}, v_{i1}, u_{i2}, v_{i2}\right)$.

- **Test 3 :** Check if $\dfrac{h_i^{d_{i2}}}{v_{i2}{}^{H_3\left(ID_i,u_{i1},v_{i1},u_{i2},v_{i2}\right)}.(h_i{}^{s_2})^{H_4\left(ID_i,u_{i1},v_{i1},u_{i2},v_{i2}\right)}} \stackrel{?}{=} v_{i1}$.

This can be verified as $\dfrac{h_i^{x'_i+r'_i.b_i+s_2.e_i}}{\left(g^{k_i.r'_i}.y_1{}^{k_i.c_i.b_i}{}^{-1}\right)^{b_i}.(h_i{}^{s_2})^{e_i}} = h_i{}^{x'_i}.y_1{}^{-k_i.c_i} = v_{i1}$

where $b_i = H_3\left(ID_i, u_{i1}, v_{i1}, u_{i2}, v_{i2}\right)$ and $e_i = H_4\left(ID_i, u_{i1}, v_{i1}, u_{i2}, v_{i2}\right)$.

Thus the components generated by the challenger are consistent with the system as the tests 1,2 and 3 are satisfied. $\qquad\square$

Session Simulation: The adversary requires the challenger to simulate shared secret keys. The challenger simulates session other than the test session. Here we mention the party which initiates the session as *owner* of the session and the other party who responds to the request of the owner as *peer*. We have to consider the following cases during the session simulation phase.

Case 1: In this case, the adversary has executed the *party corruption* query with respect to i. Hence the adversary knows the secret key of i. The adversary treats i as owner and generates the tuple $\langle u_{i1}, v_{i1}, d_{i2}, b_i, e_i, h_i{}^{s_2}, g^{t_i}, w_i + d_{i1}.H_5\left(g^{t_i}, g^{w_i}\right), g^{w_i}, ID_i\rangle$ and passes it to the challenger and asks the challenger to complete the session with j as the peer.

Case 1a: If $\tau_j = 0$, the challenger knows the secret key corresponding to j and hence executes the actual protocol and delivers the session key to the adversary.

Case 1b: If $\tau_j = 1$, the challenger does not know the secret key corresponding to j and hence simulates the session key as follows:

1. The challenger first performs the check presented in the Step 2 of the Key Agreement protocol, on $\langle u_{i1}, v_{i1}, d_{i2}, b_i, e_i, h_i{}^{s_2}, g^{t_i}, w_i + d_{i1}.H_5\left(g^{t_i}, g^{w_i}\right), g^{w_i}, ID_i\rangle$.

2. The challenger generates the parameters $\langle u_{j1} = g^{x_j}, v_{j1} = h_j{}^{x_j}, d_{j2} = x_j + r_j.b_j + s_2.e_j, b_j, e_j, h_j{}^{s_2}, g^{t_j}, w'_j + x_j.f_j, g^{w'_j}.y_1{}^{-c_j.f_j}, ID_j\rangle$, where $r_j, x_j, t_j, w'_j, f_j \in_R Z_p{}^*$, $h_j = H_1\left(ID_j\right)$, $b_j = H_3\left(ID_j, u_{j1}, v_{j1}, g^{r_j}, h_j{}^{r_j}\right)$ and $e_j = H_4\left(ID_j, u_{j1}, v_{j1}, g^{r_j}, h_j{}^{r_j}\right)$.

3. If H_5 was already queried with inputs $\left(g^{t_j}, g^{w'_j}.y_1{}^{-c_j.f_j}\right)$, generate a fresh w'_j and recompute the last but two components. With very high probability, the new $\left(g^{t_j}, g^{w'_j}.y_1{}^{-c_j.f_j}\right)$ will not result in a previously queried input set to H_5. Set $H_5\left(g^{t_j}, g^{w'_j}.y_1{}^{-c_j.f_j}\right)$ as f_j.

4. The parameters generated by the challenger, $\langle u_{j1}, v_{j1}, d_{j2}, b_j, e_j, h_j{}^{s_2}\rangle$ will satisfy **Check 1** in Step 2 of Key Agreement. This is because the parameters $\langle u_{j1}, v_{j1}, d_{j2}, b_j, e_j, h_j{}^{s_2}\rangle$ are generated in the same way as the original scheme.

5. The parameters $\langle u_{j1}, v_{j1}, d_{j2}, b_j, e_j, h_j{}^{s_2} \rangle$ also satisfy **Check 2** in the Step 2 of Key Agreement of Section 5.

$$\frac{g^{w'_j + x_j \cdot f_j}}{(g^{x_j})^{H_5\left(g^{t_j}, g^{w'_j} \cdot y_1^{-c_j \cdot f_j}\right)} \cdot (y_1)^{c_j \cdot H_5\left(g^{t_j}, g^{w'_j} \cdot y_1^{-c_j \cdot f_j}\right)}} = g^{w'_j} \cdot y_1^{-c_j \cdot f_j} = g^{w_j}.$$

6. Thus the parameters generated by the challenger, $\langle u_{j1}, v_{j1}, d_{j2}, b_j, e_j, h_j{}^{s_2} \rangle$ are consistent with that of the system.

7. The challenger sends the parameters to the adversary.

8. The challenger computes $\bar{Z}_1 = (g^{x_i} . y_1{}^{c_i} . g^{t_i})^{x_j + t_j}$ where $c_i = H_2(ID_i, u_{i1})$. It also computes $P_1 = (u_{i1} . y_1{}^{c_i} . g^{t_i})^{c_j}$ and $P_2 = y_1$ where $c_j = H_2(ID_j, u_{j1})$.

9. The challenger computes $Z_2 = v_{i1} . v_{j1}$ and $Z_3 = (g^{t_i})^{t_j}$.

10. The challenger is given access to the $DH(y_1, ., .)$ oracle, since we assume the hardness of Strong-Diffie Hellman problem. The challenger makes use of the $DH(y_1, ., .)$ Oracle to answer the query as follows:
    - The challenger finds a Z such that $DH\left(P_2, P_1, Z_1/\bar{Z}_1\right)$ (valid since $P_2 = y_1$) and $H_6(Z_1, Z_2, Z_3) = Z$, where $Z_2 = v_{i1} . v_{j1}$ and $Z_3 = (g^{t_i})^{t_j}$.
    - If a Z exists, the challenger returns Z as the shared secret key.
    - Otherwise the challenger chooses $Z \in_R Z_p{}^*$ and for any further query of the form (Z_1, Z_2, Z_3) to the H_6 Oracle, if $DH\left(P_2, P_1, Z_1/\bar{Z}_1\right)$, $Z_2 = v_{i1} . v_{j1}$ and $Z_3 = (g^{t_i})^{t_j}$, the challenger returns Z as the result to the query.

Finally the challenger returns Z as the shared secret key.

Case 2: The adversary does not know the secret key of i, the owner of the session. Here the adversary simply asks the challenger to generate a session with i as owner and j as peer.

Case 2a: The case where $\tau_i = 0$ and $\tau_j = 0$. In this case, the challenger can simulate the computations done by both the parties since the challenger knows the private key of both the owner i and the peer j.

Case 2b: The case where either $\tau_i = 1$ or $\tau_j = 1$. Without loss of generality let us consider that $\tau_i = 0$ and $\tau_j = 1$. Here the challenger knows the secret key of i but does not know the secret key of j. Hence for i the challenger will generate the session secret key as per the algorithm. For j the challenger has to simulate as follows:

1. The challenger generates the values $\langle u_{j1} = g^{x_j}, v_{j1} = h_j{}^{x_j}, d_{j2} = x_j + r_j . b_j + s_2 . e_j, b_j, e_j, h_j{}^{s_2}, g^{t_j}, w'_j + x_j . f_j, g^{w'_j} . y_1^{-c_j . f_j}, ID_j \rangle$, where $r_j, x_j, t_j, w'_j, f_j \in_R Z_p{}^*$, $h_j = H_1(ID_j)$, $b_j = H_3(ID_j, u_{j1}, v_{j1}, g^{r_j}, h_j{}^{r_j})$ and $e_j = H_4(ID_j, u_{j1}, v_{j1}, g^{r_j}, h_j{}^{r_j})$ for user j.

2. The challenger also generates the values $\langle u_{i1} = g^{x_i}, v_{i1} = h_i{}^{x_i}, d_{i2} = x_i + r_i . b_i + s_2 . e_i, b_i, e_i, h_i{}^{s_2}, g^{t_i}, w'_i + x_i . f_i, g^{w'_i} . y_1^{-c_i . f_i}, ID_i \rangle$ with i's private key for user i.

3. If H_5 was already queried with inputs $\left(g^{t_j}, g^{w'_j} . y_1^{-c_j . f_j}\right)$, generate a fresh w'_j and recompute the last but two components. With very high probability,

the new $\left(g^{t_j}, g^{w'_j}.y_1^{-c_j.f_j}\right)$ will not result in a previously queried input set to H_5. Set $H_5\left(g^{t_j}, g^{w'_j}.y_1^{-c_j.f_j}\right)$ as f_j.

4. Similarly if H_5 was already queried with inputs $\left(g^{t_i}, g^{w'_i}.y_1^{-c_i.f_i}\right)$, generate a fresh w'_i and recompute the last but two components. With very high probability, the new $\left(g^{t_i}, g^{w'_i}.y_1^{-c_i.f_i}\right)$ will not result in a previously queried input set to H_5. Set $H_5\left(g^{t_i}, g^{w'_i}.y_1^{-c_i.f_i}\right)$ as f_i.

5. The challenger computes $\bar{Z}_1 = (g^{x_i}.y_1^{c_i}.g^{t_i})^{x_j+t_j}$ where $c_i = H_2\,(ID_i, u_{i1})$. It also computes $P_1 = (u_{i1}.y_1^{c_i}.g^{t_i})^{c_j}$ and $P_2 = y_1$ where $c_j = H_2\,(ID_j, u_{j1})$.

6. The challenger computes $Z_2 = v_{i1}.v_{j1}$ and $Z_3 = (g^{t_i})^{t_j}$.

7. The challenger is given access to the $DH\,(y_1, ., .)$ oracle, since we assume the hardness of Strong-Diffie Hellman problem. The challenger makes use of the $DH\,(y_1, ., .)$ Oracle to answer the query as follows:

   - The challenger finds a Z such that $DH\left(P_2, P_1, Z_1/\bar{Z}_1\right)$ (valid since $P_2 = y_1$) and $H_6(Z_1, Z_2, Z_3) = Z$, where $Z_2 = v_{i1}.v_{j1}$ and $Z_3 = (g^{t_i})^{t_j}$.
   - If a Z exists, the challenger returns Z as the shared secret key.
   - Otherwise the challenger chooses $Z \in_R Z_p^*$ and for any further query of the form (Z_1, Z_2, Z_3) to the H_6 Oracle, if $DH\left(P_2, P_1, Z_1/\bar{Z}_1\right)$, $Z_2 = v_{i1}.v_{j1}$ and $Z_3 = (g^{t_i})^{t_j}$.

Finally the challenger returns Z as the shared secret key.

Case 2c: The case where $\tau_i = 1$ and $\tau_j = 1$. In this case the challenger does not know the secret key of both i and j. Hence the challenger has to simulate the session values for both i and j, which is done as follows:

1. The challenger generates the values $\langle u_{j1} = g^{x_j}, v_{j1} = h_j^{x_j}, d_{j2} = x_j + r_j.b_j + s_2.e_j, b_j, e_j, h_j^{s_2}, g^{t_j}, w'_j + x_j.f_j, g^{w'_j}.y_1^{-c_j.f_j}, ID_j\rangle$, where $r_j, x_j, t_j, w'_j, f_j \in_R Z_p^*$, $h_j = H_1\,(ID_j)$, $b_j = H_3\,(ID_j, u_{j1}, v_{j1}, g^{r_j}, h_j^{r_j})$ and $e_j = H_4(ID_j, u_{j1}, v_{j1}, g^{r_j}, h_j^{r_j})$ for user j.

2. The challenger also generates the values $\langle u_{i1} = g^{x_i}, v_{i1} = h_i^{x_i}, d_{i2} = x_i + r_i.b_i + s_2.e_i, b_i, e_i, h_i^{s_2}, g^{t_i}, w'_i + x_i.f_i, g^{w'_i}.y_1^{-c_i.f_i}, ID_i\rangle$, where $r_i, x_i, t_i, w'_i, f_i \in_R Z_p^*$, $h_i = H_1\,(ID_i)$, $b_i = H_3\,(ID_i, u_{i1}, v_{i1}, g^{r_i}, h_i^{r_i})$ and $e_i = H_4(ID_i, u_{i1}, v_{i1}, g^{r_i}, h_i^{r_i})$ for user i.

3. If H_5 was already queried with inputs $\left(g^{t_j}, g^{w'_j}.y_1^{-c_j.f_j}\right)$, generate a fresh w'_j and recompute the last but two components. With very high probability, the new $\left(g^{t_j}, g^{w'_j}.y_1^{-c_j.f_j}\right)$ will not result in a previously queried input set to H_5. Set $H_5\left(g^{t_j}, g^{w'_j}.y_1^{-c_j.f_j}\right)$ as f_j.

4. Similarly if H_5 was already queried with inputs $\left(g^{t_i}, g^{w'_i}.y_1^{-c_i.f_i}\right)$, generate a fresh w'_i and recompute the last but two components. With very high

probability, the new $\left(g^{t_i}, g^{w_i'}.y_1^{-c_i.f_i}\right)$ will not result in a previously queried input set to H_5. Set $H_5\left(g^{t_i}, g^{w_i'}.y_1^{-c_i.f_i}\right)$ as f_i.

5. The challenger computes $\bar{Z}_1 = (g^{x_i}.y_1^{c_i}.g^{t_i})^{x_j+t_j}$ where $c_i = H_2(ID_i, u_{i1})$. It also computes $P_1 = (u_{i1}.y_1^{c_i}.g^{t_i})^{c_j}$ and $P_2 = y_1$ where $c_j = H_2(ID_j, u_{j1})$.

6. The challenger computes $Z_2 = v_{i1}.v_{j1}$ and $Z_3 = (g^{t_i})^{t_j}$.

7. The challenger is given access to the $DH(y_1, ., .)$ oracle, since we assume the hardness of Strong-Diffie Hellman problem. The challenger makes use of the $DH(y_1, ., .)$ Oracle to answer the query as follows:
   - The challenger finds a Z such that $DH\left(P_2, P_1, Z_1/\bar{Z}_1\right)$ (valid since $P_2 = y_1$) and $H_6(Z_1, Z_2, Z_3) = Z$, where $Z_2 = v_{i1}.v_{j1}$ and $Z_3 = (g^{t_i})^{t_j}$.
   - If a Z exists, the challenger returns Z as the shared secret key.
   - Otherwise the challenger chooses $Z \in_R Z_p^*$ and for any further query of the form (Z_1, Z_2, Z_3) to the H_6 Oracle, if $DH\left(P_2, P_1, Z_1/\bar{Z}_1\right)$, $Z_2 = v_{i1}.v_{j1}$ and $Z_3 = (g^{t_i})^{t_j}$.

Finally the challenger returns Z as the shared secret key.

Test Session: The adversary impersonates as user i and sends the parameters $\langle u_{i1}, v_{i1}, d_{i2}, b_i, e_i, h_i^{s_2}, g^{t_i}, w_i + d_{i1}.H_5(g^{t_i}, g^{w_i}), g^{w_i}, ID_i\rangle$ to the challenger for session simulation. The challenger runs the H_1 Oracle with input ID_i. The test session is assumed to run between two users i and j, where adversary impersonates as i and challenger has to generate parameters for user j. If $\tau_i = 0$, it aborts. Else it does the following:

- The challenger passes the parameters $\langle u_{j1} = g^{x_j}, v_{j1} = h_j^{x_j}, d_{j2} = x_j + r_j.b_j + s_2.e_j, b_j, e_j,$ $h_j^{s_2}, D.g^{-d_{j1}}, w_j + d_{j1}.H_5\left(D.g^{-d_{j1}}, g^{w_j}\right), ID_j\rangle$ to the adversary, where d_{j1} is the private key component associated with User j which is known to the challenger, $r_j, x_j, w_j \in_R Z_p^*$, $h_j = H_1(ID_j)$, $b_j = H_3(ID_j, u_{j1}, v_{j1}, g^{r_j}, h_j^{r_j})$ and $e_j = H_4(ID_j, u_{j1}, v_{j1}, g^{r_j}, h_j^{r_j})$. The parameters passed satisfy the checks as they are generated in the way similar to the scheme. $g^{t_j} = D.g^{-d_{j1}} = g^{b-d_{j1}}$.

- The challenger performs the checks specified in *Step* 2 of the **Key Agreement** algorithm described in *Section* 5 on $\langle u_{i1}, v_{i1}, d_{i2}, b_i, e_i, h_i^{s_2}, g^{t_i}, w_i + d_{i1}.H_5(g^{t_i}, g^{w_i}), g^{w_i}, ID_i\rangle$. If the checks pass, the challenger proceeds to next step. Else, it aborts.

- The challenger returns a $Z^* \in_R Z_p^*$ as the shared secret key. This won't be a valid shared secret key. But in order to find that this is invalid the adversary should have queried the H_6 Oracle with a valid tuple (Z_1, Z_2, Z_3). Thus the challenger computes $\bar{Z}_2 = (Z_2/v_{j1})^{k_i^{-1}}$ and $\bar{Z}_3 = Z_3.(g^{t_i})^{d_{j1}}$. The challenger also computes $S = (Z_1/\bar{Z}_2\bar{Z}_3)^{c_i^{-1}}$ where $c_i = H_2(ID_i, u_{i1})$.

- Finally the challenger returns S as the solution for the CDH hard problem.

Lemma 3: The value returned by the challenger is the solution to the CDH instance of the SDH hard problem set in the beginning.

*Proof:*The challenger returns $S = \left(Z_1/\bar{Z}_2\bar{Z}_3\right)^{c_i^{-1}}$ where $c_i = H_2\left(ID_i, u_{i1}\right)$ as the solution to the hard problem.

- $S = \left(g^{(d_{i1}+t_i)(d_{j1}+b-d_{j1})}/\bar{Z}_2\bar{Z}_3\right)^{c_i^{-1}}$.

- $\bar{Z}_2 = \left(Z_2/v_{j1}\right)^{k_i^{-1}} = \left(v_{i1}.v_{j1}/v_{j1}\right)^{k_i^{-1}} = v_{i1}^{k_i^{-1}} = \left(h_i^{x_i}\right)^{k_i^{-1}} = \left(g^{b.k_i}\right)^{x_i.k_i^{-1}} = g^{b.x_i}$.(**Note :** The component $h_i = \left(g^b\right)^{k_i}$ as $\tau_i = 1$.).

- $\bar{Z}_3 = Z_3.\left(g^{t_i}\right)^{d_{j1}} = \left(g^{t_i}\right)^{(b-d_{j1})}.\left(g^{t_i}\right)^{d_{j1}} = g^{b.t_i}$.

- Therefore $S = \left(g^{(x_i+a.c_i+t_i)(d_{j1}+b-d_{j1})}/g^{b.x_i}.g^{b.t_i}\right)^{c_i^{-1}} = g^{ab}$.

Thus we have proved that the value returned by the challenger is solution to the CDH Problem. $\square$

7 Additional Security Properties

The proposed protocol offers additional security properties which we discuss informally. Formal details of these properties can be found in the full version of the paper.

Forward Secrecy: A key agreement protocol has forward secrecy, if after a session is completed and its shared secret key is erased, the adversary cannot learn it even if it corrupts the parties involved in that session. In other words, learning the private keys of parties should not affect the security of the shared secret key. Relaxing the definition of forward secrecy, we assume that the past sessions with passive adversary are the ones whose shared secret keys are not compromised. The proposed scheme offers forward secrecy.

Resistance to Reflection Attacks: A reflection attack occurs when an adversary can compromise a session in which the two parties have the same identity. A practical situation in which both parties with the same identity communicate is when a person wants to establish secure connection between her computers in the house and the one in the office. The proposed scheme is resistant to reflection attacks which can be proved by the techniques used in [5] and [11].

Resistance to Key Compromise Impersonation Attacks: Whenever a user I's private key is learned by the adversary, it can impersonate as I. A key compromise impersonation (KCI) attack can be carried out when the knowledge of I's private key allows the adversary to impersonate another party to I. Our scheme is resistant to KCI attacks. This is because in the proof, when the adversary tries to impersonate i to user j, the challenger is able to answer private key queries from the adversary corresponding to user j. Thus the resistance to KCI attacks is inbuilt in the security proof.

Resistance to Ephemeral Key Compromise Impersonation: Generally the users pick the ephemeral keys (t_i, g^{t_i}) from a pre-computed list in order to minimize online computation cost. But the problem with this approach is that the ephemeral components may be subjected to leakage. This attack considers the case when the adversary can make state-reveal queries even in the test session. [4] presents such an attack on the scheme presented by Fiore [5]. But our scheme is resistant to that type of an attack because when an adversary tries to impersonate a user j without knowing the private key of j (as in [4]), it cannot generate the components d_{j2} and the signature on g^{t_j} (We assume that w_i is erased immediately after the signature on g^{t_i} is computed and hence is not available to the adversary during state-reveal queries). Thus it is secure and resists ephemeral key compromise impersonation attack.

8   Conclusion

The main advantage of our scheme is that there is only a single round of communication between the pair of users and there is no predefined order in which messages are exchanged between the users. Moreover our scheme is secure against active adversary which can intercept and modify the messages as per will. The next advantage is that forking lemma is not used in the security reduction contributing to the tight reduction feature. This results in a reduction in the communication overhead. Our scheme also satisfies additional security attributes like forward secrecy, resistance to reflection attacks, key compromise impersonation attack and ephemeral key compromise impersonation attack. Finally our proof can also be modified to support security in the advanced CK+ model. This will be discussed in the full version of the paper.

References

1. Abe, M., Kiltz, E., Okamoto, T.: Compact cca-secure encryption for messages of arbitrary length. In: Jarecki, S., Tsudik, G. (eds.) PKC 2009. LNCS, vol. 5443, pp. 377–392. Springer, Heidelberg (2009)
2. Canetti, R., Krawczyk, H.: Analysis of key-exchange protocols and their use for building secure channels. In: Pfitzmann, B. (ed.) EUROCRYPT 2001. LNCS, vol. 2045, pp. 453–474. Springer, Heidelberg (2001)
3. Cao, X., Kou, W., Du, X.: A pairing-free identity-based authenticated key agreement protocol with minimal message exchanges. Information Sciences 180(15), 2895–2903 (2010)
4. Cheng, Q., Ma, C.: Ephemeral key compromise attack on the ib-ka protocol. IACR Cryptology ePrint Archive 2009, 568 (2009)
5. Fiore, D., Gennaro, R.: Making the diffie-hellman protocol identity-based. In: Pieprzyk, J. (ed.) CT-RSA 2010. LNCS, vol. 5985, pp. 165–178. Springer, Heidelberg (2010)
6. Goh, E.-J., Jarecki, S.: A signature scheme as secure as the diffie-hellman problem. In: Biham, E. (ed.) EUROCRYPT 2003. LNCS, vol. 2656, pp. 401–415. Springer, Heidelberg (2003)
7. Günther, C.G.: An identity-based key-exchange protocol. In: Quisquater, J.-J., Vandewalle, J. (eds.) EUROCRYPT 1989. LNCS, vol. 434, pp. 29–37. Springer, Heidelberg (1990)

8. Hafizul Islam, S.K., Biswas, G.P.: An improved pairing-free identity-based authenticated key agreement protocol based on {ECC}. Procedia Engineering 30, 499–507 (2012)
9. Katz, J., Yung, M.: Scalable protocols for authenticated group key exchange. Journal of Cryptology 20(1), 85–113 (2007)
10. Krawczyk, H.: HMQV: A high-performance secure diffie-hellman protocol. In: Shoup, V. (ed.) CRYPTO 2005. LNCS, vol. 3621, pp. 546–566. Springer, Heidelberg (2005)
11. Maurer, U.M., Wolf, S.: Diffie-hellman oracles. In: Koblitz, N. (ed.) CRYPTO 1996. LNCS, vol. 1109, pp. 268–282. Springer, Heidelberg (1996)
12. Menezes, A., van Oorschot, P.C., Vanstone, S.A.: Handbook of Applied Cryptography, ch. 14, pp. 617–618. CRC Press (1996)
13. Okamoto, T., Pointcheval, D.: The gap-problems: A new class of problems for the security of cryptographic schemes. In: Kim, K.-C. (ed.) PKC 2001. LNCS, vol. 1992, pp. 104–118. Springer, Heidelberg (2001)
14. Saeednia, S.: Improvement of gunther's identity-based key exchange protocol. Electronics Letters 36(18), 1535–1536 (2000)
15. Shamir, A.: Identity-based cryptosystems and signature schemes. In: Blakely, G.R., Chaum, D. (eds.) CRYPTO 1984. LNCS, vol. 196, pp. 47–53. Springer, Heidelberg (1985)

Appendix

Key Sanity Check: After receiving the private key from the PKG in the key extract phase, the user performs the following check to ensure the correctness of the components of the private key.

The user first computes

$$c_i = H_2\left(ID_i, u_{i1}\right)$$

$$b_i = H_3\left(ID_i, u_{i1}, v_{i1}, u_{i2}, v_{i2}\right)$$

$$e_i = H_4\left(ID_i, u_{i1}, v_{i1}, u_{i2}, v_{i2}\right)$$

Test 1: Check if $\dfrac{g^{d_{i1}}}{y_1^{H_2(ID_i, u_{i1})}} \stackrel{?}{=} u_{i1}$.

This can be verified as $\dfrac{g^{x_i + s_1 \cdot c_i}}{g^{s_1 \cdot H_2(ID_i, u_{i1})}}$ where $c_i = H_2\left(ID_i, u_{i1}\right)$. This is equal to $g^{x_i} = u_{i1}$. This check ensures the correctness of d_{i1} and u_{i1}.

Test 2: Check if $\dfrac{g^{d_{i2}}}{u_{i2}^{H_3(ID_i, u_{i1}, v_{i1}, u_{i2}, v_{i2})} \cdot y_2^{H_4(ID_i, u_{i1}, v_{i1}, u_{i2}, v_{i2})}} \stackrel{?}{=} u_{i1}$.

This can be verified as $\dfrac{g^{(x_i + r_i \cdot b_i + s_2 \cdot e_i)}}{g^{r_i \cdot H_3(ID_i, u_{i1}, v_{i1}, u_{i2}, v_{i2})} \cdot g^{s_2 \cdot H_4(ID_i, u_{i1}, v_{i1}, u_{i2}, v_{i2})}} \stackrel{?}{=} g^{x_i} = u_{i1}$, as $b_i = H_3\left(ID_i, u_{i1}, v_{i1}, u_{i2}, v_{i2}\right)$ and $e_i = H_4\left(ID_i, u_{i1}, v_{i1}, u_{i2}, v_{i2}\right)$.

This check ensures the correctness of $d_{i2}, u_{i2}, v_{i1}, v_{i2}$.

Test 3 : Check if $\dfrac{h_i^{d_{i2}}}{v_{i2}{}^{H_3(ID_i,u_{i1},v_{i1},u_{i2},v_{i2})} \cdot (h_i{}^{s_2})^{H_4(ID_i,u_{i1},v_{i1},u_{i2},v_{i2})}} = v_{i1}.$

This can be verified as $\dfrac{h_i^{x_i+r_i\cdot b_i+s_2\cdot e_i}}{(h_i{}^{r_i})^{H_3(ID_i,u_{i1},v_{i1},u_{i2},v_{i2})} \cdot (h_i{}^{s_2})^{H_4(ID_i,u_{i1},v_{i1},u_{i2},v_{i2})}} = h_i{}^{x_i} =$
v_{i1} where $b_i = H_3(ID_i, u_{i1}, v_{i1}, u_{i2}, v_{i2})$ and $e_i = H_4(ID_i, u_{i1}, v_{i1}, u_{i2}, v_{i2})$.
Test 3 ensures the correctness of $h_i{}^{s_2}$. Test 2 and Test 3 ensures that g and h_i
are raised to the same exponent x_i in u_{i1} and v_{i1} respectively.

If the received private key satisfies all the tests then it is valid.

CIL Security Proof for a Password-Based Key Exchange

Cristian Ene[1], Clémentine Gritti[2], and Yassine Lakhnech[1]

[1] Université Grenoble 1, CNRS, Verimag, France
{cristian.ene,yassine.lakhnech}@imag.fr
[2] Centre for Computer and Information Security Research
School of Computer Science and Software Engineering
University of Wollongong, Australia
cjpg967@uowmail.edu.au

Abstract. Computational Indistinguishability Logic (CIL) is a logic for reasoning about cryptographic primitives in computational model. It is sound for standard model, but also supports reasoning in the random oracle and other idealized models. We illustrate the benefits of CIL by formally proving the security of a Password-Based Key Exchange (PBKE) scheme, which is designed to provide entities communicating over a public network and sharing a short password, under a session key.

Keywords: Password-Based Key Exchange, Logic, Security Proof.

1 Introduction

Cryptography plays a central role in the design of secure and reliable systems. It consists in the conception and analysis of protocols achieving various aspects of information security such as authentication. In particular, the *provable cryptography* is defined as the conception of proofs accounting for the exact amount of security supplied by cryptographic protocols.

In the computational model, Computational Indistinguishability Logic (CIL) supports concise and intuitive proofs accross several models of cryptography. This logic features the notion of oracle system, an abstract model of interactive games in which adaptive adversaries play against a cryptographic scheme by interacting with oracles. Moreover, it states a small set of rules that capture common reasoning patterns and interface rules to connect with external reasoning. To illustrate applicability of CIL, we consider the security proof of the Password-Based Key Exchange (PBKE) protocol.

1.1 Related Work

About Security of PBKE Protocols: EKE (Encrypted Key Exchange) was introduced by Bellovin and Merritt, [1]. In their protocol, two users execute an encrypted version of the Diffie-Hellman key exchange protocol, in which each flow is encrypted using the password shared between these two users as the symmetric key. Due to the simplicity of their protocol, other protocols were proposed

W. Susilo and R. Reyhanitabar (Eds.): ProvSec 2013, LNCS 8209, pp. 59–85, 2013.

in the literature based on it, each with its own instantiation of the encryption function such that OEKE (One-Encryption Key-Exchange) protocol.

Since 2003, E. Bresson *et al.*, [3], have been working on the analysis of very efficient schemes on password-based authenticated key exchange methods, but for which actual security was an open problem. In 2012, B. Blanchet have focused on a crytpgraphic protocol verifier, called CryptoVerif, to mechanically prove OEKE.

About CIL: DCS (Distributed and Complex Systems) is working on the logic CIL for proving concrete security of cryptographic schemes. It enables reasonning about schemes directly in the computational settings. The main contribution is to support the design of proofs at a level of abstraction which allows to bridge the gap between pencil-and-paper fundamental proofs and existing pratical verification tools (see article [7]).

1.2   Contributions and Contents

For the first time, we bring out the applicability of CIL for formalizing computational proofs. The tool CIL allows us to give a new kind of analysis that has advantages over the traditional as in [3] and [9]. As we use a tool based on general and extended logic rules, the proofs are well constructed and easy to understand, and achieve good results.

The paper begins with a recall of the framework to capture cryptographic games(Section 2). The main technical contributions of the paper are: i) an extension of reasoning tools for oracle systems (Section 3); ii) a formal proof in CIL of an efficient PBKE protocol (Section 4).

2   Oracle Systems

2.1   Preliminaries

ICM: An ideal block cipher is a totally random permutation from l-bit strings to l-bit strings.

ROM: A random oracle is a mathematical function mapping every possible query to a uniformly random response from its output domain.

Miscellaneous: Let **1** to denote the unit type and (x, y) to denote pairs. For a set A, $U(A)$ defines the set of uniform distributions over A. Let _ to denote arguments that are not used or elements of tuples whose value is irrevelant in the final distribution.

2.2   Semantics

The interaction between an oracle system and an adversary proceeds in three successive phases:

- the initialization oracle sets the initial memory distributions of the oracle system;

- the adversary performs computations, updates its state and submits a query to the oracle system; the oracle system performs computations, updates its state, and replies to the adversary, which updates its state;
- the adversary outputs a result calling the finalization oracle.

During his attack, the adversary has access to the oracles, which modelize his capacities to obtain (partial) information or to execute some party of the protocol in the reality. His resources are bounded by two parameters: the number of queries he performs to the oracles and his running time.

2.3   Oracle Systems and Adversaries

Oracle systems and adversaries are modeled as stateful systems meant to interact with each another. An oracle system O is a stateful system that provides oracle access to adversaries and given by:
- sets of oracle memories and of oracles;
- a query domain, an answer domain and the related implementation;
- a distinguished initial memory, and distinguished oracles o_I for initialization and o_F for finalization.

Oracle systems O and O' are *compatible* iff they have the same sets of oracle names and the query and the answer domains of each oracle name coincide in both oracle systems. We build compatible systems out of systems we have already defined by modifying the implementation of one of the oracles.

2.4   Events

The interaction between oracle system and adversary seems as this of the pattern consisting in the query of an oracle, the computation of an answer by the oracle, and the update of its state by the adversary. This is formalized as a transition system, where a step consists in one occurence of the pattern.

Security properties abstract away from the state of adversaries and are modeled using traces. A trace is an execution sequence from which the adversary memories have been erased. The subset of traces verifying the predicate is considered to assign a probability to an event defined by a predicate.

For a step-predicate ϕ, let the event "eventually ϕ" be denoted by F_ϕ and correspond to ϕ satisfied at one step of the trace. Furthermore, the event "always ϕ", denoted by G_ϕ, is true iff ϕ is satisfied at every step of the trace. You can find an example of this concept in Appendix A.3.

For more details and examples, you can see the Appendix A or refer to the article [7].

3   Computational Indistinguishability Logic

3.1   Statements: Judgments

For an event $\mathbf{E}$, a statement $O :_\varepsilon \mathbf{E}$ is valid iff for every (k,t)-adversary A, $Pr(A \mid O : \mathbf{E}) \leq \varepsilon(k,t)$. For O and O' compatible oracle systems which expect a boolean as result, a statement $O \sim_\varepsilon O'$ is valid iff for every (k,t)-adversary A, $| Pr[A \mid O : R = \mathbf{True}] - Pr[A \mid O' : R = \mathbf{True}] | \leq \varepsilon(k,t)$. Let $\mathbf{E}$ be an event of compatible systems O and O'. A statement $O \overset{\mathbf{E}}{\sim}_\varepsilon O'$ is valid iff for every (k,t)-adversary A, $| Pr[A \mid O : R = \mathbf{True} \wedge \mathbf{E}] - Pr[A \mid O' : R = \mathbf{True} \wedge \mathbf{E}] | \leq \varepsilon(k,t)$. As $O \sim_\varepsilon O' \Leftrightarrow O \overset{\mathbf{True}}{\sim}_\varepsilon O'$, we write $O \sim_\varepsilon O'$ for the two statements. See Appendix B.1 for details.

3.2 Rules and Their Extensions

We expose briefly the rules used in our proof on Figure (1). You can find more classic and extended rules in Appendix B.1.

$$\frac{O :_{\varepsilon_2} \mathbf{E}_2 \quad O' :_{\varepsilon_1} F_{\neg\varphi} \quad O \equiv_{\mathcal{R},\varphi} O' \quad \mathbf{E}_1 \mathcal{R} \mathbf{E}_2}{O' :_{\varepsilon_1+\varepsilon_2} \mathbf{E}_1} \; UpToBad \qquad \frac{}{O :_\varepsilon F_\varphi} \; Fail$$

$$\frac{O \leq_{det,\gamma} O' \quad O :_\varepsilon \mathbf{E} \circ \pi}{O' :_\varepsilon \mathbf{E}} \; B\text{-}Det\text{-}Left \qquad \frac{O :_\varepsilon \mathbf{E} \circ C}{C[O] :_{\varepsilon'} \mathbf{E}} \; B\text{-}Sub$$

$$\frac{O \overset{\mathbf{E}_2}{\sim}_{\varepsilon_1} O' \quad \mathbf{E}_2 \Rightarrow \mathbf{E}_1 \quad O :_{\varepsilon_2} \mathbf{E}_1 \wedge \neg\mathbf{E}_2 \quad O' :_{\varepsilon_2} \mathbf{E}_1 \wedge \neg\mathbf{E}_2}{O \overset{\mathbf{E}_1}{\sim}_{\varepsilon_1+\varepsilon_2} O'} \; URCd \qquad \frac{}{O :_{\varepsilon'} F_{\varphi'}} \; Fail2$$

$$\frac{O \overset{\mathbf{E}_1 \wedge \mathbf{E}_2}{\sim}_{\varepsilon_2} O' \quad O :_{\varepsilon_1} \neg\mathbf{E}_1 \wedge \mathbf{E}_2 \quad O' :_{\varepsilon_1} \neg\mathbf{E}_1 \wedge \mathbf{E}_2}{O \overset{\mathbf{E}_2}{\sim}_{\varepsilon_1+\varepsilon_2} O'} \; FTr \qquad \frac{O \overset{\mathbf{E}_1}{\sim}_{\varepsilon_1} O' \quad O' \overset{\mathbf{E}_2}{\sim}_{\varepsilon_2} O''}{O \overset{\mathbf{E}_1 \vee \mathbf{E}_2}{\sim}_{\varepsilon_1+\varepsilon_2} O''} \; TrCd$$

$$\frac{O :_{\varepsilon_1} F_{\varphi_1} \wedge G_{\varphi_2} \quad O :_{\varepsilon_2} F_{\neg\varphi_2} \quad O \equiv_{\mathcal{R},\varphi_2} O'}{O' :_{\varepsilon_1+\varepsilon_2} F_{\varphi_1}} \; B\text{-}BisG2 \qquad \frac{O' :_\varepsilon F_{\neg\varphi_2} \wedge G_{\varphi_1} \quad O \overset{\varphi_1}{\equiv}_{\mathcal{R},\varphi_2} O'}{O \overset{G_{\varphi_1}}{\sim}_\varepsilon O'} \; I\text{-}BisCd$$

Fig. 1. Rules used in the proof (classic and extended rules). For compatible oracle systems O, O' and O'', events $\mathbf{E}$, $\mathbf{E}_1$ and $\mathbf{E}_2$ of O, O' and O'', and step-predicates φ, φ_1 and φ_2.

3.3 Contexts

A context C is an intermediary between an oracle system O and adversaries. One can compose a O-context C with O to obtain a new oracle system $C[O]$ and with a $C[O]$-adversary to obtain a new O-adversary $C \parallel A$. Procedures for contexts differ of these for oracle systems: one that transfers calls from the adversary to the oracles and another one that tranfers answers from the oracles to the adversary. See Appendix B.2.

3.4 Bisimulation

Game-based proofs proceed by transforming an oracle system into an equivalent one, or in case of imperfect simulation into a system that is equivalent up to some bad event. The notion of bisimulation-up-to is defined as two probabilistic transition systems are bisimilar until the failure of a condition on their tuple states-transitions. Bisimulations are closely related to obversational equivalence and relational Hoare logic and allow to justify proofs by simulations. Besides, bisimulations-up-to subsume the Fundamental Lemma of Victor Shoup. See Appendix B.3.

3.5   Determinization

Using the concept of automata determinization technique, the definition is based on the possibility to decompose states of a system into two components and to exhibit a distribution γ allowing to obtain the second component given the first one. See Appendix B.4.

4   CIL Security Proof for an Efficient PBKE

4.1   Preliminaries

In the computational model, messages are bitstrings, cryptographic primitives are functions from bitstrings to bitstrings and adversary is any Probabilistic Polynomial time Turing Machine.

Scheme: We denote objects describing the model:

- two sets $Users$ and $Servers$ such that $u \in [Users]$ and $s \in [Servers]$;
- for the arithmetic, $G = <g>$ is a cyclic group of l-bit prime order q and $\bar{G} = G \setminus 1_G = \{g^x \mid x \in \mathbb{Z}_q^*\}$ (g is a fixed parameter);
- for $i = \{0,1\}$, l_i is the parameter of data size for Hash function H_i;
- a set $Password$ as a small dictionary (polynomial in the security parameter), of size N, equipped with the uniform distribution.

Encryption/Decryption: E is the Encryption and D is the Decryption in the Ideal Cipher Model .

Hash Functions: There are two hash functions H_0 and H_1 in the Random Oracle Model.

We want to bound the probability for an adversary, within time t, and with less than N_u sessions with a client, N_s sessions with a server (active attacks), and asking q_H hash queries and q_E Encryption/Decryption queries, to distinguish the session key from a random key.

4.2   One-Encryption Key-Exchange (OEKE), A Password-Based Key Exchange

On Figure (2) (with a honest execution of the OEKE protocol), the protocol runs between a client u and a server s. The session key space associated to this protocol is $\{0,1\}^{l_0}$ equipped with the uniform distribution. u and s initially share a low-quality string pw, the password, from $Password$.

$$
\begin{array}{cc}
\text{Client } u & \text{Server } s \\
pw & pw \\
\text{accept} \leftarrow \text{false ; terminate} \leftarrow \text{false} & \text{accept} \leftarrow \text{false ; terminate} \leftarrow \text{false} \\
x \leftarrow [1..(q-1)] & y \leftarrow [1..(q-1)] \\
X \leftarrow g^x \xrightarrow{\;u,X\;} & Y \leftarrow g^y \\
Y \leftarrow D(pw, Y^\star) \xleftarrow{\;s,Y^\star\;} & Y^\star \leftarrow E(pw, Y) \\
K_u \leftarrow Y^x \; ; \; Auth \leftarrow H_1(Z \parallel K_u) \; ; \; sk_u \leftarrow H_0(Z \parallel K_u) & K_s \leftarrow X^y \\
\text{accept} \leftarrow \text{true} \xrightarrow{\;Auth\;} & Auth \overset{?}{=} H_1(Z \parallel K_s) \; ; \text{ if true, accept} \leftarrow \text{true} \\
& sk_s \leftarrow H_0(Z \parallel K_s) \\
\text{terminate} \leftarrow \text{true} & \text{terminate} \leftarrow \text{true}
\end{array}
$$

Fig. 2. An execution of the protocol OEKE, run by the client u and the server s. We let Z be equal to $u \parallel s \parallel X \parallel Y$.

The real game O_0^1: This game consists of: initialization and finalization oracles, Encryption/Decryption oracles, Hash oracles, oracles that simulate the protocol (named U_1, S_1, U_2 and S_2), Execute oracle, Test oracle and Reveal oracle. In the initialization oracle, the bit b is equal to 1 and hence, the Test oracle returns the real value of the session key.

$\mathrm{Imp}(o_I)() =$
     $pw \leftarrow Password;\ L_{H_0} := [];\ L_{H_1} := [];$
     $L_E := [];\ L_{pw} := [];\ L_O := [];$
     $var_X := \perp;\ var_\theta := \perp;\ var_\varphi := \perp;\ var_{sk} := \perp;$
     $b := 1$
     return **1**

$\mathrm{Imp}(E)(pw, x) =$
     if $(pw, x, \_, \_) \notin L_E$ then
         $y \leftarrow \hat{G};\ L_E := L_E.(pw, x, y, \perp);$
     endif
     return y such that $(pw, x, y, \_) \in L_E$

$\mathrm{Imp}(D)(pw, y) =$
     if $(pw, \_, y, \_) \notin L_E$ then
         $\phi \leftarrow \mathbb{Z}_q^*;\ x = g^\phi \; ;\ L_E := L_E.(pw, x, y, \phi);$
     endif
     return x such that $(pw, x, y, \_) \in L_E$

$\mathrm{Imp}(H_0)(x) =$
     if $x \notin L_{H_0}$ then
         $y \leftarrow U(l_0);\ L_{H_0} := L_{H_0}.(x, y);$
     endif
     return $L_{H_0}(x)$

$\mathrm{Imp}(H_1)(x) =$
     if $x \notin L_{H_1}$ then
         $y \leftarrow U(l_1);\ L_{H_1} := L_{H_1}.(x, y);$
     endif
     return $L_{H_1}(x)$

$\mathrm{Imp}(U_1)(u, i) =$
     $\theta \leftarrow \mathbb{Z}_q^*;\ X = g^\theta \; ;\ var_\theta[(u, i)] = (\theta, X);$
     return (u, X)

$\mathrm{Imp}(S_1)((s, j), (u, X)) =$
     $\varphi \leftarrow \mathbb{Z}_q^*;\ Y = g^\varphi;\ Y^\star = E(pw, Y);$
     $var_\varphi[(s, j)] = (\varphi, Y, Y^\star);\ var_X[(s, j)] = X;$
     $K_s = X^\varphi$
     return $(s, Y^\star)$

$\mathrm{Imp}(U_2)((u,i),(s,Y^\star)) =$
   if $var_\theta[(u,i)]! = \perp$ then
     $Y = D(pw,Y^\star);\ (\theta,X) = var_\theta[(u,i)];$
     $K_u = Y^\theta;$
     $Auth = H_1(u \parallel s \parallel X \parallel Y \parallel K_u);$
     $var_{sk}[(u,i)] = H_0(u \parallel s \parallel X \parallel Y \parallel K_u)$
   endif
   return $Auth$

$\mathrm{Imp}(S_2)((s,j),u,Auth) =$
   if $var_\varphi[(s,j)]! = \perp$ then
     $(\varphi,Y,Y^\star) = var_\varphi[(s,j)];\ X = var_X[(s,j)];$
     $K_s = X^\varphi;$
     $H' = H_1(u \parallel s \parallel X \parallel Y \parallel K_s);$
     if $H' = Auth$ then
       $var_{sk}[(s,j)] = H_0(u \parallel s \parallel X \parallel Y \parallel K_s)$
     endif
   endif
   return $\mathbf{1}$

$\mathrm{Imp}(Reveal)(p,k) =$
   if $var_{sk}[(p,k)]! = \perp$ then
     $sk := var_{sk}[(p,k)]$
   endif
   return sk

$\mathrm{Imp}(Test^1)(p,k) =$
   if $var_{sk}[(p,k)]! = \perp$ then
     $sk := var_{sk}[(p,k)]$
   endif
   return sk

$\mathrm{Imp}(Exec)((u,i),(s,j)) =$
   $\theta \leftarrow \mathbb{Z}_q^\star;\ X = g^\theta;\ \varphi \leftarrow \mathbb{Z}_q^\star;$
   $Y = g^\varphi;\ Y^\star = E(pw,Y);\ K_s = X^\varphi;\ K_u = Y^\theta;$
   $Auth = H_1(u \parallel s \parallel X \parallel Y \parallel K_u);$
   $var_{sk}[(u,i)] = H_0(u \parallel s \parallel X \parallel Y \parallel K_u)$
   return $((u,X),(s,Y^\star),Auth)$

$\mathrm{Imp}(o_F)(x) = \qquad$ return $\mathbf{1}$

The real game O_0^0: As for O_0^1, this game consists of exactly the same oracles. The differences are in the initialization oracle where $b = 0$ and in the Test oracle where is returned a random value for sk.

Summary: In a first part, we bound the probabilities that two step-predicates occur. The first one, **Cl**, is for formalizing the collisions. The second one, ϕ_{pw}, is for describing the dependence on the password in the oracles. In a second part, we write the general proof in order to obtain the indistinguishability between O_0^0 and O_0^1, considering that the two previous step-prediactes can not occur. For that, we describe the transformations of the game O_0^1, step by step, until finding a simplified game. We notice that we obtain the same thing for the game O_0^0.

These two parts are very similar: the same tranformations are made in order to obtain the wanted result. Therefore, we explain clearly the first proof and we expose briefly the second one.

N.B.: The list L_{pw} is created to simulate the oracles E and D in ICM. We suppose that the domain of E matches with the group generated by g. L_O is defined as the list stocking the tuple (oracle o, query q, answer a), writing as $L_O = L_O \cdot (o,q,a)$.

4.3   Proof for Bounding the Probability of the Step-Predicate ϕ_{pw}

C.1. Eliminating the Collisions :
We want to eliminate collisions during Hash and Encryption/Decryption processes. We formalize the small probability of that an inappropriate collision could let the adversary to find a sequence without any required effort.

Let the step-predicate **Cl** be defined on the triple $((o,q,a),m,\_)$ as the conjunction of the clauses:

- for $i = 0,1$, $o = H_i \wedge q \notin m \cdot L_{H_i} \wedge (\_,a) \in m \cdot L_{H_i}$
- $o = E \wedge (pw,q,\_,\_) \notin m \cdot L_E \wedge (\_,\_,a,\_) \in m \cdot L_E$
- $o = D \wedge (pw,\_,q,\_) \notin m \cdot L_E \wedge (\_,a,\_,\_) \in m \cdot L_E$

To complete and restrict the definition of **Cl**, let us introduce two other clauses:

- if $(pw,Y,Y_1^\star,\varphi)$ and $(pw,Y,Y_2^\star,\varphi)$ then $Y_1^\star = Y_2^\star$
- if $(pw,Y_1,Y^\star,\varphi)$ and $(pw,Y_2,Y^\star,\varphi)$ then $Y_1 = Y_2$

Since **Cl** can only be satisfied when querying H_0, H_1, E or D, applying the rule Fail2 (see Appendix B.1) allows to conclude to:

- on the hash oracles, where $l = max(l_0,l_1)$ and $q_H = q_{H_0} + q_{H_1}$, we obtain
$\varepsilon_0^1 = \frac{1}{2} \times \frac{(q_{H_0}+q_{H_1})^2}{2^l} = \frac{q_H^2}{2^{l+1}}$,
- on the Encryption/Decryption oracles, where $q_E = q_{Enc} + q_{Dec}$, we get $\varepsilon_0^2 = \frac{1}{2} \times \frac{(q_{Enc}+q_{Dec})^2}{q-1} = \frac{q_E^2}{2(q-1)}$.

Therefore, we obtain that $O_0^1 :_{\varepsilon_0} F_{\mathbf{Cl}}$ where $\varepsilon_0 = \frac{q_H^2}{2^{l+1}} + \frac{q_E^2}{2(q-1)}$. We perform the same analysis for the other game obtaining $O_0^0 :_{\varepsilon_0} F_{\mathbf{Cl}}$.

For further, at each step, we suppose there is no collision when modifying the game O_0^1. We can introduce a particular equivalence relation under the step-predicate $\neg\mathbf{Cl}$ in order to avoid the collisions, since it steps in over memories. We use the extented notion of bisimulation (for more details, see Appendix B.3). To conclude the proof, we bound the probability of such collisions (this avoids the repetition of the value ε_0 at each transformation).

C.2. Creating the independence from the password in the oracles:

We want to eliminate dependence on pw in all the oracles. We formalize the probability that the adversary guesses the good password and succeeds in the acquisition of the session key.

We define the step-predicate $\phi_{pw} = \phi_{pw1} \vee \phi_{pw2}$, where ϕ_{pw1} and ϕ_{pw2} are written as follows:

$$\phi_{pw1} = \lambda(m,\_).\ (U_2,q,\_) \in m \cdot L_O \wedge (m \cdot pw,\_,q,\perp) \in m \cdot L_E$$

$$\phi_{pw2} = \lambda(m,\_).\ (S_1,\_,a) \in m \cdot L_O \wedge (\_,a) \in m \cdot S_1 \wedge (m \cdot pw,Y,a,\_) \in m \cdot L_E$$
$$\wedge (\_ \| \_ \| \_ \| Y \| \_,a') \in m \cdot L_{H_1} \wedge (S_2,a',\_) \in m \cdot L_O$$

ϕ_{pw} steps in over memories only. We want to find the value ε_1 such that:
$O_0^1 :_{\varepsilon_1} F_{\phi_{pw}} = F_{\phi_{pw1} \vee \phi_{pw2}}$.

We transform the game O_0^1 until finding a game wherein the password is sampled in the finalization oracle. Therefore, we can obtain easily the optimal result $\frac{N_u + N_s}{N}$. Indeed, this means that the adversary can test at most one password per session.

Removing the Encryption in the oracle S_1. The unique way for the adversary to gain something is to correctly guess pw, by either sending a Y^* that is really an encryption under it of some well-chosen message or using it to decrypt Y^*. In O_1^1, we change S_1 modelizing the Encryption inside this oralce.

$$\text{Imp}(S_1)((s,j),(u,X)) = \varphi \leftarrow \mathbb{Z}_q^*; \, Y = g^\varphi; \, Y^* \leftarrow \bar{G}; \, var_\varphi[(s,j)] = (\varphi, Y, Y^*);$$
$$L_E := L_E.(pw, Y, Y^*, \varphi) \, ; \, var_X[(s,j)] = X; \, K_s = X^\varphi;$$
$$\text{return } (s, Y^*) \text{ such that } (pw, Y, Y^*, \_) \in L_E$$

In a particular case, we do not receive an exponent φ but $\bot$: that happens when Y^* has been previously obtained as a ciphertext returned by an Encryption query. Let the step-predicate **Exp** be this case:

$$\mathbf{Exp} = \lambda((o, \_, a), m, \_). \, o = S_1 \wedge (pw, \_, a, \bot) \in m \cdot L_E$$

Therefore, O_0^1 and O_1^1 are in bisimulation-up-to $\neg\mathbf{Exp}$, using as relation $\mathcal{R}'_1$ the equality on the common components of their states in $M_{\neg\mathbf{Cl}}^{O_i^1}$. Indeed, states m, m' are in relation:

- if $m, m' \in M_{\neg\mathbf{Cl}}^{O_0^1}$ or $M_{\neg\mathbf{Cl}}^{O_1^1}$, $m\mathcal{R}'_1 m'$ iff $m = m'$
- if $m \in M_{\neg\mathbf{Cl}}^{O_0^1}$ and $m' \in M_{\neg\mathbf{Cl}}^{O_1^1}$, $m\mathcal{R}'_1 m'$ iff
  - $\forall (pw, x, y, e) \in m \cdot L_E \setminus m' \cdot L_E \Rightarrow e = \bot \wedge \exists (pw, x, y, \varphi) \in m' \cdot L_E \setminus m \cdot L_E$ s.t. $x = g^\varphi$
  - $\forall (pw, x, y, e) \in m' \cdot L_E \setminus m \cdot L_E \Rightarrow e = \varphi$ s.t. $x = g^\varphi \wedge \exists (pw, x, y, \bot) \in m \cdot L_E \setminus m' \cdot L_E$

Hence, we apply the rule I-BisG2 to result in:

$$\frac{O_1^1 :_{\varepsilon_2'} F_{\mathbf{Exp}}(\wedge G_{\neg\mathbf{Cl}}) \quad O_1^1 :_{\varepsilon_1'} F_{\phi_{pw}}(\wedge G_{\neg\mathbf{Cl}}) \quad O_0^1 \overset{\neg\mathbf{Cl}}{\equiv} \mathcal{R}'_1, \neg\mathbf{Exp}\wedge\neg\phi_{pw} O_1^1}{O_0^1 :_{\varepsilon_1'+\varepsilon_2'} F_{\phi_{pw}}(\wedge G_{\neg\mathbf{Cl}})} \, I\text{-}BisG2$$

Applying the rule Fail allows to obtain $O_1^1 :_{\varepsilon_2'} F_{\mathbf{Exp}}$, where $\varepsilon_2' = \frac{N_s \times q_E}{q-1}$.

Splitting the Hash Lists. We want to be sure that u will offer a good Authenticator and s will accept it. Therefore, we modify the oracle U_2 in order to get a honest value for Y. We split the lists of the two public hash oracles H_0 and H_1 in O_2^1, introducing two private hash functions $H_2 : \{0,1\}^* \rightarrow \{0,1\}^{l_0}$ and $H_3 : \{0,1\}^* \rightarrow \{0,1\}^{l_1}$.

$\mathrm{Imp}(o_I)() =$
  $pw \leftarrow Password$
  $L_{H_0} := [];\ L_{H_1} := [];\ L_{H_2} := [];\ L_{H_3} := [];$
  $L_E := [];\ L_{pw} := [];\ L_O := [];$
  $var_X := \bot;\ var_\theta := \bot;\ var_\varphi := \bot;\ var_{sk} := \bot;$
  $b := 1$
  return $\mathbf{1}$

$\mathrm{Imp}(U_2)((u,i),(s,Y^\star)) =$
  if $var_\theta[(u,i)]! = \bot$ then
    $(\theta, X) = var_\theta[(u,i)]$
    if $\exists Y, \exists \varphi$ such that $(pw, Y, Y^\star, \varphi) \in L_E$
      $K_u = Y^\theta$;
      $Auth = H_1(u \parallel s \parallel X \parallel Y \parallel K_u);$
      $var_{sk}[(u,i)] = H_0(u \parallel s \parallel X \parallel Y \parallel K_u)$
    else
      $Y \leftarrow \bar{G};\ K_u = Y^\theta;$
      $Auth = H_3(u \parallel s \parallel X \parallel Y \parallel K_u);$
      $var_{sk}[(u,i)] = H_2(u \parallel s \parallel X \parallel Y \parallel K_u)$
    endif
  endif
  return $Auth$

O_1^1 and O_2^1 are $\mathcal{R}'_2$-bismilar up to $\neg\phi_{pw1}$. The equivalence relation $\mathcal{R}'_2$ between states m and m' is as follows:

- if $m, m' \in M^{O_1^1}_{\neg\mathbf{Cl}}$ or $M^{O_2^1}_{\neg\mathbf{Cl}}$, $m\mathcal{R}'_2 m'$ iff $m = m'$
- if $m \in M^{O_1^1}_{\neg\mathbf{Cl}}$ and $m' \in M^{O_2^1}_{\neg\mathbf{Cl}}$, $m\mathcal{R}'_2 m'$ iff $m \cdot L_{H_0} = m' \cdot (L_{H_0} \cup L_{H_2})$ and $m \cdot L_{H_1} = m' \cdot (L_{H_1} \cup L_{H_3})$

Then, applying the rule I-BisG2, we find:

$$\frac{O_2^1 :_{\varepsilon'_3} F_{\phi_{pw1}}(\wedge G_{\neg\mathbf{Cl}})\quad O_2^1 :_{\varepsilon'_4} F_{\phi_{pw}} \wedge G_{\neg\phi_{pw1}}(\wedge G_{\neg\mathbf{Cl}})\quad O_1^1 \stackrel{\neg\mathbf{Cl}}{\equiv}_{\mathcal{R}'_2, \neg\phi_{pw1}} O_2^1}{O_1^1 :_{\varepsilon'_3 + \varepsilon'_4} F_{\phi_{pw}}(\wedge G_{\neg\mathbf{Cl}})}\ \text{I-BisG2}$$

such that $\varepsilon'_3 + \varepsilon'_4 = \varepsilon'_1$. We notice that: $F_{\phi_{pw}} \wedge G_{\neg\phi_{pw1}} \Leftrightarrow F_{\phi_{pw2}}$.

Randomizing the Hash Oracles. In O_3^1, we sample the value of Y. Therefore, we no longer use the private hash functions since we internalize the hash functions in another way with the random Y. We modify the oracles U_2 and S_2.

$\mathrm{Imp}(U_2)((u,i),(s,Y^\star)) =$
  if $var_\theta[(u,i)]! = \bot$ then
    $Y \leftarrow \bar{G};\ (\_, Y, Y^\star) \in var_\varphi[(u,i)];$
    $(\theta, X) = var_\theta[(u,i)];\ K_u = Y^\theta;$
    $Auth = H_1(u \parallel s \parallel X \parallel Y \parallel K_u);$
    $var_{sk}[(u,i)] = H_0(u \parallel s \parallel X \parallel Y \parallel K_u)$
  endif
  return $Auth$

$\mathrm{Imp}(S_2)((s,j),u,Auth) =$
  if $var_\varphi[(s,j)]! = \bot$ then
    $(\varphi, Y, Y^\star) = var_\varphi[(s,j)];\ X = var_X[(s,j)];\ K_s = X^\varphi;$
    $H' = H_1(u \parallel s \parallel X \parallel Y \parallel K_s);$
    if $H' = Auth$ then
      $var_{sk}[(s,j)] = H_0(u \parallel s \parallel X \parallel Y \parallel K_s)$
    endif
  endif
  return $\mathbf{1}$

Let the step-predicate **Auth** be the conjunction of the following clauses:

- $(pw, Y, Y^\star, \varphi) \in L_E \wedge X \in var_\theta$
- for u and s, $u \parallel s \parallel X \parallel Y \parallel CDH(X,Y) \in L_{H_1}$

The adversary can not see the link between Y and $Y^\star$, except if he calls $E(pw, \_)$ or $D(pw, \_)$.

We notice that the probability that $F_{\phi pw2}$ occurs is very negligible since we suppose that the adversary can not get the password. Since we have $F_{\mathbf{Auth} \vee \phi_{pw2}} = F_{\mathbf{Auth}} \vee (F_{\phi_{pw2}} \wedge G_{\neg\mathbf{Auth}})$, we expose that $F_{\phi_{pw2}} \wedge G_{\neg\mathbf{Auth}}$ occurs with the probability ε_5' and $F_{\mathbf{Auth}}$ with ε_6'. Using the rule Fail, we get $\varepsilon_5' = \frac{N_u + N_s}{q-1}$.

We want to establish the indistinguishability between O_2^1 and O_3^1 up to $\neg\mathbf{Auth} \wedge \neg\phi_{pw2}$. We exhibit two equivalence relations $\mathcal{R}'3$ between both systems. Indeed, states m and m' are in relation:

- if $m, m' \in M_{\neg\mathbf{Cl}}^{O_2^1}$ or $M_{\neg\mathbf{Cl}}^{O_3^1}$, $m\mathcal{R}'3m'$ iff $m = m'$
- if $m \in M_{\neg\mathbf{Cl}}^{O_2^1}$ and $m' \in M_{\neg\mathbf{Cl}}^{O_3^1}$, $m\mathcal{R}'3m'$ iff $m \cdot (L_{H_0} \cup L_{H_2}) = m' \cdot L_{H_0}$ and $m \cdot (L_{H_1} \cup L_{H_3}) = m' \cdot L_{H_1}$

On the left hand, focusing on the step-predicate ϕ_{pw1}, we apply the rule I-BisG2 to result in:

$$\frac{O_3^1 :_{\varepsilon_5' + \varepsilon_6'} F_{\mathbf{Auth} \vee pw2}(\wedge G_{\neg\mathbf{Cl}}) \quad O_3^1 :_{\varepsilon_7'} F_{\phi pw1} \wedge G_{\neg\mathbf{Auth} \wedge \neg\phi pw2}(\wedge G_{\neg\mathbf{Cl}}) \quad O_2^1 \stackrel{\neg\mathbf{Cl}}{\equiv}_{\mathcal{R}'3, \neg\mathbf{Auth} \wedge \neg\phi pw2} O_3^1}{O_2^1 :_{\varepsilon_5' + \varepsilon_6' + \varepsilon_7'} F_{\phi pw1}(\wedge G_{\neg\mathbf{Cl}})} \; I\text{-}BisG2$$

such that $\varepsilon_5' + \varepsilon_6' + \varepsilon_7' = \varepsilon_3'$.

On the right hand, since we have $F_{\mathbf{Auth} \vee \phi pw2} = [F_{\mathbf{Auth}} \wedge G_{\phi pw2}] \vee [F_{\phi pw2} \wedge G_{\mathbf{Auth} \wedge \phi pw2}]$ and $O_3^1 :_0 F_{\phi pw2} \wedge G_{\mathbf{Auth} \wedge \phi pw2}(\wedge G_{\neg\mathbf{Cl}})$, we simplify the line. Focusing on the step-predicate ϕ_{pw2}, we apply the rule I-BisG2 to result in:

$$\frac{O_3^1 :_{\varepsilon_6'} F_{\mathbf{Auth}} \wedge G_{\phi pw2}(\wedge G_{\neg\mathbf{Cl}}) \quad O_3^1 :_{\varepsilon_8'} F_{\phi pw2}(\wedge G_{\neg\mathbf{Cl}}) \quad O_2^1 \stackrel{\neg\mathbf{Cl}}{\equiv}_{\mathcal{R}'3, \neg\mathbf{Auth} \wedge \neg\phi pw2} O_3^1}{O_2^1 :_{\varepsilon_6' + \varepsilon_8'} F_{\phi pw2}(\wedge G_{\neg\mathbf{Cl}})} \; I\text{-}BisG2$$

such that $\varepsilon_6' + \varepsilon_8' = \varepsilon_4'$.

We focus on the CDH problem to obtain the value of ε_6' (for more details about the Computational Diffie-Hellman assumption in G, see Appendix B.2). Hence, we write the game O_4^1 as a context C of CDH. The oracle system CDH captures the game played by an adversary to find the Diffie-Hellman instance (A, B).

We define the step-predicate $\mathbf{Auth'}$ as follows:

- $o = U_1$ s.t. $(\alpha, X) \in L_A \wedge o = S_1$ s.t. $(\beta, Y) \in L_B$
- for u and s, $u \parallel s \parallel X \parallel Y \parallel CDH(X, Y) \in L_{H_1}$

The adversary has returned a pair (R_1, R_2) that is a valid authentication when $H_1(R_1) = R_2$. Given $(\alpha, X) \in L_A$, $(\beta, Y) \in L_B$ and one CDH instance (A, B), we notice that $CDH(A, B) = CDH(X, Y)^{\alpha^{-1}\beta^{-1}}$.

Therefore, applying the rule B-Sub, we get:

$$\frac{CDH :_{\varepsilon(1_k, t)} F_{\mathbf{Auth'}} \circ C}{O_4^1 = C[CDH] :_{\varepsilon_6'} F_{\mathbf{Auth'}}} \; B\text{-}Sub$$

where $\varepsilon_6' = q_H \times \varepsilon(1_k, t)$ (see Appendix B.2).

Moreover, the games O_3^1 and O_4^1 are in perfect bisimulation. We define the equivalence relation $\mathcal{R}'_4$ between states m and m' as follows:

- if $m, m' \in M_{\neg \mathbf{Cl}}^{O_3^1}$ or $M_{\neg \mathbf{Cl}}^{O_4^1}$, $m \mathcal{R}'_4 m'$ iff $m = m'$
- if $m \in M_{\neg \mathbf{Cl}}^{O_3^1}$ and $m' \in M_{\neg \mathbf{Cl}}^{O_4^1}$, $m \mathcal{R}'_4 m'$ iff there is the equality on the common components of their states, knowing that the added lists L_A and L_B are completely determinated using the other common tables.

Then, we check the compatibility of $F_{\mathbf{Auth}} \cup F_{\mathbf{Auth'}}$ with $\mathcal{R}'_4$, i.e. that given two states $m \in M_{\neg \mathbf{Cl}}^{O_3^1}$ and $m' \in M_{\neg \mathbf{Cl}}^{O_4^1}$ in relation by $\mathcal{R}'_4$, $F_{\mathbf{Auth}}$ holds in state m iff $F_{\mathbf{Auth'}}$ holds in state m', which is obvious by the definition of the relation. Thus, applying the rule UpToBad, we find:

$$\frac{O_4^1 :_{\varepsilon_6'} F_{\mathbf{Auth'}}(\wedge G_{\neg \mathbf{Cl}}) \quad O_3^1 :_0 F_{\neg \mathbf{True}} \quad O_3^1 \stackrel{\neg \mathbf{Cl}}{\equiv}_{\mathcal{R}'_4, \mathbf{True}} O_4^1 \quad F_{\mathbf{Auth}} \mathcal{R}'_4 F_{\mathbf{Auth'}}}{O_3^1 :_{\varepsilon_6'} F_{\mathbf{Auth}}(\wedge G_{\neg \mathbf{Cl}})} \, UpToBad$$

Sorting the Password in the Finalization Oracle. We a simplified game such that all the oracles are independent of pw. We modify the finalization oracle in order to draw the password only at the end of O_5^1.

$$\mathrm{Imp}(o_F)(x) = x = pw; \text{ return } \mathbf{1}$$

The event $F_{\phi_{pw}} \circ \pi$ on O_5^1-traces is defined by $F_{\phi_{pw}} \circ \pi(\tau) = \mathbf{True}$ iff $\pi(\tau)$ verifies $F_{\phi_{pw}}$, where τ is any O_5^1-trace. Therefore, using the rule Fail, we get $O_5^1 :_{\varepsilon_1} F_{\phi_{pw}}$, where $\varepsilon_9' = \frac{N_u + N_s}{N}$. Then, applying the rule B-Det-Left, we find:

$$\frac{O_3^1 \leq_{\det, \gamma} O_5^1 \quad O_5^1 :_{\varepsilon_9'} (F_{\phi_{pw}} \circ \pi) \wedge G_{\neg \mathbf{Cl}}}{O_3^1 :_{\varepsilon_9'} F_{\phi_{pw}}(\wedge G_{\neg \mathbf{Cl}})} \, B\text{-}Det\text{-}Left$$

such that $\varepsilon_9' = \varepsilon_7' + \varepsilon_8' = \frac{N_u}{N} + \frac{N_s}{N}$. More precisely, we get $O_3^1 :_{\varepsilon_7'} F_{\phi_{pw1}}$ and $O_3^1 :_{\varepsilon_8'} F_{\phi_{pw2}}$.

To conclude, we obtain that $O_0^1 :_{\varepsilon_1} F_{\phi_{pw}}$ where $\varepsilon_1 = \frac{N_u + N_s}{N} + \frac{N_u + N_s}{q-1} + \frac{N_s q_E}{q-1} + 2 q_H \times \varepsilon(\mathbf{1}_k, t)$. We perform the same analysis for the other game obtaining that $O_0^0 :_{\varepsilon_1} F_{\phi_{pw}}$.

For further, at each step, we suppose there is no dependence on the password when modifying the game O_0^1. We can introduce a particular equivalence relation under the step-predicate $\neg \phi_{pw}$ in order to avoid a query from the adversary with the good pw, since it steps in over memories using the list L_O. From that, E and D no longer give some evidence about the password to the adversary. This process enables to avoid the repetition of the value ε_1 at each transformation in the general proof.

Proof Tree: We illustrate the proof tree for bounding the probability of the step-predicate ϕ_{pw} on Figure (3). For convenience, we understand that each event $F_{\mathbf{Predicate}}$ is associated to the event $G_{\neg \mathbf{Cl}}$ and b is the bit randomly sampled in the initialization oracle.

N.B.: Defining the step-predicate ϕ_{pw} allows us to construct a proof which seems the more general possible. Indeed, we notice that it can be applied in another password-based protocol proof. From that, we hope to get security proofs more easily since we have already met the concept.

$$I\text{-}BisG2 \quad \dfrac{O_0^b \overset{G_{\neg Cl}}{\equiv}_{R_1, \neg\mathbf{Exp} \wedge \neg\phi_{pw}} O_1^b \quad O_1^b :_{\varepsilon'_2} F_{\mathbf{Exp}} \quad I\text{-}BisG2 \dfrac{\mathbf{Tree'_1}}{O_1^b :_{\varepsilon'1} F_{\phi_{pw}}}}{O_0^b :_{\varepsilon'_1 + \varepsilon'_2} F_{\phi_{pw}}}$$

Tree'$_1$:

$$I\text{-}BisG2 \quad \dfrac{O_1^b \overset{G_{\neg Cl}}{\equiv}_{R_2, \neg\phi_{pw1}} O_2^b \quad I\text{-}BisG2 \dfrac{\mathbf{Tree'_2}}{O_2^b :_{\varepsilon'_3} F_{\phi_{pw1}}} \quad I\text{-}BisG2 \dfrac{\mathbf{Tree'_3}}{O_2^b :_{\varepsilon'_4} F_{\phi_{pw}} \wedge G_{\neg\phi_{pw1}}}}{O_1^b :_{\varepsilon'_1} F_{\phi_{pw}}}$$

Tree'$_2$:

$$I\text{-}BisG2 \quad \dfrac{O_2^b \overset{G_{\neg Cl}}{\equiv}_{R_3, \neg\mathbf{Auth} \wedge \phi_{pw2}} O_3^b \quad I\text{-}BisG2 \dfrac{\mathbf{Tree'_4}}{O_3^b :_{\varepsilon'_6} F_{\mathbf{Auth} \vee \phi_{pw2}}} \quad I\text{-}BisG2 \dfrac{\mathbf{Tree'_5}}{O_3^b :_{\varepsilon'_7} F_{\phi_{pw1}} \wedge G_{\neg\mathbf{Auth} \wedge \neg\phi_{pw2}}}}{O_2^b :_{\varepsilon'_3} F_{\phi_{pw1}}}$$

Tree'$_3$:

$$I\text{-}BisG2 \quad \dfrac{O_2^b \overset{G_{\neg Cl}}{\equiv}_{R_3, \neg\mathbf{Auth} \wedge \phi_{pw2}} O_3^b \quad I\text{-}BisG2 \dfrac{\mathbf{Tree'_4}}{O_3^b :_{\varepsilon'_6} F_{\mathbf{Auth}} \wedge G_{\phi_{pw2}}} \quad I\text{-}BisG2 \dfrac{\mathbf{Tree'_5}}{O_3^b :_{\varepsilon'_8} F_{\phi_{pw2}}}}{O_2^b :_{\varepsilon'_4} F_{\phi_{pw}} \wedge G_{\neg\phi_{pw1}} = F_{\phi_{pw2}}}$$

Tree'$_4$:

$$Up\text{-}To\text{-}Bad \quad \dfrac{O_3^b \overset{G_{\neg Cl}}{\equiv}_{R_4, \mathbf{True}} O_4^b \quad O_3^b :_0 F_{\neg\mathbf{True}} \quad F_{\mathbf{Auth}} R_4 F_{\mathbf{Auth'}} \quad B\text{-}Sub \dfrac{CDH :_{\varepsilon(1_k, t)} F_{\mathbf{Auth'}} \circ C}{O_3^b :_{\varepsilon'_6} F_{\mathbf{Auth'}}}}{O_3^b :_{\varepsilon'_6} F_{\mathbf{Auth}}}$$

Tree'$_5$:

$$B\text{-}Det\text{-}Left \quad \dfrac{O_3^b \leq_{det,\gamma} O_5^b \quad O_5^b :_{\varepsilon'_7} F_{\phi_{pw1}} \circ \pi}{O_3^b :_{\varepsilon'_7} F_{\phi_{pw1}}}$$

Tree'$_6$:

$$B\text{-}Det\text{-}Left \quad \dfrac{O_3^b \leq_{det,\gamma} O_5^b \quad O_5^b :_{\varepsilon'_8} F_{\phi_{pw2}} \circ \pi}{O_3^b :_{\varepsilon'_8} F_{\phi_{pw2}}}$$

Fig. 3. Proof Tree for the probability that the step-predicate ϕ_{pw} occurs

4.4 General Proof for the Indistinguishability between the Games O_0^0 and O_0^1.

Since the two conditions we described previously seem revelant, we transform the game O_0^1 in several steps under $G_{\neg Cl} \wedge G_{\neg\phi_{pw}}$. The description of the general proof is less developed since we use the same transformations than for the proof for bounding the probability of ϕ_{pw}. Indeed, except the last game O_5^1 using the concept of determinization, we will apply in the same order each step using in the previous proof.

Removing the Encryption in the Oracle S_1. In O_1^1, modified S_1 modelizes the Encryption inside (refer to page 67). If $Y^\star$ exists already then the exponent is equal to $\bot$. The step-predicate **Exp** defines this case (see pagerefexp).

Therefore, O_0^1 and O_1^1 are in bisimulation-up-to $\neg\mathbf{Exp}$, using as relation $\mathcal{R}_1$ the equality on the common components of their states in $M_{\neg\mathbf{Cl}\wedge\neg\phi_{pw}}^{O_1^1}$. Indeed, states m, m' are in relation:

- if $m, m' \in M_{\neg\mathbf{Cl}\wedge\neg\phi_{pw}}^{O_0^1}$ or $m, m' \in M_{\neg\mathbf{Cl}\wedge\neg\phi_{pw}}^{O_1^1}$, $m\mathcal{R}_1 m'$ iff $m = m'$
- if $m \in M_{\neg\mathbf{Cl}\wedge\neg\phi_{pw}}^{O_0^1}$, $m' \in M_{\neg\mathbf{Cl}\wedge\neg\phi_{pw}}^{O_1^1}$, $m\mathcal{R}_1 m'$ iff
  - $\forall (pw, x, y, e) \in m \cdot L_E \setminus m' \cdot L_E \Rightarrow e = \bot \wedge \exists (pw, x, y, \varphi) \in m' \cdot L_E \setminus m \cdot L_E$ s.t. $x = g^\varphi$
  - $\forall (pw, x, y, e) \in m' \cdot L_E \setminus m \cdot L_E \Rightarrow e = \varphi$ s.t. $x = g^\varphi \wedge \exists (pw, x, y, \bot) \in m \cdot L_E \setminus m' \cdot L_E$

Hence, using the rule Fail, we get $O_1^1 :_{\varepsilon_2 = \frac{N_s \times q_E}{q-1}} F_{\mathbf{Exp}}$ and we apply the rule I-BisCd to result in:

$$\frac{O_1^1 :_{\varepsilon_2} F_{\mathbf{Exp}}(\wedge G_{\neg\mathbf{Cl}} \wedge G_{\neg\phi_{pw}}) \quad O_0^1 \overset{\neg\mathbf{Cl}\wedge\neg\phi_{pw}}{\equiv}_{\mathcal{R}_1, \neg\mathbf{Exp}} O_1^1}{O_0^1 \overset{G_{\neg\mathbf{Cl}}\wedge G_{\neg\phi_{pw}}}{\sim_{\varepsilon_2}} O_1^1} \text{ I-BisCd}$$

Splitting the Hash Lists. In O_2^1, we split the lists of the hash functions. For that, we create two private hash functions H_2 and H_3 (refer to page 67).

O_1^1 and O_2^1 are $\mathcal{R}_2$-bismilar up to $\neg\phi_{pw1}$ (see page 66). We define the equivalence relation $\mathcal{R}_2$ between states m and m' as follows:

- if $m, m' \in M_{\neg\mathbf{Cl}\wedge\neg\phi_{pw}}^{O_1^1}$ or $m, m' \in M_{\neg\mathbf{Cl}\wedge\neg\phi_{pw}}^{O_2^1}$, $m\mathcal{R}_2 m'$ iff $m = m'$
- if $m \in M_{\neg\mathbf{Cl}\wedge\neg\phi_{pw}}^{O_1^1}$, $m' \in M_{\neg\mathbf{Cl}\wedge\neg\phi_{pw}}^{O_2^1}$, $m\mathcal{R}_2 m'$ iff $m \cdot L_{H_0} = m' \cdot (L_{H_0} \cup L_{H_2}) \wedge m \cdot L_{H_1} = m' \cdot (L_{H_1} \cup L_{H_3})$

We obtain $O_2^1 :_0 F\phi_{pw1}$ since we consider the independence of the password in the oracles. Then, applying the rule I-BisCd, we find:

$$\frac{O_2^1 :_0 F_{\phi_{pw1}}(\wedge G_{\neg\mathbf{Cl}} \wedge G_{\neg\phi_{pw}}) \quad O_1^1 \overset{\neg\mathbf{Cl}\wedge\neg\phi_{pw}}{\equiv}_{\mathcal{R}_2, \neg\phi_{pw1}} O_2^1}{O_1^1 \overset{G_{\neg\mathbf{Cl}}\wedge G_{\neg\phi_{pw}}}{\sim_0} O_2^1} \text{ I-BisCd}$$

Randomizing the Hash Oracles. In O_3^1, sampling Y modifies the oracles U_2 and S_2 (refer to page 68).

Auth is defined page 68 and ϕ_{pw2} page 66. We notice that the event $F_{\phi_{pw2}}$ do not occur since we suppose that the adversary can not get the password. Using the equality $F_{\mathbf{Auth}\vee\phi_{pw2}} = F_{\mathbf{Auth}} \vee (F_{\phi_{pw2}} \wedge G_{\neg\mathbf{Auth}}) = F_{\mathbf{Auth}}$, we calculate the value ε_3 of the probability that the event $F_{\mathbf{Auth}}$ occurs.

We want to establish the indistinguishability between O_2^1 and O_3^1 up to $\neg\mathbf{Auth} \wedge \neg\phi_{pw2}$. We exhibit an equivalence relation $\mathcal{R}_3$ between both systems. Indeed, states m and m' are in relation:

- if $m, m' \in M_{\neg\mathbf{Cl} \wedge \neg\phi_{pw}}^{O_2^1}$ or $m, m' \in M_{\neg\mathbf{Cl} \wedge \neg\phi_{pw}}^{O_3^1}$, $m\mathcal{R}_3 m'$ iff $m = m'$
- if $m \in M_{\neg\mathbf{Cl} \wedge \neg\phi_{pw}}^{O_2^1}$, $m' \in M_{\neg\mathbf{Cl} \wedge \neg\phi_{pw}}^{O_3^1}$, $m\mathcal{R}_3 m'$ iff $m \cdot (L_{H_0} \cup L_{H_2}) = m' \cdot L_{H_2} \wedge m \cdot (L_{H_1} \cup L_{H_3}) = m' \cdot L_{H_3}$

Hence, we apply the rule I-BisCd to result in:

$$\frac{O_3^1 :_{\varepsilon_3} F_{\mathbf{Auth} \vee \phi_{pw2}}(\wedge G_{\neg\mathbf{Cl}} \wedge G_{\neg\phi_{pw}}) \quad O_2^1 \overset{\neg\mathbf{Cl} \wedge \neg\phi_{pw}}{\equiv}_{\mathcal{R}_3, \neg\mathbf{Auth} \wedge \neg\phi_{pw2}} O_3^1}{O_2^1 \overset{G_{\neg\mathbf{Cl}} \wedge G_{\neg\phi_{pw}}}{\sim}_{\varepsilon_3} O_3^1} \; \textit{I-BisCd}$$

In the previous proof, we obtained that $O_3^1 :_{\varepsilon_6'} F_{\mathbf{Auth}}(\wedge G_{\neg\mathbf{Cl}})$. We use classic rule of Logic $O :_\varepsilon \mathbf{A} \Rightarrow O :_\varepsilon \mathbf{A} \wedge \mathbf{B}$ such that $\mathbf{A} = F_{\mathbf{Auth}}(\wedge G_{\neg\mathbf{Cl}})$ and $\mathbf{B} = G_{\neg\phi_{pw}}$. Therefore, we obtain that $O_3^1 :_{\varepsilon_6'} F_{\mathbf{Auth}}(\wedge G_{\neg\mathbf{Cl}} \wedge G_{\neg\phi_{pw}})$ where $\varepsilon_3 \leq \varepsilon_6'$.

4.5 Digest

Using four steps and the rule TrCd, we find $O_0^1 \overset{G_{\neg\mathbf{Cl}} \wedge \neg\phi_{pw}}{\sim}_{\varepsilon_2 + \varepsilon_3} O_3^1$. Similarly, we get $O_0^0 \overset{G_{\neg\mathbf{Cl}} \wedge \neg\phi_{pw}}{\sim}_{\varepsilon_2 + \varepsilon_3} O_3^0$.

To achieve the conclusion, we compare the games O_3^0 and O_3^1. At present, the adversary can not discern a random value from a real value for the session key sk. From that, he can not guess what was the bit sampled in the initialization oracle. Consequently, the latter discussion implies that the two last modified games O_3^0 and O_3^1 are in perfect bisimulation, with as a relation $\mathcal{R}_5$ the equality on the common components of their states. To conclude, we use the rule I-BisCd:

$$\frac{O_3^0 :_0 F_{\neg\mathbf{True}}(\wedge G_{\neg\mathbf{Cl}} \wedge G_{\neg\phi_{pw}}) \quad O_3^1 :_0 F_{\neg\mathbf{True}}(\wedge G_{\neg\mathbf{Cl}} \wedge G_{\neg\phi_{pw}}) \quad O_3^0 \overset{\neg\mathbf{Cl} \wedge \neg\phi_{pw}}{\equiv}_{\mathcal{R}_5, \mathbf{True}} O_3^1}{O_3^0 \overset{G_{\neg\mathbf{Cl}} \wedge G_{\neg\phi_{pw}}}{\sim_0} O_3^1} \; \textit{I-BisCd}$$

We use the rule TrCd to conclude to: $O_0^0 \overset{G_{\neg\mathbf{Cl}} \wedge G_{\neg\phi_{pw}}}{\sim}_{2\varepsilon_2 + 2\varepsilon_3} O_0^1$. Having $O_0^b :_{\varepsilon_1} F_{\phi_{pw}}$ and using the rule FTr, we get: $O_0^0 \overset{G_{\neg\mathbf{Cl}}}{\sim}_{\varepsilon_1 + 2\varepsilon_2 + 2\varepsilon_3} O_0^1$. Since $O_0^b :_{\varepsilon_0} F_{\mathbf{Cl}}$, applying the rule FTr, we obtain: $O_0^0 \sim_{\varepsilon_0 + \varepsilon_1 + 2\varepsilon_2 + 2\varepsilon_3} O_0^1$, where $\varepsilon_0 + \varepsilon_1 + 2\varepsilon_2 + 2\varepsilon_3 = \frac{q_H^2}{2^{l+1}} + \frac{q_E^2}{2(q-1)} + \frac{N_u + N_s}{N} + \frac{N_u + N_s}{q-1} + \frac{N_s q_E}{q-1} + 2q_H \times \varepsilon(1_k, t) + \frac{2N_s q_E}{q-1} + 2q_H \times \varepsilon(1_k, t)$.

General Proof Tree: We illustrate the proof tree on Figure (4). Most of the time, we use the rules I-BisCd and TrCd under the condition $G_{\neg\mathbf{Cl}} \wedge G_{\neg\phi_{pw}}$. For convenience, we understand that each event $F_{\mathbf{Predicate}}$ is associated to the event $G_{\neg\mathbf{Cl}} \wedge G_{\neg\phi_{pw}}$ and b is the bit randomly sampled in the initialization oracle.

4.6 Conclusion

We gave a manual formal proof of the OEKE protocol, as the first application of the tool CIL. This proof is well contructed under two parts; The first proof seems complicated

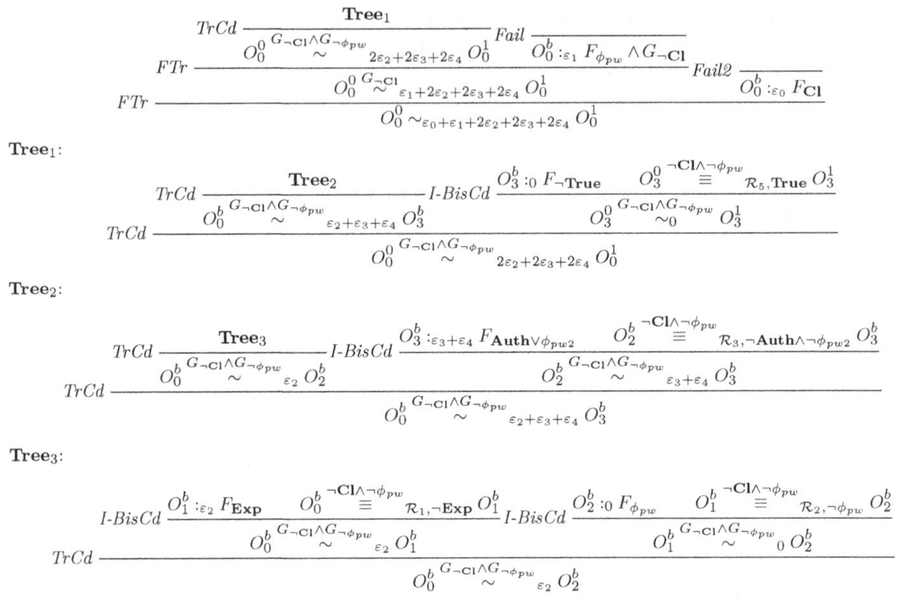

$$FTr \cfrac{FTr \cfrac{TrCd \cfrac{\textbf{Tree}_1}{O_0^0 \underset{\sim}{G_{\neg C1} \wedge G_{\neg \phi pw}} {}_{2\varepsilon_2 + 2\varepsilon_3 + 2\varepsilon_4} O_0^1} \quad Fail \cfrac{}{O_0^b :_{\varepsilon_1} F_{\phi_{pw}} \wedge G_{\neg C1}}}{O_0^0 \overset{G_{\neg C1}}{\underset{\sim}{}} {}_{\varepsilon_1 + 2\varepsilon_2 + 2\varepsilon_3 + 2\varepsilon_4} O_0^1} \quad Fail2 \cfrac{}{O_0^b :_{\varepsilon_0} F_{\textbf{C1}}}}{O_0^0 \underset{\sim}{}_{\varepsilon_0 + \varepsilon_1 + 2\varepsilon_2 + 2\varepsilon_3 + 2\varepsilon_4} O_0^1}$$

Tree$_1$:

$$TrCd \cfrac{TrCd \cfrac{\textbf{Tree}_2}{O_0^b \underset{\sim}{G_{\neg C1} \wedge G_{\neg \phi pw}} {}_{\varepsilon_2 + \varepsilon_3 + \varepsilon_4} O_3^b} \quad I\text{-}BisCd \cfrac{O_3^b :_0 F_{\neg \textbf{True}} \quad O_3^0 \overset{\neg C1 \wedge \neg \phi_{pw}}{\equiv} {}_{\mathcal{R}_5, \textbf{True}} O_3^1}{O_3^0 \underset{\sim 0}{G_{\neg C1} \wedge G_{\neg \phi pw}} O_3^1}}{O_0^0 \underset{\sim}{G_{\neg C1} \wedge G_{\neg \phi pw}} {}_{2\varepsilon_2 + 2\varepsilon_3 + 2\varepsilon_4} O_0^1}$$

Tree$_2$:

$$TrCd \cfrac{TrCd \cfrac{\textbf{Tree}_3}{O_0^b \underset{\sim}{G_{\neg C1} \wedge G_{\neg \phi pw}} {}_{\varepsilon_2} O_2^b} \quad I\text{-}BisCd \cfrac{O_3^b :_{\varepsilon_3 + \varepsilon_4} F_{\textbf{Auth} \vee \phi pw2} \quad O_2^{\neg C1 \wedge \neg \phi pw} \equiv {}_{\mathcal{R}_3, \neg \textbf{Auth} \wedge \neg \phi_{pw2}} O_3^b}{O_2^b \underset{\sim}{G_{\neg C1} \wedge G_{\neg \phi pw}} {}_{\varepsilon_3 + \varepsilon_4} O_3^b}}{O_0^b \underset{\sim}{G_{\neg C1} \wedge G_{\neg \phi pw}} {}_{\varepsilon_2 + \varepsilon_3 + \varepsilon_4} O_3^b}$$

Tree$_3$:

$$TrCd \cfrac{I\text{-}BisCd \cfrac{O_1^b :_{\varepsilon_2} F_{\textbf{Exp}} \quad O_0^b \overset{\neg C1 \wedge \neg \phi pw}{\equiv} {}_{\mathcal{R}_1, \neg \textbf{Exp}} O_1^b}{O_0^b \underset{\sim}{G_{\neg C1} \wedge G_{\neg \phi pw}} {}_{\varepsilon_2} O_1^b} \quad I\text{-}BisCd \cfrac{O_2^b :_0 F_{\phi pw} \quad O_1^{\neg C1 \wedge \neg \phi pw} \equiv {}_{\mathcal{R}_2, \neg \phi pw} O_2^b}{O_1^b \underset{\sim 0}{G_{\neg C1} \wedge G_{\neg \phi pw}} O_2^b}}{O_0^b \underset{\sim}{G_{\neg C1} \wedge G_{\neg \phi pw}} {}_{\varepsilon_2} O_2^b}$$

Fig. 4. Proof Tree for OEKE

to find the probability of one-step predicate but stays clear. As this proof is similar to the general proof, therefore the latter is concise, precise and easy to understand. We obtained a new kind of security proof for OEKE based on general and extended logic rules, instead of "writing" proofs or "rewriting" proof using CryptoVerif.

Theorem 1. *Let us consider the OEKE protocol, where Password is a finite dictionnary of size N equipped with the uniform distribution. Let A be a (k,t)-adversary against the security of OEKE within a time bound t, with less than $N_u + N_s$ interactions with the parties and asking q_H hash queries and q_E Encryption/Decryption queries. Then we have:*

$$Adv_{oeke}(A) \leq \frac{N_u + N_s}{N} + \frac{N_u + N_s}{q-1} + \frac{q_E^2}{2(q-1)} + \frac{3N_s q_E}{q-1} + \frac{q_H^2}{2^{l+1}} + 4q_H \times \varepsilon(\mathbf{1}_k, t)$$

We stayed careful of putting realistic hypothesis for elements of the proof, as for functions in ROM and ICM. We obtained the optimal term $\frac{N_u + N_s}{N}$.

N.B.: In 2003, the autors of the paper [3] recognized that their results of the reductions proof were not optimal. For technical reasons, they used a collision-resistant hash function H_1. After we began our article, in the paper [9], they proved the security of OEKE using the tool CryptoVerif. The boundary was improved relative to the former proof since they reached the optimal result $\frac{N_u + N_s}{N}$. As in these papers, we obtained the optimal term but using a new kind of analysis under CIL.

Moreover, the logic CIL is sufficiently developed: it can be used easily and efficiently to construct computational proofs.

References

1. Bellovin, S.M., Merritt, M.: Encrypted Key Exchange: Password-Based Protocols Secure Against Dictionnary Attacks. In: Proc. IEEE Computer Society Symposium on Research in Security and Privacy, pp. 72–84 (1992)
2. Bellare, M., Rogaway, P.: The AuthA Protocol for Password-Based Authenticated Key Exchange. Unpublished contribution to IEEE P1363 (2000)
3. Bresson, E., Chevassut, O., Pointcheval, D.: Security Proofs for an Efficient Password-Based Key Exchange. In: Proceedings of CCS 2003, pp. 241–250. ACM Press (2003)
4. Bellare, M., Rogaway, P.: The Security of Triple Encryption and a Framework for Code-Based Game-Playing Proofs. In: Vaudenay, S. (ed.) EUROCRYPT 2006. LNCS, vol. 4004, pp. 409–426. Springer, Heidelberg (2006)
5. Shoup, V.: Sequences of games: A Tool for Taming Complexity in Security Proofs (2004) (manuscript)
6. Halevi, S.: A plausible approach to computer-aid cryptographic proofs (2005) (manuscript)
7. Barthe, G., Daubignard, M., Kapron, B., Lakhnech, Y.: Computational Indistinguishability Logic. In: Proceedings of CCS 2010, pp. 375–386. ACM Press (2010)
8. Daubignard, M.: Formal Methods for Concrete Security Proofs. PhD thesis (2012)
9. Blanchet, B.: Automatically Verified Mechanized Proof of One-Encryption Key Exchange. In: CSF 2012 (2012)

A   Oracle Systems

A.1   Oracle Systems and Adversaries

An oracle system is a stateful system that provides oracle access to adversaries.

Definition 1. *An oracle system O is given by:*

- *sets M_O of oracle memories and N_O of oracles,*
- *for each $o \in N_O$, a query domain $In(o)$, an answer domain $Out(o)$ and an implementation $O_o : In(o) \times M_o \to D(Out(o) \times M_0)$,*
- *a distinguished initial memory $\bar{m}_o \in M_o$, and distinguished oracles o_I for initialization and o_F for finalization, such that $In(o_I) = Out(o_F) = 1$. We let $Res = In(o_F)$.*

Two oracle systems O and O' are *compatible* iff they have the same sets of oracle names, and the query and the answer domains of each oracle name coincide in both oracle systems. When building a compatible oracle system from another one, it is thus sufficient to provide its set of memories, its initial memory and the implementation of its oracles.

Adversaries interact with oracle systems by making queries and receiving answers. An exchange for an oracle system O is a triple (o, q, a) where $o \in N_o$, $q \in In(o)$ and $a \in Out(o)$. We let Xch be the set of exchanges. Initial and final exchanges are defined in the obvious way, by requiring that o is an initialization and finalization oracle respectively (the sets of these exchanges are denoted by Xch_I and Xch_F respectively). The sets Que of queries and Ans of answers are respectively defined as $\{(o, q) \mid (o, q, a) \in Xch\}$ and $\{(o, a) \mid (o, q, a) \in Xch\}$.

Definition 2. *An adversary A for an oracle system O is given by a set M_a of adversary memories, an initial memory $\bar{m}_a \in M_a$ and functions for querying and updating A : $M_a \to D(Que \times M_a)$ and $A_{\downarrow} : Xch \times M_a \to D(m_a)$.*

Informally, the interaction between an oracle system and an adversary proceeds in three successive phases: the initialization oracle sets the initial memory distributions of the oracle system and of the adversary. Then, A performs computations, updates its state and submits queries to O. In turn, O performs computations, updates its state, and replies to A, which updates its state. Finally, A outputs a result by calling the finalization oracle.

A.2   Semantics

Definition 3. *A transition system S consists of:*
- *a (countable non-empty) set M of memories (states) with a distinguished initial memory $\bar{m}$,*
- *a set $\sum$ of actions with distinguished subsets of $\sum_I$ and $\sum_F$ of initialization and finalization actions,*
- *a (partial) transition function $step : M \rightharpoonup D(\sum \times M)$.*

A partial execution sequence of S is a sequence of ζ of the form $m_0 \xrightarrow{x_1} m_1 \xrightarrow{x_2} \cdots \xrightarrow{x_k} m_k$ such that $Pr[step(m_{k-1}) = (a_k, m_k)] > 0$ for $i = 1..k$ and $x_i = (o_i, q_i, a_i)$. If $k = 1$ then ζ is a step. If $m_0 = \bar{m}$, $x_1 \in \sum_I$ and $x_k \in \sum_F$ then ζ is an execution sequence of length k. A probabilistic transition system S induces a sub-distribution on executions, denoted S, such that the probability of a finite execution sequence ζ is $Pr[S = \zeta] = \prod_{i=1}^{k} Pr[step(m_{i-1}) = (a_i, m_i)]$. A transition system is of height $k \in \mathbb{N}$ if all its executions have length at most k: in this case, S is a distribution.

Definition 4. *Let O be an oracle system and A be an O-adversary. The composition $A \,|\, O$ is a transition system such that $M = M_a \times M_o$, the initial memory is $(\bar{m}_a, \bar{m}_o)$, the set of actions is $\sum = Xch$, $\sum_I = Xch_I$ and $\sum_F = Xch_F$, and*

$$step_{A|O}(m_a, m_o) = \quad ((o,q), m_a') \leftarrow A(m_a);\ (a, m_o') \leftarrow O_o(q, m_o)\ ;\ m_a'' \leftarrow A_{\downarrow}((o,q,a), m_a');$$
$$return\ ((o,q,a), (m_a'', m_o'))$$

An adversary is called k-bounded if $A \,|\, O$ is of height k. This means that A calls the finalization oracle after less than k interactions with O. $A \,|\, O$ may be ill-defined for unbounded adversaries, since $step_{A|O}(m_a, m_o)$ may be a sub-distribution. Throughout the paper, we only consider bounded adversaries, i.e. that are k-bounded for some k.

A.3   Events

Security properties abstract away from the state of adversaries and are modeled using traces. Informally, a trace τ is an execution sequence η from which the adversary memories have been erased.

Definition 5. *Let O be an oracle system.*
- *A partial trace is a sequence τ of the form $m_0 \xrightarrow{x_1} m_1 \xrightarrow{x_2} \cdots \xrightarrow{x_k} m_k$ where $m_0..m_k \in M_O$ and $x_1..x_k \in Xch$ such that $Pr[O_{o_i}(q_i, m_{i-1}) = (a_i, m_i)] > 0$ for $i = 1..k$ and $x_i = (o_i, q_i, a_i)$. A trace is a partial trace τ such that $m_0 = \bar{m}_o$, $x_1 = (o_I, \_, \_)$ and $x_k = (o_F, \_, \_)$.*

– An O-event $\mathbf{E}$ is a predicate over O-traces, whereas an extended O-event $\mathbf{E}$ is a predicate over partial O-traces.

The probability of an (extended) event is derived directly from the definition of $A \mid O$: since each execution sequence η induces a trace $\mathcal{T}(\eta)$ simply by erasing the adversary memory at each step, one can define for each trace τ, the set $\mathcal{T}^{-1}(\tau)$ of execution sequences that are erased to τ, and for every (generalized) event $\mathbf{E}$, the probability:
$Pr[A \mid O : \mathbf{E}] = Pr[A \mid O : \mathcal{T}^{-1}(\mathbf{E})] = \sum_{\{\eta \in Exec(A|O) | \mathbf{E}(\mathcal{T}(\eta)) = \mathbf{True}\}} Pr[A \mid O : \eta]$.

Constructions and proofs in CIL use several common operations on (extended) events and traces. First, one can define the conjunction, the disjunction, etc, of events. Moreover, one can define for every predicate P over $Xch \times M_o \times M_o$ the events "eventually P" F_P and "always P" G_P that correspond to P being satisfied by one step and all steps of the trace respectively.

Reduction-based arguments require that adversaries can partially simulate behaviors. In some cases, adversaries must test whether a predicate $\varphi \subseteq Xch \times M_o \times M_o$ holds for given values. Since the adversary has no access to the oracle memory, we say that φ is *testable* iff for all x, m_1, m_1', m_2, m_2', we have $\varphi(x, m_1, m_1')$ iff $\varphi(x, m_2, m_2')$ (that is φ depends only on the exchange).

Given two traces τ and τ', we write $\tau \mathcal{R} \tau'$ iff for every $i \in [1, k]$, we have $m_i \mathcal{R} m_i'$, where: $\tau = m_0 \xrightarrow{x_1} m_1 \xrightarrow{x_2} \cdots \xrightarrow{x_k} m_k$ and $\tau' = m_0' \xrightarrow{x_1} m_1' \xrightarrow{x_2} \cdots \xrightarrow{x_k} m_k'$.

Moreover, we say that two events $\mathbf{E}$ and $\mathbf{E'}$ are $\mathcal{R}$-compatible, written $\mathbf{E} \mathcal{R} \mathbf{E'}$, iff $\mathbf{E}(\tau)$ is equivalent to $\mathbf{E'}(\tau')$ for every traces τ and τ' such that $\tau \mathcal{R} \tau'$.

B   Computational Indistinguishability Logic

B.1   Statements and Rules

As cryptographic proofs rely on assumptions, CIL manipulates sequents of the form $\Delta \Rightarrow \omega$, where Δ is a set of statements (the assumptions) and ω is a statement (the conclusion). Validity extends to sequents $\Delta \Rightarrow \omega$ in the usual manner. Given a set Δ of statements, $\models \Delta$ iff $\models \psi$ for every $\psi \in \Delta$. Then $\Delta \models \omega$ iff $\models \Delta$ implies $\models \omega$. For clarity and brevity, our presentation of CIL omits hypotheses and the standard structural and logical rules for sequent calculi.

Theorem 2. *Every sequent $\Delta \Rightarrow \varphi$ provable in CIL is also valid, i.e. $\Delta \models \varphi$.*

Judgments. CIL considers negligibility statements of the form $O :_\varphi \mathbf{E}$, where $\mathbf{E}$ is an event. A statement $O :_\varphi \mathbf{E}$ is valid, written $\models O :_\varphi \mathbf{E}$, iff for every (k, t)-adversary A, $Pr[A \mid O : \mathbf{E}] \leq \varepsilon(k, t)$.

We also consider indistinguishability statements of the form $O \sim_\varepsilon O'$, where O and O' are compatible oracle systems which expect a boolean as result. A statement $O \sim_\varepsilon O'$ is valid, written $\models O \sim_\varepsilon O'$, iff for every (k, t)-adversary A,

$$| Pr[A \mid O : R = \mathbf{True}] - Pr[A \mid O' : R = \mathbf{True}] | \leq \varepsilon(k, t)$$

where $R = \mathbf{True}$ is shorthand for $F_{\lambda(o,q,a).\, o = o_F \wedge q = \mathbf{True}}$.

Therefore, we formalize the indistinguishability of distributions yielded by systems under condition, the latter being written as an event of systems. Let $\mathbf{E}$ be an event of O

and O'. A statement $O \overset{\mathbf{E}}{\sim}_\varepsilon O'$ is valid, written $\models O \overset{\mathbf{E}}{\sim}_\varepsilon O'$, iff for every (k,t)-adversary A,

$$| Pr[A \mid O : R = \mathbf{True} \wedge \mathbf{E}] - Pr[A \mid O' : R = \mathbf{True} \wedge \mathbf{E}] | \leq \varepsilon(k,t)$$

As cryptographic proofs rely on assumptions, CIL manipulates sequents of the form $\Delta \Rightarrow \omega$, where Δ is a set of statements (the assumptions) and ω is a statement (the conclusion). Validity extends to sequents $\Delta \Rightarrow \omega$ in the usual manner. Given a set Δ of statements, $\models \Delta$ iff $\models \psi$ for every $\psi \in \Delta$. Then $\Delta \models \omega$ iff $\models \Delta$ implies $\models \omega$.

Rules. On Figures (5), (6) and (7), we expose rules that support equational reasoning and consequence in Hoare logic, rules that were extended rules found during the conception of the proofs in this article, and rules that are used mainly in the proofs in this article. Let O, O' and O'' be compatible oracle systems, $\mathbf{E}$, $\mathbf{E}_1$ and $\mathbf{E}_2$ be events of O, O' and O'', and φ, φ_1 and φ_2 be step-predicates.

$$\frac{O \sim_{\varepsilon_i} \mathbf{E}_i (i \in I) \qquad \mathbf{E} \Rightarrow \bigvee_{i \in I} \mathbf{E}_i}{O :_{\sum_{i \in I} \varepsilon_i} \mathbf{E}} \; UR \qquad \frac{}{O :_\varepsilon F_\varphi} \; Fail \qquad \frac{O :_\varepsilon F_{\neg\varphi} \qquad O \equiv_{\mathcal{R},\varphi} O'}{O \sim_\varepsilon O'} \; I\text{-}Bis$$

$$\frac{O \leq_{\det,\gamma} O' \qquad O :_\varepsilon \mathbf{E} \circ \pi}{O' :_\varepsilon \mathbf{E}} \; B\text{-}Det\text{-}Left \qquad \frac{O :_\varepsilon \mathbf{E} \circ C}{C[O] :_{\varepsilon'} \mathbf{E}} \; B\text{-}Sub \qquad \frac{O :_\varepsilon \mathbf{E}_1 \wedge G_\varphi \quad O \equiv_{\mathcal{R},\varphi} O' \quad \mathbf{E}_1 \mathcal{R} \mathbf{E}_2}{O' :_\varepsilon \mathbf{E}_2 \wedge G_\varphi} \; B\text{-}BisG$$

$$\frac{O :_{\varepsilon_2} \mathbf{E}_2 \quad O' :_{\varepsilon_1} F_{\neg\varphi} \quad O \equiv_{\mathcal{R},\varphi} O' \quad \mathbf{E}_1 \mathcal{R} \mathbf{E}_2}{O' :_{\varepsilon_1 + \varepsilon_2} \mathbf{E}_1} \; UpToBad$$

Fig. 5. Classic rules

$$\frac{O \overset{\mathbf{E}_2}{\sim}_{\varepsilon_1} O' \quad \mathbf{E}_2 \Rightarrow \mathbf{E}_1 \quad O :_{\varepsilon_2} \mathbf{E}_1 \wedge \neg \mathbf{E}_2 \quad O' :_{\varepsilon_2} \mathbf{E}_1 \wedge \neg \mathbf{E}_2}{O \overset{\mathbf{E}_1}{\sim}_{\varepsilon_1 + \varepsilon_2} O'} \; URCd \qquad \frac{}{O :_{\varepsilon'} F_{\varphi'}} \; Fail2 \qquad \frac{O \overset{\mathbf{E}_1}{\sim}_{\varepsilon_1} O' \quad O' \overset{\mathbf{E}_2}{\sim}_{\varepsilon_2} O''}{O \overset{\mathbf{E}_1 \vee \mathbf{E}_2}{\sim}_{\varepsilon_1 + \varepsilon_2} O''} \; TrCd$$

Fig. 6. Extended rules

$$\frac{O :_{\varepsilon_1} F_{\varphi_1} \wedge G_{\varphi_2} \quad O :_{\varepsilon_2} F_{\neg\varphi_2} \quad O \equiv_{\mathcal{R},\varphi_2} O'}{O' :_{\varepsilon_1 + \varepsilon_2} F_{\varphi_1}} \; B\text{-}BisG2 \qquad \frac{O' :_\varepsilon F_{\neg\varphi_2} \wedge G_{\varphi_1} \quad O \overset{\varphi_1}{\equiv}_{\mathcal{R},\varphi_2} O'}{O \overset{G_{\varphi_1}}{\sim}_\varepsilon O'} \; I\text{-}BisCd$$

$$\frac{O \overset{\mathbf{E}_1 \wedge \mathbf{E}_2}{\sim}_{\varepsilon_2} O' \quad O :_{\varepsilon_1} \neg \mathbf{E}_1 \wedge \mathbf{E}_2 \quad O' :_{\varepsilon_1} \neg \mathbf{E}_1 \wedge \mathbf{E}_2}{O \overset{\mathbf{E}_2}{\sim}_{\varepsilon_1 + \varepsilon_2} O'} \; FTr$$

Fig. 7. Rules used in the proof (extended rules)

More precisely, CIL features a rule to compute an upper-bound on the probability of an event from the number of oracle calls, and from the probability that a single oracle call triggers that event. Let φ be a predicate on $Xch \times M_o \times M_o$ and define, for every $o \in N_o$, the probability ε_o as $\max\limits_{\substack{q \in Que, m \in M_o, \\ a \in Ans, m' \in M_o}} Pr[O_o(q,m) = (a,m') \wedge \varphi((o,q,a),m,m')]$.

For every $o \in N_o$, let k_o be the maximal number of queries to o and let $\varepsilon = \sum_{o \in N_o} k_o \varepsilon_o$. CIL features the rule $\dfrac{\overline{}\; Fail}{O :_\varepsilon F_\varphi}$. But sometimes, this upper-bound is not enough convenient for the proof. We introduce another rule which keeps all the previous oracles calls triggerring the event when considering a single oracle call. CIL features the rule $\dfrac{\overline{}\; Fail2}{O :_{\varepsilon'} F_\varphi}$, where $\varepsilon' = \varepsilon \times \dfrac{\left(\sum_{o \in I} k_o\right)^2}{2}$ such that:

- k_o is the maximal number of queries of the oracle o and n is the cardinal of the set N_o
- I is the family of oracles that can ensure that the step-predicate φ can be satisfied: o can be an oracle in $N_o \setminus I$ such that $\varepsilon_o(k_{o_1}, \cdots, k_{o_n}) = 0$ or an oracle in I such that $\exists \varepsilon,\ \varepsilon_o(k_{o_1}, \cdots, k_{o_n}) = \varepsilon \times \sum_{o' \in I} k_{o'}$

B.2   Contexts

Informally, a context C is an intermediary between an oracle system O and adversaries. One can compose a O-context C with O to obtain a new oracle system $C[O]$ and with a $C[O]$-adversary to obtain a new O-adversary $C \parallel A$. Moreover, one can show that the systems $C \parallel A \mid O$ and $A \mid C[O]$ coincide in a precise mathematical sense. Despite its seemingly naivety, the relationship captures many reduction arguments used in cryptographic proofs and yields CIL rules that allow proving many schemes.

The definition of contexts is very similar to that of oracle systems, except that procedures are implemented by two functions: one that transfers calls from the adversary to the oracles and another one that tranfers answers from the oracles to the adversary (possibly after some computations).

Definition 6. *An O-context C is given by:*
- *sets M_C of context memories, an initial memory $\bar{m}_C$ and N_C of procedures*
- *for every $c \in N_C$, a query domain $In(c)$, an answer domain $Out(c)$ and two functions $C_{\overrightarrow{c}} : In(c) \times M_C \to D(Que \times M_C)$ and $C_{\overleftarrow{c}} : In(c) \times Xch \times M_C \to D(Out(c) \times M_C)$.*
- *distinguished initialization and finalization procedures c_I and c_F such that $In(c_I) = Out(c_F) = 1$, and for all x and m_c, $range(C_{\overrightarrow{c_I}}(x,m_c))(\lambda((o,\_),\_).o = o_I)$ and $range(C_{\overrightarrow{c_F}}(x,m_c))(\lambda((o,\_),\_).o = o_F)$. We let $Res_C = In(c_F)$.*

An indistinguishability context is an O-context C such that $Res_C = Res$ and $C_{\overrightarrow{c_F}}(r,m) = \delta_{((r,o_F),m)}$ for all r and m.

The sets Que_C of context queries, Ans_C of context answers and Xch_C of context exchanges are defined similarly to oracle systems. An O-context can be composed with the oracle system O or with any O-adversary A, yielding a new oracle system $C[O]$ or a new adversary $C \parallel A$. We begin by defining the composition of a context and an oracle system.

Definition 7. *The application of an O-context C to O defines an oracle system C[O] such that:*

- *the set of memories is $M_c \times M_o$ and the initial memory is $(\bar{m}_c, \bar{m}_o)$*
- *the oracles are the procedures of C and their query and answer domains are given by C. The initialization and finalization oracles are the initialization and finalization procedures of C*
- *the implementation of an oracle c is:*
  $\lambda(q_c, (m_c, m_o)). \; ((o, q_o), m'_c) \leftarrow C_{\overrightarrow{c}}(q_c, m_c) \; ; \; (a_o, m'_o) \leftarrow O_o(q_o, m_o); \; (a_c, m''_c) \leftarrow C_{\overleftarrow{c}}(q_c, (o, q_o, a_o), m'_c) \; ;$
  $\qquad return \; (a_c, (m''_c, m'_o))$

  where $\cdot \leftarrow \cdot$ notation is used for monadic composition and "return" is used for returning the result of the function.

The composition of an adversary with a context is slightly more subtle and requires that the new adversary stores the current query in its state.

Definition 8. *The application of an O-context C to a C[O]-adversary A defines an O-adversary $C \parallel A$ such that:*

- *the set of memories is $M_c \times M_a \times Que_c$ and the initial memory is $(\bar{m}_c, \bar{m}_a, \_)$*
- *the transition function is:*
  $\lambda(m_c, m_a, \_). \; ((c, q_c), m'_a) \leftarrow A(m_a) \; ; \; ((o, q), m'_c) \leftarrow C_{\overrightarrow{c}}(q_c, m_c); \; return \; ((o, q), (m'_c, m'_a, (o, q)))$
- *the update function is:*
  $\lambda((m_c, m_a, (o_c, q_c)), (o_o, q_o, a_o)). \; (a_c, m'_c) \leftarrow C_{\overleftarrow{c}}(q_c, (o_o, q_o, a_o), m_c) \; ; \; return \; (m'_c, A_{\downarrow}((o_c, q_c, a_c), m_a), \_)$

Context CDH Used in the Proofs

CDH Assumption in G

Let $G = \langle g \rangle$ be a finite cyclic group of order a l-bit prime number q, where the operation is denoted multiplicatively. We give an oracle system CDH such that:

- the memories map the variable g to the values in G and the variables α and β to the values $[1..(q-1)]$;
- for one such variable g, the initialization oracle draws uniformly at random values for α and β and outputs (g^α, g^β);
- the finalization oracle takes as input an element of G (in addition to a memory).

Bounding the number of calls of the adversary to the oracles is irrelevant. Let $\mathbf{1}_k$ be the function mapping o_I and o_F to $\mathbf{1}$. Given a negligible function ε, the $\varepsilon - CDH$ assumption holds for the group G iff for all $(\mathbf{1}_k, t)$-adversary, we have $\varepsilon - CDH \vdash$ oracle $CDH :_{\varepsilon(\mathbf{1}_k, t)} R = \mathbf{1}$.

Notation: Given g, $x \leftarrow \mathbb{Z}_q^*$ and $y \leftarrow \mathbb{Z}_q^*$, let $CDH(g^x, g^y) = g^{xy}$.

Formalization of CDH assumption: We define an oracle system CDH to capture the game played by an adversary to find the Diffie-Hellman instance (A, B). We implement this oracle as follows:

$\mathrm{Imp}_{CDH}(o_I)(g) =$
  $\alpha_0 \leftarrow \mathbb{Z}_q^* \; \beta_0 \leftarrow \mathbb{Z}_q^*; \; A := g^{\alpha_0}; \; B := g^{\beta_0};$
  $return \; (A, B)$

$\mathrm{Imp}_{CDH}(o_F)(x) =$
  $if \; x = CDH(A, B) \; then \; return \; \mathbf{1}$
  $else \; return \; \mathbf{0}$
  $endif$

Context of CDH Assumption

For this part, we write the game O_4^1 as a context C of CDH. We simulate the oracles using the random self-reducibility of the Diffie-Hellman problem, given one CDH instance (A, B).

$C_{\overrightarrow{o_I}}(x)$:
    return $(o_I, 1)$

$C_{\overleftarrow{o_I}}(x, (o, q, (A, B)))$:
    $pw \leftarrow Password$
    $L_{H_0} := []$; $L_{H_1} := []$; $L_{H_2} := []$; $L_{H_3} := []$; $L_E := []$; $L_{pw} := []$; $L_O := []$;
    $L_A := []$; $L_B := []$; $var_X := \perp$; $var_\theta := \perp$; $var_\varphi := \perp$; $var_{sk} := \perp$;
    $b := 1$
    return 1

$C_{\overrightarrow{E}}(pw, x)$:
    return $(\perp, 1)$

$C_{\overleftarrow{E}}((pw, x), (o, q, a))$:
    if $(pw, x, \_, \_) \notin L_E$ then $y \leftarrow \bar{G}$; $L_E := L_E.(pw, x, y, \perp)$ endif
    return y such that $(pw, x, y, \_) \in L_E$

$C_{\overrightarrow{D}}(pw, y)$:
    return $(\perp, 1)$

$C_{\overleftarrow{D}}((pw, y), (o, q, B))$:
    if $(pw, \_, y, \_) \notin L_E$ then $\phi \leftarrow \mathbb{Z}_q^*$; $x = g^\phi$; $L_E := L_E.(pw, x, y, \phi)$ endif
    return x such that $(pw, x, y, \_) \in L_E$

$C_{\overrightarrow{H_0}}(x)$:
    return $(\perp, 1)$

$C_{\overleftarrow{H_0}}(x, (o, q, a))$:
    if $x \notin L_{H_0}$ then $y \leftarrow U(l_0)$; $L_{H_0} := L_{H_0}.(x, y)$ endif
    return $L_{H_0}(x)$

$C_{\overrightarrow{H_1}}(x)$:
    return $(\perp, 1)$

$C_{\overleftarrow{H_1}}(x, (o, q, a))$:
    if $x \notin L_{H_1}$ then $y \leftarrow U(l_1)$; $L_{H_1} := L_{H_1}.(x, y)$ endif
    return $L_{H_1}(x)$

$C_{\overrightarrow{U_1}}(u, i)$:
    return $(\perp, 1)$

$C_{\overleftarrow{U_1}}((u, i), (o, q, A))$:
    $\alpha \leftarrow \mathbb{Z}_q^*$; $X = A^\alpha$; $var_\theta[(u, i)] = (\alpha, X)$; $var_X[(u, i)] = X$; $L_A := L_A.(\alpha, X)$
    return (u, X)

$C_{\overrightarrow{S_1}}((s, j), (u, X))$:
    return $(\perp, 1)$

$C_{\overleftarrow{S_1}}((s, j), (u, X), (o, q, B))$:
    $Y^* \leftarrow \bar{G}$; $\beta \leftarrow \mathbb{Z}_q^*$; $Y = B^\beta$; $var_\varphi[(s, j)] = (\beta, Y^*)$; $L_B := L_B.(\beta, Y)$; $var_X[(s, j)] = X$
    return (s, Y^*)

$C_{\overrightarrow{U_2}}((u, i), (s, Y^*))$:
    return $(\perp, 1)$

$C_{\overleftarrow{U_2}}((u, i), (s, Y^*), (o, q, a))$:
    if $var_\theta[(u, i)]! = \perp$ then $Y \leftarrow \bar{G}$; $(\_, Y, Y^*) = var_\varphi[(u, i)]$;
      $(\alpha, X) = var_\theta[(u, i)]$; $K_u = Y^\alpha$
      $Auth = H_1(u \parallel s \parallel X \parallel Y \parallel K_u)$; $var_{sk}[(u, i)] = H_0(u \parallel s \parallel X \parallel Y \parallel K_u)$
    endif
    return $Auth$

$C_{\overrightarrow{S_2}}((s, j), u, Auth)$:
    return $(\perp, 1)$

$C_{\overleftarrow{S_2}}((s, j), u, Auth, (o, q, B))$:
    if $var_\varphi[(s, j)]! = \perp$ then $(\beta, Y, Y^*) = var_\varphi[(s, j)]$; $X = var_X[(s, j)]$; $K_s = X^\beta$
      $H' = H_1(u \parallel s \parallel X \parallel Y \parallel K_s)$
      if $H' = Auth$ then $var_{sk}[(s, j)] = H_0(u \parallel s \parallel X \parallel Y \parallel K_s)$ endif
    endif
    return 1

$C_{\overrightarrow{Exec}}((u, i), (s, j))$:
    return $(\perp, 1)$

$C_{\overleftarrow{Exec}}((u, i), (s, j), (o, q, (A, B)))$:
    $\alpha \leftarrow \mathbb{Z}_q^*$; $X = A^\alpha$; $\beta \leftarrow \mathbb{Z}_q^*$; $Y = B^\beta$; $Y^* = E(pw, Y)$
    $Auth = H_1(u \parallel s \parallel X \parallel Y \parallel K_u)$; $var_{sk}[(u, i)] = H_0(u \parallel s \parallel X \parallel Y \parallel K_u)$
    return $((u, X), (s, Y^*), Auth)$

$C_{\overrightarrow{Reveal}}(p, k)$:
    return $(\perp, 1)$

$C_{\overleftarrow{Reveal}}((p, k), (o, q, a))$:
    if $var_{sk}[(p, k)]! = \perp$ then $sk := var_{sk}[(p, k)]$ endif
    return sk

$C_{\overrightarrow{Test^1}}(p, k)$:
    return $(\perp, 1)$

$C_{\overleftarrow{Test^1}}((p, k), (o, q, a))$:
    if $var_{sk}[(p, k)]! = \perp$ then $sk := var_{sk}[(p, k)]$ endif
    return sk

$C_{\overrightarrow{o_F}}(x)$:
    $u \parallel s \parallel X \parallel Y \parallel K \leftarrow L_{H_1}$
    if $X = (A, \alpha) \wedge Y = (B, \beta)$ then $o_F(K^{\alpha^{-1}\beta^{-1}})$ endif
    return 1

B.3   Bisimulation

Game-based proofs often proceed by transforming an oracle system into an equivalent one, or in case of imperfect simulation into a system that is equivalent up to some bad event. We reason in terms of probabilistic transition systems, using a mild extension of the standard notion of bisimulation. More specifically, we define the notion of bisimulation-up-to, where two probabilistic transition systems are bisimilar until the failure of a condition on their transitions. The definition of bisimulation is recovered by considering bisimulation-up-to the constant predicate **True**.

Let O and O' be two compatible oracle systems. For every oracle name, we let $\hat{M}$ be $M_o + M'_o$ and for every $o \in N_o$, we let $\hat{O}_o$ be the disjoint sum of O_o and O'_o, i.e. $\hat{O}_o$: $In(o) \times \hat{M} \to D(Out(o) \times \hat{M})$. We write $m \xrightarrow{(x,y)}_{>0} m'$ iff $Pr[\hat{O}_o(q, m_i) = (a, m'_i)] > 0$.

Definition 9. *Let $\varphi \subseteq Xch \times \hat{M} \times \hat{M}$ and let $\mathcal{R} \subseteq \hat{M} \times \hat{M}$ be an equivalence relation. O and O' are bisimilar-up-to φ, written $O \equiv_{\mathcal{R},\varphi} O'$, iff $\bar{m}\mathcal{R}\bar{m}'$, and for all $m_1 \xrightarrow{(o,q,a)}_{>0}$ m'_1 and $m_2 \xrightarrow{(o,q,a)}_{>0} m'_2$ such that $m_1 \mathcal{R} m_2$:*

 - *Stability: if $m'_1 \mathcal{R} m'_2$ then $\varphi((o,q,a), m_1, m'_1) \Leftrightarrow \varphi((o,q,a), m_2, m'_2)$;*
 - *Compatibility: if $\varphi((o,q,a), m_1, m'_1)$ then $Pr[\hat{O}_o(q, m_1) \in (a, C)] = Pr[\hat{O}_o(q, m_2) \in (a, C)]$ where C is the equivalence class of m'_1 under $\mathcal{R}$.*

Bisimulations are closely related to obversational equivalence and relational Hoare logic, and allow to justify proofs by simulations. Besides, bisimulations-up-to subsume the Fundamental Lemma of Victor Shoup. Then, we introduce an extension of this concept, taking account of a particular equivalence relation included in a more restricted set of memories.

Definition 10. *Let $\varphi' \subseteq \hat{M}$ and let $\hat{M}_{\varphi'} = \{m \in \hat{M} \mid \varphi'(m)\}$. Let $\varphi \subseteq Xch \times \hat{M} \times \hat{M}$ and let $\mathcal{R} \subseteq \hat{M}_{\varphi'} \times \hat{M}_{\varphi'}$ be an equivalence relation.*

O and O' are bisimilar-up-to φ, written $O \overset{\varphi'}{\equiv}_{\mathcal{R},\varphi} O'$, iff for all $\bar{m}, \bar{m}', m_1, m_2, m'_1, m'_2$ in $\hat{M}_{\varphi'}$ such that $\bar{m}\mathcal{R}\bar{m}'$, and for $m_1 \xrightarrow{(o,q,a)}_{>0} m'_1$ and $m_2 \xrightarrow{(o,q,a)}_{>0} m'_2$ such that $m_1 \mathcal{R} m_2$:

 - *Stability: if $m'_1 \mathcal{R} m'_2$ then $\varphi((o,q,a), m_1, m'_1) \Leftrightarrow \varphi((o,q,a), m_2, m'_2)$;*
 - *Compatibility: if $\varphi((o,q,a), m_1, m'_1)$ then $Pr[\hat{O}_o(q, m_1) \in (a, C)] = Pr[\hat{O}_o(q, m_2) \in (a, C)]$ where C is the equivalence class of m'_1 under $\mathcal{R}$.*

B.4   Determinization

Bisimulation is stronger than language equivalence, and can not always be used to hope from one game to another. In particular, bisimulation can not be used for eager/lazy sampling, or for extending the internal state of the oracle system. The goal of this section is to introduce a general construction, inspired from the subset construction for determinizing automata, to justify such transitions. We consider two oracles systems O and O' and assume that states $m' \in M_{o'}$ can be seen as pairs $(m, m") \in M_o \times M_{o"}$.

There are two ways to compute the probability to end up $(m, m")$ for a fixed $m"$ knowing that the step starts with a state of first component m. The first is to perform the exchange in O and then draw $m"$ according to a distribution γ. The second is to look at all possible $m"$ which γ map to m and then to perform the exchange in O'. Imposing the equality between these two ways of computing probabilities is going to compel the same equality to hold for steps, which in turn propagates to traces.

Definition 11. *Let O and O' be compatible oracle systems. O determinizes O' by γ:* $M_o \to D(M_o)$, *written* $O \leq_{det, \gamma} O'$, *iff* $M_o \times M_o" = M_o'$ *and there exists* $\bar{m}_o"$ *such that* $(\bar{m}_o, \bar{m}_o") = \bar{m}_o'$, *and* $\gamma(\bar{m}_o) = \delta_{\bar{m}_o"}$, *and* $Pr[\gamma(m_2 = m_2")]p_1 = \sum_{m_1" \in M_o"} Pr[\gamma(m_1 = m_1")]p_2(m_1")$ *for all* $m_1, m_2 \in M_o$, $m_1", m_2" \in M_o"$, *where* $p_1 = Pr[O(o_c, q, m_1) = (a, m_2)]$ *and* $p_2(m_1") = Pr[O'(o_c, q, (m_1, m_1")) = (a, (m_2, m_2"))]$).

We define a projection function π from O'-traces to O-traces by extending the projection from $M_o \times M_o"$ to M_o.

C   Proofs for Extended Rules

C.1   Proof of the Rule Fail2

Lemma 1. *Rule Fail2 defined as follows is sound:* $\overline{O :_{\varepsilon'} F_\varphi}$ *Fail2*   *where* $\varepsilon' = \varepsilon \times \dfrac{(\sum_{o \in I} k_o)^2}{2}$ *and*

- k_o *is the maximal number of queries of the oracle o and n is the cardinal of the set N_o*
- I *is the family of oracles that can ensure that the step-predicate φ can be satisfied: o can be an oracle in $N_o \setminus I$ such that $\varepsilon_o(k_{o_1}, \cdots, k_{o_n}) = 0$ or an oracle in I such that $\exists \varepsilon$, $\varepsilon_o(k_{o_1}, \cdots, k_{o_n}) = \varepsilon \times \sum_{o' \in I} k_{o'}$*

Proof. Let A be a (k, t)-adversary for oracle system O. Let φ be a step-predicate in $Xch \times \hat{M} \times \hat{M}$. We denote by T the set of traces satisfying F_φ. We recall that the event "eventually φ", written F_φ, means φ being satisfied at *one* step of a trace. Let I be the family of oracles o that can ensure that the step-predicate φ can be satisfied, $I \subseteq N_o$. We define n as the cardinal of the set N_o and for one oracle $o \in N_o$, k_o is the maximal number of its queries.

Let the trace τ in T be the sequence of the form $m_0 \xrightarrow{x_1} m_1 \xrightarrow{x_2} \cdots \xrightarrow{x_l} m_l$ where $m_0, \cdots, m_l \in M_o$ and $x_1, \cdots, x_l \in Xch$ such that $Pr[O_{o_i}(q_i, m_{i-1}) = (a_i, m_i)] > 0$ for $i = 1, \cdots, l$ and $x_i = (o_i, q_i, a_i)$. Therefore, there exists one m_{i_0} such that φ becomes satisfied, where $i_0 \in [1, \cdots, l]$.
We write two hypothesis:

- let o be an oracle in $N_o \setminus I$ such that $\varepsilon_o(k_{o_1}, \cdots, k_{o_n}) = 0$
- let o be an oracle in I such that $\exists \varepsilon$, $\varepsilon_o(k_{o_1}, \cdots, k_{o_n}) = \underset{\{\tau \in T | k_o \text{ queries}\}}{max} Pr[O_o(q, m_{l-1}) = (a, m_l)] = \varepsilon \times \sum_{o' \in I} k_{o'}$ s.t. we denote ε as the maximal number common to all oracles in I

First, we divide traces of set T in subgroups using equivalence relation. Two traces are related iff φ is true *for the first time* at step i for a query to oracle o. Classes are denoted $C(i, o, j)$, where $j = \sum_{o' \in I} k_{o'}$ is the number of good queries (i.e. the queries to oracles in I), and realize a partition of T.

Second, we let $\mathcal{T}$ be the projection mapping sequences of steps to partial traces (see for more details Section 2.4). Then, by definition, the probability that a system yields a trace τ is the sum of the probabilities that the system yields execution η projecting to τ, which we write $Pr[A \mid O : \tau] = \sum_{\{\eta \in Exec(A|O)|\mathcal{T}(\eta) = \tau\}} Pr[A \mid O : \eta]$. Let $\tau \in C(i, o, j)$. We define $\mathrm{Pref}(\eta, i)$ as the prefix of length i of partial execution η, and $\eta[i]$ its i-th step. Then, we have:

$$\sum_{\tau \in C(i,o,j)} Pr[A \mid O : \tau] = \sum_{\{\tau \in C(i,o,j)|\mathcal{T}(\eta) = \tau\}} Pr[A \mid O : \eta] \le \sum_{\{\tau \in C(i,o,j)|\mathcal{T}(\eta) = \tau\}} Pr[A \mid O : \mathrm{Pref}(\eta, i)]$$

$$= \sum_{\{\tau \in C(i,o,j)|\mathcal{T}(\eta) = \tau\}} Pr[A \mid O : \mathrm{Pref}(\eta, i-1)].Pr[A \mid O : \eta[i]]$$

$$= \sum_{\{\tau \in C(i,o,j)|\mathcal{T}(\eta) = \tau | \mathcal{T}(\eta[i]) = ((o,q,a), m, m')\}} Pr[A \mid O : \mathrm{Pref}(\eta, i-1)].Pr[O_o(q, m) = (a, m')]$$

either

$$\le \sum_{\{\tau \in C(i,o,j)|\mathcal{T}(\eta) = \tau | \mathcal{T}(\eta[i]) = ((o,q,a), m, m')\}} Pr[A \mid O : \mathrm{Pref}(\eta, i-1)] \times j.\varepsilon \le j.\varepsilon \text{ if } o \in I$$

or

$$\le \sum_{\{\tau \in C(i,o,j)|\mathcal{T}(\eta) = \tau | \mathcal{T}(\eta[i]) = ((o,q,a), m, m')\}} Pr[A \mid O : \mathrm{Pref}(\eta, i-1)] \times 0 = 0 \text{ if } o \notin I$$

Then, we use the fact that equivalence class forms a partition to conclude:

$$Pr[A \mid O : F_\varphi] = \sum_{\tau \in T} Pr[A \mid O : \tau] \sum_{i,o,j} \sum_{\tau \in C(i,o,j)} Pr[A \mid O : \tau] \le \sum_{o \in I, j} j.\varepsilon = \sum_{o \in I} \left(\sum_{o' \in I} k_{o'} \right).\varepsilon \le \varepsilon \times \frac{\left(\sum_{o \in I} k_o \right)^2}{2}$$

C.2   Proof of the Rule I-BisCd

Lemma 2. *We consider two compatible oracle systems O and O'. Let φ_1 and φ_2 be two step-predicates in $\hat{M}$ and $Xch \times \hat{M} \times \hat{M}$ respectively. The following rule is sound:*

$$\frac{O' :_\varepsilon F_{\neg \varphi_2} \wedge G_{\varphi_1} \qquad O \overset{\varphi_1}{\equiv}_{\mathcal{R}, \varphi_2} O'}{O \overset{G_{\varphi_1}}{\sim}_\varepsilon O'} \text{ I-BisCd}$$

Proof. We introduce the equivalence relation $\mathcal{R}$ such that for two states m and m' in $\hat{M}_{\varphi_1}$, we have $m\mathcal{R}m'$ and $\varphi_1(m) \wedge \varphi_1(m')$, where the step-predicate φ_1 is in $\hat{M}$ (i.e. φ_1 steps in over the memories but not over the actions in Xch). We recall that $R = \mathbf{True} \wedge G_{\varphi_1} \wedge G_{\varphi_2}$ is a compatible event. We decompose the set of traces created by $A \mid O$ and $A \mid O'$ and verifying $G_{\varphi_1} \wedge G_{\varphi_2}$ into distinct classes of equivalence of a finite number of executions $\sigma_1, \cdots, \sigma_m$, resulting in $Pr[A \mid O : R = \mathbf{True} \wedge G_{\varphi_1} \wedge G_{\varphi_2}] = \sum_{i=1}^{m} Pr[A \mid O : C_O(\sigma_i)] = \sum_{i=1}^{m} Pr[A \mid O' : C_{O'}(\sigma_i)] = Pr[A \mid O' : R = \mathbf{True} \wedge G_{\varphi_1} \wedge G_{\varphi_2}]$. Then, we conclude the rule I-BisCd since:

$$Pr[A \mid O : R = \mathbf{True} \wedge G_{\varphi_1}] - Pr[A \mid O' : R = \mathbf{True} \wedge G_{\varphi_1}]$$
$$= Pr[A \mid O : R = \mathbf{True} \wedge G_{\varphi_1} \wedge F_{\neg \varphi_2}] - Pr[A \mid O' : R = \mathbf{True} \wedge G_{\varphi_1} \wedge F_{\neg \varphi_2}]$$
$$\le max(Pr[A \mid O : R = \mathbf{True} \wedge G_{\varphi_1} \wedge F_{\neg \varphi_2}], Pr[A \mid O' : R = \mathbf{True} \wedge G_{\varphi_1} \wedge F_{\neg \varphi_2}])$$

C.3   Proof of the Rule B-BisG2

Lemma 3. *We consider two compatible oracle systems O and O'. Let φ_1 and φ_2 be two step-predicates in $Xch \times \hat{M} \times \hat{M}$. The following rule is sound:*

$$\frac{O :_{\varepsilon_1} F\varphi_1 \wedge G\varphi_2 \quad O :_{\varepsilon_2} F_{\neg\varphi_2} \quad O \equiv_{\mathcal{R},\varphi_2} O'}{O' :_{\varepsilon_1+\varepsilon_2} F\varphi_1} \; B\text{-}BisG2$$

Proof. Let φ_1 and φ_2 be step-predicates in $Xch \times \hat{M} \times \hat{M}$. The rule B-BisG2 is obtained from the combination of the rule B-BisG and a variation of this latter rule:

$$\frac{O :_{\varepsilon_1} F\varphi_1 \wedge G\varphi_2 \quad O \equiv_{\mathcal{R},\varphi_2} O'}{O' :_{\varepsilon_1} F\varphi_1 \wedge G\varphi_2} \; B\text{-}BisG \quad \frac{O :_{\varepsilon_2} \mathbf{True} \wedge F_{\neg\varphi_2} \quad O \equiv_{\mathcal{R},\varphi_2} O'}{O' :_{\varepsilon_2} \mathbf{True} \wedge F_{\neg\varphi_2}} \; B\text{-}BisG\text{-}variation$$

We are allowed to conclude since $O' :_{\varepsilon_1} F\varphi_1 \wedge G\varphi_2$ and $O' :_{\varepsilon_2} F_{\neg\varphi_2}$.

Non Observability in the Random Oracle Model

Prabhanjan Ananth and Raghav Bhaskar

Microsoft Research India,
India
prabhanjan.va@gmail.com, rbhaskar@microsoft.com

Abstract. Security proofs in the Random Oracle Model (ROM) often make use of the fact that the queries made by the adversary to the oracle are *observable* as well as the responses to those queries can be *programmed*. While, the issue of programmability of query responses has received attention in the literature, to the best of our knowledge, observability of the adversary's queries has not been identified as an artificial artefact of the Random Oracle Model. In this work, we propose a variant of ROM, in which the challenger of the security game cannot "observe" the adversary's queries to the random oracle, but can (possibly) continue to "program" the query responses. We show that this model is separable from ROM by proving that Fischlin's online extractors from [Fis05]) cannot exist when they are Non Observing. At the same time, we also show that reductions/extractors that seem to rely on observability, can sometimes achieve the same effect by programming of the responses. We also show that the schemes RSA-PFDH and Schnorr signatures are still secure with Non Observing reductions.

1 Introduction

The Random Oracle Model (ROM) was introduced by Bellare and Rogaway in [BR93] as an alternative model to study the security of cryptographic primitives and protocols. In contrast to the standard model, it assumes the availability of a random function (via an oracle) to all parties in any security game devised to study the security of a cryptographic primitive. The oracle implementing the random function (called the random oracle) returns a randomly chosen value (which it remembers for later) from the range, when queried at a new domain point. For already queried points, it returns the same value that it returned the first time around. The introduction of ROM made it possible to prove the security of many different kinds of cryptographic primitives (including digital signatures, encryption schemes etc.) for which there existed no proof in the standard model [PS00]. As truly random functions do not exist in practice, when using these primitives in the real world, the role of random oracle is played by a secure hash function. The heuristic is that secure hash functions are close enough to random oracles in their behavior, and so, the primitives continue to remain secure even under this substitution. This methodology has resulted in many provably secure (in ROM), and at the same time, practical and efficient schemes.

W. Susilo and R. Reyhanitabar (Eds.): ProvSec 2013, LNCS 8209, pp. 86–103, 2013.

Since no real world hash function is truly random, proofs in ROM have been a subject of debate by cryptographers. Public key encryption and Signature schemes have been devised such that they can be proved secure in the ROM but which become insecure as soon as the random oracle is instantiated by any real hash function [CGH04]. However, no real attacks have been demonstrated against any practical scheme that has been proved secure in ROM. This ambiguity about the *reasonability* of ROM has been of great interest to cryptographers. Furthermore, from a practical viewpoint, random oracle heuristic is the only basis for arguing the security of some of the most efficient cryptographic schemes (e.g. [PS00, BR95, BR96]). Therefore, it is of fundamental importance to understand why certain cryptographic schemes can be proved secure in the ROM while no proof of security exists for them in the standard model.

In a security game defined in ROM, the challenger (for instance, the reduction or the knowledge extractor) can simulate the random oracle for the adversary. The ability to simulate the random oracle seems to "artificially" augment the capabilities of the challenger (in comparison to a standard model challenger) in the following two ways:

- The challenger can now observe the input points at which the adversary makes queries to the random oracle. We will refer to this ability of the challenger as *observability*.
- The challenger can now control the response of the random oracle at these input points, often embedding instances of some hard problem in the response. We will refer to this ability of the challenger as *programmability*.

Both these additional capabilities of the challenger are very artifical when compared to a standard model challenger. Neither do we know of hash functions that can support such complicated programming nor do we know of a way of observing an adversary's queries to a hash function. The possibility of programming the random oracle has been exploited in constructing many security reductions and thus the programmability aspect of the ROM has attracted much attention (see [Nie02, FLR+10]). We explain some of that work later. On the other hand, even though observability is often criticized (explicitly in [Nie02]) for providing the challenger with an unreasonable ability[1], to the best of our knowledge, no formal study of this capability of the reduction has been done. Perhaps one of the most important reasons for the lack of this study is a general perception that observability is crucial to every proof in the ROM and that nothing can be achieved without it, thereby leaving no motivation to study reductions that limit observability. In this work, we study the role of observability in the construction of security proofs for several schemes. We call a reduction/extractor, which does not get to view the communication between the adversary and the random oracle, as Non Observing reduction/extractor. In the following, while we use the term reduction to explain the notion of non observability, it also refers to any entity representing the challenger in the security game (for instance extractors, simulators etc.).

---

[1] Standard model reductions would never get to see the queries made by the adversary to the hash function.

1.1   Non Observing Reductions

While in ROM, reductions often work by providing a simulation of the random oracle to the adversary, we want Non Observing reductions to operate in the presence of an external random oracle. All entities make their queries to this external random oracle which is independent of the reduction. All communication between the random oracle and the adversary is hidden from the reduction. As our focus is on restricting the observability capability of the reduction, we do let the reduction control the responses returned by the random oracle to the adversary (as long as the returned responses are uniformly distributed in the range of the random function). As shown in Figure 1, at initiation, the reduction sends a Turing machine M to the external random oracle which uses this machine to respond to the queries as follows. On receiving a query, the external random oracle, inputs "Next" to M to obtain an output r which it sends as a response to the query. We give details in Section 2. Non-Observing reductions, the way we have defined, deliberately have a fair bit of programming capability as our focus is to identify security reductions which crucially rely on Observability.

Our first result is about online extractors for NIZK-PoK proposed by Fischlin et al. in [Fis05]. The Fischlin transformation converts an interactive ZK-PoK (with some special properties) into NIZK-PoK with online extractors in the ROM. An online extractor, as defined in [Fis05], can output the witness given an acceptable proof and the queries made by the prover to the random oracle (i.e. with no rewinding). Their extractor does not need to program the random oracle responses. We introduce the notion of Non Observing extractors, which can program the responses but not observe the queries made by the adversarial prover, and then prove that they do not exist for NIZK-PoKs obtained from the Fischlin transformation. Thus, our result also rules out extractors which can neither observe random oracle queries or program the responses. Our proof idea can be extended to rule out the online extractor of [Pas03a] as well though we do not discuss this in our work. Thus, our result proves that observability is crucial for the existence of Fischlin extractor.

Our second result demonstrates the existence of extractable commitment schemes with non observing extractors. The security of the extractable commitment schemes as studied in [Pas03b] seem to rely on the fact that the extractors can observe the set of query-response pairs. We show that the capability to observe is not necessary by constructing a secure extractable commitment scheme where the extractor is not allowed to observe the queries made by the committer but only allowed to program the random oracle.

We also show that both RSA-PFDH and Schnorr signatures remain secure (under the notion of Existential Forgery with Chosen Message Attack) with Non Observing reductions. This confirms the fact that our Non Observing reductions have enough programming capabilities so as to be able to *rewind* and *embed* the challenge. Due to space constraints, we present these results (RSA-PFDH and Schnorr) in our full version [AB12].

1.2   Related Work

As part of this ongoing scrutiny of ROM, weaker versions of the Random Oracle model have been proposed. We briefly survey the most relevant ones:

- Micali and Reyzin [MR98] initiated the study of the security of signing with weak hashing by considering hash functions for which an adversary can fix arbitrarily the input-output values at polynomially many inputs.
- Nielsen [Nie02] proposed a variant of the random oracle model where the random oracle is not programmable. In this model, one cannot program or set the value that the random oracle returns to any arbitrary value. He establishes separation results between proofs in the (programmable) random oracle model and non-programmable random oracle model
- Liskov [Lis06] proposed models for weak hash functions where there exist the random oracle and the additional oracles that break some properties of the ROM. He listed several such oracles that provide, for example, collisions. He also proposed a general construction of a hash function from weak hash functions. Pasini and Vaudenay [PV07] applied Liskov's idea to the security analysis of digital signature schemes. They considered the security of hash-then-sign type signature schemes in the random oracle model with an additional oracle that returns first-preimages. Numayama, Isshiki and Tanaka [NIT08] studied the security of the Full Domain Hash signature scheme, as well as three variants thereof in weakened random oracle models.
- Mironov [Mir06] relaxed the collision-resistant requirement of hash functions in hash-and-sign constructions, without addressing the need for a random oracle. He notably revisited two popular signature schemes, DSA and PSS-RSA, and proposed variants based only on the target-collision resistant property of the underlying hash function. Their proofs of security, while still dependent on random oracles, only require *short-input ones*. In [HK06], Halevi and Krawczyk proved similar results.
- Unruh [Unr07] pointed out the fact that it might be more realistic to consider random oracles with auxiliary input. The auxiliary input models the fact that adversary at times has access to certain information about the hash function (e.g. collisions) before the initiation of the protocol. He showed that the RSA-OAEP encryption scheme [BR95] is secure in the random oracle model even in the presence of oracle-dependent auxiliary inputs
- [FLR+10] was the first work to examine the programmability by (black-box) reductions in ROM and proposed three variants of reduction in ROM: Fully-Programming Reductions, Non-Programming Reductions and Randomly-Programming Reductions. Our work is similar in spirit but for the property of observability in black-box reductions in ROM.

2   Modelling Non Observability

In this section, we formally define the notion of Non Observability via reductions in ROM, though as before, the discussion also applies to extractors. As

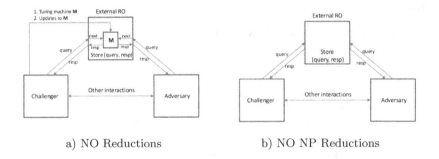

a) NO Reductions   b) NO NP Reductions

Fig. 1. Non Observing (NO) reductions can return responses to adversary's queries without actually observing the query. Non Observing, Non Programming (NO NP) reductions can neither observe the queries nor influence the responses.

discussed in the introduction, a non observing reduction cannot observe the interaction between the adversary and the random oracle, though it can continue to 'influence' the query responses. Modelling how the reduction can influence the responses returned by the oracle machine while ensuring that the reduction can get no 'information' about the queries of the adversary is tricky. One way of modelling it is as follows: The reduction sends a (stateful) Turing machine M to the external oracle. On receiving a query q from the adversary, M is executed by the oracle machine on input q to obtain an element r. The value r is then sent to the adversary as a response. Also, M needs to be programmed in such a way that for a repeat query, the same response is returned. Unfortunately, this approach does not work because consider a machine M designed in a way, such that on receiving a "pecial' query from the reduction, all the queries made by the adversary till then are revealed. Thus, even though the reduction did not actually "see" the queries made by the adversary it still gets information about the queries made by the adversary through the machine M. The problem with the previous approach was that the response returned to a query could depend upon all the queries made till then. We can rectify this problem by forcing the condition that the machine M should return responses from a list which is fixed before the adversary makes any query. We allow the reduction to program this list before the random oracle is initiated. This again allows the reduction to learn several bits of the adversary's queries as follows: M can output a list of size $2^\ell \cdot q_h$, where the reduction wants to learn some ℓ bits of the query and q_h is the maximum number of queries that the adversary can make. The machine returns a response for each query from a bucket of size 2^ℓ based on its ℓ bits. The reduction, can make special formatted queries to learn all the returned responses and thus learn ℓ bits of each query made by the adversary. The problem with this approach is that the machine M is allowed to maintain state. We can fix this problem by requiring M to be stateless. Thus, the reduction sends a stateless machine M along with a list L such that for every query q the following is done: $M(q, L)$ is executed to obtain r. It is verified whether r is in L before sending it to the adversary. This seems to do better than the previous approaches, in that the machine can no longer return responses which are correlated to the queries made till that point. But even this approach does not work! For two different queries q_1 and q_2, $M(q_1, L)$ and $M(q_2, L)$ can give the same answer which might help the adversary in distinguishing between a pure random oracle from M because in a pure random oracle model this can happen only with negligible probability. To circumvent these problems, we present a model, defined in the next subsection, which seems to not only capture non observability reasonably well but also is a more natural transition from (programmable and observable) ROM.

2.1   Our Model

A Non Observing reduction works in the presence of an external random oracle which is beyond its control. The adversary and other parties make queries directly to this external random oracle and receive the responses from it. All communication between the adversary and the random oracle is hidden from everyone else. For every instantiation of a random oracle, the reduction can send a Turing machine M to the oracle. This machine is used by the external random oracle to answer its queries in the following manner: When a random oracle receives a query, which it has never answered before[2], it forwards a request to machine M using the "Next" message. The machine M, at this point, can provide a response chosen uniformly at random from the range of the random function. On receiving a response from M, the oracle stores the (query, response) pair for future use and returns the response to the adversary. The reduction is also allowed to send updates in the form of query-response pairs to the external oracle during the lifetime of its exection. This update procedure, allows the reduction to dynamically adjust its responses to the random oracle queries. As the reduction may be interacting with the adversary through other channels (for instance it may be simulating a signature oracle for the adversary), this way, it can use its knowledge from the other channels in returning the response. The external machine, maintains consistency of the stored list, by ensuring that the list is not updated with a new response for a already stored query. The reduction can also send queries of its own to the random oracle. In case of it being a fresh query, the oracle will answer it just like an adversary's fresh query, else it will return a response using the stored (query, response) pairs. We show this in Figure 1. Before we formally define the model, we present some preliminaries.

For a cryptographic primitive S with the security property Π_S, let $\mathsf{Adv}_S^{\Pi}(\mathcal{A})$ be defined as the success probability of the adversary $\mathcal{A}$ in violating the security property Π_S. For an oracle adversary $\mathcal{A}^{\mathcal{O}}$, the probability $\mathsf{Adv}_S^{\Pi}(\mathcal{A}^{\mathcal{O}})$ is taken over the random coins of the oracle $\mathcal{O}$ as well. More formally, $\mathsf{Adv}_S^{\Pi}(\mathcal{A}^{\mathcal{O}})$ is the weighted average of the Adv parameters when instantiated with specific oracles and the weights correspond to the probabilities that the corresponding specific oracles are chosen. We say that an adversary $\mathcal{A}$ Π_S-breaks S if there

---

[2] The external random oracle can check this by maintaining list of all returned query-response pairs.

exists a polynomial $p(\cdot)$ such that $\mathsf{Adv}_{\mathsf{S}}^{\Pi}(\mathcal{A}) > 1/p(n)$ for infinitely many n. Consider cryptographic primitives S and f with security properties Π_{S} and Π_f respectively. Let $\mathcal{A}$ denote an attacker on the primitive S and let $\mathcal{R}$ denote a reduction from f to S, i.e., $\mathcal{R}$ uses $\mathcal{A}$ to attack primitive f. We will denote by $\mathcal{O}$ to denote a random oracle that chooses a response uniformly at random from its range and by $\mathcal{O}(M)$ an oracle that uses the machine M produced by reduction $\mathcal{R}$ to provide the responses to its queries. We will use $\mathcal{R}^{\boxed{\mathcal{A}^{\mathcal{O}(M)}}}$ to denote the fact that the reduction has black box access to $\mathcal{A}$ and that the interaction between $\mathcal{A}$ and $\mathcal{O}(\mathcal{M})$ is hidden from $\mathcal{R}$. Further, $\mathcal{R}^{\boxed{\mathcal{A}^{\mathcal{O}(M)}},\mathcal{O}(M)}$ denotes such a reduction which also has oracle access to $\mathcal{O}(\mathcal{M})$.

Definition 1. *There exists a black-box Non Observing reduction from f to S if there exists a machine $\mathcal{R}$ that outputs M with the property that if $\mathcal{A}^{\mathcal{O}(M)}$ Π_{S} -breaks S, making $q_{\mathcal{O}}$ queries to the oracle $\mathcal{O}(M)$, then $\mathcal{R}^{\boxed{\mathcal{A}^{\mathcal{O}(M)}},\mathcal{O}(M)}$ Π_f-breaks f.*

We define a Non Observing Non Programming reduction as a Non Observing reduction that can no longer provide the responses to the oracle. Thus, such a reduction works with oracle $\mathcal{O}$ rather than $\mathcal{O}(M)$. See Figure 1 for a diagramatic representation of the reduction.

Definition 2. *There exists a black-box Non Observing Non Programming reduction from f to S if there exists a PPT ITM machine $\mathcal{R}$ with the property that if $\mathcal{A}^{\mathcal{O}}$ Π_{S}-breaks S, making $q_{\mathcal{O}}$ queries to the oracle $\mathcal{O}$, then $\mathcal{R}^{\boxed{\mathcal{A}^{\mathcal{O}}},\mathcal{O}}$ Π_f-breaks f.*

3 Preliminaries

Let $\lambda \in \mathbb{N}$ be the security parameter. We say that a function is *negligible* in λ if it is asymptotically smaller than the inverse of any fixed polynomial. More precisely, a function $\eta(\lambda)$ from non-negative integers to reals is called negligible in λ if for every constant $c > 0$, $\exists \lambda_c$ such that $\forall \lambda > \lambda_c$, $|\eta(\lambda)| < \lambda^{-c}$. Otherwise, $\eta(\lambda)$ is said to be *non-negligible* in λ.

3.1 Fischlin Transformation

We now describe the preliminaries to understand Fischlin transformation. Fischlin transformation converts a Fiat-Shamir proof of knowledge to a non interactive proof of knowledge. We describe Fiat-Shamir proof of knowledge below.

Definition 3. *A Fiat Shamir proof of knowledge (with $l(k)$-bit challenges) for relation W is pair (P, V) of probabilistic polynomial time algorithms $P = (P_0, P_1)$, $V = (V_0, V_1)$ with the following properties. [Completeness.] For any parameter k, any $(x, w) \in W_k$, any $(P(x, w), V_0(x)) \to (\alpha, \beta, \gamma)$ it holds $V_1(x, \alpha, \beta, \gamma) = 1$.*

[Commitment Entropy.] *For parameter* k, *for any* $(x, w) \in W_k$, *the min-entropy of* $P_0(x, w) \rightarrow \alpha$ *is superlogarithmic in* k.

[Public Coin.] *For any* k, *any* $(x, w) \in W_k$ *any* $\alpha \leftarrow P_0(x, w)$ *the challenge* $V_0(x, \alpha) \rightarrow \beta$ *is uniform on* $\{0, 1\}^{l(k)}$.

[Unique responses.] *For any probabilistic polynomial time algorithm* A, *for parameter* k *and* $A(k) \rightarrow (x, \alpha, \beta, \gamma, \gamma')$ *we have, as a function of* k,

$$Pr[V_1(x, \alpha, \beta, \gamma) = V_1(x, \alpha, \beta, \gamma') = 1 \wedge \gamma \neq \gamma'] \approx 0$$

[Special Soundness.] *There exists a probabilistic polynomial time algorithm* K, *the knowledge extractor, such that for any* k, *any* $(x, w) \in W_k$, *any pairs* (α, β, γ), $(\alpha, \beta', \gamma')$ *with* $V_1(x, \alpha, \beta, \gamma) = V_1(x, \alpha, \beta', \gamma') = 1$ *and* $\beta \neq \beta'$, *for* $K(x, \alpha, \beta, \gamma, \beta', \gamma') \rightarrow w'$ *it holds* $(x, w') \in W_k$.

[Honest-Verifier Zero-Knowledge.] *There exists a probabilistic polynomial time algorithm* Z, *the zero-knowledge simulator, such that for any pair of probabilistic polynomial time algorithms* $D = (D_0, D_1)$ *the following distributions are computationally indistinguishable:*

- Let $D_0(k) \rightarrow (x, w, \delta)$ *and* $(P(x, w), V_0(x)) \rightarrow (\alpha, \beta, \gamma)$ *if* $(x, w) \in W_k$ *and* $\perp \rightarrow (\alpha, \beta, \gamma)$ *otherwise. Output* $D_1(\alpha, \beta, \gamma, \delta)$.
- Let $D_0(k) \rightarrow (x, w, \delta)$ *and* $Z(x, YES) \rightarrow (\alpha, \beta, \gamma)$ *if* $(x, w) \in W_k$ *and* $Z(x, NO) \rightarrow (\alpha, \beta, \gamma)$. *Output* $D_1(\alpha, \beta, \gamma, \delta)$.

If a Fiat-Shamir proof of knowledge in addition to the above properties has a polynomial sized challenge space (that is, the challenge space is of the size $p(k)$ for some polynomial p) then it satisfies a property termed as Special Zero Knowledge, which is described below.

Definition 4 (Special Zero-Knowledge). *There exists a probabilistic polynomial time algorithm* X, *the special zero-knowledge simulator, such that for any pair of probabilistic polynomial-time algorithms* $D = (D_0, D_1)$ *the following distributions are computationally indistinguishable: (-) Let* $(x, w, ch, \delta) \leftarrow D_0(k)$ *and* $(com, ch, resp) \leftarrow (P(x, w), V_0(x, ch))$ *if* $(x, w) \in W_k$ *and* $(com, ch, resp) \leftarrow \perp$ *else. Output* $D_1(com, ch, resp, \delta)$. *(-) Let* $(x, w, ch, \delta) \leftarrow D_0(k)$ *and* $(com, ch, resp) \leftarrow Z(x, ch, YES)$ *if* $(x, w) \in W_k$ *and* $(com, ch, resp) \leftarrow Z(x, ch, NO)$ *else. Output* $D_1(com, ch, resp, \delta)$.

The Fischlin transformation is shown to be secure by arguing that if there exists a PPT adversary that violates the soundness then there exists a PPT algorithm that given a valid input instance (corresponding to the relation for which the protocol is defined) outputs a witness for that instance with non-negligible probability. In other words, the security of the Fischlin transformation is based on the assumption that given a valid input instance, drawn from some distribution, it is hard to obtain a witness for the instance. This is formalised in the following assumption.

Definition 5. *A relation W is said to have a one-way instance generator $\mathcal{I}$ if for any parameter k algorithm $\mathcal{I}$ returns in probabilistic polynomial time $(x, w) \in W_k$, but such that for any probabilistic polynomial time algorithm, termed as inverter, I, for $(x, w) \in \mathcal{I}(1^k)$ and $I(x) \to w'$ the probability $P((x, w') \in W_k)$ is negligible in k.*

3.2   Commitment Schemes

In this section, we recall the definition of commitment schemes in the random oracle model. A commitment scheme consists of three PPT algorithms: Commit, Decommit and Verify which are as described below. The committer executes the Commit algorithm during the commit phase and it executes the Decommit algorithm during the reveal phase. Consider a random oracle H.

- Commit(m, r): It takes the message m and chooses randomness r to derive a commitment c using the random oracle H.
- Decommit(c): The commitment c is opened by outputting m and r.
- Verify(m, r, c): It verifies whether c is indeed the output of (m, r) using the random oracle H.

A commitment scheme is said to satisfy two main properties: namely, hiding and binding. The computational hiding property says that distributions of the commitments corresponding to two different messages are computationally indistinguishable. The computational binding property says that a probabilistic polynomial time committer can open a commitment to two different values only with negligible probability.

4   Non Observing Online Extractors

In this section, we explore online extractors in the non observability framework. The construction of online extractors in Non Interactive Zero Knowledge Proofs of Knowledge (NIZK-PoK) was studied by [Fis05] though it was first discussed in [SG98]. Informally, an online extractor can extract a witness for an input instance, given a proof (accepted by an honest verifier) and all the queries made by the prover to the random oracle. The online extractors deviate from the traditional extractors in that rewinding is not necessary to extract the witness. As remarked in [Fis05], rewinding leads to loose security reductions and hence online extractors can be useful to obtain tighter security results.

The formal definition of online extractors for a non interactive zero knowledge proof of knowledge is given below.

Definition 6 (Online Extractor). *[Fis05] There exists a probabilistic polynomial time algorithm K such that the following holds for any algorithm A. Let $\mathcal{O}$ be a random oracle, $(x, \pi) \leftarrow A^{\mathcal{O}}(k)$ and $Q_{\mathcal{O}}(A)$ be the sequence of queries of A to $\mathcal{O}$. Let $w \leftarrow K(x, \pi, Q_{\mathcal{O}}(A))$. Then as a function of k,*

$$Pr[(x, w) \notin W_k \wedge V^{\mathcal{O}}(x, \pi) = 1] \approx 0$$

In the above definition, the online extractor does not have any power to choose the random oracle. In other words, the extractor is not allowed to program the random oracle. We first describe the result from [Fis05] which gives the construction of online extractors. [Fis05] gave a transformation, termed as Fischlin transformation, to convert an interactive proof of knowledge (defined as Fiat Shamir Proof of knowledge; see definition 3 in Section 3) to a NIZK-PoK which has an online extractor.

Fischlin transformation converts a 3-message interactive ZKPoK (P_{FS}, V_{FS}) to a non interactive ZKPoK (P^H, V^H), where H is the random oracle, as follows. P^H executes logarithmically many copies, denoted by r, of the underlying prover P_{FS}. In each execution it gets the commitment com_i from P_{FS}. In the ith execution, P^H then sequentially checks whether there exists any challenge ch_i from 0 to $2^t - 1$ such that $H(\text{com}, i, ch_i, resp_i)$ has all its last b bits as 0, where b is typically logarithmic in the security parameter and $resp_i$ is the response returned by the ith copy of P_{FS} on challenge ch_i. If no such challenge exists then P^H picks the challenge ch_i for which $H(\text{com}, i, ch_i, resp_i)$ is minimum among all other challenges. Finally, P^H composes the proof $(com_i, ch_i, resp_i)_{1 \leq i \leq r}$. The verifier V_{FS} on input $x, (com_i, ch_i, resp_i)_{1 \leq i \leq r}$ checks whether V_{FS} accepts the proof $(x, com_i, ch_i, resp_i)$ for all $1 \leq i \leq r$. And also, it checks whether the last b bits of summation of $H(\text{com}, i, ch_i, resp_i)$ is at most logarithmic in the security parameter. We formally describe the Fischlin transformation below.

Definition 7 (Fischlin Transformation). *[Fis05] Let H be a random oracle. Let (P_{FS}, V_{FS}) be an interactive Fiat-Shamir proof of knowledge with challenges of $\ell = \ell(k) = O(log(k))$ bits for relation W. Define the parameters b, r, S, t (as functions of k) for the number of test bits, repetitions, maximum sum and trial bits such that $br = \omega(logk)$, $2^{t-b} = \omega(logk)$, b, r, $t = O(logk)$, $S = O(r)$ and $b \leq t \leq \ell$. Define the following non-interactive proof system for relation W in the random oracle model, where the random oracle maps to b bits.*

- ***Prover.*** *The prover P^H on input (x,w) first runs the prover $P_{FS}(x, w)$ in r independent repetitions to obtain r commitments $com_1, \cdots, com_r$. Let $\text{com} = (com_1, \cdots, com_r)$. Then P_H does the following, either sequentially or in parallel for each repetition i. For each $ch_i = 0, 1, 2, \cdots, 2^t - 1$ (viewed as t-bit strings) it lets P_{FS} compute the final responses $resp_i = resp_i(ch_i)$ by rewinding, until it finds the first one such that $H(x, \text{com}, i, ch_i, resp_i) = 0^b$; if no such tuple is found then P^H picks the first one for which the hash value is minimal among all 2^t hash values. The prover finally outputs $\pi = (com_i, ch_i, resp_i)_{i=1,2,\ldots,r}$.*
- ***Verifier.*** *The verifier V^H on input x and $\pi = (com_i, ch_i, resp_i)_{i=1,2,\ldots,r}$ accepts if and only if $V_{1,FS}(x, com_i, ch_i, resp_i) = 1$ for each $i = 1, 2, \cdots, r$, and if $\Sigma_{i=1}^r H(x, \text{com}, ch_i, resp_i) \leq S$.*

We first give an intuitive description of the proof of online extractability of the above transformation. Consider an adversary who, on input x, has produced a proof π without having a witness for x. Let Q be the set of queries made by the adversary to the random oracle. We first claim that there cannot exist two queries (com, $i, ch_i, resp_i$) and (com, $i, ch_i^*, resp_i^*$) in Q such that both $(com_i, ch_i, resp_i)$ and $(com_i, ch_i^*, resp_i^*)$ are accepted by the verifier V_{FS}. If there existed two such queries then by the special soundness property of (P_{FS}, V_{FS}), the witness can be extracted. The extraction can be done by the online extractor since he can observe the queries made by the adversary. Hence, once the commitment tuple is fixed the adversary can query the random oracle for one particular challenge ch_i for i from 1 to r. Let s_i be the value output by the random oracle for the challeng e ch_i. Using simple probability arguments it can be shown that the summation of s_i for all the repetitions is negligible. Thus, for a given commitment tuple adversary succeeds with negligible probability in producing an accepting proof corresponding to that tuple. Since, adversary can try only polynomially many commitment tuples he can succeed in producing an accepting proof only with negligible probability.

The capability of the online extractor to extract the witness comes from crucial fact that the extractor can observe the queries made by the prover. If the extractor is not allowed to see the queries made by the prover and not allowed to program the random oracle then it can be seen that the extractor cannot extract the witness from the proof. In other words, there does not exist an online extractor for any NIZKPoK that neither programs the random oracle nor observes the queries made by the prover. The reason is that, if such an extractor were to exist then a malicious verifier can simply run the extractor to get the witness thus contradicting the zero knowledge property of the protocol. The same is not clear when the extractor is allowed to program the random oracle. More precisely, we want to understand whether there exist online extractors for NIZKPoK which are allowed do some limited programming of the random oracle but not allowed to observe. We term this class of online extractors as non observing online extractors and formally define them below.

Definition 8 (Non Observing Online Extractors). *There exists a probabilistic polynomial time algorithm $K = (K_1, K_2)$ such that for large enough k the following holds for any algorithm A. There exists a polynomial $p(k)$ such that $(M, aux) \leftarrow K_1(k, p(k))$ and $(x, \pi) \leftarrow A^{\mathcal{O}(M)}(k)$ making $q_{\mathcal{O}} \leq p(k)$ queries to the oracle $\mathcal{O}(M)$. Then we have that $w \leftarrow K_2^{\mathcal{O}(M)}(x, \pi, M, aux)$. Then as a function of k,*

$$Pr[(x, w) \notin W_k \wedge V^{\mathcal{O}(M)}(x, \pi) = 1] \approx 0$$

We first show that there is a NIZKPoK which has a non observing extractor in the random oracle model. Consider a NIZKPoK (P, V) in the common reference string model. Construction of NIZKPoK in the common reference string model has been well studied in literature. See [DSP92] for one such example. The fact that (P, V) is a NIZKPoK means that it has an extractor $E = (E_0, E_1)$ which executes as follows. On input security parameter, E_0 produces a pair of strings (σ, aux). Let π be an acceptable proof produced by an adversary A on input x as well as σ. Then, E_1 on input (x, π, σ, aux) outputs a witness w for x with non negligible probability. We construct (P^*, V^*) in the random oracle model from (P, V) as follows. P^* on input x, queries the random oracle on the point

x to get the response σ. P^* then executes $P(x,\sigma)$ to obtain π. The verifier V^*, on receiving π, first queries x to the random oracle to get σ and then executes $V(x,\pi,\sigma)$. V^* then outputs whatever V outputs. We can construct a non observing online extractor $E^* = (E_0^*, E_1^*)$ as follows. Consider an adversarial prover A. Let q_O be the number of queries made by the adversary. E_0^* executes E_0 for q_O times to obtain the strings $\big((\sigma_1, aux_1), \dots, (\sigma_{q_O}, aux_{q_O})\big)$. E_0^* then constructs a Turing machine M which on being invoked for the ith time with input $next$ outputs the string σ_i. E_0^* then sends the Turing machine M to the random oracle. After receiving the proof π from an adversary A, E_1^* then queries x to the random oracle to obtain σ_i and then it executes $E_1(x, \pi, \sigma_i, aux_i)$ to obtain w. From the extractability property of (P,V), it follows that if π is an acceptable proof then E^* outputs a witness for x with non negligible probability. This shows the existence of a NIZKPoK having non observing extractors.

The natural question to ask now is whether this is true for all NIZKPoK in the random oracle model. That is, whether there exists non observing online extractors for all NIZKPoK. We show that this is not true. In fact, we show that all the NIZKPoKs that are obtained from the Fischlin transformation do not have non observing online extractors. We formalize this result in the following theorem.

Theorem 1. *Consider a relation W having a one-way instance generator $\mathcal{I}$. Let (P^H, V^H) be a non-interactive zero-knowledge proof of knowledge obtained by applying the Fischlin transformation to an interactive Fiat-Shamir proof of knowledge, (P_{FS}, V_{FS}) defined for the relation W. Then, there does not exist a Non Observing extractor for (P^H, V^H)* [3].

Proof: We show that if a Non Observing online extractor K exists for (P^H, V^H) then we can construct an algorithm B, termed as inverter, which does the following. It takes as input x where x is produced by the one way instance generator, $\mathcal{I}$. It then outputs a witness w for x with non-negligible probability such that $(x, w) \in W$. This contradicts the fact that $\mathcal{I}$ is a one-way instance generator for the relation W. We now give the construction of B. The algorithm B on input x executes the following steps.

Step 1) B first executes K_1 to get the Turing machine M which is passed on to the random oracle. It then makes $2^t r$ queries to a copy of M to obtain a list L. The reason why the size of the list is set to $2^t r$ is because the honest prover makes at most $2^t r$ queries. Note, the list L is the same as the first $2^t r$ responses returned by $\mathcal{O}(M)$.

Step 2) B chooses the r challenges $ch_i, i \in [1, r]$ by looking up the list L. As B has access to the list L of hash responses, it can figure out the exact challenges which an honest prover will include in his proof by

---

[3] We say that there does not exist a non observing online extractor for a proof system if for every PPT extractor there exists a PPT adversarial prover such that the probability that the adversarial prover produces an accepting proof and at the same time the non observing extractor cannot extract a witness is non-negligible.

imitating the honest prover's strategy. B considers the first 2^t elements in the list L which $K_1(1^k)$ outputs. If there is an element whose least significant b bits are 0 (if there are many such elements pick the one with the least index in L), then B assigns ch'_1 to be its index else assign ch'_1 to be the index of the minimum among the first 2^t elements. If $(ch'_1)^{th}$ element corresponds to an element whose least significant b bits are 0, then B repeats the process to compute ch'_2 starting from the $(\beta'_1 + 1)^{th}$ element of L. Whereas if $(ch'_1)^{th}$ element corresponds to the smallest element in the first 2^t elements, repeat the above process starting from the $(2^t + 1)^{th}$ element of the list. Thus, using the above approach B computes ch'_i, for all $i \in [1, r]$. Assign ch_i to be ch'_i if $i = 1$ else $ch_i = ch'_i - ch'_{i-1}$.

Step 3) B executes the special zero knowledge simulator, Z, of the interactive Fiat-Shamir proof of knowledge, (P_{FS}, V_{FS}), at (x, ch_i, YES) to obtain com_i and $resp_i$ for all $i \in [1, r]$. Let $\text{com} = (com_1, \dots, com_r)$.

Step 4) B makes ch'_r queries to the random oracle $\mathcal{O}(M)$ as follows. At query numbers $ch'_i, \forall i \in [1, r]$ it queries the oracle with $(x, \text{com}, i, ch_i, resp_i)$. At all other points it queries the oracle at $(x, \text{com}, 1, 0, 0)$, where com is a r-sized vector with each element chosen randomly from the commitment space.

Finally, B produces $\pi_B = ((com_1, ch_1, resp_1), (com_2, ch_2, resp_2), \dots, (com_r, ch_r, resp_r))$ as the proof. The following lemma proves that no probabilistic polynomial time algorithm (even with access to the Turing machine M) can distinguish proof π_B from a proof $\pi_{P^{\mathcal{O}(L)}}$ produced by an honest prover $P^{\mathcal{O}(M)}$, where $P^{\mathcal{O}(M)}$ is same as the prover P^H but with random oracle H replaced with $\mathcal{O}(M)$.

Lemma 1. *Let D be a probabilistic polynomial time algorithm. The following two distributions are indistinguishable.*

- *$K_1(1^k, 2^t r) \to M$. B is executed with input (x, M) and oracle access to $\mathcal{O}(M)$ which then outputs π_B. Output $D^{\mathcal{O}(M)}(x, M, \pi_B)$.*
- *$K_1(1^k, 2^t r) \to M$. $P^{\mathcal{O}(M)}$ is executed with input x, w and oracle access to $\mathcal{O}(M)$ which then outputs $\pi_{P^{\mathcal{O}(M)}}$. Output $D^{\mathcal{O}(M)}(x, M, \pi_{P^{\mathcal{O}(M)}})$.*

Proof. B's strategy of producing the challenges and the special zero knowledge property ensure that the distributions of π_B is computationally indistinguishable from $\pi_{P^{\mathcal{O}(M)}}$ and thus D cannot distinguish the proof transcript π_B from $\pi_{P^{\mathcal{O}(M)}}$. But as the queries made to the random oracle by B are different from that of an honest prover, D could try guessing the queries. We show below that this happens with negligible probability. Let the set of queries made by $P^{\mathcal{O}(M)}$ (respectively, B) to $\mathcal{O}(M)$ during its execution be $Query_{P^{\mathcal{O}(M)}}$ (resp. $Query_B$). Denote the set of responses returned by $\mathcal{O}(M)$ corresponding to $Query_{P^{\mathcal{O}(M)}}$ (resp. $Query_B$) by $Resp_{P^{\mathcal{O}(M)}}$ (resp. $Resp_B$). To prove the theorem, we first make the claim that $Resp_{P^{\mathcal{O}(M)}}$ is in fact the same as $Resp_B$. This follows from the description of B and $P^{\mathcal{O}(M)}$. Let $\pi_{P\mathcal{O}(M)} = (com_i, ch_i, resp_i)_{1 \leq i \leq r}$ and $\pi_B = (com_i', ch_i', resp_i')_{1 \leq i \leq r}$. We then claim that in both the cases, if the distinguisher makes a query q to $\mathcal{O}(M)$ then q belongs to $(Query_{P\mathcal{O}(M)} \backslash \{(com_1, \cdots, com_r, i, ch_i, resp_i) : 1 \leq i \leq r\})$ (resp. q belongs to $(Query_B \backslash \{(com_1', \cdots, com_r', i, ch_i', resp_i')\})$ with negligible probability. To prove this claim, consider the following cases.

Case 1. $P^{\mathcal{O}(M)}$: Without loss of generality let q be equal to $(com_1, \cdots, com_r, i, ch, resp)$ for some $i \in \{1, \ldots, r\}$. Since $q \in (Query_{P\mathcal{O}(M)} \backslash \{(com_1, \cdots, com_r, i, ch_i, resp_i) : 1 \leq i \leq r\})$, it should happen that $(com_i, ch, resp)$ is an accepting transcript (this is because the honest prover follows the protocol and hence all its queries correspond to accepting transcripts). We now have two accepting transcripts $(com_i, ch_i, resp_i)$ (from $\pi_{P\mathcal{O}(M)}$) and $(com_i, ch, resp)$ using which we can extract a witness for x. Using this observation, we can construct a polynomial time procedure which can extract a witness from the input instance. Now, we make the observation that we could have executed the zero knowledge simulator to obtain π_{Sim} (which is indistinguishable from $\pi_{P\mathcal{O}(M)}$) and then using the strategy of D (in a non black box way) to find q we could then extract a witness for the input instance. Since such an approach gives us a probabilistic polynomial time algorithm to compute the witness, our assumption that the considered relation has a one-way instance generator is violated.

Case 2. B: Consider the query $q' = (com_1'', \ldots, com_r'', 0, 0, 0)$ in the set $(Query_B \backslash \{(com_1', \cdots, com_r'), i, ch_i', resp_i'\})$. The probability that $q' = q$ is negligible since $com_1'', \ldots, com_r''$ is picked uniformly at random.

From the above two cases it can be inferred that the distributions $D^{\mathcal{O}(M)}(x, L, \pi_{P\mathcal{O}(M)})$ and $D^{\mathcal{O}(M)}(x, L, \pi_B)$ are indistinguishable. □

Now, consider the following probabilistic polynomial time algorithm.

Input: Instance x obtained as the output of the one-way instance generator $\mathcal{I}$.
Output: Witness w.
1. $K_1(1^k, 2^t r) \rightarrow M$.
2. $B^{\mathcal{O}(M)}(x, M) \rightarrow \pi_B$.
3. $K_2^{\mathcal{O}(M)}(x, M, \pi_B) \rightarrow w$.

Using Lemma 4 and the construction of B, it can be seen that the above algorithm outputs w with non-negligible probability for input x such that $(x, w) \in W$ contradicting the assumption that W has a one-way instance generator. Thus, Non Observing online extractors do not exist for (P^H, V^H).

5   Extractable Commitment Schemes

The notion of extractable commitment schemes has been studied [Pas03b, ACP09] in the common reference string model as well as the random oracle model.

Extractable commitments are commitment schemes equipped with an additional algorithm, called the *extractor*, which can recover the committed value given the commitment as well as the trapdoor to the CRS (in the CRS model) or given access to the queries to the random oracle made by the committer to generate the commitment. In this section, we study extractable commitments in the random oracle model. If the extractor is allowed to observe the queries made by the committer then there is a simple commitment scheme as described in [Pas03b]. We give an example of an non interactive extractable commitment scheme where the extractor is allowed the program the random oracle but not allowed to observe the queries made by the committer to the random oracle. We now define the notion of extractable commitment schemes in the random oracle model when the extractor is non-observing.

Definition 9. *Consider a non-interactive commitment scheme (C, R) defined in the random oracle model where C is the committer and R is the receiver. We say (C, R) is an extractable commitment scheme with non observing extractors if there exists a PPT extractor $K = (K_1, K_2)$ which does the following. The algorithm K_1 on input security parameter ouputs a Turing machine M along with auxillary information aux. Let the output of the committer with access to $\mathcal{O}(M)$ be the commitment c. Then, K_2 on input (c, M, aux) and access to the random oracle $\mathcal{O}(M)$ outputs m with probability negligibly close to the probability that the committer succeeds in decommitting to m.*

We now describe our extractable commitment scheme. Consider the random oracle H mapping from $\{0, 1\}^*$ to $\{0, 1\}^n$, where n is some polynomial in the security parameter. Let $k_1 < n$ and k_2 be polynomials in the security parameter.

ExtCom

Commit phase:
On input m, the committer picks a value R from $\{0, 1\}^{k_2}$ uniformly at random. It then sends the queries $(m, R, 1), \ldots, (m, R, l)$ to H to receive the responses $(h'_1, \ldots, h'_l)$, where l is the length of m. It then picks a non-zero key K from the space $\{0, 1\}^{n-k_1} \setminus \{0^{n-k_1}\}$ uniformly at random [4]. It then computes $(h_1, \ldots, h_l)$ as follows: $h_i = h'_i$ if $m_i = 0$ (m_i denotes the ith bit of m) else $h_i = h'_i \oplus (K||0^{k_1})$. It then sends $(h_1, \ldots, h_l)$ as the commitment.

Reveal phase:
The committer sends (m, R, K) as the decommitment. Let the input received by the receiver during the commit phase be $(h_1, \ldots, h_l)$. The receiver accepts if the following conditions are satisfied.
1. $K \neq 0$.
2. $H(m, R, i) = h_i$ if $m_i = 0$, else $H(m, R, i) \oplus (K||0^{k_1}) = h_i$.

---

[4] This means that it picks a *non-zero* key from the space $\{0, 1\}^{n-k_1}$ uniformly at random.

We now show that the above commitment scheme satisfies both the hiding and the binding properties. We first show that the commitment scheme satisfies computational hiding property. Observe that the only way for the adversary to distinguish the commitments corresponding to two different messages is when it queries the random oracle on the message which is contained in the commitment. Since the adversary runs in polynomial time the probability that it guesses R (picked by the committer) correctly is negligible, since R is polynomial in the security parameter. This shows that no PPT adversary can distinguish commitments corresponding to two different messages. We now show that the extractable commitment scheme satisfies the binding property. Let m_1 and m_2 be two distinct messages which correspond to the opening of a commitment $c = (h_1, \ldots, h_l)$. Without loss of generality, assume that the ith bit of m_1 is different from the ith bit of m_2. Also assume that the ith bit of m_1 is 1 while the ith bit of m_2 is 0. Since c can be opened to both m_1 and m_2, this means that $H(m_1, R, i) \oplus (K \| 0^{k_1}) = H(m_2, R, i)$. In other words, the last k_1 bits of $H(m_1, R, i)$ is the same as the last k_1 bits of $H(m_2, R, i)$. But this can happen only with probability $\frac{1}{2^{k_1}} = negl(k)$ which in turn means that with negligible probability the commitment c can be opened to both m_1 and m_2 for any two distinct messages m_1 and m_2. This shows that the commitment scheme satisfies binding property.

The following theorem shows that the above described commitment scheme is a secure extractable commitment scheme even when the extractor is non observing, as per Definition 9.

Theorem 2. *ExtCom is an extractable commitment scheme secure in the random oracle model. Further, the extractor in the commitment scheme is non-observing.*

Proof. We demonstrate the existence of an extractor K for the commitment scheme **ExtCom** which succeeds in extracting the message from the commitment with non-negligible probability. To do this, we crucially use the fact that the extractor can program the random oracle. Further, the extractor we construct is a non-observing one: the extractor cannot see the interaction between the oracle and the adversary. We now define the extractor K which is decomposed into algorithms K_1 and K_2.

K_1 picks a list L of responses of length q_h uniformly at random. It then constructs a machine M which does the following. On being invoked for the ith time with the *next* query, M outputs the ith entry in the list L. Note that M is a stateful machine and so can store the number of times it has been invoked till now. K_1 then sends M to the oracle $\mathcal{O}$. We now define K_2: On input a commitment $(h_1, \ldots, h_l)$ along with the Turing machine M and oracle access to $\mathcal{O}(M)$, K_2 does the following. It executes $M(next)$ for q_h times to get a list L. It then computes a message m such that for all $i = 1, \ldots, l$ it assigns the ith bit of m to be 0 *if* h_i is found in L else it assigns m_i to be 1. It then outputs m.

We claim that, with overwhelming probability the output of K_2 is the same as the message decommitted by the sender during the reveal phase. More precisely, if the sender successfully decommits to m then K outputs m' such that $m' = m$

with overwhelming probability. To prove this claim, we first consider the event that $m_i' \neq m_i$ for some i from $1, \ldots, l$. To show that this event is negligible, observe that it suffices to show that the event $resp_i = resp_j \oplus (K \| 0^{k_1})$ is negligible for any non-zero K, where $resp_i, resp_j$ are any two responses returned by the machine M. This follows from the following two cases: if $resp_i = resp_j$ then $resp_i \neq resp_j \oplus (K \| 0^{k_1})$ since K is non-zero and if $resp_i \neq resp_j$ then $resp_i$ can be same as $resp_j \oplus (K \| 0^{k_1})$ with negligible probability since the probability that the last k_1 bits of $resp_i$ and $resp_j$ are the same is $\frac{1}{2^{k_1}}$ (because the responses returned by M are picked uniformly at random). This proves that $resp_i = resp_j \oplus (K \| 0^{k_1})$ with negligible probability which further proves that the probability that $m' \neq m$ is negligible. This completes the proof.   □

These ideas can be extended further, in a straightforward manner, to construct plaintext aware encryption schemes having non observing plaintext extractors.

References

[AB12]   Ananth, P., Bhaskar, R.: Non observability in the random oracle model. IACR ePrint (2012)

[ACP09]   Abdalla, M., Chevalier, C., Pointcheval, D.: Smooth projective hashing for conditionally extractable commitments. In: Halevi, S. (ed.) CRYPTO 2009. LNCS, vol. 5677, pp. 671–689. Springer, Heidelberg (2009)

[BR93]   Bellare, M., Rogaway, P.: Random Oracles are Practical: A Paradigm for Designing Efficient Protocols. In: Proceedings of the First ACM Conference on Computer and Communications Security, pp. 62–73 (1993)

[BR95]   Bellare, M., Rogaway, P.: Optimal Asymmetric Encryption. In: De Santis, A. (ed.) EUROCRYPT 1994. LNCS, vol. 950, pp. 92–111. Springer, Heidelberg (1995)

[BR96]   Bellare, M., Rogaway, P.: The exact security of digital signatures - how to sign with RSA and rabin. In: Maurer, U.M. (ed.) EUROCRYPT 1996. LNCS, vol. 1070, pp. 399–416. Springer, Heidelberg (1996)

[CGH04]   Canetti, R., Goldreich, O., Halevi, S.: The Random Oracle Methodology, Revisited. J. Assoc. Comput. Mach. 51(4), 557–594 (2004)

[DSP92]   De Santis, A., Persiano, G.: Zero-knowledge proofs of knowledge without interaction. In: Proceedings of the 33rd Annual Symposium on Foundations of Computer Science, pp. 427–436. IEEE (1992)

[Fis05]   Fischlin, M.: Communication-efficient non-interactive proofs of knowledge with online extractors. In: Shoup, V. (ed.) CRYPTO 2005. LNCS, vol. 3621, pp. 152–168. Springer, Heidelberg (2005)

[FLR+10]   Fischlin, M., Lehmann, A., Ristenpart, T., Shrimpton, T., Stam, M., Tessaro, S.: Random oracles with(out) programmability. In: Abe, M. (ed.) ASIACRYPT 2010. LNCS, vol. 6477, pp. 303–320. Springer, Heidelberg (2010)

[HK06]   Halevi, S., Krawczyk, H.: Strengthening Digital Signatures Via Randomized Hashing. In: Dwork, C. (ed.) CRYPTO 2006. LNCS, vol. 4117, pp. 41–59. Springer, Heidelberg (2006)

[Lis06]   Liskov, M.: Constructing an Ideal Hash Function from Weak Ideal Compression Functions. In: Biham, E., Youssef, A.M. (eds.) SAC 2006. LNCS, vol. 4356, pp. 358–375. Springer, Heidelberg (2007)

[Mir06]   Mironov, I.: Collision-Resistant No More: Hash-and-Sign Paradigm Revisited. In: Yung, M., Dodis, Y., Kiayias, A., Malkin, T. (eds.) PKC 2006. LNCS, vol. 3958, pp. 140–156. Springer, Heidelberg (2006)

[MR98]   Micali, S., Reyzin, L.: Signing with Partially Adversarial Hashing. Technical Report 575, MIT/LCS/TM (1998)

[Nie02]   Nielsen, J.B.: Separating Random Oracle Proofs from Complexity Theoretic Proofs: The Non-committing Encryption Case. In: Yung, M. (ed.) CRYPTO 2002. LNCS, vol. 2442, pp. 111–126. Springer, Heidelberg (2002)

[NIT08]   Numayama, A., Isshiki, T., Tanaka, K.: Security of Digital Signature Schemes in Weakened Random Oracle Models. In: Cramer, R. (ed.) PKC 2008. LNCS, vol. 4939, pp. 268–287. Springer, Heidelberg (2008)

[Pas03a] Pass, R.: On deniability in the common reference string and random oracle model. In: Boneh, D. (ed.) CRYPTO 2003. LNCS, vol. 2729, pp. 316–337. Springer, Heidelberg (2003)

[Pas03b] Pass, R.: On deniability in the common reference string and random oracle model. In: Boneh, D. (ed.) CRYPTO 2003. LNCS, vol. 2729, pp. 316–337. Springer, Heidelberg (2003)

[PS00]   Pointcheval, D., Stern, J.: Security Arguments for Digital Signatures and Blind Signatures. J. Cryptology 13(3), 361–396 (2000)

[PV07]   Pasini, S., Vaudenay, S.: Hash-and-Sign with Weak Hashing Made Secure. In: Pieprzyk, J., Ghodosi, H., Dawson, E. (eds.) ACISP 2007. LNCS, vol. 4586, pp. 338–354. Springer, Heidelberg (2007)

[SG98]   Shoup, V., Gennaro, R.: Securing threshold cryptosystems against chosen ciphertext attack. In: Nyberg, K. (ed.) EUROCRYPT 1998. LNCS, vol. 1403, pp. 1–16. Springer, Heidelberg (1998)

[Unr07]   Unruh, D.: Random Oracles and Auxiliary Input. In: Menezes, A. (ed.) CRYPTO 2007. LNCS, vol. 4622, pp. 205–223. Springer, Heidelberg (2007)

Indistinguishability against Chosen Ciphertext Verification Attack Revisited: The Complete Picture

Angsuman Das[1], Sabyasachi Dutta[2], and Avishek Adhikari[2]

[1] Department of Mathematics,
St. Xavier's College, Kolkata, India
angsumandas054@gmail.com
[2] Department of Pure Mathematics,
University of Calcutta, Kolkata, India
{saby.math,avishek.adh}@gmail.com

Abstract. The knowledge that whether a purported ciphertext is valid or not may leak sufficient information to mount practical attacks on public key cryptosystem, e.g., Bleichenbacher's attack on RSA-PKCS#1, Hall-Goldberg-Schneier's "reaction attack" on both McEliece and Ajtai-Dwork cryptosystems. A notion called indistinguishability against chosen ciphertext verification attack (IND-CCVA) has been introduced in the literature, where the adversary has access to a chosen ciphertext verification oracle (not the full decryption oracle), to address those cryptographic functionalities where IND-CPA security is not sufficient and IND-CCA security is more than necessary. Some of the implications and separations between CPA, CCA and CCVA notions are known, while the rest are still open. In this paper we provide non-trivial constructions of schemes (existing/ new) to resolve all the open issues, thus providing a complete picture. We also introduce a slightly stronger attack, called Adaptive Chosen Ciphertext Decryption/Verification Attack (CCA1.5), where the adversary gets an access to a decryption oracle in the first query phase and a ciphertext verification oracle in the second query phase. We argue that this attack is more realistic than usual CCA2 attack. In fact, it lies between CCA1 and CCA2 security as well as between CCVA2 and CCA2 security. In this regard, inter-relationships between the proposed CCA1.5 notion with existing notions are established. Moreover, it is shown that any group homomorphic cryptosystem is CCA1.5 under some reasonable assumption, thereby providing another motivation for studying this particular type of attack scenario.

Keywords: Chosen Ciphertext Attack, Chosen Ciphertext Verification Attack, Homomorphic Cryptosystems.

1 Introduction

The notion of indistinguishability of ciphertexts under adaptive chosen ciphertext attack has been well-accepted all over for designing pubic-key cryptosystems

W. Susilo and R. Reyhanitabar (Eds.): ProvSec 2013, LNCS 8209, pp. 104–120, 2013.

for general cryptographic purposes. However, for the advanced and more useful applications e.g., electronic voting, cloud computing etc., the encryption scheme should allow computation on encrypted messages. Unfortunately, IND-CCA2 security forbids computation on encrypted data and hence many useful functionalities, like homomorphic encryption schemes, can never achieve this level of security. No doubt, this is the security that an encryption scheme deserves in general, but not the one suited for computing on encrypted databases. To the other extremity lies the notion of IND-CPA security and more or less all of the known and existing schemes [19,9,15] which are efficient too, achieve this level of security. But one can never be sure to use IND-CPA secure schemes in a larger set up for the dire consequences they may cause because of their "additional unforeseen features" that one may fail to notice but the adversary may not. As for example, the knowledge that whether a purported ciphertext is valid or not may leak sufficient information to mount practical attacks on public key cryptosystem, e.g., Bleichenbacher's attack on RSA-PKCS#1 [4], Hall-Goldberg-Schneier's "reaction attack" on both McEliece and Ajtai-Dwork cryptosystems [12], Joye-Quisquater-Yung's attack on EPOC [14]. Although almost all of the known IND-CCA secure schemes till date, starting from [17,22] to more recent [10,11,21,6,18,8], have a validity check step embedded in the decryption algorithm to achieve some sort of plaintext awareness but, Bleichenbacher's attack [4] is an eye-opener to the fact that merely a validity check set up does not guarantee security. This serves as one of the motivations to study those cryptosystems which remain secure when adversary has access to such a validity checking "judge" oracle or chosen ciphertext verification oracle. The definition of chosen ciphertext verification attack (CCVA) closely resembles CCA2, the major difference being that the adversary will not have access to the full decryption oracle but rather a judge oracle that will simply output whether or not a ciphertext is "legal". In fact, CCVA is a practical attack as many protocols such as RSA PKCS#1 etc, inform the adversary over the network whenever it submits an illegal or invalid ciphertext, rather than requiring the adversary to have physical access to the decryption box.

The notion of indistinguishability against (both adaptive and non-adaptive) chosen ciphertext verification attack (IND-CCVA) was first introduced in [16], under the name of "illegal ciphertext attack" (IND-ICA) to explore and quantify the gap between practical attacks in [4], [14] and more formal and theoretical frameworks in [2]. A similar kind of attack, called "reaction attack" was discussed in [12] in connection with McEliece and Ajtai-Dwork cryptosystems. The name CCVA was used in [20], where the authors considered only adaptive attacks.[1] CCVA attacks and security against it in symmetric key setting can be found in [13].

1.1   Our Results

While finding the relationship among the notions of indistinguishability against CPA, CCA1, CCA2, CCVA1 and CCVA2 attacks, it was shown in [16] and

---

[1] We will be using this terminology for the rest of the paper.

[20] that only the trivial implications hold (e.g., IND-CCA2 $\Rightarrow$ IND-CCVA2 $\Rightarrow$ IND-CCVA1 and IND-CCA1 $\Rightarrow$ IND-CCVA1 and so on). Apart from that others were either shown or conjectured to be separations (See Figure 1). In this present work, we resolve all of them by showing them to be strict separations.

We also introduce a relatively stronger and yet practical attack, termed as Adaptive Chosen Ciphertext Decryption/Verification Attack (CCA1.5) and security against it. In CCA1.5 attack, the adversary gets access to a decryption oracle in the first query phase and a ciphertext verification or validity checking oracle in the second query phase. In fact, it is quite plausible that the adversary had gained access to decryption box during "lunchtime" and later wants to attack a ciphertext when he can only check the validity of ciphertexts over the network with no more access to the full decryption box. In this connection, we study inter-relationships with respect to indistinguishability of encryptions among the proposed CCA1.5 notion with existing CCA1, CCA2, RCCA2 and CCVA2 notions.

Moreover, it is shown that a slight modification of a group homomorphic cryptosystem [1] yields another group homomorphic cryptosystem which is IND-CCA1.5 secure. In fact, as far as the knowledge of authors, till date, this is the strongest security achievable for any group homomorphic cryptosystems, the previous best being IND-CCA1 security discussed in [1].

The complete picture showing previous and our work is given in Figure 1. A hatched arrow means seperation and a regular arrow is an implication. The dotted arrows shows previous results from [16], [20], the bold arrows are the new results and regular arrows indicates the trivial implications. Each number refers to the theorem or corollary that justifies the separation. All the constructions in this paper are given in standard model.

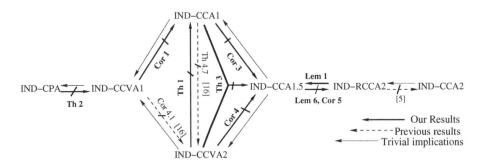

Fig. 1. The Complete Picture

2   Definitions and Preliminaries

Definition 1. *A public-key encryption scheme $\Pi = (\mathcal{K}, \mathcal{E}, \mathcal{D})$ consists of three probabilistic polynomial-time algorithms with the length of their inputs: a key* *generation algorithm* $\mathcal{K}$, *an encryption algorithm* $\mathcal{E}$ *and a decryption algorithm* $\mathcal{D}$ *such that*

1. $\mathcal{K}$ *takes as input a security parameter* k *and outputs a public key-private key pair* (pk, sk).
2. $\mathcal{E}$ *takes as input a message* m *from the message space* $\mathcal{M}$ *and the public-key* pk *to output* $c = \mathcal{E}_{pk}(m)$, *the encryption of* m.
3. $\mathcal{D}$ *takes as input the corresponding private key* sk *and a ciphertext* c *to output either a message* m *when* $c = \mathcal{E}_{pk}(m)$ *or a special failure symbol* $\bot$.

Remark 1. This definition of PKE differs from those in which the decryption algorithm may return a random value for inputs which can not be generated by the encryption algorithm. In our definition, only the feasible outputs of encryption algorithm are decrypted to their corresponding plaintexts and for the rest, a special symbol $\bot$ is returned.

Definition 2. *[11] Let* $\Pi = (\mathcal{K}, \mathcal{E}, \mathcal{D})$ *be a public-key encryption scheme with message space* $\mathcal{M}$, *ciphertext space* $\mathcal{C}$ *and randomness space* COINS. *For given* (pk, sk), $x \in \mathcal{M}$ *and* $y \in \mathcal{C}$, *define*

$$\Gamma(x, y) = \Pr[h \in_R \text{COINS} : y = \mathcal{E}_{pk}(x, h)].$$

We say that Π *is* γ-*uniform if for any* (pk, sk), *any message* $x \in \mathcal{M}$ *and any ciphertext* $y \in \mathcal{C}$, $\Gamma(x, y) \leq \gamma$.

Now, we review the existing notions of security of public key cryptosystems like indistinguishability against CPA, CCA [17,22], CCVA [16,20] attacks and the proposed notion of CCA1.5 by presenting the formalizations of these attacks, where the goal of the attack is to distinguish encryptions. All the definitions are framed in terms of an interactive experiment or game between two abstract parties, a challenger $\mathcal{C}$ and an adversary $\mathcal{A}$ as follows:

- **Set up:** $\mathcal{C}$ picks $(PK, SK) \leftarrow KeyGen$ and gives PK to $\mathcal{A}$.
- **Query Phase I:** $\mathcal{A}$ is given access to an oracle $\mathcal{O}(\cdot)$.
- **Challenge Phase:** $\mathcal{C}$ flips a random coin $b \leftarrow \{0, 1\}$ and receives from $\mathcal{A}$ two plaintexts $\text{msg}_0, \text{msg}_1$. $\mathcal{C}$ computes $c^* \leftarrow Enc_{PK}(\text{msg}_b)$, and gives c^* to $\mathcal{A}$.
- **Query Phase II:** $\mathcal{A}$ is given access to the oracle $\mathcal{O}(\cdot)$.
- **Output Phase:** $\mathcal{A}$ outputs a bit b'. The *advantage of* $\mathcal{A}$ in this game is given by $\text{Adv}_{\mathcal{A}} = 2Pr[b = b'] - 1$.

By using different predicates for $\mathcal{O}$, different levels of security are obtained:

Security	$\mathcal{O}(c)$
CPA	no decryption queries in both phases.
CCA1 [17]	decryption queries only in 1st phase.
CCA2 [22]	decryption queries in both phases, but $c \neq c^*$.
RCCA2 [5]	decryption queries for those $\mathcal{D}(c) \notin \{\text{msg}_0, \text{msg}_1\}$. If $\mathcal{D}(c) \in \{\text{msg}_0, \text{msg}_1\}$, oracle returns a special symbol "test".
CCVA1 [16]	validity of ciphertexts can be checked only in the 1st phase.
CCVA2 [16,20]	validity of ciphertexts can be checked in both phases.
CCA1.5	decryption queries in 1st phase and verification queries in 2nd.

If all probabilistic polynomial time (p.p.t.) adversaries $\mathcal{A}$ have a negligible advantage $\mathsf{Adv}_\mathcal{A}$, then we deem the cryptosystem secure against that attack scenario.

Remark 2. It is to be noted that in an encryption scheme, like Elgamal [9], Paillier [19] etc., any string in the ciphertext space $\mathcal{C}$ is a valid ciphertext, i.e., $\mathcal{E}_{pk}(\mathcal{M}) = \mathcal{C}$. In that case, the notions of IND-CPA, IND-CCVA1 and IND-CCVA2 are all equivalent. But as in most of the standard cryptosystems not all ciphertexts are valid, they have a validity check step in the decryption algorithm. In this work, we consider those cryptosystems where $\mathcal{E}_{pk}(\mathcal{M}) \subsetneq \mathcal{C}$.

Given the definitions of IND-CCVA1, IND-CCVA2 and IND-CCA1.5, we expect that it fits logically within the framework of the existing definitions of IND-CPA, IND-CCA1 and IND-CCA2. Apart from the trivial implications, some others were shown as strict seperations in [16,20] (See Figure 1). But, some of the questions like whether

- IND-CCVA1 $\Rightarrow$ IND-CCA1 or not?   • IND-CCVA2 $\Rightarrow$ IND-CCA1 or not?
- IND-CPA $\Rightarrow$ IND-CCVA1 or not?   • IND-CPA $\Rightarrow$ IND-CCA1 or not?

were either left unaddressed or unresolved. In fact, as far as the knowledge of the authors, the last one was an open problem since the evolution of notion of chosen ciphertext attacks in case of PKE's where *the decryption oracle returns $\perp$ for any invalid ciphertext* (as in Definition 1). Though in [2], authors showed that IND-CPA $\not\Rightarrow$ IND-CCA1, but that was shown for cryptosystems which decrypts and leaks information when malformed or illegal ciphertexts are queried upon.

3   Implications and Separations: Constructions and Proofs

Apart from the trivial implications as discussed in the above section, we show that IND-RCCA2 security implies IND-CCA1.5 security.

Lemma 1. *IND-RCCA2 $\Rightarrow$ IND-CCA1.5.*

Proof. Let Π be an IND-RCCA2 secure PKE. If possible, let $\mathcal{A}$ be an IND-CCA1.5 adversary against Π. We construct an IND-RCCA2 adversary $\mathcal{B}$ against Π using $\mathcal{A}$ as a subroutine. $\mathcal{B}$ takes as input the public key pk of Π and restricted decryption oracle, $\mathcal{O}_R(\cdot)$, as in the RCCA2 game. $\mathcal{A}$ is fed with pk and a decryption oracle for the IND-CCA1.5 game, $\mathcal{O}_{1.5}(\cdot)$, simulated by $\mathcal{B}$ as follows: In the first query phase, when $\mathcal{A}$ queries $\mathcal{O}_{1.5}(\cdot)$ with c, $\mathcal{B}$ returns $\mathcal{O}_R(c)$ to $\mathcal{A}$. (Note that in the first query phase, both the oracles are same, i.e., both of them either output $m = \mathsf{Dec}(c)$ or an invalid symbol $\perp$, when the ciphertext c is not a valid one.) In the challenge phase, $\mathcal{A}$ outputs two messages m_0 and m_1, which $\mathcal{B}$ passes to the IND-RCCA2 challenger $\mathcal{C}$. $\mathcal{C}$ outputs $c^* = \mathsf{Enc}(m_b)$ to $\mathcal{B}$, which in return is passed on to $\mathcal{A}$. In the second query phase, $\mathcal{O}_{1.5}(\cdot)$ responds to the queries of $\mathcal{A}$ as follows:

$$\mathcal{O}_{1.5}(c) = \begin{cases} \text{``valid''}, & \text{if } c = c^* \text{ or } \mathcal{O}_R(c) = m \text{ or } \mathsf{test} \\ \text{``invalid''}, & \text{if } \mathcal{O}_R(c) = \perp \end{cases}$$

(Note that $\mathcal{A}$ can even query the challenge ciphertext c^*.) In the guess phase, $\mathcal{A}$ outputs a bit b', which $\mathcal{B}$ passes to $\mathcal{C}$. As the simulation of $\mathcal{O}_{1.5}(\cdot)$ in both the phases is perfect, we have $\mathsf{Adv}_\mathcal{A} = \mathsf{Adv}_\mathcal{B}$.

However, the converse of this lemma is not true, which is exhibited later by Lemma 6 and Corollary 5.

In the rest of this section, we first provide constructions (existing/new) to prove that all the four open problems are strict separations. We also construct schemes to seperate the notion of IND-CCA1.5 security from the other existing ones. The first construction was used in [3], but in a different motivation. We show that the same construction can be used to show that IND-CCVA2 security does not imply IND-CCA1 security. The second construction is a new one which shows that IND-CPA security does not imply IND-CCVA1. The third one is an example of a scheme which is IND-CCA1.5 secure but not IND-CCA2. In fact, this construction indicates that any group homomorphic cryptosystem can be converted into another group homomorphic one which achieves IND-CCA1.5 security. At this junction, it is worth mentioning that though it seems intuitively that IND-CCVA2 and IND-CCA1 security taken together implies IND-CCA1.5 security, but it is not so, as demonstrated in the fourth construction. On the other hand, we show that Cramer-Shoup (CS) lite scheme, which was previously known to be both IND-CCVA2 and IND-CCA1 secure, is also secure in IND-CCA1.5 sense. Lastly, we give a non-homomorphic variant of CS lite which achieves IND-CCA1.5 security to show that the class of IND-CCA1.5 secure schemes contains non-homomorphic schemes too.

Construction-I: Let $\Pi = (\mathsf{Gen}, \mathsf{Enc}, \mathsf{Dec})$ be a cryptosystem with message space $\mathcal{M}$ and ciphertext space $\{0,1\}^k$. We construct another cryptosystem $\overline{\Pi} = (\overline{\mathsf{Gen}}, \overline{\mathsf{Enc}}, \overline{\mathsf{Dec}})$ which is IND-CCVA2 secure but not IND-CCA1 secure, with same message space $\mathcal{M}$ and ciphertext space as $\{0,1\}^{k+1}$, using Π and an one-way permutation f on $\mathcal{M}$. (See Figure 2)

Two things are to be observed over here. Firstly, it is evident that the scheme is consistent i.e., $\overline{\mathsf{Dec}}(\overline{\mathsf{Enc}}(m)) = m$ for all $m \in \mathcal{M}$. Secondly, not all $k+1$ bit strings are valid ciphertexts for $\overline{\Pi}$ e.g., the strings starting with 1 except $1||1^k$.

Lemma 2. $\overline{\Pi}$ is IND-CCVA2 secure if Π is γ-uniform & IND-CCVA2 secure and f is one-way, i.e., if $\overline{A}$ be an IND-CCVA2 adversary against $\overline{\Pi}$ with winning

$\overline{\mathsf{Gen}} : 1^n$	$\overline{\mathsf{Enc}} : m \in \mathcal{M},\ \overline{pk}$	$\overline{\mathsf{Dec}} : \overline{c},\ \overline{sk},$
$\mathsf{Gen}(1^n) \to (pk, sk)$	If $Y = f(m)$	Parse $\overline{c} = (s||c),\ s \in \{0,1\}$
Choose $\mathsf{M}_{weak} \in_R \mathcal{M}$	output $\overline{c} = (1||1^k)$	If $s = 0$, output $\mathsf{Dec}(sk, c)$
$Y = f(\mathsf{M}_{weak})$	else output, $\overline{c} = (0||c)$	If $s = 1$, $c = 1^k$,
$\overline{pk} = (pk, f, Y)$	where $c = \mathsf{Enc}(pk, m)$	output M_{weak}
$\overline{sk} = (sk, \mathsf{M}_{weak})$		Else output $\bot$

Fig. 2. Construction-I

probability ϵ, then there exists either an IND-CCVA2 adversary $\mathcal{A}$ against Π or an inverting algorithm $\mathcal{I}$ for f such that

$$\Pr[\mathcal{I}\ wins] + \Pr[\mathcal{A}\ wins] \geq (1 - q\gamma)\epsilon,$$

where q is the number of decryption queries made by $\mathcal{A}$.

Proof. Let $\overline{\mathcal{A}}$ be an IND-CCVA2 adversary against $\overline{\Pi}$. Using $\overline{\mathcal{A}}$ as a subroutine, we construct either an IND-CCVA2 adversary $\mathcal{A}$ against Π or an algorithm $\mathcal{I}$ which inverts Y under f (i.e., find M_{weak} from Y, f).

As an input, $\mathcal{A}$ takes pk of Π and a chosen ciphertext verification oracle, $\mathcal{O}_\Pi(\cdot)$. $\mathcal{I}$ takes as input Y and f. $\overline{\mathcal{A}}$ is simulated with $\overline{pk} = (pk, f, Y)$ and a chosen ciphertext verification oracle, $\mathcal{O}_{\overline{\Pi}}$. When a ciphertext verification query, $\overline{c}$, is made by $\overline{\mathcal{A}}$, $\mathcal{O}_{\overline{\Pi}}$ responds as following:

1. Parse $\overline{c}$ as $s||c$, where $s \in \{0,1\}$.
2. If $s = 0$, return $\mathcal{O}_\Pi(c)$.
3. If $s = 1$ and $c = 1^k$, return "valid".
4. Else, return "invalid".

This simulation of $\mathcal{O}_{\overline{\Pi}}$ is perfect, except the case when $\overline{c} = (0||c)$ and $c = \mathsf{Enc}(pk, \mathsf{M}_{weak})$. Observe that $c = \mathsf{Enc}(pk, \mathsf{M}_{weak})$ is a valid ciphertext for Π but $0||c$ is not a valid ciphertext for $\overline{\Pi}$. Hence, $\mathcal{O}_\Pi$ will render c as valid and and as a result the simulated $\mathcal{O}_{\overline{\Pi}}$ will incorrectly declare $0||c$ as valid. Now, since Π is γ-uniform, the probability that the simulation of $\mathcal{O}_{\overline{\Pi}}$ is incorrect is at most γ. If q queries are made to the $\mathcal{O}_{\overline{\Pi}}$, the probability that it answers correctly is

$$(1 - \gamma)^q \geq (1 - q\gamma).$$

Now, in the challenge phase, $\overline{\mathcal{A}}$ outputs two messages m_0 and m_1 to $\mathcal{A}$. If either $f(m_0)$ or $f(m_1)$ is equal to Y, then $\mathcal{A}$ aborts the game (hence, $\overline{\mathcal{A}}$ wins) and $\mathcal{I}$ outputs the corresponding m_i for which $f(m_i) = Y$ and thereby inverting f. If neither of $f(m_0)$ and $f(m_1)$ equals Y, $\mathcal{A}$ sends m_0, m_1 to the IND-CCVA2 challenger $\mathcal{C}$ of Π as the challenge plaintexts. $\mathcal{C}$ randomly chooses a bit $b \in \{0,1\}$ and sends $c^* = \mathsf{Enc}(pk, m_b)$ to $\mathcal{A}$ and $\mathcal{A}$ passes $\overline{c}^* = (0||c^*)$ to $\overline{\mathcal{A}}$ as the challenge ciphertext. The second query phase is simulated exactly in the same way as that in first phase. (Note that here even the challenge ciphertext can be queried). Finally, in the guess phase, $\mathcal{A}$ returns the answer b' given by $\overline{\mathcal{A}}$ to $\mathcal{C}$.

Let ϵ be the probability with which $\overline{\mathcal{A}}$ wins the real IND-CCVA2 game. Now, in the simulated game, , provided $\mathcal{O}_{\overline{\Pi}}$ answers correctly, $\overline{\mathcal{A}}$ wins if either $\mathsf{M}_{weak} \in \{m_0, m_1\}$ (i.e., $\mathcal{I}$ wins) or $b' = b$ (i.e., $\mathcal{A}$ wins) i.e.,

$$\Pr[\mathcal{I}\ wins] + \Pr[\mathcal{A}\ wins] \geq (1 - q\gamma)\epsilon$$

Lemma 3. $\overline{\Pi}$ *is not IND-CCA1 secure.*

Proof. We construct an IND-CCA1 adversary $\overline{\mathcal{A}}$ against $\overline{\Pi}$ as follows: $\overline{\mathcal{A}}$ queries the decryption oracle in the first phase with $(1||1^k)$ to get M_{weak} and he sets $m_0 = \mathsf{M}_{weak}$ and $m_1 \in \mathcal{M} \setminus \{\mathsf{M}_{weak}\}$ and sends it to the IND-CCA1 challenger. Once, $\overline{\mathcal{A}}$ gets the challenge ciphertext, he can determine whether it is the encryption of m_0 or m_1 simply by looking at the first bit of the challenge ciphertext.

Theorem 1. *IND-CCVA2 $\not\Rightarrow$ IND-CCA1.*

Proof. The theorem follows from Lemma 2 and 3.

Corollary 1. *IND-CCVA1 $\not\Rightarrow$ IND-CCA1.*

Proof. As Construction-I is IND-CCVA2 secure (by Lemma 2), it is IND-CCVA1 secure. But it is not IND-CCA1 secure (by Lemma 3).

Corollary 2. *IND-CPA $\not\Rightarrow$ IND-CCA1.*

Proof. As Construction-I is IND-CCVA2 secure (by Lemma 2), it is IND-CPA secure. But it is not IND-CCA1 secure (by Lemma 3).

Corollary 3. *IND-CCA1 $\not\Rightarrow$ IND-CCA1.5.*

Proof. If IND-CCA1 implies IND-CCA1.5, which in turn implies IND-CCVA2, it follows that IND-CCA1 implies IND-CCVA2. But this is not the case by Theorem 4.7 [16] or Section 6.3 [20].

Corollary 4. *IND-CCVA2 $\not\Rightarrow$ IND-CCA1.5.*

Proof. If IND-CCVA2 implies IND-CCA1.5, which in turn implies IND-CCA1, it follows that IND-CCVA2 implies IND-CCA1. But this is not the case by Theorem 1.

Construction-II: Let $\Pi = (\mathsf{Gen}, \mathsf{Enc}, \mathsf{Dec})$ be an IND-CPA secure cryptosystem with message space $\mathcal{M} = \{0,1\}^l$ and ciphertext space $\{0,1\}^k$. We construct another cryptosystem $\overline{\Pi} = (\overline{\mathsf{Gen}}, \overline{\mathsf{Enc}}, \overline{\mathsf{Dec}})$ (See Figure 3), which is IND-CPA secure but not IND-CCVA1 secure with same message space $\mathcal{M}$ and ciphertext space as $\{0,1\}^{k+1}$, using Π and an one-way permutation f on $\mathcal{M}$. Here, by $\hat{i}, m[i]$ and $c(k-1)$, we mean $(k-1)$-bit representation of i, i-th bit of m and first $k-1$ bits of c respectively.

Observe that unlike the previous construction where M_{weak} has only one possible ciphertext $1||1^k$, here M_{weak} has l possible ciphertexts.

$\overline{\mathsf{Gen}} : 1^n$	$\overline{\mathsf{Enc}} : m \in \{0,1\}^l,\ \overline{pk}$	$\overline{\mathsf{Dec}} : \overline{c} \in \{0,1\}^{k+1},\ \overline{sk},$
$\mathsf{Gen}(1^n) \to (pk, sk)$	If $Y = f(m)$	Parse $\overline{c} = (s\|\|c),\ s \in \{0,1\}$
$\mathsf{M}_{weak} \in_R \{0,1\}^l$	$\quad$ Choose $i \in_R \{1,2,\ldots,l\}$	If $s = 0$, output $\mathsf{Dec}(sk, c)$
$Y = f(\mathsf{M}_{weak})$	$\quad$ Output $\overline{c} = (1\|\|\hat{i}\|\|m[i])$	If $s = 1$, $c(k-1) = \hat{i}$,
$\overline{pk} = (pk, f, Y)$	Else output $\overline{c} = (0\|\|c)$,	$\quad$ and $\mathsf{M}_{weak}[i] = c[k]$
$\overline{sk} = (sk, \mathsf{M}_{weak})$	$\quad$ where $c = \mathsf{Enc}(pk, m)$	$\quad$ output M_{weak}
		Else output $\perp$

Fig. 3. Construction-II

Lemma 4. $\overline{\Pi}$ *is IND-CPA secure if* Π *is IND-CPA secure and* f *is one-way.*

Proof. See Appendix A.2.

Lemma 5. $\overline{\Pi}$ *is not IND-CCVA1 secure.*

Proof. We construct an IND-CCVA1 adversary $\overline{\mathcal{A}}$ against $\overline{\Pi}$. $\overline{\mathcal{A}}$ queries the ciphertext verification oracle, $\mathcal{O}_{\overline{\Pi}}$ in the first phase as follows:

- For $i = 1$ to l

  do $\begin{cases} \text{Query } c_i = (1||\hat{i}||0) \text{ to } \mathcal{O}_{\overline{\Pi}} \\ \text{If } \mathcal{O}_{\overline{\Pi}}(c_i) = \text{``valid''}, \text{ set } m[i] = 0 \\ \text{Else, set } m[i] = 1 \end{cases}$

- Return $\mathsf{M}_{weak} = (m[1]||m[2]||m[3]||\cdots||m[l])$.

Now, in the challenge phase, $\overline{\mathcal{A}}$ sets $m_0 = \mathsf{M}_{weak}$ and $m_1 \in \mathcal{M} \setminus \{\mathsf{M}_{weak}\}$ and sends it to the challenger. Once it receives the challenge ciphertext, $\overline{\mathcal{A}}$ considers its first bit. If it is 0, $\overline{\mathcal{A}}$ returns m_1 and if it is 1, $\overline{\mathcal{A}}$ returns m_0. The correctness of the attack is obvious.

Theorem 2. *IND-CPA* $\not\Rightarrow$ *IND-CCVA1.*

Proof. The theorem follows from Lemma 4 and 5.

Construction-III: We recall that Paillier cryptosystem [19] and GBD cryptosystem [15] are two group homomorphic encryption schemes which have been proved to be IND-CCA1 secure under a new class of problem called *Splitting Oracle-Assisted Subgroup Membership Problem* (SOAP) in [1]. But as mentioned earlier, in these schemes, $\mathcal{E}_{pk}(\mathcal{M}) = \mathcal{C}$ and hence the notions of IND-CPA, IND-CCVA1 & IND-CCVA2 are all equivalent and IND-CCA1 & IND-CCA1.5 are equivalent.

Let $\Pi = (\mathsf{Gen}, \mathsf{Enc}, \mathsf{Dec})$ be the Paillier (or GBD) cryptosystem with message space $\mathcal{M}$ and ciphertext space as $\{0,1\}^k$. We construct a scheme $\overline{\Pi} = (\overline{\mathsf{Gen}}, \overline{\mathsf{Enc}}, \overline{\mathsf{Dec}})$ (See Figure 4), which is IND-CCA1.5 secure but not IND-CCA2 secure, with same message space $\mathcal{M}$ and ciphertext space as $\{0,1\}^{k+1}$, where $\mathcal{E}_{pk}(\mathcal{M}) \subsetneq \mathcal{C}$ and .

Clearly, the scheme $\overline{\Pi}$ is consistent and $\mathcal{E}_{pk}(\mathcal{M}) \subset \mathcal{C}$.

$\overline{\mathsf{Gen}} : 1^n$	$\overline{\mathsf{Enc}} : m \in \mathcal{M},\ \overline{pk}$	$\overline{\mathsf{Dec}} : \bar{c},\ \overline{sk},$
$\mathsf{Gen}(1^n) \to (pk, sk)$	Output $\bar{c} = (0||c)$	Parse $\bar{c} = (s||c),\ s \in \{0,1\}$
$\overline{pk} = pk$	where $c = \mathsf{Enc}(pk, m)$	If $s = 0$, output $\mathsf{Dec}(sk, c)$
$\overline{sk} = sk$		If $s = 1$, Output $\perp$

Fig. 4. Construction-III

Lemma 6. $\overline{\Pi}$ *is IND-CCA1.5 secure.*

Proof. By Theorem 5 in [1], Π is IND-CCA1. Also as it is trivial to distinguish valid ciphertexts from invalid ciphertexts (by just looking at the most significant bit) in $\overline{\Pi}$, CCVA oracle does not give any extra advantage to the adversary in the second (any) query phase. Hence, $\overline{\Pi}$ is IND-CCA1.5 secure.

Lemma 7. $\overline{\Pi}$ *is not IND-CCA2 secure.*

Proof. As the original cryptosystem Π, is group homomorphic and $\overline{\Pi}$ just concatenate 0 with the original ciphertext, an IND-CCA2 adversary $\overline{\mathcal{A}}$ against $\overline{\Pi}$ runs as follows: $\overline{\mathcal{A}}$ removes the most significant bit i.e., 0 from the challenge ciphertext $\overline{c^*}$ to get c^*. Now, as c^* is a malleable ciphertext (Π is homomorphic), so is $\overline{c^*} = 1||c^*$. Thus, $\overline{\Pi}$ is not NM-CCA2 secure and hence not IND-CCA2 secure (by Theorem 3.3 in [2]).

Lemma 8. $\overline{\Pi}$, *when instantiated with Paillier Scheme (say) as Π, is not NM-CPA secure.*

Proof. Recall that a Paillier ciphertext looks like $c = g^m \cdot r^n \bmod n^2$. Formally we can specify an adversary $\overline{\mathcal{A}}$ that breaks NM-CPA security of $\overline{\Pi}$ with probability 1. Given a ciphertext $0||c$ of a message m, $\overline{\mathcal{A}}$ outputs $(R, 0||c')$ where $c' = c \cdot g^{m'} \bmod n^2$ is the ciphertext of $m + m'$ and R describes the binary relation defined by $R(m_1, m_2) = 1$ iff $m_2 = m_1 + m' \bmod n^2$.

Corollary 5. $\overline{\Pi}$, *as in Lemma 8, is not IND-RCCA2 secure.*

Proof. By Lemma 8, $\overline{\Pi}$ is not NM-CPA secure and hence not NM-RCCA2 secure. In [5], authors showed that NM-RCCA2 and IND-RCCA2 are equivalent for super-polynomial size message space, which is the case for the message space of $\overline{\Pi}$. Thus, $\overline{\Pi}$ is not IND-RCCA2 secure.

Construction-IV: Let $\Pi = (\mathsf{Gen}, \mathsf{Enc}, \mathsf{Dec})$ be an IND-CCA2 secure cryptosystem with message space $\mathcal{M} = \{0,1\}^{k+k_0}$ and ciphertext space $\{0,1\}^l$. We construct another cryptosystem $\overline{\Pi} = (\overline{\mathsf{Gen}}, \overline{\mathsf{Enc}}, \overline{\mathsf{Dec}})$ (See Figure 5) with message space $\{0,1\}^k$ and ciphertext space as $\{0,1\}^{l+k_3+1}$, using Π, an one-way permutation f on $\{0,1\}^k$ and a pseudo-random function family $G : \{0,1\}^{k_1} \times \{0,1\}^{k_2} \to \{0,1\}^{k_3}$, where $k_0 = k_1 + k_2$.

Lemma 9. $\overline{\Pi}$ *is not IND-CCA1.5 secure.*

Proof. We construct an IND-CCA1.5 adversary $\overline{\mathcal{A}}$ against $\overline{\Pi}$. $\overline{\mathcal{A}}$ queries the decryption oracle, $\mathcal{O}_{\overline{\Pi}}$ in the first phase with $1||1^{l+k_3}$ to get M_{weak}. Now, in the challenge phase, $\overline{\mathcal{A}}$ sets $m_0 = \mathsf{M}_{weak}$ and $m_1 \in \mathcal{M} \setminus \{\mathsf{M}_{weak}\}$ and sends it to the challenger. Once it receives the challenge ciphertext c^*, $\overline{\mathcal{A}}$ first checks if $c^* = 1||1^{l+k_3}$ or not. If it is, $\overline{\mathcal{A}}$ outputs m_0. If not, $\overline{\mathcal{A}}$ just flips the last bit of c^* to get c' and queries the verification oracle with c'. If it returns valid, $\overline{\mathcal{A}}$ returns m_1 and if it returns invalid, $\overline{\mathcal{A}}$ returns m_0. The correctness of the attack is obvious.

114   A. Das, S. Dutta, and A. Adhikari

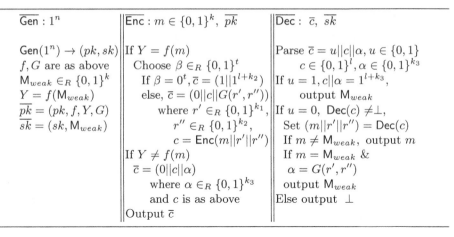

Fig. 5. Construction-IV

Lemma 10. $\overline{\Pi}$ *is IND-CCVA2 secure if*

1. Π *is IND-CCA2 and*
2. f *is one-way.*

Proof. Let $\overline{\mathcal{A}}$ be an IND-CCVA2 adversary against $\overline{\Pi}$. We construct either an IND-CCA2 adversary $\mathcal{A}$ against Π or an inversion algorithm $\mathcal{I}_f$ for f using $\overline{\mathcal{A}}$ as a subroutine. As an input, $\mathcal{A}$ takes pk and an oracle access to the decryption oracle of Π. $\mathcal{I}_f$ takes as input f, Y. $\mathcal{A}$ chooses a pseudo-random function family $G : \{0,1\}^{k_1} \times \{0,1\}^{k_2} \to \{0,1\}^{k_3}$ and simulates $\overline{\mathcal{A}}$ with $\overline{pk} = (pk, f, Y, G)$. The verification queries of $\overline{\mathcal{A}}$ are responded as follows: In the query phase, if $\overline{\mathcal{A}}$ queries $1||1^{l+k_3}$, simulator returns "valid". If $\overline{\mathcal{A}}$ queries a ciphertext of the form $\overline{c} = (u||c||\alpha)$, $\mathcal{A}$ queries its decryption oracle with c to get either $(m||r'||r'')$ or $\bot$. Now, if $f(m) = Y$, $\mathcal{A}$ stops the game and $\mathcal{I}_f$ outputs m. If $f(m) \neq Y$, simulator returns "valid". If $\bot$ occurs, simulator returns "invalid". In the challenge phase, $\overline{\mathcal{A}}$ outputs two k-bit strings m_0 and m_1 to $\mathcal{A}$. If either of $f(m_0)$ or $f(m_1)$ equals Y, $\mathcal{A}$ aborts the game and $\mathcal{I}_f$ returns m_0 or m_1 accordingly. If not, $\mathcal{A}$ randomly chooses $r_0, r_1 \in \{0,1\}^{k_0}$ and sends $m_0||r_0, m_1||r_1$ to the IND-CCA2 challenger $\mathcal{C}$. $\mathcal{C}$ randomly chooses a bit $b \in \{0,1\}$ and encrypts $m_b||r_b$ to output $c^* = $ Enc$(m_b||r_b)$ as the challenge ciphertext for $\mathcal{A}$. $\mathcal{A}$ returns $\overline{c^*} = (0||c^*||\alpha)$ to $\overline{\mathcal{A}}$ as the challenge ciphertext, where $\alpha \in_R \{0,1\}^{k_3}$. Second verification query phase is simulated as that of the first one. Finally in the guess phase, $\overline{\mathcal{A}}$ returns a bit b' and $\mathcal{A}$ outputs the same bit b' as its guess to $\mathcal{C}$.

Lemma 11. $\overline{\Pi}$ *is IND-CCA1 secure if*

1. Π *is IND-CCA2,*
2. G *is a pseudo-random function family.*

Proof. See Appendix A.3.

Theorem 3. *IND-CCVA2 + IND-CCA1 $\nRightarrow$ IND-CCA1.5.*

Proof. It follows immediately from Lemma 9, 10 and 11.

Cramer-Shoup Lite: We show that the Cramer-Shoup lite scheme (Figure 6) which was previously known to be IND-CCA1 and IND-CCVA2 secure is also IND-CCA1.5 secure.

Gen : 1^k	Enc : $m \in \mathcal{G}$, pk	Dec : (u, v, e, w), sk,
Choose a prime q of length k	Choose $r \in_R \mathbb{Z}_q$	If $w = u^a v^b$,
Choose $\mathcal{G} = \langle g_1 \rangle = \langle g_2 \rangle$	Compute	output $e/(u^x v^y)$
of order q	$u = g_1^r, v = g_2^r,$	Else output $\perp$
Choose $x, y, a, b \in_R \mathbb{Z}_q$	$e = h^r \cdot m, w = c^r$	
Set $h = g_1^x g_2^y, c = g_1^a g_2^b$	Output (u, v, e, w)	
Set $pk = (g_1, g_2, h, c),$		
$sk = (x, y, a, b)$		

Fig. 6. Cramer-Shoup Lite

Lemma 12. *Cramer-Shoup lite is not IND-CCA2 secure.*

Proof. See Lemma 1 of Section 4.1 of [20].

Theorem 4. *Cramer-Shoup lite is IND-CCA1.5 secure if DDH assumption holds in $\mathcal{G}$.*

Proof. See Appendix A.1.

Theorem 5. *IND-CCA1.5 $\nRightarrow$ IND-CCA2.*

Proof. It follows immediately from Lemma 12 and Theorem 4.

Another Cramer-Shoup Lite Variant: In this construction (Figure 7), we show that class of IND-CCA1.5 secure schemes contains non-homomorphic schemes too.

Lemma 13. *Cramer-Shoup lite variant is not IND-CCA2 secure.*

Proof. Similar to that of Lemma 12.

Theorem 6. *Cramer-Shoup lite variant is IND-CCA1.5 secure if DDH assumption holds in $\mathcal{G}$.*

Proof. Similar to that of Theorem 4.

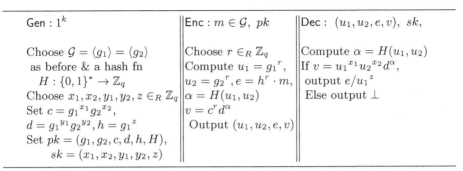

Fig. 7. Cramer-Shoup Lite Variant

4 Conclusion and Open Issues

The idea of chosen ciphertext verification attack was introduced in [16] to find marriage between practical methods of cryptographic attack, such as the Bleichenbacher's attack [4], and theoretical definitions of security, as presented in [2]. This work provides the complete picture of chain of inter-relationships among CCVA, CCA1.5 attacks and existing attacks, like CPA, CCA1, RCCA2 and CCA2, from indistinguishability point of view for better understanding of these security notions. However, the notion of non-malleability under this new attack and the relationships among NM-CCVA1, NM-CCVA2, NM-CCA1.5 and IND-CCVA1, IND-CCVA2, IND-CCA1.5 are still unaddressed and can be an interesting topic for future research.

Acknowledgements. The second author's research is funded by CSIR PhD Fellowship, Govt. of India, Grant no - 09/028(0808)/2010-EMR-I. The authors would like to thank Sumit Kumar Pandey of C.R.Rao Institute, Hyderabad for some fruitful discussions in the initial phase of the work and the anonymous reviewers of ProvSec 2013 for their comments and suggestions.

References

1. Armknecht, F., Katzenbeisser, S., Peter, A.: Group homomorphic encryption: characterizations, impossibility results, and applications. Design, Codes and Cryptography (2012), doi:10.1007/s10623-011-9601-2
2. Bellare, M., Desai, A., Pointcheval, D., Rogaway, P.: Relations among notions of security for public-key encryption schemes. In: Krawczyk, H. (ed.) CRYPTO 1998. LNCS, vol. 1462, pp. 26–45. Springer, Heidelberg (1998)
3. Bellare, M., Hofheinz, D., Kiltz, E.: Subtleties in the Definition of IND-CCA: When and How Should Challenge-Decryption be Disallowed?,
   eprint.iacr.org/2009/418.pdf
4. Bleichenbacher, D.: Chosen ciphertext attacks against protocols based on the RSA encryption standard PKCS #1. In: Krawczyk, H. (ed.) CRYPTO 1998. LNCS, vol. 1462, pp. 1–12. Springer, Heidelberg (1998)

5. Canetti, R., Krawczyk, H., Nielsen, J.B.: Relaxing Chosen-Ciphertext Security. In: Boneh, D. (ed.) CRYPTO 2003. LNCS, vol. 2729, pp. 565–582. Springer, Heidelberg (2003)
6. Coron, J.-S., Handschuh, H., Joye, M., Paillier, P., Pointcheval, D., Tymen, C.: GEM: A Generic Chosen-Ciphertext Secure Encryption Method. In: Preneel, B. (ed.) CT-RSA 2002. LNCS, vol. 2271, pp. 263–276. Springer, Heidelberg (2002)
7. Cramer, R., Shoup, V.: A Practical Public Key Cryptosystem Provably Secure against Adaptive Chosen Ciphertext Attack. In: Krawczyk, H. (ed.) CRYPTO 1998. LNCS, vol. 1462, pp. 13–25. Springer, Heidelberg (1998)
8. Das, A., Adhikari, A.: An Efficient IND-CCA2 secure Paillier-based cryptosystem. Information Processing Letters 112, 885–888 (2012)
9. Elgamal, T.: A Public Key Cryptosystem and A Signature Scheme Based on Discrete Logarithms. IEEE Trans. on Information Theory, IT-31(4), 469–472 (1985)
10. Fujisaki, E., Okamoto, T.: How to Enhance the Security of Public-Key Encryption at Minimum Cost. In: Imai, H., Zheng, Y. (eds.) PKC 1999. LNCS, vol. 1560, pp. 53–68. Springer, Heidelberg (1999)
11. Fujisaki, E., Okamoto, T.: Secure Integration of Asymmetric and Symmetric Encryption Schemes. In: Wiener, M. (ed.) CRYPTO 1999. LNCS, vol. 1666, pp. 537–554. Springer, Heidelberg (1999)
12. Hall, C., Goldberg, I., Schneier, B.: Reaction attacks against several public-key cryptosystem. In: Varadharajan, V., Mu, Y. (eds.) ICICS 1999. LNCS, vol. 1726, pp. 2–12. Springer, Heidelberg (1999)
13. Hu, Z.Y., Sun, F.C., Jiang, J.C.: Ciphertext verification security of symmetric encryption schemes. Sci. China Ser. F-Inf. Sci. 52(9), 1617–1631 (2009)
14. Joye, M., Quisquater, J.-J., Yung, M.: On the Power of Misbehaving Adversaries and Security Analysis of the Original EPOC. In: Naccache, D. (ed.) CT-RSA 2001. LNCS, vol. 2020, pp. 208–222. Springer, Heidelberg (2001)
15. Nieto, J.M.G., Boyd, C., Dawson, E.: A Public Key Cryptosystem Based On A Subgroup Membership Problem. Designs, Codes and Cryptography 36, 301–316 (2005)
16. Krohn, M.: On the Definitions of Cryptographic Security: Chosen-Ciphertext Attack Revisited. Undergraduate Thesis, Harvard University (1999), pdos.csail.mit.edu/~max/docs/uthesis.pdf
17. Naor, M., Yung, M.: Public-key cryptosystems provably secure against chosen ciphertext attacks. In: 22nd ACM STOC, pp. 427–437. ACM Press (May 1990)
18. Okamoto, T., Pointcheval, D.: REACT: Rapid Enhanced-Security Asymmetric Cryptosystem Transform. In: Naccache, D. (ed.) CT-RSA 2001. LNCS, vol. 2020, pp. 159–174. Springer, Heidelberg (2001)
19. Paillier, P.: Public-Key Cryptosystems Based on Composite Degree Residuosity Classes. In: Stern, J. (ed.) EUROCRYPT 1999. LNCS, vol. 1592, pp. 223–238. Springer, Heidelberg (1999)
20. Kumar Pandey, S., Sarkar, S., Prasad Jhanwar, M.: Relaxing IND-CCA: Indistinguishability against Chosen Ciphertext Verification Attack. In: Bogdanov, A., Sanadhya, S. (eds.) SPACE 2012. LNCS, vol. 7644, pp. 63–76. Springer, Heidelberg (2012)
21. Pointcheval, D.: Chosen-Ciphertext Security for Any One-Way Cryptosystem. In: Imai, H., Zheng, Y. (eds.) PKC 2000. LNCS, vol. 1751, pp. 129–146. Springer, Heidelberg (2000)
22. Rackoff, C., Simon, D.: Noninteractive zero-knowledge proof of knowledge and chosen ciphertext attack. In: 22nd Annual ACM Symposium on Theory of Computing, pp. 427–437 (1990)

A   Appendix: Proofs

A.1   Proof of Theorem 4

The proof goes exactly on the same line as the proof of CCA1 security of Cramer-Shoup lite or CCA2 security of Cramer-Shoup scheme [7], i.e., if an adversary is able to break the IND-CCA1.5 security, then it can be used to solve the DDH problem. We therefore give only the description of the simulator.

Let us assume, there is an adversary $\mathcal{A}$ which can break the IND-CCA1.5 security of the scheme. Using $\mathcal{A}$, we can construct an algorithm $\mathcal{B}$ that solves the DDH problem. $\mathcal{B}$ takes as input a tuple (g_1, g_2, u, v). $\mathcal{B}$ solves the DDH problem by interacting with $\mathcal{A}$ in IND-CCA1.5 game as follows:

1. **Simulation of Gen**
   - Choose $x, y, a, b \in_R \mathbb{Z}_q$ and set $h = g_1{}^x g_2{}^y, c = g_1{}^a g_2{}^b$.
   - Set public key as (g_1, g_2, h, c) and make it available to $\mathcal{A}$ and keep x, y, a, b secret.
2. **Simulation of Decryption Oracle (Phase-I) and Verification Oracle (Phase II)**
   - Knowledge of x, y, a, b enables $\mathcal{B}$ to answer the queries of $\mathcal{A}$ in both the phases.
3. **Simulation of Challenge Ciphertext**
   - $\mathcal{A}$ chooses m_0, m_1 and sends it to $\mathcal{B}$.
   - $\mathcal{B}$ chooses a bit $\beta \in_R \{0, 1\}$ and sets $e = u^x v^y \cdot m_\beta$, $w = u^a v^b$.
   - $\mathcal{B}$ returns (u, v, e, w) as the challenge ciphertext to $\mathcal{A}$.
4. **Guess Phase**
   - $\mathcal{A}$ returns a bit β' to $\mathcal{B}$.
   - If $\beta = \beta'$, $\mathcal{B}$ declares the instance to be a valid DDH tuple, else declares it to be an invalid tuple.

This completes the description of $\mathcal{B}$. It is clear that the simulation is almost perfect and hence the result follows.

A.2   Proof of Lemma 4

Let $\overline{\mathcal{A}}$ be an IND-CPA adversary against $\overline{\Pi}$. Using $\overline{\mathcal{A}}$ as a subroutine, we construct either an IND-CPA adversary $\mathcal{A}$ against Π or an algorithm $\mathcal{I}$ which inverts Y under f (i.e., find M_{weak} from Y, f).

As an input, $\mathcal{A}$ takes pk of Π and $\mathcal{I}$ takes Y and f. $\overline{\mathcal{A}}$ is simulated with $\overline{pk} = (pk, f, Y)$. In the challenge phase, $\overline{\mathcal{A}}$ outputs two messages m_0, m_1 to $\mathcal{A}$. If either $f(m_0)$ or $f(m_1)$ is equal to Y, then $\mathcal{A}$ aborts the game and $\mathcal{I}$ outputs the corresponding m_i for which $f(m_i) = Y$ and thereby inverting f. If neither of $f(m_0)$ and $f(m_1)$ equals Y, $\mathcal{A}$ sends m_0, m_1 to the IND-CPA challenger $\mathcal{C}$ of Π as the challenge plaintexts. $\mathcal{C}$ randomly chooses a bit $b \in \{0, 1\}$ and sends $c^* = \mathsf{Enc}(pk, m_b)$ to $\mathcal{A}$ and $\mathcal{A}$ passes $\overline{c}^* = (0||c^*)$ to $\overline{\mathcal{A}}$ as the challenge ciphertext. Finally, in the guess phase, $\mathcal{A}$ returns the answer b' given by $\overline{\mathcal{A}}$ to $\mathcal{C}$.

Let E denote the event that either $f(m_0)$ or $f(m_1)$ is equal to Y. Then probability that $\mathcal{I}$ successfully inverts f is $\Pr[\mathsf{E}]$ i.e., $\mathsf{Adv}_{\mathcal{I}} = \Pr[\mathsf{E}]$. Hence, it follows that

$$\mathsf{Adv}_{\overline{\mathcal{A}}} = \mathsf{Adv}_{\mathcal{A}} + \mathsf{Adv}_{\mathcal{I}}.$$

A.3 Proof of Lemma 11

Let δ be the maximum probability with which a p.p.t. adversary can distinguish between a random string and a particular output of G. Let $\overline{A}$ be an IND-CCA1 adversary against $\overline{\Pi}$. We construct an IND-CCA2 adversary $\mathcal{A}$ against Π using $\overline{A}$ as a subroutine. As an input, $\mathcal{A}$ takes pk and an oracle access to the decryption oracle of Π. $\mathcal{A}$ chooses an one-way permutation f on $\{0,1\}^k$, a pseudo-random function family $G : \{0,1\}^{k_1} \times \{0,1\}^{k_2} \to \{0,1\}^{k_3}$ and $\mathsf{M}_{weak} \in_R \{0,1\}^k$ and sets $Y = f(\mathsf{M}_{weak})$. $\overline{A}$ is fed with $\overline{pk} = (pk, f, Y, G)$. The queries of $\overline{A}$ are answered as follows: In the first phase, when $\overline{A}$ queries a ciphertext $\overline{c} = (u||c||\alpha)$, usual decryption algorithm $\overline{\mathsf{Dec}}$ is run to return the corresponding plaintext. (Note that simulator queries the decryption oracle of Π to decrypt c.) In the challenge phase, $\overline{A}$ outputs two k-bit strings m_0 and m_1 to $\mathcal{A}$. Now, two cases may arise:

- **Case 1: (Neither of m_0 and m_1 is M_{weak})** In this case, $\mathcal{A}$ randomly chooses $r_0, r_1 \in \{0,1\}^{k_0}$ and sends $m_0||r_0, m_1||r_1$ to the IND-CCA2 challenger $\mathcal{C}$. $\mathcal{C}$ randomly chooses a bit $b \in \{0,1\}$ and encrypts $m_b||r_b$ to output $c^* = \mathsf{Enc}(m_b||r_b)$ as the challenge ciphertext for $\mathcal{A}$. $\mathcal{A}$ returns $\overline{c^*} = (0||c^*||\alpha)$ to $\overline{A}$ as the challenge ciphertext, where $\alpha \in_R \{0,1\}^{k_2}$.
- **Case 2: (One of m_0 and m_1 is M_{weak})** In this case, $\mathcal{A}$ randomly chooses $r \in \{0,1\}^{k_0}$ and sends $m_0||r, m_1||r$ to the IND-CCA2 challenger $\mathcal{C}$. $\mathcal{C}$ randomly chooses a bit $b \in \{0,1\}$ and encrypts $m_b||r$ to output $c^* = \mathsf{Enc}(m_b||r)$ as the challenge ciphertext for $\mathcal{A}$. $\mathcal{A}$ returns $\overline{c^*} = (0||c^*||\alpha)$ to $\overline{A}$ as the challenge ciphertext, where $\alpha = G(r', r''), r = r'||r''$.

Finally in the guess phase, $\overline{A}$ returns a bit b' and $\mathcal{A}$ outputs the same bit b' as its guess to $\mathcal{C}$.

Now, if **Case 1** occurs, then $\overline{c^*}$ is indeed a valid ciphertext for $\overline{A}$, and clearly $\mathsf{Adv}_{\mathcal{A}} = \mathsf{Adv}_{\overline{A}}$.

Let us consider $\overline{A}$'s view in this simulated game, if **Case 2** occurs.

If $m_b = \mathsf{M}_{weak}$, i.e., $\mathsf{M}_{weak}||r$ is encrypted by $\mathcal{C}$, then $\overline{c^*}$ is indeed a valid ciphertext. But, in $\overline{A}$'s view, $\overline{c^*}$ is a valid ciphertext with probability $1 - \frac{1}{2^t}$. (As, $1||1^{l+k_3}$ is also a valid ciphertext for M_{weak} occuring with probability $\frac{1}{2^t}$.)

On the other hand, if $m_b \neq \mathsf{M}_{weak}$, then α (the last k_3 bit of $\overline{c^*}$) should have been a random string, instead of a particular output of G. So, in $\overline{A}$'s view, $\overline{c^*}$ is a valid ciphertext with probability $(1 - \delta)$.

Thus, if **Case 2** occurs, in any case, $\overline{c^*}$ is a valid ciphertext in $\overline{A}$'s view with probability

$$= \frac{1}{2}\left(1 - \frac{1}{2^t}\right) + \frac{1}{2}(1 - \delta) = 1 - \frac{\delta}{2} - \frac{1}{2^{t+1}}.$$

Now, we define

H be the event that $\overline{c^*}$ is a valid ciphertext in $\overline{A}$'s view;

$\mathcal{A}_{\mathsf{win}}$ be the event that $\mathcal{A}$ wins the IND-CCA2 game;

$\overline{A}_{\mathsf{win}}^{\mathsf{sim}}$ be the event that $\overline{A}$ wins the simulated game and

$\overline{A}_{\mathsf{win}}^{\mathsf{real}}$ be the event that $\overline{A}$ wins the real IND-CCA1 game.

Note that $\Pr[\overline{A}_{\mathsf{win}}^{\mathsf{sim}}|H] = \Pr[\overline{A}_{\mathsf{win}}^{\mathsf{real}}]$. Thus we have,

$$\Pr[\mathcal{A}_{\mathsf{win}}] = \Pr[\overline{\mathcal{A}}_{\mathsf{win}}^{\mathsf{sim}} \wedge H] = \Pr[\overline{\mathcal{A}}_{\mathsf{win}}^{\mathsf{sim}}|H] \cdot \Pr[H] = \Pr[\overline{\mathcal{A}}_{\mathsf{win}}^{\mathsf{real}}] \cdot \Pr[H].$$

Thus, $\mathsf{Adv}_{\mathcal{A}} = 2\Pr[\mathcal{A}_{\mathsf{win}}] - 1 = 2\Pr[\overline{\mathcal{A}}_{\mathsf{win}}^{\mathsf{real}}] \cdot \Pr[H] - 1 = \Pr[\overline{\mathcal{A}}_{\mathsf{win}}^{\mathsf{real}}] \cdot \left(2 - \delta - \frac{1}{2^t}\right) - 1$

$= \left(2\Pr[\overline{\mathcal{A}}_{\mathsf{win}}^{\mathsf{real}}] - 1\right) - \left(\delta + \frac{1}{2^t}\right)\Pr[\overline{\mathcal{A}}_{\mathsf{win}}^{\mathsf{real}}] = \mathsf{Adv}_{\overline{\mathcal{A}}} - \left(\delta + \frac{1}{2^t}\right)\Pr[\overline{\mathcal{A}}_{\mathsf{win}}^{\mathsf{real}}]$

$\geq \mathsf{Adv}_{\overline{\mathcal{A}}} - \left(\delta + \frac{1}{2^t}\right)$

Combining both **Case 1** and **Case 2**, we have $\mathsf{Adv}_{\mathcal{A}} \geq \mathsf{Adv}_{\overline{\mathcal{A}}} - \left(\delta + \frac{1}{2^t}\right).$

Input-Aware Equivocable Commitments
and UC-secure Commitments with Atomic Exchanges

Ioana Boureanu and Serge Vaudenay

Ecole Polytechnique Fédérale de Lausanne (EPFL)
{ioana.boureanu,serge.vaudenay}@epfl.ch

Abstract. We define a new primitive, *input-aware equivocable commitment*, baring similar hardness assumptions as plaintext-aware encryption and featuring equivocability. We construct an actual input-aware equivocable commitment protocol, based on a flavor of Diffie-Hellman assumptions allowing adversarially chosen domain parameters. On a parallel front, and since our commitment is extractable and equivocable in a straight-line way, we show that our commitment enjoys UC-security, when *atomic exchanges* are available as a UC setup. We further compare our protocol and our UC setup with similar, existing ones (i.e., in terms of efficiency, assumptions needed, etc.). Finally, we show that cryptography becomes UC-realizable in a natural way when participants are able to have "close encounters" or when atomic exchanges can be enforced onto the communication.

1 Introduction

An attractive, neat way to prove security of a protocol is to show that it realizes an ideal functionality [26,1,3,19] modelling a primitive. In this sense, a normal starting point is the well-known framework of Canetti's, i.e., the universal composability (UC) [7]. There are several versions of the UC framework (from [7] to [8]); slight differences are operated in the communication model, the order of quantifiers in the UC proofs, etc. In this paper, we will follow the original universal composability model, i.e., the one in [7], summarised below.

At a high level, a UC proof that a protocol is secure (in the bare UC model) means to show that no environment machine, $\mathcal{Z}$, can distinguish between the execution in the "real world" from the execution in the "ideal world". The "ideal world" contains "dummy" parties, the "target" ideal functionality (that the protocol is emulating) and the "ideal" adversary, I. These "dummy" parties simply send their inputs to the ideal functionality and wait for the response which they write on their output tapes. The environment $\mathcal{Z}$ gives the inputs to the parties and reads their local outputs and can communicate with I. The "real world" contains actual protocol participants, the environment $\mathcal{Z}$, the "real adversary" $\mathcal{A}$. The "ideal" adversary I or the "real" adversary $\mathcal{A}$ can corrupt protocol-parties, in which case the adversary will see the input of such a party, all communication sent to it, and $\mathcal{A}$ can decide its output. The communication channels between participants is assumed to be secure. So far, this perfectly describes the bare UC model which is often referred to as the *UC plain* model. In the UC plain model, several essential cryptographic protocols (e.g., commitments) are not realizable. Thus, the formalism is enhanced with some extra functionality, i.e., a *setup functionality*. Such an "empowering" add-on to the UC plain models yields the so-called *UC hybrid* models.

W. Susilo and R. Reyhanitabar (Eds.): ProvSec 2013, LNCS 8209, pp. 121–138, 2013.

UC Plain Models and Commitments. In the context of UC, we recall that if multiple commitments are UC-realized, then any multiparty computation can be UC-realized [11]. The UC functionality for single commitment is normally referred to as $\mathcal{F}_{COM}$ and can be assimilated to an ideal safe where to store the commitment. Another common functionality $\mathcal{F}_{MCOM}$ can deal with multiple commitments. Note that the general impossibility result of realizing UC commitment in the plain UC model is strongly linked to the notion of relay attacks.

UC Hybrid Models & Commitments. To achieve UC-secure (multiple) commitments, different UC setups have been used. We recall that UC-secure multi-commitment are generally realizable as follows: with a common reference string (CRS) setup [11], or with a public-key infrastructure (PKI) using a trusted party to manage the correct knowledge of respective public/secret keys [2], or with Katz's tamper-resistant hardware token [23] (under the computational Diffie-Hellman assumption and a static adversarial model), or with similar tokens to Katz's but susceptible to more powerful attacks [12], or with hardware tokens similar to those in [23], but used in a "receiver-empowering" fashion to minimize the computational assumptions. More recently, Damgård *et al.* [15] UC-realized multiple commitments by using a setup assumption that relaxes the tamper-resistant hardware token to a functionality that models the partial isolation and limited communication-power of a party. Unlike previous protocols, the protocol of Damgård's *et al.* [15] is in fact a general construction, relying on the following fact: if a functionality of isolated parties is available, then witness indistinguishable proofs of knowledge (WI PoK) can be realized, which further provide a PKI and make UC multiple commitments possible. In this setting, the UC-realization relies on the existence of one-way permutations and dense public key, IND-CPA secure encryption schemes with pseudorandom ciphertexts, but the adversarial model is strong (i.e., active and adaptive). In their paper, Damgård *et al.* [15] fully compare their functionality with that of tamper-evident hardware devices; we refer the reader to [15] for this comparison.

UC Augmented Models & Commitments. In fact, a UC-like scenario that made commitment possible is that of a communication augmented with pre-specified delays: i.e., the timing model of Kalai's *et al.* [22]. The assumptions under which multi-party computation becomes possible in this model are similar to some of the aforementioned assumptions for UC commitments with setups, i.e., the existence of enhanced trapdoor permutations and dense cryptosystems. However, whilst commitment in itself is not an issue anymore (i.e., the relay is prevented), Kalai's *et al.* [22] state that their model has the drawback of not being usable with protocols that employ time themselves (e.g., distance-bounding protocols [6]). But this may be unfortunate: as we will see further (i.e., in Section 3.2), time-sensitive protocols can in fact be themselves tightly linked to UC-secure protocols and their realization.

Our Justification for UC Hybrid Models with Atomic Exchanges. Summing up the above paragraphs, we can see that the ℓ-isolated parties of Damgård's *et al.* [15] can clearly be viewed as a restriction of the UC communication, as much as Kalai's *et al.* [22] model can. Thus, the former can also prevent relay attacks; moreover, ℓ-isolated parties do allow (and, in fact, facilitate) the composition of/with protocols that involve time themselves. And, as we envisage the usage of timed protocols (e.g., distance-bounding protocols [6]), thus setting *à la* Kalai with delayed messages would be difficult to handle in our context. So, we embark on the approach of using UC setups, rather than augmentation of models with time/delays. In order to realize UC (multiple) commitments (and thus all multi-party computation as per [11]), we will invoke a UC-setup similar to the recent ℓ-isolated parties of Damgård's *et al.* To this end, we put forward a UC setup called $\mathcal{F}_{atomic}$. By *atomic exchanges* we mean the communication between protocol parties produced via their interaction with $\mathcal{F}_{atomic}$.

Our functionality $\mathcal{F}_{atomic}$ is similar to the "ℓ-isolated parties" setup of Damgård *et al.* [15]. The intuition behind is that the $\mathcal{F}_{atomic}$ functionality allows two parties to have an elementary, "fully isolated" exchange of *just one* message each. This can be viewed as a specialization of the $\mathcal{F}_{\ell\text{-isolated}}$ functionality of Damgård's *et al.* [15] (namely, with $\ell = 0$ and an exchanges limited to two messages in "one-round"). On the one hand, it is not clear how to realize $\mathcal{F}_{0-isolate}$ using $\mathcal{F}_{atomic}$. Intuitively, we need several instances of $\mathcal{F}_{atomic}$ and it would mean to pass information from one to the other using non-malleable encryption. So, $\mathcal{F}_{atomic}$ may be weaker than $\mathcal{F}_{0-isolate}$. On the other hand, $\mathcal{F}_{atomic}$ may be simpler to implement. For instance, the responder may be subject to several constraints such as time-bound to respond (like in NFC tags in distance-bounding [6]), or may be in a tamper proof token (such as the one by Katz [23]), or may result from a "close encounter".

Extrapolating PAW. In parallel, in this paper, we will define *input-aware equivocable commitments* (outside the UC model), a scheme akin in its characteristics to plaintext-aware encryption [14,21,31]. Our definition also includes equivocability, which is crucial for UC-security. We propose a specific protocol that implements this scheme under special types Diffie-Hellman assumptions. I.e., one such assumption is an extension of the DH regular knowledge assumption to be required to hold in any group [17]. In our case, the DH knowledge assumption needed is supposed to hold further in any adversarially chosen group (which is a weaker assumption than assuming it holds in any group). Also, in our UC setting, such a scheme can be employed in, e.g., concurrent RFID/NFC-based contactless payment protocols [25] where some computation is to be done *atomically* (i.e., by the RFID/NFC tag alone) and the final result needs to be "independent" for other simultaneous such computations.

UC Commitments and Their Assumptions. UC multiple commitments are possible under the different UC-setups. A short list of such setups is as follows: 1. Katz's tamper-resistant hardware tokens [23] (where under the computational Diffie-Hellman assumption and a static adversarial model); 2. similar tokens to Katz's but susceptible to more powerful attacks [12]; 3. hardware tokens similar to those in [23], but used in an asymmetric fashion to minimize the computational assumptions [28]; 4. the more recent [15] relaxation of the tamper-resistant hardware tokens to a functionality modelling the partial isolation and limited communication power of a party (under the assumptions of one-way permutations and dense public key, IND-CPA secure encryption schemes with pseudorandom ciphertexts, but the adversarial model is strong (i.e., active and adaptive).

There are some UC lines [10,16] in which the ideas underlying the ideal-world simulation of (multiple) commitment can be loosely linked to the one that we are going to put forward. Firstly, in [10], Canetti *et al.* achieve a $\mathcal{F}_{MCOM}$-realization with non-erasing parties, in the CRS-hybrid model using an encryption scheme obviously samplable[14]. In this case, the trick that allows I to run its simulations (i.e., that gives I the oblivious-sampling coins for its ciphertext) is to sample ciphertexts without running the encryption algorithm. Note that an encryption obviously samplable (with respect to chosen-ciphertext attacks) [14] is possible under the Decisional Diffie-Hellman (DDH) assumption. Similarly, our protocol is possible if some special Diffie-Hellman assumptions are used.

Using several instances of $\mathcal{F}_{COM}$, ZK is UC-realized in the $\mathcal{F}_{COM}$-hybrid model [10] by mainstream ideas: by repeating t times, in parallel, Blum's protocol for Hamiltonian-Cycles (HC) [4], where the commitments of the provers are calls to $\mathcal{F}_{COM}$. Damgård and Nielsen [16] construct ZK more efficiently, but in a similar way, using the SAT protocol which proves satisfiability of boolean circuits. Along similar lines, our one-bit commitment can be used to $\mathcal{F}_{atomic}$-UC realize ZK in the same complexity as the Canetti's *et al.* [10]. In Appendix A we included a discussion about some further, "unconventional" commitments.

Our Contribution. In this paper, we introduce the notion of input-aware equivocable commitment, i.e., commitments that include both extractability and equivocability. We further propose some extensions of the Diffie-Hellman hardness assumptions or of the discrete logarithm hardness assumption, for the case where the adversary can maliciously select the group structure. We call it an *adversarially-chosen group* extension of the DH assumption. We propose the $\mathcal{F}_{atomic}$ functionality as a new setup assumption. This is a new, easy to implement UC setup, drawing upon un-aided local computation. Finally, we propose an input-aware equivocable commitment in the plain model, which we then prove to UC-realize $\mathcal{F}_{COM}$ in presence of the $\mathcal{F}_{atomic}$ setup.

2   Input-Aware Commitments in Classical Cryptography

In this section, we formalize the notion of input-aware equivocable commitments and present one protocol. On our way to doing so, we specify different flavors of Diffie-Hellman (DH) assumptions.

2.1   Commitment Scheme

The following definition reiterates the usual meaning of a commitment scheme in conformity with traditional (i.e., non-composable) cryptography.

Definition 1 (Commitment Scheme). *A bit-commitment scheme in terms of a security parameter λ is a pair of polynomially bounded protocols*
$((S_{COM}, R_{COM}), (S_{OPEN}, R_{OPEN}))$ *where S_{COM} has an input bit b, and R_{OPEN} has an output bit $\bar{b}$. The protocols may abort. The*

$$S_{COM}(1^\lambda, b; r_S) \leftrightarrow R_{COM}(1^\lambda; r_R)$$

execution[1] is called the commitment phase. *For simplicity, 1^λ is omitted from the notation. Let View_S, respectively View_R, denote the view of S_{COM}, respectively the view of R_{COM}. The*

$$S_{OPEN}(\mathsf{View}_S; r'_S) \leftrightarrow R_{OPEN}(\mathsf{View}_R; r'_R)$$

---

[1] This execution is understood as any standard interactive system [20].

execution is called the opening phase. *It produces the final output from R, i.e.,* $\bar{b}$. *A commitment scheme is expected to be* correct: *i.e., when correctly executed, no protocol aborts and* $\bar{b} = b$.

The following definition completes the above by formalizing the usual requirements of a commitment scheme in conformity with traditional (i.e., non-composable) cryptography.

Definition 2 (The Hiding Property). *A commitment scheme is said to be* hiding *if the following holds. For any polynomially bounded* R^*_{COM}, *if* $S_{COM}(b; r_S) \leftrightarrow R^*_{COM}(r_R)$ *ends up with the final view* View_R *for* R^*_{COM}, *then* $\mathsf{View}_R | b = 0$ *and* $\mathsf{View}_R | b = 1$ *are computationally indistinguishable.*

In the above, $\mathsf{View}_R | b = x$ (with $x \in \{0, 1\}$) denotes the marginal distribution (over all random coins and inputs) of View_R as a random variable, conditioned to the event $b = x$. Note that we can assume without loss of generality that R^*_{COM} is deterministic (since r_R could be hard-coded in it).

Definition 3 (The Binding Property). *A commitment scheme is said to be* binding *if the following holds. For any polynomially bounded* S^*_{COM} *and* S^*_{OPEN}, *if the* $S^*_{COM}(r_S) \leftrightarrow R_{COM}(r_R)$ *and then the* $S^*_{OPEN}(\mathsf{View}_S; r'_S) \leftrightarrow R_{OPEN}(\mathsf{View}_R; r'_R)$ *experiment occur, then* $\min(\Pr[\bar{b} = 0 | r_S, r_R], \Pr[\bar{b} = 1 | r_S, r_R]) = \mathsf{negl}(\lambda)$, *where this probability is taken in the random choices of* S^*_{OPEN} *and* R_{OPEN}.

This means that once the commitment is made (i.e., r_S and r_R are fixed), S^*_{OPEN} cannot open to both $\bar{b} = 0$ and $\bar{b} = 1$. We recall that $f(\lambda) = \mathsf{negl}(\lambda)$ means that for all $c > 0$, we have $f(\lambda) = O(\lambda^{-c})$.

2.2 Diffie-Hellman Assumptions

In this subsection, we specify several Diffie-Hellman assumptions.

Definition 4 (DH Key Generator). *A DH key is a tuple* $K = (G, q, g)$ *such that G is a group, q is a prime dividing the order of G, g is an element of G of order q. A DH key-generator is a ppt. algorithm Gen producing DH keys K such that* $|K| = Poly(\log q)$ *and the operations (i.e., multiplication, comparison, and membership checking in the group* $\langle g \rangle$ *generated by g) over their domain can be computed in time* $Poly(\log q)$. *We say that* (S, S') *is a valid K-DH pair for* g^σ *if* $S \in \langle g \rangle$ *and* $S' = S^\sigma$, *where* $\sigma \in \mathbb{Z}_q$. *Given* $K = (G, q, g)$, *we define a function* DH_K *with a variable number of inputs from G by* $\mathsf{DH}_K(g^{x_1}, \ldots, g^{x_n}) = g^{x_1 \cdots x_n}$.

An example of a DH key is $(\mathbb{Z}_p^*, q, g)$ where p and q are primes and $p = 2q + 1$, $g \in QR(p)$, $g \neq 1$.

We now strengthen the Decisional Diffie-Hellman (DDH) assumption. Below, we use an arbitrary ppt. algorithm $\mathcal{B}$ generating some coins ρ and a state state. Such coins ρ and/or state state will be sometimes used as auxiliary inputs to some ITMs in the security games formalized below.

Definition 5 (DDH Asmpt. in an Adversarially-Chosen Group (ag-DDH$_{\text{Gen}}$)). *The* ag-DDH$_{\text{Gen}}$ *assumption over a domain of DH keys $\mathcal{K}$ states that for any ppt. algorithms $\mathcal{A}$ and $\mathcal{B}$ in the next game, $\Pr[b = \bar{b}] - \frac{1}{2} = \mathsf{negl}(\lambda)$:*

1: $(\rho, \mathsf{state}) := \mathcal{B}(1^\lambda; r_\mathcal{B})$
2: $K := Gen(1^\lambda; \rho)$
3: define (G, q, g) from K
4: pick $\alpha, \beta, \gamma \in_U \mathbf{Z}_q$
5: $A := g^\alpha; B := g^\beta; C_0 := g^\gamma; C_1 := g^{\alpha\beta}$
6: pick $b \in_U \{0, 1\}$
7: $\bar{b} := \mathcal{A}(1^\lambda, \mathsf{state}, A, B, C_b; r)$

The probability stands over the random coins $r_\mathcal{B}$, r, $b \in_U \{0, 1\}$ and $\alpha, \beta, \gamma \in_U \mathbf{Z}_q$ and is negligible in terms of $\log q$. $\mathcal{A}$ (and $\mathcal{B}$) run in ppt. in terms of $\log q$.

It should be clear that ag-CDH$_{\text{Gen}}$, the computational version of this problem can be defined as well.

Definition 6 (CDH^n Asmpt. in an Adversarially-Chosen Group (ag-CDH$_{\text{Gen}}^n$)). *The* ag-CDH$_{\text{Gen}}^n$ *assumption over a domain of DH keys $\mathcal{K}$ states that for any ppt. algorithms $\mathcal{A}$ and $\mathcal{B}$ in the next game, the probability that $S_0 = DH_K(A, B, S_1, \ldots, S_n)$ and that $S_i \neq 1$ for $i = 1, \ldots, n$ is negligible:*

1: $(\rho, \mathsf{state}) := \mathcal{B}(1^\lambda; r_\mathcal{B})$
2: $K := Gen(1^\lambda; \rho)$
3: define (G, q, g) from K
4: pick $\alpha, \beta \in_U \mathbf{Z}_q$
5: $A := g^\alpha; B := g^\beta$
6: $(S_0, S_1, \ldots, S_n) := \mathcal{A}(1^\lambda, \mathsf{state}, A, B; r)$

The probability stands over the random coins $r_\mathcal{B}$, r, and $\alpha, \beta \in_U \mathbf{Z}_q$. The probability is negligible in terms of $\log q$. $\mathcal{A}$ (and $\mathcal{B}$) run in ppt. in terms of $\log q$.

The standard Diffie-Hellman computational problem corresponds to the CDH^0 problem. Clearly, the CDH^n assumption implies the CDH^{n-1} assumption for all $n > 0$, but the opposite implication is an open problem. In what follows, we will use the CDH^1 assumption.

We now similarly strengthen the Diffie-Hellman knowledge (DHK0) assumption (for a summary the latter, refer to [17]).

Definition 7 (DHK0 Asmpt. in an Adversarially-Chosen Group (ag-DHK0$_{\text{Gen}}$)). *The* ag-DHK0$_{\text{Gen}}$ *assumption over a domain of DH keys $\mathcal{K}$ states that for any ppt. algorithm $\mathcal{A}$ and $\mathcal{B}$ in the next game, there is a polynomially bounded algorithm $\mathcal{E}$ such that the probability of the below experiment outputting 1 is negligible:*

1: $(\rho, \mathsf{state}) := \mathcal{B}(1^\lambda; r_\mathcal{B})$
2: $K := Gen(1^\lambda; \rho_\lambda)$
3: define (G, q, g) from K
4: pick $\sigma \in_U \mathbf{Z}_q$
5: $(S, S') := \mathcal{A}(1^\lambda, \mathsf{state}, g^\sigma; r)$
6: if (S, S') is not a valid K-DH pair for g^σ, then return 0

7: $s := \mathcal{E}(1^\lambda, \text{state}, g^\sigma, r)$
8: *if* $S = g^s$, *then return 0*
9: *return 1*

The probability stands over the random coins $r_{\mathcal{B}}$, r *and* $\sigma \in_U \mathbf{Z}_q$ *and is negligible in terms of* $\log q$. *The running time of* $\mathcal{E}$ *(and* $\mathcal{B}$*) is ppt. in terms of* $\log q$.

This assumption means that whatever the algorithm producing valid DH pairs for a random g^σ with σ unknown, this algorithm must know the discrete logarithm of their components except for some negligible cases.

The algorithm $\mathcal{B}$ used in the games above is denoted as the *biotope* algorithm.

What distinguishes these assumptions from the mainstream DDH and DHK0 assumptions [17] is that these should hold for all K selected by a ppt. biotope algorithm (even by a malicious one) and not only for some K which is randomly selected by an honest participant. In fact, when selecting a DH key without a CRS in a two party protocol, the above assumption must hold for any maliciously selected K (since we ignore a priori which party is honest). Hence, the name we use: DH assumptions in an adversarially-chosen group. As we mentioned in the introduction, the latter assumption is a special case of the DH knowledge assumption required to hold in any group, or, equivalently, for any $\mathcal{B}$ and $r_{\mathcal{B}}$. Such assumptions were originally introduced by Dent in [17]. Here, we do not require the assumption to hold in any group, but rather in those groups G for which we can produce a seed for *Gen* to use in generating G, or equivalently, for any, $\mathcal{B}$ on average over $r_{\mathcal{B}}$.

In the next, for readability purposes, we will omit the additional-input 1^λ from the inputs of the machines that take it, its presence being implicit.

2.3 Input-Aware Equivocable Bit-Commitment

Definition 8 (Input-Aware Equivocable Commitment Scheme). *An* input-aware equivocable bit-commitment (IAEC) scheme *is a commitment scheme* $((S_{COM}, R_{COM}), (S_{OPEN}, R_{OPEN}))$ *as per Def. 1, with the following additional properties. Let b denote the input of S_{COM}, $\bar{b}$ be the output of R_{OPEN} or R^*_{OPEN}, and View_S, respectively* View_R, *be the view of S_{COM} or S^*_{COM} and, respectively, of R_{COM} or R^*_{COM} in the commitment phase.*

- *(sender input-awareness aka extractability) For any polynomially bounded algorithms S^*_{COM} and S^*_{OPEN}, there is a polynomially bounded algorithm* Extract *such that the following holds. When running the commitment phase*

$$S^*_{COM}(r_S) \leftrightarrow R_{COM}(r_R),$$

  followed by the opening phase

$$S^*_{OPEN}(\text{View}_S; r'_S) \leftrightarrow R_{OPEN}(\text{View}_R; r'_R),$$

  the next holds with probability $1 - \text{negl}(\lambda)$, *taken over the random* r_S, r'_S, r_R, r'_R:
  - $\bar{b} = \text{Extract}(\text{View}_S)$ *and no protocol aborts,*
  - *or* Extract(View_S) *aborts and the commitment phase as well,*
  - *or the opening phase aborts.*

– *(receiver self-equivocability) For any polynomially bounded algorithm R^*_{COM} and R^*_{OPEN}, there is a polynomially bounded algorithm Equiv such that the following holds. When running the commitment phase*

$$S_{COM}(b; r_S) \leftrightarrow R^*_{COM}(r_R),$$

followed by the flipping a coin b' to run the opening phase

$$\begin{cases} S_{OPEN}(\text{View}_S; r'_S) \leftrightarrow R^*_{OPEN}(\text{View}_R; r'_R), & \text{if } b' = b \\ \text{Equiv}(b', \text{View}_R; r'_S) \leftrightarrow R^*_{OPEN}(\text{View}_R; r'_R), & \text{if } b' = 1 - b, \end{cases}$$

it all results in a final view View'_R of R^*_{OPEN} and this is such that $\text{View}'_R | b = 0$ and $\text{View}'_R | b = 1$ are computationally indistinguishable over the random r_S, r_R, r'_R, r'_S and b'.

The above definition implies the classical notions of security (i.e., notions of hiding and binding commitments as per Defs. 2, 3). Equivocability already says that $\text{View}_R | b = 0$ and $\text{View}_R | b = 1$ are indistinguishable since View_R is included in View'_R; so the commitment is hiding. Furthermore, a malicious sender who could open a commitment to both $b = 0$ and $b = 1$ with a probability which is negligible would contradict $\bar{b} = \text{Extract}(\text{View}_S)$; so, the commitment is binding.

We will now construct an IAEC based on the ag-DHK0$_{\text{Gen}}$, the ag-DDH$_{\text{Gen}}$ and the ag-CDH$^1_{\text{Gen}}$ assumptions. We denote it as protocol Π_{Gen} (see Fig. 1). As per Section 3.2, the label "atomic" in Fig. 1, applies only in the context of the use of a UC functionality for atomic exchanges when building the protocol to be UC-secure. It shall be ignored in the current section.

Protocol Π_{Gen}

The commitment phase (i.e., to be described by the S_{COM} and R_{COM} protocols) works as follows.

1. S generates ρ for *Gen*, i.e., it does $K := Gen(\rho)$, and S sends ρ to R.
2. Then, R also computed $K := Gen(\rho)$ and R selects[2] some $\alpha \in \mathbf{Z}^*_q$ and sends $X_0 := g^\alpha$ to S.
3. S verifies[3] that $X_0 \in \langle g \rangle$, selects $x \in \mathbf{Z}^*_q$, calculates $X := g^x$ and $X' := X_0^x$, and sends X, X' to R. S picks $\beta \in \mathbf{Z}^*_q$ and calculates $Y_0 := g^\beta$. S sends Y_0 to R.
4. R verifies that $X \in \langle g \rangle$, $X' = X^\alpha$, and that $Y_0 \in \langle g \rangle$. Then, R selects $y \in \mathbf{Z}^*_q$ and calculates $Y := g^y$ and $Y' := Y_0^y$. Then, R sends Y, Y', and α to S. Then, R selects some $z_0, z_1 \in \mathbf{Z}^*_q$ and calculates Z_0 and Z_1 as follows: $Z_i := g^{z_i}$, for $i \in \{0,1\}$. The R party sends Z_0 and Z_1 to S.
5. The party S verifies that $Y, Z_0, Z_1 \in \langle g \rangle$, that $Y' = Y^\beta$, and that $X_0 = g^\alpha$. S further selects $r \in \mathbf{Z}_q$ and sends $U := g^r$, $V := Z_b X^r$ and β to R, where b is the bit that S is in the process of committing to.
6. R verifies that $U, V \in \langle g \rangle$ and that $Y_0 = g^\beta$.

---

[2] All occurrences of "selects" in this description denote "picks uniformly".

[3] If a verification fails, then the party running it aborts.

Sender   Receiver

commitment phase

input: b

pick ρ and set $K := Gen(1^\lambda,\rho)$ $\xrightarrow{\quad \rho \quad}$ set $K := Gen(1^\lambda,\rho)$

$X_0 \overset{?}{\in} \langle g \rangle$ $\xleftarrow{\text{atomic: } X_0}$ $\alpha \in_U \mathbf{Z}_q^*, X_0 := g^\alpha$

$x \in_U \mathbf{Z}_q^*, X := g^x, X' := X_0^x$ $\xrightarrow{\quad X,X' \quad}$ $X \overset{?}{\in} \langle g \rangle, X' \overset{?}{=} X^\alpha$

$\beta \in_U \mathbf{Z}_q^*, Y_0 := g^\beta$ $\xleftarrow{\text{atomic: } Y_0}$ $Y_0 \overset{?}{\in} \langle g \rangle$

$Y \overset{?}{\in} \langle g \rangle, Y' \overset{?}{=} Y^\beta, X_0 \overset{?}{=} g^\alpha$ $\xleftarrow{\quad Y,Y',\alpha \quad}$ $y \in_U \mathbf{Z}_q^*, Y := g^y, Y' := Y_0^y$

$Z_0, Z_1 \overset{?}{\in} \langle g \rangle$ $\xleftarrow{\quad Z_0,Z_1 \quad}$ $z_0, z_1 \in_U \mathbf{Z}_q^*, Z_0 := g^{z_0}, Z_1 := g^{z_1}$

$r \in_U \mathbf{Z}_q, U := g^r, V := Z_b X^r$ $\xrightarrow{\quad U,V,\beta \quad}$ $U, V \overset{?}{\in} \langle g \rangle, Y_0 \overset{?}{=} g^\beta$

opening phase

set $b' := b$ $\xrightarrow{\quad b' \quad}$

$\gamma \in_U \mathbf{Z}_q^*$ $\xleftarrow{\quad U',V' \quad}$ $s \in_U \mathbf{Z}_q, U' := U^y g^s, V' := V^y X^s$

$W := g^\gamma, W' := \left(V'U'^{-x}\right)^\gamma$ $\xrightarrow{\quad W,W' \quad}$

$U' \overset{?}{=} Y^r g^s, (V'Y^{-xr}X^{-s})^\gamma \overset{?}{=} W'$ $\xleftarrow{\quad s \quad}$

$\xrightarrow{\quad \gamma \quad}$ $W \overset{?}{=} g^\gamma, W' \overset{?}{=} Z_{b'}^{y\gamma}$

Fig. 1. Input-aware Equivocable Commitment Protocol Π_{Gen}

The opening phase (i.e., to be described by the $\mathcal{S}_{OPEN}$ and $\mathcal{R}_{OPEN}$ protocols) works as follows.

1. S sends a bit b' with $b' = b$.
2. Then, R selects $s \in \mathbf{Z}_q$ and calculates $U' := U^y g^s$ and $V' := V^y x^s$. Then, R sends U' and V' to S.
3. S selects $\gamma \in \mathbf{Z}_q^*$ and calculates $W := g^\gamma$ and $W' := (V'U'^{-x})^\gamma$. Then, S sends W,W' to R.
4. R sends s to S.
5. S verifies that $U' = Y^r g^s$ and $(V'Y^{-xr}X^{-s})^\gamma = W'$. Then, R sends γ to S.
6. S verifies that $W = g^\gamma, W' = Z_{b'}^{y\gamma}$ and outputs $\bar{b} := b'$.

The commitment is an ElGamal encryption (U,V) of Z_b with a self-made public key X. The opening uses the homomorphic properties of the encryption to transform (U,V) into an encryption of Z_b^y such that the following holds: if $Z_{b'}$ were not the correct decryption of (U,V), then decrypting $Z_{b'}^y$ would require to know y or $z_{b'}$ (since $Z_{b'}^y = (g^{z_{b'}})^y$ is equal to the "public" $W'^{\frac{1}{\gamma}}$). The trick is that keys X and Y are declared in such a way that the DHK0 assumption would make the corresponding secret-keys x and y extractable by using input-aware equivocable techniques when given the appropriate coins. Indeed, x would allow to extract b from the commitment and y would allow to equivocate.

Theorem 9. *Under the* ag-CDH$_{Gen}^1$, DDH$_{Gen}$, *and* ag-DHK0$_{Gen}$ *assumptions, the protocol* Π_{Gen} *above is an input-aware equivocable bit-commitment.*

Proof (space-constrained sketch). Since the polynomial-time bound and the correctness are trivial, we only have to construct Extract and Equiv.

Sender Input-Awareness. Let S^*_{COM} and S^*_{OPEN} be some malicious commitment and opening algorithms, respectively. We define two algorithms $\mathcal{A}$ and $\mathcal{B}$ as follows. The algorithm $\mathcal{B}$ simulates the experiment $S^*_{COM}(r_S) \leftrightarrow R_{COM}(r_R)$ up to the moment before S^*_{COM} receives X_0, when $\mathcal{B}$ stops. Then, as per dictated by the ag-DHK0$_{Gen}$ game, $\mathcal{B}$ sets ρ and state according to the experiment he just took part in. That is ρ would be as generated in $S^*_{COM}(r_S) \leftrightarrow R_{COM}(r_r)$ and state would be the current view of S^*_{COM} with its coins limited to its run so far, i.e., limited to a prefix $\bar{r}_s$ of the whole set of coins r_s ($r_s := \bar{r}_s \| \overline{\overline{r}_s}$). Then the output (X, X') of S^*_{COM} with input state, augmented with the message X_0 and the coins $\overline{\overline{r}_s}$ defines $\mathcal{A}(\text{state}, X_0; \overline{\overline{r}_s})$. By the ag-DHK0$_{Gen}$ assumption, there must exist some algorithm $\mathcal{E}(\text{state}, X_0; \overline{\overline{r}_s})$ such that —except for negligible cases— $\mathcal{E}(\text{state}, X_0; \overline{\overline{r}_s})$ outputs x satisfying that $X = g^x$, or R_{COM} rejects (X, X').

Now, let $r_s = \bar{r}_s \| \overline{\overline{r}_s}$ be the coins in Views and state, X_0, Z_0, Z_1 as above be in Views. We now define Extract(Views) as follows. Let $\rho := S^*_{COM}(r_S)$ and $(X, X') := S^*_{COM}(X_0; r_S)$. Except in negligible cases, $x = \mathcal{E}(1^\lambda, \text{state}, X_0; r_S)$ is such that $X = g^x$. If (U, V) is valid, Extract can compute $Z = VU^{-x}$ and compare Z to Z_0 and to Z_1. If there is no match, then we return $\perp$. Otherwise, we return b as per the match $Z_b = Z$. Note that $\Pr[Z_0 = Z_1]$ is negligible, so there is a unique match.

Now, we need to show the soundness of this procedure, i.e., S^*_{OPEN} cannot open to something different from $b = \text{Extract(Views)}$. For this, we show that S^*_{COM} and S^*_{OPEN} could define an adversary for ag-CDH$^1_{Gen}$. We will use a rewinding technique to define this adversary. (Note that extraction is straight-line. It is only the adversary showing that extraction is sound which is using rewinding.)

To define the adversary (using the created ρ) receiving A and B from outside, we first simulate the experiment until we get β. Then, we rewind it but inject $Y = A$ instead of some Y with a known discrete logarithm. We can also compute $Y' = Y^\beta$ thanks to getting β. Similarly, we flip a coin $\tilde{b}$ and inject $Z_{\tilde{b}} = g^{z_{\tilde{b}}}$ with $z_{\tilde{b}}$ random and $Z_{1-\tilde{b}} = B$. Clearly, β is bound to be unchanged. Since Views has a correct distribution, we can still run $b = \text{Extract(Views)}$ and $x = \mathcal{E}(1^\lambda, \text{state}, X_0, r_S)$. If $b \neq \tilde{b}$, this is bad luck and we restart. Since S^*_{COM} sees no information about $\tilde{b}$, bad luck happens with probability $\frac{1}{2}$ and we do not have to restart too much until we are in the lucky $b = \tilde{b}$ case.

Then, the adversary continues to simulate the opening. If $b' = b$, the adversary aborts. Otherwise, the adversary must simulate some genuine (U', V'). We know that $V = g^{z_b}U^x$. The regular receiver would send a random $U' = U^y g^s$ and some $V' = Y^y X^s$ connected to U' with the relation $V' = Y^{z_b}(U')^x$. So, the simulator could just pick U' at random and compute $V' = Y^{z_b}(U')^x$ since he knows $z_b = z_{\tilde{b}}$ and x. He then obtains from S^*_{OPEN} some (W, W'). With a genuine receiver sending s, we obtain γ such that

$$\text{DH}(A, B, W) = \text{DH}(Y, Z_{1-b}, g^\gamma) = Z^{y\gamma}_{1-b}$$

So, to make the receiver accept, the (W, W') pair we must satisfy $\text{DH}(A, B, W) = W'$ even before providing s. Due to the ag-CDH$^1_{Gen}$ assumption, this happens with negligible probability. So, in the genuine experiment, either the experiment aborts, or $b' = \text{Extract(Views)}$, or $W' \neq \text{DH}_K(Y, Z_{1-b'}, W)$, thus making R_{OPEN} aborts.

Receiver Self-Equivocability. Let R^*_{COM} and R^*_{OPEN} be some malicious commitment and opening algorithms. We define two algorithms $\mathcal{A}$ and $\mathcal{B}$ as follows. The algorithm $\mathcal{B}$ simulates the experiment $S_{COM}(r_S) \leftrightarrow R^*_{COM}(r_R)$ until the moment before R^*_{COM} receives Y_0 and then $\mathcal{B}$ stops. As before, $\mathcal{B}$ will produce his needed ρ as in the experiment $S_{COM}(r_S) \leftrightarrow R^*_{COM}(r_R)$ and state as the current view of R^*_{COM}, limiting his coins r_R to $\overline{r_R}$, i.e., to those used so far, where $r_R := \overline{r_R}\|\overline{\overline{r_R}}$. Then the output (Y,Y') of R^*_{COM} with input state, augmented with the message Y_0 and the coins $\overline{\overline{r_R}}$ defines $\mathcal{A}(\text{state}, Y_0; \overline{\overline{r_R}})$. Due to the ag-DHK0$_{\text{Gen}}$ assumption, there must exist some algorithm $\mathcal{E}$ such that, except for negligible cases, $\mathcal{E}(\text{state}, Y_0; \overline{\overline{r_R}})$ produces y satisfying $Y = g^y$, or S_{COM} rejects (Y,Y').

We define all messages as in the $S_{COM}(b; r_S) \leftrightarrow R^*_{COM}(r_R)$ experiment from the view View$_S$. Note that running $S_{COM}(b; r_S)$ also defines ρ.

We define Equiv$(b', \text{View}_R; r'_S)$ by sending out b', receiving U', V', computing $y = \mathcal{E}(\text{state}, Y_0; \overline{\overline{r_R}})$ constructed like above, computing $Z^y_{b'}$ and producing the pair (W, W') such that $W' = \text{DH}_K(Y, Z_{b'}, W)$, by $W = g^\gamma$ and $W' = \left(Z^y_{b'}\right)^\gamma$.

The view of R includes $\rho, X, X', Y_0, U, V, \beta, b', W, W', \gamma$. In all cases, W, W', γ can be simulated by R with the same distribution, as well as Y_0, β. Since α is produced by R, X' can be simulated as well. Finally, the view reduces to (ρ, X, U, V, b'). Indeed, distinguishing $b = 0$ from $b = 1$ with b' random reduces to the semantic security of the ElGamal cryptosystem. As proven in [5], this reduces to the Decisional Diffie-Hellman (DDH) problem. $\qquad\square$

3 UC-Secure (Input-Aware Equivocable) Commitment with a "Mild" Setup

In Subsection 3.1, we introduce the UC functionality called $\mathcal{F}_{atomic}$, which is needed as UC setup for the UC-realization of our (IAEC) commitment. The actual UC-realization of commitment is shown in Subsection 3.2; some discussions about this realization and its relationships with existing lines of UC-realization of commitment are also included.

3.1 UC Setup Functionality for Atomic Exchanges

We will now present a UC functionality that models *one* exchange of messages between two parties, one of which is in complete isolation; hence, the name *atomic* exchange. The restriction to one exchange makes this functionality a specialization of the $\mathcal{F}_{\ell-\text{isolate}}$ of Damgård's *et al.* [15]. Also, differently from [15], the functionality below draws strictly upon the user on which the limited communication is enforced; in that sense, in the functionality below, this user can update its algorithm sent to the functionality several times before the actual computation is made.

The $\mathcal{F}_{atomic}$ Functionality of Atomic Exchanges. Let *poly* be a polynomial. Assume two parties A and B that would like to have an atomic exchange, i.e., A would normally send m to B and, without outside help, B would have to respond with m'. Mainly, this lack of outside help and the *one* exchange are the core of the $\mathcal{F}_{atomic}$ functionality.

Request for Atomicity. The participant B sends a message $(\textbf{atomic}, A, B, M)$ to $\mathcal{F}_{atomic}$, where M denotes description of the Turing machine[4] run by B. The functionality $\mathcal{F}_{atomic}$

---

[4] We assume that this machine is deterministic.

parses the message and stores (A, B, M). Any other tuple including the same (A, B) is erased.[5] A special case is where the participant B sends the message $(\textbf{atomic}, A, B, \bot)$, which counts for an abortion of the atomic session.

Challenge an Atomic Response. The participant A can send the command $(\textbf{challenge}, A, B, m)$ to $\mathcal{F}_{atomic}$. In this case, the functionality verifies the existence of a tuple (A, B, M). If the corresponding register is empty or if $M = \bot$, then the functionality sends a reject message to A and to the ideal adversary. Otherwise, the machine proceeds as follows. It runs $M(m)$ for no more than $poly(|m|)$ steps, finally storing the result in m'. Then, it sends $(\textbf{challenge-issued}, A, B, m)$ to B and $(\textbf{response}, A, B, m')$ to A. The (A, B, M) tuple is then erased.

Again, this functionality models the fact that B does not communicate with another participant in between receiving m and producing his response m', that before "being asked" to compute m in isolation the participant can update his machine and that this computation/communication is supposed to capture one exchange only. As we said in the introduction and in the related-work, this functionality is a specialization of the $\mathcal{F}_{\ell-\text{isolated}}$ in [15], where $\ell = 0$, the exchange is reduced to one message per each of the two parties involved and where the machine of the "computing-party" can be updated before the need for the computation is imminent. In that sense, one cannot say clearly if our functionality is weaker or stronger than the $\mathcal{F}_{\ell-\text{isolated}}$ functionality in [15].

Further, we note that this sort of setup is sufficient for bypassing a relay attack of the sort that lead to the impossibility of UC-commitments in the plain model. In the same time, especially for the cases where only two parties are involved (e.g., the aforementioned mutually independent commitments [24]), this sort of setup is suitable to bypass the known malleability problems.

In practice, a possible way to implement such an atomic-exchange functionality is given by distance-bounding protocols [6]. This is one of the actual methods implemented to prevent relay attacks [18]. Namely, to achieve the atomic-exchange, the two concerned parties can use –in an initial/certain part of the communication– a distance-bounding protocol (or a slight modification of such a protocol, which still considers the time-of-flight of the messages in accepting/rejecting them). I.e., the correct answer could have been produced only and solely by the close-by partner, otherwise the distance-bound would be broken.

To easily specify protocols using atomic exchanges, the $(\textbf{challenge}, A, B, m)$ query by A it simply denoted "`atomic:` m". It is followed by the message answering $M(m)$ by B, due to an abuse of notation. This implicitly means that B must have committed M to $\mathcal{F}_{atomic}$ before.

3.2 UC-realization of Commitment in the $\mathcal{F}_{atomic}$-hybrid Model

It is easy to see that any input-aware equivocable commitment UC-realizes commitment using $\mathcal{F}_{0-\text{isolate}}$: we just have to run S and R in isolation. Here, we strengthen the result by relying on $\mathcal{F}_{atomic}$ only. The Π_{Gen} protocol, presented in Fig. 1 also requires some messages to be exchanged atomically, i.e., using the $\mathcal{F}_{atomic}$ functionality. This means

---

[5] Note that –by the above– B can resend this command to $\mathcal{F}_{atomic}$, possibly with a different machine-description M.

that if R wants S to compute X, X' on his own based upon S's view and the fresh receipt of X_0, then they establish an *atomic exchange*: S cooperates in this and sends (several) (**atomic**, $R, S,$ algo_of_S) to $\mathcal{F}_{atomic}$, where algo_of_S computes (X, X') from the (hard-coded) partial view of S and the input X_0. We consider only the last deposited algo_of_S. Then, R sends (**challenge**, R, S, X_0) to $\mathcal{F}_{atomic}$, which will eventually send X_0 to S and X, X' to R, with $(X, X') := $ algo_of_S(X_0) with algo_of_S running up to $poly(|X_0|)$ in time. The same goes for the $Y_0 \mapsto (Y, Y')$ atomic exchange.

We are now going to prove that the Π_{Gen} protocol UC-realizes commitment.

Theorem 10. *Under the* ag-CDH$^1_{\text{Gen}}$, DDH$_{\text{Gen}}$, *and* ag-DHK0$_{\text{Gen}}$ *assumptions, in the* $\mathcal{F}_{atomic}$-*hybrid UC model in the presence of static, non-adaptive adversaries, the protocol* Π_{Gen} *UC-realizes* $\mathcal{F}_{\text{COM}}$.

The proof is very similar to the one of Th. 9. We construct an ideal adversary I by using the straight-line extraction of b (when the sender is corrupted) or the straight-line equivocation (when the receiver is corrupted). In the first case, we use the extracted b to commit to it. In the latter case, I simulates the commitment to a dummy bit b to R^*_{COM}, then we use the equivocation once b' is opened by the functionality to simulate the opening to b'.

We note that the constructed I does not require rewinding. However, to prove that I works well, we do rewind algorithms, but this is allowed. The (sketch of) proof is given in Appendix B.

Discussions about the UC-realization of $\mathcal{F}_{COM}$ *by* Π_{Gen}. We underline that, as per Fig. 1, after the initialization phase, the two parties involved are in the position where they share (amongst other things) the tuple (X, Y). This part can be separated and viewed realizing itself a particular key-sharing functionality (call it $\mathcal{G}$) in a $\mathcal{F}_{atomic}$-hybrid UC model. Then, the UC-realization in Th. 10 can be cast as follows: "in the $\mathcal{G}$-hybrid UC model in the presence of static, non-adaptive adversaries, the protocol Π'_{Gen} (i.e., Π_{Gen} without its init phase exchanging X and Y) UC-realizes $\mathcal{F}_{COM}$ (if the ag-DHK0$_{\text{Gen}}$ assumption, the ag-DDH$_{\text{Gen}}$ and the ag-CDH$^1_{\text{Gen}}$ assumption hold)."

The formulation above renders our result visibly closer to the result in [15]. Namely, if a setup functionality restricting the communication is available, then this leads to some key-establishment, which then leads to the UC-realization of commitment. However, the difference between our approach here and the one in [15] is that secret extraction is integrated based on input-awareness, and we do not need to run a multi-round protocol in isolation: only an elementary challenge-response one. Finally, this indicates that cryptography becomes UC-realizable in a natural way when participants are able to have "close encounters" to exchange public-key material.

ZK is UC-realized in the $\mathcal{F}_{COM}$-hybrid model [10] by mainstream ideas: by repeating t times, in parallel, Blum's protocol for Hamiltonian-Cycles (HC) [4], where the commitments of the provers are calls to $\mathcal{F}_{COM}$. Thus, our one-time one-bit-commitment can be used to UC realize ZK in the same complexity as the Canetti's *et al.*

Damgård and Nielsen UC-realize a commitment UC-functionality called $\mathcal{F}_{HCOM}$ [16], for homomorphic commitment. This functionality is slightly different from the original $\mathcal{F}_{MCOM}$; there the difference stems from the increased efficiency sought and, most importantly, from the way to achieve equivocability and extractability for the ideal adversary I. In the introduction, we recalled the so-called UC-"mixed commitments" [16] by Damgård and Nielsen, which achieve their equivocability and extractability for the ideal adversary I by basing their commitment on two, disjoint sets of keys: the E-keys (for the perfectly hiding property and equivocability by I), and on the X-keys (for the perfectly binding property and extractability by I). For the simulation to work, only a part of the key (formed of E-keys [16], used for the perfectly hiding property and equivocability by I) is placed in the reference string. The Damgård and Nielsen commitments are inherently based on non-erasure Σ-protocols and their security against lunchtime opening [16], i.e., roughly, an adversary is unable to produce an arbitrary opening for a commitment, even if he sees several fake commitments under E-keys and can adaptively specify how these ones should be opened. One such commitment protocol is based on the p-subgroup assumption [29] and another assumes hardness of the decisional composite residuosity problem [30] used in Paillier's cryptosystem. We believe that our construction can be extended also exploiting the Paillier encryption, to commit to more than one bit. Damgård and Nielsen [16] construct ZK efficiently using their commitments on top of the SAT protocol which proves satisfiability of boolean circuits.

Using our approach, we can further realize a PKI in a natural way. What we need is to establish a link between each participant and a central authority, then UC-realize key registration based on commitment using standard proof-of-knowledge techniques. Based on the PKI, we can realize multiparty computation. Our technique also makes it easier to realize 2-party computation is a light way.

4   Conclusions

In this paper, we formalized two special kinds of Diffie-Hellman assumptions, formalized an input-aware equivocable scheme and exhibits a protocol Π_{Gen} that provably implements the scheme under the aforementioned assumptions. These objects and proofs have been done along traditional lines, i.e., outside of a particular framework like Canetti's UC model.

We presented a UC (setup) functionality called $\mathcal{F}_{atomic}$ (which allows two parties to have a short, "fully isolated" exchange of *just one* message each). We gave the necessary proofs to show that a slight modification of our protocol Π_{Gen} UC-realizes commitments. This is possible without the need of a PKI, i.e., with the mere separation of an initialization phase (using just 2 atomic exchanges) and allows the two parties involved to establish two private, public key-pairs.

Finally, we also herein discussed the relevance and efficiency of our protocol, on a stand-alone basis as well as a protocol realizing other primitives, e.g., ZK.

References

1. Backes, M., Pfitzmann, B., Waidner, M.: A general composition theorem for secure reactive systems. In: Naor, M. (ed.) TCC 2004. LNCS, vol. 2951, pp. 336–354. Springer, Heidelberg (2004)
2. Barak, B., Canetti, R., Nielsen, J.B., Pass, R.: Universally composable protocols with relaxed set-up assumptions. In: Proc. of the 45th Annual IEEE Symposium on Foundations of Computer Science, FOCS 2004, pp. 186–195. IEEE Computer Society, Washington, DC (2004)

3. Beaver, D.: Foundations of secure interactive computing. In: Feigenbaum, J. (ed.) CRYPTO 1991. LNCS, vol. 576, pp. 377–391. Springer, Heidelberg (1992)
4. Blum, M.: How to prove a theorem so no one else can claim it. In: An Address to the Int. Congress of Mathematicians (August 1986)
5. Boneh, D.: The Decision Diffie-Hellman Problem. In: Buhler, J.P. (ed.) ANTS 1998. LNCS, vol. 1423, pp. 48–63. Springer, Heidelberg (1998)
6. Brands, S., Chaum, D.: Distance-Bounding Protocols (Extended Abstract). In: Helleseth, T. (ed.) EUROCRYPT 1993. LNCS, vol. 765, pp. 344–359. Springer, Heidelberg (1994)
7. Canetti, R.: A Unified Framework for Analyzing Security of Protocols. In: Electronic Colloquium on Computational Complexity (ECCC), vol. 8(16) (2001)
8. Canetti, R.: Universally composable security: A new paradigm for cryptographic protocols. Cryptology ePrint Archive, Report 2000/067 (2005), http://eprint.iacr.org/
9. Canetti, R., Dakdouk, R.R.: Towards a theory of extractable functions. In: Reingold, O. (ed.) TCC 2009. LNCS, vol. 5444, pp. 595–613. Springer, Heidelberg (2009)
10. Canetti, R., Fischlin, M.: Universally Composable Commitments. In: Kilian, J. (ed.) CRYPTO 2001. LNCS, vol. 2139, pp. 19–41. Springer, Heidelberg (2001)
11. Canetti, R., Lindell, Y., Ostrovsky, R., Sahai, A.: Universally Composable Two-Party and Multi-Party Secure Computation. In: The 34th Annual ACM Symposium on Theory of Computing (STOC 2002), pp. 494–503 (2002)
12. Chandran, N., Goyal, V., Sahai, A.: New Constructions for UC Secure Computation Using Tamper-Proof Hardware. In: Smart, N.P. (ed.) EUROCRYPT 2008. LNCS, vol. 4965, pp. 545–562. Springer, Heidelberg (2008)
13. Cimato, S., Galdi, C., Persiano, G. (eds.): SCN 2002. LNCS, vol. 2576. Springer, Heidelberg (2003)
14. Cramer, R., Shoup, V.: A practical public key cryptosystem provably secure against adaptive chosen ciphertext attack. In: Krawczyk, H. (ed.) CRYPTO 1998. LNCS, vol. 1462, pp. 13–25. Springer, Heidelberg (1998)
15. Damgård, I., Nielsen, J.B., Wichs, D.: Universally composable multiparty computation with partially isolated parties. In: Reingold, O. (ed.) TCC 2009. LNCS, vol. 5444, pp. 315–331. Springer, Heidelberg (2009)
16. Damgård, I.B., Nielsen, J.B.: Perfect hiding and perfect binding universally composable commitment schemes with constant expansion factor. In: Yung, M. (ed.) CRYPTO 2002. LNCS, vol. 2442, pp. 581–596. Springer, Heidelberg (2002)
17. Dent, A.W. The hardness of the DHK problem in the generic group model (2006) a.dent@rhul.ac.uk13277 (received April 24, 2006), (last revised May 9, 2006)
18. Drimer, S., Murdoch, S.J.: Keep your enemies close: distance bounding against smartcard relay attacks. In: Proc. of 16th USENIX Security Symposium on USENIX Security Symposium, SS 2007, pp. 7:1–7:16. USENIX Association, Berkeley (2007)
19. Goldreich, O., Micali, S., Wigderson, A.: Proofs that yield nothing but their validity and a methodology of cryptographic protocol design. In: 27th Annual Symposium on Foundations of Computer Science, pp. 174–187 (October 1986)
20. Goldwasser, S., Micali, S., Rackoff, C.: The knowledge complexity of interactive proof-systems. In: Proc. of the Seventeenth Annual ACM Symposium on Theory of Computing, STOC 1985, pp. 291–304. ACM, New York (1985)
21. Herzog, J.C., Liskov, M., Micali, S.: Plaintext awareness via key registration. In: Boneh, D. (ed.) CRYPTO 2003. LNCS, vol. 2729, pp. 548–564. Springer, Heidelberg (2003)
22. Kalai, Y.T., Lindell, Y., Prabhakaran, M.: Concurrent general composition of secure protocols in the timing model. In: Proc. of the Thirty-Seventh Annual ACM Symposium on Theory of Computing, STOC 2005, pp. 644–653. ACM, New York (2005)

23. Katz, J.: Universally Composable Multi-party Computation Using Tamper-Proof Hardware. In: Naor, M. (ed.) EUROCRYPT 2007. LNCS, vol. 4515, pp. 115–128. Springer, Heidelberg (2007)

24. Liskov, M., Lysyanskaya, A., Micali, S., Reyzin, L., Smith, A.: Mutually independent commitments. In: Boyd, C. (ed.) ASIACRYPT 2001. LNCS, vol. 2248, pp. 385–401. Springer, Heidelberg (2001)

25. Mayes, K., Cobourne, S., Markantonakis, K.: Near field technology in challenging environments. In: Smart Card Technology Int., NFC and Contactless, pp. 65–69 (2011)

26. Micali, S., Rogaway, P.: Secure computation (abstract). In: Feigenbaum, J. (ed.) CRYPTO 1991. LNCS, vol. 576, pp. 392–404. Springer, Heidelberg (1992)

27. Welzl, E., Montanari, U., Rolim, J.D.P. (eds.): ICALP 2000. LNCS, vol. 1853. Springer, Heidelberg (2000)

28. Moran, T., Segev, G.: David and Goliath Commitments: UC Computation for Asymmetric Parties Using Tamper-Proof Hardware. In: Smart, N.P. (ed.) EUROCRYPT 2008. LNCS, vol. 4965, pp. 527–544. Springer, Heidelberg (2008)

29. Okamoto, T., Uchiyama, S.: A new public-key cryptosystem as secure as factoring. In: Nyberg, K. (ed.) EUROCRYPT 1998. LNCS, vol. 1403, pp. 308–318. Springer, Heidelberg (1998)

30. Paillier, P.: Public-key cryptosystems based on composite degree residuosity classes. In: Stern, J. (ed.) EUROCRYPT 1999. LNCS, vol. 1592, pp. 223–238. Springer, Heidelberg (1999)

31. Teranishi, I., Ogata, W.: Relationship between standard model plaintext awareness and message hiding. IEICE Trans. Fundam. Electron. Commun. Comput. Sci. E91-A, 244–261 (2008)

32. Ventre, C., Visconti, I.: Message-aware commitment schemes (2008) (unpublished manuscript)

A   "Unconventional" Commitments: A Comparison

The notion of input-aware commitments (IAC) was studied before under the name of extractable commitments [13]. This was carried mainly in the CRS model, in [27,13], as part of zero-knowledge proofs. Unlike the scheme to follow, these commitments did not contain an explicit notion of equivocability, in the standard lines, i.e., outside the UC framework. Thus, we sometimes refer to them as *IAC* (input-aware commitments) as opposed to *IAEC* (input-aware equivocable commitments).

Canetti *et al.* [9] applied known commitment-constructions from injective one-way functions and from pseudorandom generators to get extractable commitments (i.e., IAC) when the underlying primitives used are extractable. We dissociate ourselves from this method and rely instead on hardness assumptions[6].

In the above sense, we use a stronger knowledge guarantee, which brings us closer to an (unpublished) result by Ventre and Visconti [32] in which they construct extractable commitments (i.e., IAC) from plaintext-aware encryption schemes, using certain hardness assumptions. However, our construction is not from PAW encryption directly, yet it bears similar assumptions to such encryption schemes [14], but it is also equivocable, i.e., it is an IAEC.

---

[6] Extractable functions abstract away from specific e.g., number-theoretic assumptions like the knowledge of exponents and are cast in a complexity-theoretic setting.

Further, we mention that primitives similar to input-aware equivocable commitments have been explored before by Damgård and Nielsen (i.e., mixed commitments) inside the UC framework, UC-realizing an ideal functionality $\mathcal{F}_{HCOM}$ of homomorphic commitment [16] in the CRS-hybrid UC model. Here, the formalization is different, the protocol more specific, the scheme is initially cast upon traditional lines. We only eventually show that we UC-realize the normal, ideal functionality of commitment, i.e., not the homomorphic version, using not a CRS, but a different setup. Namely, we show that our specialized commitment protocol is UC-realizable in the UC hybrid model with the $\mathcal{F}_{atomic}$ setup. More precisely, we will show that the thus-wise realized protocol UC-emulates the ideal functionality of commitment $\mathcal{F}_{COM}$ (not $\mathcal{F}_{HCOM}$). The protocol from Damgård and Nielsen [16] is sometimes extractable, sometimes equivocable, but not both. This depends on what the simulator needs in UC-security. (See more technical details on page 134.) In the plain model, Damgård and Nielsen's commitment is therefore not extractable nor equivocable. This is essentially different from the protocol advanced herein. Indeed, one of the ideas in this paper also lies in introducing new techniques of extractability of the "real" committed bit by the ideal adversary. Our protocol enjoys both extractability and equivocability, at the same time, even outside of the UC framework.

When compared to constructions from Damgård et al. [15], one advantage of our input-aware equivocable commitment is that it integrates the secret key extraction and becomes feasible with $\mathcal{F}_{atomic}$ efficiently. (In [15], the entire prover protocol of a WI ℓ-PoK scheme must be run in isolation.)

Another notion to thwart relay attack in commitment protocols is the notion of mutually independent commitments [24].

B   Proof of Th. 10

Proof (sketch). Given a real-world adversary $\mathcal{A}$ in the UC model with atomic-exchange setup, we construct a UC ideal adversary I as follows.

A. We first treat the case where only S is corrupted by $\mathcal{A}$ and it is denoted as S^*. I simulates S^*, $\mathcal{F}_{atomic}$ and R_{COM} internally, and I lets S^* interact with Z externally (so that Z cannot distinguish I's run from the real-world experiment).

The simulation by I together with Z defines an algorithm $\mathcal{B}$, which stops before $\mathcal{F}_{atomic}$ receives X_0 from R_{COM} (as per the games defining the DDH and DHK0 assumptions). The algorithm $\mathcal{B}$ defines ρ and state, the latter being the current view of S^*. Like before, in state, we restrict to the coins $\overline{r_{\mathcal{A}}}$ that S^* has used so far. Let the unused coins by S^* be denoted $\overline{\overline{r_{\mathcal{A}}}}$. The next step of the simulation defines from state the last algorithm that S^* would have sent to $\mathcal{F}_{atomic}$ such that $\mathcal{A}(\text{state}, X_0; \overline{\overline{r_{\mathcal{A}}}})$ would produce (X, X'), using solely on the view of $\mathcal{A}$ since in fact X, X' should be the output m' of $\mathcal{F}_{atomic}$. By the assumptions we use, we now have another algorithm $\mathcal{E}(\text{state}, X_0; \overline{\overline{r_{\mathcal{A}}}})$ that yields x such that $X = g^x$ or R_{COM} aborts[7]. Thus, our constructed I can simply run $\mathcal{E}(\text{state}, X_0; \overline{\overline{r_{\mathcal{A}}}})$ by using the view of S^*. As I goes on in the simulation of R_{COM}, it can extract the committed bit b from (U, V) thanks to x and send this bit to $\mathcal{F}_{COM}$. As in Th. 9, we can show that the opening to $1 - b$ would contradict the assumptions.

B. When R is corrupted by $\mathcal{A}$, we denote it as R^*. The simulation works as follows. I simulates R^*, $\mathcal{F}_{atomic}$ and $S_{COM}(b_0)$ (for an arbitrary bit b_0) internally, and I lets R^*

---

[7] If M aborts in real life, we assume it outputs a special value such that the protocol itself finishes.

interact with $\mathcal{Z}$ externally (so that $\mathcal{Z}$ cannot distinguish I's run from the real-world experiment).

The simulation by I together with $\mathcal{Z}$ defines an algorithm $\mathcal{B}$, which runs until the moment before $\mathcal{F}_{atomic}$ receives Y_0 from S_{COM} and then $\mathcal{B}$ stops. As before, $\mathcal{B}$ will produce ρ and state as the current view of R^*, limiting his coins $r_{\mathcal{A}}$ to $\overline{r_{\mathcal{A}}}$, i.e., to those used so far, where $r_{\mathcal{A}} := \overline{r_{\mathcal{A}}} \| \overline{\overline{r_{\mathcal{A}}}}$. Then the output (Y, Y') of $\mathcal{F}_{atomic}$ (on the algorithm sent to it by R^*) can be seen as the output of $\mathcal{A}$ with input state. Augmented with the message Y_0 and the coins $\overline{\overline{r_{\mathcal{A}}}}$, it defines $\mathcal{A}(\text{state}, Y_0; \overline{\overline{r_{\mathcal{A}}}})$. Due to the ag-DHK0$_{\mathsf{Gen}}$ assumption, there must exist some algorithm $\mathcal{E}$ such that, except for negligible cases, $\mathcal{E}(\text{state}, Y_0; \overline{\overline{r_{\mathcal{A}}}})$ produces y satisfying $Y = g^y$, or S_{COM} rejects (Y, Y'). Note that as before, the pair (Y, Y') is produced by using solely on the view of R^* (since the message Y_0 is tagged as atomic). So, our constructed I can again simply run $\mathcal{E}(\text{state}, Y_0; \overline{\overline{r_{\mathcal{A}}}})$. Then, the adversary I can either simulate S_{OPEN} (if $b = b_0$) or, otherwise, simulate Equiv using y.

The argument of the indistinguishability between the two worlds (the real one and the simulated one by I) follows the exact same arguments as those in the proof of Th. 9. □

Towards Anonymous Ciphertext Indistinguishability with Identity Leakage[*]

Tsz Hon Yuen[1], Cong Zhang[1], Sherman S.M. Chow[2], and Joseph K. Liu[3]

[1] Department of Computer Science
The University of Hong Kong, Hong Kong
{thyuen,czhang2}@cs.hku.hk
[2] Department of Information Engineering
The Chinese University of Hong Kong, Hong Kong
sherman@ie.cuhk.edu.hk
[3] Institute for Infocomm Research, Singapore
ksliu@i2r.a-star.edu.sg

Abstract. Key escrow is a major drawback of identity-based encryption (IBE). The key generation centre (KGC) can generate the user secret key of any user by using the master secret key and the user's identity. This paper presents a systematic study of what it takes to prevent a malicious KGC from decrypting a ciphertext encrypted for an honest user, which covers the case for certificateless encryption, and shows the impossibility of ideal escrow-free IBE, unless there is uncertainty in the user's identity.

Our study also explains the underpinning idea of anonymous ciphertext indistinguishability (ACI), formalized by Chow in PKC 2009. An ACI-secure IBE prevent a KGC (or any logical entity which get holds of the master secret key, such as the collusion of a number of authorities holding the sufficient number of master secret's shares) from decrypting if it does not know the intended recipient of the ciphertext, a guarantee that none of the existing attempts in the literature can provide.

The notion of ACI crucially relies on the privacy of user's identity in the eyes of the KGC. The only privacy leakage allowed in Chow's model is via querying an embedded-identity encryption oracle. In this paper, we strengthen his model to allow arbitrary bounded leakage of the recipient's identity. We also give a generic construction on how to achieve this notion when the identity has enough entropy.

Keywords: identity-based encryption, anonymous ciphertext indistinguishability, key escrow, leakage.

1 Introduction

In traditional public key cryptography, each user generates his own public key and secret key. People have to obtain digital certificates, which bind their public

---

[*] The first author is supported by the HKU Small Project Funding under Grant No. 201109176192. The third author is supported by the Early Career Scheme and the Early Career Award of the Research Grants Council, Hong Kong SAR (CUHK 439713), and Direct Grant (4055018) of the Chinese University of Hong Kong.

W. Susilo and R. Reyhanitabar (Eds.): ProvSec 2013, LNCS 8209, pp. 139–153, 2013.

keys with their identities, from a trusted certificate authority. A certificate can be used to verify that a public key belongs to an individual.

In 1984, Shamir [1] introduced the concept of identity-based cryptography. In an identity-based cryptosystem, the user public key is the identity, which can be the name of a person, an email address, the name of an organisation, etc. Comparing with traditional public key cryptography, the advantage of identity-based cryptography is to avoid the distribution of public key certificates. The person who wants to encrypt a message or to verify a signature only needs to know the identity of the other party.

In identity-based cryptography, the identity-based secret key is generated by a trusted third party called key generation centre (KGC) who holds a master secret key. In most identity-based signatures or encryption schemes, a high trust is placed on the KGC. This condition is not appropriate in some real world scenarios. A malicious KGC can sell users' identity-based secret keys, sign messages or decrypt ciphertexts on behalf of users without being confronted in a law court. This is known as the *key escrow problem*.

1.1   Impossibility Result

Ideally, an identity-based encryption that is free from the escrow problem is one such that a malicious KGC cannot decrypt any ciphertext when it is given the ciphertext and its identity of its intended recipient. We call this IBE as the *ideal escrow-free IBE*. By the original definition of IBE [2], an ideal escrow-free IBE does not exist intuitively. However, to the best of the authors' knowledge, *there is no formal proof* that such a system does or does not exist. This paper gives the impossibility result of an ideal escrow-free IBE.

We first formalize the notion for an ideal escrow-free IBE. Subsequently, we provide a weak security model for ideal escrow-free IBE. Finally, we prove that ideal escrow-free IBE is not secure even in a weak security model. Therefore it is not possible to construct an ideal escrow-free IBE scheme secure in a model which is stronger than our proposed model.

To circumvent this impossibility result, we need to look into the encryption process or the key generation process. The inclusion of auxiliary information for the encryption process is one possible approach, which matches with several attempts in the literature. Cryptosystems such as certificateless cryptosystems [3,4,5], certificate-based cryptosystems [6] and self-certified cryptosystems [7] are proposed to solve the key-escrow problem. They can be viewed as a combination of public key cryptography and identity-based cryptography. Unfortunately, these cryptosystems are *no longer* identity-based — the encryptor or the verifier has to know the user public key in addition to the user identity.

1.2   Towards Escrow-Free Identity-Based Encryption

The second possibility to circumvent the impossibility result is to consider the omission of information required for the identity-based secret key generation process. Different from prior attempts to be reviewed in the next subsection, the security model of Anonymous Ciphertext Indistinguishability (ACI-KGC) proposed by Chow in 2009 [8] aims to disallow any adversary with the master secret key from decrypting the ciphertext. The guarantee provided by ACI is that, without the knowledge of the challenge identity ID^*, the adversary is still not able to distinguish the encrypted message.

An immediate concern is that the KGC in traditional identity-based cryptosystem must need to know all users' identity to perform its job. To address this problem, Chow put forth an anonymous key-issuing architecture (with an accompanying protocol for his proposed ACI-KGC secure IBE scheme) which separates the tasks of authenticating the users and issuing the identity-based secret keys to the users. Now, there is a certificate authority (known as identity-certifying authority, or ICA [8]) who authenticates the user and issues a blinded form of certificate. Subsequently, this blinded certificate can be presented to the KGC to obtain an identity-based secret key, without the KGC learning the identity involved.

Under the assumption that the KGC will not collude with the ICA, the normal function of an identity-based cryptosystem is not affected even we do not want the KGC to learn the users' identities. However, partial information about the target identity may still be known to the malicious KGC via other means. For the case of using email address as the identity, the KGC may easily guess the alias of "xxx@ie.cuhk.edu.hk" or "yyy@cs.hku.hk" as its target, given only the second half of the identity.

Correspondingly, we introduce the identity leakage oracle which leaks about the target identity, on top of the embedded-identity encryption oracle of existing ACI-KGC notion. In the security game, the adversary can additionally query an arbitrary function f and obtains $f(\mathsf{ID}^*)$, where f is reasonably restricted. It models the case that the adversary may obtain partial information of the target identity, other than the form of ciphertext provided by the encryption oracle. In other words, we are consider the indistinguishability of partially anonymous ciphertexts. Finally, we propose an efficient and generic construction built from any normal ACI-KGC secure IBE scheme.

1.3   Related Solutions of the Key-Escrow Problem

Boneh and Franklin [2] proposed a threshold extension of identity-based encryption (IBE) scheme in which multiple KGCs jointly compute the master secret key. No single KGC has the knowledge of the master secret key and hence users are protected unless a large number of KGCs are corrupted. However, this approach requires extra communication cost between users and different KGCs. Also note that the new privacy-preserving key-issuing architecture proposed by Chow can be actually built on top of this threshold KGC structure.

Goyal [9] proposed a different approach for the identity-based secret key generation, which is done via the interaction between the KGC and the user. When the key generation procedure is run twice, the outputs will be different with a high probability. Therefore, the KGC can be caught when there exist two different identity-based secret keys for the same identity. Au *et al.* [10] further proposed an extension that the secret key of the KGC can even be extracted when the user secret keys are generated honestly. However, it is possible for a malicious KGC to create a working user secret key which is in a format different from what produced by an honest execution of secret key generation [10]. There is also no measure preventing the KGC from selling a signed message / decrypted ciphertext, without being detected. To address this issue, Goyal *et al.* [11] proposed the black-box accountable-authority IBE to blame a malicious KGC selling a decoder box which can decrypt a ciphertext with non-negligible probability; Yuen *et al.* [12] proposed the escrow-free identity-based signature to blame a malicious KGC selling a signed message.

Roadmap

In the next section, we provide the basic framework and security notions of IBE. In §3, we present our definition of ideal escrow-free IBE. We demonstrate that it is not possible to achieve ideal escrow-free IBE by showing an adversary that can always win in a weak security model. In §4, we survey on what is the best possible protection for users if such ideal escrow-free IBE is not achievable. In §5, we demonstrate the gap between the ideal (but not instantiable) security model and the existing models. We give a new security model and a generic construction. Finally, §6 concludes the paper.

2 Backgrounds

We first review the security model of identity-based encryption in [2].

2.1 Identity-Based Encryption

An IBE scheme has four polynomial-time algorithms, namely **Setup**, **Extract**, **Enc**, **Dec**.

- **Setup:** On input a security parameter 1^λ, it generates a master public key mpk (including the message space $\mathcal{M}$, and the identity space $\mathcal{I}$), and a master secret key msk.
- **Extract:** On input mpk, msk and an identity ID, the KGC outputs the identity-based secret key sk_{ID}.
- **Enc:** On input mpk, ID and a message m, it outputs a ciphertext C.
- **Dec:** On input mpk, ID, sk_{ID} and C, it outputs a message m or outputs $\perp$ if the ciphertext is not valid.

2.2 Security Notions

Correctness. The *correctness* is defined as follows:

$$\mathbf{Dec}(\mathsf{mpk}, \mathsf{ID}, sk_{ID}, \mathbf{Enc}(\mathsf{mpk}, \mathsf{ID}, m)) = m.$$

where sk_{ID} is the output of **Extract**(mpk, msk, ID), and (mpk, msk) $\leftarrow$ **Setup**(1^λ).

Confidentiality. The common security model of IBE is the indistinguishability against adaptive identity, adaptive chosen ciphertext attack (IND-ID-CCA) security. An adversary $\mathcal{A}$ is given the master public key and the access to two oracles: Extract Oracle and Dec Oracle. The adversary $\mathcal{A}$ picks two challenge messages and a challenge identity. The challenger encrypts one of the messages under the challenge identity. The adversary $\mathcal{A}$ has to distinguish which message the challenger encrypted.

It is defined as the following game:

1. Setup. The challenger $\mathcal{C}$ runs $(\mathsf{mpk}, \mathsf{msk}) \leftarrow \mathbf{Setup}(1^\lambda)$. The adversary $\mathcal{A}$ is given mpk from the challenger $\mathcal{C}$.
2. $\mathcal{A}$ is allowed to query the following oracles adaptively:
   - Extract Oracle: On input an identity ID, the oracle returns $sk_{\mathsf{ID}} \leftarrow \mathbf{Extract}(\mathsf{mpk}, \mathsf{msk}, \mathsf{ID})$.
   - Dec Oracle: On input an identity ID and a ciphertext C, the oracle returns $m/\perp \leftarrow \mathbf{Dec}(\mathsf{mpk}, \mathsf{ID}, sk_{\mathsf{ID}}, C)$.
3. Challenge. $\mathcal{A}$ picks two messages of equal length $m_0^*, m_1^* \in \mathcal{M}$ and an identity $\mathsf{ID}^* \in \mathcal{I}$ and sends them to $\mathcal{C}$. $\mathcal{C}$ picks a random bit $b \in \{0, 1\}$. $\mathcal{C}$ computes the challenge ciphertext $C^* \leftarrow \mathbf{Enc}(\mathsf{mpk}, \mathsf{ID}^*, m_b^*)$ and send C^* to $\mathcal{A}$.
4. $\mathcal{A}$ is allowed to query the above oracles adaptively.
5. Output. Finally $\mathcal{A}$ outputs a bit b'.

We require that ID^* has never been submitted to the Extract Oracle, and (ID^*, C^*) has never been submitted to the Dec Oracle. $\mathcal{A}$ wins the game if $b' = b^*$. We say that the advantage of $\mathcal{A}$ is the probability of $\mathcal{A}$ winning minus half. We say that an IBE is IND-ID-CCA secure if no polynomial time adversary wins the above game with non-negligible advantage.

Weaker Security Models. There are a few security models proposed for IBE which are weaker than the IND-ID-CCA security. If the adversary $\mathcal{A}$ is not allowed to query the Dec Oracle, then the model is changed from the CCA (chosen ciphertext attack) to CPA (chosen plaintext attack).

If the adversary $\mathcal{A}$ is required to give the challenge identity ID^* at the Setup phase of the game, then the model is changed from the adaptive identity (ID) attack to selective identity (sID) attack.

3 Systematic Study of Ideal Escrow-Free IBE

In order to avoid the key escrow problem from a powerful KGC who knows all public information, ciphertexts, identities and the master secret key, a user must have a private sequence of random coin toss which is not known by the KGC. Otherwise, the KGC can just play the role of the user and runs the **Extract** and **Dec** algorithms completely by himself. We suppose the user computes a private secret usk and an optional public auxiliary information upk from the random coin toss in the **UserSetup** algorithm. We define an "ideal escrow-free IBE" as an IBE scheme which a malicious KGC cannot decrypt any ciphertext even if he knows the master secret key and the recipient identity.

3.1   Ideal Escrow-Free IBE

An ideal escrow-free IBE scheme has five polynomial-time algorithms, namely **Setup, UserSetup, Extract, Enc, Dec.**

- **Setup:** On input a security parameter 1^λ, it generates a master secret key msk and a master public key mpk (including the message space $\mathcal{M}$, and the identity space $\mathcal{I}$).
- **UserSetup:** On input the master public key mpk, and (optionally) an identity ID, a user generates a secret usk and an (optional) public auxiliary information upk. This algorithm is probabilistic, i.e., the user has his own secret randomness.
- **Extract:** This is an efficient interactive protocol $(\mathbf{Extract}_p, \mathbf{Extract}_u)$ between the KGC and the user. The common input are mpk, upk, and an identity ID. The KGC's algorithm $\mathbf{Extract}_p$ has a private input which is msk. Additionally, the KGC may use a sequence of random coin tosses as private input.
  At the end of the protocol, the user will receive an identity-based secret key sk_{ID} from the KGC. The user's algorithm $\mathbf{Extract}_u$ has a private output of $\mathsf{usk}_{\mathsf{ID}}$, which is generated from usk and sk_{ID}. The output can also be $\perp$ if the secret key that he receives is not valid.
- **Enc:** On input mpk, ID and a message m, it outputs a ciphertext C.
- **Dec:** On input mpk, ID, $\mathsf{usk}_{\mathsf{ID}}$, and C, it outputs a message m or outputs $\perp$ if it is not valid.

Our current definition of ideal escrow-free IBE defines that the **Enc** algorithm does not take upk as the input. Since upk is the public information which is only determined after the user's involvement, it would violates the concept of IBE if the **Enc** algorithm takes upk as the input. As a result, we define the *correctness* as follows:

Correctness.

$$\mathbf{Dec}(\mathsf{mpk}, \mathsf{ID}, \mathsf{usk}_{\mathsf{ID}}, \mathbf{Enc}(\mathsf{mpk}, \mathsf{ID}, m)) = m.$$

where $\mathsf{usk}_{\mathsf{ID}}$ is the output of $\mathbf{Extract}_u(\mathsf{mpk}, \mathsf{upk}, \mathsf{ID}, \mathsf{usk})$ interacting with the algorithm $\mathbf{Extract}_p(\mathsf{mpk}, \mathsf{upk}, \mathsf{ID}, \mathsf{msk})$, and $(\mathsf{usk}, \mathsf{upk}) \leftarrow \mathbf{UserSetup}(\mathsf{mpk}, \mathsf{ID})$, and $(\mathsf{mpk}, \mathsf{msk}) \leftarrow \mathbf{Setup}(1^\lambda)$.

3.2   Security Notions

We define our "KGC one-wayness" (OW-KGC) security model where an adversary $\mathcal{A}$ wants to decrypt a challenge ciphertext. $\mathcal{A}$ acts as the role of a malicious KGC. In the security game, the adversary $\mathcal{A}$ is given the master public key, master secret key and the auxiliary information of the challenger user. The challenger $\mathcal{C}$ picks a challenge message and a challenge identity. The challenger encrypts the message under the challenge identity. The adversary $\mathcal{A}$ is given the ciphertext and the challenge identity. $\mathcal{A}$ has to output the message that the challenger encrypted. More formally, consider the following OW-KGC game:

1. Setup. The challenger $\mathcal{C}$ computes $(\mathsf{mpk}, \mathsf{msk}) \leftarrow \mathbf{Setup}(1^\lambda)$ and $(\mathsf{usk}, \mathsf{upk}) \leftarrow \mathbf{UserSetup}(\mathsf{mpk})$. $\mathcal{A}$ is given $(\mathsf{mpk}, \mathsf{msk}, \mathsf{upk})$ from the challenger $\mathcal{C}$.
2. Challenge. $\mathcal{C}$ picks a random message $m^* \in \mathcal{M}$ and a random identity $\mathsf{ID}^* \in \mathcal{I}$. $\mathcal{C}$ computes the challenge ciphertext $C^* \leftarrow \mathbf{Enc}(\mathsf{mpk}, \mathsf{ID}^*, m^*)$.
3. Output. $\mathcal{A}$ is given ID^* and C^*. Finally $\mathcal{A}$ outputs a message m'.

$\mathcal{A}$ wins the game if $m' = m^*$. We say that an ideal escrow-free IBE is OW-KGC secure if no polynomial time adversary wins the above game with non-negligible probability.

3.3 Comparison

Chow's Definition. In Chow's IBE framework [8], the **Setup** algorithm is divided into two sub-algorithms. One is a trusted initialization algorithm which takes into a security parameter and outputs some public parameters, such as the elliptic curve and the bilinear map context to be used by the cryptosystem. The master secret key and the master public key pair will be generated by another algorithm which takes the public parameters as input. This separation is needed for proving his IBE scheme to achieve ACI-KGC security.

The reason of defining our version of OW-KGC model is that we want to show that a probabilistic polynomial time adversary $\mathcal{A}$ can always wins in this model. Hence, we consider a weaker model where the adversary is given the master secret key, instead of having the flexibility to generate the master secret key by its own. Another difference from Chow's OW-KGC notion [8] is that we additionally equip $\mathcal{A}$ with upk.

Standard Users Attacks. We compare the above OW-KGC security with the common security model of IBE. Except that the master secret key is given to the adversary, the above OW-KGC game is a relatively weak model when compared with the IND-ID-CCA model in §2.2:

- All parameters are chosen by the challenger, but not the adversary $\mathcal{A}$.
- $\mathcal{A}$ is not given any oracle access.
- $\mathcal{A}$ has to output m^* instead of distinguishing between two messages.

We compare the security models in Table 1. If we extended the existing models, e.g. the IND-ID-CPA model, from users attack to KGC attack, i.e., the adversary is given the master secret key msk (in order to model the key escrow problem), we can see that our OW-KGC model is the weakest model among possible extension of existing models.

Table 1. Different security models of IBE: we compare whether msk is given to the adversary; what can the adversary or the challenger select in the game; which oracle can the adversary access or what it can learn; and what does the adversary output

Models	msk	Adversary selects	Challenger selects	Adversary knows/can access	Output
IND-ID-CCA	$\times$	m_0, m_1, ID^* in Challenge	$\mathsf{mpk}, \mathsf{msk}$ in Setup b^* in Challenge	Extract Oracle Dec Oracle	b'
IND-sID-CCA	$\times$	ID^* in Setup, $m_0,$ m_1 in Challenge	$\mathsf{mpk}, \mathsf{msk}$ in Setup b^* in Challenge	Extract Oracle Dec Oracle	b'
IND-ID-CPA	$\times$	m_0, m_1, ID^* in Challenge	$\mathsf{mpk}, \mathsf{msk}$ in Setup b^* in Challenge	Extract Oracle	b'
OW-KGC	$\checkmark$	$\times$	$\mathsf{mpk}, \mathsf{msk}$ in Setup ID^*, m^* in Challenge	ID^*	m'

3.4 Impossibility Result

Now, we are ready to show that all ideal escrow-free IBE schemes are not OW-KGC secure. Therefore ideal escrow-free IBE is not secure in any security model which are stronger than the OW-KGC security model, including the IND-ID-CPA, IND-sID-CCA and IND-ID-CCA if the master secret key is given to the adversary.

Theorem 1. *All ideal escrow-free IBE schemes are not OW-KGC secure.*

Proof. Recall our correctness definition,

$$\mathbf{Dec}(\mathsf{mpk}, \mathsf{ID}^*, \mathsf{usk}_{\mathsf{ID}^*}, \mathbf{Enc}(\mathsf{mpk}, \mathsf{ID}^*, m)) = m.$$

While $\mathsf{usk}_{\mathsf{ID}}$ is supposed to be the private output of $\mathbf{Extract}_u$, recall that $\mathbf{Enc}$ does not take upk as part of the input, any $\mathsf{usk}_{\mathsf{ID}}$ which is the output of $\mathbf{Extract}_u(\mathsf{mpk}, \mathsf{upk}, \mathsf{ID}, \mathsf{usk})$ interacting with $\mathbf{Extract}_p(\mathsf{mpk}, \mathsf{upk}, \mathsf{ID}, \mathsf{msk})$ should satisfy the correctness of decryption for every possible $(\mathsf{usk}, \mathsf{upk})$ generated by **UserSetup**. Therefore, the adversary $\mathcal{A}$ can just firstly run **UserSetup**, then run both $\mathbf{Extract}_u$ and $\mathbf{Extract}_p$ by himself and get a working usk_{ID^*}. Hence, $\mathcal{A}$ always wins the OW-KGC game.

3.5 Exceptional Case

The above proof simply falls apart when **Enc** is allowed to take upk as part of the input. For example, we let $\mathcal{E}$ be a public key encryption scheme and let pk be a public key. The user sets the upk as $(\mathcal{E}, pk)$. During **Enc**, the "message" of the ideal escrow-free IBE is the output of $\mathcal{E}_{pk}(m)$, therefore a malicious KGC cannot obtain m without the corresponding secret key of $(\mathcal{E}, pk)$. This covers the cases of certificateless encryption[3,4,5] and certificate-based encryption [6]. For example, some existing generic constructions of certificateless encryption carefully utilized such a multi-encryption approach [13,5]. Unfortunately, encryption is no longer identity-based.

4   Alternative Methods to Protect the IBE Users

Apart from changing the framework of IBE, another possible approach is to further restrict the adversary's power in OW-KGC. Looking into the security definition again, $\mathcal{A}$ is given mpk, msk, upk, ID^* and C^*. Clearly, mpk and C^* must be given to $\mathcal{A}$. To model KGC attack, $\mathcal{A}$ should also be equipped with msk. One may consider restricting the knowledge of msk, as in the leakage attack and related key attack. The only other possibility we may hope for is withholding ID^* (and upk) from the adversary's knowledge. That leads to the notion of anonymous ciphertext indistinguishability [8].

4.1   Anonymous Ciphertext Indistinguishability

One may ask if the malicious KGC does not know the recipient identity, can it distinguish the encrypted message? If the KGC cannot distinguish the encrypted message and the number of possible identities are exponential to the security parameter, then the KGC cannot generate all identity-based secret keys to decrypt it in polynomial time. Therefore, the encrypted message is protected as long as the recipient identity is anonymous. Then, the ciphertext can be sent by anonymous network like Tor to ensure the recipient anonymity in practice.

Chow [8] formalized the above idea by proposing a new security notion called "anonymous ciphertext indistinguishability" against the KGC (ACI-KGC). It is similar to the traditional IND-ID-CCA security that the adversary has to distinguish between two messages from the challenge ciphertext. In the definition of ACI-KGC, the adversary is allowed to choose the master secret key, instead of the challenge identity in the IND-ID-CCA. The challenge identity is unknown to the adversary. Nevertheless, the adversary has accesses to an embedded-identity oracle, which creates ciphertext for adversarially chosen message, for this unknown identity.

4.2   Leakage-Resilient IBE

A possible attack to the IBE is the side-channel leakage of the master secret key and the identity-based secret keys. Side-channel attacks are practical attacks on the physical implementation of the cryptosystems. In the case of IBE, a honest KGC may leak some (partial) information about the master secret key, by timing attack, differential power analysis, cold boot attack, etc. Leakage-Resilient IBE was proposed to provide certain degree of protection under side-channel attacks.

Lewko *et al.* [14] proposed the first leakage-resilient identity-based encryption (LR-IBE) with master secret key leakage. In the security game, the adversary is allowed to ask a leakage oracle with an arbitrary function f, and the oracle outputs $f(\mathsf{msk})$. In order to avoid trivial attacks, the length of overall leakage bits are bounded (which is strictly less than the size of msk). They also proposed the continual leakage model, such that periodic updates on the master secret key is possible. Then the leakage bound only applies on the leakage size between updates, and the overall leakage is unbounded throughout the lifetime of the

Table 2. Different leakage models of IBE: we compare whether the msk is given to the adversary; what can the adversary select in the game; what can the challenger select in the game; which oracle can the adversary access or what it learns; and what does the adversary output. For LR-IBE, some part of the msk is known to the adversary by the leak oracle, but no polynomial time adversary should be able to calculate the entire msk with non-negligible probability.

Models	msk	Adversary selects	Challenger selects	Adversary knows/asks	Output
OW-KGC	$\sqrt{}$	$\times$	mpk, msk in Setup ID^*, m^* in Challenge	ID^*	m'
ACI-KGC	$\sqrt{}$	m_0, m_1 in Challenge	mpk, msk in Setup b^*, ID^* in Challenge	Enc Oracle	b'
LR-IBE	?	m_0, m_1, ID^* in Challenge	mpk, msk in Setup b^* in Challenge	Leak Oracle $f(msk)$, Extract, Update Oracle	b'
RKA-IBE	$\times$	m_0, m_1, ID^* in Challenge	mpk, msk in Setup b^* in Challenge	Extract Oracle, **Extract**(mpk, ID, ϕ(msk))	b'

system. The adversary may even obtain the leakage of the randomness used in the update process.[1]

Yuen et al. [15] further proposed the LR-IBE with auxiliary input model. It means that the adversary can obtain the leakage $f(msk)$ as long as f is an hard-to-invert function. Therefore, even if the leakage f is a one-way permutation, which information-theoretically leaks the entire entropy of the msk, the IBE scheme remains secure. They also extends the model to continual auxiliary input, such that the "hard-to-invert" restriction only applies between the periodic updates of the msk.

4.3   Related-Key-Attack-Secure IBE

Another possible attack on the KGC is fault injection [16,17]. It can induce modifications in a hardware-stored key, such that the KGC may run the normal key extraction protocols with modified keys. The Φ-related-key attack (RKA) model was proposed to offer protection against these malicious modification. In this model, the adversary is allowed to ask the Extract Oracle with input ID and a function ϕ. The oracle outputs **Extract**(mpk, ID, ϕ(msk)). All functions ϕ must belong to a set of pre-defined function Φ. The adversary is not allowed to ask the oracle with input ID = ID^* and ϕ is the identity map.

Bellare et al. [18] proposed a method to convert some IBE schemes into RKA-secure IBE schemes, including the Boneh-Franklin IBE and the Waters IBE. The set of functions Φ is the Affine space and the set of polynomials respectively.

---

[1] Note that the above statements also holds for the identity-based secret keys in leakage-resilient IBE. Since we now only interested in the leakage of msk, we ignore the discussion about the leakage of identity-based secret keys.

5 Partially-Anonymous Ciphertext Indistinguishability

From the result of previous section, we showed that OW-KGC secure IBE is impossible to construct. The LR-IBE and RKA-IBE notions only consider the case that adversary is attacking a honest KGC instead of being a malicious KGC by itself. The only notion which considers active and malicious KGC is the ACI-KGC security. We investigate if there exists a reasonable security model which is in the spirit of ACI-KGC, and yet allows achievable construction unlike OW-KGC.

5.1 Generalized ACI-KGC Model

We consider the assumption underlying ACI-KGC model a bit too strong in the sense that the challenge identity is completely unknown to the KGC. For example, the KGC is responsible to generate identity-based secret keys to users having identities as their email address. If the malicious KGC is interested in stealing some research results or grant proposals from a university, it will try to decrypt ciphertext using identities like "zzz@uni.edu". Therefore, the partial identity information, like the last part of the email address may be known or easily guessed by the KGC. In this case, the ciphertext can at most be partially anonymous.

We propose the new notion of identity leakage with the existing ACI-KGC model. Like the leakage-resilient IBE, the adversary is allowed to obtain a leakage of the challenge identity. For simplicity, we consider bounded leakage in this model. Even the adversary can obtain partial information about this challenge identity, it cannot win the ACI-KGC security game. We give the formal construction as follows:

1. Setup. The challenger $\mathcal{C}$ computes $(\mathsf{mpk}, \mathsf{msk}) \leftarrow \textbf{Setup}(1^\lambda)$ and picks a random identity $\mathsf{ID}^* \in \mathcal{I}$. $\mathcal{A}$ is given (mpk, msk) from the challenger $\mathcal{C}$.
2. Oracle. $\mathcal{A}$ is allowed to ask:
   (a) Enc Oracle: On input a message m, the oracle returns $C \leftarrow \textbf{Enc}(\mathsf{mpk}, \mathsf{ID}^*, m)$.
   (b) LeakID Oracle: On input f, the oracle returns $f(\mathsf{ID}^*)$.
3. Challenge. $\mathcal{A}$ sends two messages $m_0^*, m_1^* \in \mathcal{M}$ to $\mathcal{C}$. $\mathcal{C}$ picks a random bit b and returns the challenge ciphertext $C^* \leftarrow \textbf{Enc}(\mathsf{mpk}, \mathsf{ID}^*, m_b^*)$ to $\mathcal{A}$.
4. Output. Finally $\mathcal{A}$ outputs a bit b'.

$\mathcal{A}$ wins the game if $b' = b$ and the size of Leak Oracle output $|f(\mathsf{ID}^*)|$ is less than some parameter ℓ. The advantage of $\mathcal{A}$ is

$$Adv_{\mathcal{A}}(\lambda, \ell) = |\Pr[\mathcal{A} \text{ wins}] - 1/2|.$$

We say that an IBE is ℓ-identity-leakage secure against ACI-KGC attack if for all polynomial time adversary $\mathcal{A}$ it is true that $Adv_{\mathcal{A}}(\lambda, \ell) \leq \mathsf{negl}(\lambda)$.

Selective Security. We also propose a weaker variant of the *selective* security model such that the adversary must submit the set of possible LeakID Oracle query before the Setup phase. We call this ℓ-identity-leakage selective security against ACI-KGC attack.

5.2 Construction

We propose a generic construction which can convert an ACI-KGC secure IBE to additionally allow identity-leakage. Suppose (**Setup, Extract, Enc, Dec**) is an ACI-KGC and IND-ID-CPA secure IBE with identity space as a cyclic group $\mathbb{G}$ with prime order p. We give a new IBE scheme as:

- **Setup'**: On input 1^λ, the KGC runs (mpk, msk) $\leftarrow$ **Setup**(1^λ) and picks a random n group elements $h_1, h_2, \ldots, h_n \in \mathbb{G}$. The master public key mpk' = (mpk, $h_1, \ldots, h_n$) and the master secret key msk' = msk. The new identity space is $\mathbb{Z}_p^n$ [2].
- **Extract'**: On input (mpk', msk') and an identity ID = $(I_1, \ldots, I_n) \in \mathbb{Z}_p^n$, the KGC computes $Y = \prod_{i=1}^n h_i^{I_i}$ and outputs $sk_{\text{ID}} \leftarrow$ **Extract**(mpk, msk, Y).
- **Enc'**: On input mpk', ID and a message m, it computes $Y = \prod_{i=1}^n h_i^{I_i}$ and outputs $C \leftarrow$ **Enc**(mpk, Y, m).
- **Dec'**: On input mpk', sk_{ID} and a ciphertext C, it outputs $m \leftarrow$ **Dec**(mpk, sk_{ID}, C).

A possible instantiation is the Boneh-Franklin IBE [2], in which the identity space is an arbitrary string. This scheme is also proven to be ACI-KGC secure in Chow's PhD thesis [19].

Theorem 2. *Our scheme is ℓ-identity-leakage selective secure against ACI-KGC attack if $(n-1)\log p - \ell = \omega(\log \lambda)$ and the underlying IBE scheme is ACI-KGC secure.*

Proof. We prove the security of our scheme by the transition between two security games:

- Game 0: It is the same as the ℓ-identity-leakage ACI-KGC security game.
- Game 1: It is the same as Game 0, except the Enc Oracle output and the challenge ciphertext is encrypted under the same identity uniformly chosen from random, and is independent to the identity leaked in LeakID Oracle.

We first show that no probabilistic polynomial time adversary can distinguish between the two games. We use the following simplified lemma based on Lemma B.7 in [20], while considering a single row vector only, instead of a matrix in [20].

---

[2] Note that the identity space is larger than a typical one of a traditional IBE.

Lemma 1. *Let the integer n be polynomial in the security parameter λ. Let* Leak $: \{0,1\}^* \to \{0,1\}^\ell$ *be an arbitrary function with ℓ-bit output. For randomly sampled $\boldsymbol{A}, \boldsymbol{V} \in \mathbb{Z}_p^n$ and $U \in \mathbb{Z}_p$, the statistical distance between:*

$$(\mathsf{Leak}(\boldsymbol{A}), \boldsymbol{V}, \langle \boldsymbol{A}, \boldsymbol{V} \rangle), \quad (\mathsf{Leak}(\boldsymbol{A}), \boldsymbol{V}, U),$$

is negligible as long as $(n-1)\log p - \ell = \omega(\log \lambda)$.

Consider the simulator $\mathcal{B}$ is given the selective LeakID Oracle query f (which can be composed of all leak function input) by the adversary $\mathcal{A}$. $\mathcal{B}$ obtains $f(\boldsymbol{A}), \boldsymbol{V}$ and T which is either $\langle \boldsymbol{A}, \boldsymbol{V} \rangle$ or a random element U in $\mathbb{Z}_p$.

Denote $\boldsymbol{V} = (v_1, \ldots, v_n)$. $\mathcal{B}$ picks a generator $g \in \mathbb{G}$ and sets $h_i = g^{v_i}$ for $i \in [1, n]$ in the mpk. When the LeakID Oracle is asked, $\mathcal{B}$ answers it by using $f(\boldsymbol{A})$.

$\mathcal{B}$ computes $\mathbf{Enc}(\mathsf{mpk}, g^T, \cdot)$ to answer the Enc Oracle and to calculate the challenge ciphertext. If T is the inner product $\langle \boldsymbol{A}, \boldsymbol{V} \rangle$, then $\mathcal{B}$ simulates the Game 0. Otherwise, $\mathcal{B}$ simulates the Game 1 since g^U corresponds to some random challenge identity I^* which is unknown to $\mathcal{B}$. As long as $(n-1)\log p - \ell = \omega(\log \lambda)$, no probabilistic polynomial time adversary can distinguish between these two games.

Lemma 2. *The advantage of $\mathcal{A}$ in the* Game 1 *is negligible if the underlying IBE scheme is ACI-KGC secure.*

Proof. The simulator $\mathcal{B}$ is given mpk' from the challenger of the underlying IBE scheme. $\mathcal{B}$ randomly picks $h_1, \ldots h_n \in \mathbb{G}$ and returns $\mathsf{mpk} = (\mathsf{mpk}', h_1, \ldots, h_n)$ to the adversary $\mathcal{A}$. $\mathcal{B}$ randomly picks $\mathsf{ID}^* \in \mathbb{Z}_p^n$. For all Enc Oracle queries, $\mathcal{B}$ forwards $\mathcal{A}$'s query to its challenger and forwards the answer to $\mathcal{A}$. For all LeakID Oracle queries, $\mathcal{B}$ can answer it using ID^*.

In the challenge phase, $\mathcal{A}$ submits two messages m_0^* and m_1^*. $\mathcal{B}$ sends them to its challenger and obtains a challenge ciphertext C^*. $\mathcal{B}$ returns C^* to $\mathcal{A}$. Note that C^* is independent of ID^*. Finally, $\mathcal{B}$ uses the answer from $\mathcal{A}$ to reply to its challenger. If $\mathcal{A}$ has non-negligible advantage in Game 1, then $\mathcal{B}$ breaks the ACI-KGC security of the underlying IBE. $\square$

Theorem 3. *Our scheme is IND-ID-CPA secure if the underlying IBE scheme is IND-ID-CPA and the discrete logarithm assumption holds in $\mathbb{G}$.*

Proof. Suppose the discrete logarithm of $g_1 \in \mathbb{G}$ to the base $g_2 \in \mathbb{G}$ is hard. The simulator $\mathcal{B}$ is given mpk' from the challenger of the underlying IBE scheme. $\mathcal{B}$ randomly picks $\alpha_i, \beta_i \in \mathbb{Z}_p$ for $i \in [1, n]$. $\mathcal{B}$ sets $h_i = g_1^{\alpha_i} g_2^{\beta_i}$. $\mathcal{B}$ returns $\mathsf{mpk} = (\mathsf{mpk}', h_1, \ldots, h_n)$ to the adversary $\mathcal{A}$.

For all Extract Oracle queries, $\mathcal{B}$ forwards $\mathcal{A}$'s query to its challenger and forwards the answer to $\mathcal{A}$. Observe that if $\mathcal{A}$ can query two different identities $\mathsf{ID}_1 = (I_1, \ldots, I_n)$ and $\mathsf{ID}_2 = (I_1', \ldots, I_n')$ such that $Y = \prod_{i=1}^n h_i^{I_i} = \prod_{i=1}^n h_i^{I_i'}$, then $\mathcal{B}$ can solve the discrete logarithm as follows. Note that

$$\prod_{i=1}^n (g_1^{\alpha_i} g_2^{\beta_i})^{I_i} = \prod_{i=1}^n (g_1^{\alpha_i} g_2^{\beta_i})^{I_i'}$$

$$\Rightarrow g_1^{\sum_{i=1}^n \alpha_i (I_i - I_i')} = g_2^{\sum_{i=1}^n \beta_i (I_i' - I_i)}$$

Since $I_i \neq I_i'$ for some $i \in [1, n]$, the discrete logarithm of g_1 and g_2 can be computed.

In the challenge phase, $\mathcal{A}$ submits two messages m_0^* and m_1^* and a challenge identity ID^*. $\mathcal{B}$ sends them to its challenger and obtains a challenge ciphertext C^*. $\mathcal{B}$ returns C^* to $\mathcal{A}$. Finally, $\mathcal{B}$ uses the answer from $\mathcal{A}$ to reply to its challenger. If $\mathcal{A}$ has non-negligible advantage, then $\mathcal{B}$ breaks the IND-ID-CPA security of the underlying IBE.

6 Conclusion

In this paper, we presented the model for an ideal escrow-free identity-based encryption. We defined a weak security model OW-KGC. If we model the key-escrow problem as "giving the master secret key to the adversary", then we can extend the existing IBE security models easily. These extended IBE models are all stronger than our OW-KGC model.

Subsequently, we demonstrated that all IBE schemes are insecure in this weak model. Therefore, we conclude that an ideal escrow-free IBE scheme is insecure in any model that is stronger than the OW-KGC model.

After that, we review the existing alternative methods to provide protection against malicious KGC or honest KGC under attacks. We identify a gap between the existing ACI-KGC model and the ideal escrow-free IBE model.

Finally, we formalize the identity-leakage model for ACI-KGC and give an efficient and generic construction. However, this construction can only achieve selective-leakage security. It is easy to come up with a leakage-query after seeing the master public key which will render the scheme totally insecure. Moreover, it requires the identity to have enough entropy. Indeed, if the identity has enough entropy, one may consider a slightly more secure model in which the user secret key is also given to the adversary, since we can extract the entropy from the identity to perform another layer of encryption. We left the construction in the full security model as an interesting open problem.

References

1. Shamir, A.: Identity-based cryptosystems and signature schemes. In: Blakely, G.R., Chaum, D. (eds.) CRYPTO 1984. LNCS, vol. 196, pp. 47–53. Springer, Heidelberg (1985)
2. Boneh, D., Franklin, M.: Identity-based encryption from the weil pairing. In: Kilian, J. (ed.) CRYPTO 2001. LNCS, vol. 2139, pp. 213–229. Springer, Heidelberg (2001)
3. Al-Riyami, S.S., Paterson, K.G.: Certificateless public key cryptography. In: Laih, C.-S. (ed.) ASIACRYPT 2003. LNCS, vol. 2894, pp. 452–473. Springer, Heidelberg (2003)
4. Chow, S.S.M.: Certificateless Encryption. In: Identity-Based Cryptography, pp. 135–155. IOS Press (2008)
5. Dent, A.W.: A Survey of Certificateless Encryption Schemes and Security Models. Int. J. Inf. Sec. 7(5), 349–377 (2008)

6. Gentry, C.: Certificate-based encryption and the certificate revocation problem. In: Biham, E. (ed.) EUROCRYPT 2003. LNCS, vol. 2656, pp. 272–293. Springer, Heidelberg (2003)

7. Girault, M.: Self-certified public keys. In: Davies, D.W. (ed.) EUROCRYPT 1991. LNCS, vol. 547, pp. 490–497. Springer, Heidelberg (1991)

8. Chow, S.S.M.: Removing escrow from identity-based encryption. In: Jarecki, S., Tsudik, G. (eds.) PKC 2009. LNCS, vol. 5443, pp. 256–276. Springer, Heidelberg (2009)

9. Goyal, V.: Reducing trust in the PKG in identity based cryptosystems. In: Menezes, A. (ed.) CRYPTO 2007. LNCS, vol. 4622, pp. 430–447. Springer, Heidelberg (2007)

10. Au, M.H., Huang, Q., Liu, J.K., Susilo, W., Wong, D.S., Yang, G.: Traceable and retrievable identity-based encryption. In: Bellovin, S.M., Gennaro, R., Keromytis, A.D., Yung, M. (eds.) ACNS 2008. LNCS, vol. 5037, pp. 94–110. Springer, Heidelberg (2008)

11. Goyal, V., Lu, S., Sahai, A., Waters, B.: Black-box accountable authority identity-based encryption. In: CCS 2008, pp. 427–436. ACM (2008)

12. Yuen, T.H., Susilo, W., Mu, Y.: How to construct identity-based signatures without the key escrow problem. Int. J. Inf. Sec. 9(4), 297–311 (2010)

13. Chow, S.S.M., Boyd, C., González Nieto, J.M.: Security-Mediated Certificateless Cryptography. In: Yung, M., Dodis, Y., Kiayias, A., Malkin, T. (eds.) PKC 2006. LNCS, vol. 3958, pp. 508–524. Springer, Heidelberg (2006)

14. Lewko, A., Rouselakis, Y., Waters, B.: Achieving leakage resilience through dual system encryption. In: Ishai, Y. (ed.) TCC 2011. LNCS, vol. 6597, pp. 70–88. Springer, Heidelberg (2011)

15. Yuen, T.H., Chow, S.S.M., Zhang, Y., Yiu, S.M.: Identity-based encryption resilient to continual auxiliary leakage. In: Pointcheval, D., Johansson, T. (eds.) EUROCRYPT 2012. LNCS, vol. 7237, pp. 117–134. Springer, Heidelberg (2012)

16. Boneh, D., DeMillo, R.A., Lipton, R.J.: On the importance of checking cryptographic protocols for faults (extended abstract). In: Fumy, W. (ed.) EUROCRYPT 1997. LNCS, vol. 1233, pp. 37–51. Springer, Heidelberg (1997)

17. Biham, E., Shamir, A.: Differential fault analysis of secret key cryptosystems. In: Kaliski Jr., B.S. (ed.) CRYPTO 1997. LNCS, vol. 1294, pp. 513–525. Springer, Heidelberg (1997)

18. Bellare, M., Paterson, K.G., Thomson, S.: RKA security beyond the linear barrier: IBE, encryption and signatures. In: Wang, X., Sako, K. (eds.) ASIACRYPT 2012. LNCS, vol. 7658, pp. 331–348. Springer, Heidelberg (2012)

19. Chow, S.S.M.: New Privacy-Preserving Architectures for Identity-/Attribute-based Encryption. PhD thesis, New York University (2010)

20. Dodis, Y., Lewko, A.B., Waters, B., Wichs, D.: Storing Secrets on Continually Leaky Devices. In: Ostrovsky, R. (ed.) FOCS 2011, pp. 688–697. IEEE (2011)

k-time Proxy Signature: Formal Definition and Efficient Construction

Weiwei Liu, Guomin Yang, Yi Mu, and Jiannan Wei

School of Computer Science and Software Engineering,
University of Wollongong, Wollongong, NSW 2522, Australia
{wl265,jw903}@uowmail.edu.au, {gyang,ymu}@uow.edu.au

Abstract. Proxy signature, which allows an original signer to delegate his/her signing right to another party (or proxy signer), is very useful in many applications. Conventional proxy signature only allows the original signer to specify in the warrant the validity time period of the delegation but not the number of proxy signatures the proxy signer can generate. To address this problem, in this paper, we provide a formal treatment for *k-time proxy signature*. Such a scheme allows a designated proxy signer to produce only a fixed number of proxy signatures on behalf of the original signer. We provide the formal definitions and adversary models for k-time proxy signature, and propose an efficient construction which is *provably secure* against different types of adversaries.

Keywords: proxy signature, restricted delegation, secret sharing.

1 Introduction

Proxy signature is a special type of digital signature, and is very useful in many real-world applications. In a proxy signature scheme, an original signer (or delegator) can delegate his/her signing right to a proxy signer. Thereafter, the proxy signer can sign documents on behalf of the original signer.

The first proxy signature scheme was proposed by Mambo, Usuda and Okamoto in 1996 [14]. In their work they classified proxy signatures into three main categories, namely full delegation, partial delegation, and delegation by warrant. Partial delegation proxy signature schemes can be further divided into proxy-protected and proxy-unprotected schemes according to whether a verifier can decide the proxy signature is generated by a proxy signer or the original signer. Shortly after that, Kim et al. [10] proposed a new type of proxy signature combining partial delegation and warrant. They further showed that such a combination can provide a higher level of security. Since then many proxy signature schemes based on partial delegation and warrant have been proposed (e.g., [12,24,20,23,25]).

Many extensions on proxy signature have also been proposed according to different application needs, such as threshold proxy signature [28,26,13], blind proxy signature [27,4,2], one-time proxy signature [15,21], ring proxy signature

W. Susilo and R. Reyhanitabar (Eds.): ProvSec 2013, LNCS 8209, pp. 154–164, 2013.

[22,1,7], and so on. Threshold proxy signature, also known as multi-proxy signature, enables an original signer to delegate his signing right to multiple proxy signers. The proxy signers need to work together in order to produce a valid proxy signature on behalf of the original signer. One-time proxy signature puts strict restrictions on the signing capability of a proxy signer, who is only allowed to generate one valid proxy signature on behalf of the original signer. Blind proxy signature allows a user to obtain a valid signature on a message in a way that the proxy signer learns neither the message nor the resulting signature, and ring proxy signature allows a proxy signer to hide his/her identity among a group of possible signers.

Proxy signature and its extended variants have been found very useful in many practical applications, such as distributed systems [16], grid computing [6], and mobile agent applications [12]. However, one of the key issues in proxy signature is to ensure that a proxy signer will not misuse the signing right obtained from an original signer. In the seminal work by Mambo et al. [14], a validity period is specified in a warrant in order to restrict the signing capability of a proxy signer. This approach has been used in almost all the following works on proxy signature. However, if the proxy signer is malicious, even in a very short time, the malicious proxy signer can still produce as many proxy signatures as he/she wishes. To address this problem, in this paper, we provide a formal and comprehensive treatment for k-time proxy signature where the proxy signer can only generate a fixed number of proxy signatures on behalf of the original signer.

There have been a number of works (e.g., [3,9,18,11]) on restricting the signing capability of a signer in normal digital signature schemes. In [9], Hwang et al. proposed a multiple-time digital signature scheme, which gives an upper bound on the number of signatures a signer can produce. Shortly after that, Pieprzyk et al. [18] proposed a more general multiple-time signature scheme based on one-way functions and cover-free families. Kim et al. [11] then extended multiple-time signature to a new primitive named metered signature, which allows a signer to produce a fixed number of signatures in a designated time period.

However, a formal and complete treatment for multi-time (or k-time) proxy signature is still missing. In [15], Mehta and Harn proposed a one-time proxy signature scheme, which is less useful than a more general k-time proxy signature scheme. There is a multi-time proxy signature scheme presented in [5], however, no formal security model or proof has been provided. In [8], Hong and Chen presented a multiple-time proxy signature scheme based on a binary hash tree. However, their security analysis is incomplete since it does not cover all the possible attacks against a multiple-time proxy signature scheme.

In this paper, we provide a formal and complete treatment for multi-time (or k-time) proxy signature schemes. We first provide a formal security model for such schemes. In our model, we will consider three types of adversaries, namely outsiders, proxy signer, and original signer. Our model aims to capture the exact security goal of a k-time proxy signature scheme, that is only a proxy signer, who has been delegated the signing right from an original signer, can produce *at most* k valid proxy signatures. We then propose a new k-time proxy signature scheme based on the Schnorr signature scheme and verifiable secret sharing. In our scheme, the original signer can specify in the warrant the number of proxy signatures a proxy signer can produce. If the proxy signer produces more than predetermined number of proxy signatures, his/her private key can be computed by the public. That means the original signer does not need to monitor the behavior of the proxy signer. It is worth noting that such a feature is not supported in Hong and Chen's scheme [8]. In their scheme, the proxy signer's private key can only be computed by the original signer rather than by any third party verifier when the proxy signer misbehaves.

Paper Outline. The rest of the paper is organized as follows. We introduce the definition of k-time proxy signature in Section 2. A formal security model for k-time proxy signature is presented in Section 3. We then give our new proxy signature scheme in Section 4 and prove its security in Section 5. The paper is concluded in Section 6.

2 k-time Proxy Signature

A k-time (or multi-time) proxy signature scheme consists of a tuple of algorithms $(\mathcal{ST}, \mathcal{KG}, \mathcal{DSK}\ \mathcal{PKG}, \mathcal{PS}, \mathcal{PV}, \mathcal{R})$:

- Setup–($\mathcal{ST}$): This algorithm takes 1^κ as input where κ is a security parameter and returns the public parameters *params*.
- KeyGen–($\mathcal{KG}$): The Key Generation algorithm takes *params* as input and outputs a user key pair (pk, sk).
- DskGen–($\mathcal{DKG}$): This algorithm takes (sk_o, pk_o, pk_p, m_w) as input and outputs a delegation key dsk. Here m_w denotes a warrant which specifies the predetermined number of proxy signatures that can be generated by the proxy signer.
- PskGen–($\mathcal{PKG}$): This algorithm takes dsk and sk_p as input and outputs a proxy signing key psk.
- ProSig–($\mathcal{PS}$): The proxy signing algorithm takes the proxy signing key psk and a message m in the message space $\mathbb{M}$ as input, and outputs a proxy signature σ.
- ProVer–($\mathcal{PV}$): The proxy signature verification algorithm takes the public keys pk_o and pk_p, a warrant m_w, a message m, and a proxy signature σ as input, and outputs either 1 or 0.
- Reveal–($\mathcal{R}$): Given pk_o, pk_p, a warrant m_w, and $k+1$ different message and proxy signature pairs, where k is the number specified in the warrant m_w, this algorithm either outputs a private key sk_p of the proxy signer or a special symbol '$\perp$'.

Correctness. We require that for any message space $\mathbb{M} \subseteq \{0,1\}^*$ and any security parameter $\kappa \in \mathbb{N}$, if *params* $\leftarrow \mathcal{ST}(1^\kappa)$, $(sk_o, pk_o) \leftarrow \mathcal{KG}(params)$, $(sk_p, pk_p) \leftarrow \mathcal{KG}(params)$, $dsk \leftarrow \mathcal{DKG}(sk_o, pk_o, pk_p, m_w)$, $psk \leftarrow \mathcal{PKG}(dsk, sk_p)$, then

$$\mathcal{PV}(pk_o, pk_p, m_w, m, \mathcal{PS}(psk, m)) = 1.$$

3   Security Model

In a k-time proxy signature scheme, the security consideration is different from that for the traditional proxy signature [25] or k-time signature [9]. According to the definition, the security of a k-time proxy signature should be defined in three aspects, which are summarized below.

1. Type I: the Type I attacker $\mathcal{A}_I$ (an outsider) possesses the public keys of the original signer and the proxy signer, and tries to forge a proxy signature.
2. Type II: the Type II attacker $\mathcal{A}_{II}$ (proxy signer) possesses the public keys of the original signer and the proxy signer. In addition, he also possesses the private key sk_p. We can further divide $\mathcal{A}_{II}$ into $\mathcal{A}_{II1}$ and $\mathcal{A}_{II2}$. $\mathcal{A}_{II1}$ tries to forge a valid proxy signature without obtaining delegation from the original signer, and $\mathcal{A}_{II2}$ has a valid delegation from the original signer and tries to produce more than predetermined number of proxy signatures.
3. Type III: the Type III attacker $\mathcal{A}_{III}$ (the original signer) possesses the public keys of the original signer and the proxy signer. In addition, he has the private key sk_o of the original signer. $\mathcal{A}_{III}$ tries to forge a valid proxy signature without knowing the private key sk_p of the proxy signer.

It is obvious that if a k-time proxy signature scheme is secure against $\mathcal{A}_{II}$ and $\mathcal{A}_{III}$, it is also secure against $\mathcal{A}_I$. So we will only focus on the adversarial models with regards to $\mathcal{A}_{II}$ and $\mathcal{A}_{III}$ in the rest of this paper.

Before we formally define each adversarial model, we first introduce two types of queries that may appear in the models:

- Delegation query: $\mathcal{A}$ can query the delegation oracle $\mathcal{O}_{DKG}(sk_o, pk_o, pk_p, \cdot)$ with any warrant m_w. The corresponding delegation key dsk is then generated and returned to $\mathcal{A}$.
- Proxy signing query: $\mathcal{A}$ can query the proxy signing oracle $\mathcal{O}_{PS}(psk, \cdot)$ with any message m of his choice. A valid proxy signature on m is generated and returned to $\mathcal{A}$.

3.1   Type II1 Adversary

We define the adversarial game between a Type II1 adversary $\mathcal{A}_{II1}$ and an simulator $\mathcal{S}$ as follows:

- **Setup:** The Simulator $\mathcal{S}$ runs $\mathcal{ST}$ to generate public parameters *params*.
- **KeyGen** The Simulator $\mathcal{S}$ runs $\mathcal{KG}$ to generate the key pairs of the original signer (sk_o, pk_o) and a proxy signer (sk_p, pk_p). $\mathcal{S}$ sends pk_o, pk_p and sk_p to the adversary $\mathcal{A}_{II1}$.
- **Delegation queries:** $\mathcal{A}_{II1}$ chooses any warrant m_w of his/her choice and queries the delegation oracle $\mathcal{O}_{DKG}$. $\mathcal{S}$ generates the delegation key $dsk \leftarrow \mathcal{DKG}(sk_o, pk_o, pk_p, m_w)$ and returns dsk to $\mathcal{A}_{II1}$.

- **Proxy signing queries:** $\mathcal{A}_{II1}$ chooses a warrant m_w and a message m, and queries the proxy signing oracle $\mathcal{O}_{PS}$. If m_w has appeared in a Delegation Query, a special symbol '$\perp$' is returned to $\mathcal{A}$. Otherwise, $\mathcal{S}$ generates $dsk \leftarrow \mathcal{DKG}(sk_o, pk_o, pk_p, m_w)$, $psk \leftarrow \mathcal{PKG}(dsk, sk_p)$, $\sigma \leftarrow \mathcal{PS}(psk, m)$, and returns σ to $\mathcal{A}_{II1}$.
- Finally, $\mathcal{A}_{II1}$ outputs (m_w^*, m^*, σ^*). We say $\mathcal{A}_{II1}$ wins the game if
  - $\mathcal{PV}(pk_o, pk_p, m_w^*, m^*, \sigma^*) = 1$;
  - $\mathcal{A}_{II1}$ did not make a query to $\mathcal{O}_{DKG}$ on m_w^*;
  - $\mathcal{A}_{II1}$ did not make a query to $\mathcal{O}_{PS}$ on (m_w^*, m^*).

Define the advantage of a Type II1 adversary as

$$Adv_{\mathcal{A}_{II1}}^{cwcma}(\kappa) = \Pr[\mathcal{A}_{II1} \text{ Wins the game}].$$

Definition 1. *We say a k-time proxy signature scheme is secure against the Type II1 chosen warrant and chosen message attacks if for any probabilistic polynomial time $\mathcal{A}_{II1}$, $Adv_{\mathcal{A}_{II1}}^{cwcma}(\kappa)$ is negligible in κ.*

3.2 Type II2 Adversary

We define the adversarial game between a Type II2 adversary $\mathcal{A}_{II2}$ and an simulator $\mathcal{S}$ as follows:

- **Setup:** The Simulator $\mathcal{S}$ runs $\mathcal{ST}$ to generate public parameters *params*.
- **KeyGen** The Simulator $\mathcal{S}$ runs $\mathcal{KG}$ to generate the key pairs of an original signer (sk_o, pk_o) and a proxy signer (sk_p, pk_p). $\mathcal{S}$ sends pk_o, pk_p and sk_p to the adversary $\mathcal{A}_{II2}$.
- **Delegation queries:** $\mathcal{A}_{II2}$ chooses any warrant m_w of his/her choice and queries the delegation oracle $\mathcal{O}_{DKG}$. $\mathcal{S}$ generates the delegation key $dsk \leftarrow \mathcal{DKG}(sk_o, pk_o, pk_p, m_w)$ and returns dsk to $\mathcal{A}_{II2}$.
- Finally, $\mathcal{A}_{II2}$ outputs a warrant m_w which contains a predetermined number k, and $k + 1$ message-signature pairs (m_i, σ_i) $(1 \leq i \leq k+1)$ where $m_i \neq m_j$ for $i \neq j$. We say $\mathcal{A}_{II2}$ wins the game if
  - $\mathcal{PV}(pk_o, pk_p, m_w, m_i, \sigma_i) = 1$ for all $i \in [1, k+1]$;
  - $\mathcal{R}(pk_o, pk_p, m_w, (m_1, \sigma_1), \cdots, (m_{k+1}, \sigma_{k+1})) = \perp$.

Define the advantage of a Type II2 adversary as

$$Adv_{\mathcal{A}_{II2}}^{cwa}(\kappa) = \Pr[\mathcal{A}_{II2} \text{ Wins the game}].$$

Definition 2. *We say a k-time proxy signature scheme is secure against the Type II2 chosen warrant attacks if for any probabilistic polynomial time $\mathcal{A}_{II2}$, $Adv_{\mathcal{A}_{II2}}^{cwa}(\kappa)$ is negligible in κ.*

3.3 Type III Adversary

The adversarial game between a Type III adversary $\mathcal{A}_{III}$ and an simulator $\mathcal{S}$ is defined as follows:

- **Setup:** The Simulator $\mathcal{S}$ runs $\mathcal{S}$ to generate public parameters *params* and gives *params* to the adversary.
- **KeyGen** The Simulator $\mathcal{S}$ runs $\mathcal{KG}$ to generate the key pairs of the original signer (sk_o, pk_o) and a proxy signer (sk_p, pk_p). $\mathcal{S}$ sends sk_o, pk_o and pk_p to the adversary $\mathcal{A}_{III}$.
- **Proxy signing queries:** $\mathcal{A}_{III}$ queries the proxy signing oracle $\mathcal{O}_{PS}$ by providing a warrant m_w generated according to the scheme, a valid delegation key dsk for m_w, and a message m. $\mathcal{S}$ generates $psk \leftarrow \mathcal{PKG}(dsk, sk_p)$, $\sigma \leftarrow \mathcal{PS}(psk, m)$, and returns σ to $\mathcal{A}_{III}$.
- Finally, $\mathcal{A}_{III}$ outputs (m_w^*, m^*, σ^*). We say $\mathcal{A}_{III}$ wins the game if
  - $\mathcal{PV}(pk_o, pk_p, m_w^*, m^*, \sigma^*) = 1$;
  - For any warrant m_w with a predetermined number k, $\mathcal{A}_{III}$ makes at most k proxy signing queries;
  - $\mathcal{A}_{III}$ did not make a query to $\mathcal{O}_{PS}$ on (m_w^*, m^*).

Define the advantage of a Type III adversary as

$$Adv_{\mathcal{A}_{III}}^{cma}(\kappa) = \Pr[\mathcal{A}_{III} \text{ Wins the game}].$$

Definition 3. *We say a k-time proxy signature scheme is secure against the Type III chosen message attacks if for any probabilistic polynomial time $\mathcal{A}_{III}$, $Adv_{\mathcal{A}_{III}}^{cma}(\kappa)$ is negligible in κ.*

4 A New *k*-time Proxy Signature Scheme

In this section, we present a new *k*-time proxy signature scheme based on the Discrete Logarithm Problem and secret sharing.

Discrete Logarithm Problem (DLP): Let G denote a group of prime order q, and g a generator of G. Given a random element $y \in G$, compute $x \in \mathbb{Z}_q$ such that $y = g^x$.

Our *k*-time proxy signature scheme works as follows:

1. $\mathcal{ST}$: given a security parameter $\kappa \in \mathbb{N}$, generate the parameters *params* = (G, g, q) such that $|q| = \kappa$ and a hash function $H : \{0, 1\}^* \rightarrow \mathbb{Z}_q$.
2. $\mathcal{KG}$: randomly choose $x \in \mathbb{Z}_q$ and compute $y = g^x$. Output $(sk, pk) = (x, y)$.
3. $\mathcal{DKG}$: given a warrant $m_w = (k, B = \{b_1, b_2, \cdots, b_k\})^1$, where k is a number selected by the original signer and $b_i = g^{a_i}$ ($1 \leq i \leq k$) are generated by the proxy signer and sent to the original singer via a secure channel, the original signer first chooses a random number $k_o \in \mathbb{Z}_q$, and then computes $K_o = g^{k_o}$, $\sigma_o = sk_o \cdot h(m_w \| K_o) + k_o \bmod q$. The original signer then sets $dsk = (K_o, \sigma_o)$ as the delegation key for m_w.

---

[1] It is worth noting that we can put additional information, such as the validity time period and the type of message the proxy signer is allowed to sign, in the warrant.

4. $\mathcal{PKG}$: given a delegation key $dsk = (K_o, \sigma_o)$ for a warrant m_w, the proxy signer computes $S_p = \sigma_o + sk_p \bmod q$ and outputs the proxy signing key $psk = (K_o, S_p, sk_p)$.

5. $\mathcal{PS}$: given a message m to be signed, and a proxy signing key $psk = (K_o, S_p, sk_p)$, the proxy signer chooses a random number $k_p \in \mathbb{Z}_q$, and computes $K_p = g^{k_p}$ and $\sigma_p = S_p \cdot h(h(m_w\|K_o)\|m\|K_p) + k_p \bmod q$. The proxy signer also computes $f(\omega) = sk_p + a_1\omega + a_2\omega^2 + ... + a_k\omega^k \bmod q$ where $\omega = h(m_w, m, \sigma_p)$. The proxy signature is $\sigma = (K_o, K_p, \sigma_p, f(\omega))$.

6. $\mathcal{PV}$: given public keys pk_o and pk_p, a warrant $m_w = (k, B = \{b_1, b_2, \cdots, b_k\})$, a message m and a proxy signature $\sigma = (K_o, K_p, \sigma_p, f(\omega))$, the verifier checks if the following equation holds
   - $g^{\sigma_p} = K_p \cdot (pk_p \cdot K_o \cdot pk_o^{h(m_w\|K_o)})^{h(h(m_w\|K_o)\|m\|K_p)}$;
   - $g^{f(\omega)} = pk_p \cdot b_1^{\omega} \cdot b_2^{\omega^2} \cdots b_k^{\omega^k}$.

   If both equations hold, output 1; otherwise, output 0.

7. $\mathcal{R}$: given $pk_o, pk_p, m_w = (k, B = \{b_1, b_2, \cdots, b_k\})$, and $k+1$ message signature pairs (m_i, σ_i), solve the following equations

$$f(\omega_1) = sk_p + a_1\omega_1 + a_2\omega_1^2 + ... + a_k\omega_1^k$$
$$f(\omega_2) = sk_p + a_1\omega_2 + a_2\omega_2^2 + ... + a_k\omega_2^k$$
$$\cdots$$
$$f(\omega_{k+1}) = sk_p + a_1\omega_{k+1} + a_2\omega_{k+1}^2 + ... + a_k\omega_{k+1}^k$$

for variables $(sk_p, a_1, \cdots, a_k)$. If a solution is found, output sk_p, otherwise, output '$\perp$'.

The correctness of the scheme can be verified as follows

$$
\begin{aligned}
g^{\sigma_p} &= g^{S_p \cdot h(h(m_w\|K_o)\|m\|K_p) + k_p} \\
&= (g^{\sigma_o + sk_p})^{h(h(m_w\|K_o)\|m\|K_p)} \cdot g^{k_p} \\
&= (g^{sk_o \cdot h(m_w\|K_o) + k_o} \cdot g^{sk_p})^{h(h(m_w\|K_o)\|m\|K_p)} \cdot K_p \\
&= (pk_o^{h(m_w\|K_o)} \cdot K_o \cdot pk_p)^{h(h(m_w\|K_o)\|m\|K_p)} \cdot K_p \\
g^{f(\omega)} &= g^{sk_p + a_1\omega + a_2\omega^2 + ... + a_k\omega^k} \\
&= pk_p \cdot (g^{a_1})^{\omega} \cdot (g^{a_2})^{\omega^2} \cdots (g^{a_k})^{\omega^k} \\
&= pk_p \cdot b_1^{\omega} \cdot b_2^{\omega^2} \cdots b_k^{\omega^k}
\end{aligned}
$$

5 Security Analysis

In this section we analyse the security of the above k-time proxy signature scheme against $\mathcal{A}_{II}$ and $\mathcal{A}_{III}$ adversaries.

Theorem 1. *The proposed k-time proxy signature scheme is secure against the Type II1 chosen warrant and chosen message attacks if the Discrete Logarithm Problem is hard.*

Proof. The proof is by contradiction. Given an adversary $\mathcal{A}_{II1}$ that can win the Type $II1$ game, we construct another algorithm $\mathcal{B}$ that can solve the DLP.

Given $(g, y^* = g^{x^*})$ for some unknown $x^* \in \mathbb{Z}_q$, $\mathcal{B}$ simulates the Type II1 game for $\mathcal{A}_{II1}$ as follows. $\mathcal{B}$ sets the original signer's public key as $pk_o = y^*$ and maintains a H-table to record all the hash queries and the corresponding answers.

Hash Queries: For each hash query with an input message msg, $\mathcal{B}$ first checks the H-table:

- If there exists an item (msg, h) in the H-table, where msg refers to the messages queried before, $\mathcal{B}$ returns h as the answer to $\mathcal{A}_{II1}$.
- Otherwise, $\mathcal{B}$ chooses a random $h \in \mathbb{Z}_q$, sends h to $\mathcal{A}_{II1}$ as the answer for the hash query, and adds (msg, h) into the H-table.

Delegation Queries: When $\mathcal{A}_{II1}$ makes a delegation query on a warrant $m_w = (k, B = (b_1, b_2, \cdots, b_k))$, $\mathcal{B}$ answers the query as follows.

- Choose randomly $h_o, \sigma_o \in \mathbb{Z}_q$, compute $K_o = g^{\sigma_o}/pk_o^{h_o}$, and set $h(m_w \| K_o) = h_o$ by adding $(m_w \| K_o, h_o)$ into the H-table.
- Return (K_o, σ_o) as the delegation key to $\mathcal{A}_{II1}$.

Proxy Signing Queries: When $\mathcal{A}_{II1}$ makes a proxy signing query on a warrant $m_w = (k, B = (b_1, b_2, \cdots, b_k))$, and a message m, $\mathcal{B}$ responds the query as follows:

- Generate a delegation key $dsk = (K_o, \sigma_o)$ for the warrant m_w by applying the same approach as described in answering delegation queries.
- Use the derived dsk and sk_p to produce the proxy signing key psk by running the $\mathcal{PKG}$ algorithm, and then use psk to generate the proxy signature for message m by running the $\mathcal{PS}$ algorithm.

Assume $\mathcal{A}_{II1}$ can forge a valid proxy signature $\sigma^* = (K_o^*, K_p^*, \sigma_p^*, f(\omega^*))$ for a warrant m_w^* and a message m^* such that

$$g^{\sigma_p^*} = K_p^* \cdot (pk_p \cdot K_o^* \cdot pk_o^{h(m_w^* \| K_o^*)})^{h(h(m_w^* \| K_o^*) \| m^* \| K_p^*)}.$$

Then according to the Forking Lemma [19], by rewinding the adversary and providing a new hash value for $h(m_w^* \| K_o^*) \| m^* \| K_p^*$, $\mathcal{B}$ can obtain $S_p^* = \sigma_o^* + sk_p$ mod q and $\sigma_o^* = S_p^* - sk_p$ mod q which satisfies

$$g^{\sigma_o^*} = K_o^* \cdot pk_o^{h^*}$$

where $h^* = h(m_w^* \| K_o^*)$.

After that, $\mathcal{B}$ repeats the above simulation for $\mathcal{A}_{II1}$ except that a new value $\hat{h}^*$ is chosen as the hash value for $m_w^* \| K_o^*$. Again, due to the Forking Lemma, $\mathcal{B}$ can obtain a new $\hat{\sigma}_o^*$ which satisfies

$$g^{\hat{\sigma}_o^*} = K_o^* \cdot pk_o^{\hat{h}^*}.$$

$\mathcal{B}$ can then compute $x^* = sk_o = (\sigma_o^* - \hat{\sigma}_o^*)/(h^* - \hat{h}^*)$ and solve the Discrete Logarithm Problem. This completes the proof for Theorem 1.

Theorem 2. *The proposed k-time proxy signature scheme is secure against the Type II2 chosen warrant attacks.*

Proof. According to our scheme, if a signature $\sigma = (K_o, K_p, \sigma_p, f(\omega))$ is valid with regards to a warrant $m_w = (k, B = (b_1, b_2, \cdots, b_k))$ and message m , then

$$g^{f(\omega)} = pk_p \cdot b_1{}^{\omega} \cdot b_2{}^{\omega^2} \cdots b_k{}^{\omega^k}.$$

Suppose an adversary $\mathcal{A}_{II2}$ have produced $k+1$ proxy signatures with regards to a warrant m_w and different messages $\{m_1, m_2, \cdots, m_{k+1}\}$, then we have

$$\begin{cases} f(\omega_1) = sk_p + a_1\omega_1 + a_2\omega_1^2 + \ldots + a_k\omega_1^k \\ f(\omega_2) = sk_p + a_1\omega_2 + a_2\omega_2^2 + \ldots + a_k\omega_2^k \\ \ldots \\ f(\omega_{k+1}) = sk_p + a_1\omega_{k+1} + a_2\omega_{k+1}^2 + \ldots + a_k\omega_{k+1}^k \end{cases}$$

where $\omega_i = h(m_w, m_i, \sigma_{p_i})$ for $1 \leq i \leq k+1$. Since the hash function is modelled as a random oracle, each ω_i is a random element in $\mathbb{Z}_q$. Therefore, with overwhelming probability, the reveal algorithm $\mathcal{R}$ can recover the unique solution $(sk_p, a_1, a_2, \cdots, a_k)$ that satisfies the above equations.

Theorem 3. *The proposed k-time proxy signature scheme is secure against the Type III chosen message attacks if the Discrete Logarithm Problem is hard.*

Proof. The proof is similar to the proof for Theorem 1, that is, if there exists an adversary $\mathcal{A}_{III}$ which can win the Type III game, we can construct another algorithm $\mathcal{B}$ which can solve the Discrete Logarithm Problem.

Given $(g, y^* = g^{x^*})$ where $x^* \in \mathbb{Z}_q$ is randomly chosen from $\mathbb{Z}_q$, $\mathcal{B}$ simulates the Type III game for $\mathcal{A}_{III}$ as follows. $\mathcal{B}$ generates sk_o, pk_o and sets the proxy signer's public key as $pk_p = y^*$. $\mathcal{B}$ answers hash queries by maintaining a H-table as in the proof of Theorem 1.

When a new warrant m_w with a predetermined number k is to be created, $\mathcal{B}$ generates the values of $B = (b_1, b_2, \cdots, b_k)$ as follows. $\mathcal{B}$ randomly chooses $\omega_i, s_i \in \mathbb{Z}_q$ for $1 \leq i \leq k$. Then based on the result in [17], $\mathcal{B}$ can calculate $b_i(1 \leq i \leq k) \in G$ that satisfies $g^{s_i} = y^* \cdot \prod_{j=1}^{k} b_j^{\omega_i^j}$ for all $1 \leq i \leq k$. $\mathcal{B}$ saves the values of $\{\omega_i, s_i\}_{1 \leq i \leq k}$ with regards to m_w for later use.

Proxy Signing Queries: To answer the ℓ-th ($1 \leq \ell \leq k$) proxy signing query on a warrant m_w, $\mathcal{B}$ first finds out the values of (ω_ℓ, s_ℓ) that have been computed when generating the warrant m_w. $\mathcal{B}$ then computes the proxy signature as follows:

- Randomly choose $\sigma_p, \tau \in \mathbb{Z}_q$;
- Compute $K_p = g^{\sigma_p}/(pk_p \cdot K_o \cdot pk_o^{h(m_w \| K_o)})^\tau$;
- Set $h(h(m_w \| K_o) \| m \| K_p) = \tau$;
- Set $h(m_w \| m \| \sigma_p) = \omega_\ell$;
- Return $\sigma = (K_o, K_p, \sigma_p, s_\ell)$.

It is easy to verify that σ can successfully pass the signature verification.

Suppose $\mathcal{A}_{III}$ outputs a forgery $(m_w^*, m^*, \sigma^* = (K_o^*, K_p^*, \sigma_p^*, s^*))$ which satisfies

$$g^{\sigma_p^*} = K_p^* \cdot (y^* \cdot K_o^* \cdot pk_o^{h(m_w^* \| K_o^*)})^{h(h(m_w^* \| K_o^*) \| m^* \| K_p^*)}$$

where $dsk^* = (K_o^*, \sigma_o^*)$ is the delegation key provided by $\mathcal{A}_{III}$ for the warrant m_w^*. According to the Forking Lemma, by rewinding $\mathcal{A}_{III}$ and providing a new hash value of $h(h(m_w^* \| K_o^*) \| m^* \| K_p^*)$, $\mathcal{B}$ can obtain another valid signature $\hat{\sigma}^* = (K_o^*, K_p^*, \hat{\sigma}_p^*, \hat{s}^*))$ for (m_w^*, m^*). Then $\mathcal{B}$ can derive

$$S_p^* = (\sigma_p^* - \hat{\sigma}_p^*)/(h^* - \hat{h}^*) \bmod q$$

where h^* and $\hat{h}^*$ are the hash values for $h(m_w^* \| K_o^*) \| m^* \| K_p^*$ in the two executions. Finally, $\mathcal{B}$ can compute $x^* = S_p^* - \sigma_o^* \bmod q$ and solve the DLP.

6 Conclusion

In this paper, we presented a formal security model and an efficient construction of k-time proxy signature scheme. Our model has considered different types of potential adversaries against a k-time proxy signature scheme, and is to date the first complete formal security model for such schemes. We then presented a practical k-time proxy signature scheme based on the Schnorr signature and verifiable secret sharing. One interesting feature of our scheme is that the proxy signer's secret key can be discovered by the public if the proxy signer misbehaves. We also provided formal security proofs to demonstrate that the proposed scheme is provably secure in the proposed security model. We leave the problem of constructing a secure k-time proxy signature scheme without random oracles as our future work.

References

1. Awasthi, A.K., Lal, S.: ID-based ring signature and proxy ring signature schemes from bilinear pairings. arXiv preprint cs/0504097 (2005)
2. Awasthi, A.K., Lal, S.: Proxy blind signature scheme. Transaction on Cryptology 2(1), 5–11 (2005)
3. Bicakci, K., Tsudik, G., Tung, B.: How to construct optimal one-time signatures. Computer Networks 43(3), 339–349 (2003)
4. Chen, X., Zhang, F., Kim, K.: ID-based multi-proxy signature and blind multisignature from bilinear pairings. Proceedings of KIISC 3, 11–19 (2003)
5. Choi, C.-J., Kim, Z., Kim, K.: Schnorr signature scheme with restricted signing capability and its application. In: Proc. of CSS (2003)
6. Foster, I.T., Kesselman, C., Tsudik, G., Tuecke, S.: A security architecture for computational grids. In: ACM Conference on Computer and Communications Security, pp. 83–92 (1998)
7. Herranz, J., Sáez, G.: New identity-based ring signature schemes. In: López, J., Qing, S., Okamoto, E. (eds.) ICICS 2004. LNCS, vol. 3269, pp. 27–39. Springer, Heidelberg (2004)

8. Hong, X., Chen, K.: Secure multiple-times proxy signature scheme. Computer Standards and Interfaces 31(1), 19–23 (2009)
9. Hwang, J.Y., Kim, H.-J., Lee, D.H., Lim, J.I.: Digital signature schemes with restriction on signing capability. In: Safavi-Naini, R., Seberry, J. (eds.) ACISP 2003. LNCS, vol. 2727, pp. 324–335. Springer, Heidelberg (2003)
10. Kim, S., Park, S., Won, D.: Proxy signatures, revisited. In: Han, Y., Quing, S. (eds.) ICICS 1997. LNCS, vol. 1334, pp. 223–232. Springer, Heidelberg (1997)
11. Kim, W.-H., Yoon, H., Cheon, J.H.: Metered signatures: How to restrict the signing capability. Journal of Communications and Networks 12(3), 201–208 (2010)
12. Lee, B., Kim, H., Kim, K.: Strong proxy signature and its applications. In: Proc. of SCIS, pp. 603–608 (2001)
13. Liu, J., Huang, S.: Identity-based threshold proxy signature from bilinear pairings. Informatica 21(1), 41–56 (2010)
14. Mambo, M., Usuda, K., Okamoto, E.: Proxy signatures for delegating signing operation. In: Proceedings of the 3rd ACM Conference on Computer and Communications Security, CCS 1996, pp. 48–57 (1996)
15. Mehta, M., Harn, L.: Efficient one-time proxy signatures. In: IEE Proceedings of the Communications, vol. 152, pp. 129–133. IET (2005)
16. Clifford Neuman, B.: Proxy-based authorization and accounting for distributed systems. In: ICDCS, pp. 283–291 (1993)
17. Pedersen, T.P.: Distributed provers with applications to undeniable signatures. In: Davies, D.W. (ed.) EUROCRYPT 1991. LNCS, vol. 547, pp. 221–242. Springer, Heidelberg (1991)
18. Pieprzyk, J., Wang, H., Xing, C.: Multiple-time signature schemes against adaptive chosen message attacks. In: Matsui, M., Zuccherato, R.J. (eds.) SAC 2003. LNCS, vol. 3006, pp. 88–100. Springer, Heidelberg (2004)
19. Pointcheval, D., Stern, J.: Security proofs for signature schemes. In: Maurer, U.M. (ed.) EUROCRYPT 1996. LNCS, vol. 1070, pp. 387–398. Springer, Heidelberg (1996)
20. Wang, G.: Designated-verifier proxy signature schemes. In: Sasaki, R., Qing, S., Okamoto, E., Yoshiura, H. (eds.) SEC. IFIP AICT, vol. 181, pp. 409–423. Springer, Heidelberg (2005)
21. Wang, T., Wei, Z.: One-time proxy signature based on quantum cryptography. Quantum Information Processing 11(2), 455–463 (2012)
22. Wei, B., Zhang, F., Chen, X.: Ring proxy signatures. Journal of Electronics (China) 25(1), 108–114 (2008)
23. Wu, W., Mu, Y., Susilo, W., Seberry, J., Huang, X.: Identity-based proxy signature from pairings. In: Xiao, B., Yang, L.T., Ma, J., Muller-Schloer, C., Hua, Y. (eds.) ATC 2007. LNCS, vol. 4610, pp. 22–31. Springer, Heidelberg (2007)
24. Xu, J., Zhang, Z., Feng, D.: ID-based proxy signature using bilinear pairings. In: Chen, G., Pan, Y., Guo, M., Lu, J. (eds.) ISPA-WS 2005. LNCS, vol. 3759, pp. 359–367. Springer, Heidelberg (2005)
25. Yu, Y., Mu, Y., Susilo, W., Sun, Y., Ji, Y.: Provably secure proxy signature scheme from factorization. Mathematical and Computer Modelling 55, 1160–1168 (2012)
26. Zhang, F., Kim, K.: Efficient ID-based blind signature and proxy signature from bilinear pairings. In: Safavi-Naini, R., Seberry, J. (eds.) ACISP 2003. LNCS, vol. 2727, pp. 312–323. Springer, Heidelberg (2003)
27. Zhang, F., Safavi-Naini, R., Lin, C.-Y.: New proxy signature, proxy blind signature and proxy ring signature schemes from bilinear pairing. IACR Cryptology ePrint Archive, 104 (2003)
28. Zhang, K.: Threshold proxy signature schemes. In: Okamoto, E. (ed.) ISW 1997. LNCS, vol. 1396, pp. 282–290. Springer, Heidelberg (1998)

Anonymous Signcryption against Linear Related-Key Attacks

Hui Cui, Yi Mu, and Man Ho Au

School of Computer Science and Software Engineering,
University of Wollongong, Wollongong, NSW 2522, Australia
hc892@uowmail.edu.au, {ymu,aau}@uow.edu.au

Abstract. A related-key attack (RKA) occurs when an adversary tampers the private key stored in a cryptographic hardware device and observes the result of the cryptographic primitive under this modified private key. In this paper, we concentrate on the security of anonymous signcryption schemes under related-key attacks, in the sense that a signcryption system should contain no information that identifies the sender of the signcryption and the receiver of the message, and yet be decipherable by the targeted receiver. To achieve this, we consider our anonymous signcryption scheme being semantically secure against chosen ciphertext and related-key attacks (CC-RKA), existentially unforgeable against chosen message and related-key attacks (CM-RKA), and anonymous against chosen ciphertext and related-key attacks (ANON-RKA). Specifically, we require that an anonymous signcryption scheme remains secure even when an adversary is allowed to access the signcryption oracle and the designcryption oracle on linear shifts of the private keys of the sender and the receiver, respectively. After reviewing some basic definitions related to our construction, based on the existing work on cryptographic primitives in the setting of related-key attacks, we give a concrete anonymous signcryption scheme from BDH which achieves CC-RKA security, CM-RKA security, ANON-RKA security in the random oracle model.

Keywords: Signcryption, CC-RKA, CM-RKA, Anonymity.

1 Introduction

In recent decades, physical attacks like side channel attacks [29] that exploit information leakage from the implementation of an algorithm are becoming increasingly popular and come in a large variety, where an adversary observes some "physical output" of a computation (such as radiation, power, temperature, running time), in addition to the "logical output" of the computation. In some of these situations, the adversary might get some partial information about private key through certain physical methods, which are referred to as key-leakage attacks. However, such attacks are not anticipated by the designer of the system and, correspondingly, not taken into account when arguing its security. Since modern notions of security, such as semantic security [17] and CCA security [30]

W. Susilo and R. Reyhanitabar (Eds.): ProvSec 2013, LNCS 8209, pp. 165–183, 2013.

in encryption systems, is formulated in a very desired way that the adversary can fully control almost all aspects of the system (that is, the adversary is able to encrypt messages and decrypt ciphertexts at its choice), but have no access to the private keys of the entities in the communication. Unfortunately, this assumption is too ideal to satisfy in the above scenarios.

To achieve such security requirements, it requires to capture security under the context where some information of the private key are leaked to the adversary. In this paper, we consider a special case of such attacks, where an adversary tampers the private key stored in a cryptographic hardware device and observes the result of the cryptographic primitive under this modified private key, called related-key attack (RKA) [16,8]. The key here could be a signing key of a certificate authority or a decryption key of an encryption scheme. In related-key attacks, the adversary attempts to break a cryptographic system by invoking it with several private keys satisfying some known relations.

Although the RKA security has been achieved in various cryptographic primitives, there are few considering anonymity, which requires that the identities of participants should not be leaked during the communication [1]. With this in mind, in this work, we propose an approach for anonymous signcryption secure against related-key attacks. Suppose the signcryption system is composed of algorithms, public parameters, as well as private and public key pairs of the sender and the receiver respectively, of which the private and public keys are subject to related-key attacks, and the public parameters are system-wide, i.e., they are set beforehand and independent of users. In a protocol run, all these parameters are possible to be tampered when distributed via a public channel.

For an anonymous signcryption system, the designcryption needs the private key of the receiver while the signcryption needs the private key of the sender, hence we consider related-key attacks on private keys of both sides: chosen ciphertext attack security under related-key attack (CC-RKA), chosen message attack security under related-key attack (CM-RKA), as well as anonymity under chosen ciphertext attack and related-key attack (ANON-RKA). The designcryption oracle is forbidden when the signcryption is equal to the challenged signcryption and the derived receiver's private key matches the original one. Also, the signcryption oracle will not be executed if the given plaintext is equal to the challenged plaintext and the derived sender's private key matches the original one. Note that we define our model on the basis of the definitions in [7,8,33].

To begin with, we need to solve a problem how to designcrypt a signcryption C with the private key $\phi(sk_R)$, where ϕ denotes a linear shift. This can be achieved with key homomorphism [33], which can reduce a signcryption scheme against related-key attacks with chosen ciphertext attack security and anonymity to a general chosen ciphertext attack secure and anonymous signcryption scheme with additional properties that the designcryption of a signcryption C with the private key $\phi(sk_R)$ equals the designcryption of another signcryption C' with the original private key sk_R. To consider the security one step further, key homomorphism fails when the signcryption C' equals the challenge signcryption in the chosen ciphertext attack security and anonymity games. Anyway, with the adaptive trapdoor relations mentioned in [22,32,33], this event will never happen, which can simply formulate that the challenge signcryption is an invalid signcryption for any receiver's private key $sk'_R \neq sk_R$, such that a valid signcryption with the public parameters decides a consistent private key uniquely. Next, we should consider to signcrypt a plaintext m with the private key $\phi(sk_S)$, where ϕ denotes a linear shift, yet the case where the plaintext m in the signcryption C' equals the plaintext in the output signcryption where $\phi(sk_S) \neq sk_S$. We adopt a collision resistant hash function in the signcryption, which disables the adversary to output a valid signcryption for any sender's private key $sk'_S \neq sk_S$. In this way, a valid signcryption with public parameters can only be constructed by a correct private key.

1.1   Related Work

Signcryption, introduced by Zheng [35] in 1997, is a cryptographic primitive "Signcryption" to combine the functions of digital signature and encryption in a single step with a cost lower than that required by signature-then-encryption approach. In 2002, Baek, Steinfeld, and Zheng [5] formalized and defined security notions for signcryption, which are similar to the chosen ciphertext attack security and chosen message attack security. The notion was first defined by Jee Hea An, Yevgeniy Dodis, Tal Rabin [3], where an adversary not only access the public keys of both the sender and the receiver but also know the private key of the sender, which later was extended to the security properties of signcryption [28,25]. Malone-Lee [28] proposed the first identity-based signcryption scheme, and claimed that their scheme achieves both privacy and unforgeability. Libert and Quisquater [25] pointed out that the scheme in [28] is not semantically secure in privacy as the signature of the message is not hidden in the signcrypted message, and proposed a signcryption scheme with ciphertext anonymity [26] based on gap Diffie-Hellman assumption, but Yang, Wong and Deng [34] found that it is not secure. Chow et al. [15] designed an identity-based signcryption scheme with public verifiability and forward security. Concurrently, Boyen [14] extended the security model in [28] via adding three new security notions: ciphertext unlinkability, ciphertext authentication and ciphertext anonymity. In addition, there are also some works concentrating on efficiency [6,23,24]. Barreto et al. [6] constructed an identity-based signcryption scheme which greatly improves the efficiency. Chung et al. [23] described a key privacy preserving signcryption scheme with high efficiency and simple design, and then they extended it to a ring signcryption scheme based on the technique due to Boneh et al. [13].

   In 2004, Micali and Reyzin [29] put forward a comprehensive framework for modeling security against side-channel attacks, which relies on the assumption that there is no leakage of information in absence of computation. Halderman et al. [19] in 2008 described a set of attacks violating the assumption of the framework of Micali and Reyzin. Specially speaking, their "cold boot" attacks showed that a significant fraction of the bits of a cryptographic key can be recovered if the key is ever stored in memory, of which the framework was modeled by

Akavia, Goldwasser and Vaikuntanathan [2]. Similarly, fault injection techniques can be used to falsify, inducing the internal state of the devices being modified, if given physical access to the hardware devices [11]. Bellare and Kohno [9] investigated related-key attacks from a theoretical point of view and presented an approach to formally handle the notion of related-key attacks. Followed the approach in [9], Lucks [27] presented some constructions for block ciphers and pseudorandom function generators. To solve the open problem in related-secret security whether or not related-key secure blockciphers exist, in 2010, Bellare and Cash [7] provided the first constructions to create related-secret pseudorandom bits. On the basis of the work in [7], Applebaum, Harnik, and Ishai [4] put forward some RKA secure symmetric encryption schemes, which can be used in garbled circuits in secure computation. In [8], Bellare, Cash and Miller found the approaches to build high-level primitives secure against related-key attacks like signatures, CCA secure public-key encryption, identity-based encryption, based on RKA secure pseudorandom functions. So far, efforts have been made to achieve RKA security about cryptographic systems such as signatures [18,10], CCA secure public-key encryption [33,10], identity-based encryption [10], in the setting of related-key deriving function being a class of constant functions, linear functions, affine functions, and polynomial functions.

The remainder of this paper is organized as follows. In Section 2, we briefly present the concepts associated to this work and our defined security model of RKA secure signcryption. In Section 3, we review the bilinear pairs and the complexity assumptions. In Section 4, we propose a specific construction of RKA secure signcryption from BDH, and prove its security in the random oracle model. Finally, we conclude this paper in Section 5.

2   Preliminaries

Firstly, we briefly describe the framework of signcryption, and some concepts related to RKA security. Then we details the security definitions of signcryption schemes with anonymity in the setting of related-key attacks.

2.1   Signcryption

Let $\mathcal{M}$ be the message space. An signcryption scheme is composed of the following four algorithms [24]: Setup, Keygen, Signcrypt, Designcrypt.

- Setup(1^λ) → $params$: Taking a security parameter λ as input, this algorithm outputs the public parameters $params$.
- Keygen(1^λ, $params$) → $(sk_R, pk_R),(sk_S, pk_S)$: Taking a security parameter λ and the public parameters $params$ as input, this algorithm outputs two private and public key pairs (sk_R, pk_R), (sk_S, pk_S).
- Signcrypt(1^λ, $params$, m, sk_S, pk_R) → C: Taking a security parameter λ, the public parameters $params$, a plaintext $m \in \mathcal{M}$, the private key sk_S and the public key pk_R as input, this algorithm outputs a signcryption C.

– Designcrypt(1^λ, *params*, C, sk_R, pk_S) $\rightarrow m/\bot$: Taking a security parameter λ, the public parameters *params*, a signcryption C, the private key sk_R, and the public key pk_S as input, this algorithm first computes a message and signature pair (m, σ) with sk_R, and checks its validity with pk_S. Then it outputs either $m \in \mathcal{M}$ for a valid signcryption, or $\bot$ in case of a invalid signcryption.

We require that a signcryption system is correct, meaning that if *params* $\leftarrow$ Setup(1^λ), (sk_R, pk_R),$(sk_S, pk_S) \leftarrow$ Keygen(1^λ, *params*) and $C \leftarrow$ Signcrypt(1^λ, *params*, m, sk_S, pk_R), then $m \leftarrow$ Designcrypt(1^λ, *params*, C, sk_R, pk_S).

2.2 RKA Security

Related-Key Deriving Functions. Our definition follows the notion of related-key deriving functions given in [9]. Briefly speaking, a class $\varPhi$ of related-key deriving functions ϕ: $sk_u \rightarrow sk_u$ is a finite set of functions with the same domain and range, which map a key to a related key. Additionally, $\varPhi$ should allow an efficient membership test, and ϕ should be efficiently computable. Note that in this paper, we only consider the class $\varPhi^+$ as linear shifts.

The family $\varPhi^+$. Any function $\phi : Z_q^* \rightarrow Z_q^*$ in this class is indexed by $\triangle \in Z_q^*$, where $\phi_\triangle(sk_u) := sk_u + \triangle$.

Informally, we consider a secure anonymous signcryption scheme against related-key attacks to be semantically secure against chosen ciphertext and related-key attacks (CC-RKA), existentially unforgeable against chosen message and related-key attacks (CM-RKA), and anonymous against related-key attacks in the sense that a signcryption should contain no information that identifies the sender of the signcryption and the receiver of the message (ANON-RKA), and yet be decipherable by the targeted receiver.

CC-RKA Security. A signcryption scheme is semantically secure against chosen ciphertext and related-key attacks (CC-RKA security) if no probabilistic polynomial-time adversary has a non-negligible advantages in the following game.

– Initialization. The challenger algorithm $\mathcal{B}$ runs *params* $\leftarrow$ Setup(1^k), and (sk_R, pk_R),$(sk_S, pk_S) \leftarrow$ Keygen(1^λ, *params*). Algorithm $\mathcal{B}$ gives the public parameters *params*, the private and public key pair (sk_S, pk_S), and the public key pk_R to the adversary algorithm $\mathcal{A}$.
– Phase 1. Algorithm $\mathcal{A}$ issues a series of queries to RKA.Designcrypt oracle. On input a signcryption C, and a related-key deriving function $\phi \in \varPhi$, algorithm $\mathcal{B}$ runs $(m, \sigma) \leftarrow$ Designcrypt(1^λ, *params*, C, $\phi(sk_R)$), and sends (m, σ) to algorithm $\mathcal{A}$. Note that as sk_S is given to algorithm $\mathcal{A}$, we remove the queries to RKA.Signcrypt oracle.
– Challenge. Algorithm $\mathcal{A}$ outputs two messages $M_0^*, M_1^* \in \mathcal{M}$, $|M_0^*| = |M_1^*|$, on which it wishes to be challenged. Algorithm $\mathcal{B}$ chooses a random $d \in \{0, 1\}$, and runs $C^* \leftarrow$ Signcrypt(1^λ, *params*, m_d, sk_S, pk_R). Algorithm $\mathcal{B}$ sends C^* as the designcryption to algorithm $\mathcal{A}$.

- Phase 2. Algorithm $\mathcal{A}$ continues to adaptively issue queries to RKA.Designcrypt oracle. On input a signcryption C, and a related-key deriving function $\phi \in \Phi$, with the constraint $(\phi(sk_R), C) \neq (sk_R, C^*)$, algorithm $\mathcal{B}$ responds as in Phase 1.
- Output. Algorithm $\mathcal{A}$ outputs its guess $d' \in \{0, 1\}$ for d and wins the game if $d' = d$.

We define algorithm $\mathcal{A}$'s advantage in this game to be

$$\text{Adv}_{\mathcal{A}}^{\text{CC-RKA}}(\lambda) \overset{\text{def}}{=} |\Pr[d = d'] - 1/2|.$$

CM-RKA Security. A signcryption scheme is existentially unforgeable against chosen message and related-key attacks (CM-RKA security) if no probabilistic polynomial-time adversary has a non-negligible advantages in the following game.

- Initialization. The challenger algorithm $\mathcal{B}$ runs $params \leftarrow$ Setup(1^k), and $(sk_R, pk_R), (sk_S, pk_S) \leftarrow$ Keygen($1^\lambda, params$). Algorithm $\mathcal{B}$ gives the public parameters $params$, the private and public key pair (sk_R, pk_R), and the public key pk_S to the adversary algorithm $\mathcal{A}$.
- Phase 1. Algorithm $\mathcal{A}$ issues a series of queries to RKA.Signcrypt oracle. On input a message $m \in \mathcal{M}$, and a related-key deriving function $\phi \in \Phi$, algorithm $\mathcal{B}$ runs $C \leftarrow$ Signcrypt($1^\lambda, params, m, \phi(sk_S), pk_R$), and sends C to algorithm $\mathcal{A}$. Note that as sk_R is given to algorithm $\mathcal{A}$, we remove the queries to RKA.Designcrypt oracle.
- Output. Algorithm $\mathcal{A}$ outputs a signcryption C^*, and wins the game if $(m^*, \sigma^*) \leftarrow$ Designcrypt($1^\lambda, params, C^*, sk_R$), and $true \leftarrow$ Verify($1^\lambda, params, m^*, \sigma^*$).

ANON-RKA Security. A signcryption scheme is anonymous against chosen ciphertext and related-key attacks (ANON-RKA security) if no probabilistic polynomial-time adversary has a non-negligible advantages in the following game.

- Initialization. The challenger algorithm $\mathcal{B}$ runs $params \leftarrow$ Setup(1^k), and $(sk_{R,0}, pk_{R,0}), (sk_{S,0}, pk_{S,0}) \leftarrow$ Keygen($1^\lambda, params$), $(sk_{R,1}, pk_{R,1}), (sk_{S,1}, pk_{S,1}) \leftarrow$ Keygen($1^\lambda, params$), respectively. Algorithm $\mathcal{B}$ gives the public parameters $params$, the private and public key pairs $(sk_{S,0}, pk_{S,0})$, $(sk_{S,1}, pk_{S,1})$, and the public keys $pk_{R,0}, pk_{R,1}$ to the adversary algorithm $\mathcal{A}$.
- Phase 1. Algorithm $\mathcal{A}$ issues a series of queries to RKA.Designcrypt oracle. On input $sk_S \in \{sk_{S,0}, sk_{S,1}\}$, $pk_R \in \{pk_{R,0}, pk_{R,1}\}$, a signcryption C, and a related-key deriving function $\phi \in \Phi$, algorithm $\mathcal{B}$ runs $(m, \sigma) \leftarrow$ Designcrypt($1^\lambda, params, C, \phi(sk_R)$), and sends (m, σ) to algorithm $\mathcal{A}$. Note that as $sk_{S,0}, sk_{S,1}$ are given to algorithm $\mathcal{A}$, we remove the queries to RKA.Signcrypt oracle.
- Challenge. Algorithm $\mathcal{A}$ outputs a message $M^* \in \mathcal{M}$ on which it wishes to be challenged. Algorithm $\mathcal{B}$ chooses random $d, e \in \{0, 1\}$, and runs $C^* \leftarrow$ Signcrypt($1^\lambda, params, m, sk_{S,d}, pk_{R,e}$). Algorithm $\mathcal{B}$ sends C^* as the designcryption to algorithm $\mathcal{A}$.

- Phase 2. Algorithm $\mathcal{A}$ continues to adaptively issue queries to RKA.Designcrypt oracle. On input $sk_S \in \{sk_{S,0}, sk_{S,1}\}$, $pk_R \in \{pk_{R,0}, pk_{R,1}\}$, a signcryption C, and a related-key deriving function $\phi \in \Phi$, with the constraint $(\phi(sk_{R,d}), C) \neq (sk_{R,d}, C^*)$, algorithm $\mathcal{B}$ responds as in Phase 1.
- Output. Algorithm $\mathcal{A}$ outputs its guess d', $e' \in \{0,1\}$ for d, e, and wins the game if $d' = d$ and $e' = e$.

We define algorithm $\mathcal{A}$'s advantage in this game to be

$$\mathrm{Adv}_{\mathcal{A}}^{\mathrm{ANON\text{-}RKA}}(\lambda) \stackrel{\mathrm{def}}{=} |\Pr[d = d' \wedge e = e'] - 1/4|.$$

3   Bilinear Maps and Complexity Assumptions

In this section, we review a few facts related to groups with efficiently computable bilinear maps, and the security assumptions that our new schemes based on.

3.1   Bilinear Maps

Let G and G_T be two multiplicative cyclic groups of prime order q. Let g be a generator of G, and $\hat{e} : G \times G \to G_T$ be a bilinear map with the following properties [12,20,21]: (1) Bilinear: for all $g \in G$ and a, $b \in Z_q^*$, we have $\hat{e}(g^a, g^b) = \hat{e}(g,g)^{ab}$; (2) Non-degenerate: $\hat{e}(g,g) \neq 1$.

We say that G is a bilinear group if the group action in G can be computed efficiently and there exists a group G_T and an efficiently computable bilinear map $\hat{e} : G \times G \to G_T$ as above.

3.2   Complexity Assumptions

Computational DL. The computational Discrete Logarithm (DL) problem is that for any probabilistic polynomial-time algorithm, it is difficult to compute b given (g, g^b), where $g \in G$, $b \in Z_q^*$ are chosen independently and uniformly at random.

Computational BDH. The computational bilinear Diffie-Hellman (BDH) problem is that for any probabilistic polynomial-time algorithm, it is difficult to compute $\hat{e}(g,g)^{abc}$ given (g, g^a, g^b, g^c), where $g \in G$, a, b, $c \in Z_q^*$ are chosen independently and uniformly at random.

Decisional BDH. The decisional bilinear Diffie-Hellman (BDH) problem is that for any probabilistic polynomial-time algorithm, it is difficult to distinguish $(g, g^a, g^b, g^c, \hat{e}(g,g)^{abc})$ from (g, g^a, g^b, g^c, Z), where $g \in G$, $Z \in G_T$, a, b, $c \in Z_q^*$ are chosen independently and uniformly at random.

4 Anonymous Signcryption from RKA Security

In this section, we propose a specific anonymous signcryption scheme in the setting of related-key attacks, and analyze its CC-RKA, CM-RKA and ANON-RKA security.

4.1 Techniques in Our Solution

To achieve key homomorphism [33], we make use of a class of functions with an additional input (namely tag), called adaptive trapdoor relations [22,32], which is easy to compute and invert with tag, but hard to invert without tag.

More specifically, our adaptive trapdoor relation F_{pk_u} satisfies the following features.

- Generation. This is a randomized algorithm G that outputs a pair (pk_u, sk_u) on input a security parameter λ.
- Sampling. On input pk_u and tag, this randomized algorithm F outputs $(\theta, F_{pk_u}(tag, \theta))$ for a random θ.
- Inversion. For all tag, y and (pk_u, sk_u), this efficient algorithm F' computes $F'(sk_u, tag, y) = F_{pk_u}^{-1}(tag, y)$.
- One-wayness. For a stateful adversary $\mathcal{A}$, it holds that

$$\Pr\left[\theta = \theta' \,\middle|\, \begin{array}{l} tag^* \leftarrow \mathcal{A}(1^\lambda). \\ (pk_u, sk_u) \leftarrow G(1^\lambda). \\ (\theta, y) \leftarrow F(pk_u, tag^*). \\ \theta' \leftarrow \mathcal{A}^{F_{pk_u}^{-1}(\cdot,\cdot)}(pk_u, y). \end{array}\right]$$

is a negligible function in λ, where adversary $\mathcal{A}$ is allowed to query $F_{pk_u}^{-1}(\cdot, \cdot)$ on any tag different from tag^*.

Key Homomorphism. Let Φ be a set of related-key deriving functions. We say that F_{pk_u} is Φ-key homomorphic if there is a probabilistic polynomial-time algorithm T such that $F'(\phi(sk_u), tag, y) = F'(sk_u, tag, T(\phi, tag, y))$ holds with overwhelming probability for all $\phi \in \Phi$, sk_u, tag and y.

4.2 Construction

Let $\hat{e} : G \times G \to G_T$ be a bilinear map over a bilinear group G of prime order q with a generator $g \in G$. The scheme is described as follows.

- Setup. To generate the system public parameters, this algorithm works as follows.
  1. Chooses random $\beta, \gamma \in Z_q^*$, and computes $g_1 = g^\beta$, $g_2 = g^\gamma$.
  2. Chooses collision resistant hash functions $H_0 : G^2 \to G$, $H : G^2 \to Z_q^*$, $H' : G^5 \times G_T^2 \to Z_q^*$.
  3. Outputs the public parameters $(g, g_1, g_2, H_0, H, H')$.

- Keygen. To generate two private and public key pairs for receiver R and sender S respectively, the system chooses random x_R, $x_S \in Z_q^*$ as the private keys, and computes $Y_R = g^{x_R}$, $Y_S = g^{x_S}$ as the public keys.
- Signcrypt. To signcrypt a message $m \in G_T$ for receiver R, sender S runs as follows.
  1. Chooses a random $r \in Z_q^*$, and computes $\mu = g^r$, $\theta = g_1^r$.
  2. Chooses a random $e \in Z_q^*$, and computes $tag = g^e$.
  3. Computes $\psi = \hat{e}(\theta, g_2) \cdot m$, and

$$\tau = (Y_R \cdot g_1{}^{H(\mu, tag)})^r \cdot H_0(\mu, Y_R{}^r),$$
$$\sigma = e - x_S \cdot H'(\mu, \tau, \psi, Y_R{}^r, Y_R{}^{x_S}, tag, m),$$

  4. Outputs the signcryption $C = (\mu, \tau, \psi, tag, \sigma)$.
- Designcrypt. To designcrypt a signcrypiton C from sender S, receiver R runs as follows.
  1. Computes θ as $\theta = (\frac{\tau}{H_0(\mu, \mu^{x_R})} \cdot \mu^{-x_R})^{\frac{1}{H(\mu, tag)}}$. If $\hat{e}(\theta, g) = \hat{e}(\mu, g_1)$, computes $m = \psi / \hat{e}(\theta, g_2)$, and outputs $(\mu, \tau, \psi, m, tag, \sigma)$. Otherwise, it outputs $\bot$.
  2. Check the validity of σ via $tag = g^\sigma \cdot Y_S{}^{H'(\mu, \tau, \psi, \mu^{x_R}, Y_S{}^{x_R}, tag, m)}$. If the equation holds, it outputs m. Otherwise, it outputs $\bot$.

4.3   Proof of Security

We analyze the security of our proposed signcryption scheme against related-key attacks by reducing its CC-RKA security, CM-RKA security, and ANON-RKA security under the security games defined in Section 2.

Theorem 1. *Assume that the decisional BDH assumption holds in G, G_T, the computational BDH problem holds in G, G_T, then our signcryption scheme is CC-RKA secure regarding linear related-key deriving functions ϕ^+ in the random oracle model.*

Let $(\mu^*, \tau^*, \psi^*, tag^*, \sigma^*)$ be the challenge signcryption of the message M_d given to algorithm $\mathcal{A}$ by algorithm $\mathcal{B}$. Denote Failure by the event that algorithm $\mathcal{A}$ issues $(\mu^*, \tau^*, \psi^*, Y_1, Y_2, M_0)$ or $(\mu^*, \tau^*, \psi^*, Y_1, Y_2, M_1)$ to random oracle H', and (μ, Y_1) to random oracle H_0, where $\hat{e}(Y_1, g) = \hat{e}(Y_R, \mu^*)$.

In what follows we prove that if the event Failure does not occur, then our signcryption scheme is CC-RKA secure. We conclude this proof by showing that the event Failure has a negligible probability to occur.

Lemma 1. *If the decisional BDH assumption holds in G, G_T, and the event Failure does not happen, then our signcryption scheme is CC-RKA secure.*

Proof. Suppose that algorithm $\mathcal{A}$ is an adversary algorithm against the CC-RKA security of our signcrypiton scheme, then we can construct a challenger algorithm $\mathcal{B}$ that solves the decisional BDH problem, which is given input a BDH instance

(g, g^a, g^b, g^c, Z) and outputs 1 (Z is $\hat{e}(g,g)^{abc}$) or 0 (Z is a random element in G_T).

Initialization. To simulate the system parameters, algorithm $\mathcal{B}$ runs as follows.

1. Chooses a collision resistant hash function $H : G^2 \to Z_q^*$.
2. Chooses a random $e^* \in Z_q^*$, computes $tag^* = g^{e^*}$.
3. Chooses a random $x_S \in Z_q^*$, computes computes $Y_S = g^{x_S}$.
4. Chooses a random $x_r \in Z_q^*$, computes $Y_R = (g^b)^{-H(g^c, tag^*)} g^{x_r}$. Note that $x_R = \log_g Y_R = -b \cdot H(g^c, tag^*) + x_r$ is unknown to algorithm $\mathcal{B}$.
5. Sends the public parameters $(g, g_1, g_2, H_0, H, H')$ of which $g_1 = g^b$, $g_2 = g^a$, H_0, H' are the random oracles controlled by algorithm $\mathcal{B}$, receiver R's public key Y_R, and sender S's public and private key pair (x_S, Y_S) to algorithm $\mathcal{A}$.

H_0-**query.** At any time algorithm $\mathcal{A}$ can query the random oracle on (μ, Y_1). Algorithm $\mathcal{B}$ maintains a list L_{H_0} of tuples $((\mu, Y_1), H_0(\mu, Y_1))$ which is initially empty. When algorithm $\mathcal{A}$ issues a hash query on Y, algorithm $\mathcal{B}$ responds as follows.

- If (μ, Y_1) already appears in list L_{H_0}, algorithm $\mathcal{B}$ responds with $H_0(\mu, Y_1)$.
- Otherwise, algorithm $\mathcal{B}$ chooses a random $t_i \in Z_q^*$, sets $H_0(\mu, Y_1) = t_i$, and adds $((\mu, Y_1), t_i)$ to list L_{H_0}.

H'-**query.** At any time algorithm $\mathcal{A}$ can query the random oracle on $(\mu, \tau, \psi, Y_1, Y_2, tag, m)$. Algorithm $\mathcal{B}$ maintains a list $L_{H'}$ of tuples $((\mu, \tau, \psi, Y_1, Y_2, tag, m), H'(\mu, \tau, \psi, Y_1, Y_2, tag, m))$ which is initially empty. When algorithm $\mathcal{A}$ issues a hash query on $(\mu, \tau, \psi, Y_1, Y_2, tag, m)$, algorithm $\mathcal{B}$ responds as follows.

- If $(\mu, \tau, \psi, Y_1, Y_2, tag, m)$ already appears in list $L_{H'}$, algorithm $\mathcal{B}$ responds with $H'(\mu, \tau, \psi, Y_1, Y_2, tag, m)$.
- Otherwise, algorithm $\mathcal{B}$ chooses a random $s_i \in Z_q^*$, sets $H'(\mu, \tau, \psi, Y_1, Y_2, tag, m) = s_i$, sends s_i to algorithm $\mathcal{A}$, and adds $((\mu, \tau, \psi, Y_1, Y_2, tag, M), s_i)$ to list $L_{H'}$.

Phase 1. Algorithm $\mathcal{A}$ adaptively issues the RKA designcryption queries to algorithm $\mathcal{B}$. For a query (C, ϕ) to RKA.Designcrypt oracle where $C = (\mu, \tau, \psi, tag, \sigma)$, algorithm $\mathcal{B}$ responds as follows.

1. Algorithm $\mathcal{B}$ computes θ' with $\phi(x_R)$. To see how algorithm $\mathcal{B}$ obtains θ without x_R, we rewrite τ such that

$$\frac{\tau}{t_i} = (Y_R \cdot g_1^{H(\mu, tag)})^r = \mu^{-b \cdot H(g^c, tag^*) + x_r + b \cdot H(\mu, tag)}$$

$$= (\mu^b)^{H(\mu, tag) - H(g^c, tag^*)} \cdot \mu^{x_r} = \theta^{H(\mu, tag) - H(g^c, tag^*)} \cdot \mu^{x_r}$$

$$\Rightarrow \theta = \left(\frac{\tau}{t_i \cdot \mu^{x_r}}\right)^{\frac{1}{H(\mu, tag) - H(g^c, tag^*)}}.$$

On the other hand,

$$\theta' = (\frac{\tau}{t_i} \cdot \mu^{-(x_R+\triangle)})^{\frac{1}{H(\mu,tag)}} = ((\frac{\tau}{t_i} \cdot \mu^{-\triangle}) \cdot \mu^{-x_R})^{\frac{1}{H(\mu,tag)}}$$

$$= \theta \cdot (\mu^{-\triangle})^{\frac{1}{H(\mu,tag)}}.$$

Note that this reflects how key homomorphism works in the adaptive trap-door relation [33].

2. If $\hat{e}(\theta', g) = \hat{e}(\mu, g_1)$, algorithm $\mathcal{B}$ outputs $m = \psi/\hat{e}(\theta', g_2)$. Otherwise, it outputs $\perp$.

Challenge. Algorithm $\mathcal{A}$ outputs two messages $M_0, M_1 \in G_T$ on which it wishes to be challenged. Algorithm $\mathcal{B}$ chooses random $s^*, t^* \in Z_q^*$, a random $d \in \{0,1\}$, sets $\mu^* = g^c$, and computes

$$\tau^* = (g^c)^{x_r} \cdot t^*, \quad \psi^* = Z \cdot M_d, \quad \sigma^* = e^* - x_S \cdot s^*.$$

Algorithm $\mathcal{B}$ outputs the signcryption $C^* = (\mu^*, \tau^*, \psi^*, tag^*, \sigma^*)$, and adds $((\mu^*, \tau^*, \psi^*, Y_R^c, Y_R^{x_S}, M_d), s^*)$ to list $L_{H'}$, $((\mu, Y_R^c), t^*)$ to list L_{H_0}.

Phase 2. Algorithm $\mathcal{A}$ adaptively issues the RKA designcryption queries to algorithm $\mathcal{B}$. For a query (C, ϕ) to RKA.Designcrypt oracle where $C = (\mu, \tau, \psi, tag, \sigma)$, algorithm $\mathcal{B}$ responds as follows.

- $H(\mu, tag) \neq H(g^c, tag^*)$. Algorithm $\mathcal{B}$ responds as in Phase 1.
- $H(\mu, tag) = H(g^c, tag^*)$, and $(\mu, \tau, \psi, \sigma) \neq (\mu^*, \tau^*, \psi^*, \sigma^*)$. If algorithm $\mathcal{B}$ accepts this signcryption, it means algorithm $\mathcal{A}$ breaks the security of the CM-RKA security of our scheme, which we will analyze later. Therefore, algorithm $\mathcal{B}$ outputs $\perp$ except with negligible probability.
- $H(\mu, tag) = H(g^c, tag^*)$, and $(\mu, \tau, \psi, \sigma) = (\mu^*, \tau^*, \psi^*, \sigma^*)$ and $\phi(x_R) \neq x_R$. If algorithm $\mathcal{B}$ accepts this signcryption, it means algorithm $\mathcal{A}$ can output $\phi \in \Phi$ such that $(\frac{\tau^*}{t^*} \cdot (\mu^*)^{-\phi(x_R)})^{\frac{1}{H(g^c,tag^*)}} \neq \perp$. That is, $\hat{e}(\theta', g) = \hat{e}(\mu, g_1)$, to guarantee this,

$$(\frac{\tau^*}{t^*} \cdot (\mu^*)^{-x_R})^{\frac{1}{H(g^c,tag^*)}} = (\frac{\tau^*}{t^*} \cdot (\mu^*)^{-\phi(x_R)})^{\frac{1}{H(g^c,tag^*)}} \Rightarrow x_R = \phi(x_R)$$

should hold. Therefore, algorithm $\mathcal{B}$ outputs $\perp$ except with negligible probability.

In fact this is the one-wayness property of the adaptive trapdoor relation, which on the other hand reflects how the key fingerprint property, which is indispensable according to the definitions given in [7,4,33], works in our construction.

Note that (C, ϕ) satisfying $H(\mu, tag) = H(g^c, tag^*)$, $(\mu, \tau, \psi, \sigma) = (\mu^*, \tau^*, \psi^*, \sigma^*)$ and $\phi(x_R) = x_R$, is not allowed by the definition of the CC-RKA security game.

Output. Algorithm $\mathcal{A}$ outputs a guess $d' \in \{0,1\}$. If $d = d'$, algorithm $\mathcal{A}$ wins the game, and algorithm $\mathcal{B}$ outputs 1 indicating $Z = \hat{e}(g,g)^{abc}$. Otherwise, algorithm $\mathcal{B}$ outputs 0 indicating Z is random in G_T.

Let ϵ be the advantage that algorithm $\mathcal{A}$ breaks the CC-RKA security of the above game. We can see that if algorithm $\mathcal{B}$'s input tuple is (g, g^a, g^b, g^c, Z) where $Z = \hat{e}(g,g)^{abc}$, then algorithm $\mathcal{A}$'s view of this simulation is identical to the real attack, thus algorithm $\mathcal{A}$'s probability in outputting $d' = d$ must satisfy $\Pr[d = d'] = 1/2 + \epsilon$. On the other hand, if algorithm $\mathcal{B}$'s input tuple (g, g^a, g^b, g^c, Z) where $Z \in G_T$, then algorithm $\mathcal{A}$'s advantage is nil and thus $\Pr[d' = d] = 1/2$. To sum up, algorithm $\mathcal{B}$'s probability in solving the decisional BDH problem is

$$\Pr[\mathcal{B}(g,g^a,g^b,g^c,Z)] = 1/2 \cdot (1/2 + \epsilon) + 1/2 \cdot 1/2 = 1/2 + \epsilon/2.$$

In the following, we prove that the event Failure has a negligible probability to occur due to the security of the computational DH problem hiding in hash function H'.

Lemma 2. *If the computational BDH problem holds in G, G_T, then the event Failure happens with a negligible probability.*

Proof. Given algorithm $\mathcal{A}$ for which the event Failure happens with a noticeable probability, we construct an algorithm $\mathcal{B}'$ that solves the computational BDH problem. Specifically, we consider the following game where algorithm $\mathcal{B}'$ solves the computational BDH problem. Suppose that algorithm $\mathcal{B}'$ is given a random tuple (g, g^a, g^b, g^c) as input and outputs $\hat{e}(g,g)^{abc}$.

Initialization. The same as in Lemma 1.

H_0-query. At any time algorithm $\mathcal{A}$ can query the random oracle on (μ, Y_1). Algorithm $\mathcal{B}$ maintains a list L_{H_0} of tuples $((\mu, Y_1), H_0(\mu, Y_1))$ which is initially empty. When algorithm $\mathcal{A}$ issues a hash query on (μ, Y_1), algorithm $\mathcal{B}$ responds as follows.

- If $\hat{e}(Y_1, g) = \hat{e}(Y_R, g^c)$, algorithm $\mathcal{B}$ solves the computational BDH problem immediately. To see this, we have

$$Y_1 = Y_R{}^c = (g^{bc})^{-H(g^c, tag^*)} g^{c \cdot x_r}$$

$$\Rightarrow g^{bc} = (\frac{Y_1}{g^{c \cdot x_r}})^{-\frac{1}{H(g^c, tag^*)}} \Rightarrow \hat{e}(g,g)^{abc} = \hat{e}(g^a, g^{bc}).$$

- If (μ, Y_1) already appears in list L_{H_0}, algorithm $\mathcal{B}$ responds with $H_0(\mu, Y_R{}^r)$.
- Otherwise, algorithm $\mathcal{B}$ chooses a random $t_i \in Z_q^*$, sets $H_0(\mu, Y_1) = t_i$, and adds $((\mu, Y_1), t_i)$ to list L_{H_0}.

H'-query. At any time algorithm $\mathcal{A}$ can query the random oracle on $(\mu, \tau, \psi, Y_1, Y_2, tag, m)$, Algorithm $\mathcal{B}$ maintains a list $L_{H'}$ of tuples $((\mu, \tau, \psi, Y_1, Y_2, tag, m), H'(\mu, \tau, \psi, Y_1, Y_2, tag, m))$ which is initially empty. When algorithm $\mathcal{A}$ issues a hash query on $(\mu, \tau, \psi, Y_1, Y_2, tag, m)$, algorithm $\mathcal{B}$ responds as follows.

- If $\hat{e}(Y_1, g) = \hat{e}(Y_R, g^c)$, the same as that in H_0 query.
- If $(\mu, \tau, \psi, Y_1, Y_2, tag, m)$ already appears in list $L_{H'}$, algorithm $\mathcal{B}$ responds with $H'(\mu, \tau, \psi, Y_1, Y_2, tag, m)$.
- Otherwise, algorithm $\mathcal{B}$ chooses a random $s_i \in Z_q^*$, sets $H'(\mu, \tau, \psi, Y_1, Y_2, tag, m) = s_i$, sends s_i to algorithm $\mathcal{A}$, and adds $((\mu, \tau, \psi, Y_1, Y_2, tag, m), s_i)$ to list $L_{H'}$.

Phase 1. The same as in Lemma 1.

Challenge. Algorithm $\mathcal{A}$ outputs two messages $M_0, M_1 \in G_T$ on which it wishes to be challenged. Algorithm $\mathcal{B}'$ chooses random $r^*, s^*, t^* \in Z_q^*$, and computes

$$\mu^* = g^{r^*}, \quad \tau^* = (Y_R \cdot g_1^{H(\mu^*, tag^*)})^{r^*} \cdot t^*,$$
$$\psi^* = \hat{e}(g_1, g_2)^{r^*} \cdot M_d, \quad \sigma^* = e^* - x_S \cdot s^*,$$

Algorithm $\mathcal{B}$ outputs the signcryption $C^* = (\mu^*, \tau^*, \psi^*, tag^*, \sigma^*)$, and adds $((\mu^*, \tau^*, \psi^*, Y_R^{r^*}, Y_R^{x_S}, tag^*, M_d), s^*)$ to list $L_{H'}$, $(Y_R^{r^*}, t^*)$ to list L_{H_0}.

Phase 2. The same as in Lemma 1.

Lemma 1 makes sure that as long as the event Failure does not happen, then our signcryption scheme preserves CC-RKA security. Lemma 2 guarantees that as long as the event Failure does not happen, algorithm $\mathcal{B}'$ is the same as algorithm $\mathcal{B}$ such that algorithm $\mathcal{A}$ cannot differentiate between algorithm $\mathcal{B}$ and algorithm $\mathcal{B}'$.

This completes the proof of CC-RKA security of our signcryption scheme.

Theorem 2. *Assume that the computational DL problem holds in G, then our signcryption scheme is CM-RKA secure regarding linear related-key deriving functions ϕ^+ in the random oracle.*

Proof. Suppose that algorithm $\mathcal{A}$ is an adversary breaks the CM-RKA security of our signcrypiton scheme, we construct algorithm $\mathcal{B}$ that solves the computational DL problem which is given input a random tuple (g, g^b) and outputs b.

Initialization. To simulate the system parameters, algorithm $\mathcal{B}$ runs as follows.

1. Chooses collision resistant hash functions $H_0 : G^2 \rightarrow G$, $H : G^2 \rightarrow Z_q^*$,
2. Chooses a random $a \in Z_q^*$, computes $g_2 = g^a$, and then chooses a random $x_R \in Z_q^*$, computes $Y_R = g^{x_R}$, and a random $x_s \in Z_q^*$, computes $Y_S = (g^b)^{x_s}$. Note that $x_S = \log_g Y_S = b \cdot x_s$, which is unknown to algorithm $\mathcal{B}$.
3. Sends the public parameters $(g, g_1, g_2, H_0, H, H')$ of which $g_1 = g^b$, where H' is a random oracle controlled by algorithm $\mathcal{B}$, receiver R's public and private key pair (x_R, Y_R), and sender S's public key Y_S to algorithm $\mathcal{A}$.

H'-**query.** At any time algorithm $\mathcal{A}$ can query the random oracle on $(\mu, \tau, \psi, Y_1, Y_2, tag, m)$. Algorithm $\mathcal{B}$ maintains a list $L_{H'}$ of tuples $((\mu, \tau, \psi, Y_1, Y_2, tag, m), H'(\mu, \tau, \psi, Y_1, Y_2, tag, m))$ which is initially empty. When algorithm $\mathcal{A}$ issues a hash query on $(\mu, \tau, \psi, Y_1, Y_2, tag, m)$, algorithm $\mathcal{B}$ responds as follows.

- If $(\mu, \tau, \psi, Y_1, Y_2, tag, m)$ already appears in list $L_{H'}$, algorithm $\mathcal{B}$ responds with $H'(\mu, \tau, \psi, Y_1, Y_2, tag, m)$.
- Otherwise, algorithm $\mathcal{B}$ chooses a random $s_i \in Z_q^*$, sets $H'(\mu, \tau, \psi, Y_1, Y_2, tag, m) = s_i$, sends s_i to algorithm $\mathcal{A}$, and adds $((\mu, \tau, \psi, Y_1, Y_2, tag, m), s_i)$ to list $L_{H'}$.

Phase 1. Algorithm $\mathcal{A}$ adaptively issues the RKA signcryption queries to algorithm $\mathcal{B}$. Once algorithm $\mathcal{A}$ queries (m, ϕ) to RKA.Signcrypt oracle, algorithm $\mathcal{B}$ responds as follows.

1. Chooses a random $r \in Z_q^*$, and computes $\mu = g^r$.
2. Chooses random $\sigma, s_i \in Z_q^*$, and computes $tag = g^\sigma \cdot Y_S{}^{s_i}$, $\tau = (Y_R \cdot g_1{}^{H(\mu, tag)})^r \cdot H_0(\mu, Y_R{}^r)$, and $\psi = \hat{e}(g_1{}^r, g_2) \cdot m$.
3. Outputs the signcryption $C = (\mu, \tau, \psi, tag, \sigma)$, and adds $((\mu, \tau, \psi, Y_R{}^r, Y_R{}^{x_S + \triangle}, tag, m), s_i)$ to list $L_{H'}$.

Output. Algorithm $\mathcal{A}$ outputs a signcryption $C^* = (\mu^*, \tau^*, \psi^*, tag^*, \sigma^*)$, and algorithm $\mathcal{B}$ designcrypts it following the designcryption algorithm. If this is a valid signcryption, from the Forking Lemma in [31], after a polynomial replay attack of algorithm $\mathcal{A}$, we obtain two valid signcryption $(\mu^*, \tau^*, \psi^*, tag^*, \sigma^*)$ and $(\mu^*, \tau^*, \psi^*, tag^*, \sigma)$ with $s_i \neq s^*$, from which we have

$$tag^* = g^{\sigma^*} \cdot Y_S{}^{s^*} = g^\sigma \cdot Y_S{}^{s_i} \Rightarrow Y_S = g^{\frac{\sigma - \sigma^*}{s^* - s_i}} \Rightarrow b = \frac{\sigma - \sigma^*}{x_s \cdot (s^* - s_i)}.$$

That is, algorithm $\mathcal{B}$ solves the computational DL problem.

This completes the proof of CM-RKA security of our signcryption scheme.

Theorem 3. *Assume that the computational BDH assumption holds in G, G_T, then our signcryption scheme is ANON-RKA secure regarding linear related-key deriving functions ϕ^+ in the random oracle model.*

Proof. This part is similar to that of Theorem 1. Denote Failure by the event that algorithm $\mathcal{A}$ issues $(\mu^*, \tau^*, \psi^*, Y_1, Y_2, M^*)$ to random oracle H', and (μ, Y_1) to random oracle H_0, where $\hat{e}(Y_1, g) = \hat{e}(Y_R, \mu^*)$. We firstly prove that if the event Failure does not occur, our signcryption scheme is ANON-RKA secure; then conclude it by that the event Failure has a negligible probability to occur.

Suppose there is an adversary algorithm $\mathcal{A}$ against the anonymity of our RKA secure signcryption scheme. We construct a challenge algorithm $\mathcal{B}$ that solves the computational BDH problem, which is given a random tuple (g, g^a, g^b, g^c) as input and outputs $Z = \hat{e}(g, g)^{abc}$.

Initialization. To simulate the system parameters, algorithm $\mathcal{B}$ runs as follows.

1. Chooses a collision resistant hash function $H : G^2 \to Z_q^*$.
2. Chooses a random $e^* \in Z_q^*$, computes $tag^* = g^{e^*}$.
3. Chooses random $x_{S,0}, x_{S,1} \in Z_q^*$, computes $Y_{S,0} = g^{x_{S,0}}$, $Y_{S,1} = g^{x_{S,1}}$.
4. Chooses random $x_{r,0}, x_{r,1} \in Z_q^*$, computes $Y_{R,0} = (g^b)^{-H(g^c, tag^*)} g^{x_{r,0}}$, $Y_{R,1} = (g^b)^{-H(g^c, tag^*)} g^{x_{r,1}}$.
5. Sends $(g, g_1, g_2, H_0, H, H', (x_{S,0}, Y_{S,0}), (x_{S,0}, Y_{S,1}), Y_{R,0}, Y_{R,1})$ to algorithm $\mathcal{A}$, where $g_1 = g^b$, $g_2 = g^a$, H_0, H' are the random oracles controlled by algorithm $\mathcal{B}$.

H_0-**query.** At any time algorithm $\mathcal{A}$ can query the random oracle on (μ, Y_1). Algorithm $\mathcal{B}$ maintains a list L_{H_0} of tuples $((\mu, Y_1), H_0(\mu, Y_1))$ which is initially empty. When algorithm $\mathcal{A}$ issues a hash query on (μ, Y_1), algorithm $\mathcal{B}$ responds as follows.

- If $\hat{e}(Y_1, g) = \hat{e}(Y_{R,e}, g^c)$ for $e \in \{0, 1\}$, algorithm $\mathcal{B}$ solves the computational BDH problem immediately. To see this, we have

$$Y_1 = Y_{R,e}{}^c = (g^{bc})^{-H(g^c, tag^*)} g^{c \cdot x_r}$$
$$\Rightarrow g^{bc} = (\frac{Y_1}{g^{c \cdot x_r}})^{-\frac{1}{H(g^c, tag^*)}} \Rightarrow \hat{e}(g, g)^{abc} = \hat{e}(g^a, g^{bc}).$$

- If (μ, Y_1) already appears in list L_{H_0}, algorithm $\mathcal{B}$ responds with $H_0(\mu, Y_1)$.
- Otherwise, algorithm $\mathcal{B}$ chooses a random $t_i \in Z_q^*$, sets $H_0(\mu, Y_1) = t_i$, and adds $((\mu, Y_1), t_i)$ to list L_{H_0}.

H'-**query.** At any time algorithm $\mathcal{A}$ can query the random oracle on $(\mu, \tau, \psi, Y_1, Y_2, tag, m)$. Algorithm $\mathcal{B}$ maintains a list $L_{H'}$ of tuples $((\mu, \tau, \psi, Y_1, Y_2, tag, m), H'(\mu, \tau, \psi, Y_1, Y_2, tag, m))$ which is initially empty. When algorithm $\mathcal{A}$ issues a hash query on $(\mu, \tau, \psi, Y_1, Y_2, tag, m)$, algorithm $\mathcal{B}$ responds as follows.

- If $\hat{e}(Y_1, g) = \hat{e}(Y_{R,e}, g^c)$ for $e \in \{0, 1\}$, the same as that in H_0 query.
- If $(\mu, \tau, \psi, Y_1, Y_2, tag, m)$ already appears in list $L_{H'}$, algorithm $\mathcal{B}$ responds with $H'(\mu, \tau, \psi, Y_1, Y_2, tag, m)$.
- Otherwise, algorithm $\mathcal{B}$ chooses a random $s_i \in Z_q^*$, sets $H'(\mu, \tau, \psi, Y_1, Y_2, tag, m) = s_i$, sends s_i to algorithm $\mathcal{A}$, and adds $((\mu, \tau, \psi, Y_1, Y_2, tag, m), s_i)$ to list $L_{H'}$.

Phase 1. Algorithm $\mathcal{A}$ chooses (x_S, Y_R), where $x_S \in \{x_{S,0}, x_{S,1}\}$, $Y_R \in \{Y_{R,0}, Y_{R,1}\}$, and adaptively issues the RKA designcryption queries to algorithm $\mathcal{B}$. For a query (C, ϕ) to RKA.Designcrypt oracle where $C = (\mu, \tau, \psi, tag, \sigma)$, algorithm $\mathcal{B}$ responds as follows.

1. Algorithm $\mathcal{B}$ computes θ' with $\phi(x_R)$. To see how algorithm $\mathcal{B}$ obtains θ without x_R, we rewrite τ such that

$$\frac{\tau}{t_i} = (Y_R \cdot g_1{}^{H(\mu,tag)})^r = \mu^{-b \cdot H(g^c,tag^*) + x_r + b \cdot H(\mu,tag)}$$

$$= (\mu^b)^{H(\mu,tag) - H(g^c,tag^*)} \cdot \mu^{x_r} = \theta^{H(\mu,tag) - H(g^c,tag^*)} \cdot \mu^{x_r}$$

$$\Rightarrow \theta = (\frac{\tau}{t_i \cdot \mu^{x_r}})^{\frac{1}{H(\mu,tag) - H(g^c,tag^*)}}.$$

On the other hand,

$$\theta' = (\frac{\tau}{t_i} \cdot \mu^{-(x_R + \triangle)})^{\frac{1}{H(\mu,tag)}} = ((\frac{\tau}{t_i} \cdot \mu^{-\triangle}) \cdot \mu^{-x_R})^{\frac{1}{H(\mu,tag)}}$$

$$= \theta \cdot (\mu^{-\triangle})^{\frac{1}{H(\mu,tag)}}.$$

2. If $\hat{e}(\theta', g) = \hat{e}(\mu, g_1)$, algorithm $\mathcal{B}$ outputs $m = \psi/\hat{e}(\theta', g_2)$. Otherwise, it outputs $\perp$.

Challenge. Algorithm $\mathcal{A}$ outputs a message $M^* \in G_T$ on which it wishes to be challenged. Algorithm $\mathcal{B}$ chooses random $s^*, t^* \in Z_q^*$, $d, e \in \{0, 1\}$, $Z \in G_T$, sets $\mu^* = g^c$, and computes

$$\tau^* = (g^c)^{x_{r,e}} \cdot t^*, \quad \psi^* = Z \cdot M^*, \quad \sigma^* = e^* - x_{S,d} \cdot s^*.$$

Algorithm $\mathcal{B}$ outputs the signcryption $C^* = (\mu^*, \tau^*, \psi^*, tag^*, \sigma^*)$, and adds $((\mu^*, \tau^*, \psi^*, (Y_{R,e})^c, Y_{R,e}{}^{x_{S,d}}, tag^*, M^*), s^*)$ to list $L_{H'}$, $((g^c, (Y_{R,e})^c), t^*)$ to list L_{H_0}.

Phase 2. Algorithm $\mathcal{A}$ chooses (x_S, Y_R), where $x_S \in \{x_{S,0}, x_{S,1}\}$, $Y_R \in \{Y_{R,0}, Y_{R,1}\}$, and adaptively issues the RKA designcryption queries to algorithm $\mathcal{B}$. For a query (C, ϕ) to RKA.Designcrypt oracle where $C = (\mu, \tau, \psi, tag, \sigma)$, algorithm $\mathcal{B}$ responds as follows.

- $H(\mu, tag) \neq H(g^c, tag^*)$. Algorithm $\mathcal{B}$ responds as in Phase 1.
- $H(\mu, tag) = H(g^c, tag^*)$, and $(\mu, \tau, \psi, \sigma) \neq (\mu^*, \tau^*, \psi^*, \sigma^*)$. If algorithm $\mathcal{B}$ accepts this signcryption, it means algorithm $\mathcal{A}$ breaks the security of the CM-RKA security of our scheme. Therefore, algorithm $\mathcal{B}$ outputs $\perp$ except with negligible probability.
- $H(\mu, tag) = H(g^c, tag^*)$, $(\mu, \tau, \psi, \sigma) = (\mu^*, \tau^*, \psi^*, \sigma^*)$ and $\phi(x_R) \neq x_R$. If algorithm $\mathcal{B}$ accepts this signcryption, it means algorithm $\mathcal{A}$ can output $\phi \in \Phi$ such that $(\frac{\tau^*}{t^*} \cdot (\mu^*)^{-\phi(x_R)})^{\frac{1}{H(g^c,tag^*)}} \neq \perp$. That is, $\hat{e}(\theta', g) = \hat{e}(\mu, g_1)$. To guarantee this,

$$(\frac{\tau^*}{t^*} \cdot (\mu^*)^{-x_R})^{\frac{1}{H(g^c,tag^*)}} = (\frac{\tau^*}{t^*} \cdot (\mu^*)^{-\phi(x_R)})^{\frac{1}{H(g^c,tag^*)}} \Rightarrow x_R = \phi(x_R)$$

should hold. Therefore, algorithm $\mathcal{B}$ outputs $\perp$ except with negligible probability.

Analysis. Algorithm $\mathcal{A}$ has negligible probability to issue (g^c, Y_1) to random oracle H_0 such that $\hat{e}(Y_1, g) = \hat{e}(g^c, Y_{R,e})$ for $e \in \{0, 1\}$. If so, algorithm $\mathcal{B}$ can solve the computational BDH problem immediately. On the other hand, without the value of $H_0(\mu, Y_{R,e}{}^c)$, algorithm $\mathcal{A}$ has no idea about the identity of receiver R from the challenge signcryption C^*. Likewise, algorithm $\mathcal{A}$ has negligible probability to issue $(\mu^*, \tau^*, \psi^*, Y_1, Y_2, M^*)$ to random oracle H' such that $\hat{e}(Y_1, g) = \hat{e}(g^c, Y_{R,e})$; otherwise, algorithm $\mathcal{B}$ can solve the computational BDH problem immediately. Obviously, without the value of $H'(\mu^*, \tau^*, \psi^*, Y_{R,e}{}^c, Y_{R,e}{}^{x_{S,d}}, M^*)$, algorithm $\mathcal{A}$ cannot distinguish the identity of sender S from the challenge signcryption C^* via verification.

This completes the proof of ANON-RKA security of our signcryption scheme.

5 Conclusions

With the development of information technology, there has been a great interest in anonymous systems. On the other hand, traditional security notions cannot meet the requirements in the scenarios where the adversaries might get some partial information about private keys through certain physical methods. Motivated by the above, following the work in [8,33], in this paper, we focus on the construction of anonymous signcryption schemes secure against related-key attacks. We put forward a specific anonymous signcryption scheme from BDH under the setting of related-key attacks, where an adversary can subsequently observe the outcome of the signcryption and designcryption algorithms under a series of modified private keys of the sender and the receiver (related to the original private keys of the sender and the receiver), respectively. On the basis of the work in [10,33], we define the security model for anonymous signcryption systems which can resist related-key attacks while maintaining chosen ciphertext attack security (CC-RKA security), chosen message attack security (CM-RKA security) and anonymity, in the sense that a signcryption should contain no information that identifies the sender of the signcryption and the receiver of the message (ANON-RKA), where an adversary is allowed to issue queries to designcryption oracle on linear shifts of the private key of the receiver, and signcryption oracle on linear shifts of the private key of the sender.

References

1. Abdalla, M., Bellare, M., Catalano, D., Kiltz, E., Kohno, T., Lange, T., Malone-Lee, J., Neven, G., Paillier, P., Shi, H.: Searchable encryption revisited: Consistency properties, relation to anonymous IBE, and extensions. In: Shoup, V. (ed.) CRYPTO 2005. LNCS, vol. 3621, pp. 205–222. Springer, Heidelberg (2005)
2. Akavia, A., Goldwasser, S., Vaikuntanathan, V.: Simultaneous hardcore bits and cryptography against memory attacks. In: Reingold, O. (ed.) TCC 2009. LNCS, vol. 5444, pp. 474–495. Springer, Heidelberg (2009)
3. An, J.H., Dodis, Y., Rabin, T.: On the security of joint signature and encryption. In: Knudsen, L.R. (ed.) EUROCRYPT 2002. LNCS, vol. 2332, pp. 83–107. Springer, Heidelberg (2002)

4. Applebaum, B., Harnik, D., Ishai, Y.: Semantic security under related-key attacks and applications. In: ICS. Tsinghua University Press (2011)
5. Baek, J., Steinfeld, R., Zheng, Y.: Formal proofs for the security of signcryption. In: Naccache, D., Paillier, P. (eds.) PKC 2002. LNCS, vol. 2274, pp. 80–98. Springer, Heidelberg (2002)
6. Barreto, P.S.L.M., Libert, B., McCullagh, N., Quisquater, J.-J.: Efficient and provably-secure identity-based signatures and signcryption from bilinear maps. In: Roy, B. (ed.) ASIACRYPT 2005. LNCS, vol. 3788, pp. 515–532. Springer, Heidelberg (2005)
7. Bellare, M., Cash, D.: Pseudorandom functions and permutations provably secure against related-key attacks. In: Rabin, T. (ed.) CRYPTO 2010. LNCS, vol. 6223, pp. 666–684. Springer, Heidelberg (2010)
8. Bellare, M., Cash, D., Miller, R.: Cryptography secure against related-key attacks and tampering. In: Lee, D.H., Wang, X. (eds.) ASIACRYPT 2011. LNCS, vol. 7073, pp. 486–503. Springer, Heidelberg (2011)
9. Bellare, M., Kohno, T.: A theoretical treatment of related-key attacks: RKA-PRPS, RKA-PRFS, and applications. In: Biham, E. (ed.) EUROCRYPT 2003. LNCS, vol. 2656, pp. 491–506. Springer, Heidelberg (2003)
10. Bellare, M., Paterson, K.G., Thomson, S.: RKA security beyond the linear barrier: IBE, encryption and signatures. In: Wang, X., Sako, K. (eds.) ASIACRYPT 2012. LNCS, vol. 7658, pp. 331–348. Springer, Heidelberg (2012)
11. Biham, E.: New types of cryptoanalytic attacks using related keys (extended abstract). In: Helleseth, T. (ed.) EUROCRYPT 1993. LNCS, vol. 765, pp. 398–409. Springer, Heidelberg (1994)
12. Boneh, D., Franklin, M.: Identity-based encryption from the weil pairing. In: Kilian, J. (ed.) CRYPTO 2001. LNCS, vol. 2139, pp. 213–219. Springer, Heidelberg (2001)
13. Boneh, D., Gentry, C., Lynn, B., Shacham, H.: Aggregate and verifiably encrypted signatures from bilinear maps. In: Biham, E. (ed.) EUROCRYPT 2003. LNCS, vol. 2656, pp. 416–432. Springer, Heidelberg (2003)
14. Boyen, X.: Multipurpose identity-based signcryption (a swiss army knife for identity-based cryptography). In: Boneh, D. (ed.) CRYPTO 2003. LNCS, vol. 2729, pp. 383–399. Springer, Heidelberg (2003)
15. Chow, S.S.M., Yiu, S.-M., Hui, L.C.K., Chow, K.P.: Efficient forward and provably secure id-based signcryption scheme with public verifiability and public ciphertext authenticity. In: Lim, J.-I., Lee, D.-H. (eds.) ICISC 2003. LNCS, vol. 2971, pp. 352–369. Springer, Heidelberg (2004)
16. Gennaro, R., Lysyanskaya, A., Malkin, T., Micali, S., Rabin, T.: Algorithmic tamper-proof (ATP) security: Theoretical foundations for security against hardware tampering. In: Naor, M. (ed.) TCC 2004. LNCS, vol. 2951, pp. 258–277. Springer, Heidelberg (2004)
17. Goldwasser, S., Micali, S.: Probabilistic encryption and how to play mental poker keeping secret all partial information. In: STOC, pp. 365–377. ACM (1982)
18. Goyal, V., O'Neill, A., Rao, V.: Correlated-input secure hash functions. In: Ishai, Y. (ed.) TCC 2011. LNCS, vol. 6597, pp. 182–200. Springer, Heidelberg (2011)
19. Halderman, J.A., Schoen, S.D., Heninger, N., Clarkson, W., Paul, W., Calandrino, J.A., Feldman, A.J., Appelbaum, J., Felten, E.W.: Lest we remember: Cold boot attacks on encryption keys. In: USENIX Security Symposium, pp. 45–60. USENIX Association (2008)
20. Joux, A.: A one round protocol for tripartite diffie-hellman. In: Bosma, W. (ed.) ANTS 2000. LNCS, vol. 1838, pp. 385–394. Springer, Heidelberg (2000)

21. Joux, A., Nguyen, K.: Separating decision diffie-hellman from computational diffie-hellman in cryptographic groups. J. Cryptology 16(4), 239–247 (2003)
22. Kiltz, E., Mohassel, P., O'Neill, A.: Adaptive trapdoor functions and chosen-ciphertext security. In: Gilbert, H. (ed.) EUROCRYPT 2010. LNCS, vol. 6110, pp. 673–692. Springer, Heidelberg (2010)
23. Li, C.K., Yang, G., Wong, D.S., Deng, X., Chow, S.S.M.: An efficient signcryption scheme with key privacy. In: López, J., Samarati, P., Ferrer, J.L. (eds.) EuroPKI 2007. LNCS, vol. 4582, pp. 78–93. Springer, Heidelberg (2007)
24. Li, C.K., Yang, G., Wong, D.S., Deng, X., Chow, S.S.M.: An efficient signcryption scheme with key privacy and its extension to ring signcryption. Journal of Computer Security 18(3), 451–473 (2010)
25. Libert, B., Quisquater, J.-J.: New identity based signcryption schemes from pairings. IACR Cryptology ePrint Archive 2003, 23 (2003)
26. Libert, B., Quisquater, J.-J.: Efficient signcryption with key privacy from gap diffie-hellman groups. In: Bao, F., Deng, R., Zhou, J. (eds.) PKC 2004. LNCS, vol. 2947, pp. 187–200. Springer, Heidelberg (2004)
27. Lucks, S.: Ciphers secure against related-key attacks. In: Roy, B., Meier, W. (eds.) FSE 2004. LNCS, vol. 3017, pp. 359–370. Springer, Heidelberg (2004)
28. Malone-Lee, J.: Identity-based signcryption. IACR Cryptology ePrint Archive 2002, 98 (2002)
29. Micali, S., Reyzin, L.: Physically observable cryptography (extended abstract). In: Naor, M. (ed.) TCC 2004. LNCS, vol. 2951, pp. 278–296. Springer, Heidelberg (2004)
30. Naor, M., Yung, M.: Public-key cryptosystems provably secure against chosen ciphertext attacks. In: STOC, pp. 427–437. ACM (1990)
31. Pointcheval, D., Stern, J.: Security proofs for signature schemes. In: Maurer, U.M. (ed.) EUROCRYPT 1996. LNCS, vol. 1070, pp. 387–398. Springer, Heidelberg (1996)
32. Wee, H.: Efficient chosen-ciphertext security via extractable hash proofs. In: Rabin, T. (ed.) CRYPTO 2010. LNCS, vol. 6223, pp. 314–332. Springer, Heidelberg (2010)
33. Wee, H.: Public key encryption against related key attacks. In: Fischlin, M., Buchmann, J., Manulis, M. (eds.) PKC 2012. LNCS, vol. 7293, pp. 262–279. Springer, Heidelberg (2012)
34. Yang, G., Wong, D.S., Deng, X.: Analysis and improvement of a signcryption scheme with key privacy. In: Zhou, J., López, J., Deng, R.H., Bao, F. (eds.) ISC 2005. LNCS, vol. 3650, pp. 218–232. Springer, Heidelberg (2005)
35. Zheng, Y.: Digital signcryption or how to achieve cost (Signature & encryption) << cost(Signature) + cost(Encryption). In: Kaliski Jr., B.S. (ed.) CRYPTO 1997. LNCS, vol. 1294, pp. 165–179. Springer, Heidelberg (1997)

Improved Authenticity Bound of EAX, and Refinements

Kazuhiko Minematsu[1], Stefan Lucks[2], and Tetsu Iwata[3]

[1] NEC Corporation, Japan
k-minematsu@ah.jp.nec.com
[2] Bauhaus-Universität Weimar, Germany
stefan.lucks@uni-weimar.de
[3] Nagoya University, Japan
iwata@cse.nagoya-u.ac.jp

Abstract. EAX is a mode of operation for blockciphers to implement an authenticated encryption. The original paper of EAX proved that EAX is unforgeable up to $O(2^{n/2})$ data with one verification query. However, this generally guarantees a rather weak bound for the unforgeability under multiple verification queries, i.e., only $(2^{n/3})$ data is acceptable.

This paper provides an improvement over the previous security proof, by showing that EAX is unforgeable up to $O(2^{n/2})$ data with multiple verification queries. Our security proof is based on the techniques appeared in a paper of FSE 2013 by Minematsu et al. which studied the security of a variant of EAX called EAX-prime. We also provide some ideas to reduce the complexity of EAX while keeping our new security bound. In particular, EAX needs three blockcipher calls and keep them in memory as a pre-processing, and our proposals can effectively reduce three calls to one call. This would be useful when computational power and memory are constrained.

Keywords: Authenticated encryption, EAX, security bound.

1 Introduction

EAX [5] is a mode of operation for blockciphers proposed by Bellare, Rogaway and Wagner at FSE 1994. It implements an authenticated encryption with associated data, AEAD for short. EAX has been standardized by ISO/IEC [2] and included in some popular software libraries [1,8,9]. In FSE 2013, Minematsu, Lucks, Morita, and Iwata [13] investigated a variant of EAX defined by ANSI C12.22, called EAX-prime. They showed that EAX-prime is totally broken if the 'cleartext' part of the input is as short as a single block or shorter. At the same time, the authors proved EAX-prime is secure if cleartexts are required to be longer than a single block.

In this paper, we study the implications of [13] to the original EAX. Though the original EAX has already been proved to be secure, the security bound provided by [5], in particular the authenticity bound, does not show the standard

W. Susilo and R. Reyhanitabar (Eds.): ProvSec 2013, LNCS 8209, pp. 184–201, 2013.
© Springer-Verlag Berlin Heidelberg 2013

birthday-type security when the adversary is allowed to make multiple verification queries. More formally, the original bound is $O(\sigma^2/2^n + 1/2^\tau)$ where σ denotes the total input blocks, n denotes the block size, and τ denotes the tag length, *if the number of verification queries is one*. From the well-known result of [3], this bound generally implies $O(q_v\sigma^2/2^n + q_v/2^\tau)$ when the number of verification queries is $q_v \geq 1$, hence the provable security is degraded, roughly from $2^{n/2}$ to $2^{n/3}$, assuming $q_v \approx \sigma$. We note that, since many systems in practice do accept multiple verification queries, the analysis for this case is relevant. Based on the idea of [13], we provide an improved authenticity bound for EAX, namely $O(\sigma^2/2^n + q_v/2^\tau)$, hence the security up to $2^{n/2}$ data. When $n = 128$, this means that the provable security is improved from 43 bits to 64 bits. In addition, we prove our new bound in a slight more general setting than the original specification, in the sense that the empty header is acceptable, which is plausible in practice.

We note that the technical difficulty in handling the multiple verification queries comes from the fact that the reject symbol returned from the decryption oracle may leak some information about the secret key, and hence this may have impact on the choice of the subsequent encryption and decryption queries. Furthermore, nonces used in encryption queries can be reused for decryption queries, or vice versa. In this case, we may not have "fresh" randomness in order to show that the success probability of the last decryption query is small.

We also provide ideas to reduce the computation overhead of EAX, which we assume the primal goal of EAX-prime. In EAX, three blockcipher calls are required in advance to the actual processing, and this may make it less attractive to constrained devices. In our proposals, the overhead is reduced to one blockcipher call while keeping the security bound that we proved for the original EAX. This also achieves a more memory-efficient, faster operation than the original. In this respect our proposal can be seen as a provably-secure alternative to EAX-prime having no input-length restriction.

The main technical point in our proposals is the generation of five mask values, originally generated from three blockcipher calls. We propose three mask-generation methods, where the first one is based on the constant Galois field multiplication similar to [14], and the second and third ones are based on the word permutation and XOR. The underlying problem has a relationship to word-oriented LFSR [18] discussed by Chakraborty and Sarkar [7] and by Krovetz and Rogaway [11].

2   Preliminaries

Notations. For a binary string X, $|X|$ denotes the bit length of X. For a positive integer n we define $|X|_n \overset{\text{def}}{=} \max\{1, \lceil |X|/n \rceil\}$. The first s bits of X for $|X| \geq s$ is written as $\text{msb}_s(X)$. Let ε denote the empty string, which is a binary string of length 0. Thus we have $|\varepsilon| = 0$ and $|\varepsilon|_n = 1$. The set of all finite-length binary strings, including ε, is denoted by $\{0,1\}^*$. Let $\mathbb{N} = \{0, 1, \dots\}$. If $X \in \mathcal{X}$ is uniformly chosen from $\mathcal{X}$ we write $X \overset{\$}{\leftarrow} \mathcal{X}$. For $X, Y \in \{0,1\}^*$, their concatenation is denoted by $X\|Y$ or XY. A sequence of a zeros (ones) is denoted by 0^a (1^a). Following [5], let $[i]_n$ denote a standard n-bit encoding of integer $i \geq 0$, e.g., $[2]_n$ denotes $0^{n-2}10$. Let $(\{0,1\}^n)^{>0}$ denote the set of strings of length $n, 2n, \ldots$. For $X, Y \in \{0,1\}^n$, $X + Y$ or $X - Y$ is defined as an addition or a subtraction modulo 2^n.

For $X \in \{0,1\}^*$, let $X[1]\|X[2]\| \ldots \|X[m] \xleftarrow{n} X$ denote the partition into n-bit blocks, i.e., we have $m = |X|_n$ and $|X[i]| = n$ for $i < m$ and $|X[m]| \leq n$. For $X, Y \in \{0,1\}^*$, let $X \oplus_{\text{end}} Y$ be the XOR of the shorter variable into the end of the longer one: i.e. $X \oplus_{\text{end}} Y = (0^{|Y|-|X|}\|X) \oplus Y$ if $|Y| \geq |X|$ and otherwise $X \oplus_{\text{end}} Y = X \oplus (0^{|X|-|Y|}\|Y)$.

Random Function. The set of all functions $\{0,1\}^n \to \{0,1\}^m$ is denoted by $\text{Func}(n,m)$. We will write $\text{Func}(n)$ to mean $\text{Func}(n,n)$. The set of all permutations over $\{0,1\}^n$ is denoted by $\text{Perm}(n)$. Following [13], we define a uniform random function (URF) as a random function uniformly distributed over $\text{Func}(n,m)$ for some n and m. A URF is denoted by R, assuming n and m are clear from the context. In a similar manner we define a uniform random permutation (URP) as a random permutation uniformly distributed over $\text{Perm}(n)$ for some n. A URP is denoted by P.

Field with 2^n Points. We may view $X \in \{0,1\}^n$ as a coefficient vector of the polynomial of $\text{GF}(2^n)$, yielding a one-to-one mapping. By writing $2X$ we mean the multiplication of the generator of $\text{GF}(2^n)$ and X over $\text{GF}(2^n)$. Here, $2(2L)$ is denoted by $4L$ or 2^2L. The operation $2X$ is called *doubling*, and is efficiently implemented by one-bit shift with constant XOR, see e.g. [10].

3 Provable Security of EAX

3.1 Specification of EAX

We first define the authenticated encryption, AE in short (or more formally, AE with associated data (AEAD)). The encryption function of an AE scheme accepts the nonce N, the header (also called associated data) H, and the plaintext M and generates the ciphertext C and the tag T. The decryption (verification) function accepts N, H, C, and T, and generates the decrypted plaintext M if (N, C, T) is valid, or the flag $\perp$ if invalid.

The specification EAX is shown in Fig. 1. EAX is based on an n-bit block-cipher, E, where the key of E is written as K. EAX taking a blockcipher E and using the τ-bit tag for $\tau \leq n$ is denoted by $\text{EAX}[E, \tau]$. The encryption and decryption functions are written as $\text{EAX-}\mathcal{E}_{K,\tau}$ and $\text{EAX-}\mathcal{D}_{K,\tau}$, or $\text{EAX-}\mathcal{E}_K$ and $\text{EAX-}\mathcal{D}_K$ if τ is clear from the context.

In $\text{EAX}[E, \tau]$, we assume that $N, H, M \in \{0,1\}^*$ with $N \neq \varepsilon$. In the original specification, N and H are assumed to be non-empty (see Section 6 of [4]). However, this paper slightly generalizes the setting, allowing H to be empty[1].

---

[1] This setting allows (N, H, M) with $H = \varepsilon$ and $M = \varepsilon$ as a valid, though artificial, input to the encryption function.

Algorithm EAX-$\mathcal{E}_{K,\tau}(N, H, M)$	Algorithm EAX-$\mathcal{D}_{K,\tau}(N, H, C, T)$
1. $\underline{N} \leftarrow \mathrm{CMAC}_K^{(0)}(N)$ 2. $\underline{H} \leftarrow \mathrm{CMAC}_K^{(1)}(H)$ 3. $C \leftarrow \mathrm{CTR}_K(\underline{N}, M)$ 4. $\underline{T} \leftarrow \underline{N} \oplus \underline{H} \oplus \mathrm{CMAC}_K^{(2)}(C)$ 5. $T \leftarrow \mathrm{msb}_\tau(\underline{T})$ 6. **return** (C, T)	1. $\underline{N} \leftarrow \mathrm{CMAC}_K^{(0)}(N)$ 2. $\underline{H} \leftarrow \mathrm{CMAC}_K^{(1)}(H)$ 3. $\underline{T} \leftarrow \underline{N} \oplus \underline{H} \oplus \mathrm{CMAC}_K^{(2)}(C)$ 4. $\widehat{T} \leftarrow \mathrm{msb}_\tau(\underline{T})$ 5. **if** $\widehat{T} \neq T$ **return** $\perp$ 6. **else** $M \leftarrow \mathrm{CTR}_K(\underline{N}, C)$ 7. **return** M

Algorithm $\mathrm{CMAC}_K^{(i)}(M)$ (for $i \in \{0, 1, 2\}$)	Algorithm $\mathrm{CBC}_K(I, M)$
1. $L \leftarrow E_K([0]_n),\ L' \leftarrow E_K([1]_n),\ L'' \leftarrow E_K([2]_n)$ 2. $D \leftarrow 2L,\ Q \leftarrow 4L$ 3. **if** $M = \varepsilon$ **return** $E_K([i]_n \oplus D)$ 4. **else** 5. **if** $i = 0$ **return** $\mathrm{CBC}_K(L, \mathrm{pad}(M; D, Q))$ 6. **if** $i = 1$ **return** $\mathrm{CBC}_K(L', \mathrm{pad}(M; D, Q))$ 7. **if** $i = 2$ **return** $\mathrm{CBC}_K(L'', \mathrm{pad}(M; D, Q))$	1. $M[1]\|M[2]\| \cdots \|M[m] \stackrel{n}{\leftarrow} M$ 2. $C[0] \leftarrow I$ 3. **for** $i \leftarrow 1$ **to** m **do** $\quad C[i] \leftarrow E_K(M[i] \oplus C[i-1])$ 4. **return** $C[m]$
	Algorithm $\mathrm{pad}(M; B_1, B_2)$
Algorithm $\mathrm{CTR}_K(\underline{N}, M)$	1. **if** $|M| \in \{n, 2n, 3n, \dots, \}$ 2. **then return** $M \oplus_{\mathrm{end}} B_1$ 3. **else return**
1. $m \leftarrow \lceil |M| \rceil_n$ 2. $S \leftarrow E_K(\underline{N})\|E_K(\underline{N}+1)\| \cdots \|E_K(\underline{N}+m-1)$ 3. $C \leftarrow M \oplus \mathrm{msb}_{|M|}(S)$ 4. **return** C	$\quad (M\|10^{n-1-(|M| \bmod n)}) \oplus_{\mathrm{end}} B_2$

Fig. 1. (Upper) The encryption and decryption algorithms of EAX$[E, \tau]$. Here H and M can be the empty string, ε, while $H \neq \varepsilon$ was originally required in [5]. (Lower) Component algorithms of EAX$[E, \tau]$. For CBC_K, $|M| \in \{n, 2n, \dots\}$.

The plaintext M can be empty, and in that case the corresponding C is also empty. The ciphertext C has the same length as the corresponding plaintext, M, and the tag T is τ bits.

In [5] the definition of $\mathrm{CMAC}_K^{(i)}(M)$ is simpler than ours, namely $\mathrm{CMAC}_K^{(i)}(M) \stackrel{\mathrm{def}}{=} \mathrm{CMAC}_K([i]_n\|M)$. Here, $\mathrm{CMAC}_K(M)$ denotes the original CMAC, defined as $\mathrm{CBC}_K(\mathrm{pad}(M; D, Q))$. Our definition is equivalent and we employ it to emphasize the three redundant E_K calls, L, L', and L'', and make explicit the computation of $\mathrm{CMAC}_K^{(i)}(\varepsilon)$ with them.

3.2 Security Notions

The security of AE can be defined by two notions, privacy and authenticity [5,15]. In defining them, let $\mathcal{A}^{O_1, O_2, \dots, O_c}$ denote the adversary $\mathcal{A}$ accessing c oracles, $O_1, \dots, O_c$, in an arbitrarily order. If O_i and O_j are oracles having the same input and output domains, we say they are compatible. Let AE$[\tau]$ be an AE compatible with EAX having τ-bit tag. The encryption and decryption algorithms are AE-$\mathcal{E}_\tau$ and AE-$\mathcal{D}_\tau$. If $\mathcal{A}$ is a CPA-adversary against AE$[\tau]$, it accesses AE-$\mathcal{E}_\tau$. The encryption queries made by $\mathcal{A}$ are written as $(N_1, H_1, M_1), \dots, (N_q, H_q, M_q)$, where the number of queries, q, is a parameter of $\mathcal{A}$. We also consider $\sigma_{\mathsf{X}} \stackrel{\mathrm{def}}{=} \sum_{i=1}^q |X_i|_n$

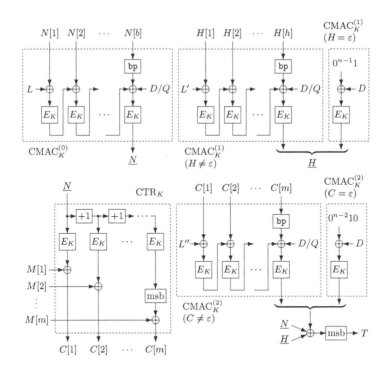

Fig. 2. The encryption algorithm of EAX. The specification is extended to accept $H = \varepsilon$. In the figure, $\mathtt{bp}(x) = x$ if $|x| = n$ and $\mathtt{bp}(x) = x\|10^{n-1-(|x| \bmod n)}$ if $|x| < n$.

for $\mathsf{X} \in \{N, H, M\}$, and assume a parameter list $(q, \sigma_N, \sigma_H, \sigma_M)$ to define the resource of $\mathcal{A}$.

Let \$ denote the random-bit oracle, which takes (N, H, M) and returns $(C, T) \xleftarrow{\$} \{0,1\}^{|M|} \times \{0,1\}^\tau$. Then the privacy of AE for CPA-adversary $\mathcal{A}$ is defined as

$$\mathrm{Adv}_{\mathsf{AE}[\tau]}^{\mathrm{priv}}(\mathcal{A}) \overset{\mathrm{def}}{=} \Pr[K \xleftarrow{\$} \mathcal{K} : \mathcal{A}^{\mathsf{AE}\text{-}\mathcal{E}_\tau} \Rightarrow 1] - \Pr[\mathcal{A}^{\$} \Rightarrow 1]. \tag{1}$$

Here, $\mathcal{A}$ is nonce-respecting, i.e., all N_is chosen by $\mathcal{A}$ are distinct.

To define the authenticity, we assume a CCA-adversary $\mathcal{A}$ against $\mathsf{AE}[\tau]$. It accesses $\mathsf{AE}\text{-}\mathcal{E}_\tau$ and $\mathsf{AE}\text{-}\mathcal{D}_\tau$. The set of encryption queries is denoted by $(N_1, H_1, M_1), \ldots, (N_q, H_q, M_q)$, and the set of decryption queries is denoted by $(\widetilde{N}_1, \widetilde{H}_1, \widetilde{C}_1, \widetilde{T}_1), \ldots, (\widetilde{N}_{q_v}, \widetilde{H}_{q_v}, \widetilde{C}_{q_v}, \widetilde{T}_{q_v})$. We assume a parameter list $(q, q_v, \sigma_N, \sigma_H, \sigma_M, \sigma_{\widetilde{N}}, \sigma_{\widetilde{H}}, \sigma_{\widetilde{C}})$ to define the attack resource, where $\sigma_{\mathsf{Y}} = \sum_{i=1}^{q_v} |\mathsf{Y}_i|_n$ for $\mathsf{Y} \in \{\widetilde{N}, \widetilde{H}, \widetilde{C}\}$, in addition to σ_N, σ_H, and σ_M. The authenticity of AE is defined as

$$\mathrm{Adv}_{\mathsf{AE}[\tau]}^{\mathrm{auth}}(\mathcal{A}) \overset{\mathrm{def}}{=} \Pr[K \xleftarrow{\$} \mathcal{K} : \mathcal{A}^{\mathsf{AE}\text{-}\mathcal{E}_\tau, \mathsf{AE}\text{-}\mathcal{D}_\tau} \text{ forges }], \tag{2}$$

where $\mathcal{A}$ forges if it receives a bit string (not $\perp$) from AE-$\mathcal{D}_\tau$ for a non-trivial query $(\widetilde{N}_i, \widetilde{H}_i, \widetilde{C}_i, \widetilde{T}_i)$ for some $1 \leq i \leq q_v$. Here $(\widetilde{N}_i, \widetilde{H}_i, \widetilde{C}_i, \widetilde{T}_i)$ is non-trivial if any encryption query-response pair $(N_j, H_j, M_j, C_j, T_j)$ obtained before satisfies $(\widetilde{N}_i, \widetilde{H}_i, \widetilde{C}_i, \widetilde{T}_i) \neq (N_j, H_j, C_j, T_j)$. We remark that CCA-adversary is always nonce-respecting with respect to encryption queries. This implies that, we can have $N_i = \widetilde{N}_j$ or $\widetilde{N}_i = \widetilde{N}_j$ for some i and j. In the security proofs we use the following notion. Let F_K and $G_{K'}$ be two compatible keyed functions with $K \in \mathcal{K}$ and $K' \in \mathcal{K}'$. Then

$$\mathrm{Adv}_{F,G}^{\mathrm{cpa}}(\mathcal{A}) \overset{\mathrm{def}}{=} \Pr[K \xleftarrow{\$} \mathcal{K} : \mathcal{A}^{F_K} \Rightarrow 1] - \Pr[K' \xleftarrow{\$} \mathcal{K}' : \mathcal{A}^{G_{K'}} \Rightarrow 1]. \quad (3)$$

Note that this definition can be naturally extended when $G_{K'}$ is substituted with the random-bit oracle compatible to F_K.

3.3 Security Bounds

Original Bounds. We denote EAX using an n-bit URP as a blockcipher by $\mathrm{EAX}[\mathrm{Perm}(n), \tau]$ and the corresponding encryption and decryption functions by EAX-$\mathcal{E}_\mathsf{P}$ and EAX-$\mathcal{D}_\mathsf{P}$. Similarly, the subscript K in the component algorithms is substituted with P, e.g. $\mathrm{CMAC}_\mathsf{P}^{(i)}$. We focus on the security bounds for $\mathrm{EAX}[\mathrm{Perm}(n), \tau]$ as the computational counterparts for $\mathrm{EAX}[E, \tau]$ are trivial.

In [5], Bellare et al. introduced *data complexity* denoted by σ, which is slightly different from our parameters[2]. The provided bounds are as follows. Note that these theorems assume $H \neq \varepsilon$.

Theorem 1 ([5]). *Fix $\tau \in \{1, \ldots, n\}$. Let $\mathcal{A}$ be the CPA-adversary against $\mathrm{EAX}[\mathrm{Perm}(n), \tau]$ with data complexity σ. Then the privacy is bounded as $\mathrm{Adv}_{\mathrm{EAX}[\mathrm{Perm}(n), \tau]}^{\mathrm{priv}}(\mathcal{A}) \leq 9.5\sigma^2/2^n$.*

Theorem 2 ([5]). *Fix $\tau \in \{1, \ldots, n\}$. Let $\mathcal{A}$ be the CCA-adversary against $\mathrm{EAX}[\mathrm{Perm}(n), \tau]$ with data complexity σ and $q_v = 1$. Then the authenticity is bounded as $\mathrm{Adv}_{\mathrm{EAX}[\mathrm{Perm}(n), \tau]}^{\mathrm{auth}}(\mathcal{A}) \leq 11\sigma^2/2^n + 1/2^\tau$.*

Our Bounds. The privacy bound of Theorem 1 is the standard birthday bound security. The bound is tight in the sense that there is an adversary that meets the stated security bound up to a constant factor. However, the authenticity bound of Theorem 2 is not satisfactory as it requires $q_v = 1$. There is a known result [3] proving that, if authenticity bound of a scheme for one verification query is ϵ, authenticity bound for c verification queries is bounded by $c\epsilon$, for any $c > 1$. Applying this result to Theorem 2, we have $\mathrm{Adv}_{\mathrm{EAX}[\mathrm{Perm}(n), \tau]}^{\mathrm{auth}}(\mathcal{A}) \leq 11q_v\sigma^2/2^n + q_v/2^\tau$ for $q_v \geq 1$, implying that the security is guaranteed up to $2^{n/3}$ data when $q_v \approx \sigma$. Now we show an improved authenticity bound for EAX that provides security up to $2^{n/2}$ data even for $q_v \geq 1$, with an extended specification allowing $H = \varepsilon$.

---

[2] According to [5], σ is defined as "the sum of the lengths of all strings encoded in the adversary's oracle queries, plus the total number of all of these strings".

Theorem 3. *Fix* $\tau \in \{1, \ldots, n\}$. *Let* $\mathcal{A}$ *be the CCA-adversary against* EAX[Perm(n), τ] *with parameter list* $(q, q_v, \sigma_N, \sigma_H, \sigma_M, \sigma_{\widetilde{N}}, \sigma_{\widetilde{H}}, \sigma_{\widetilde{C}})$. *Let* $\sigma_{\mathrm{auth}} = \sigma_N + \sigma_H + \sigma_M + \sigma_{\widetilde{N}} + \sigma_{\widetilde{H}} + \sigma_{\widetilde{C}}$. *Then we have*

$$\mathrm{Adv}^{\mathrm{auth}}_{\mathrm{EAX[Perm}(n),\tau]}(\mathcal{A}) \leq \frac{18.5\sigma^2_{\mathrm{auth}} + 4.5}{2^n} + \frac{q_v}{2^\tau}.$$

Note that σ_{auth} is largely the same as the plain σ of Theorems 1 and 2. Theorem 3 shows that EAX preserves birthday-type security in the authenticity notion for any $q_v \geq 1$, rather than for $q_v = 1$, only.

As we extended the specification to allow $H = \varepsilon$, a corresponding privacy bound should also be given in principle. For completeness we show the privacy bound in this extended specification.

Theorem 4. *Fix* $\tau \in \{1, \ldots, n\}$. *Let* $\mathcal{A}$ *be the CPA-adversary against* EAX[Perm(n), τ] *who has parameter list* $(q, \sigma_N, \sigma_H, \sigma_M)$. *Let* $\sigma_{\mathrm{priv}} = \sigma_N + \sigma_H + \sigma_M$. *Then we have* $\mathrm{Adv}^{\mathrm{priv}}_{\mathrm{EAX[Perm}(n),\tau]}(\mathcal{A}) \leq (18.5\sigma^2_{\mathrm{priv}} + 4.5)/2^n$.

The proofs of the above theorems are provided in Section 5.1.

4 Refinements of EAX

EAX needs three blockcipher calls in advance to the actual processing, namely $L = E_K([0]_n)$, $L' = E_K([1]_n)$, and $L'' = E_K([2]_n)$. They are used as masks for the initial block of CMAC. In addition, CMAC itself needs two masks for the last block, namely $2L$ and $4L$, hence five mask values in total. To achieve the fastest operation, these mask values, at least the first three ones, must be kept in memory while processing. This fact implies that EAX is not ultimately optimized, in particular for short messages, when the amount of pre-processing is critical. This is possible due to some practical reasons, e.g., a huge number of keys, or frequent key changes. In addition retaining many mask values in memory may not be desirable for constrained devices, such as low-end micro-controllers or tiny hardware.

We propose a refinement of EAX, which we call EAX$^+$, to minimize these drawbacks. We note that EAX seems to have a design philosophy for keeping the algorithm of CMAC intact, and our proposal does not follow this design philosophy in return for the efficiency gain.

Specifically, EAX$^+$ changes the definitions of five mask values so that they are simple functions of $L = E_K([0]_n)$. EAX$^+$ also sets some initial counter bits off to suppress carry bit propagation. This is the technique used by SIV [16] and EAX-prime to simplify the implementation of the counter mode. These changes affect the definitions of two internal components, CMAC$^{(i)}$ and CTR. EAX$^+$ uses CMAC$^{+(i)}$ and CTR$^+$, as shown in Fig. 3, instead of CMAC$^{(i)}$ and CTR of Fig. 1. For simplicity Fig. 3 assumes $n = 128$ for fixing the constant adjusting the initial counter, however other values of n are possible. In CMAC$^{+(i)}$, the five mask values are denoted by $A(0)$, $A(1)$, $A(2)$, D, and Q, and they are functions of $L = E_K([0]_n)$ denoted by $g_{A(0)}$, $g_{A(1)}$, and so on. In the following, we give three concrete masking schemes.

Scheme 1: Use GF Doubling. The first scheme, which we call EAX_1^+, uses the following masks. Here, $3L$ denotes $2L \oplus L$.

$$A(0) = 3L, \qquad A(1) = 2 \cdot 3L, \qquad A(2) = 2^2 \cdot 3L,$$
$$D = 2L, \qquad Q = 2^2 L$$

This keeps the definitions of CMAC masks for the last blocks (D and Q). Note that we have $A(0) = 2L \oplus L$, $A(1) = 2^2 L \oplus 2L$, and $A(2) = 2^3 L \oplus 2^2 L$. Any mask is efficiently computed by holding $X = L$ and $Y = 2^2 L$, as we have $A(0) = 2X \oplus X$, $A(1) = Y \oplus 2X$, $A(2) = 2Y \oplus Y$, $D = 2X$, and $Q = Y$. Each mask computation requires at most one doubling and one XOR.

Scheme 2: Use Sum of Four Quarters of L. The second scheme, which we call EAX_2^+, assumes that n is divisible by 4, and uses operations over $\text{GF}((2^{n/4})^4)$. We write $L = (L_1, L_2, L_3, L_4)$ where $L_i \in \text{GF}(2^{n/4})$. The masks are as follows.

$$A(0) = (L_1, L_2, L_3, L_4), \quad A(1) = (L_*, L_1, L_2, L_3), \quad A(2) = (L_4, L_*, L_1, L_2),$$
$$D = (L_3, L_4, L_*, L_1), \qquad Q = (L_2, L_3, L_4, L_*),$$

where $L_* = L_1 \oplus L_2 \oplus L_3 \oplus L_4$. The scheme is efficient, in particular for software, since it is merely a combination of $n/4$-bit word permutations and XORs. Specifically, any mask can be efficiently computed by holding L and L_*, which are $5n/4$ bits in total.

Scheme 3: Use Two Sums. The third scheme, which we call EAX_3^+, is another instance using word permutation and XOR. The masks are;

$$A(0) = (L_1, L_2, L_3, L_4), \quad A(1) = (L_2, L_\sharp, L_4, L_\flat), \quad A(2) = (L_\sharp, L_1, L_\flat, L_3),$$
$$D = (L_3, L_\flat, L_2, L_1), \qquad Q = (L_4, L_3, L_\sharp, L_2),$$

where $L_\sharp = L_1 \oplus L_2$ and $L_\flat = L_3 \oplus L_4$. The mask generation is a simple word permutation by holding L, $L_\sharp$, and $L_\flat$. Even if we only hold L, each mask is computed by at most 2 XORs of words and a permutation, and the number of word XORs required for generating all masks from L is 6.

The following theorem shows the security of these schemes.

Theorem 5. *For $j \in \{1, 2, 3\}$, let $\text{EAX}_j^+[\text{Perm}(n), \tau]$ be EAX_j^+ using n-bit URP. For any j we have*

$$\text{Adv}_{\text{EAX}_j^+[\text{Perm}(n), \tau]}^{\text{priv}}(\mathcal{A}) \leq \frac{15\sigma_{\text{priv}}^2}{2^n}, \text{ and}$$

$$\text{Adv}_{\text{EAX}_j^+[\text{Perm}(n), \tau]}^{\text{auth}}(\mathcal{A}) \leq \frac{15\sigma_{\text{auth}}^2}{2^n} + \frac{q_v}{2^\tau}.$$

Algorithm $\mathrm{CMAC}^{+(i)}_K(M)$	**Algorithm** $\mathrm{CTR}^+_K(\underline{N}, M)$
1. $L \leftarrow E_K([0]_n)$	1. $m \leftarrow \lceil M \rceil_n$
2. **for** $i = 0, 1, 2$ **do** $A(i) \leftarrow g_{A(i)}(L)$	2. $\underline{N}^\wedge \leftarrow \underline{N} \wedge (1^{n-64} \| 01^{31} \| 01^{31})$
3. $D \leftarrow g_D(L),\ Q \leftarrow g_Q(L)$	3. $S \leftarrow E_K(\underline{N}^\wedge) \| E_K(\underline{N}^\wedge + 1) \|$
4. **if** $M = \varepsilon$ **return** $E_K([i]_n \oplus D)$	$\cdots \| E_K(\underline{N}^\wedge + m - 1)$
5. **else return**	4. $C \leftarrow M \oplus \mathrm{msb}_{\lvert M \rvert}(S)$
$\mathrm{CBC}_K(A(i), \mathrm{pad}(M; D, Q))$	5. **return** C

Fig. 3. Our refinement of EAX, EAX$^+$. Here, CMAC$^{+(i)}$ for $i \in \{0, 1, 2\}$ and CTR$^+$ are used instead of CMAC$^{(i)}$ and CTR, and other functions are not changed. The definitions of $g_A(i)$, g_D, and g_Q are written in Section 4, yielding the three versions.

The proof idea of Theorem 5 is given in Section 5.2. The complete proof will be given in the full version [12]. We can build variants of these schemes by applying a permutation $\mathbb{P}$ that commutes with respect to XOR, i.e. $\mathbb{P}(x) \oplus \mathbb{P}(y) = \mathbb{P}(x \oplus y)$, to all masks. An example is a regular matrix over $\mathrm{GF}(2^{n/a})^a$ for a being a factor of n, and a variant using such masks will have the same bounds as Theorem 5.

We note that [13] suggested some variants of EAX-prime that are provably secure without input-length restriction. However the proposals of [13] focuses on the black-box usage of EAX-prime. As a result the proposals of [13] are not as efficient as ours, or require a stronger security assumption on the blockcipher.

5   Security Proofs

5.1   Proofs of Theorem 3 and Theorem 4

OMAC-Extension. In proving Theorems 3 and 4, we observe that the most part are quite the same as those given for EAX-prime [13], which is based on the original proof of EAX [5] with extensions taken from [10].

We therefore concentrate on the most involved part: the pseudorandomness of OMAC-extension. Other parts will be briefly described.

OMAC-extension is a set of functions obtained by decomposing EAX [5,13]. Formally, we define OMAC-extension[3] as a set of three functions using an n-bit URP, P, obtained from EAX[Perm$(n), \tau$]. It is denoted by OMAC-e[P] $=$ (OMAC-e[P]$^{(0)}$, OMAC-e[P]$^{(1)}$, OMAC-e[P]$^{(2)}$). See Figs. 4 and 7 in Appendix B. Here, OMAC-e[P]$^{(0)}$ is a function that takes (N, d), where $d = \lceil M \rceil_n$ ($d = \lceil C \rceil_n$) for encryption (decryption), and produces $\underline{N}$ and the d-block keystream before truncation, i.e., S of Fig. 1. Similarly, OMAC-e[P]$^{(1)}$ takes H, and OMAC-e[P]$^{(2)}$ takes C. We may view OMAC-e[P] as single function taking (t, X, d) as input and

---

[3] Our OMAC-extension does not need the auxiliary output mask as in the proof of EAX-prime [13]. This is because of the difference in the processing for one-block inputs.

outputs OMAC-e[P]$^{(t)}(X, d)$ when $t = 0$ and OMAC-e[P]$^{(t)}(X)$ when $t = 1, 2$, assuming d is a default value.

Similarly to Proposition 1 of [13], we have the following proposition.

Proposition 1. *For any fixed τ, there exist deterministic procedures, $f_e(\cdot)$ and $f_d(\cdot)$, that use OMAC-e[P] as a black-box and perfectly simulate EAX-$\mathcal{E}_P$ and EAX-$\mathcal{D}_P$. That is, we have EAX-$\mathcal{E}_P \equiv f_e$(OMAC-e[P]) and EAX-$\mathcal{D}_P \equiv f_d$(OMAC-e[P]).*

Here, $F \equiv G$ means the equivalence of the output probability distribution functions for F and G, i.e. $\Pr[F(x_1) = y_1, \ldots, F(x_q) = y_q] = \Pr[G(x_1) = y_1, \ldots, G(x_q) = y_q]$ for any fixed possible $x_1, \ldots, x_q$ and $y_1, \ldots, y_q$.

Then we need to evaluate the indistinguishability between OMAC-e[P] and a set of three random functions $\mathbb{RND} = (\mathbb{RND}^{(0)}, \mathbb{RND}^{(1)}, \mathbb{RND}^{(2)})$, where $\mathbb{RND}^{(i)}$ is compatible with OMAC-e[P]$^{(i)}$. Here $\mathbb{RND}^{(0)}(X, d)$ samples $Y \xleftarrow{\$} (\{0,1\}^n)^{d_{\max}+1}$ and outputs $\mathrm{msb}_{n(d+1)}(Y)$ if X is new, where $d_{\max}$ is the largest possible value of d determined by the game we consider.

To bound the indistinguishability, we further break down OMAC-e[P] into a set of 19 small functions, $\mathbf{Q} = \{\mathbf{Q}_i\}_{i=1,\ldots,19}$.

Definition 1. *Let $\mathbf{Q}_i : \{0,1\}^n \to \{0,1\}^n$ for $i \in \{1, 2, \ldots, 19\} \setminus \{3, 4, 5, 6\}$ and let $\mathbf{Q}_j : \{0,1\}^n \times \mathbb{N} \to (\{0,1\}^n)^{>0}$ for $j = 3, 4, 5, 6$. We define*

$$\mathbf{Q}_1(x) \overset{\text{def}}{=} \mathsf{P}(L \oplus x) \oplus \mathrm{Rnd}_1, \qquad \mathbf{Q}_2(x) \overset{\text{def}}{=} \mathsf{P}(\mathrm{Rnd}_1 \oplus x) \oplus \mathrm{Rnd}_1,$$

$$\mathbf{Q}_3(x, d) \qquad\qquad\qquad\qquad \mathbf{Q}_4(x, d)$$

$$\overset{\text{def}}{=} G_\mathsf{P}(\mathsf{P}(2L \oplus \mathrm{Rnd}_1 \oplus x), d), \qquad \overset{\text{def}}{=} G_\mathsf{P}(\mathsf{P}(4L \oplus \mathrm{Rnd}_1 \oplus x), d),$$

$$\mathbf{Q}_5(x, d) \overset{\text{def}}{=} G_\mathsf{P}(\mathsf{P}(L \oplus 2L \oplus x), d), \qquad \mathbf{Q}_6(x, d) \overset{\text{def}}{=} G_\mathsf{P}(\mathsf{P}(L \oplus 4L \oplus x), d),$$

$$\mathbf{Q}_7(x) \overset{\text{def}}{=} \mathsf{P}(L' \oplus x) \oplus \mathrm{Rnd}_2, \qquad \mathbf{Q}_8(x) \overset{\text{def}}{=} \mathsf{P}(\mathrm{Rnd}_2 \oplus x) \oplus \mathrm{Rnd}_2,$$

$$\mathbf{Q}_9(x) \overset{\text{def}}{=} \mathsf{P}(2L \oplus \mathrm{Rnd}_2 \oplus x), \qquad \mathbf{Q}_{10}(x) \overset{\text{def}}{=} \mathsf{P}(4L \oplus \mathrm{Rnd}_2 \oplus x),$$

$$\mathbf{Q}_{11}(x) \overset{\text{def}}{=} \mathsf{P}(L' \oplus 2L \oplus x), \qquad \mathbf{Q}_{12}(x) \overset{\text{def}}{=} \mathsf{P}(L' \oplus 4L \oplus x),$$

$$\mathbf{Q}_{13}(x) \overset{\text{def}}{=} \mathsf{P}(L'' \oplus x) \oplus \mathrm{Rnd}_3, \qquad \mathbf{Q}_{14}(x) \overset{\text{def}}{=} \mathsf{P}(\mathrm{Rnd}_3 \oplus x) \oplus \mathrm{Rnd}_3,$$

$$\mathbf{Q}_{15}(x) \overset{\text{def}}{=} \mathsf{P}(2L \oplus \mathrm{Rnd}_3 \oplus x), \qquad \mathbf{Q}_{16}(x) \overset{\text{def}}{=} \mathsf{P}(4L \oplus \mathrm{Rnd}_3 \oplus x),$$

$$\mathbf{Q}_{17}(x) \overset{\text{def}}{=} \mathsf{P}(L'' \oplus 2L \oplus x), \qquad \mathbf{Q}_{18}(x) \overset{\text{def}}{=} \mathsf{P}(L'' \oplus 4L \oplus x),$$

$$\mathbf{Q}_{19}(x) \overset{\text{def}}{=} \mathsf{P}(2L \oplus x),$$

where P is an n-bit URP, and $L = \mathsf{P}([0]_n)$, $L' = \mathsf{P}([1]_n)$, and $L'' = \mathsf{P}([2]_n)$. Also, Rnd_1, Rnd_2 and Rnd_3 are independent n-bit random sequences, and $G_\mathsf{P}(v, d)$ is v if $d = 0$ and $(v\|\mathsf{P}(v)\|\mathsf{P}(v + 1)\|\cdots\|\mathsf{P}(v + (d - 1)))$ if $d > 0$. The sampling procedures for $\mathsf{P}, \mathrm{Rnd}_j$ for $j = 1, 2, 3$ are shared for all $\mathbf{Q}_i s$.

We treat $\mathbf{Q}$ as a tweakable function with tweak $t \in \{1, \ldots, 19\}$ by writing $\mathbf{Q}(t, x, d) = \mathbf{Q}_t(x, d)$ when $t \in \{3, 4, 5, 6\}$ and otherwise $\mathbf{Q}(t, x, d) = \mathbf{Q}_t(x)$. We observe that OMAC-e[P] can be simulated with black-box accesses to $\mathbf{Q}$.

Algorithm OMAC-e[P] :
Initialization
00      $L \leftarrow \mathsf{P}([0]_n)$, $L' \leftarrow \mathsf{P}([1]_n)$, $L'' \leftarrow \mathsf{P}([2]_n)$
On query $(t, X, d) \in \{0, 1, 2\} \times \{0, 1\}^* \times \mathbb{N}$
10      $X[1]\|X[2]\|\cdots\|X[m] \overset{n}{\leftarrow} X$
11   **if** $|X| \bmod n \neq 0$ **or** $X = \varepsilon$ **then** $w \leftarrow 1$, **else** $w \leftarrow 0$
12   **if** $t = 0$
13   **if** $1 \leq |X| \leq n$ **then** $Y \leftarrow \mathsf{P}(\mathtt{bp}(X) \oplus L \oplus 2^{w+1}L)$; **return** Y
14   **else** $Y[1] \leftarrow \mathsf{P}(L \oplus X[1])$
15   **for** $i = 1$ to $m - 2$ **do** $Y[i+1] \leftarrow \mathsf{P}(Y[i] \oplus X[i+1])$
16          $Y \leftarrow \mathsf{P}(Y[m-1] \oplus \mathtt{bp}(X[m]) \oplus 2^{w+1}L)$
17   **if** $d = 0$ **return** Y $\ast$
18   **for** $j = 0$ to $d - 1$ **do** $S[j+1] \leftarrow \mathsf{P}(Y + j)$
19   **return** $Y\|S[1]S[2]\cdots S[d]$
20   **if** $t = 1$
21   **if** $|X| = 0$ **then** $Y' \leftarrow \mathsf{P}(2L \oplus [1]_n)$; **return** Y'
22   **if** $1 \leq |X| \leq n$ **then** $Y' \leftarrow \mathsf{P}(\mathtt{bp}(X) \oplus L' \oplus 2^{w+1}L)$; **return** Y'
23   **else** $Y'[1] \leftarrow \mathsf{P}(L' \oplus X[1])$
24   **for** $i = 1$ to $m - 2$ **do** $Y'[i+1] \leftarrow \mathsf{P}(Y'[i] \oplus X[i+1])$
25          $Y' \leftarrow \mathsf{P}(Y'[m-1] \oplus \mathtt{bp}(X[m]) \oplus 2^{w+1}L)$
26   **return** Y'
27   **if** $t = 2$
28   **if** $|X| = 0$ **then** $Y'' \leftarrow \mathsf{P}(2L \oplus [2]_n)$; **return** Y''
29   **if** $1 \leq |X| \leq n$ **then** $Y'' \leftarrow \mathsf{P}(\mathtt{bp}(X) \oplus L'' \oplus 2^{w+1}L)$; **return** Y''
30   **else** $Y''[1] \leftarrow \mathsf{P}(L'' \oplus X[1])$
31   **for** $i = 1$ to $m - 2$ **do** $Y''[i+1] \leftarrow \mathsf{P}(Y''[i] \oplus X[i+1])$
32          $Y'' \leftarrow \mathsf{P}(Y''[m-1] \oplus \mathtt{bp}(X[m]) \oplus 2^{w+1}L)$
33   **return** Y''

Fig. 4. OMAC-extension using an n-bit URP, P

For example, when we want to simulate the computation of OMAC-e$[\mathsf{P}](0, N, 2)$ for $|N| = 3n$, we first parse N into n-bit blocks, i.e., $N[1]\|N[2]\|N[3] \overset{n}{\leftarrow} N$ and then proceed as $Y[1] \leftarrow \mathbf{Q}_1(N[1])$, and $Y[2] \leftarrow \mathbf{Q}_3(N[2] \oplus Y[1])$, and $Y[3]\|S[1]S[2] \leftarrow \mathbf{Q}_5(N[3] \oplus Y[2], 2)$. Note that, $\mathbf{Q}_{19}$ is only used to simulate $\mathrm{CMAC}_K^{(1)}$ given $H = \varepsilon$, or $\mathrm{CMAC}_K^{(2)}$ given $C = \varepsilon$, i.e., to compute $\mathsf{P}(2L \oplus [1]_n)$ or $\mathsf{P}(2L \oplus [2]_n)$.

We next define $\widetilde{\mathbf{Q}} = \{\widetilde{\mathbf{Q}}_i\}_{i=1,\ldots,19}$. For all $i = 1, \ldots, 19$, $\widetilde{\mathbf{Q}}_i$ is compatible to $\mathbf{Q}_i$.

Definition 2. *Let* P_i *for* $i = 1, 2, 7, 8, 13, 14$ *be six independent n-bit URPs, and let* R_j *for* $j \in \{9, \ldots, 19\} \setminus \{13, 14\}$ *be nine independent n-bit URFs, and let* R_j *for* $j = 3, 4, 5, 6$ *be four independent URFs with n-bit input and $(d_{\max} + 1)n$-bit output. Using them we define*

$$\widetilde{\mathbf{Q}}_i(x) \overset{\mathrm{def}}{=} \mathsf{P}_i(x), \text{ for } i = 1, 2, 7, 8, 13, 14$$

$$\widetilde{\mathbf{Q}}_j(x, d) \overset{\mathrm{def}}{=} \mathsf{R}_j^{d+1}(x), \text{ for } j = 3, 4, 5, 6$$

$$\widetilde{\mathbf{Q}}_h(x) \overset{\mathrm{def}}{=} \mathsf{R}_h(x), \text{ for } h = 9, \ldots, 12, 15, \ldots, 19,$$

where $\mathsf{R}_i^{d+1}(x) = \mathtt{msb}_{n(d+1)}(\mathsf{R}_i(x))$ *for* $i = 3, 4, 5, 6$. *Here* $d_{\max}$ *is the maximum possible value of queried d, which will be determined by the underlying game and adversary's parameter.*

```
Algorithm ℂ𝔹ℂ (given d_max):
Initialization
00      for i = 1, 2, 7, 8, 13, 14 do P_i ⸠← Perm(n)
01      for j = 3, 4, 5, 6 do R_j ⸠← Func(n, d_max)
02      for k = 9, 10, 11, 12, 15, 16, 17, 18, 19 do R_k ⸠← Func(n)
On query (t, X, d) ∈ {0, 1, 2} × {0, 1}* × ℕ
10      X[1]‖X[2]‖···‖X[m] ⸠← X
11      if |X| mod n ≠ 0 or X = ε then w ← 1, else w ← 0
12      if t = 0
13          if m = 1 and d = 0 return Y ← R¹_{5+w}(bp(X))
14          if m = 1 and d > 0 return Y‖S[1]‖S[2]‖···‖S[d] ← R^{d+1}_{5+w}(bp(X))
15          Y[1] ← P_1(X[1])
16          for i = 1 to m − 2 do Y[i + 1] ← P_3(Y[i] ⊕ X[i + 1])
17          if d = 0 then Y ← R¹_{5+w}(Y[m − 1] ⊕ bp(X[m])); return Y
18          else Y‖S[1]‖S[2]‖···‖S[d] ← R^{d+1}_{5+w}(Y[m − 1] ⊕ bp(X[m]))
19          return Y‖S[1]‖S[2]‖···‖S[d]
20      if t = 1
21          if X = ε then Y′ ← R_19([1]_n); return Y′
22          else if m = 1 then Y′ ← R_{11+w}(bp(X)); return Y′
23          else Y′[1] ← P_7(X[1])
24          for i = 1 to m − 2 do Y′[i + 1] ← P_8(Y′[i] ⊕ X[i + 1])
25          Y′ ← R_{9+w}(Y′[m − 1] ⊕ bp(X[m]))
26          return Y′
27      if t = 2
28          if X = ε then Y″ ← R_19([2]_n); return Y″
29          else if m = 1 then Y″ ← R_{17+w}([2]_n); return Y″
30          else Y″[1] ← P_13(X[1])
31          for i = 1 to m − 2 do Y″[i + 1] ← P_14(Y″[i] ⊕ X[i + 1])
32          Y″ ← R_{15+w}(Y″[m − 1] ⊕ bp(X[m]))
33          return Y″
```

Fig. 5. Modified CBC-MAC

A function compatible to $\mathbf{Q}$ is said to have $\mathbf{Q}$ profile. An adversary querying a function of $\mathbf{Q}$ profile is characterized by the number of queries, q, and the number of total output n-bit blocks for $t \in \{3, 4, 5, 6\}$, σ_{out}. The next lemma shows the CPA-advantage in distinguishing $\mathbf{Q}$ and $\widetilde{\mathbf{Q}}$.

Lemma 1. *Let $\mathcal{A}$ be the adversary querying a function of $\mathbf{Q}$ profile with parameter list (q, σ_{out}). Then we have*

$$\text{Adv}^{\text{cpa}}_{\mathbf{Q}, \widetilde{\mathbf{Q}}}(\mathcal{A}) \leq \frac{(4.5q^2 + 10\sigma_{\text{out}}q + \sigma^2_{\text{out}} + 4.5)}{2^n}.$$

The proof is in Appendix A.

The remaining part of the proof is almost the same as the proof of EAX-prime. We define the Modified CBC-MAC, $\mathbb{CBC}$, which is compatible with OMAC-e[P] and consists of three functions shown in Fig. 5. Here, $R^i_j(X)$ for $j = 3, 4, 5, 6$ denotes $\text{msb}_{n \cdot i}(R_j(X))$. Then, we obtain the following proposition and lemma as counterparts of Proposition 2 and Lemma 2 of [13]. The proofs are similar, thus omitted.

Proposition 2. *There exists a procedure $h(\cdot)$ that uses $\mathbf{Q}$ as a black box and perfectly simulates OMAC-e[P], i.e. $h(\mathbf{Q}) \equiv$ OMAC-e[P]. Moreover, we have $h(\widetilde{\mathbf{Q}}) \equiv \mathbb{CBC}$ for this $h(\cdot)$.*

Lemma 2. *Let $\mathcal{A}$ be an adversary querying a function of OMAC-e profile, and let σ_{in} denote the number of total blocks of queries made by $\mathcal{A}$. Then, $\text{Adv}_{\text{CBC,RND}}^{\text{cpa}}(\mathcal{A}) \leq 3\sigma_{in}^2/2^n$.*

Our PRIV bound is derived by combining Propositions 1 and 2 and Lemma 2 in the same manner to [13]. In proving AUTH bound, let EAX be the AE algorithm compatible to $\text{EAX}[\text{Perm}(n)]$ using $f_e(\text{RND})$ and $f_d(\text{RND})$ for the encryption and decryption algorithms. We let $\mathcal{A}$ be the CCA-adversary with parameter list $(q, q_v, \sigma_N, \sigma_H, \sigma_M, \sigma_{\widetilde{N}}, \sigma_{\widetilde{H}}, \sigma_{\widetilde{C}})$. Then we have

$$\text{Adv}_{\text{EAX}}^{\text{auth}}(\mathcal{A}) \leq q_v/2^\tau. \tag{4}$$

with almost the same proof as Eq. (14) of [13].

In the last step, we combine Propositions 1 and 2, and Lemmas 1 and 2, and Eq. (4) in the same way as Eq. (15) to (22) of [13], and obtain the AUTH bound of Theorem 3. To give an idea, the coefficient of σ_{auth} comes from a sum of coefficients in Lemmas 1 and 2, i.e. $(4.5 + 10 + 1) + 3$.

5.2 Proof Idea of Theorem 5

The proof of Theorem 5 is quite the same as those of Theorems 3 and 4. The difference is in Lemma 1. To have a counterpart of Lemma 1, we change the definitions of OMAC-e[P] and $\mathbf{Q}$, and evaluate the indistinguishability of $\mathbf{Q}$ from $\widetilde{\mathbf{Q}}$, where the definition of $\widetilde{\mathbf{Q}}$ does not change (though we skip the definitions of modified functions : see the full version [12]). Let $A(i) = g_{A(i)}(L)$ for $i = 0, 1, 2$, $D = g_D(L)$ and $Q = g_Q(L)$ be the mask functions using $L \in \{0,1\}^n$. Let $\mathcal{M}_1 = \{A(0), A(1), A(2)\}$ and $\mathcal{M}_2 = \{D, Q\}$ and $\mathcal{M} = \mathcal{M}_1 \cup \mathcal{M}_2$. It turns out that the modified version of $\mathbf{Q}$ and $\widetilde{\mathbf{Q}}$ are indistinguishable if the following conditions are satisfied;

1. $\max_{X \in \mathcal{M}, c \in \{0,1\}^n} \Pr[X = c] \leq 1/2^n$
2. $\max_{X, X' \in \mathcal{M}, X \neq X', c \in \{0,1\}^n} \Pr[X \oplus X' = c] \leq 1/2^n$
3. $\max_{X, X' \in \mathcal{M}_1, X \neq X', c \in \{0,1\}^n} \Pr[X \oplus X' \oplus D = c] \leq 1/2^n$
4. $\max_{X, X' \in \mathcal{M}_1, X \neq X', c \in \{0,1\}^n} \Pr[X \oplus X' \oplus Q = c] \leq 1/2^n$
5. $\max_{X, X' \in \mathcal{M}_1, X \neq X', c \in \{0,1\}^n} \Pr[X \oplus X' \oplus D \oplus Q = c] \leq 1/2^n$

Here all probabilties are defined over $L \xleftarrow{\$} \{0,1\}^n$.

In fact, for any instance of EAX^+, we observe that all five conditions are satisfied.

Proposition 3. *For any $j = 1, 2, 3$, the mask-generation of EAX_j^+ satisfies the above five conditions.*

Here is the rough proof sketch. For EAX_1^+, the first and second conditions hold true, as X and $X \oplus X'$ (for $X \neq X'$) can be written as an element of $\text{GF}(2^n)$, $c \cdot L$, with a non-zero constant c. We then observe that $A(0) \oplus A(1) = 2^2L \oplus L$, $A(0) \oplus A(2) = 2^3L \oplus 2^2L \oplus 2L \oplus L$, and $A(1) \oplus A(2) = 2^3L \oplus 2L$. Any of these sums is not included in $\{D, Q, D \oplus Q\}$, which is $\{2L, 2^2L, 2^2L \oplus 2L\}$. This shows that the third to fifth conditions are satisfied.

For EAX_2^+ and EAX_3^+, each mask generation function can be defined as a matrix-vector multiplication with a 4×4 matrix over $\text{GF}(2^{n/4})$. For instance, $g_{A(1)}$ of EAX_2^+ is a $\text{GF}(2^{n/4})$ multiplication with

$$\begin{pmatrix} 1 & 1 & 1 & 1 \\ 1 & 0 & 0 & 0 \\ 0 & 1 & 0 & 0 \\ 0 & 0 & 1 & 0 \end{pmatrix}.$$

The five conditions can be verified by computing the rank (over $\text{GF}(2^{n/4})$) of the corresponding sums of the matrices, and seeing that the rank is full. We confirmed this by software.

6 Conclusion

In this paper, we have presented an improved authenticity bound for EAX, an authenticated encryption mode proposed by Bellare, Rogaway and Wagner. While the original bound guarantees the standard birthday-type security in the case of one verification query, we proved the birthday-type security in the case of multiple verification queries. We also showed refinements of EAX for reducing the amounts of pre-processing blockcipher calls and working memory, which will be useful for constrained devices.

Acknowledgments. The authors thank the anonymous reviewers for helpful comments.

References

1. Bouncy Castle, http://www.bouncycastle.org/
2. Information technology - Security techniques - Authenticated encryption. ISO/IEC 19772:2009 (2009)
3. Bellare, M., Goldreich, O., Mityagin, A.: The Power of Verification Queries in Message Authentication and Authenticated Encryption. Cryptology ePrint Archive, Report 2004/309 (2004), http://eprint.iacr.org/
4. Bellare, M., Rogaway, P., Wagner, D.: The EAX Mode of Operation (A Two-Pass Authenticated-Encryption Scheme Optimized for Simplicity and Efficiency), http://www.cs.ucdavis.edu/~rogaway/papers/eax.pdf
5. Bellare, M., Rogaway, P., Wagner, D.: The EAX Mode of Operation. In: Roy, Meier (eds.) [17], pp. 389–407
6. Black, J.A., Rogaway, P.: CBC MACs for Arbitrary-Length Messages: The Three-Key Constructions. In: Bellare, M. (ed.) CRYPTO 2000. LNCS, vol. 1880, pp. 197–215. Springer, Heidelberg (2000)
7. Chakraborty, D., Sarkar, P.: A general construction of tweakable block ciphers and different modes of operations. IEEE Transactions on Information Theory 54(5), 1991–2006 (2008)

8. Dai, W.: Crypto++ Library, http://www.cryptopp.com/

9. Gladman, B.: http://www.gladman.me.uk/

10. Iwata, T., Kurosawa, K.: OMAC: One-Key CBC MAC. In: Johansson, T. (ed.) FSE 2003. LNCS, vol. 2887, pp. 129–153. Springer, Heidelberg (2003)

11. Krovetz, T., Rogaway, P.: The Software Performance of Authenticated-Encryption Modes. In: Joux, A. (ed.) FSE 2011. LNCS, vol. 6733, pp. 306–327. Springer, Heidelberg (2011)

12. Minematsu, K., Lucks, S., Iwata, T.: Improved Authenticity Bound of EAX, and Refinements. Full-version of Provable Security 2013 (2013), http://eprint.iacr.org/

13. Minematsu, K., Lucks, S., Morita, H., Iwata, T.: Attacks and Security Proofs of EAX-Prime. Pre-proceedings of Fast Software Encryption 2013 (2013), full-version available at http://eprint.iacr.org/2012/018

14. Rogaway, P.: Efficient Instantiations of Tweakable Blockciphers and Refinements to Modes OCB and PMAC. In: Lee, P.J. (ed.) ASIACRYPT 2004. LNCS, vol. 3329, pp. 16–31. Springer, Heidelberg (2004)

15. Rogaway, P.: Nonce-Based Symmetric Encryption. In: Roy, Meier (eds.) [17], pp. 348–359

16. Rogaway, P., Shrimpton, T.: A Provable-Security Treatment of the Key-Wrap Problem. In: Vaudenay, S. (ed.) EUROCRYPT 2006. LNCS, vol. 4004, pp. 373–390. Springer, Heidelberg (2006)

17. Roy, B., Meier, W. (eds.): FSE 2004. LNCS, vol. 3017. Springer, Heidelberg (2004)

18. Zeng, G., Han, W., He, K.: High Efficiency Feedback Shift Register: σ-LFSR. Cryptology ePrint Archive, Report 2007/114 (2007), http://eprint.iacr.org/

A   Proof of Lemma 1

Let $\mathbf{Q}^{\mathbf{r}} = \{\mathbf{Q}_i^{\mathbf{r}}\}_{i=1,\ldots,19}$ be the set of 19 functions defined in the same way as $\mathbf{Q}$ but the internal n-bit URP, P, is substituted with n-bit URF, R. From the PRF/PRP switching lemma (e.g. [6]), we have

$$\mathsf{Adv}^{\mathsf{cpa}}_{\mathbf{Q},\mathbf{Q}^{\mathbf{r}}}(\mathcal{A}) \leq (q + \sigma_{\mathsf{out}} + 3)^2 / 2^{n+1}, \tag{5}$$

for any adversary $\mathcal{A}$ with parameter list $(q, \sigma_{\mathsf{out}})$. Let $\mathbf{R} = \{\mathbf{R}_i\}_{i=1,\ldots,19}$ be defined in the same way as $\widetilde{\mathbf{Q}}$, except that $\mathbf{R}_i$ for $i = 1, 2, 7, 8, 13, 14$ are independent n-bit URFs. That is, each $\mathbf{R}_i$ is compatible to $\mathbf{Q}_i$ and outputs are completely random. We consider the advantage in distinguishing between $\mathbf{Q}$ and $\mathbf{R}$. Then, let $\mathsf{mask}(i, L, L', L'', \mathsf{Rnd}_1, \mathsf{Rnd}_2, \mathsf{Rnd}_3)$ be the input masking value used by $\mathbf{Q}_i$. The value of $\mathsf{mask}(i, L, L', L'', \mathsf{Rnd}_1, \mathsf{Rnd}_2, \mathsf{Rnd}_3)$ for each i is defined as follows.

Similarly let $\mathsf{omask}(t, \mathsf{Rnd}_1, \mathsf{Rnd}_2, \mathsf{Rnd}_3)$ be the outer masking value, defined as Rnd_1 if $t \in \{1, 2\}$ and Rnd_2 if $t \in \{7, 8\}$ and Rnd_3 if $t \in \{13, 14\}$ and otherwise 0^n. We may abbreviate $\mathsf{mask}(i, L, L', L'', \mathsf{Rnd}_1, \mathsf{Rnd}_2, \mathsf{Rnd}_3)$ to $\mathsf{mask}(i)$, and $\mathsf{omask}(j, \mathsf{Rnd}_1, \mathsf{Rnd}_2, \mathsf{Rnd}_3)$ to $\mathsf{omask}(j)$. Here, $\mathsf{P}(\mathsf{mask}(i) \oplus x) \oplus \mathsf{omask}(i)$ corresponds to $\mathbf{Q}_i(x)$ when $i \neq 3, 4, 5, 6$ and $\mathsf{msb}_n(\mathbf{Q}_i(x, d))$ when $i = 3, 4, 5, 6$. From

$i=1$	2	3	4	5	6	7
L	Rnd_1	$2L \oplus \mathrm{Rnd}_1$	$4L \oplus \mathrm{Rnd}_1$	$L \oplus 2L$	$L \oplus 4L$	L'
$i=8$	9	10	11	12	13	14
Rnd_2	$2L \oplus \mathrm{Rnd}_2$	$4L \oplus \mathrm{Rnd}_2$	$L' \oplus 2L$	$L' \oplus 4L$	L''	Rnd_3
$i=15$	16	17	18	19		
$2L \oplus \mathrm{Rnd}_3$	$4L \oplus \mathrm{Rnd}_3$	$L'' \oplus 2L$	$L'' \oplus 4L$	$2L$		

the property of Galois field it is easy to see that

$$\max_{1 \leq i < j \leq 19, \delta \in \{0,1\}^n} \Pr[\mathrm{mask}(i) \oplus \mathrm{mask}(j) = \delta] \leq 1/2^n \tag{6}$$

$$\max_{1 \leq i \leq 19, \delta \in \{0,1\}^n} \Pr[\mathrm{mask}(i) = \delta] \leq 1/2^n \tag{7}$$

where both probabilities are defined by the independent uniform samplings of L, L', L'', and Rnd_i for $i = 1, 2, 3$.

For any adversary querying $\mathbf{Q^r}$ or $\mathbf{R}$, let (t_i, X_i, d_i) be the i-th query. Without loss of generality, we assume d_i is fixed to 0 whenever $t_i \notin \{3, 4, 5, 6\}$, and all queries are distinct, i.e. $(t_i, X_i, d_i) \neq (t_j, X_j, d_j)$ for any $1 \leq i < j \leq q$, and when $t_i = 19$, X_i is fixed to $[1]_n$ or $[2]_n$. For query (t, X, d), we define $XE = X \oplus \mathrm{mask}(t)$ which is an actual input to the underlying random function when $\mathbf{Q^r}$ is queried.

Fig. 6 in Appendix B defines two games, $\mathrm{Game}\mathbf{Q^r}$ and $\mathrm{Game}\mathbf{R}$, and it is easy to observe that $\mathrm{Game}\mathbf{Q^r}$ perfectly simulates $\mathbf{Q^r}$. Note that $\mathrm{Game}\mathbf{R}$ behaves identically to $\mathbf{R}$, as Y is $V \oplus \mathrm{omask}(t, \mathrm{Rnd}_1, \mathrm{Rnd}_2, \mathrm{Rnd}_3)$ and V is uniform and independent of $\mathrm{Rnd}_1, \mathrm{Rnd}_2$. Because a collision in (t, X, d) is not allowed the output of $\mathrm{Game}\mathbf{R}$ is always independent and uniformly random. We define the flag bad and set it when two inputs with input maskings collide. Then both games are identical until bad gets set to $\mathtt{true}$, thus $\mathrm{Adv}^{\mathrm{cpa}}_{\mathbf{Q^r}, \mathbf{R}}(\mathcal{A})$ is bounded by

$$\Pr[\mathcal{A}^{\mathrm{Game}\mathbf{Q^r}} \Rightarrow 1] - \Pr[\mathcal{A}^{\mathrm{Game}\mathbf{R}} \Rightarrow 1] \leq \Pr[\mathcal{A}^{\mathrm{Game}\mathbf{R}} \text{ sets } bad]. \tag{8}$$

That is, what we need is to bound the last probability.

We first focus on bad at line 13. The probability of this event is not increased by an adaptive choice of queries, since outputs are completely random and independent of XE for both games until bad sets. The existence of $\mathrm{omask}(t)$ in the output does not help, since it is XORed to a perfectly random value. Thus we fix all queries and measure the probability of bad.

Let us assume bad first occurs at line 13 with the i-th query, (t_i, X_i, d_i). We define XE_i and $Y_{i,h} \stackrel{\mathrm{def}}{=} Y_i + h$ as the corresponding internal variables appeared in the i-th run of the game (where the latter only appears when $t_i \in \{3, 4, 5, 6\}$ and $d_i \geq 1$). We must have one of the three sub-events,

- $XE_i = XE_j$ for $i \leq q$, $j < i$, or
- $XE_i \in \{[0]_n, [1]_n, [2]_n\}$ for $i \leq q$ or
- $XE_i = Y_j + h$ for $i \leq q$ and $j < i$ and $0 \leq h \leq d_j - 1$.

From Eqs. (6) and (7) the first and the last sub-events occur with probability at most $1/2^n$, and the middle one with probability at most $3/2^n$. We next focus on bad at line 18, which implies the occurrence of one of the three sub-events (when $t_i, t_j \in \{3, 4, 5, 6\}$),

- $Y_i + h = XE_j$ for some $i \leq q$, $j \leq i$, $0 \leq h \leq d_i - 1$ or
- $Y_i + h \in \{[0]_n, [1]_n, [2]_n\}$ for some $i \leq q$ and $0 \leq h \leq d_i - 1$, or
- $Y_i + h = Y_j + h'$ for some $(i, h) \neq (j, h')$, $i, j \leq q$ and $0 \leq h \leq d_i - 1$ and $0 \leq h' \leq d_j - 1$.

As Y_i is random and independent of all previous variables, we have

$$\Pr[Y_i + h = X_j] = \max_\delta \Pr[Y_i = \delta - h] = 1/2^n. \tag{9}$$

Now we have $\Pr[Y_i + h \in \{[0]_n, [1]_n, [2]_n\}] \leq 3/2^n$ and $\Pr[Y_i + h = Y_j + h'] \leq 1/2^n$. By counting the number of sub-events, we have

$$\Pr[\mathcal{A}^{\text{GameR}} \text{ sets } bad] \leq \underbrace{\binom{q}{2} \frac{1}{2^n}}_{XE_i = XE_j} + \underbrace{\frac{3q}{2^n}}_{XE_i \in \{[0]_n, [1]_n, [2]_n\}} + \underbrace{\frac{\sigma_{\text{out}} q}{2^n}}_{\substack{XE_i = Y_j + h \\ \text{for both } i < j \text{ and } j \leq i}}$$

$$+ \underbrace{\frac{3\sigma_{\text{out}}}{2^n}}_{Y_i + h \in \{[0]_n, [1]_n, [2]_n\}} + \underbrace{\binom{\sigma_{\text{out}}}{2} \frac{1}{2^n}}_{Y_i + h = Y_j + h'} \tag{10}$$

$$\leq \frac{(0.5q^2 + 6\sigma_{\text{out}} q + 0.5\sigma_{\text{out}}^2)}{2^n}. \tag{11}$$

We also need to evaluate the distinguishing advantage of $\mathbf{R}$ and $\widetilde{\mathbf{Q}}$. The difference between them is that $\mathbf{R}$ uses n-bit URFs when t is in $\{1, 2, 7, 8, 13, 14\}$ while $\widetilde{\mathbf{Q}}$ uses n-bit URPs. For other values of t their behaviors are identical and independent of the responses obtained when $t = 1, 2, 7, 8, 13, 14$. Combining this observation and the PRP/PRF switching lemma we have

$$\text{Adv}_{\mathbf{R}, \widetilde{\mathbf{Q}}}^{\text{cpa}}(\mathcal{A}) \leq q^2/2^{n+1}. \tag{12}$$

Combining Eqs. (5), (12), (11), and (8), we have

$$\text{Adv}_{\mathbf{Q}, \widetilde{\mathbf{Q}}}^{\text{cpa}}(\mathcal{A}) \leq \text{Adv}_{\mathbf{Q}, \mathbf{Q}^r}^{\text{cpa}}(\mathcal{A}) + \text{Adv}_{\mathbf{Q}^r, \mathbf{R}}^{\text{cpa}}(\mathcal{A}) + \text{Adv}_{\mathbf{R}, \widetilde{\mathbf{Q}}}^{\text{cpa}}(\mathcal{A}) \tag{13}$$

$$\leq \frac{(q + \sigma_{\text{out}} + 3)^2}{2^{n+1}} + \frac{0.5q^2 + 6\sigma_{\text{out}} q + 0.5\sigma_{\text{out}}^2}{2^n} + \frac{q^2}{2^{n+1}} \tag{14}$$

$$\leq \frac{4.5q^2 + 10\sigma_{\text{out}} q + \sigma_{\text{out}}^2 + 4.5}{2^n}, \tag{15}$$

which concludes the proof.

B   Supplemental Figures

Initialization
00      $L \leftarrow \rho([0]_n) \overset{\$}{\leftarrow} \{0,1\}^n$, $L' \leftarrow \rho([1]_n) \overset{\$}{\leftarrow} \{0,1\}^n$, $L'' \leftarrow \rho([2]_n) \overset{\$}{\leftarrow} \{0,1\}^n$
01      $\mathrm{Rnd}_1 \overset{\$}{\leftarrow} \{0,1\}^n$, $\mathrm{Rnd}_2 \overset{\$}{\leftarrow} \{0,1\}^n$, $\mathrm{Rnd}_3 \overset{\$}{\leftarrow} \{0,1\}^n$
On query $(t, X, d) \in \{0,1,2\} \times \{0,1\}^* \times \mathbb{N}$
10      $XE \leftarrow \mathrm{mask}(t, L, L', L'', \mathrm{Rnd}_1, \mathrm{Rnd}_2, \mathrm{Rnd}_3) \oplus X$
11      $Y \overset{\$}{\leftarrow} \{0,1\}^n$
12      $V \leftarrow Y \oplus \mathrm{omask}(t, \mathrm{Rnd}_1, \mathrm{Rnd}_2, \mathrm{Rnd}_3)$
13   **if** $XE \in \mathrm{Dom}(\rho)$ **then** bad $\leftarrow$ true,
$\boxed{V \leftarrow \rho(XE), Y \leftarrow V \oplus \mathrm{omask}(t, \mathrm{Rnd}_1, \mathrm{Rnd}_2, \mathrm{Rnd}_3)}$
14   **else** $\rho(XE) \leftarrow V$
15   **if** $t \notin \{3,4,5,6\}$ **or** $t \in \{3,4,5,6\}$ **and** $d = 0$ **then return** Y
16   **for** $i = 0$ **to** $d - 1$ **do**
17              $S[i+1] \overset{\$}{\leftarrow} \{0,1\}^n$
18   **if** $V + i \in \mathrm{Dom}(\rho)$ **then** bad $\leftarrow$ true, $\boxed{S[i+1] \leftarrow \rho(V+i)}$
19   **else** $\rho(V+i) \leftarrow S[i+1]$
20   **return** $Y \| S[1] \| S[2] \| \cdots \| S[d]$

Fig. 6. Game$\mathbf{Q^r}$ contains the boxed arguments, while Game$\mathbf{R}$ does not

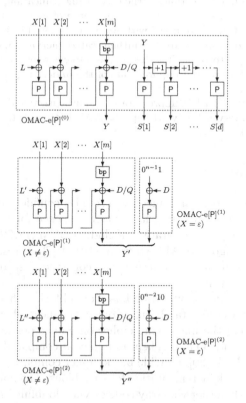

Fig. 7. OMAC-extension in the proofs of Theorems 3 and 4

The Security of the OCB Mode of Operation without the SPRP Assumption

Kazumaro Aoki and Kan Yasuda

NTT Secure Platform Laboratories, Japan
{aoki.kazumaro,yasuda.kan}@lab.ntt.co.jp

Abstract. OCB is an efficient, rate-1, single-key block-cipher mode of operation for nonce-based authenticated encryption. The OCB mode uses the block-cipher inverse for decryption, and existing security proofs of OCB are all based on the assumption that the underlying cipher is a strong pseudo-random permutation (SPRP). In this work, this assumption is substantially weakened. Namely, we show that, for the security of OCB, we only need to assume that the cipher is a) secure as a plain *PRP* (under chosen-plaintext attacks), and b) *unpredictable*, which is a notion strictly weaker than being pseudo-random, under chosen-ciphertext attacks. We also point out that, in the case of tag truncation, our security reduction would become "better" (in the sense of assumptions we have to make) if OCB were equipped with *two* independent block-cipher keys. To our knowledge, in the area of authenticated encryption, our result is the first example to show that the number of keys makes a fundamental difference in the essential requirements of the underlying cipher.

Keywords: SPRP, PRP, unpredictability, authenticated decryption, integrity, nonce, forward-only attempt, backward attempt, tag truncation, key separation.

1 Introduction

Authenticated encryption simultaneously provides confidentiality and integrity of digital data. Numerous schemes have been proposed for this purpose, many of which use a block cipher in iteration, including CCM [12,22,27], EAX [4] and GCM [18,21]. The ongoing CAESAR competition [7] represents the fact that nowadays it is still a main area of research to construct fast and secure schemes of authenticated encryption.

To date, of these modes of operation based on a block cipher, OCB [13,24,25], proposed by Rogaway et al., stands out as one of the most efficient constructions. OCB is rate-1, calling the underlying cipher only once per message block. The computational overhead of OCB is kept minimal, as compared to confidentiality-only modes such as ECB [20]. Outside block-cipher computations, OCB requires just a few xors and mask incrementation for each block. The mask incrementation can be done efficiently either via Gray code or via "doubling" in the binary field. The original OCB [25] and the latest OCB3 [13] employ Gray code, whereas OCB2 [24] uses doubling.

W. Susilo and R. Reyhanitabar (Eds.): ProvSec 2013, LNCS 8209, pp. 202–220, 2013.

Unfortunately OCB has its drawbacks. One of its major disadvantages is that its security has to rely on a relatively strong assumption about the underlying block cipher—namely, that of strong pseudo-random permutation (SPRP). The notion of SPRP requires the cipher to behave like a random permutation under chosen-plaintext and chosen-ciphertext attacks. This contrasts sharply with some rate-2 constructions such as GCM [18, 21] whose security can be proven under the plain PRP assumption [11, 18], which requires the cipher to behave like a random permutation under just chosen-plaintext attacks.

Motivation and Intuition behind Our Work. At the first glance the difference in the requirements between OCB and GCM seems "natural," as OCB utilizes the block-cipher inverse for decryption but GCM never calls the block-cipher inverse. This would have been indeed "natural" if the block-cipher inverse were used for the purpose of making the decryption process of OCB "look random."

However, that is not the case. Actually, the decryption of OCB does not need to look random at all; it only needs to ensure the integrity of the ciphertext. This pertinent observation raises the following question:

Is SPRP absolutely necessary for the Security of OCB?

The motivation behind the current work is to answer this question. Our answer is negative. The strong requirement of SPRP is not essential for the security of OCB. The intuition is that, in the syntax of authenticated encryption, the decryption process always outputs just the reject symbol "⊥" unless the tag integrity is verified. Note that ⊥ does not leak any information about the plaintext. Therefore, it seems that the inverse cipher $E_K(\cdot)$ does not have to be so strong but needs to be just "sufficiently secure" to ensure integrity. We demonstrate that such an intuition is indeed correct.

Our Contributions. In this work, we show that the SPRP requirement can be considerably relaxed. Specifically, we show that OCB is secure if the underlying cipher is:

1. secure as a plain *pseudo-random permutation* (PRP) under chosen-plaintext attacks, *and*
2. *unpredictable* under chosen-plaintext and chosen-ciphertext attacks.

Recall that unpredictability is the *very* notion of integrity. Roughly speaking, we are assuming the integrity of the underlying primitive in order to prove the integrity of the OCB mode of operation, which seems a natural and reasonable reduction of security.

We do not "lose" security by weakening the assumptions about the underlying block cipher. We obtain an integrity bound which ensures essentially the same birthday security as the previous bound based on SPRP.

Furthermore, in the paper we explore deeper implications of our security results. These are:

- *Tag Truncation.* The unpredictability assumption needs to be "enhanced" if the tag is truncated; that is, we have to assume that the truncated function (rather than the cipher itself) is unpredictable.
- *Key Separation.* However, if we are allowed to use independent keys for encryption and authentication, then we can prove the security of the (two-key) OCB without the enhanced assumption, even when the tag is truncated. We only need to assume that the *cipher* is unpredictable.

The reason behind the key separation is as follows. We use a key $K1$ for encryption and another key $K2$ for tag generation. Then since $K2$ is never used in decryption, the inverse $E_{K2}^{-1}(\cdot)$ is never invoked. This means that we can treat $E_{K2}(\cdot)$ as a random permutation (by the PRP assumption). Then the security is "preserved" even if we truncate tag output (up to degradation). We believe that, in the field of authenticated encryption, this is the first result to show that the number of keys may make a fundamental difference in the assumptions we have to make about the underlying cipher.

Organization of the Paper. In Sect. 2, we explain the technical background to this paper. We review the OCB mode of operation in Sect. 3. Security notions are defined in Sect. 4, and security proofs are given in Sect. 5. In Sect. 6, we describe how to handle associated data while keeping our security results valid. In Sect. 7 we provide discussions on our integrity bound, on the tag truncation, and on the key separation. We conclude the paper in Sect. 8.

2   Background

In this section, we describe the technical background to the current work. In particular, we focus on revealing the differences between the security notions, which help us grasp clearly the full significance of our results.

Gap between PRP and SPRP. There exists a significant gap separating the notion of PRP from that of SPRP. We give several examples that illustrate the gap.

Luby and Rackoff [16, 17] showed that three-round Feistel Network (using random round functions) is sufficient to construct a PRP, while four rounds are necessary to construct an SPRP. That is, such a three-round Feistel cipher is secure in the sense of PRP but insecure in the sense of SPRP.

To highlight the gap, we construct a block cipher that is PRP but certainly not SPRP. Let $E_K : \{0,1\}^n \to \{0,1\}^n$ be a block cipher with $K \in \{0,1\}^k$. Put $X_0 := E_K^{-1}(0^n)$. Given a random string $r \in \{0,1\}^{n/2}$, set $Y_0 := E_K(0^{n/2}\|r)$. We define a block cipher $E'_{K,r} : \{0,1\}^n \to \{0,1\}^n$ as

$$E'_{K,r}(X) := \begin{cases} 0^n & \text{if } X = 0^{n/2}\|r, \\ Y_0 & \text{if } X = X_0, \text{ and} \\ E_K(X) & \text{otherwise.} \end{cases}$$

We see that $E'_{K,r}(\cdot)$ is a secure PRP up to about $2^{n/2}$ queries if $E_K(\cdot)$ is a secure PRP. However, it is absolutely not an SPRP, since an adversary can easily distinguish it from a random permutation by just making a single query 0^n to the inverse oracle.

The gap between PRP and SPRP does not remain theoretical but appear in cryptanalysis of actual block ciphers. For example, Wagner [26] introduced the boomerang attack on block ciphers. The boomerang attack is a framework based on differential cryptanalysis. The framework is inherently an adaptive chosen-ciphertext attack. Indeed, the full AES-192 and AES-256 (with the full key space) were first cryptanalyzed using the boomerang attack [5]. The attack shows that AES-192/256 are not SPRP (though in the related-key setting). However, AES-192/256 remains as a secure PRP, because the attack has to make inverse queries.

Gap between Pseudo-Randomness and Unpredictability. We explain the substantial gap between being pseudo-random and being just unpredictable. First, observe that the former implies the latter, with a loss of $1/2^n$, where n is the output size of the function [2]. The latter does not imply the former, and efficiently constructing the former from the latter is not easy [19]. There are numerous efficient modes of operation whose security proof relies on the pseudo-randomness of the underlying block cipher. On the other hand, modes of operation whose security relies on the unpredictability of the underlying cipher seem harder to construct (e.g. [8–10, 14]).

Here, the aforementioned counterexample $E'_{K,r}(\cdot)$ is also instructive. Assume that $E_K(\cdot)$ is an SPRP, rather than just a PRP. Still, $E'_{K,r}(\cdot)$ is not a secure SPRP; the same attack applies. However, we notice that $E'_{K,r}$ is unpredictable under chosen-ciphertext attacks, meaning that an adversary cannot output a pair (X^*, Y^*) satisfying $Y^* = E'_{K,r}(X^*)$ such that the query X^* has not been made to the $E'_{K,r}(\cdot)$ oracle and the query Y^* has not been made to the $E'^{-1}_{K,r}(\cdot)$ oracle.

This counterexample serves to clarify the importance of our results. According to previous proofs, the security of the OCB mode constructed of such a non-SPRP block cipher $E'_{K,r}(\cdot)$ could not be guaranteed. On the other hand, our proof demonstrates that the OCB with such $E'_{K,r}(\cdot)$ actually generates a secure scheme of authenticated encryption.

Tweakable Ciphers. Recalling the previous security proofs of OCB modes [13, 24, 25], we see that, to a greater or less extent, these proofs can be recaptured by the framework of *tweakable ciphers* [15]. Tweakable ciphers are tightly tied together with the notion of pseudo-randomness, namely PRP and/or SPRP.

Our proofs also use techniques from the framework of tweakable ciphers, but we do so carefully, so that we separate the block-cipher inverse $E_K^{-1}(\cdot)$ from the framework of tweakable ciphers. In other words, we are forced to restrict the usage of tweakable ciphers to PRP, because we do not assume SPRP about the cipher. Whenever we have to deal with the block-cipher inverse, we use the

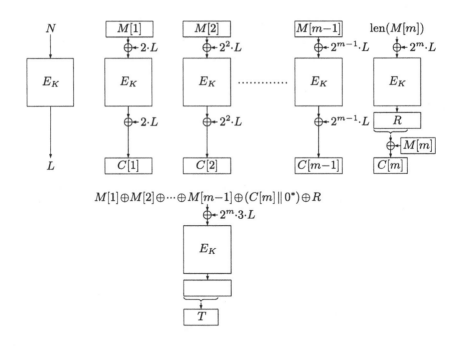

Fig. 1. OCB2 Encryption

Algorithm 1. OCB2 Encryption $\mathcal{E}_K(N, M)$

Input: a nonce $N \in \{0,1\}^n$, a message $M \in \{0,1\}^*$, a key $K \in \{0,1\}^k$
Output: a ciphertext $C \in \{0,1\}^*$, a tag $T \in \{0,1\}^n$
1 $(C, R) \leftarrow \mathrm{Enc}_K^{+1}(N, M); T \leftarrow \mathrm{Auth}_K(N, M, C, R)$
2 **return** (C, T)

---

framework of message authentication codes. This is made possible owing to the unpredictability that we assume about the underlying block cipher.

3   Review of OCB

In this section we review the OCB mode of operation. For the sake of simplicity, we choose OCB2 (our results apply to other versions of OCB). At the moment we assume that the tag size is not truncated. Algorithms 1 and 2 define the encryption and decryption processes of the OCB2 mode, respectively. The algorithms call an n-bit block cipher $E_K : \{0,1\}^n \rightarrow \{0,1\}^n$ with $K \in \{0,1\}^k$. The subroutines are defined in Algorithms 3 and 4. Figure 1 describes the OCB2 encryption.

We choose an appropriate irreducible polynomial. For example, when $n = 128$, we can choose $f(u) := u^{128} \oplus u^7 \oplus u^2 \oplus u \oplus 1 \in \mathrm{GF}(2)[u]$ to represent the finite

---

Algorithm 2. OCB2 Decryption $\mathcal{D}_K(N, C, T)$

Input: a nonce $N \in \{0,1\}^n$, a ciphertext $C \in \{0,1\}^*$, a tag $T \in \{0,1\}^n$,
   a key $K \in \{0,1\}^k$
Output: a message $M \in \{0,1\}^*$ or a special symbol $\perp$
1 $(M, R) \leftarrow \mathrm{Enc}_K^{-1}(N, C)$; $T' \leftarrow \mathrm{Auth}_K(N, M, C, R)$
2 **if** $T = T'$ **then return** M **else return** $\perp$

Algorithm 3. $\mathrm{Enc}_K^{\pm 1}(N, X)$ Subroutine

Input: a nonce $N \in \{0,1\}^n$, data $X \in \{0,1\}^*$, a key $K \in \{0,1\}^k$
Output: data $Y \in \{0,1\}^*$, a mask $R \in \{0,1\}^n$
1 $L \leftarrow E_K(N)$
2 **if** $X = \varepsilon$ **then**   /* empty data */
3 | $Y \leftarrow \varepsilon$
4 | $\Delta \leftarrow 2 \cdot L$
5 | $R \leftarrow E_K(\Delta \oplus 0)$
6 **else**   /* non-empty */
7 | $X[1] \,\|\, X[2] \,\|\, \cdots \,\|\, X[x] \xleftarrow{n} X$
8 | **for** $i = 1$ **to** $x - 1$ **do**
9 | | $\Delta \leftarrow 2^i \cdot L$ /* multiplication in GF(2^n) */
10 | | $Y[i] \leftarrow E_K^{\pm 1}(\Delta \oplus X[i]) \oplus \Delta$
11 | **end**
12 | $\Delta \leftarrow 2^x \cdot L$
13 | $r \leftarrow \mathrm{len}(X[x])$
14 | $R \leftarrow E_K(\Delta \oplus r)$
15 | $Y[x] \leftarrow \mathrm{msb}_r(R) \oplus X[x]$
16 | $Y \leftarrow Y[1] \,\|\, Y[2] \,\|\, \cdots \,\|\, Y[x]$
17 **end**
18 **return** (Y, R)

---

field GF(2^{128}). The dot $\cdot$ represents a multiplication in the field. Multiplication by '2' means that by u, and multiplication by '3' means that by $u \oplus 1$. A non-negative integer is represented as a bit string using a natural conversion. The leftmost bit is the most significant bit. The function $\mathrm{msb}_i(X)$ outputs the leftmost (significant) i bits of the string X.

Given a non-empty string X, the notation $X[1]\|X[2]\|\cdots\|X[x] \xleftarrow{n} X$ represents the partitioning operation into n-bit strings; we have

$$X[1]\|X[2]\|\cdots\|X[x] = X,$$

where $|X[i]| = n$ for $1 \leq i \leq x - 1$ and $1 \leq |X[x]| \leq n$. The function $\mathrm{len}(X)$ returns the bit length of a string $X \in \{0,1\}^*$. The returned value is a non-negative integer.

Given a string X, the notation $X\|0^*$ means padding a minimum number of zero bits so that the bit length of the resulting string becomes divisible by n. No bit is padded if X is the null string ε.

Algorithm 4. $\text{Auth}_K(N, M, C, R)$ Subroutine

Input: a nonce $N \in \{0,1\}^n$, a message $M \in \{0,1\}^*$, a ciphertext $C \in \{0,1\}^*$,
    a mask $R \in \{0,1\}^n$, a key $K \in \{0,1\}^k$
Output: a tag $T \in \{0,1\}^n$

1 **if** $M = \varepsilon$ **then**   /* empty message */
2 $\quad | \quad \Sigma \leftarrow R$
3 **else**   /* non-empty */
4 $\quad | \quad M[1] \parallel M[2] \parallel \cdots \parallel M[m] \xleftarrow{n} M$
5 $\quad | \quad C[1] \parallel C[2] \parallel \cdots \parallel C[m] \xleftarrow{n} C$
6 $\quad | \quad \Sigma \leftarrow M[1] \oplus M[2] \oplus \cdots \oplus M[m-1] \oplus (C[m] \parallel 0^*) \oplus R$
7 **end**
8 $\Delta \leftarrow 2^m \cdot 3 \cdot L$
9 $T \leftarrow E_K(\Delta \oplus \Sigma)$
10 **return** T

4 Security Definitions

Basically, we follow the security notions used in the work of OCB [13, 24, 25]. The notion of PRP and that of unpredictability are the standard ones used in, for example, [8, 24].

PRP Assumption. We assume that our underlying block cipher E is a pseudo-random permutation (PRP). We give an adversary A (an oracle machine) access either to the cipher oracle $E_K(\cdot)$ or to the random permutation oracle $\pi(\cdot)$, where the key K is chosen at random from the key space $\{0,1\}^k$ and the permutation π is chosen at random from the set of permutations over $\{0,1\}^n$. We write $A^{\mathcal{O}(\cdot)}$ for the value returned by A after its interaction with oracle $\mathcal{O}(\cdot)$. We define

$$\text{Adv}_E^{\text{prp}}(A) := \Pr_K[A^{E_K(\cdot)} = 1] - \Pr_\pi[A^{\pi(\cdot)} = 1],$$

where the probabilities are taken over the random coins used by the oracles and also over internal coins of A, if any. We fix a model of computation and a method of encoding in order to measure the time complexity of an adversary A. We define $\text{Adv}_E^{\text{prp}}(t, q) := \max_A \text{Adv}_E^{\text{prp}}(A)$, where max is taken over adversaries A whose time complexity is at most t and whose query complexity is at most q queries to the oracle.

Similarly, we define the SPRP advantage $\text{Adv}_E^{\text{prp}\pm1}(A)$, where the adversary is given access also to the inverse oracle, $E_K^{-1}(\cdot)$ or $\pi^{-1}(\cdot)$. The quantity $\text{Adv}_E^{\text{prp}\pm1}(t, q)$ is defined in the same way, where q denotes the maximum number of oracle queries. Sometimes we write $\text{Adv}_E^{\text{prp}\pm1}(t, q_{+1}, q_{-1})$, where q_{+1} is the maximum number of forward queries and q_{-1} that of inverse queries (so we have $q = q_{+1} + q_{-1}$).

Unpredictability under Chosen-Ciphertext Attacks. This is the other property that we need to assume about the cipher. We give an adversary A

access to the forward oracle $E_K(\cdot)$ and to the inverse oracle $E_K^{-1}(\cdot)$. We often write $A^{E_K^{\pm 1}(\cdot)}$ to mean $A^{E_K(\cdot), E_K^{-1}(\cdot)}$. We demand the adversary to output a forgery attempt $(X^*, Y^*) \leftarrow A^{E_K^{\pm 1}(\cdot)}$ after its interaction with oracles. We define

$$\mathrm{Adv}_E^{\mathrm{mac}\pm 1}(A) := \Pr\left[A^{E_K^{\pm 1}(\cdot)} \text{ forges}\right],$$

where "forges" means that $E_K(X^*) = Y^*$ where X^* has not been asked to the $E_K(\cdot)$ oracle and Y^* not to the $E_K^{-1}(\cdot)$ oracle. The quantity $\mathrm{Adv}_E^{\mathrm{mac}\pm 1}(t, q)$ is defined similarly.

Confidentiality Definition. We give an adversary A access either to the encryption oracle $\mathcal{E}_K(\cdot, \cdot)$ or to the random oracle $\$(\cdot, \cdot)$. The $\mathcal{E}_K(\cdot, \cdot)$ oracle takes (N, M) as its input and returns (C, T). The $\$(\cdot, \cdot)$ oracle takes (N, M) as its input and returns a random string of the length $|M| + n$. The adversary needs to be *nonce-respecting*; we demand that an adversary A never repeats the same N in its queries. We define the privacy advantage as

$$\mathrm{Adv}_{\mathcal{E}}^{\mathrm{priv}}(A) := \Pr_K\left[A^{\mathcal{E}_K(\cdot, \cdot)} = 1\right] - \Pr_{\$}\left[A^{\$(\cdot, \cdot)} = 1\right].$$

We define $\mathrm{Adv}_{\mathcal{E}}^{\mathrm{priv}}(t, \sigma) := \max_A \mathrm{Adv}_{\mathcal{E}}^{\mathrm{priv}}(A)$, where the max runs over adversaries A who consumes time at most t, the total length of queries being at most σ blocks. A block is n bits, and the length of a query (N, M) is $1 + \lceil |M|/n \rceil$ blocks.

Integrity Definition. Again we give an adversary A access to the encryption oracle $\mathcal{E}_K(\cdot, \cdot)$. The adversary needs to be nonce-respecting. We demand the adversary to output a forgery attempt $(N^*, C^*, T^*) \leftarrow A^{\mathcal{E}_K(\cdot, \cdot)}$ after its interaction with the oracle. The value N^* can be old. We define

$$\mathrm{Adv}_{\mathcal{E}}^{\mathrm{int}}(A) := \Pr_K\left[A^{\mathcal{E}_K(\cdot, \cdot)} \text{ forges}\right],$$

where "forges" means that $\mathcal{D}_K(N^*, C^*, T^*)$ returns some $M^* \neq \bot$ and the query (N^*, M^*) has not been made to the $\mathcal{E}_K(\cdot)$ oracle. The quantity $\mathrm{Adv}_{\mathcal{E}}^{\mathrm{int}}(t, \sigma)$ is defined similarly, except that this time the total length of queries σ contains the length of (N^*, C^*, T^*).

Security of Tweakable Ciphers. We give an adversary A access either to the tweakable-cipher oracles $E_{K,i}(\cdot)$ or to an ideal oracles $\pi_i(\cdot)$, where the key K is chosen at random from the key space $\{0, 1\}^k$ and the tweaks i are specified by the adversary A within the tweak space $\mathcal{T}$. The permutations π_i $(i \in \mathcal{T})$ are independently chosen at random from the set of permutations over $\{0, 1\}^n$. We define

$$\mathrm{Adv}_E^{\widetilde{\mathrm{prp}}}(A) := \Pr_K\left[A^{E_{K,i}(\cdot)} = 1\right] - \Pr_{\pi_i}\left[A^{\pi_i(\cdot)} = 1\right],$$

where the probabilities are taken over the random coins used by the oracles and also over internal coins of A, if any. We define $\mathrm{Adv}_E^{\widetilde{\mathrm{prp}}}(t, q) := \max_A \mathrm{Adv}_E^{\widetilde{\mathrm{prp}}}(A)$, where max is taken over adversaries A whose time complexity is at most t and whose query complexity is at most q queries to the oracle.

Similarly, we define the SPRP version $\mathrm{Adv}_E^{\widetilde{\mathrm{prp}}\pm 1}(A)$, where the adversary is given access also to the inverse oracles, $E_{K,i}^{-1}(\cdot)$ or $\pi_i^{-1}(\cdot)$. Also, the quantity $\mathrm{Adv}_E^{\widetilde{\mathrm{prp}}\pm 1}(t, q)$ is defined in the same way as before, where q denotes the maximum number of oracle queries. Again, we may write $\mathrm{Adv}_E^{\widetilde{\mathrm{prp}}\pm 1}(t, q_{+1}, q_{-1})$, where q_{+1} is the maximum number of forward queries and q_{-1} that of inverse queries.

5   Security Proofs of OCB without SPRP

This section is devoted to security proofs. We prove the security of OCB based on the weaker-than-SPRP assumptions.

5.1   Confidentiality of OCB without SPRP

The original proofs of confidentiality of OCB [25], OCB2 [24], OCB3 [13] all rely on the sole assumption that the underlying block cipher is a PRP. This is strongly related to the fact that the definition of confidentiality does not involve the block-cipher inverse $E_K^{-1}(\cdot)$. Specifically, the following theorem holds:

Theorem 1 (Confidentiality of OCB2 Based on PRP). *We have*

$$\mathrm{Adv}_{\mathrm{OCB2}[E]}^{\mathrm{priv}}(t, \sigma) \leq \mathrm{Adv}_E^{\mathrm{prp}}(t', 2\sigma) + \frac{9.5\sigma^2}{2^n},$$

where t' is about t plus 2σ times the time to compute $E_K(\cdot)$.

Proof. For the sake of completeness, here we include the proof of OCB2's privacy based on just the PRP (rather than SPRP) assumption. Recall that Rogaway [24] proves OCB2's privacy in the case of ideal tweakable ciphers:

Lemma 1 (Confidentiality of OCB2 Based on an Ideal Tweakable Cipher). *Let π be an ideal tweakable cipher yielding independently random permutations $\pi_{i,j}^N : \{0,1\}^n \to \{0,1\}^n$ for tweaks $(N, i, j) \in \{0,1\}^n \times \{1, 2, \ldots, 2^{n/2}\} \times \{0,1\}$. Then we have*

$$\mathrm{Adv}_{\mathrm{OCB2}[\pi]}^{\mathrm{priv}}(t, \sigma) = 0,$$

where t is arbitrary and $\sigma \leq 2^{n/2}$. The CPA security is required when π is replaced with an actual tweakable cipher.

Therefore, it remains to prove the CPA security of the XEX[E] construction, based on the PRP assumption of the block cipher E. The following guarantees this:

Lemma 2 (XEX CPA-Security Based on PRP). *We have*

$$\mathrm{Adv}_{\mathrm{XEX}[E]}^{\widetilde{\mathrm{prp}}}(t, q) \leq \mathrm{Adv}_E^{\mathrm{prp}}(t', 2q) + \frac{9.5q^2}{2^n},$$

where t' is about t plus $2q$ times the time to compute $E_K(\cdot)$.

Proof. Rogaway [24] proves that the XEX construction is a CCA-secure tweakable cipher if the underlying block cipher is a secure SPRP. More specifically, Rogaway [24] proves

$$\mathrm{Adv}_{\mathrm{XEX}[E]}^{\widetilde{\mathrm{prp}}\pm 1}(t, q_{+1}, q_{-1}) \leq \mathrm{Adv}_E^{\mathrm{prp}\pm 1}(t', 2q_{+1} + q_{-1}, q_{-1}) + \frac{9.5(q_{+1} + q_{-1})^2}{2^n},$$

where q_{+1} denotes the maximum number of forward queries and q_{-1} that of inverse queries (Rogaway [24] gives an inequality in terms of $q = q_{+1} + q_{-1}$, but his proof [24] directly implies the above refined inequality). Now setting $q_{-1} := 0$ yields the desired inequality.   □

Now, by setting $q = \sigma$, we obtain Theorem 1 by combining the above two lemmas.   □

5.2 Integrity of OCB without SPRP

We now prove the integrity of OCB. For the sake of easy presentation, we prove our results for OCB2 [24] without tag truncation. Similar results apply to other versions of OCB.

Before we proceed, we give some definitions. These definitions play important roles in our proofs.

Forward-Only Attempts and Backward Attempts. Let (N^*, C^*, T^*) be the adversary's output (forgery attempt). Write $C^* = C^*[1]\|C^*[2]\|\cdots\|C^*[c^*]$. We call (N^*, C^*, T^*) *forward-only* if the blocks $C^*[1]$, $C^*[2]$, ..., $C^*[c^* - 1]$ are the values returned by the oracle on a previous query (N^*, M°) with some $M^\circ \in \{0, 1\}^*$. That is, if we write (C°, T°) for the value returned by the oracle on this query (N^*, M°) and $C^\circ = C^\circ[1]\|C^\circ[2]\|\cdots\|C^\circ[c^\circ]$, then forward-only means $c^* \leq c^\circ$ and $C^*[1] = C^\circ[1]$, $C^*[2] = C^\circ[2]$, ..., $C^*[c^* - 1] = C^\circ[c^* - 1]$. We also define any (N^*, C^*, T^*) with a single-block C^* as a forward-only attempt. We call (N^*, C^*, T^*) *backward* otherwise. If (N^*, C^*, T^*) is a backward attempt, then C^* must contain at least two blocks.

"Index α." Let (N^*, C^*, T^*) be a backward attempt, so that C^* consists of two or more blocks. Let us write $C^* = C^*[1]\|C^*[2]\|\cdots\|C^*[c^*]$. We shall define an index α as follows. If N^* is new, then set $\alpha := 1$. If N^* is old, then let (N^*, M°) be the previous query and (C°, T°) the value returned by the oracle. Write $C^\circ = C^\circ[1]\|C^\circ[2]\|\cdots\|C^\circ[c^\circ]$. We define α to be the smallest index such that $C^*[\alpha] \neq C^\circ[\alpha]$. Note that $\alpha \leq c^* - 1$.

Algorithm 5. Verification of Backward Attempt (N^*, C^*, T^*)

---

1 **if** N^* *is new and* $N^* \in \textbf{input}(E)$ **then**
2 $\quad\mid\quad$ NonceColl $\leftarrow 1$; **return** 1   /* let adversary win */
3 **end**
4 $L^* \leftarrow E_K(N^*)$; $C^*[1] \parallel C^*[2] \parallel \cdots \parallel C^*[c^*] \overset{n}{\leftarrow} C^*$
5 **for** *each* $i(\neq \alpha) \in \{1, 2, \ldots, c^* - 1\}$ **do**
6 $\quad\mid\quad \Delta \leftarrow 2^i \cdot L^*$; add $\Delta \oplus C^*[i]$ to **output**(E)
7 **end**
8 $\Delta \leftarrow 2^{c^*} \cdot L^*$; $r \leftarrow \text{len}\big(C^*[c^*]\big)$; $R \leftarrow E_K(\Delta \oplus r)$
9 add T^* to **output**(E)
10 **if** $2^\alpha \cdot L^* \oplus C^*[\alpha] \in \textbf{output}(E)$ **then**
11 $\quad\mid\quad$ OutColl $\leftarrow 1$; **return** 1   /* let adversary win */
12 **end**
13 **for** $i = 1$ **to** $c^* - 1$ **do**
14 $\quad\mid\quad \Delta \leftarrow 2^i \cdot L^*$; $M^*[i] \leftarrow E_K^{-1}\big(\Delta \oplus C^*[i]\big) \oplus \Delta$ /* inverse cipher */
15 **end**
16 $\Delta \leftarrow 2^{c^*} \cdot 3 \cdot L^*$; $\Sigma \leftarrow M^*[1] \oplus M^*[2] \oplus \cdots \oplus M^*[c^* - 1] \oplus \big(C^*[c^*] \parallel 0^*\big) \oplus R$
17 **if** $\Delta \oplus \Sigma \in \textbf{input}(E)$ **then**
18 $\quad\mid\quad$ SumColl $\leftarrow 1$; **return** 1   /* let adversary win */
19 **end**
20 $T' \leftarrow E_K(\Delta \oplus \Sigma)$
21 **if** $T^* = T'$ **then**   /* successful forgery */
22 $\quad\mid\quad$ TagColl $\leftarrow 1$; **return** 1
23 **end**
24 **return** 0

Theorem 2 (Integrity of OCB2, without Tag Truncation). *We have*

$$\text{Adv}^{\text{int}}_{\text{OCB2}}(t, \sigma) \leq 3 \,\text{Adv}^{\text{prp}}_E(t', 2\sigma) + 3\sigma \,\text{Adv}^{\text{mac}\pm 1}_E(t', 2\sigma) + \frac{24.5\sigma^2}{2^n},$$

where t' *is about* t *plus* 2σ *times the time to compute* $E_K^{\pm 1}(\cdot)$.

Proof. The proof of this theorem is a mixture of information-theoretic notions (related to PRP) and complexity-theoretic notions (mainly related to MAC± 1). This is unlike usual proofs of block-cipher-based modes of operation, where the two kinds of notions are clearly separated in two stages. The mixture might look strange but is the core of our proofs.

Let A be an adversary trying to break the integrity of OCB2. Adversary A may be adaptive and/or randomized. We assume that the total length of queries made by A is at most σ. Let (N^*, C^*, T^*) be adversary A's output. Let $q \leq \sigma$ denote the number of queries that A has made at this point.

If (N^*, C^*, T^*) is a forward-only attempt, then the verification process of (N^*, C^*, T^*) does not involve the block-cipher inverse $E_K^{-1}(\cdot)$. So we can bound the forgery probability as follows. We first replace the block-cipher calls with random permutations $\pi^N_{i,j}$, which costs us $\text{Adv}^{\text{prp}}_E(t', 2\sigma) + 9.5\sigma^2/2^n$ by Lemma 2.

The random permutation $\pi_{i,1}^{N^*}$ producing T^* in response to the forward-only attempt (N^*, C^*, T^*) has been never invoked before, and hence for any value T^* the probability that the output value becomes equal to T^* is at most $1/2^n$. In total, the success probability of a forward-only attempt is bounded by

$$\mathrm{Adv}_E^{\mathrm{prp}}(t', 2\sigma) + \frac{9.5\sigma^2}{2^n} + \frac{1}{2^n},$$

where t' is, throughout the paper, about t plus 2σ times the time to compute $E_K^{\pm 1}(\cdot)$.

Hence, it remains to treat the case where (N^*, C^*, T^*) is a backward attempt. We run the adversary as $(N^*, C^*, T^*) \leftarrow A^{\mathcal{E}_K(\cdot)}$, maintaining two sets $\mathbf{input}(E)$ and $\mathbf{output}(E)$. The set $\mathbf{input}(E)$ records all input values to $E_K(\cdot)$ and output values from $E_K^{-1}(\cdot)$. Vice versa for $\mathbf{output}(E)$. We then verify the integrity of (N^*, C^*, T^*) according to Algorithm 5. We let the adversary win if she successfully sets one of the four flags. Obviously we have

$$\begin{aligned}
\Pr[\mathbf{TagColl}] \leq{}& \Pr[\mathbf{TagColl} \wedge \overline{\mathbf{SumColl}}] \\
&+ \Pr[\mathbf{SumColl} \wedge \overline{\mathbf{OutColl}}] \\
&+ \Pr[\mathbf{OutColl} \wedge \overline{\mathbf{NonceColl}}] + \Pr[\mathbf{NonceColl}],
\end{aligned}$$

and we shall evaluate each of these probabilities.

- **NonceColl.** This is an event in which the adversary outputs a fresh N^* such that N^* collides with some previous input value to $E_K(\cdot)$. Note that this event can be described without calling the block-cipher inverse $E_K^{-1}(\cdot)$. Therefore, it turns out that we can bound this probability, within the framework of tweakable ciphers [24, Theorem 7], based on the assumption that E is a PRP. We become generous and let A win if it causes a collision of input values, not only at the time of a backward attempt but at any time during the game, even while making queries to oracle $\mathcal{E}_K(\cdot)$. We first replace $E_K(\cdot)$ with a random permutation π, and then replace π with a random function φ. This costs us $\mathrm{Adv}_E^{\mathrm{prp}}(t', \sigma+q) + 0.5(\sigma+q+1)(\sigma+q)/2^n \leq \mathrm{Adv}_E^{\mathrm{prp}}(t', 2\sigma) + 4\sigma^2/2^n$, by the PRP-PRF switching lemma (e.g. [3]). Observe that there are at most $\sigma + q \leq 2\sigma$ calls to φ (for encrypting nonces, for encrypting messages and for producing tags). A collision of input values are one of the following events:

  - $N' = 2^i \cdot 3^j \cdot L \oplus X$,
  - $2^{i'} \cdot 3^{j'} \cdot L' \oplus X' = N$, or
  - $2^{i'} \cdot 3^{j'} \cdot L' \oplus X' = 2^i \cdot 3^j \cdot L \oplus X$,

  where the query with N' is made after the one with N. Note that L and L' are random values not seen by the adversary as long as $\overline{\mathbf{NonceColl}}$, and $N, i, j, X, N', i', j', X'$ are independent from L and L'. Under the event $\overline{\mathbf{NonceColl}}$, what A observes is the output values of a random function φ, and these returned values do not affect the probability that one of the above three equations holds. Therefore, we may assume that A is non-adaptive,

---

Algorithm 6. Forger B attacking $E_K^{\pm 1}(\cdot)$

---

1 **initialize** input(E) /* record input of $E_K(\cdot)$ and output of $E_K^{-1}(\cdot)$ */
2 **run** $(N^*, C^*, T^*) \leftarrow A^{\mathcal{E}_K(\cdot, \cdot)}$ /* simulate A's oracle using $E_K(\cdot)$ */
3 **if** (N^*, C^*, T^*) *is not a backward attempt* **then**
4 $\quad$ | $\quad$ abort
5 **else**
6 $\quad$ | $\quad$ $L^* \leftarrow E_K(N^*)$; $C^*[1] \parallel C^*[2] \parallel \cdots \parallel C^*[c^*] \xleftarrow{n} C^*$
7 $\quad$ | $\quad$ **for** *each* $i(\neq \alpha) \in \{1, 2, \ldots, c^* - 1\}$ **do**
8 $\quad$ | $\quad$ | $\quad$ compute $M^*[i]$ by making a query to $E_K^{-1}(\cdot)$
9 $\quad$ | $\quad$ **end**
10 $\quad$ | $\quad$ compute R by making a query to $E_K(\cdot)$
11 $\quad$ | $\quad$ choose uniformly at random $X \leftarrow$ input(E) /* reduction degrades */
12 $\quad$ | $\quad$ $M^*[\alpha] \leftarrow X \oplus 2^{c^*} \cdot 3 \cdot L^* \oplus (C^*[c^*] \parallel 0^*) \oplus R \oplus \bigoplus_{i \neq \alpha, i < c^*} M^*[i]$
13 $\quad$ | $\quad$ **return** $(2^\alpha \cdot L \oplus M^*[\alpha], 2^\alpha \cdot L \oplus C^*[\alpha])$ /* forgery attempt on $E_K^{\pm 1}(\cdot)$ */
14 **end**

---

and the overall probability of an input collision (after becoming generous to the adversary) is at most

$$\sum_{\alpha=1}^{2\sigma} \frac{\alpha}{2^n} \leq \frac{4\sigma^2}{2^n}.$$

- **OutColl$\wedge\overline{\text{NonceColl}}$.** This is an event in which $2^\alpha \cdot L^* \oplus C^*[\alpha]$ collides with some previous output value of $E_K(\cdot)$. Again, similarly to the previous case, note that this event can be described without the block-cipher inverse $E_K^{-1}(\cdot)$. We can first replace $E_K(\cdot)$ with a random permutation $\pi(\cdot)$ and then with a random function $\varphi(\cdot)$. This costs us $\text{Adv}_E^{\text{prp}}(t', 2\sigma) + 4\sigma^2/2^n$. We can then observe that the previous output values must be either a) $L \leftarrow E_K(N)$, b) $2^i \cdot L \oplus C[i]$ or c) $T \leftarrow E_K(2^m \cdot 3 \cdot L \oplus \Sigma)$. In any event, under the condition $\overline{\text{NonceColl}}$, even though adversary A may well be adaptive (and may have chosen C^* adaptively), adversary A has learned nothing about the value L^*. The values returned by the random function φ do not affect the probability of guessing L^*. So the probability is at most

$$\sum_{\alpha=1}^{\ell^*} \frac{2\sigma}{2^n} \leq \frac{2\sigma^2}{2^n},$$

where ℓ^* denotes the block length of C^*.

- **SumColl$\wedge\overline{\text{OutColl}}$.** Using A as a subroutine, we shall construct a forger B that attacks the unpredictability of $E_K^{\pm 1}(\cdot)$. See Algorithm 6 for the definition of adversary B. Under the event $\overline{\text{OutColl}}$, we see that $2^\alpha \cdot L \oplus C^*[\alpha]$ must be a new output value. We can compute its preimage by making queries to the $E_K^{\pm 1}(\cdot)$ oracle, which yields a forgery. Note that there is a loss factor of $1/(\sigma + q)$, because B has to make a guess of the value X. Overall, we can bound the probability as $\Pr\left[\mathbf{SumColl} \wedge \overline{\mathbf{OutColl}}\right] \leq (\sigma + q) \operatorname{Adv}_E^{\text{mac}\pm 1}(t', \sigma + q) \leq 2\sigma \operatorname{Adv}_E^{\text{mac}\pm 1}(t', 2\sigma)$.

- **TagColl**$\wedge$**SumColl**. This event directly implies a forgery of the block cipher. We can easily compute $\Pr\left[\mathbf{TagColl} \wedge \overline{\mathbf{SumColl}}\right] \leq \operatorname{Adv}_E^{\text{mac}\pm 1}(t', 2\sigma)$.

We can now sum up the probabilities as

$$
\begin{aligned}
\operatorname{Adv}_{\text{OCB2}}^{\text{int}}(A) \leq{}& \operatorname{Adv}_E^{\text{prp}}(t', 2\sigma) + \frac{9.5\sigma^2}{2^n} + \frac{1}{2^n} \\
&+ \operatorname{Adv}_E^{\text{prp}}(t', 2\sigma) + \frac{4\sigma^2}{2^n} + \frac{4\sigma^2}{2^n} \\
&+ \operatorname{Adv}_E^{\text{prp}}(t', 2\sigma) + \frac{4\sigma^2}{2^n} + \frac{2\sigma^2}{2^n} \\
&+ 2\sigma \operatorname{Adv}_E^{\text{mac}\pm 1}(t', 2\sigma) \\
&+ \operatorname{Adv}_E^{\text{mac}\pm 1}(t', 2\sigma) \\
\leq{}& 3 \operatorname{Adv}_E^{\text{prp}}(t', 2\sigma) + 3\sigma \operatorname{Adv}_E^{\text{mac}\pm 1}(t', 2\sigma) + \frac{24.5\sigma^2}{2^n},
\end{aligned}
$$

as desired. $\square$

6 AEAD (AE with Associated Data)

Rogaway [23] discusses a generic way ("ciphertext translation") to handle associated data (AD) $A \in \{0,1\}^*$ with an AE scheme that does not have an AD input. Specifically, given a MAC $F_{K'} : \{0,1\}^* \to \{0,1\}^n$ which is PRF-secure (indistinguishable from a random function $\Phi : \{0,1\}^* \to \{0,1\}^n$, where $\{0,1\}^*$ is treated as the set of strings whose length is at most $2^{n/2}$ blocks; the quantities $\operatorname{Adv}_F^{\text{prf}}(A)$ and $\operatorname{Adv}_F^{\text{prf}}(t,\sigma)$ are defined in the natural way) with a secret key K', we can construct an AEAD scheme OCB2$[E]$-F as follows:

$$
\text{OCB2}[E]\text{-}F_{K,K'}^N(A, M) := \begin{cases} (C, T) & \text{if } A = \varnothing, \\ (C, T \oplus V) & \text{otherwise,} \end{cases}
$$

where $(C, T) \leftarrow \text{OCB2}[E]_K^N(M)$ and $V \leftarrow F_{K'}(A)$. Here, K and K' are assumed to be independent. Regarding the security of this combined scheme, we have

$$
\operatorname{Adv}_{\text{OCB2}[E]\text{-}F}^{\text{priv}}(t, \sigma) \leq \operatorname{Adv}_{\text{OCB2}[E]}^{\text{priv}}(t', \sigma) + \operatorname{Adv}_F^{\text{prf}}(t', \sigma), \tag{1}
$$

$$
\operatorname{Adv}_{\text{OCB2}[E]\text{-}F}^{\text{int}}(t, \sigma) \leq \operatorname{Adv}_{\text{OCB2}[E]}^{\text{int}}(t', \sigma) + \operatorname{Adv}_F^{\text{prf}}(t', \sigma), \tag{2}
$$

where t' is about t plus the time to compute OCB2 and F on these inputs. Now, if we realize F using for example PMAC [6] based on the block cipher E, then our results carry over to this AEAD scheme, because the PRF security of PMAC can be proven based on the PRP assumption of the underlying cipher E [6].

Rogaway [24] introduces PMAC1 and combines it with OCB2 via ciphertext translation. This results in a single-key AEAD scheme, The definition of PMAC1

Algorithm 7. $\mathrm{PMAC1}_K(A)$

Input: associated data $A(\neq \varnothing) \in \{0,1\}^*$, a key $K \in \{0,1\}^k$
Output: a value $V \in \{0,1\}^n$
1   $L \leftarrow E_K(0)$
2   $\Sigma \leftarrow 0$
3   $A[1] \parallel A[2] \parallel \cdots \parallel A[a] \xleftarrow{n} A$
4   **for** $i = 1$ **to** $a - 1$ **do**
5 | $\Delta \leftarrow 2^i \cdot 3^2 \cdot L$ /* multiplication in $\mathrm{GF}(2^n)$ */
6 | $B[i] \leftarrow E_K(\Delta \oplus A[i])$
7 | $\Sigma \leftarrow \Sigma \oplus B[i]$
8   **end**
9   **if** $|A[a]| = n$ **then**
10 | $\Delta \leftarrow 2^a \cdot 3^3 \cdot L$
11 | $\Sigma \leftarrow \Sigma \oplus A[a]$
12   **else**
13 | $\Delta \leftarrow 2^a \cdot 3^4 \cdot L$
14 | $\Sigma \leftarrow \Sigma \oplus (A[a] \parallel 10^*)$
15   **end**
16   $V \leftarrow E_K(\Delta \oplus \Sigma)$
17   **return** V

---

is given in Algorithm 7. For the single-key OCB2+PMAC1 (using the same block-cipher key K), (1) is relatively easily proven, as we can apply the tweakable cipher framework which essentially separates the key between OCB2 and PMAC1. On the other hand, unfortunately, (2) for OCB2+PMAC1 is not immediate. The difficulty lies in the fact that we are unable to completely separate the PRP part (which goes down to information-theoretic notion) from the MAC ± 1 part (which remains within the complexity-theoretic notion). However, the integrity of OCB2+PMAC1 can be proven (without SPRP) in essentially the same way as our proof of integrity of OCB2. The proof would not need much modification and hence is omitted.

7   Further Discussion

In this section we dicuss the implications of our security results. We first closely compare our integrity bound with the previous one that is based on the SPRP assumption. We then explore the problem of tag truncation and the separation of block-cipher keys.

Comparison with the Previous Bound. Table 1 compares our integrity bound with the one obtained in [24] for OCB2 based on the SPRP assumption. One might wonder that our bound is qualitatively worse, because of the constant 3σ in front of $\mathrm{Adv}_E^{\mathrm{mac}}(\cdot)$. This is not the case, because in general $\mathrm{Adv}_E^{\mathrm{mac}}(\cdot)$ is significantly smaller than $\mathrm{Adv}_E^{\mathrm{prp}}(\cdot)$. Essentially, our bound gives a birthday

Table 1. Comparison of OCB2 integrity bounds, where τ denotes the tag length. Note that the work [24] allows only a single attempt of forgery, whereas we allow multiple attempts.

Assumptions	Bounds	Source
SPRP	$\mathrm{Adv}_E^{\mathrm{sprp}}(t', 2\sigma) + \dfrac{9.5\sigma^2}{2^n} + \dfrac{2^{n-\tau}}{(2^n - 1)}$	[24]
PRP + MAC	$3\,\mathrm{Adv}_E^{\mathrm{prp}}(t', 2\sigma) + 3\sigma\,\mathrm{Adv}_E^{\mathrm{mac}}(t', 2\sigma) + \dfrac{24.5\sigma^2}{2^n}$	This work

security comparable to the previous bound that is based on SPRP. We refer to [1, 9, 19] for detailed discussion on the difference between $\mathrm{Adv}_E^{\mathrm{mac}}(\cdot)$ and $\mathrm{Adv}_E^{\mathrm{prp}}(\cdot)$.

Tag Truncation. If one wants to prove the security of OCB2 based on the weaker-than-SPRP assumptions for the cases where the tag size is truncated to $\tau < n$ bits, then one needs to assume that the function $E'_K : \{0,1\}^n \to \{0,1\}^\tau$ defined naturally from E_K is unpredictable when given access to the oracles $E_K^{\pm 1}(\cdot)$. This assumption, of course, is stronger than assuming that the cipher $E_K : \{0,1\}^n \to \{0,1\}^n$ itself is unpredictable. The stronger assumption seems inevitable, since we are reducing the event **TagColl** $\wedge$ $\overline{\textbf{SumColl}}$ directly to the unpredictability of the truncated function $E'_K : \{0,1\}^n \to \{0,1\}^\tau$.

Two-Key OCB2. Interestingly, however, we could circumvent the aforementioned stronger assumption if we are allowed to use two different keys. Figure 2 describes a two-key version of OCB2 (note that the mask is just Λ, not $2^m \cdot 3 \cdot \Lambda$). The security proof becomes a bit easier for this construction, and the bound becomes slightly better (by a constant factor). Moreover, since the inverse $E_{K2}^{-1}(\cdot)$ is never used in the algorithm, we can replace $E_{K2}(\cdot)$ with a random permutation π_2, independent of the key $K1$. Therefore, for this two-key construction, we do not need to assume the stronger unpredictability; we can prove the security of the two-key OCB2 based on the original weaker-than-SPRP assumption about the underlying cipher.

The trick is that we are able to measure the degradation of security caused by truncating the output of a PRP function. We cannot do the same for an unpredictable function. This seems to be the first example of an authenticated-encryption mode in which the number of keys makes a fundamental difference in the assumptions about the underlying block cipher.

We are *not* proposing the two-key version over the original OCB. There is of course performance issues with the two-key version. The two-key OCB2 is expected to perform asymptotically the same as compared to OCB2, since the main operation is the same and the other operations are done in a constant time. On the other hand, there exist engineering issues. The two-key version obviously needs twice the size of secure memory. Also, the two-key version needs to redo the key scheduling of the underlying cipher when changing to the second key.

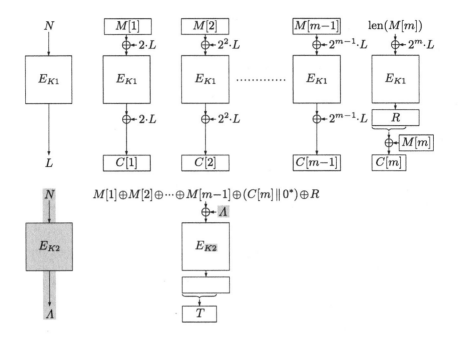

Fig. 2. Two-key OCB2 encryption: Places in gray are the differences from the original OCB2

Moreover, the nonce N needs to be kept till the end of encryption process, in order to compute the tag. Nonetheless, the two-key OCB2 is both practically efficient and theoretically intriguing at the same time.

8   Conclusion

In this paper, we have proven that the OCB mode of operation is secure if the underlying cipher is a PRP and unpredictable. The original proof of privacy carries over. For integrity, we have provided a new proof, in which we applied the framework of tweakable ciphers to forward evaluation of ciphers and the framework of message authentication codes to backward evaluation.

Our integrity bound is essentially the same as the birthday bound obtained in the previous work based on the SPRP assumption. So we do not "lose" security for assuming less about the underlying cipher. Moreover, we have presented a number of examples to illustrate the gap between our assumptions and the conventional SPRP, thereby clarifying the significance of our new security reduction.

Lastly, we pointed out that we would need a stronger assumption in case of tag truncation. However, we also presented a two-key version of OCB2, which circumvents the stronger assumption and remains secure based on the PRP and unpredictability of the underlying cipher. The two-key OCB2 is practically efficient and might deserve extra attention for its added security.

Acknowledgments. We would like to thank the anonymous reviewers for valuable comments. We are also grateful to Shoichi Hirose and Reza Reyhanitabar for helping us revise the paper.

References

1. An, J.H., Bellare, M.: Constructing VIL-MACs from FIL-MACs: Message authentication under weakened assumptions. In: Wiener, M. (ed.) CRYPTO 1999. LNCS, vol. 1666, pp. 252–269. Springer, Heidelberg (1999)
2. Bellare, M., Goldreich, O., Mityagin, A.: The power of verification queries in message authentication and authenticated encryption. Cryptology ePrint Archive: Report 2004/309 (2004)
3. Bellare, M., Rogaway, P.: The security of triple encryption and a framework for code-based game-playing proofs. In: Vaudenay, S. (ed.) EUROCRYPT 2006. LNCS, vol. 4004, pp. 409–426. Springer, Heidelberg (2006)
4. Bellare, M., Rogaway, P., Wagner, D.: The EAX mode of operation. In: Roy, B., Meier, W. (eds.) FSE 2004. LNCS, vol. 3017, pp. 389–407. Springer, Heidelberg (2004)
5. Biryukov, A., Khovratovich, D.: Related-key cryptanalysis of the full AES-192 and AES-256. In: Matsui, M. (ed.) ASIACRYPT 2009. LNCS, vol. 5912, pp. 1–18. Springer, Heidelberg (2009)
6. Black, J.A., Rogaway, P.: A block-cipher mode of operation for parallelizable message authentication. In: Knudsen, L.R. (ed.) EUROCRYPT 2002. LNCS, vol. 2332, pp. 384–397. Springer, Heidelberg (2002)
7. CAESAR: Competition for authenticated encryption: Security, applicability, and robustness (2013), http://competitions.cr.yp.to/caesar.html
8. Dodis, Y., Pietrzak, K., Puniya, P.: A new mode of operation for block ciphers and length-preserving MACs. In: Smart, N.P. (ed.) EUROCRYPT 2008. LNCS, vol. 4965, pp. 198–219. Springer, Heidelberg (2008)
9. Dodis, Y., Steinberger, J.: Message authentication codes from unpredictable block ciphers. In: Halevi, S. (ed.) CRYPTO 2009. LNCS, vol. 5677, pp. 267–285. Springer, Heidelberg (2009)
10. Dodis, Y., Steinberger, J.: Domain extension for MACs beyond the birthday barrier. In: Paterson, K.G. (ed.) EUROCRYPT 2011. LNCS, vol. 6632, pp. 323–342. Springer, Heidelberg (2011)
11. Iwata, T., Ohashi, K., Minematsu, K.: Breaking and repairing GCM security proofs. In: Safavi-Naini, R., Canetti, R. (eds.) CRYPTO 2012. LNCS, vol. 7417, pp. 31–49. Springer, Heidelberg (2012)
12. Jonsson, J.: On the security of CTR + CBC-MAC. In: Nyberg, K., Heys, H.M. (eds.) SAC 2002. LNCS, vol. 2595, pp. 76–93. Springer, Heidelberg (2003)
13. Krovetz, T., Rogaway, P.: The software performance of authenticated-encryption modes. In: Joux, A. (ed.) FSE 2011. LNCS, vol. 6733, pp. 306–327. Springer, Heidelberg (2011)
14. Lee, J., Steinberger, J.: Multi-property-preserving domain extension using polynomial-based modes of operation. In: Gilbert, H. (ed.) EUROCRYPT 2010. LNCS, vol. 6110, pp. 573–596. Springer, Heidelberg (2010)
15. Liskov, M., Rivest, R.L., Wagner, D.: Tweakable block ciphers. In: Yung, M. (ed.) CRYPTO 2002. LNCS, vol. 2442, pp. 31–46. Springer, Heidelberg (2002)

16. Luby, M., Rackoff, C.: How to construct pseudo-random permutations from pseudo-random functions. In: Williams, H.C. (ed.) CRYPTO 1985. LNCS, vol. 218, pp. 447–447. Springer, Heidelberg (1986)
17. Luby, M., Rackoff, C.: How to construct pseudorandom permutations from pseudorandom functions. SIAM J. Comput. 17(2), 373–386 (1988)
18. McGrew, D.A., Viega, J.: The security and performance of the Galois/Counter Mode (GCM) of operation. In: Canteaut, A., Viswanathan, K. (eds.) INDOCRYPT 2004. LNCS, vol. 3348, pp. 343–355. Springer, Heidelberg (2004)
19. Naor, M., Reingold, O.: From unpredictability to indistinguishability: A simple construction of pseudo-random functions from MACs (extended abstract). In: Krawczyk, H. (ed.) CRYPTO 1998. LNCS, vol. 1462, pp. 267–282. Springer, Heidelberg (1998)
20. NIST: DES modes of operation. FIPS Publication 81 (1980)
21. NIST: Recommendation for block cipher modes of operation: Galois/Counter Mode (GCM) for confidentiality and authentication. Special Publication 800-38D (2007)
22. NIST: Recommendation for block cipher modes of operation: The CCM mode for authentication and confidentiality. Special Publication 800-38C (2007)
23. Rogaway, P.: Authenticated-encryption with associated-data. In: ACM CCS 2002, pp. 98–107. ACM Press (2002)
24. Rogaway, P.: Efficient instantiations of tweakable blockciphers and refinements to modes OCB and PMAC. In: Lee, P.J. (ed.) ASIACRYPT 2004. LNCS, vol. 3329, pp. 16–31. Springer, Heidelberg (2004)
25. Rogaway, P., Bellare, M., Black, J., Krovetz, T.: OCB: A block-cipher mode of operation for efficient authenticated encryption. In: Reiter, M.K., Samarati, P. (eds.) ACM CCS 2001, pp. 196–205. ACM (2001)
26. Wagner, D.: The boomerang attack. In: Knudsen, L.R. (ed.) FSE 1999. LNCS, vol. 1636, pp. 156–170. Springer, Heidelberg (1999)
27. Whiting, D., Housley, R., Ferguson, N.: AES encryption & authentication using CTR mode & CBC-MAC. IEEE P802.11 doc 02/001r2 (2002)

A Short Universal Hash Function from Bit Rotation, and Applications to Blockcipher Modes

Kazuhiko Minematsu

NEC Corporation, 1753 Shimonumabe, Nakahara-Ku, Kawasaki, Japan
k-minematsu@ah.jp.nec.com

Abstract. In this paper we propose a new universal hash function based on bit rotation. The proposed scheme, called Circulant hash, is a variant of the classical random matrix-based hash of Carter and Wegman, called H_3, and Toeplitz hash by Krawczyk. However, Circulant hash has a smaller key space and the proved differential probability is not implied by the previous analyses on these functions.

Since Circulant hash is an almost XOR-universal hash function for balanced input/output, it may not be a perfect substitute for H_3 and Toeplitz hash. However, we show that Circulant hash is a useful tool for blockcipher modes, specifically as an alternative to Galois field constant multiplications. We provide some illustrative examples of the constructions of tweakable blockcipher and vector-input pseudorandom function using Circulant hash. Our schemes are as efficient as previous ones using GF constant multiplications, and provide some unique features.

Keywords: Bit rotation, Toeplitz hash, Blockcipher Mode.

1 Introduction

Bit rotation is one of the most basic operations appearing in numerous fields of computer science. In case of cryptography, bit rotation mainly serves as a basic tool for building cryptographic primitives [4, 6, 14, 31, 40]. This paper shows that bit rotation also offers a powerful tool in the field of provable security. We propose a simple bit rotation-based function, called Circulant hash, and show that it is ϵ-almost XOR universal (ϵ-AXU) hash function if the length of input vector satisfies certain conditions. As the name suggests, it is basically a matrix-vector product of a random circulant matrix over GF(2) and the input vector. Circulant hash can be seen as a variant of classical random matrix-based hash of Carter and Wegman [10], called H_3, or Toeplitz hash by Krawczyk [19], with a restriction to square matrix. One can also take it as an extension of Data-dependent rotation (DDR) by Rivest [29]. However, Circulant hash has a smaller key space than H_3 and Toeplitz hash, while much larger input space than DDR of the same key length.

Despite the simple look, proving the differential probability (i.e. the AXU bias) of Circulant hash is non-trivial. We prove that, for Circulant hash using κ-bit key

W. Susilo and R. Reyhanitabar (Eds.): ProvSec 2013, LNCS 8209, pp. 221–238, 2013.

and $(\kappa-1)$-bit input and κ-bit output, the differential probability is at most $2/2^{\kappa}$, if κ is a special prime (see Definition 1 and Lemma 1). This result is not implied by the previous analyses on H_3, Toeplitz hash, and DDR [10, 11, 19, 30, 37, 38]. In fact, our finding is based on an old paper by Daykin [12] discussing how to derive the rank of a matrix over a finite field, which has been overlooked by the cryptography community, to the best of our knowledge.

Circulant hash realizes an ϵ-AXU hash function having almost balanced input and output. When compared with square Toeplitz hash, Circulant hash has a reduced key length and hardware complexity, hence is a better substitute when (almost) square Toeplitz hash has been used, such as [9, 22, 23]. In contrast, even though we can basically extend the input length via tree hashing [10], it may not be appropriate for very long inputs.

We then show that Circulant hash provides a powerful tweaking tool for block-cipher modes. In the field of blockcipher modes, the constant multiplication over a Galois Field (GF) has been widely used as a tweaking tool [13, 16, 28, 33, 35]. We provide some illustrative examples showing that, Circulant hash can be an alternative to GF constant multiplication, or even more useful in some cases. We choose two illustrative applications. The first application is tweakable blockci-pher (TBC) [21] based on a blockcipher. A previous TBC scheme called XEX [33] utilizes constant GF multiplications for efficient sequential tweak update. We build TBC using Circulant hash instead of constant GF multiplication. It allows efficient sequential tweak update as well, and also effectively handles certain non-sequential tweak update without using a precomputation, which may be useful in the real-world applications of TBC.

The second application is vector-input pseudorandom function (PRF). Rog-away and Shrimpton [35] proposed a concrete instantiation of vector-input PRF, called S2V, using a string-input PRF with a post-processing based on constant GF multiplications. In S2V, the computations of string-input PRFs are par-allelizable, however the post-processing is logically serial. We show that, the post-processing can be replaced with (an decomposed form of) Circulant hash, which is essentially bit rotations and is fully parallelizable. Our proposal keeps the most features of S2V while achieves a faster parallel computation. Moreover, it enables powerful incremental update using the previous output (i.e., it is an incremental message authentication code (MAC) [5]), which is impossible with S2V. One can also use our result to build a fast, parallelizable short-input PRF.

These two examples imply that we can build a Circulant hash-based counter-parts for the most of previous blockcipher modes utilizing GF constant multipli-cations, and the each of the resulting scheme exhibits some unique advantages.

2   Preliminaries

Let $\{0,1\}^n$ be the space of n-bit strings, and let $\{0,1\}^*$ be the space of all binary strings, including the empty string, ε. A bit length of a binary string X is written as $|X|$. We define $|X|_n \overset{\text{def}}{=} \lceil |X|/n \rceil$. Here $|\varepsilon| = 0$. The first (last) c bits of X is denoted by $\mathsf{msb}_c(X)$ ($\mathsf{lsb}_c(X)$). We write $\mathbb{N}_c$ to denote

$\{1, 2, \ldots, c\}$. A concatenation of two strings, X and Y, is written as $X\|Y$ or simply XY. A sequence of i zeros is written as 0^i. An i-bit left rotation of n-bit string $X = (X[1]\|X[2]\|\ldots\|X[n])$ is written as $X \lll i = (X[i+1]\|\ldots\|X[n]\|X[1]\|\ldots\|X[i])$. For $X, Y \in \{0,1\}^*$ with $|X| \le |Y|$, let $X \oplus_{\text{end}} Y$ be the XOR of X into the end of Y, i.e. $X \oplus_{\text{end}} Y = (0^{|Y|-|X|}\|X) \oplus Y$. For $X \in \{0,1\}^*$, let $X[1]\|X[2]\|\ldots\|X[m] \xleftarrow{n} X$ denote the n-bit block partitioning of X, i.e., $X[1]\|X[2]\|\ldots\|X[m] = X$ where $m = |X|_n$, and $|X[i]| = n$ for $i < m$ and $|X[m]| \le n$.

If X is uniformly distributed over set $\mathcal{X}$, we write $X \xleftarrow{\$} \mathcal{X}$. The set of all functions having n-bit inputs and m-bit outputs is denoted by $\text{Func}(n, m)$ and the set of all n-bit permutations is denoted by $\text{Perm}(n)$. A keyed function F with key $K \in \mathcal{K}$, input domain $\mathcal{X}$, and output domain $\mathcal{Y}$ is written as $F : \mathcal{K} \times \mathcal{X} \to \mathcal{Y}$. We may write $F_K : \mathcal{X} \to \mathcal{Y}$ if the existence of key is obvious. A pair of two keyed functions, $F : \mathcal{K} \times \mathcal{X} \to \mathcal{Y}$ and $G : \mathcal{K}' \times \mathcal{X} \to \mathcal{Y}$, are said to be compatible (the key spaces are not necessarily the same).

We define the uniform random function (URF) $R : \{0,1\}^n \to \{0,1\}^m$ as the keyed function with a key being uniform over $\text{Func}(n, m)$. The n-bit uniform random permutation (URP), $P : \{0,1\}^n \to \{0,1\}^n$ is a keyed permutation with a key being uniform over $\text{Perm}(n)$. Note that the notion of URF can be extended to the case that input domain is an infinite set, say, $\{0,1\}^*$, by using the lazy sampling. The inverse of keyed permutation E_K (P) is written as E_K^{-1} (P^{-1}).

We define the two classes of universal hash function.

Definition 1. *For $H_K : \mathcal{X} \to \mathcal{Y}$, if $\Pr[H_K(x) = H_K(x')] \le \epsilon$ for any distinct $x, x' \in \mathcal{X}$, H_K is ϵ-almost universal (ϵ-AU). If $\mathcal{Y} = \{0,1\}^n$ and $\Pr[H_K(x) \oplus H_K(x') = c] \le \epsilon$ for any distinct $x, x' \in \mathcal{X}$ and $c \in \{0,1\}^n$, H_K is ϵ-almost XOR universal (ϵ-AXU).*

Note that if H_K is ϵ-AXU it is also ϵ-AU.

Pseudorandom Function. For a pair of compatible keyed function $F : \mathcal{K} \times \mathcal{X} \to \mathcal{Y}$ and $G : \mathcal{K}' \times \mathcal{X} \to \mathcal{Y}$ and an adversary A who performs (possibly adaptive) chosen-plaintext queries and makes a binary output, we write

$$\text{Adv}^{\text{cpa}}_{F,G}(A) \stackrel{\text{def}}{=} \Pr[K \xleftarrow{\$} \mathcal{K} : A^{F_K} \Rightarrow 1] - \Pr[K' \xleftarrow{\$} \mathcal{K}' : A^{G_{K'}} \Rightarrow 1]$$

where $K \xleftarrow{\$} \mathcal{K} : A^{F_K} \Rightarrow 1$ denotes the event that A outputs 1 by querying F_K, when $K \xleftarrow{\$} \mathcal{K}$ is the underlying key sampling. Using URF compatible to $F_K : \{0,1\}^n \to \{0,1\}^m$, R, we write $\text{Adv}^{\text{prf}}_{F_K}(A)$ to denote $\text{Adv}^{\text{cpa}}_{F_K,R}(A)$, which means $\Pr[K \xleftarrow{\$} \mathcal{K} : A^{F_K} \Rightarrow 1] - \Pr[R \xleftarrow{\$} \text{Func}(n, m) : A^R \Rightarrow 1]$.

The definition of $\text{Adv}^{\text{prf}}_{F_K}(A)$ may be extended when F_K takes variable-length input in $\{0,1\}^*$. In this case the underlying R is replaced with $\$$ oracle that outputs independent and random value for any new input; for colliding inputs, the outputs are the same.

3   Universal Hash Function from Bit Rotation

3.1   Constructions Based on Matrix-Vector Product

In [10], Carter and Wegman introduced the idea of universal hash function and provided several examples. Among them a function called H_3 is particularly relevant to our proposal. Suppose we need a universal hash function of η-bit input and κ-bit output. The key of H_3 is a binary $\kappa \times \eta$ matrix, $\mathbb{M}$, whose elements are independent and random. Hence the key length is $\eta \cdot \kappa$ bits. For input vector $x \in \{0,1\}^\eta$, the output of H_3 is a matrix-vector product over GF(2), written as $\mathbb{M} \cdot x^T$, where x^T denotes the column vector of x.

Clearly H_3 provides $1/2^\kappa$-AXU[1] for any positive κ and η. Krawczyk [19] showed a variant of H_3 with reduced key bits, called Toeplitz hash. In Toeplitz hash the key is randomly sampled to specify the $\kappa \times \eta$ Toeplitz matrix over GF(2), $\mathbb{M}_T^{(\kappa,\eta)}$. For input $x \in \{0,1\}^\eta$ the κ-bit output is computed as the matrix-vector product over GF(2), i.e. $y = \mathbb{M}_T^{(\kappa,\eta)} \cdot x^T$. As $\mathbb{M}_T^{(\kappa,\eta)}$ has $(\kappa + \eta - 1)$ independent bits to be specified (i.e. the first column and row vectors), the key length is reduced to $(\kappa + \eta - 1)$ bits. This keyed function has η-bit input and κ-bit output, and is $1/2^\kappa$-AXU [19].

In this paper, we present a new variant of H_3 having even reduced key space from Toeplitz, applicable when η is close to κ. The idea is to use a random circulant matrix, which requires only key of κ bits.

Definition 2. *Let κ be a positive integer. The Circulant hash (CLH for short) is a keyed function* : $\{0,1\}^\kappa \times \{0,1\}^{\kappa-1} \to \{0,1\}^\kappa$ *defined as*

$$\mathrm{CLH}_\kappa(K,x) = \bigoplus_{1 \le i \le \kappa-1:\ x[i]=1} (K \lll (i-1)),$$

where $x = (x[\kappa-1] \| \ldots \| x[1])$ and $x[i] \in \{0,1\}$.

For example, $\mathrm{CLH}_\kappa(K, 0^{\kappa-1}) = 0^\kappa$, and $\mathrm{CLH}_\kappa(K, 0^{\kappa-4}\|101) = K \oplus (K \lll 2)$. It is easy to see that $\mathrm{CLH}_\kappa(K,x)$ is equivalent to a matrix-vector product over GF(2), represented as $\mathbb{M}_C^{(\kappa,\kappa-1)} \cdot \overline{x}^T$, where $\mathbb{M}_C^{(\kappa,\kappa-1)}$ denotes the first $\kappa - 1$ columns of circulant matrix of order κ whose first column vector is the key K and $\overline{x}^T \in \{0,1\}^{\kappa-1}$ is the transposed input of $\overline{x} = (x[1]\| \ldots \| x[\kappa-1])$.

Despite the simple look, proving ϵ-AXU for CLH_κ turns out to be quite nontrivial. The fact that random matrix works fine with H_3 does not necessarily mean the goodness of reduced-key variants. For example, when $\kappa = 5$, we can see (by an exhaustive search) that $\mathrm{CLH}_5(K,x) \oplus \mathrm{CLH}_5(K,x')$ for any $x \ne x$ contains at least 4 independent bits of K, resulting in $1/2^4$-AXU, which is close to the theoretical minimum, $1/2^5$. However, when $\kappa = 8$, $\mathrm{CLH}_8(K,x) \oplus \mathrm{CLH}_8(K,x')$ has only 2 independent bits when $x \oplus x' = (1,0,1,0,1,0,1)$, thus the probability is $1/2^2$. When $\kappa = 7$, $\mathrm{CLH}_7(K,x) \oplus \mathrm{CLH}_7(K,x')$ with $x \oplus x' = (1,1,1,0,1,0)$ has 3 independent bits. This arises a natural question on the condition of κ that assures ϵ-AXU for a small ϵ. The following lemma shows the answer.

---

[1]   [10] only proved that it is $1/2^\kappa$-AU, but it is easily extended to AXU.

Lemma 1. *Let $K \overset{\$}{\leftarrow} \{0,1\}^\kappa$. We have*

$$\max_{\substack{c \in \{0,1\}^\kappa, \\ x,x' \in \{0,1\}^{\kappa-1}, \; x \neq x'}} \Pr_K[\mathrm{CLH}_\kappa(K,x) \oplus \mathrm{CLH}_\kappa(K,x') = c] \leq \frac{2}{2^\kappa}, \quad and$$

$$\max_{c \in \{0,1\}^\kappa, \; x \in \{0,1\}^{\kappa-1} \setminus \{0^{\kappa-1}\}} \Pr_K[\mathrm{CLH}_\kappa(K,x) = c] \leq \frac{2}{2^\kappa},$$

when κ is prime and 2 is the primitive root modulo κ, which we call p*-prime.*

Proof. We first observe that $\mathrm{CLH}_\kappa(K,x) \oplus \mathrm{CLH}_\kappa(K,x') = \mathrm{CLH}_\kappa(K, x \oplus x')$, hence the first claim is proved by showing the maximum of probability $\Pr[\mathrm{CLH}_\kappa(K,x) = c]$ for all $c \in \{0,1\}^\kappa$ and $x \in \{0,1\}^{\kappa-1} \setminus \{0^{\kappa-1}\}$, i.e. proving the second claim also proves the first. Now, let $\mathbb{R}$ be $\kappa \times \kappa$ GF(2)-matrix defined as

$$\mathbb{R} = \begin{bmatrix} 0 & 1 & 0 & \ldots & 0 \\ 0 & 0 & 1 & \ldots & 0 \\ \vdots & \vdots & \vdots & \vdots & \vdots \\ 0 & 0 & 0 & \ldots & 1 \\ 1 & 0 & 0 & \ldots & 0 \end{bmatrix}. \tag{1}$$

Then we have $(K \lll i)^T = \mathbb{R}^i \cdot K^T$, where $\cdot$ is the matrix-vector multiplication over GF(2), and $\mathbb{R}^i$ denotes the matrix exponentiation over GF(2) (i.e. $\mathbb{R}^3 = \mathbb{R} \times \mathbb{R} \times \mathbb{R}$ with matrix multiplication $\times$). Here we define $\mathbb{R}^0$ as the identity matrix, thus $\mathbb{R}^0 \cdot K^T$ means $(K \lll 0) = K$.

From the theory of linear systems, we have

$$\Pr[\mathrm{CLH}_\kappa(K,x) = c]$$

$$= \Pr_K\left[\sum_{1 \leq i \leq \kappa-1 : x[i]=1} \mathbb{R}^i \cdot K = c\right] = \Pr_K\left[\left(\sum_{1 \leq i \leq \kappa-1 : x[i]=1} \mathbb{R}^i\right) \cdot K = c\right]$$

$$= \frac{\left|k \in \{0,1\}^\kappa : \left(\sum_{i:x[i]=1} \mathbb{R}^i\right) \cdot k = c\right|}{2^\kappa} \tag{2}$$

$$\leq \frac{2^{\kappa - \mathrm{rank}\left(\sum_{i:x[i]=1} \mathbb{R}^i\right)}}{2^\kappa} = \frac{1}{2^{\mathrm{rank}\left(\sum_{i:x[i]=1} \mathbb{R}^i\right)}}, \tag{3}$$

where K is uniform over $\{0,1\}^\kappa$ and the matrix sums are over GF(2), and rank(M) denotes the rank of matrix M over GF(2). Hence, we have to prove that $\mathrm{rank}(\sum_{i \in \mathcal{I}} \mathbb{R}^i) \leq \kappa - 1$ for any nonempty $\mathcal{I} \subseteq \{0, \ldots, \kappa - 2\}$.

For a finite field $\mathscr{F}$, let M be the matrix over $\mathscr{F}$. Let $\mathscr{F}[\mathrm{M}]$ be the set of all (nonempty) univariate polynomials for M with coefficients in $\mathscr{F}$. For instance $\mathscr{F}[\mathrm{M}]$ contains $a \cdot \mathrm{M}^2 + b \cdot \mathrm{M}^1 + c \cdot \mathrm{M}^0$, where $a,b,c \in \mathscr{F}$ and addition and multiplication are defined over $\mathscr{F}$. The corresponding $\mathscr{F}$-polynomial is

$f(x) = ax^2 + bx + c$. Specifically, we let $\mathscr{F} = \mathrm{GF}(2)$ and $\mathbb{M} = \mathbb{R}$, then $\sum_{i \in \mathcal{I}} \mathbb{R}^i$ is a member of $\mathrm{GF}(2)[\mathbb{R}]$. We then apply a useful formula of Daykin [12] which provides the $\mathscr{F}$-rank of a square matrix in $\mathscr{F}[\mathbb{M}]$ for any field $\mathscr{F}$ and matrix $\mathbb{M}$. Using Theorem 1 and Section 5 of [12], for any $f[\mathbb{R}] \in \mathrm{GF}(2)[\mathbb{R}]$ we have

$$\mathrm{rank}(f(\mathbb{R})) = \kappa - \mathrm{DegL}(x^\kappa - 1, f(x)) \qquad (4)$$

where $\mathrm{DegL}(g(x), g'(x))$ denotes the degree of largest common factor of $\mathrm{GF}(2)$-polynomials, g and g'. Here, $x^\kappa - 1$ is factored into $(x-1)(x^{\kappa-1} + x^{\kappa-2} + \cdots + x + 1)$, where addition and subtraction are XOR, for any n. The latter factor is called the all-one polynomial (AOP). Because the degree of $f(\mathbb{R})$ we consider is at most $\kappa - 2$, if AOP of degree $\kappa - 1$ is irreducible over $\mathrm{GF}(2)$, $\mathrm{rank}(f(\mathbb{R}))$ is at least $\kappa - 1$. Here, Wah et al. [39] proved that over $\mathrm{GF}(2)$-AOP of degree m is irreducible if and only if $m+1$ is prime and 2 is the primitive root modulo $m+1$. This proves the second claim, and thus concludes the proof. □

Lemma 1 shows that if κ satisfies the conditions, CLH_κ with $K \xleftarrow{\$} \{0,1\}^\kappa$ is $2/2^\kappa$-AXU, and that $\mathrm{CLH}_\kappa^+ : \{0,1\}^\kappa \times (\{0,1\}^{\kappa-1} \times \{0,1\}^\kappa) \to \{0,1\}^\kappa$ defined as $\mathrm{CLH}_\kappa^+(K, (x_1, x_2)) = \mathrm{CLH}_\kappa(K, x_1) \oplus x_2$ is $2/2^\kappa$-AU. As a slight extension of the lemma, if K is not uniform but $\max_k \Pr[K = k] \leq 1/2^p$ holds for some p, then the resulting CLH is $2/2^p$-AXU.

For example, $3, 5, 11, 13,$ and 19 are p-primes. Larger values can be easily derived (e.g.) from the table [2] or by using software. Table 1 shows some examples, where $\kappa_{<2^i}$ ($\kappa_{>2^i}$) denotes the largest (smallest) κ being p-prime smaller (larger) than 2^i. It is worth noting that for many cases there exists a p-prime close to a power of two.

Table 1. Examples of p-primes

$\kappa_{<2^5}$	$\kappa_{>2^5}$	$\kappa_{<2^6}$	$\kappa_{>2^6}$	$\kappa_{<2^7}$	$\kappa_{>2^7}$	$\kappa_{<2^8}$	$\kappa_{>2^8}$	$\kappa_{<2^9}$	$\kappa_{>2^9}$	$\kappa_{<2^{10}}$	$\kappa_{>2^{10}}$	$\kappa_{<2^{11}}$	$\kappa_{>2^{11}}$
29	37	61	67	107	131	227	269	509	523	1019	1061	2029	2053

3.2 Useful Variants

The output and key lengths of CLH are prime, however we frequently need a function of n-bit output with n-bit key, for n being a power of two. For this purpose, we define two variants of CLH.

Definition 3. *Let* $\kappa \leq n \leq \lambda$. *Let* $f_{n,\kappa}^1 : \{0,1\}^n \times \mathbb{N}_{\kappa-1} \to \{0,1\}^n$ *and* $f_{n,\lambda}^2 : \{0,1\}^n \times \mathbb{N}_{\lambda-1} \to \{0,1\}^n$, *where*

$$f_{n,\kappa}^1(K, i) = (\mathrm{msb}_\kappa(K) \lll i) \| 0^{n-\kappa},$$
$$f_{n,\lambda}^2(K, i) = \mathrm{msb}_n(K \| 0^{\lambda-n} \lll i),$$

and we define $\mathrm{CLH}'_{n,\kappa} : \{0,1\}^n \times \{0,1\}^{\kappa-1} \to \{0,1\}^n$ and $\mathrm{CLH}''_{n,\kappa} : \{0,1\}^n \times \{0,1\}^{\lambda-1} \to \{0,1\}^n$ as

$$\mathrm{CLH}'_{n,\kappa}(K,x) \overset{\mathrm{def}}{=} \bigoplus_{1\leq i\leq\kappa-1:\ x[i]=1} f^1_{n,\kappa}(K,i), \quad \text{for } x = (x[\kappa-1]\|\ldots\|x[1]),$$

and

$$\mathrm{CLH}''_{n,\lambda}(K,x) \overset{\mathrm{def}}{=} \bigoplus_{1\leq i\leq\lambda-1:\ x[i]=1} f^2_{n,\lambda}(K,i), \quad \text{for } x = (x[\lambda-1]\|\ldots\|x[1]).$$

Note that $\mathrm{CLH}'_{n,\kappa}(K,x)$ and $\mathrm{CLH}''_{n,\lambda}(K,x)$ are respectively equivalent to $\mathrm{CLH}_\kappa(\mathrm{msb}_\kappa(K),x)\|0^{n-\kappa}$ and $\mathrm{msb}_n(\mathrm{CLH}_\lambda(K\|0^{\lambda-n},x))$, and when $\kappa = n = \lambda$, they are the same as the original CLH_κ. Both $f^1_{n,\kappa}(K,i)$ and $f^2_{n,\lambda}(K,i)$ can be computed with two shifts and one logic operation.

We have the following lemma.

Lemma 2. *Let K be uniform over $\{0,1\}^n$. For $\kappa \leq n \leq \lambda$ we have*

$$\max_{\substack{c\in\{0,1\}^n, \\ x,x'\in\{0,1\}^{\kappa-1},\ x\neq x'}} \Pr_K[\mathrm{CLH}'_{n,\kappa}(K,x) \oplus \mathrm{CLH}'_{n,\kappa}(K,x') = c] \leq \frac{2}{2^\kappa}, \quad and$$

$$\max_{\substack{c\in\{0,1\}^n, \\ x\in\{0,1\}^{\kappa-1}\setminus\{0^{\kappa-1}\}}} \Pr_K[\mathrm{CLH}'_{n,\kappa}(K,x) = c] \leq \frac{2}{2^\kappa},$$

$$\max_{\substack{c\in\{0,1\}^n, \\ x,x'\in\{0,1\}^{\lambda-1},\ x\neq x'}} \Pr_K[\mathrm{CLH}''_{n,\lambda}(K,x) \oplus \mathrm{CLH}''_{n,\lambda}(K,x') = c] \leq \frac{2}{2^{2n-\lambda}}, \quad and$$

$$\max_{\substack{c\in\{0,1\}^n, \\ x\in\{0,1\}^{\lambda-1}\setminus\{0^{\lambda-1}\}}} \Pr_K[\mathrm{CLH}''_{n,\lambda}(K,x) = c] \leq \frac{2}{2^{2n-\lambda}},$$

when κ and λ are p-primes.

The proof of Lemma 2 is a simple extension of the proof of Lemma 1 (the bound of the last two claims are obtained as $(2/2^n) \cdot 2^{\lambda-n} = 2/2^{2n-\lambda}$), hence omitted. For example, $\mathrm{CLH}'_{64,61}(K,x)$ and $\mathrm{CLH}''_{64,71}(K,x)$ implement about 64-bit input/output space with differential probability $1/2^{60}$, and $\mathrm{CLH}''_{128,131}(K,x)$ implements 130-bit input, 128-bit output space with differential probability $1/2^{124}$.

3.3 Notes

Relation to DDR. The keyed DDR, defined as $\mathrm{DDR}(K,x) \overset{\mathrm{def}}{=} (K \lll x)$ for $x \in \{0,\ldots,\kappa-1\}$ with $|K| = \kappa$, is $2/2^\kappa$-AXU if κ is prime [11]. However, the $\log|K|$ input space is too small for most practical applications. With CLH, we can extend the input space from $\log|K|$ to $|K|/2$.

Toeplitz Hash with LFSR. In generation of $\kappa \times \eta$ Toeplitz matrix, Krawczyk [19] also suggested to use the $(\kappa + \eta - 1)$-bit output of κ-bit linear feedback shift register (LFSR). If the initial seed of LFSR is uniformly chosen from $\{0,1\}^\kappa$ and the feedback polynomial is uniformly chosen from the set of *all irreducible polynomials*, the resulting Toeplitz hash is $2\eta/2^\kappa$-AXU [3, 19]. In this case the key can be represented as a pair of κ-bit strings, K_1 and K_2, where K_1 specifies the coefficients of feedback polynomial and K_2 specifies the initial seed of LFSR. The hardware implementation requires an κ-bit accumulator register and an κ-bit LFSR [19]. As pointed out by [26, 36] the K_1's distribution is not uniform over $\{0,1\}^\kappa$ and is hard to determine if κ is large, say, 80.

Compared with $\kappa \times \kappa$ square Toeplitz hash, CLH can roughly halve the key bits. Table 2 provides a comparison of Toeplitz and Circulant hashs for the accumulator-based hardware implementation. It shows that, as an AXU hash function of balanced I/O, CLH provides a smaller footprint while keeping the small differential probability (DP). This will be useful for some applications, e.g. [9, 22, 23].

Extending Input Length. When we want to extend input length, we can use Tree hashing [10] with CLH_κ^+ of Section 3.1, in a similar manner to Badger [8]. At the cost of logarithmic key increase, we can process a long input with small circulant matrices. Effectiveness of such implementation is an interesting future topic.

Table 2. Comparison of Toeplitz and Circulant hashs for accumulator-based hardware implementation. $DP = \epsilon$ means that the function is ϵ-AXU. For Circulant hash we require κ to be a p-prime.

Function	I/O (bit)	Key (bit)	ShReg (bit)	ShReg Feedback	DP
Toeplitz (LFSR) [19]	κ/κ	2κ	κ	Key-dep. IRPoly	$2\kappa/2^\kappa$
Toeplitz (Naive) [19]	κ/κ	$2\kappa - 1$	$2\kappa - 1$	Nothing	$1/2^\kappa$
Circulant (This paper)	$\kappa - 1/\kappa$	κ	κ	Rotation	$2/2^\kappa$

4   Tweakable Blockcipher

We describe how to use CLH for blockcipher modes of operations. Our first target is tweakable blockcipher (TBC), proposed by Liskov et al. [21].

4.1   Definition of Tweakable Blockcipher

TBC is a keyed permutation with auxiliary input called tweak. Formally, a ciphertext of a TBC, $\widetilde{E}_K : \mathcal{M} \times \mathcal{T} \to \mathcal{M}$, is $C = \widetilde{E}_K(M, T)$ for plaintext $M \in \mathcal{M}$ and tweak $T \in \mathcal{T}$. The encryption, $\widetilde{E}_K$, must be a keyed permutation over $\mathcal{M}$ for every $T \in \mathcal{T}$, and the decryption is defined as $\widetilde{E}_K^{-1}(C, T) = M$ with $\widetilde{E}_K^{-1} : \mathcal{M} \times \mathcal{T} \to \mathcal{M}$. We here assume $\mathcal{M} = \{0,1\}^n$ for some fixed n and $\mathcal{T}$ is a certain finite set. TBC works as a building-block of blockcipher modes for various purposes [13, 15, 21, 27, 33].

To define the security, let $\mathrm{Perm}(\mathcal{T}, n)$ be the set of all mappings from $\mathcal{T}$ to n-bit permutations. The size of $\mathrm{Perm}(\mathcal{T}, n)$ is $|\mathrm{Perm}(n)|^{|\mathcal{T}|}$. The sampling $\widetilde{\mathsf{P}} \xleftarrow{\$} \mathrm{Perm}(\mathcal{T}, n)$ implements a set of independent n-bit URPs indexed by $T \in \mathcal{T}$, where $\widetilde{\mathsf{P}}$ and $\widetilde{\mathsf{P}}^{-1}$ have the same interfaces as $\widetilde{E}_K$ and $\widetilde{E}_K^{-1}$. The security notion for $\widetilde{E}_K$ is the indistinguishability from $\widetilde{\mathsf{P}}$ under a chosen-ciphertext attack (CCA), that is,

$$\mathsf{Adv}_{\widetilde{E}}^{\mathsf{tsprp}}(\mathsf{A})$$

$$\stackrel{\text{def}}{=} \Pr[K \xleftarrow{\$} \mathcal{K} : \mathsf{A}^{\widetilde{E}_K, \widetilde{E}_K^{-1}} \Rightarrow 1] - \Pr[\widetilde{\mathsf{P}} \xleftarrow{\$} \mathrm{Perm}(\mathcal{T}, n) : \mathsf{A}^{\widetilde{\mathsf{P}}, \widetilde{\mathsf{P}}^{-1}} \Rightarrow 1], \quad (5)$$

where A^{O_1, O_2} denotes the adversary A querying two oracles, O_1 and O_2, in an arbitrary order.

4.2   Previous Constructions

Liskov et al. [21] showed how to build a secure TBC in the sense of Eq. (5), using $E_K : \mathcal{M} \to \mathcal{M}$ and an ϵ-AXU hash, $H_L : \mathcal{T} \to \mathcal{M}$, for independent keys, K and L. Extending the idea of [21], Rogaway proposed a one-key variant called XEX [33] using $\mathrm{GF}(2^n)$ constant multiplications. Let $\alpha_1, \ldots, \alpha_k$ be the distinct non-zero elements of $\mathrm{GF}(2^n)$ called bases. For each α_i we define the set of allowed indices, $\mathbb{I}_i \subseteq \mathbb{Z}$, which is an integer interval (e.g. $\mathbb{I}_i = [0 \ldots 10]$). The tweak space of (basic) XEX is $\mathcal{T} = \mathcal{T}_1 \times \mathcal{T}_2$ with $\mathcal{T}_1 = \mathbb{I}_1 \times \cdots \times \mathbb{I}_k$, $\mathcal{T}_2 = \{0,1\}^n$, and it is defined as

$$\mathrm{XEX}[E_K](M, T) = E_K(M \oplus \Gamma \cdot E_K(T_2)) \oplus \Gamma \cdot E_K(T_2), \quad (6)$$

where tweak is $T = (T_1, T_2)$ with $T_1 = (i_1, \ldots, i_k)$ and $\Gamma = \alpha_1^{i_1} \cdot \alpha_2^{i_2} \cdots \alpha_k^{i_k}$, and the multiplications are over $\mathrm{GF}(2^n)$. The multiplication $\Gamma \cdot E_K(T_2)$ is also over $\mathrm{GF}(2^n)$ by seeing $E_K(T_2)$ as a coefficient vector of a polynomial in $\mathrm{GF}(2^n)$. The security in terms of Eq. (5) is proved when bases and $\mathcal{T}_1$ satisfy some conditions (see [33]). The point of such construction is that the sequential update of a component index of T_1, i.e., $i_j \to i_j + 1$ for some j, can be quite efficient if we cache the previous value of Γ, because it is essentially the multiplication of the cached Γ by α_j. Typically we set $\alpha_1 = 2$ (the primitive element) since the multiplication by 2 is particularly simple. In this case the update procedure is called "doubling".

Alternatively, based on [21], we could simply use GF multiplication. Assuming n-bit tweak T and n-bit second key[2] L, we take a multiplication of L and T, denoted by $L \cdot T$, and encrypt as $E_K(M \oplus L \cdot T) \oplus L \cdot T$. By precomputing all powers of L, i.e. $L, 2L, \ldots, 2^{n-1}L$, $L \cdot T$ is computed as $L \cdot T = \oplus_{i:T[i]=1} 2^{i-1}L$, where $T[i]$ denotes the i-th bit of T for $i = 1, \ldots, n$. Thanks to the precomputed powers of L, this scheme enables an efficient incrementation of T using Gray code (see Section 4.3).

---

[2] With a slight modification one can generate L from K in a similar manner to XEX, see [25] (Section 5).

4.3   Tweakable Blockcipher Using CLH

We present a single-key TBC based on CLH, in a similar manner to XEX.

Definition 4. *Let* $\kappa \leq n \leq \lambda$. *Let* E_K *be an n-bit blockcipher. The single-key TBCs, XEX-R1$[E_K]$ and XEX-R2$[E_K]$, are defined as*

$$\text{XEX-R1}[E_K](M,T) \overset{\text{def}}{=} E_K(M \oplus \Gamma_1) \oplus \Gamma_1, \text{ and },$$

$$\text{XEX-R2}[E_K](M,T) \overset{\text{def}}{=} E_K(M \oplus \Gamma_2) \oplus \Gamma_2,$$

where $\Gamma_1 = \text{CLH}'_{n,\kappa}(E_K(T_2), T_1)$ *and* $\Gamma_2 = \text{CLH}''_{n,\lambda}(E_K(T_2), T_1)$.
    Here, a tweak is $T = (T_1, T_2) \in \mathcal{T} = \mathcal{T}_1 \times \mathcal{T}_2$ *with* $\mathcal{T}_2 = \{0,1\}^n$. *XEX-R1 has* $\mathcal{T}_1 = \{0,1\}^{\kappa-1} \setminus \{0^{\kappa-1}, 0^{\kappa-2}1\}$. *XEX-R2 has* $\mathcal{T}_1 = \{0,1\}^{\lambda-1} \setminus \{0^{\lambda-1}, 0^{\lambda-2}1\}$.

When the underlying blockcipher is a URP, the security of our schemes are proved as follows. The computational counterparts are trivial.

Theorem 1. *Suppose κ and λ are p-primes. Let* P *be an n-bit URP, and let* A *be an adversary against TBC, using q CCA-queries. Then we have*

$$\text{Adv}^{\text{tsprp}}_{\text{XEX-R1[P]}}(A) \leq \left(\frac{6}{2^{\kappa}} + \frac{4}{2^n}\right) q^2, \quad \text{Adv}^{\text{tsprp}}_{\text{XEX-R2[P]}}(A) \leq \left(\frac{8}{2^{2n-\lambda}} + \frac{2}{2^n}\right) q^2.$$

Proof. See Appendix A.

When $n = 128$, XEX-R1 with $\kappa = 107$ provides about 52-bit security with 106-bit tweak, and XEX-R2 with $\lambda = 131$ provides about 61-bit security with 130-bit tweak.

Properties. Our proposals enable efficient sequential updates of T_1. For simplicity, let us assume $\kappa = n$. Then, since CLH_κ is XOR-linear, the computation of $\text{CLH}_\kappa(L, T_1')$ using $\text{CLH}_\kappa(L, T_1)$ (for $L = E_K(T_2)$) is easy if the hamming weight of $T_1 \oplus T_1'$ is small. To fully utilize this property we can use Gray code in a similar manner to the previous works [20,34], which is as follows. We first take $T_1 \in \mathcal{T}_1$ as a positive integer, thus $2 \leq T_1 \leq 2^{\kappa-1} - 1$, and we modify Definition 4 so that the input to CLH is Gray code of T_1, $\text{gc}(T_1)$. This causes no security degradation since Gray code is a permutation and $\text{gc}(0^{\kappa-1}) = 0^{\kappa-1}$ and $\text{gc}(0^{\kappa-2}1) = 0^{\kappa-2}1$. Let $Z = \text{CLH}_\kappa(L, \text{gc}(T_1 - 1))$ and $Z' = \text{CLH}_\kappa(L, \text{gc}(T_1))$. We want to compute Z' using Z. From the property of Gray code we have

$$Z' = Z \oplus \text{CLH}_\kappa(L, \text{gc}(T_1) \oplus \text{gc}(T_1 - 1))$$
$$= Z \oplus \text{CLH}_\kappa(L, (0\ldots01 \ll \text{ntz}(T_1))) = Z \oplus (L \lll (\text{ntz}(T_1) + 1)),$$

where $\text{ntz}(v)$ denotes the number of trailing zero for v (e.g. $\text{ntz}(0100) = 2$). This can be quite efficient; most CPUs natively support an ntz instruction and there exist fast generic methods [1]. Moreover, this does not require any precomputation on L or additional blockcipher calls. In general, the computation of $\text{CLH}_\kappa(L, \text{gc}(T_1'))$ from $\text{CLH}_\kappa(L, \text{gc}(T_1))$ is fast as long as the weight of

$gc(T_1) \oplus gc(T_1')$ is small. That is, we can easily "jump" to such T_1'. Though conceptually a similar operation is possible with XEX using multiple bases, ours seems to have more flexibility. The above method can be easily extended to the case $\kappa < n$ or $n < \lambda$, using $\mathrm{CLH}_{n,\kappa}'$ or $\mathrm{CLH}_{n,\lambda}''$, where the latter needs to keep κ-bit output before truncation. We remark that jump operation with Gray code trick is also possible with a TBC construction described in the last of Section 4.2, that is, mask is generated by $\mathrm{GF}(2^n)$ multiplication based on the precomputed powers, $\{2^i L\}_{i=0,\dots,n-1}$.

In summary, our CLH enables incremental tweak update and certain non-incremental (jump) update without precomputation, while the basic form of doubling enables only incremental update. GF multiplication using precomputed powers enables both incremental and non-incremental updates, though the cost of precomputation and memory can be problematic, in particular for constrained devices.

If our TBCs replace blockcipher modes where internal tweak update is mostly sequential (e.g. OCB, PMAC [33], and XTS [13]), ours enable additional functionalities, such as selective decryption, without harming the efficiency of normal operation. If we built an online cipher using TBC [27], internal TBC has random tweaks. In [27], using GF multiplication is suggested, however using CLH' or CLH'' may be another option.

Software Results. According to our experiments, even random input to CLH is manageable. We implement $\mathrm{CLH}_{64,61}'$ on Intel Xeon E5620 (2.4GHz) and 64-bit Windows OS, using C with `ntz` instruction, called `BitScanForward`. It processes random inputs using 22 cycles per byte (cpb). For random inputs with weight 16 it runs at about 7.5 cpb, and for sequential update with Gray code, it runs at below 0.5 cpb. The same performance can be obtained for parallel computing of two $\mathrm{CLH}_{64,61}'$ functions by using XMM registers and SSE intrinsics. For reference, a naive C implementation of doubling function, $\mathrm{dbl}_L(i) = 2^i L$ for $L \in \mathrm{GF}(2^{64})$, runs at 1.38 cpb for $i = 1$, 18.6 cpb for $i = 10$, and 52.5 cpb for $i = 30$ on the same platform.

5   Vector-Input PRF

5.1   Construction of S2V-R

For string $X[i] \in \{0,1\}^*$ with $i = 1,\dots,\ell$, we call $X = (X[1],\dots,X[\ell])$ a *vector*. Let $\{0,1\}^{**} \stackrel{\text{def}}{=} \bigcup_{\ell=0,1,2,\dots} \{(X[1],\dots,X[\ell]) : X[i] \in \{0,1\}^*\}$, i.e. the set of all vectors. Note that $\{0,1\}^{**}$ includes the empty vector (which contains no string) which is denoted by ε_v. Rogaway and Shrimpton [35] called a PRF of input domain $\{0,1\}^{**}$ a vector-input PRF (vPRF). They showed how to build vPRF: $\{0,1\}^{**} \to \{0,1\}^n$ from a string-input PRF, sPRF: $\{0,1\}^* \to \{0,1\}^n$ such as CMAC [16]. Their construction, called S2V, is used as a component of a deterministic AE (DAE) called SIV. S2V uses GF constant multiplications in a different way from XEX of Section 4. For reference it is presented in Appendix

---

Algorithm S2V-R$[f, F_K](X[1], \ldots, X[\ell]), 0 \leq \ell \leq t - 1$

1. $S \leftarrow 0^n$, $L \leftarrow F_K(0^n)$
2. **if** $\ell = 0$ **then return** $F_K(f(L, t))$
3. **for** $i \leftarrow 1$ **to** $\ell - 1$ **do** $S \leftarrow S \oplus f(F_K(X[i]), i)$
4. **if** $|X[\ell]| \geq n$ **then** $V \leftarrow (S \oplus f(L, t - 1)) \oplus_{\text{end}} X[\ell]$
5. **else** $V \leftarrow S \oplus f(L, t) \oplus X[\ell] \| 10^*$
6. **return** $F_K(V)$

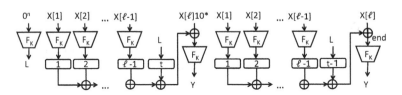

Fig. 1. Vector-input PRF using $F_K : \{0, 1\}^* \rightarrow \{0, 1\}^n$ and post-processing $f : \{0, 1\}^n \times \mathbb{N}_t \rightarrow \{0, 1\}^n$. In the lower figure, the box with $i = 1, 2, \ldots$ denotes the post-processing $f(*, i)$.

B. Building a vPRF from an sPRF is basically possible by first applying an invertible function (encoding) $g : \{0, 1\}^{**} \rightarrow \{0, 1\}^*$ to the input vector then applying the sPRF to the encoded string. However, as explained by [35], S2V has a number of practical advantages over this naive construction.

This section shows a new S2V-like vPRF. Our vPRF, which we call S2V-R, can be based on any sPRF, $F_K : \{0, 1\}^* \rightarrow \{0, 1\}^n$. The pseudo-code and the figure are given in Fig. 1, where $X[i] \| 10^*$ denotes the padding, $X[i] \| 10^{n-1-|X[i]|}$ for $0 \leq |X[i]| \leq n - 1$. The key component of our proposal is the post-processing function, $f : \{0, 1\}^n \times \mathbb{N}_t \rightarrow \{0, 1\}^n$, applied to the outputs of underlying sPRF. Here, t denotes the maximum post-processing variations and each vector can contain at most $t - 1$ strings. We show that, f can be a (variant of) unit computation of CLH_κ, i.e., a bit rotation of the input.

Let $\mathsf{R}_{**} : \{0, 1\}^{**} \rightarrow \{0, 1\}^n$ be the vector-input URF. For security notion of a vector-input keyed function, $F_K : \{0, 1\}^{**} \rightarrow \{0, 1\}^n$, we write $\mathrm{Adv}_{F_K}^{\mathrm{prf}}(\mathsf{A})$ to mean the indistinguishability of F_K from R_{**} under a CPA-adversary $\mathcal{A}$. The security bound of our proposal is as follows.

Theorem 2. *Let* $f : \{0, 1\}^n \times \mathbb{N}_t \rightarrow \{0, 1\}^n$ *be a post-processing function satisfying*

$$\max_{\mathcal{I} \subseteq \mathbb{N}_t, \mathcal{I} \neq \emptyset, c \in \{0,1\}^n} \Pr\left[U \xleftarrow{\$} \{0, 1\}^n : \bigoplus_{i \in \mathcal{I}} f(U, i) = c \right] \leq p_f$$

for $1/2^n \leq p_f \leq 1$. *Let* $\mathsf{R} : \{0, 1\}^* \rightarrow \{0, 1\}^n$ *be URF, and let* S2V-R$[f, \mathsf{R}]$ *be* S2V-R *using* f *and* R. *Let* A *be an adversary querying* S2V-R$[f, \mathsf{R}]$ *with* q

chosen-plaintext queries and the total number of component strings among q queries being σ_s. Then we have

$$\mathrm{Adv}^{\mathrm{prf}}_{\text{S2V-R}[f,\mathrm{R}]}(\mathsf{A}) \le (2q\sigma_s + q^2)p_f.$$

Corollary 1. *For* $n = 128$, *we define* S2V-R1$[F_K]$ *and* S2V-R2$[F_K]$ *as* S2V-R$[f^1_{128,107}, F_K]$ *and* S2V-R$[f^2_{128,131}, F_K]$ *using* $f^1_{128,107}$ *and* $f^2_{128,131}$ *of Definition 3. Then,* S2V-R1 *can accept a vector of 105 strings, with security bound* $(4q\sigma_s + 2q^2)/2^{107}$, *and* S2V-R2 *can accept a vector of 129 strings, with security bound* $(2q\sigma_s + q^2)/2^{124}$.

The proof of Theorem 2 will be given in the full version. The proof of Corollary 1 is obtained by Theorem 2 and Lemma 2.

5.2   Properties of S2V-R

Basic Points. We could implement S2V-R with F_K being (e.g.) CMAC-AES or HMAC-SHA2. If $L = F_K(0^n)$ is precomputed S2V-R$[f, F_K]$ requires one F_K invocation to process one string. These features are shared with the original S2V. The acceptable number of component strings in a vector is largely the same as S2V, which accepts at most $n - 1$ strings. One can build a DAE using S2V-R in the same manner as SIV.

In sequential computation, the computation cost of S2V-R is basically the same as S2V. A difference arises in parallel computation. As well as S2V, the computations of $F_K(X[i])$ in S2V-R are parallelizable. Moreover, S2V-R allows the parallel computation of the post-processing after $F_K(X[i])$, namely bit rotations, while those of S2V is sequential constant multiplications (See Appendix B). This implies that our proposal enables a faster parallel computation. We remark that a variant using a powering-based post-processing, e.g., $f(x, i) = 2^i x$, is also possible. This has the same parallelizability as S2V-R1 or S2V-R2, however the computation cost is much higher.

Short-Input PRF. When we implement F_K by an n-bit blockcipher, E_K, the resulting S2V-R$[f, E_K]$ is a PRF accepting short inputs, i.e. at most $n(t-1)$ bits. For instance, S2V-R2 of Corollary 1 accepts $16 \cdot 128 = 2$Kbyte inputs, which is enough for most of the packet communications[3]. In case of the parallel processing, S2V-R2 with blockcipher is advantageous compared to PMAC, as PMAC needs serial mask computation of $2^i E_K(0^n)$ for $i = 1, \ldots, 128$, or, needs 2Kbyte memory to store the precomputed masks. In hardware (parallel) implementation, the post-processing of S2V-R1 and S2V-R2 are just wires, hence quite fast and small.

Incremental Update. One unique feature of S2V is that it efficiently handles static (invariant) strings. More generally, once we have computed the

---

[3] For example IPSec authenticates packets of 43 to 1.5K Bytes.

output for an input vector $(X[1], \ldots, X[\ell])$ and cached the outputs of F, $\{F_K(X[1]), \ldots, F_K(X[\ell-1])\}$, the output computation for the next input, $(X'[1], \ldots, X'[\ell'])$, requires only the computations of $F_K(X'[i])$ for all $X'[i] \notin \{X[1], \ldots, X[\ell-1]\}$. That is, a restricted form of incremental update. An incremental update for vPRF is particularly valuable when component strings can be long. Our S2V-R shares this feature. Moreover, if the post-processing is commutative (i.e. $f(f(x, i), j) = f(f(x, j), i) = f(x, i+j)$), as with S2V-R1, we can say much more about the incremental operation. Suppose the last string is at most n bits and F_K is invertible for n-bit inputs, which is satisfied with (e.g.) CMAC. Then, S2V-R allows the incremental update from previous outputs, without caching the internal F_K outputs. As well as PMAC [7], this update is secure under the basic security notion for incremental update defined by [5]. For example, suppose we have $Y = \text{S2V-R}[f, F_K](X)$ for $X = (X[1], \ldots, X[\ell])$ with $X[i] \in \{0, 1\}^*$ for $i \leq \ell - 1$ and $|X[\ell]| \leq n$. Let us write $X_{<i} = X[1] \| \cdots \| X[i-1]$ and $X_{>i} = X[i+1] \| \cdots \| X[\ell]$. Then, the output computation for a new vector, $(X_{<i} \| X'[i] \| X_{>i})$ for some $X'[i] \neq X[i]$, can be done as

1. $V' \leftarrow F_K^{-1}(Y)$
2. $V' \leftarrow V' \oplus f(F_K(X[i]), i) \oplus f(F_K(X'[i]), i)$
3. $Y' \leftarrow F_K(V')$,

where F_K^{-1} denotes the inversion for n bits. Namely, we can handle the `replace` operation written as $X \to (X_{<i} \| X'[i] \| X_{>i})$. Similarly, `truncate`, $X \to X_{<\ell}$, and `append`, $X \to X \| X'[\ell+1]$, are efficiently handled. We remark that the same (block-wise) update operations are also supported by PMAC [7,33].

Thanks to the nature of rotation, we can do even more. When $X\|[\ell]\| = n$, `insert` operation, $X \to X'[1]\|X$, is also possible as

1. $V' \leftarrow F_K^{-1}(Y) \oplus f(L, t-1) \oplus X[\ell]$
2. $V' \leftarrow f(V', 1) \oplus f(F_K(X[1]), 1) \oplus f(L, t-1) \oplus X[\ell]$
3. $Y' \leftarrow F_K(V')$,

where $L = F_K(0^n)$. Generally, if we insert a string $X'[i]$ before $X[i]$, the update requires $\min\{i, \ell - i\}$ F_K calls with few additional F_K and F_K^{-1} calls, thus we can save *at least* the half of F_K calls. One more example, `merge` operation, which means the output computation for $X\|X'$ using $Y_1 = \text{S2V-R}[f, F_K](X)$ and $Y_2 = \text{S2V-R}[f, F_K](X')$, also possible with few F_K calls. There should be more examples of practical, application-specific incremental operations that can be handled by S2V-R, and the set of these update operations can offer a very powerful incremental vPRF beyond the ability to handle static strings.

6   Conclusion

This paper has presented Circulant hash, a simple keyed hash function consisting of bit rotations and XORs. We showed that it is ϵ-AXU for ϵ close to the minimum if the length of rotated vectors satisfies certain conditions. Circulant hash can be a good alternative to the famous Toeplitz hash in case we need an

ϵ-AXU hash of balanced I/O lengths. We also showed that Circulant hash works as a powerful tweaking tool for blockcipher modes, and presented two illustrative examples for tweakable blockcipher and vector-input PRF.

Acknowledgments. The author would like to thank Norifumi Kamiya for the discussion on the work of Daykin. The author also would like to thank Mohammad Reza Reyhanitabar for constructive suggestions, and the anonymous reviewers for many useful comments, in particular for pointing out H_3 function of Carter and Wegman.

References

1. Chess Programming Wiki, http://chessprogramming.wikispaces.com/
2. The On-Line Encyclopedia of Integer Sequences: A046145 Smallest primitive root of n, or 0 if no root exists, http://oeis.org/A046145/
3. Alon, N., Goldreich, O., Håstad, J., Peralta, R.: Simple Constructions of Almost k-Wise Independent Random Variables. In: FOCS, pp. 544–553. IEEE Computer Society (1990)
4. Aumasson, J.P., Henzen, L., Meier, W., Phan, R.C.W.: SHA-3 proposal BLAKE, Round 2 (2009)
5. Bellare, M., Goldreich, O., Goldwasser, S.: Incremental cryptography and application to virus protection. In: Leighton, F.T., Borodin, A. (eds.) STOC, pp. 45–56. ACM (1995)
6. Bernstein, D.J.: The Salsa20 Family of Stream Ciphers. In: Robshaw, Billet (eds.) [32], pp. 84–97
7. Black, J., Rogaway, P.: A Block-Cipher Mode of Operation for Parallelizable Message Authentication. In: Knudsen (ed.) [18], pp. 384–397
8. Boesgaard, M., Christensen, T., Zenner, E.: Badger – A Fast and Provably Secure MAC. In: Ioannidis, J., Keromytis, A.D., Yung, M. (eds.) ACNS 2005. LNCS, vol. 3531, pp. 176–191. Springer, Heidelberg (2005)
9. Bösch, C., Guajardo, J., Sadeghi, A.-R., Shokrollahi, J., Tuyls, P.: Efficient Helper Data Key Extractor on FPGAs. In: Oswald, E., Rohatgi, P. (eds.) CHES 2008. LNCS, vol. 5154, pp. 181–197. Springer, Heidelberg (2008)
10. Carter, L., Wegman, M.N.: Universal Classes of Hash Functions. J. Comput. Syst. Sci. 18(2), 143–154 (1979)
11. Contini, S., Yin, Y.L.: On differential properties of data-dependent rotations and their use in MARS and RC6 (Extended Abstract). In: Proceedings of the Second AES Candidate Conference, pp. 230–239 (2000)
12. Daykin, D.E.: On the Rank of the Matrix f(A) and the Enumeration of Certain Matrices over a Finite Field. Journal of the London Mathematical Society s1-35(1), 36–42 (1960)
13. Dworkin, M.: Recommendation for Block Cipher Modes of Operation: The XTS-AES Mode for Confidentiality on Storage Devices. Special Publication 800-38E pp. 175–182 (2010)
14. Ferguson, N., Lucks, S., Schneier, B., Whiting, D., Bellare, M., Kohno, T., Callas, J., Walker, J.: The Skein Hash Function Family. Submission to the NIST SHA-3 Competition, Round 2 (2009)

15. Fleischmann, E., Forler, C., Lucks, S.: McOE: A Family of Almost Foolproof On-Line Authenticated Encryption Schemes. In: Canteaut, A. (ed.) FSE 2012. LNCS, vol. 7549, pp. 196–215. Springer, Heidelberg (2012)

16. Iwata, T., Kurosawa, K.: OMAC: One-Key CBC MAC. In: Johansson, T. (ed.) FSE 2003. LNCS, vol. 2887, pp. 129–153. Springer, Heidelberg (2003)

17. Jetchev, D., Özen, O., Stam, M.: Understanding Adaptivity: Random Systems Revisited. In: Wang, X., Sako, K. (eds.) ASIACRYPT 2012. LNCS, vol. 7658, pp. 313–330. Springer, Heidelberg (2012)

18. Knudsen, L.R. (ed.): EUROCRYPT 2002. LNCS, vol. 2332. Springer, Heidelberg (2002)

19. Krawczyk, H.: LFSR-based Hashing and Authentication. In: Desmedt, Y.G. (ed.) CRYPTO 1994. LNCS, vol. 839, pp. 129–139. Springer, Heidelberg (1994)

20. Krovetz, T., Rogaway, P.: The Software Performance of Authenticated-Encryption Modes. In: Joux, A. (ed.) FSE 2011. LNCS, vol. 6733, pp. 306–327. Springer, Heidelberg (2011)

21. Liskov, M., Rivest, R.L., Wagner, D.: Tweakable Block Ciphers. In: Yung, M. (ed.) CRYPTO 2002. LNCS, vol. 2442, pp. 31–46. Springer, Heidelberg (2002)

22. Ma, X., Xu, F., Xu, H., Tan, X., Qi, B., Lo, H.K.: Postprocessing for quantum random number generators: entropy evaluation and randomness extraction (2012), http://arxiv.org/abs/1207.1473

23. Maes, R., Tuyls, P., Verbauwhede, I.: Low-Overhead Implementation of a Soft Decision Helper Data Algorithm for SRAM PUFs. In: Clavier, C., Gaj, K. (eds.) CHES 2009. LNCS, vol. 5747, pp. 332–347. Springer, Heidelberg (2009)

24. Maurer, U.M.: Indistinguishability of Random Systems. In: Knudsen (ed.) [18], pp. 110–132

25. Minematsu, K.: Improved Security Analysis of XEX and LRW Modes. In: Biham, E., Youssef, A.M. (eds.) SAC 2006. LNCS, vol. 4356, pp. 96–113. Springer, Heidelberg (2007)

26. Nguyen, L.H., Roscoe, A.W.: Simple construction of epsilon-biased distribution. Cryptology ePrint Archive, Report 2012/429 (2012), http://eprint.iacr.org/

27. Rogaway, P., Zhang, H.: Online Ciphers from Tweakable Blockciphers. In: Kiayias, A. (ed.) CT-RSA 2011. LNCS, vol. 6558, pp. 237–249. Springer, Heidelberg (2011)

28. Ristenpart, T., Rogaway, P.: How to Enrich the Message Space of a Cipher. In: Biryukov, A. (ed.) FSE 2007. LNCS, vol. 4593, pp. 101–118. Springer, Heidelberg (2007)

29. Rivest, R.L.: The RC5 Encryption Algorithm. In: Preneel, B. (ed.) FSE 1994. LNCS, vol. 1008, pp. 86–96. Springer, Heidelberg (1995)

30. Rivest, R.L.: The invertibility of the xor of rotations of a binary word. Int. J. Comput. Math. 88(2), 281–284 (2011)

31. Rivest, R.L., Robshaw, M.J.B., Yin, Y.L.: Rc6 as the aes. In: AES Candidate Conference, pp. 337–342 (2000)

32. Robshaw, M., Billet, O. (eds.): New Stream Cipher Designs. LNCS, vol. 4986. Springer, Heidelberg (2008)

33. Rogaway, P.: Efficient Instantiations of Tweakable Blockciphers and Refinements to Modes OCB and PMAC. In: Lee, P.J. (ed.) ASIACRYPT 2004. LNCS, vol. 3329, pp. 16–31. Springer, Heidelberg (2004)

34. Rogaway, P., Bellare, M., Black, J., Krovetz, T.: OCB: a block-cipher mode of operation for efficient authenticated encryption. In: Reiter, M.K., Samarati, P. (eds.) ACM Conference on Computer and Communications Security, pp. 196–205. ACM (2001)

35. Rogaway, P., Shrimpton, T.: A provable-security treatment of the key-wrap problem. In: Vaudenay, S. (ed.) EUROCRYPT 2006. LNCS, vol. 4004, pp. 373–390. Springer, Heidelberg (2006)
36. Sarkar, P.: A new multi-linear universal hash family. Designs, Codes and Cryptography pp. 1–17, http://dx.doi.org/10.1007/s10623-012-9672-8, 10.1007/s10623-012-9672-8
37. Stankovski, P., Hell, M., Johansson, T.: Analysis of Xorrotation with Application to an HC-128 Variant. In: Susilo, W., Mu, Y., Seberry, J. (eds.) ACISP 2012. LNCS, vol. 7372, pp. 419–425. Springer, Heidelberg (2012)
38. Thomsen, S.S.: Cryptographic hash functions. PhD thesis, Technical University of Denmark (2008)
39. Wah, P., Wang, M.Z.: Realization and application of the Massey-Omura lock. Digital Commnucation, International Zurich Seminar, 175–182 (1984)
40. Wu, H.: The Stream Cipher HC-128. In: Robshaw, Billet (eds.) [32], pp. 39–47

A   Proof of Theorem 1

We use a result of Minematsu [25][4]. We first show the proof for XEX-R1. Let us write $h(V, t_1) = \text{CLH}'_{n,\kappa}(V, t_1)$ for $V \in \{0,1\}^n$ and $t_1 \in \mathcal{T}_1$. Then the tweakable encryption of Theorem 1 can be written as $\widetilde{E}_K(M, T) = E_K(M \oplus h(E_K(T_2), T_1)) \oplus h(E_K(T_2), T_1)$, which fits into the model discussed by [25]. First, we have to bound

$$\gamma \overset{\text{def}}{=} \max_{t_1 \in \mathcal{T}_1, c \in \{0,1\}^n} \Pr[h(V, t_1) = c],$$

$$\epsilon \overset{\text{def}}{=} \max_{t_1 \neq t'_1 \in \mathcal{T}_1, c \in \{0,1\}^n} \Pr[h(V, t_1) \oplus h(V, t'_1) = c], \text{ and}$$

$$\rho \overset{\text{def}}{=} \max_{t_1 \in \mathcal{T}_1, c \in \{0,1\}^n} \Pr[h(V, t_1) \oplus V = c],$$

where probabilities are defined over $V \overset{\$}{\leftarrow} \{0,1\}^n$ and $\mathcal{T}_1 = \{0,1\}^{\kappa-1} \setminus \{0^{\kappa-1}, 0^{\kappa-2}1\}$. For γ, the probability is at most the maximum point probability of $\text{CLH}'_{n,\kappa}(V, t_1)$ for $t_1 \neq 0^{\kappa-1}$. As V is uniform, we have $\gamma = 2/2^\kappa$ from Lemma 1. Then, ϵ is equivalent to $\Pr[\text{msb}_\kappa(h(V, t_1) \oplus h(V, t'_1)) = \text{msb}_\kappa(c)]$, which is at most $2/2^\kappa$ from Lemma 1. For ρ, let $V = V_l \| V_r$ and $c = c_l \| c_r$ with $|V_l| = |c_l| = \kappa$ and $|V_r| = |c_r| = n - \kappa$. Then we have

$$\Pr[h(V, t_1) \oplus V = c] = \Pr[\text{CLH}_\kappa(V_l, t_1) \oplus \text{CLH}_\kappa(V_l, 0^{\kappa-2}\|1) = c_l, V_r = c_r].$$

Since $\mathcal{T}_1$ does not contain $0^{\kappa-2}\|1$ and that V_l and V_r are independent and random, the probability of the right hand side is at most $2/2^\kappa \cdot 1/2^{n-\kappa} = 2/2^n$ from Lemma 2. Combining Lemma 2 and Theorem 4 of [25] with the result $(\gamma, \epsilon, \rho) = (2/2^\kappa, 2/2^\kappa, 2/2^n)$, we obtain the bound of TSPRP-advantage being $(2\epsilon + \gamma + \rho + 2/2^n)q^2 = (6/2^\kappa + 2.5/2^n)q^2$.

For proving the bound for XEX-R2, we similarly have $\gamma, \epsilon \leq 2/2^{2n-\lambda}$ from Lemma 2. For ρ, since $V = \text{CLH}''_{n,\lambda}(V, 0^{\lambda-2}\|1)$ and $t_1 = 0^{\lambda-2}\|1$ is excluded, we obtain $\rho \leq 2/2^{2n-\lambda}$.

---

[4] This result is obtained by using Maurer's random system method [24], and the result does not suffer from a flaw of a theorem of [24] recently found by Jetchev et al. [17].

B String-to-Vector (S2V) PRF

Fig. 2 shows the String-to-Vector (S2V) PRF [35]. Here $2S$ denotes the GF doubling over $GF(2^n)$.

Algorithm $S2V[F_K](X[1], \ldots, X[\ell])$

1. **if** $\ell = 0$ **then return** $F_K(0^{n-1}1)$
2. $S \leftarrow F_K(0^n)$
3. **for** $i \leftarrow 1$ **to** $\ell - 1$ **do** $S \leftarrow 2S \oplus F_K(X[i])$
4. **if** $|X[\ell]| \geq n$ **then** $V \leftarrow S \oplus_{\text{end}} X[\ell]$ **else** $V \leftarrow 2S \oplus X[\ell] \| 10^*$
5. **return** $F_K(V)$

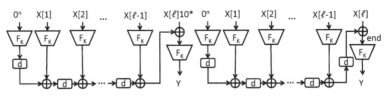

Fig. 2. S2V vector-input PRF using $F_K : \{0,1\}^* \to \{0,1\}^n$. The box with "d" in the lower figure denotes the GF doubling.

How to Remove the Exponent GCD in HK09[*]

Xianhui Lu, Bao Li, and Yamin Liu

Institute of Information Engineering of Chinese Academy of Sciences, Beijing,
100093, China
{xhlu,ymliu,lb}@is.ac.cn

Abstract. To improve the decapsulation efficiency of HK09 (proposed
by Hofheinz and Kiltz in Eurocrypt 2009), we propose a new skill to remove the exponent GCD operation. In the proposed scheme, the decapsulation efficiency is improved by 38.9% (instantiated over the semi-smooth
subgroup) and the efficiency of encapsulation is dropped by 5.7%.

Keywords: public key encryption, chosen ciphertext security, factoring.

1 Introduction

Based on the Blum-Goldwasser encryption (BG84) [2], Hofheinz and Kiltz proposed the first practical IND-CCA (Chosen Ciphertext Attack) secure public
key encryption scheme from the factoring assumption [7](HK09) in the standard
model. The BG84 scheme is IND-CPA (Chosen Plaintext Attack) secure under
the factoring assumption. To achieve IND-CCA security, Hofheinz and Kiltz used
the famous All-But-One skill [6,3,4,8], which was widely used in the construction
of IND-CCA secure encryption schemes.

The skill of HK09 was later generalized to the extractable hash proof system
by Wee in [13]. In [13], Wee also proposed a conceptually simpler variant of
HK09 which is more modular but less efficient (there is a linear blow-up in both
ciphertext overhead and public key size over HK09).

The efficiency of HK09 was later improved by Mei [11] and Lu [9,10]. In [11],
the authors instantiated HK09 over the semi-smooth subgroup and also proposed
an ElGamal style variant of HK09. Briefly, semi-smooth subgroup consider the
modulus of $N = PQ = (2p'p+1)(2q'q+1)$, where (p', q') are prime numbers large
enough but much smaller than (P, Q), and (p, q) are product of distinct prime
numbers smaller than a bound. The unique subgroup of QR_N (the quadratic
residuosity group) with order $p'q'$ is called semi-smooth subgroup. Since $p'q'$ is
much smaller than the order of QR_N, schemes instantiated over semi-smooth
subgroup are more efficient. In [9] the authors proposed a tradeoff between the

---

[*] Supported by the National Basic Research Program of China (973
project)(No.2013CB338002), the National Nature Science Foundation of China
(No.61070171, No.61272534), the Strategic Priority Research Program of Chinese
Academy of Sciences under Grant XDA06010702, IIE's Cryptography Research
Project (No.Y3Z0024103, Y3Z0027103).

W. Susilo and R. Reyhanitabar (Eds.): ProvSec 2013, LNCS 8209, pp. 239–248, 2013.
© Springer-Verlag Berlin Heidelberg 2013

efficiency of encapsulation and decapsulation of HK09. The efficiency of decapsulation was improved by 38.9% and the efficiency of encapsulation was dropped by 11.4% (instantiated over the semi-smooth subgroup). In [10] the authors improved the decapsulation efficiency at the price of a slightly increased key size. The decapsulation efficiency is improved by 32% (instantiated over the quadratic residuosity group) or 57.6% (instantiated over the semi-smooth subgroup) and the encapsulation efficiency remains the same.

1.1   Motivation

The ciphertext of HK09 is $(R = g^{\mu 2^{l_K + l_H}}, S = |g^{\mu t}X^{\mu}|)$, the encapsulated key is $K = \mathrm{BBS}_r(g^{\mu 2^{l_H}})$, where l_K is the length of K, l_H is the length of the hash value $t = \mathrm{H}(R)$, $\mathrm{BBS}_r()$ is a Blum-Blum-Shub pseudorandom generator [1]. Since the exponent inversion can not be computed directly for hidden order group, the decapsulation algorithm computes $g^{\mu 2^{l_H}}$ by using Shamir's GCD (greatest common divisor) in the exponent algorithm [12].

One of the skills to improve the efficiency of HK09 is to remove the exponent GCD operation in the decapsulation. In [9] the authors derive the encapsulated key from $g^{\mu t 2^{l_H}}$ and compute $K = \mathrm{BBS}_r((S/R^\rho)^{2^{l_H}})$ directly. In [10] the authors remove the computation of exponent GCD by hiding g^μ instead of $g^{\mu t}$ into S.

The above skills to remove the exponent GCD operation also have some drawbacks. The skill used in [9] causes a loose security reduction and the skill used in [10] increases the size of the key.

An interesting question is, how can we remove the exponent GCD operation while maintain the key size and the security reduction complexity?

1.2   Our Contribution

We propose a new method to remove the exponent GCD operation in HK09. The decapsulation efficiency is improved by 38.9% (instantiated over the semi-smooth subgroup) and the efficiency of encapsulation is dropped by 5.7%.

Our main idea is to directly embed g^μ into S. Concretely, the ciphertext is $(R = g^{\mu 2^{l_K}}, S = |g^\mu X^{\mu t}|)$, the encapsulated key is $K = \mathrm{BBS}_N(g^\mu)$, where $g \in \mathrm{QR}_N, X = g^{x 2^{l_K}}, x \in [(N-1)/4]$ is the private key. Thus, the decapsulation computes $g^\mu = S/R^{xt}$ directly.

One of the main difficulties in the security proof is the construction of the challenge ciphertext. According the All-But-One skill, the simulator needs to set $X = g^{x 2^{l_K}} g^{-1/t^*}$. Unfortunately, the simulator can not compute $1/t^*$ since he does not know the factoring of N. Our solution is to choose $h \in QR_N$ and set $g = h^{t^*}$. Thus the simulator can set $X = g^{x 2^{l_K}} h^{-1}$.

The other difficulty in the security reduction is the simulation of the decapsulation operation. When the adversary submits a ciphertext $(R = g^{\mu 2^{l_K}}, S = |g^\mu X^{\mu t}|)$, the simulator can compute $(S/R^{xt})^{t^*} = g^{\mu(t^* - t)}$ and then get $g^{\mu 2^c}$, where $2^c = gcd(2^{l_K}, (t^* - t))$. If $c \geq 1$, the simulator can not compute g^μ. To solve this problem we use the same skill as in [7]. Briefly, the simulator sets $R = g^{\mu 2^l K + l_H}$ and computes $K = \text{BBS}_N(g^{\mu 2^l H})$.

Compared with the scheme in [9], the encapsulation of our new scheme is more efficient and the efficiency of decapsulation remains the same. More importantly, the security reduction of our new scheme is tighter. Compared with the scheme in [10], their scheme is more efficient, while the key of our new scheme is shorter.

We remark that our new variant can be instantiated over the semi-smooth subgroup using the technique in [11]. The resulting scheme is more efficient than that over the QR_N group.

1.3   Outline

In section 2 we review the definition of key encapsulation mechanism and target collision resistant hash function. In section 3 we propose our new variant of HK09. Finally we give the conclusion in section 4.

2   Definitions

In describing probabilistic processes, $x \xleftarrow{R} X$ denotes that x is sampled according to the distribution X. If S is a finite set, $s \xleftarrow{R} S$ denotes that s is sampled from the uniform distribution on S. If A is a probabilistic algorithm and x an input, then $A(x)$ denotes the output distribution of A on input x. Thus, we write $y \xleftarrow{R} A(x)$ to denote of running algorithm A on input x and assigning the output to the variable y.

2.1   Key Encapsulation Mechanism

A key encapsulation mechanism consists of the following algorithms:

- KEM.KeyGen(1^k): A probabilistic polynomial-time key generation algorithm takes as input a security parameter (1^k) and outputs a public key PK and a secret key SK. We write (PK, SK) ← KEM.KeyGen(1^k)
- KEM.Enc(PK): A probabilistic polynomial-time encapsulation algorithm takes as input the public key PK, and outputs a pair (K, ψ), where $K \in K_D$ (K_D is the key space) is a key and ψ is a ciphertext. We write (K, ψ) ← KEM.Enc(PK)
- KEM.Dec(SK, ψ): A decapsulation algorithm takes as input a ciphertext ψ and the secret key SK. It returns a key K. We write K ← KEM.Dec(SK, ψ).

We require that for all (PK,SK) output by KEM.KeyGen(1^k), all $(K, \psi) \in$ [KEM.Enc(PK)], we have KEM.Dec(SK, ψ)=K.

Now we review the IND-CCA (Indistinguishability against adaptive chosen ciphertext attack) security of KEM. Note that we use the definition in [8] which is simpler than the original definition in [5].

Definition 1. *A KEM scheme is secure against adaptive chosen ciphertext attacks if the advantage of any adversary in the following game is negligible in the security parameter k.*

1. The adversary queries a key generation oracle. The key generation oracle computes $(PK, SK) \leftarrow KEM.KeyGen(1^k)$ and responds with PK.
2. The adversary queries an encapsulation oracle. The encapsulation oracle computes:

$$b \xleftarrow{R} \{0, 1\}, (K_1, \psi^*) \leftarrow KEM.Enc(PK), K_0 \xleftarrow{R} K_D,$$

   and responds with (K_b, ψ^*).
3. The adversary makes a sequence of calls to the decapsulation oracle. For each query the adversary submits a ciphertext ψ, and the decapsulation oracle responds with $KEM.Dec(SK, \psi)$. The only restriction is that the adversary can not request the decapsulation of ψ^*.
4. Finally, the adversary outputs a guess b'.

The adversary's advantage in the above game is $Adv_A^{cca}(k) = |\Pr[b' = 1|b = 1] - \Pr[b' = 1|b = 0]|$. If a KEM is secure against adaptive chosen ciphertext attacks defined in the above game we say it is IND-CCA secure.

2.2   Target Collision Resistant Hash Function

Now we review the definition of target collision resistant (TCR) hash function. We say that a function $H : X \to Y$ is a TCR hash function, if given a random preimage $x \in X$, it is hard to find $x' \neq x$ with $H(x') = H(x)$. Concretely, the advantage of an adversary $\mathcal{A}$ is defined as:

$$Adv_A^{tcr}(k) = \Pr[x \xleftarrow{R} X, x' \leftarrow A(x) : x \neq x' \wedge H(x) = H(x')].$$

We say H is a TCR hash function if $Adv_A^{tcr}(k)$ is negligible.

3   New Variant of HK09

Our new variant of HK09 is described as follows.

– KeyGen: The key generation algorithm chooses uniformly at random a Blum integer $N = PQ = (2p+1)(2q+1)$, where P, Q, p, q are prime numbers, then computes:

$$g \xleftarrow{R} QR_N, x \xleftarrow{R} [(N-1)/4], X \leftarrow g^{x2^{l_K+l_H}},$$

$$pk \leftarrow (N, g, X), sk \leftarrow x,$$

where $H : QR_N \to \{0, 1\}^{l_H}$ is a TCR hash function, l_H is the bit length of the output value of H, l_K is the bit length of the encapsulated key K, .

- Encapsulation: Given pk, the encapsulation algorithm computes:

$$\mu \xleftarrow{R} [(N-1)/4], R \leftarrow g^{\mu 2^{l_K}+l_H}, t \leftarrow H(R), S \leftarrow \left|(gX^t)^{\mu}\right|,$$

$$K \leftarrow \mathrm{BBS}_N(g^{\mu 2^{l_H}}),$$

where $\mathrm{BBS}_N(\alpha) = \mathrm{LSB}(\alpha), \cdots, \mathrm{LSB}(\alpha^{2^{l_K-1}})$, $\mathrm{LSB}(\alpha)$ denotes the least significant bit of α.
- Decapsulation: Given a ciphertext (R, S) and sk, the decapsulation algorithm verifies $R \in Z_N^*, S \in Z_N^* \cap [(N-1)/2]$, then computes:

$$t \leftarrow H(R), \rho \leftarrow xt,$$

$$\text{if } \left(\frac{S}{R^\rho}\right)^{2^{l_K}+l_H} = R \text{ then computes } K \leftarrow \mathrm{BBS}_N\left(\frac{S^{2^{l_H}}}{R^{\rho 2^{l_H}}}\right),$$

$$\text{else returns the rejection symbol } \perp.$$

The correctness of the scheme above can be verified as follows:

$$\left(\frac{S^{2^{l_H}}}{R^{\rho 2^{l_H}}}\right) = \left(\frac{|(gX^t)^{\mu}|^{2^{l_H}}}{(g^{\mu 2^{l_K}+l_H})^{xt 2^{l_H}}}\right) = \left(\frac{|(g(g^{x2^{l_K}+l_H})^t)^{\mu}|^{2^{l_H}}}{(g^{\mu 2^{l_K}+l_H})^{xt 2^{l_H}}}\right) = g^{\mu 2^{l_H}}.$$

We remark that, similar to [10], if pq is added to the private key, the efficiency of decapsulation can be improved by computing $\rho = xt \mod pq$. It is clear that our new variant above can also be instantiated over semi-smooth subgroup using the technique in [11]. In this case, x is selected from $2^{l_{p'}+l_{q'}+\lambda}$, where $l_{p'}$ is the length of p', $l_{q'}$ is the length of q', λ is a parameter for security level. If $p'q'$ is added to the private key, the efficiency of decapsulation can be further improved by selecting x from $[p'q']$ instead of $2^{l_{p'}+l_{q'}+\lambda}$.

3.1   Security Proof

Theorem 1. *If factoring N is hard and H is a TCR hash function, then the new variant is IND-CCA secure.*

The proof is similar to that of HK09, in which the reduction is divided into two phases. First, the BBS distinguisher is reduced to the factoring assumption. Then, the IND-CCA security of the scheme is reduced to the BBS distinguisher. The experiment for the BBS distinguish problem is defined as:

$$\mathrm{Adv}_{\mathcal{A}}^{\mathrm{BBS}} = |\Pr[\mathcal{A}(N, z, \mathrm{BBS}_N(u)) = 1] - \Pr[A(N, z, U) = 1]|,$$

where N is a Blum integer ($N = PQ, P = 2p+1, Q = 2q+1$, p and q are prime numbers), $u \in QR_N$, $z = u^{2^{l_K}}$, U is a random bit string of length l_K.

Given Theorem 2 in [7], it is clear that we only need to prove the following theorem.

Theorem 2. *If it is hard to distinguish* $(N, z, \mathrm{BBS}_N(u))$ *from* (N, z, U) *and* H *is a TCR hash function, then the new variant is IND-CCA secure.*

Proof. Suppose that an adversary $\mathcal{A}$ can break the IND-CCA security of the new variant. To prove the theorem, we construct an adversary $\mathcal{B}$ to distinguish $(N, z, \mathrm{BBS}_N(u))$ from (N, z, U). The construction of $\mathcal{B}$ is described as follows.

Setup: On receiving (N, z, V), where $V = U$ or $V = \mathrm{BBS}_N(u)$, the adversary $\mathcal{B}$ computes:

$$t^* \leftarrow H(z), h \xleftarrow{R} \mathrm{QR}_N, g \leftarrow h^{t^*}, x \xleftarrow{R} [(N-1)/4],$$

$$X \leftarrow g^{x 2^{l_K + l_H}} h^{-1}, pk \leftarrow (N, g, X).$$

The adversary $\mathcal{B}$ sends pk to adversary $\mathcal{A}$.

Challenge: The adversary $\mathcal{B}$ constructs the challenge ciphertext as follows.

$$R^* \leftarrow z, S^* \leftarrow \left| R^{*x t^*} \right|, K^* \leftarrow V.$$

Let $R^* = g^{\mu^* 2^{l_K + l_H}}$, the correctness of the challenge ciphertext can be verified as follow:

$$
\begin{aligned}
S^* &= \left| R^{*x t^*} \right| \\
&= \left| g^{\mu^* 2^{l_K + l_H} (x t^*)} \right| \\
&= \left| g^{\mu^*} g^{\mu^* 2^{l_K + l_H} x t^*} g^{-\mu^*} \right| \\
&= \left| g^{\mu^*} (g^{x 2^{l_K + l_H}} h^{-1})^{\mu^* t^*} \right| \\
&= \left| g^{\mu^*} X^{\mu^* t^*} \right| \\
&= \left| (g X^{t^*})^{\mu^*} \right|.
\end{aligned}
\tag{1}
$$

Decapsulation: On receiving the decapsulation query (R, S), the adversary $\mathcal{B}$ verifies $R \in Z_N^*, S \in Z_N^* \cap [(N-1)/2]$, then computes:

$$t \leftarrow H(R).$$

Then the adversary $\mathcal{B}$ considers three cases:

Case 1: $t \neq t^*$. In this case, the adversary $\mathcal{B}$ acts as:

$$\text{if } \left(\frac{S}{R^{xt}} \right)^{t^* 2^{l_K + l_H}} = R^{(t^* - t)} \text{ computes:}$$

$$2^c = \gcd(t^* - t, 2^{l_K + l_H}) = a(t^* - t) + b 2^{l_K + l_H},$$

$$\text{returns } K \leftarrow \mathrm{BBS}_N \left(\left(\left(S R^{-xt} \right)^{t^* a} R^b \right)^{2^{l_H - c}} \right),$$

$$\text{else returns the rejection symbol } \perp.$$

Since $t \neq t^*$ we have $0 < c < l_H$. Let $R = g^{\mu 2^{l_K + l_H}}$, the correctness of the verification equation can be verified as follows:

$$
\begin{aligned}
\left(\frac{S}{R^{zt}}\right)^{t^* 2^{l_K + l_H}} &= \left(\frac{(gX^t)^\mu}{g^{\mu z t 2^{l_K + l_H}}}\right)^{t^* 2^{l_K + l_H}} \\
&= \left(\frac{(gg^{zt 2^{l_K + l_H}} h^{-t})^\mu}{g^{\mu z t 2^{l_K + l_H}}}\right)^{t^* 2^{l_K + l_H}} \\
&= ((gh^{-t})^\mu)^{t^* 2^{l_K + l_H}} \\
&= (g^{t^*} g^{-t})^{\mu 2^{l_K + l_H}} \\
&= g^{(t^* - t)\mu 2^{l_K + l_H}} \\
&= R^{(t^* - t)}.
\end{aligned}
\tag{2}
$$

The correctness of K can be verified as follows:

$$
\begin{aligned}
K &= \mathrm{BBS}_N \left(\left((SR^{-zt})^{t^* a} R^b\right)^{2^{l_H - c}}\right) \\
&= \mathrm{BBS}_N \left(\left(\left(\frac{(gX^t)^\mu}{g^{\mu z t 2^{l_K + l_H}}}\right)^{t^* a} R^b\right)^{2^{l_H - c}}\right) \\
&= \mathrm{BBS}_N \left(\left(\left(\frac{(gg^{zt 2^{l_K + l_H}} h^{-t})^\mu}{g^{\mu z t 2^{l_K + l_H}}}\right)^{t^* a} R^b\right)^{2^{l_H - c}}\right) \\
&= \mathrm{BBS}_N \left(\left(((gh^{-t})^\mu)^{t^* a} R^b\right)^{2^{l_H - c}}\right) \\
&= \mathrm{BBS}_N \left(\left(g^{\mu(t^* - t)a} g^{\mu 2^{l_K + l_H} b}\right)^{2^{l_H - c}}\right) \\
&= \mathrm{BBS}_N \left(\left(g^{\mu(a(t^* - t) + b2^{l_K + l_H})}\right)^{2^{l_H - c}}\right) \\
&= \mathrm{BBS}_N \left(\left(g^{\mu 2^c}\right)^{2^{l_H - c}}\right) \\
&= \mathrm{BBS}_N \left(g^{\mu 2^{l_H}}\right).
\end{aligned}
\tag{3}
$$

Case 2: $t = t^*, R \neq R^*$. Denote this case as an event $\mathrm{bad}_{\mathrm{tcr}}$. Since H is a TCR hash function, we have $\Pr[\mathrm{bad}_{\mathrm{tcr}}] \leq \mathrm{Adv}_C^{\mathrm{tcr}}$.

Case 3: $t = t^*, R = R^*, S \neq S^*$. In this case, if $S^2 \neq R^{2zt}$ return the rejection symbol $\bot$. If $S^2 = R^{2zt}$, we have $|S| = S \neq S^* = |S^*|$ and $S^2 = R^{2zt} = R^{*2zt^*} = S^{*2}$. Then, $S \neq \pm S^*$ and $S^2 - S^{*2} = (S + S^*)(S - S^*) = 0$. Thus $\mathcal{B}$ can factor N directly by computing $\gcd(N, S + S^*)$ or $\gcd(N, S - S^*)$.

Guess: On receiving b' from adversary $\mathcal{A}$, the adversary $\mathcal{B}$ outputs b'.

This finishes the construction of the adversary $\mathcal{B}$. We claim that the distribution of simulated public key and the challenge ciphertext are almost identical in the simulation above and the IND-CCA game.

Lemma 1. *There exists an event* $\mathrm{bad}_{\mathrm{key}}$ *such that, conditioned on* $\neg \mathrm{bad}_{\mathrm{key}}$ *the public key and the challenge ciphertext are identically distributed in simulation and the IND-CCA game. Concretely,*

$$\Pr[\text{bad}_{\text{key}}] \leq \frac{5}{2^{k-1}},$$

where k is the parameter of security level.

Since the proof of the lemma above is very similar to that of lemma 1 in [7], we omit the detail.

It is clear that, unless bad_{tcr} or bad_{key} occurs, $\mathcal{B}$ perfectly simulates the real IND-CCA game. To be concrete:

$$\begin{aligned}
\text{Adv}_{\mathcal{B}}^{\text{BBS}} &= \text{Adv}_{\mathcal{A}}^{\text{cca}} - \Pr[\text{bad}_{\text{tcr}}] - \Pr[\text{bad}_{\text{key}}] \\
&\geq \text{Adv}_{\mathcal{A}}^{\text{cca}} - \text{Adv}_{\mathcal{C}}^{\text{tcr}} - \frac{5}{2^{k-1}}.
\end{aligned} \tag{4}$$

This completes the proof of theorem 2.   □

3.2   Efficiency

In this section, we analyze the efficiency of our new variant and compare it with the previous schemes in [7,11,9,10]. Note that, all of these schemes can be instantiated over the QR_N group or the semi-smooth subgroup. For the sake of clarity, these two cases are discussed respectively.

The Case of QR_N Group. The efficiency of schemes in [7,11,9,10] and our variant is listed in table 1, where HK09 is the scheme in [7], E-HK is the ElGamal style variant of HK09 in [11], LLML2011 is the variant of HK09 in [9], LLML2012 is the variant of HK09 in [10] and NEW is the proposed variant. The parameters are the same as those in [7,11,9,10], $l_N = 1024, l_K = l_H = 80$.

Table 1. Schemes instantiated over the QR_N group

	Encapsulate(mul)	Decapsulate(mul)	SK (bits)	PK (bits)
HK09	$3272(3l_N + l_K + 1.5l_H)$	$2376(1.5l_N + 4l_K + 6.5l_H)$	l_N	$2l_N$
E-HK	$4808(4.5l_N + l_K + 1.5l_H)$	$2043(1.5 \times 1.2l_N + 2.5l_H)$	$2l_N$	$3l_N$
LLML2011	$3432(3l_N + 2l_K + 2.5l_H)$	$1816(1.5l_N + l_K + 2.5l_H)$	l_N	$2l_N$
LLML2012	$3272(3l_N + l_K + 1.5l_H)$	$1736(1.5l_N + l_K + 1.5l_H)$	$2l_N$	$3l_N$
NEW	$3352(3l_N + l_K + 2.5l_H)$	$1816(1.5l_N + l_K + 2.5l_H)$	l_N	$2l_N$

The encapsulation of our variant can first compute $A = g^\mu$, which requires $1.5l_N$ multiplications. Then, the computation of $B = X^{\mu t}$ requires $1.5l_N + 1.5l_H$ multiplications. Finally, the computations of $R = A^{2^{l_K + l_H}} = g^{2^{l_K + l_H}\mu}$ and $K = \text{BBS}_N(A^{2^{l_K}})$ require $l_K + l_H$ multiplications. Thus, the encapsulation requires $3l_N + l_K + 2.5l_H$ multiplications. The decapsulation computes $D = R^\rho$, which requires $1.5l_N + 1.5l_H$ multiplications (the length of $\rho = xt$ is $l_N + l_H$). Then computes $(S/D)^{2^{l_K + l_H}}$ and $K = \text{BBS}_N((S/D)^{2^{l_H}})$, which require $l_K + l_H$ multiplications. We have that the decapsulation requires $1.5l_N + l_K + 2.5l_H$

multiplications. Note that, the decapsulation can be improved by adding pq to the private key and computing $\rho = xt \bmod pq$. As a result, the decapsulation requires $1.5l_N + l_K + l_H$ multiplications.

The Case of Semi-smooth Subgroup Group. The efficiency of schemes in [7,11,9,10] and our variant is listed in table 2, where S-HK is the instantiation of HK09, S-E-HK is the instantiation of E-HK, S-LLML2011 is the instantiation of LLML2011, S-LLML2012 is the instantiation of LLML2012 and S-NEW is the instantiation of our new variant. The parameters are the same as those in [7,11,9], $l_K = l_H = 80, l_{p'} = l_{q'} = 160, \lambda = 80, l_e = l_{p'} + l_{q'} + \lambda = 400, l_{e'} = l_{p'} + l_{q'} = 320$.

Table 2. Schemes instantiated over the semi-smooth subgroup

	Encapsulate(mul)	Decapsulate(mul)	SK (bits)	PK (bits)
S-HK	$1400(3l_e + l_K + 1.5l_H)$	$1440(1.5l_e + 4l_K + 6.5l_H)$	l_e	$2l_N$
S-E-HK	$2000(4.5l_e + l_K + 1.5l_H)$	$920(1.5 \times 1.2l_e + 2.5l_H)$	$2l_e$	$3l_N$
S-LLML2011	$1560(3l_e + 2l_K + 2.5l_H)$	$880(1.5l_e + l_K + 2.5l_H)$	l_e	$2l_N$
S-LLML2012	$1400(3l_e + l_K + 1.5l_H)$	$800(1.5l_e + l_K + 1.5l_H)$	$2l_e$	$3l_N$
S-NEW	$1480(3l_e + l_K + 2.5l_H)$	$880(1.5l_e + l_K + 2.5l_H)$	l_e	$2l_N$

Note that, the private key of schemes instantiated over semi-smooth subgroup is selected from $[2^{l_{p'} + l_{q'} + \lambda}]$. When $p'q'$ is added to the private key, the decapsulation efficiency can be improved by selecting the private key from $[p'q']$.

4   Conclusion

We proposed a new method to remove the exponent GCD operation in HK09, which improves the decapsulation without increasing the key size. The decapsulation efficiency is improved by 38.9% (instantiated over the semi-smooth subgroup) and the efficiency of encapsulation is dropped by 5.7%. Compared with previous skill in [9] to remove the exponent GCD operation, the security reduction of our new scheme is tighter. Compared with the skill in [10], their scheme is more efficient, while the key of our new scheme is shorter. We proved that the proposed variant is IND-CCA secure under the factoring assumption.

References

1. Blum, L., Blum, M., Shub, M.: A simple unpredictable pseudo-random number generator. SIAM J. Comput. 15(2), 364–383 (1986)
2. Blum, M., Goldwasser, S.: An probabilistic public key encryption scheme which hides all partial information. In: Blakely, G.R., Chaum, D. (eds.) CRYPTO 1984. LNCS, vol. 196, pp. 289–299. Springer, Heidelberg (1985)
3. Boneh, D., Boyen, X.: Efficient selective-ID secure identity-based encryption without random oracles. In: Cachin, C., Camenisch, J.L. (eds.) EUROCRYPT 2004. LNCS, vol. 3027, pp. 223–238. Springer, Heidelberg (2004)

4. Boyen, X., Mei, Q., Waters, B.: Direct chosen ciphertext security from identity-based techniques. In: ACM Conference on Computer and Communications Security, pp. 320–329. ACM (2005)

5. Cramer, R., Shoup, V.: Design and analysis of practical public-key encryption schemes secure against adaptive chosen ciphertext attack. SIAM J. Comput. 33, 167–226 (2004), http://dl.acm.org/citation.cfm?id=953065.964243

6. Dolev, D., Dwork, C., Naor, M.: Non-malleable cryptography (extended abstract). In: STOC, pp. 542–552. ACM (1991)

7. Hofheinz, D., Kiltz, E.: Practical chosen ciphertext secure encryption from factoring. In: Joux, A. (ed.) EUROCRYPT 2009. LNCS, vol. 5479, pp. 313–332. Springer, Heidelberg (2009)

8. Kiltz, E.: Chosen-ciphertext secure key-encapsulation based on gap hashed diffie-hellman. In: Okamoto, T., Wang, X. (eds.) PKC 2007. LNCS, vol. 4450, pp. 282–297. Springer, Heidelberg (2007)

9. Lu, X., Li, B., Mei, Q., Liu, Y.: Improved tradeoff between encapsulation and decapsulation of HK09. In: Wu, C.-K., Yung, M., Lin, D. (eds.) Inscrypt 2011. LNCS, vol. 7537, pp. 131–141. Springer, Heidelberg (2012)

10. Lu, X., Li, B., Mei, Q., Liu, Y.: Improved efficiency of chosen ciphertext secure encryption from factoring. In: Ryan, M.D., Smyth, B., Wang, G. (eds.) ISPEC 2012. LNCS, vol. 7232, pp. 34–45. Springer, Heidelberg (2012)

11. Mei, Q., Li, B., Lu, X., Jia, D.: Chosen ciphertext secure encryption under factoring assumption revisited. In: Catalano, D., Fazio, N., Gennaro, R., Nicolosi, A. (eds.) PKC 2011. LNCS, vol. 6571, pp. 210–227. Springer, Heidelberg (2011)

12. Shamir, A.: On the generation of cryptographically strong pseudo-random sequences. In: Even, S., Kariv, O. (eds.) ICALP 1981. LNCS, vol. 115, pp. 544–550. Springer, Heidelberg (1981)

13. Wee, H.: Efficient chosen-ciphertext security via extractable hash proofs. In: Rabin, T. (ed.) CRYPTO 2010. LNCS, vol. 6223, pp. 314–332. Springer, Heidelberg (2010)

Translation-Randomizable Distributions via Random Walks[*]

Nirattaya Khamsemanan[1] and William E. Skeith III[2]

[1] SIIT, Thammasat University
nirattaya@siit.tu.ac.th
[2] The City College of New York, CUNY
wes@cs.ccny.cuny.edu

Abstract. This work continues the search for viable intractability assumptions over *infinite groups*. In particular, we study the possibility of phrasing random self-reducibility properties for infinite groups in an analogous manner to the case of finite groups with the uniform distribution. As a first step, it is natural to look for distributions which are *translation-invariant, i.e.,* the probability of an event and its translate by a group element are the same (as is the case for the uniform distribution). Indeed, this approach has been considered in cryptographic literature by Lee [18], who introduced the concept of *right invariance*. However, we argue a number of shortcomings for its applicability to cryptography, showing in particular that any computational problem defined on a right-invariant distribution will not yield a better (weaker) intractability assumption than some problem defined over a finite group with the uniform distribution.

Perhaps the problem is simply that translation invariance is too strong of a property to ask of a distribution over an infinite group. Any such distribution is necessarily non-atomic, and the atomic approximations introduced by [18] (*universally right invariant distributions*) are still insufficient to deliver the desired complexity reductions. However, if a family of distributions is *randomizable* via translation, this may in fact suffice: one could translate an arbitrary instance by a sample from a known distribution, and obtain a *related instance* distributed according to a desired base distribution (or something statistically close) – highly analogous to the mode of operation of many random self reductions in cryptography.

Using a novel approach based on random walks, we construct families of such distributions, which are *translation-randomizable* over *infinite groups*. The main ingredients in our construction are *recurrence* (meaning a random walk will invariably return to its origin), and *shortcut sampling*, which asserts the existence of an efficient method for sampling a long (super-polynomial length) walk. Given a suitable group with these properties (for instance $\mathbb{Z}$), we demonstrate how one may formulate problems with random self reducibility properties akin to the familiar setting of finite groups and the uniform distribution.

---

[*] See [17] for the full version. Work supported in part by NSF grant CNS 1117675 and DPST Research Fund Grant number 041/2555.

W. Susilo and R. Reyhanitabar (Eds.): ProvSec 2013, LNCS 8209, pp. 249–270, 2013.

Keywords: Random self-reducibility, Random walks, Right-invariance, Non-commutative cryptography, Infinite groups, Recurrent groups.

1   Introduction

Motivation. The modern approach to cryptography builds an array of protocols and functionalities for which violating security requires the solving of an instance of a computational problem that is believed to be intractable. Early works exhibiting this approach include the famous results of [9] and [25]. Yet as vitally important as cryptography has become, we still have but a small handful of intractability assumptions on which the majority of our protocols rely. Without alternate assumptions, a breakthrough in factoring algorithms, or perhaps in quantum computing could be devastating. Hence, efforts are underway in the community to find new sources of computationally difficult problems upon which cryptographic protocols can be built.

In spite of what seems to be an abundance of difficult computational problems (*cf.* the theory of NP-completeness), we are still suffering from a shortage of viable intractability assumptions. But perhaps the reason is simple: problems which are difficult in the *worst case* are generally not sufficient for cryptographic use. Cryptography demands problems with a difficult *average case*. Indeed, one of the crucially important observations of [13] that led to a proper formalization of security was that *probabilistic modeling* is a necessary ingredient for any sensible definition.

Background. One intriguing approach that's been offered is the use of *group theoretic* problems to fill the gap. There are many difficult computational problems in group theory (as well as many algorithmically unsolvable problems), yet very few group-theoretic cryptographic schemes have withstood scrutiny by the community. As noted in the work of Lee [18], part of the difficulty is that many such problems involve *infinite* groups. Once infinite sets are involved, it is no longer clear how to proceed with probabilistic modeling, since the discrete uniform distribution does not make sense on an infinite set. One especially troubling consequence of not having a uniform distribution is that one must forgo one of the key tools used by cryptographers for reasoning about average case hardness—*random self reducibility.* The uniform distribution was assumed in nearly all definitions of random self-reducibility, *e.g.*, [1,7,10], and unfortunately does not make sense on an infinite set.

To address this problem, [18] attempts to provide an analog of the uniform distribution which makes sense for infinite groups. The author began by introducing the notion of a *right-invariant distribution,* for which the probability of any event was unchanged by translation by a group element. The idea is that this would in some sense allow for random sampling by translating an arbitrary instance by a sample from the distribution—a process found in many random self reductions for number-theoretic problems. However, clearly such a distribution on an infinite group must be non-atomic. Thus, [18] also considered some relaxations of this notion termed *universally right-invariant distributions* which, up to finite quotients, are randomizable by right translations. The hope was that this concept would provide a framework for reasoning about the average case complexity of problems in the theory of infinite groups, and more importantly, to lead the way toward new computational problems with random self-reducibility properties, and ultimately, viable intractability assumptions.

Our Contributions. Our work continues the search for intractability assumptions based on problems in infinite groups. We give both positive and negative results: on the negative side, we show some major obstacles to applying right invariance towards formulating random self reducibility on infinite groups; on the positive side, we develop and analyze an altogether new approach using random walks on *recurrent* groups, which provides families of translation-randomizable distributions which could make the foundation for a rigorous approach to proving random self-reducibility properties over infinite domains. We explain in more detail below.

The first of our main contributions is the observation that the concept of right-invariance is unlikely to produce intractability assumptions that are better (*i.e., weaker*) than an assumption involving a problem on finite groups with the uniform distribution. In particular, we show (Observation 1) that

1. Right-invariant distributions on an infinite group do not provide sufficient basis to even reason about the average-case hardness of a problem, unless one imposes additional assumptions.
2. Furthermore, if one imposes these additional assumptions, then the new problem will yield an intractability assumption that is no weaker than a related assumption regarding a problem on a *finite group* with the *uniform distribution*.

Thus, it seems unlikely that right-invariance will aide cryptographers in leveraging the complexity of infinite groups — at least not directly.[1] Perhaps this helps explain why we've not seen right-invariance appear in the literature for some time now, in spite of how intriguing an idea it is.

As such, we explore alternative solutions to the problem. The second of our main contributions is a new approach based on random walk distributions which provides translation-randomizable distributions on certain classes of infinite groups. Indeed, a number of researchers have already considered employing random walks toward cryptographic ends (*e.g.,* [16, 18]), yet in many ways, our approach is fundamentally different. We take a moment now to highlight these differences. Note that most prior work has considered groups in which the n-balls (in the metric space defined by the Cayley graph) grow quickly, *e.g.,* free groups. While at first glance this seems sensible, as it provides an efficient method to sample from a high-entropy distribution on the group, it is not without issues. In particular, the multiplication operation in such groups is somewhat transparent, and perhaps this has been an important factor leading to the cryptanalysis of

---

[1] It may nevertheless be the case that the corresponding assumption over a finite group is novel in itself.

many such schemes. See for example [4,11,19], and in particular work on "length based attacks", *e.g.*, [15,22]. Colloquially, one might say that there's usually "not enough cancellation", or in terms of the Cayley graph, they are too "tree-like". Following this intuition, we look toward groups with a more opaque operation on elements. One class of groups which in some sense may be thought of as a closer relative to finite groups, are those which carry *recurrent random walks* (see [27] for an in-depth survey). In contrast to braid groups and free groups, random walks on the generators of a recurrent group will invariably return to the identity element. Intuitively, this gives some sense as to the opaqueness of the group operation,[2] and similarity to the finite case. However, there is one glaring issue with recurrent groups: the n-balls in the Cayley graph of such a group will generally grow polynomially (in fact, quadratically; see [27, Prop. 3.23]). Thus, to sample from a set of cryptographically significant size, *we cannot actually take the steps of the random walk*, leading us to the notion of "shortcut sampling", which we present in Section 4.2. We show (Proposition 3) that this property, combined with recurrence, yields a family of translation-randomizable distributions *on an infinite group*, which in some sense was one of the main goals that right-invariance failed to achieve. While we do show explicit examples of groups which satisfy the above properties, we remark that this merely sets the stage for generalized random self reducibility; we do not as of yet have candidate problems to offer.

Organization. Section 2 contains a review of the notion of *right invariance* from [18]. Section 3 contains some elementary results on the role of right invariance in formulating computational problems. In particular, we illustrate a number of its shortcomings as a tool in the search for new intractability assumptions based on group theory. Section 4 studies the concept of shortcut sampleable random walks, and their potential for reasoning about average care hardness of computational problems on infinite groups. Section 5 concludes with a discussion of future work. A reference of basic notation and ideas from the measure-theoretic approach to probability can be found in the appendix (Section A).

2   Review of Right Invariance

Here we review the basic concept of *right invariance*, introduced in [18]. We begin with a high-level overview, and then present the ideas more formally in 2.2.

2.1   High-Level Remarks

In some sense, the work of [18] tries to find a suitable analogue of the uniform distribution on an infinite group. Motivated by random self reducibility properties (abbr. "RSR") of a number of computational problems over finite groups[3],

---

[2] Such a strong property is certainly not necessary, but it may be sufficient.

[3] Classic examples in finite groups include the discrete log problem and the RSA problem.

the author is in search of distributions on groups that are preserved under right translation. The uniform distribution $\mathbf{U}$ on a finite group G has the following useful property: for any $x, r \in G$,

$$\Pr[\mathbf{U} = r] = \Pr[\mathbf{U} = rx]. \tag{1}$$

Lee tries to find an analog of this property for infinite groups. Roughly put, a distribution $\mathbf{P}$ on a group G has the property of *right invariance* if for any event $E \subset G$ which has a defined probability, and for any $x \in G$, we will have that

$$\mathbf{P}(E) = \mathbf{P}(Ex). \tag{2}$$

A few remarks are in order. First, note that the distribution is not necessarily atomic. In fact, if $\mathbf{P}$ were to define a probability for every element, then Equation (2) would be impossible to satisfy for an infinite group. Furthermore, on a finite group, this property uniquely determines the uniform distribution. Hence, more general probability distributions defined for some σ-algebra over G are studied. Second, notice that in the finite case, Equation (1) actually says more: it gives a way convert an *arbitrary* instance into a *random* instance, and moreover, in a "lossless" manner. That is, given an arbitrary instance x, by sampling $r \xleftarrow{\$} \mathbf{U}$ and multiplying, the translated element rx is distributed uniformly, and given r, x is recoverable from rx. The analog of this property for the infinite case does not immediately follow from right invariance—after all, the distribution on G will in general not be atomic! We'll return to this idea later on, but first we review the work of [18] in more detail, and put formal definitions in place for the main objects of our discussion.

2.2 Details of Right Invariance

In what follows, G denotes a group, and $\mathcal{G}$ will denote a σ-algebra on G. The basic definition of *right invariance* is the following.

Definition 1. *Let* $(G, \mathcal{G}, \mathbf{P})$ *be a probability space. An event* $E \in \mathcal{G}$ *is called* right invariant *if for all* $x \in G$ *it holds that* $Ex \in \mathcal{G}$ *and* $\mathbf{P}(E) = \mathbf{P}(Ex)$. *The space* $(G, \mathcal{G}, \mathbf{P})$ *is called* right invariant *if every event in* $\mathcal{G}$ *is right invariant.*

This property can be expressed a little more cleanly using random variables. For an element $x \in G$, define a random variable T_x from the measure space to itself by right translation.[4] Right invariance simply asserts that all of these random variables are equivalent; that is, for all $x, x' \in G$ we have $T_x \equiv T_{x'}$. As it turns out, just the required closure property (*i.e.*, that translation is measurable) already imposes some interesting restrictions. [18] makes the following definition and observation.

Definition 2. *A* σ*-algebra* $\mathcal{G}$ *is called* RIGHT-CLOSED *if for every* $E \subset G$ *and for every* $x \in G$, $E \in \mathcal{G} \implies Ex \in \mathcal{G}$.

---

[4] Note that this requires the translation of every measurable set to be measurable; see Definition 2.

Lemma 1 ([18]). *Let* $M_{\mathcal{G}} = \bigcap_{\{E \in \mathcal{G} \mid 1 \in E\}} E$. *Then* $M_{\mathcal{G}} \triangleleft G$.

The above lemma states that the closure in the algebra of the identity element is always a normal subgroup. The significance of this is that one can always find a nice generating set for a right-closed σ-algebra over a group: the cosets of $M_{\mathcal{G}}$ partition the space, and hence there is nothing smaller. The rest of the algebra can be built up from countable unions of these cosets. Notice also that a group acts transitively on the cosets of any subgroup via translation. Hence if you are interested in finding a probability distribution $\mathbf{P}$ on this algebra that is invariant under translation, you have essentially one choice: all cosets must have weight equal to the inverse of the index. *I.e.*, for every coset K we must have $\mathbf{P}(K) = 1/[G : M_{\mathcal{G}}]$. Thus, we have a bijection between right-invariant probability distributions and finite index normal subgroups of G.

This makes the difficulties arising from infinite groups a little more clear. One seems to have very limited choices for right-invariant probability distributions: if the subgroup $M_{\mathcal{G}}$ has infinite index, then you can not assign any right-invariant distribution on the algebra, and if it is finite, then you have only one choice for the distribution which may not be very natural. Moreover, no such distribution on an infinite group is atomic, so if one plans to sample individual elements as problem instances, numerous technical problems arise (this is discussed in detail in Section 3). [18] tries to remedy this unfortunate state of affairs by introducing the concept of *universally right invariant* distributions. Roughly speaking, these are *atomic* distributions that are well-behaved with respect to *all finite quotients*. More formally, we have:

Definition 3. *An atomic probability distribution* $\mathbf{P}$ *on a group G is called* UNI-VERSALLY RIGHT INVARIANT *if for every $H < G$ with $[G : H] < \infty$ and for every $x \in G$ one has that* $\mathbf{P}(H) = \mathbf{P}(Hx)$.

Although a universally right invariant distribution would produce right invariant distributions for every finite quotient, it is still not clear how this applies to probabilistic modeling, since it leaves no apparent way to randomize actual instances – only cosets. Moreover, it is shown that any finitely generated group G with an infinite number of finite index subgroups will fail to have such an atomic distribution, which ruled out many of the infinite groups which have been experimented with in cryptography. To resolve the latter problem, a relaxation of the definition is considered which demands only statistical closeness to a right invariant measure. The motivation is a result of [8] regarding random walks on free groups, which states that $\sum_{Hx \in F/H} \left| \bar{\mu}_k(Hx) - [F : H]^{-1} \right| \in o(c^{-k})$. Here, $\bar{\mu}_k$ is a distribution on the free group coming from random walks of length bounded below by k. See [18] for the precise definition of "random-walk"—essentially one stops with probability s, and otherwise takes a random step along $X \cup X^{-1}$ (but not in the direction from which you just came) where each of the remaining $2|X| - 1$ generators are taken with equal probability $\frac{1-s}{2|X|-1}$. Hence for small enough s, (*i.e.*, for long enough walks) this distribution gives you something close to a universally right invariant measure on a free group.

3   Right Invariance and Computational Problems

Keeping in mind the goal of finding new intractability assumptions based on the theory of infinite groups, we explore in more detail the ways in which right invariance might be of use, but mainly we focus on several ways in which it *will not*. As we will see shortly, there are some intrinsic problems with formulating the notion of "difficult on average" in a setting that involves general probability distributions.

3.1   A Definitional Observation

Average-case complexity has been studied in the literature in a number of contexts, for example [3,5,6,14,20], yet none of these works adequately address the situation we face in formulating cryptographic assumptions from the theory of infinite groups. To begin, much of the literature focused on problems which are *tractable* on average, whereas cryptography is concerned more with problems that are **not** tractable, and in a strong sense.[5] The work of [12] does provide a formulation of the desired cryptographic notion of *hard on average* for a number of specific settings, however, this formulation does not consider problems which are defined on infinite instance sets, but rather problems that are defined on an infinite family of *finite* sets.[6] As such, all problems are defined over the uniform distribution; there is no need to consider more general probability distributions. Unfortunately, our premise does not afford us the convenience of the uniform distribution, since our sets of instances are infinite.[7] We investigate here the possibility of extending the definition of [12] to more general settings.

For our more general notion of average-case hardness to be the object of rational study, we would hope that, at a minimum, the notion is well-defined. We'll first present natural (although somewhat minimalistic) definitions which are analogues of those found in, for example [14,20], and are required to formulate the idea of *average-case hardness* in our setting. We then demonstrate that right invariant distributions are not sufficient to formulate computational problems for which the average-case hardness is even well defined.

The first required definition is that of a randomized computational problem. Several variations have appeared in the literature (*e.g.*, Levin's *distributional*

---

[5] Here, "intractable" is not just the negation of "tractable", but rather specifies that for sufficiently large instances, the probability of any efficient adversary succeeding is bounded by a negligible function. The negation of being tractable would just state that there is some infinite sequence of instance sizes which are difficult.

[6] The set of all finite length strings is naturally partitioned by length into finite sets, and instances of a specific length are generated according to the uniform distribution.

[7] Note that in number-theoretic settings, it is usually the size of the group that determines the size of instances (*i.e.*, the security parameter). However, most infinite groups which have been considered for cryptographic use have been finitely generated, and thus are all of the same size in terms of cardinality (they are all countably infinite). Thus, a different metric must be used for infinite groups; often it is the size of a generating set that is used for the security parameter.

problems, and Gurevich's *randomized decision problems*), and each definition consisted of some coupling of a traditional search or decision problem with a probability distribution on the instances. We remark that the distribution on the instances was required to satisfy certain properties; either the cumulative distribution function had to be efficiently computable, or efficiently sampleable (the latter asserts the existence of an efficient procedure that produces elements of the instance set with the desired probability distribution). Our main departure from these works is in the types of distributions we consider. In particular, the prior works always considered *atomic* distributions, and in one way or another, involved the discrete uniform distribution. Here is yet another variation, molded into our context. It is intentionally oversimplified, as it serves primarily as a "straw man" for our discussion.

Definition 4. *We define a* RANDOMIZED DECISION PROBLEM *to be a family of (distribution, language) pairs* $((\Omega_n, \mathcal{B}_n, \mathbf{P}_n), \alpha_n)$ *where*

- *The sets* $\{\Omega_n\}_{n \in \mathbb{N}}$ *correspond to the problem instances.*
- $(\Omega_n, \mathcal{B}_n, \mathbf{P}_n)$ *are probability distributions on the sets of instances , such that the distributions* $(\Omega_n, \mathcal{B}_n, \mathbf{P}_n)$ *are efficiently sampleable.*
- $\alpha_n : \Omega_n \longrightarrow \{0, 1\}$ *is a family of functions describing the "yes" instances.*

A few remarks are in order:

- We consider "abstract" problems, in which we do not demand that the instances are encoded as binary strings. This is intentional, as it simplifies the discussion, and is not needed to illustrate the main results.
- The distributions on instances are of the more general measure theoretic variety, and are efficiently sampleable. The latter requirement states that there exists $S \in$ PPT such that S generates elements of the sample space according to the specified distribution.
- We follow the definitions of [12], and use a parameterized set of instance distributions, as opposed to having a single universe of instances with a size function, for example as is the work of [14]. However, such a space of instances could be viewed as the disjoint union of all the sets Ω_n.

We will use the term *atomic randomized computational problem* to refer to the usual case in which the distribution on instances is atomically defined. Next, we *attempt* a definition of what it means to be difficult on average in our context, and then explore some of the inherent issues. One natural extension in the spirit of [12] is the following.

Definition 5. *Let* $((\Omega_n, \mathcal{B}_n, \mathbf{P}_n), \alpha_n)$ *be a randomized decision problem, as in Definition 4. We say that* $((\Omega_n, \mathcal{B}_n, \mathbf{P}_n), \alpha_n)$ *is* HARD ON AVERAGE *if for every algorithm* $\mathcal{A} \in$ PPT, *and for every polynomial* p, *then for all sufficiently large* n,

$$\Pr\left[\mathcal{A}(\mathbf{P}_n) = \alpha_n(\mathbf{P}_n)\right] < \frac{1}{2} + \frac{1}{p(n)}.$$

Consider the following observation, which states that allowing non-atomic distributions in the definition of a randomized computational problem necessarily introduces problems for which the average case hardness is not well defined.

Observation 1. *If there exists any atomic randomized computational problem which is hard on average, then the notion of* HARD ON AVERAGE *for general (non-atomic) randomized computational problems is not well defined.*

Put another way, to assert the average-case hardness of a randomized computational problem, then the σ-algebra $\mathcal{B}$ must be 2^{Ω}, the full σ-algebra on the set of instances. Failing to do so will either (1) leave the problem underspecified, or (2) require an additional assumption that, irrespective of the sampling algorithm, every version of the problem is polynomial-time equivalent.

The gist of Observation 1 is that in the non-atomic case, there may in fact be many efficient procedures to sample elements according to $\mathbf{P}_n$, and different sampling algorithms may have complete influence over the difficulty of the problem. The following example, while indeed contrived, illustrates the potential issues.

Example 1. For concreteness, we'll use the Quadratic Residuosity problem [13], although the following construction is fairly generic. The set of instances is the subgroup $H < \mathbb{Z}_N$ of index 2, consisting of all elements with Jacobi symbol $+1$, where $N = pq$ is the product of two primes. We'll let $\alpha : H \longrightarrow \{0, 1\}$ denote the "answer map" that takes each instance to a binary value indicating whether or not the input has a square root modulo N. Now modify the original problem so that the set of instances is $H' = H \times \mathbb{Z}_2$, and for a pair (x, b), the answer is just that of the first coordinate: $\alpha(x, b) = \alpha(x)$. We'll now define a right invariant, non-atomic probability distribution on H' as follows. Let $\mathcal{B}$ denote the σ-algebra generated by the sets

$$\{\{x\} \times \mathbb{Z}_2 \mid x \in H\}.$$

Define a natural probability space over $\mathcal{B}$ by setting $\mathbf{P}(\{x\} \times \mathbb{Z}_2) = \frac{1}{|H|}$ for every $x \in H$. Right invariance of the distribution follows easily from the fact that translation by a group element $(x, b) \in H'$ will permute the first and second coordinates individually.

We now specify two different sampling algorithms on H' that will completely determine the difficulty of the problem, and yet produce the same probability distribution on the events in $\mathcal{B}$. Moreover, both of these sampling algorithms are *efficiently computable* with only public information. As in the cryptosystem application of [13], let $\eta \in H$ be a quadratic non-residue which is publicly known. The first algorithm samples a uniform $y \xleftarrow{\$} H$ and uniform $b \xleftarrow{\$} \{0, 1\}$ and then outputs the instance $(y^2 \eta^b, b)$. The second algorithm samples y and b identically to the first, yet outputs the instance (y, b). It is easy to see that the first coordinate in uniformly distributed in both cases, and thus both algorithms efficiently sample according to $\mathbf{P}$. However, the computational difficulty of the corresponding problems is completely different (assuming that quadratic residuosity is hard).

In summary, we see that in order to make an assertion about the average case hardness of a computational problem, the definition must include an atomic probability distribution on the instances. Else, additional assumptions are required regarding the computational equivalence of different sampling algorithms that yield the same overall distribution $\mathbf{P}_n$. The following section discusses applications of this observation to right-invariance.

3.2   Consequences for Right Invariance

One aim of right invariance was to express random self reducibility properties for computational problems over infinite groups, which would hopefully enrich the sources of intractability assumptions available for cryptographic use. In light of the above observation, right invariance seems unlikely to succeed in this goal. To begin, note that you can never have an atomic distribution on an infinite group that is right invariant. So, any right invariant distribution is necessarily non-atomic, and thus is not suitable for discussing average case complexity or random self reducibility. There is also the concept of *universally right invariant* (Definition 3), which is an atomic distribution that approximates a right invariant distribution, but this too is not without issues. In the following, we consider 3 potential use-cases of right invariant, or universally right invariant distributions for formulating cryptographic intractability assumptions, and highlight the issues with each. We'll stick with the notation of the previous section, and let $(\Omega = I, \mathcal{B}, \mathbf{P})$ denote the set of instances, the σ-algebra, and the probability measure respectively. G will denote the group over which the problem is defined.

$(\mathcal{B}, \mathbf{P})$ *is Right Invariant, $G = I$.* Since the sample space is the same as the set of instances, this will fit nicely with the formulation of most problems in computational group theory. However, as shown in Example 1, this will leave you with either an underspecified distribution, and no way to discuss average case complexity, or it will require the additional assumption that all efficient sampling algorithms are equivalent. In the former case, the detraction is obvious, so let us consider the latter case: *Even if the assumption holds and all efficient sampling algorithms are indeed equivalent, right invariance still does not yield intractability assumptions which are weaker than assumptions on a finite group with the uniform distribution.* Consider the following: if all sampling methods are equivalent, then we may select a single representative of each coset of $M_{\mathcal{G}}$ (the closure in $\mathcal{B}$ of the identity of G) and define our sampling algorithm to return each of these designated representatives with probability $1/[G : M_{\mathcal{G}}]$. We can now view the situation not as a problem defined over G, but rather defined over the quotient group[8] $G/M_{\mathcal{G}}$, which is finite, with the uniform distribution on instances. Thus, the assumption on the infinite group is in fact **no weaker** of an assumption than some assumption over a finite group with the uniform distribution, and therefore seems unlikely to produce new sources of intractability assumptions.

---

[8] We can redefine multiplication if necessary.

($\mathcal{B}, \mathbf{P}$) *is Right Invariant, instances are no longer elements.* If the instances are identified with the cosets that generate the σ-algebra, then this approach provides the benefit that you are able to randomize the instances. However, there are a number of obvious drawbacks. To begin with, this does not seem to be compatible with the description of many problems in computational group theory. Moreover, if the instances are identified with cosets, then it seems that the problem is actually defined on a finite quotient group, $G/M_{\mathcal{G}}$, with the uniform distribution being used for sampling the instances. This is of course the familiar setting for cryptography, and thus does not seem to be useful in providing new sources of intractability assumptions.

($\mathcal{B}, \mathbf{P}$) *is Universally Right Invariant, $I = G$.* Since the σ-algebra is now atomic, there are no concerns about differences in sampling algorithms, however, this comes at a very steep price: any universally right-invariant distribution, is *not* actually right-invariant, and thus the instances cannot be randomized via translation, leaving no apparent way to express random self reducibility. The only kind of randomization property that is guaranteed is relative to finite quotients, which again does not yield new assumptions, as discussed in the prior cases.

Moreover, it was shown that very few of the infinite groups which have been considered for cryptographic use will have a universally right invariant distribution to begin with. The work of [16] shows that certain random walk distributions will be very close approximations to universally right invariant distributions, however this result applies *only to free groups*, which as we have noted do not seem suitable for cryptography.

4   Random Walks, Recurrence, and Shortcut Sampling

Given the apparent difficulties of applying right-invariance to the search for intractability assumptions, we explore here the idea of using random walk distributions to phrase generalized random self-reductions on groups. We begin by defining a new notion (*shortcut-sampleable*) and then show how that property, on a suitable (yet possibly infinite) group yields a family of distributions which are randomizable via translation. Such distributions could provide a framework for proving random self-reductions on an infinite group, much in the same way as the uniform distribution on a finite group. We begin with some basic facts and definitions about random walks.

4.1   Random Walks and Recurrence

Generalities. A RANDOM WALK is simply a Markov chain, which can be specified by a (finite, or countable) state space X, an initial state, and a matrix of probabilities $P : X \times X \to [0, 1]$ which, via the (x, y) entry, determines the probability of moving from x to y in a single step. Following [27], we will denote the (x, y) entry of the matrix by the lower case $p(x, y)$. Note that the n-th matrix power P^n corresponds to the n-step random walk; *i.e.,* the probability of reaching y from x after n steps is the (x, y) entry of P^n, which we denote by $p^{(n)}(x, y)$. A Markov chain is called IRREDUCIBLE if $\forall x, y \in X, \exists n \in \mathbb{N}$ such that $p^{(n)}(x, y) > 0$. We consider only irreducible chains. We denote by Z_n the X-valued random variable describing the position of the walk after n steps. We define the GREEN FUNCTION as follows:

$$G(x, y|z) = \sum_{n=0}^{\infty} p^{(n)}(x, y) z^n. \tag{3}$$

The Green function has the following interpretation: $G(x, y|1) = G(x, y)$ is the expected number of visits to y when starting at x.

Definition 6. *A Markov chain is called* RECURRENT *if* $G(x, y) = \infty$ *for some* $x, y \in X$. *If the chain is not recurrent, it is said to be* TRANSIENT.

It is also useful to consider the random variable describing the number of steps until y is reached from x. We define $\mathbf{s}^y = \min \{n \geq 0 \mid Z_n = y\}$ as the STOPPING TIME, and set $f^{(n)}(x, y) = \Pr[\mathbf{s}^y = n]$, and $F(x, y|z) = \sum_{n=0}^{\infty} f^{(n)}(x, y) z^n$. We denote $F(x, y|1)$ by $F(x, y)$. Recurrence may also be formulated in terms of F: it is equivalent to the condition $F(x, y) = 1$. As it turns out, recurrence / transience is well defined, independent of the points x, y.

Fact 2. *If a chain is recurrent, then in fact we have* $G(x, y) = \infty$ *and* $F(x, y) = 1 \ \forall x, y \in X$.

Walks on Graphs and Groups. There are several natural ways to adapt random walks to a graph structure. Suppose X is the vertex set of a graph, and let us denote adjacency in the graph by $x \sim y$.

Definition 7. *The* SIMPLE RANDOM WALK *on* X *is defined by*

$$p(x, y) = \begin{cases} \dfrac{1}{\deg(x)} & \text{if } x \sim y \\ 0 & \text{else.} \end{cases}$$

Now suppose that G is a discrete group, with $S \subset G$ a finite set of generators. Recall the CAYLEY GRAPH of G relative to S is a natural graph structure on G which places an edge between x, y if and only if $x^{-1}y \in S$. In this way, we can consider random walks on finitely generated groups in the same terms as we have for graphs. Unless stated otherwise, it will be understood that a random walk on (G, S) refers to the simple random walk on the corresponding Cayley graph, starting at 1_G.

Definition 8. *A simple random walk on the Cayley graph of a group* G *relative to the set of generators* S *is called* LAZY *if* $1_G \in S$.

Laziness is useful for sidestepping situations in which the random walks are periodic (that is, when elements are only connected by paths of the same modular character, *e.g.*, all paths from x to y in $\mathbb{Z}^d$ have the same length modulo 2). Note that a walk is recurrent if and only if its corresponding lazy version is.

4.2   Shortcut Sampling

The idea of using random walks for sampling group elements in a cryptographic context has been considered in a number of prior works, *e.g.*, [16, 18]. However, generally speaking these attempts have only considered using random walks on groups for which the n-balls in the Cayley graph grow very quickly. Our intuition is that many of these groups are fundamentally unsuitable for cryptography, primarily due to a lack of "opacity" in the group operation. Roughly speaking, we mean that if given a fixed, random generating set, and a product of the generators, there are very few ways to factor an element in terms of those generators. Colloquially, one might say that there's usually "not enough cancellation", or in terms of the Cayley graph, they are too "tree-like". Following this intuition, we look towards groups with smaller growth rates; more specifically, recurrent groups, which (see [27, Prop. 3.23]) have n-balls that are quadratically bounded.[9] As a consequence of this small rate of growth, we must forgo the ability to efficiently sample from a set of cryptographically significant size by actually taking the steps of a random walk, and must find an alternative. Intuitively, our idea is simple: a random walk is *shortcut-sampleable* if one can efficiently (poly-logarithmic time in the walk's length) sample the distribution. More formally, we have the following, where Δ represents the statistical distance.

Definition 9. *A Markov chain X is said to be* SHORTCUT-SAMPLEABLE *if there exists a probabilistic algorithm W such that $\Delta(W(n, k), Z_n) < 2^{-k}$, and such that W runs in polynomial time in both $\log n$ and k.*

Remark 1. Note that Definition 9 will generally preclude chains corresponding to simple random walks on groups for which the n-balls (and hence $\operatorname{supp}(Z_n)$) have super-polynomial growth: in this case the $\log n$ time constraint won't leave time to even write the output.

The notion is general, but for some familiar examples, this will concretely amount to "sampling exponents" of generators according to a specific distribution, rather than walking along the generators themselves. We will study the specific case of the integers in some detail, as what happens there illustrates much of our intuition.

Consider the random walk on $\mathbb{Z}$ over the symmetric generating set $\{\pm 1\}$. In this case

$$\Pr[Z_n = i] = \begin{cases} \dfrac{\dbinom{n}{(n+i)/2}}{2^n}, & \text{if } i \equiv n \mod 2 \\ 0, & \text{else.} \end{cases} \tag{4}$$

Proposition 1. *The random walk on $\mathbb{Z}$ is shortcut-sampleable according to definition 9.*

---

[9] We remark however, that there are irregular trees which both exhibit exponential growth and carry a recurrent walk. See [27, Ex. 6.16] for example.

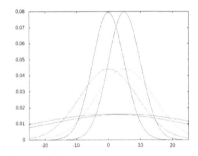

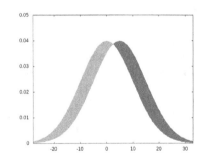

(a) Random walk distributions on $\mathbb{Z}$ with different means converge with increasing length.

(b) Illustration of ℓ^1 distance in terms of CDF's. L^1 of normal approximation shown above for clarity.

Fig. 1. Convergence of walk distributions on $\mathbb{Z}$: long walks can "forget" their starting point.

Proof. Due to space constraints, we defer the proof to the full version [17]. However, the result can be accomplished via a fairly straightforward application of inverse transform sampling.

Remark 2. At first glance, the walk from Eq. 4 appears less than perfect for sampling cryptographic instances, as it seems too clumped around 0. However, as we take longer walks, the variance will grow linearly (Z_n will have variance $\frac{n}{4}$) and since we are able to shortcut-sample very long walks, we can flatten the distribution quite effectively in a sizable neighborhood around 0. This point, among others, is illustrated in figure 1a.

Remark 3. The above distribution will assign no mass to points k for which $k \not\equiv n$ mod 2. As we've noted above, this can be remedied by using a lazy walk, or alternatively by only considering n of the same parity. We will generally take the latter approach, as the lazy walk approach complicates the analysis somewhat, and since for application of the results this presents no major obstacles.

4.3   Translation-Randomizable Distributions

Here we demonstrate families of translation-randomizable distributions, which may form a foundation for generalized random self reducibility. We show an explicit example (the integers), and then demonstrate randomization via translation properties for any shortcut-sampleable random walk on a recurrent group (although certain rates of convergence will vary from group to group).

Intuition. The first observation is that a random walk is, by definition, a Markov process. Thus, it has no "memory" and its future depends only on its current state. For example, the distribution of Z_n conditioned upon returning to the origin after k steps is precisely Z_{n-k}. Now suppose that we are given an arbitrary state $x \in X$, corresponding to some problem instance. We would hope that by taking a long walk away from x, we could (statistically) drown out all information about x, and be left with a random instance—that is, an instance distributed as a random walk from the origin. The intuition is that *if the group is recurrent*, then with good probability, you will hit the origin somewhere[10] early in the walk (see Fact 2), and thus the resulting distribution must be close to the walk from the origin, as the only difference between the two is a (relatively) small amount of length. As we show below (Proposition 3), this is indeed what happens, although in general it seems difficult to bound the rates of convergence. We do, however, show tight bounds for the random walk on $\mathbb{Z}$. Finally, we note the similarity with the notion of *ergodicity*, which would indeed be highly applicable here. The issue is of course that almost none of the random walks over infinite groups are positive recurrent[11] which is a requisite property for ergodicity. As we'll see, in spite of the integers being null recurrent (the expected time of a walk to return to the origin is infinite), they very much meet our needs in terms of their random walk distributions.

Example: the integers. Let Z_n denote the distribution after n steps starting at 0, and let Z_n^x denote the n-step walk distribution starting at x, and suppose[12] that $x \equiv 0 \mod 2$.

Proposition 2. *For Z_n, Z_n^x as above,* $\lim_{n \to \infty} \Delta(Z_n, Z_n^x) = 0$. *Moreover, setting* $n = \Omega(|x|^4)$ *gives* $\Delta(Z_n, Z_n^x) = \mathcal{O}(1/|x|)$.

Proof. First note that by symmetry, we can assume without loss of generality that $x \geq 0$. In this case, observe that again by symmetry in the distributions about their means, we have

$$\Delta(Z_n, Z_n^x) = \Psi(x/2) - \Psi(-x/2) \tag{5}$$

where Ψ denotes the cumulative distribution function of Z_n. See figure 1b. Noting that $Z_n(y)$ is maximized at $y = 0$, to bound the difference in Ψ values from (5), it suffices to bound $Z_n(0)$. Using Stirling's approximation to the factorial:

$$\Delta(Z_n, Z_n^x) = \Psi(x/2) - \Psi(-x/2) \leq x Z_n(0) \tag{6}$$

$$= x \frac{\binom{n}{n/2}}{2^n} \tag{7}$$

$$\approx \frac{x(\frac{n}{e})^n}{2^n (\frac{n}{2e})^n \sqrt{\pi n}} \tag{8}$$

$$= \frac{x}{\sqrt{\pi n}}. \tag{9}$$

---

[10] Since the walk is too long to actually take the steps, one cannot be sure precisely where this happened; and indeed if this were possible, it would of course imply an efficient algorithm for solving the problem.

[11] That is, the expected number of steps to return to the origin is finite.

[12] If not, then of course the statistical distance will be 1. However, this is easily remedied in applications, for example by using lazy random walks.

It is easy to show that the error in the final expression (introduced by the use of Stirling) will be at most a factor of e. The proposition then follows at once from Equation (9). □

Towards more general results. We show here that the above proposition (2) regarding the integers generalizes to some extent. In particular, we show (Proposition 3) that any recurrent group has the property that a long random walk is able to "statistically drown-out" its starting point. We remark that although there are fairly powerful *local limit theorems* which demonstrate asymptotic convergence of the values of $p^{(n)}(x, y)$ (see [27, Ch. III]), these do not suffice for our purposes, since they do not necessarily yield convergence in ℓ^1.[13] Ultimately, we would like tight bounds on the rate of convergence. Our result does not immediately yield such bounds, however, the hypotheses of the proposition are rather mild. It may of course be possible to say more in specific cases of interest (*e.g.,* Proposition 2). For convenience, we first introduce the following property, which as it turns out, is satisfied by the lazy random walk on *any* finitely generated group.

Definition 10. *We say that a sequence $\{s_n\}_{n=0}^{\infty}$ in a metric space is* WINDOW-CAUCHY *if for every $c, \epsilon > 0, \exists n_0 \in \mathbb{N}$ such that*

$$n > n_0 \implies \sup_{0 \leq i < j \leq c} d(s_{n+i}, s_{n+j}) < \epsilon.$$

Lemma 2. *Let $\{Z_n\}_{n=0}^{\infty}$ be the distributions of n-step, lazy random walks on any finitely-generated group X. Then $\{Z_n\}_{n=0}^{\infty}$ is window-Cauchy.*

Proof. Due to space constraints, we defer the proof to the full version [17].

Using the window-Cauchy property, we now show that in any recurrent group, a sufficiently long walk is always able to "forget" its starting point. Note: when it is clear from context, we will omit braces when writing the inverse image of a singleton set, for example $\pi^{-1}(\{y\})$ will be written as $\pi^{-1}(y)$.

Proposition 3. *Let Z_n, Z_n^x be the distributions of the n-step, lazy random walks on a recurrent group X, starting at the identity element and x, respectively. Then $\lim_{n \to \infty} \Delta(Z_n, Z_n^x) = 0$.*

We sketch the proof below; the full details can be found in [17].

Proof sketch: Note that while Z_n^x is naturally defined on the set of states X, we can also view Z_n^x in terms of the *trajectory space*, $X^{\mathbb{N}_0}$ and the product σ-algebra induced by 2^X. The distribution $\mathbb{P}_x$ on $X^{\mathbb{N}_0}$ is given by the Kolmogorov extension theorem. In this case, the mass function for Z_n^x can be expressed as

$$\Pr[Z_n^x = y] = \mathbb{P}_x(\pi_n^{-1}(y)) \tag{10}$$

---

[13] The convergence is proved only point-wise, and if rates of convergence are given, they usually hold only for a small neighborhood of the mean.

where $\pi_n : X^{\mathbb{N}_0} \longrightarrow X$ denotes the nth projection. While we are primarily interested in the Z_n^x distributions, defined on X, it will be convenient to condition on the actual steps of the walk that led to a particular outcome. Thus, for any event $E \subseteq X^{\mathbb{N}_0}$ and any $n \in \mathbb{N}_0$, we define a distribution $\mathbb{P}_x^n(\cdot \mid E)$ on X as follows:

$$\Pr\left[\mathbb{P}_x^n(\cdot \mid E) = y\right] = \mathbb{P}_x(E \cap \pi_n^{-1}(y))/\mathbb{P}_x(E). \tag{11}$$

That is, $\mathbb{P}_x^n(\cdot \mid E)$ represents the probability of arriving at y after n steps, given some conditions E on the actual steps taken. Now consider the set $A_k = (X \setminus \{1_X\})^k \times X \times \cdots$ corresponding to all walks which have avoided 1_X after k steps. Since X is recurrent, we know that $F(x, 1_X) = 1$, and hence $\lim_{k \to \infty} \mathbb{P}_x(\mathbf{s}^{1_X} > k) = 0$ so that $\lim_{k \to \infty} \mathbb{P}_x(A_k) = 0$. Let B_k denote the complement of A_k: that is, the walks which have passed through 1_X at some point in the first k steps. Partition B_k as $B_k = \bigvee_{j=0}^k F_j$ where $F_j = A_j \cap \pi_j^{-1}(1)$. Now for $m > k$, we may condition Z_m^x on A_k, B_k:

$$Z_m^x = \mathbb{P}_x^m = \mathbb{P}_x^m(\cdot \mid A_k)\mathbb{P}_x(A_k) + \mathbb{P}_x^m(\cdot \mid B_k)\mathbb{P}_x(B_k) \tag{12}$$

$$= \mathbb{P}_x^m(\cdot \mid A_k)\mathbb{P}_x(A_k) + \mathbb{P}_x(B_k) \sum_{j=0}^k \mathbb{P}_x^m(\cdot \mid F_j)\mathbb{P}_x(F_j \mid B_k). \tag{13}$$

Notice that $\mathbb{P}_x^m(\cdot \mid F_j) = Z_{m-j}$. Thus, we've expressed the distribution $\mathbb{P}_x^m(\cdot \mid B_k)$ as a convex combination of $\{Z_{m-i}\}_{i \leq k}$. From the window-Cauchy property and a straightforward application of Jensen's inequality, the last sum in (13) will in fact be close to Z_m. Finally, since the contribution from the A_k prefixes is small, it follows (again using convexity of the norm) that Z_m is close to Z_m^x for sufficiently large m. Complete details can be found in [17]. $\square$

Note that while Lemma 2 shows that lazy walks of differing lengths will rapidly converge in ℓ^1 (see equation (9)), this does not necessarily give us a strong rate of convergence for walks with different origins (Proposition 3), which depends also on the rate of convergence for $\lim_{k \to \infty} \mathbb{P}_x(A_k)$ towards 0. For cryptographic application, stronger results on the rates of convergence, similar to equation (9), are generally desirable. However, looking ahead towards random self-reducibility, such a strong rate of convergence may not always be necessary: if for example, we are using the framework to argue a random self reduction for a *search problem*, then we may have an efficient procedure to check the results of an oracle (think DLP or RSA), and thus if given a polynomial lower bound for sampling the correct distribution, the oracle will work *often enough*. Moreover, for such problems this may also allow one to side-step the recurrence requirement.

Towards generalized random self-reducibility. We now outline some definitions for generalized random self-reducibility, as well as sufficient conditions to argue such a property over suitable random walk distributions. We begin with distributional problems, reminiscent of those in the works of [5, 6, 14, 20].

Definition 11. *A* DISTRIBUTIONAL PROBLEM *is a tuple* $(I, A, \alpha : I \longrightarrow A)$ *together with a* size function $|\cdot| : I \longrightarrow \mathbb{N}$, *and a family of distributions* $\{\mathcal{I}_N\}_{N=0}^{\infty}$ *on* I *such that* $\operatorname{supp}(\mathcal{I}_N) \subseteq \{x \in I \mid |x| \leq N\}$.

In the above, I represents the set of instances, A, the space of answers ($A = \{0, 1\}$ for a decision problem), and α maps each instance to its answer.

Remark 4. Note that the notation $|\cdot|$ used for the size function is being re-purposed; up until this point, it was frequently used to denote the Cayley graph metric, or the length of a walk; it is now being used in the complexity theoretic sense as the length of a binary representation.

Definition 12. *For a distributional problem as above, we'll define the* ADVAN-TAGE *of an algorithm* $\mathcal{A}$ *to be*

$$\mathsf{Adv}_{\mathcal{A}}(N) = \left| \Pr_{\substack{x \xleftarrow{\$} \mathcal{I}_N, \\ \text{coins}(\mathcal{A})}} [\mathcal{A}(x) = \alpha(x)] - \frac{1}{|\alpha(\operatorname{supp}(\mathcal{I}_N))|} \right|.$$

Definition 13. *Let* (I, A, α) *be a distributional problem as above. The problem is said to be* QUASI RANDOM SELF-REDUCIBLE *if there exists* $\tau, \xi \in$ PPT *such that*

1. *(Randomization)* $\forall x \in I$, *the distribution of* $\tau(x)$ *is statistically close to* $\mathcal{I}_{|\tau(x)|}$.
2. *(Reconstruction)* *With high probability,* $\xi(x, r, \alpha(\tau(x))) = x$, *where* r *denotes auxiliary information used by* τ *to construct its sample.*

The idea for proving random self reductions in this framework is simple, and highly analogous to the way things work over finite groups and the uniform distribution. Suppose that we are given an oracle Ω which solves a distributional problem with polynomial advantage $\epsilon(N)$. Suppose also that the $\mathcal{I}_N$ are shortcut sampleable random walk distributions, and moreover, that by keeping track of the random selections in the algorithm, we're able to sample instances *with known answers*. Lastly, suppose that the problem has a sort of "homomorphic" property; say the answer function commutes with the group operation. If given an arbitrary instance x, we could effectively randomize it by taking a long walk away from it, thus creating an element xr which is distributed statistically close to $\mathcal{I}_N$ for some $N > |x|$. Now invoke the oracle on xr, and with good probability, it will return $\alpha(xr) = \alpha(x)\alpha(r)$, from which we can solve for $\alpha(x)$. There are a few small concessions in contrast to the finite case: we lose some of Ω's advantage since the distribution isn't exactly the same as what it expects, and the reduction will cost some extra time, since we are invoking Ω on a larger input than x. Nevertheless, the conclusions are essentially identical: an efficient procedure solving instances according to some fixed distribution implies an efficient procedure for solving arbitrary instances.

5   Conclusions and Future Work

In the continued search for viable intractability assumptions from combinatorial group theory, we have made progress in several directions: both positive, and negative. On the negative side, we have demonstrated a number of substantial obstacles to using right-invariance toward this end; on the other hand, we have introduced a new, alternative framework which allows one to phrase random self-reductions for computational problems over infinite groups in a way that's highly analogous to the finite case and the uniform distribution. While these preliminary results do not immediately yield cryptographic application, they nevertheless seem to take a small step towards understanding this difficult and important problem. Along the way, we have also demonstrated interesting properties of random walk distributions for recurrent groups (Proposition 3) which, to the best of our knowledge, were not known prior to this work. In addition to the obvious question of finding a cryptographically interesting instantiation of our construction, other directions for future work may include the following topics:

- Is the converse of Proposition 3 true?
- Right-invariance, as well as our new notion of shortcut-sampleable distributions, both focus on a *particular type of randomization procedure*: translation by a group element. Perhaps by considering other types of self-mappings on the instances, one could formulate more general "randomizable distributions" over infinite groups to attain the desired effect (that the probability of the image under this mapping is the same as the preimage).
- Although right-invariance may not produce weaker intractability assumptions than a corresponding problem on a finite group, it may be the case that this corresponding problem nevertheless turns out to be novel and interesting. [18] has already provided some work in characterizing such groups, but it may be useful to explore their finite quotients. Furthermore, if one relaxes the distribution to be statistically close (as illustrated in Section 2.2), then there seems to be a rich class of groups and distributions to study.

Acknowledgments. We are grateful to Rosario Gennaro for a number of helpful discussions. This work was supported in part by NSF grant CNS 1117675 and DPST Research Fund Grant number 041/2555. The authors would also like to thank Associate Professor Dr. Bunyarit Uyyanonvara who has served as a mentor under DPST Research Fund.

References

1. Abadi, M., Feigenbaum, J., Kilian, J.: On hiding information form an oracle. J. Comput. Syst. Sci. 39, 21–50 (1989),
   http://citeseerx.ist.psu.edu/viewdoc/summary?doi=10.1.1.35.5151
2. Agrawal, S., Gentry, C., Halevi, S., Sahai, A.: Discrete gaussian leftover hash lemma over infinite domains. Cryptology ePrint Archive, Report 2012/714 (2012),
   http://eprint.iacr.org/

3. Ben-David, S., Chor, B., Goldreich, O., Luby, M.: On the theory of average case complexity. Journal of Computer and system Sciences 44(2), 193–219 (1992)
4. Blackburn, S.R., Galbraith, S.D.: Cryptanalysis of two cryptosystems based on group actions. In: Lam, K.-Y., Okamoto, E., Xing, C. (eds.) ASIACRYPT 1999. LNCS, vol. 1716, pp. 52–61. Springer, Heidelberg (1999)
5. Blass, A., Gurevich, Y.: On the reduction theory for average case complexity. In: Schönfeld, W., Börger, E., Kleine Büning, H., Richter, M.M. (eds.) CSL 1990. LNCS, vol. 533, pp. 17–30. Springer, Heidelberg (1991)
6. Blass, A., Gurevich, Y.: Matrix transformation is complete for the average case. SIAM Journal on Computing 24(1), 3–29 (1995)
7. Blum, M., Micali, S.: How to generate cryptographically strong sequences of pseudo-random bits. SIAM J. Comput. 13, 850–864 (1984), http://portal.acm.org/citation.cfm?id=2054.2068
8. Borovik, A., Myasnikov, A., Shpilrain, V.: Measuring sets in infinite groups. Contemporary Mathematics 298, 21–42 (2002)
9. Diffie, W., Hellman, M.E.: New directions in cryptography. IEEE Transactions on Information Theory IT-22(6), 644–654 (1976)
10. Feigenbaum, J., Fortnow, L.: On the random-self-reducibility of complete sets. SIAM Journal on Computing 22, 994–1005 (1991), http://www.cs.uchicago.edu/~fortnow/papers/rsr.pdf
11. Gennaro, R., Micciancio, D.: Cryptanalysis of a pseudorandom generator based on braid groups. In: Knudsen, L.R. (ed.) EUROCRYPT 2002. LNCS, vol. 2332, pp. 1–13. Springer, Heidelberg (2002)
12. Goldreich, O.: Foundations of Cryptography: Basic Tools. Cambridge University Press, New York (2000)
13. Goldwasser, S., Micali, S.: Probabilistic encryption. JCSS 28(2), 270–299 (1984)
14. Gurevich, Y.: Average case completeness. Journal of Computer and System Sciences 42(3), 346–398 (1991)
15. Hughes, J., Tannenbaum, A.: Length-based attacks for certain group based encryption rewriting systems. arXiv preprint cs/0306032 (2003)
16. Kapovich, I., Myasnikov, A., Schupp, P., Shpilrain, V.: Average-case complexity and decision problems in group theory. Advances in Mathematics 190(2), 343–359 (2005)
17. Khamsemanan, N., Skeith, W.E.: Translation-randomizable distributions via random walks. Tech. rep., The City College of New York, CUNY (2013)
18. Lee, E.: Right-invariance: A property for probabilistic analysis of cryptography based on infinite groups. In: Lee, P.J. (ed.) ASIACRYPT 2004. LNCS, vol. 3329, pp. 103–118. Springer, Heidelberg (2004)
19. Lee, E., Park, J.H.: Cryptanalysis of the public-key encryption based on braid groups. In: Biham, E. (ed.) EUROCRYPT 2003. LNCS, vol. 2656, pp. 477–490. Springer, Heidelberg (2003)
20. Levin, L.: Problems, complete in average instance. In: Proceedings of the Sixteenth Annual ACM Symposium on Theory of Computing, p. 465. ACM (1984)
21. Mairesse, J., Mathéus, F.: Randomly growing braid on three strands and the manta ray. The Annals of Applied Probability, 502–536 (2007)
22. Myasnikov, A.D., Ushakov, A.: Length based attack and braid groups: Cryptanalysis of anshel-anshel-goldfeld key exchange protocol. In: Okamoto, T., Wang, X. (eds.) PKC 2007. LNCS, vol. 4450, pp. 76–88. Springer, Heidelberg (2007)
23. Pak, I.: Random walks on groups: strong uniform time approach. Ph.D. thesis, Harvard University (1997)

24. Pak, I.: Random walks on finite groups with few random generators. Electron. J. Probab 4, 1–11 (1999)
25. Rivest, R., Shamir, A., Adleman, L.: A method for obtaining digital signatures and public-key cryptosystems. Communications of the ACM 21, 120–126 (1978)
26. Schuler, R., Yamakami, T.: Structural average case complexity. In: Shyamasundar, R.K. (ed.) FSTTCS 1992. LNCS, vol. 652, pp. 128–139. Springer, Heidelberg (1992)
27. Woess, W.: Random Walks on Infinite Graphs and Groups. Cambridge University Press, New York (2000)
28. Yamakami, T.: Polynomial time samplable distributions. Journal of Complexity 15(4), 557–574 (1999)

A   Notation, Terminology, Etc.

Here we review some common notation and concepts from probability. We assume some familiarity with the standard measure-theoretic view of probability.

σ-algebras. A collection $\mathcal{B}$ of subsets of a sample space Ω is a σ-ALGEBRA in Ω if it satisfies the following:

1. $\Omega \in \mathcal{B}$
2. If $E \in \mathcal{B}$ then $\Omega - E \in \mathcal{B}$.
3. If $E_1, E_2, ..., \in \mathcal{B}$ then $\cup_{i=1}^{\infty} E_i \in \mathcal{B}$.

A pair $(\Omega, \mathcal{B})$ is called a MEASURABLE SPACE. Each $E \in \mathcal{B}$ is called a MEASURABLE SET. The special case in which $\mathcal{B} = 2^{\Omega}$, is referred to as the ATOMIC σ-ALGEBRA.

Probability Spaces. We define a PROBABILITY SPACE as a triple $(\Omega, \mathcal{B}, \mathbf{P})$ consisting of a sample space Ω, a σ-algebra $\mathcal{B} \subset 2^{\Omega}$ and a probability measure $\mathbf{P}$ which maps events $E \in \mathcal{B}$ to real numbers in $[0, 1]$, such that $\mathbf{P}$ is countably additive, and such that $\mathbf{P}(\Omega) = 1$.

Distributions and Random Variables. Let $(\Omega, \mathcal{B}, \mathbf{P})$ be a probability space, and let $(R, \mathcal{R})$ be a measurable space ($\mathcal{R}$ is a σ-algebra on the set R). We define a RANDOM VARIABLE simply to be a measurable map $X : \Omega \longrightarrow R$.[14] That is to say, for every $S \in \mathcal{R}$, we have $X^{-1}(S)$ is an event. We remark that this definition generalizes the definition typically found in statistics (in which random variables are constrained to take values in $\mathbb{R}$).

For a random variable $X : \Omega \longrightarrow R$, we define the DISTRIBUTION of X (denoted μ_X) as the induced probability measure on $(R, \mathcal{R})$. That is, $\mu_X(S) = \mathbf{P}(X^{-1}(S))$. We consider two random variables X, Y to be equivalent (written $X \equiv Y$) if they induce the same distribution; that is, if $\mu_X = \mu_Y$. When there is no risk of confusion, we will often write $X(S)$ to denote $\mu_X(S)$, the probability of S under the induced distribution.

---

[14] Recall that a measurable map is just a function f for which $f^{-1}(S)$ is measurable for every measurable S in the range.

Unless otherwise stated, $\mathbf{U}(S)$ will denote the uniform distribution on a finite set S, or more simply, just $\mathbf{U}$ when the set is clear from the context. In a probabilistic statement, we will denote that a variable x is sampled according to the distribution X by writing $x \xleftarrow{\$} X$. For a finite set S, $x \xleftarrow{\$} S$ is shorthand for $x \xleftarrow{\$} \mathbf{U}(S)$. It is important to note that this only applies to *atomic distributions*; we will at times consider probability spaces for which singleton sets are *not measurable*, and thus there is no clear meaning for "sampling an element".

When random variables appear in probability statements, it will be understood that the probability is taken over selection of an element from that distribution. For example, $\Pr[\mathbf{U} = x]$ is synonymous with

$$\Pr_{r \xleftarrow{\$} \mathbf{U}} [r = x].$$

Again, we stress that this only applies to the atomic setting, in which a probability is defined for each element of the sample space.

RKA Secure PKE Based
on the DDH and HR Assumptions[*]

Dingding Jia[1,2], Xianhui Lu[1], Bao Li[1], and Qixiang Mei[3]

[1] Institute of Information Engineering,
Chinese Academy of Sciences, Beijing, China
[2] University of Chinese Academy of Sciences, Beijing, China
[3] College of Information, Guangdong Ocean University
{ddjia,xhlu,lb}@is.ac.cn, nupf@163.com

Abstract. In this paper, we prove the security against related key attacks of two public key encryption schemes in the standard model. The first scheme is a variation of the scheme (KYPS09) presented by Kiltz, Pietrzak et al. in Eurocrypt 2009. While KYPS09 has been proved CCA secure under the DDH assumption, we show that it is not secure against related key attacks when the class of related key functions includes affine functions. We make a modification on KYPS09 and prove that the resulted scheme is secure against related key attacks in which the related key functions could be affine functions. We also prove the security against related key attacks of the scheme presented by Hofheinz and Kiltz in Crypto 2009 based on the HR assumption. The security proofs rely heavily on a randomness extractor called 4-wise independent hash functions.

Keywords: related key attack, 4-wise independent hash assumption, DDH assumption, HR assumption.

1 Introduction

Since "cold-boot" attacks demonstrated a practical threat to cryptography systems [13], researchers have contributed much effort to constructing schemes against side channel attacks. Among these attacks there is one kind called related key attacks (RKA), which means that attackers can modify keys stored in the memory and observe the outcome of the cryptographic primitive under this modified key [10,8].

In this work we study public key encryption (PKE) schemes against chosen ciphertext RKA (CC-RKA), which is formulated by Bellare et al. [4]. Following the original theory given by Bellare and Kohoo [5], the definition is parameterized

---

[*] This work is Supported by the National Basic Research Program of China (973 project)(No.2013CB338002), the National Nature Science Foundation of China (No.61070171, No.61272534), the Strategic Priority Research Program of Chinese Academy of Sciences under Grant XDA06010702 and IIE's Cryptography Research Project (No. Y3Z0027103, No.Y3Z0024103).

W. Susilo and R. Reyhanitabar (Eds.): ProvSec 2013, LNCS 8209, pp. 271–287, 2013.
© Springer-Verlag Berlin Heidelberg 2013

by the class of Φ functions that the adversary can apply to the secret key. As denoted by Bellare et al. [7], let S be the secret key space. If S is a group, $\Phi^{\text{lin}} = \{\phi_a\}_{a \in S}$ is used to denote the class of linear functions; if S is a ring, $\Phi^{\text{affine}} = \{\phi_{a,b}\}_{a,b \in S}$ is used to denote the class of affine functions; $\Phi^{\text{poly}(d)}$ is used to denote the class of polynomial functions bounded by degree d.

Bellare, Cash and Miller [4] showed that CC-RKA secure PKE can be transformed from RKA secure pseudorandom functions (PRF) and RKA secure identity based encryption (IBE) separately for the same class of Φ. In [3] Bellare and Cash gave a framework of building RKA secure PRFs for $\Phi = \Phi^{\text{lin}}$. In [7] Bellare, Paterson and Thomson gave a framework of building RKA secure IBE for $\Phi = \Phi^{\text{poly}(d)}$. So by combining [4] and [3] we can get Φ-CC-RKA secure PKE for $\Phi = \Phi^{\text{lin}}$; and by combining [4] and [7] we can get Φ-CC-RKA secure PKE for $\Phi = \Phi^{\text{poly}(d)}$. In [19] Wee proposed a framework of constructing Φ-CC-RKA secure PKE from adaptive trapdoor relations for $\Phi = \Phi^{\text{lin}}$.

In [19] Wee pointed out that the Cramer-Shoup CCA secure construction [11] can not achieve CC-RKA security through their approach, since the property that the secret key has some residual entropy given only its evaluation on a non-DDH tuple makes it impossible to fulfill "finger-printing". However, whether all variants of the Cramer-Shoup construction can not achieve CC-RKA secure is still an open problem. Is "finger-printing" a necessary condition of CC-RKA security for PKE?

Our Result. In this work we prove the Φ-CC-RKA security of two PKE schemes for $\Phi = \Phi^{\text{affine}}$ in the standard model.

- The first scheme is based on the DDH assumption, and it achieves Φ-CC-RKA security by making a modification to the CCA secure PKE proposed by Kiltz et al. [16], which is a variant of the Cramer-Shoup construction. As in [16], here we use 4-wise independent hash functions as a randomness extractor. In the appendix we give a successful RKA attack on the PKE scheme in [16] when Φ includes affine functions. By applying the 4-wise independent hash function to more group elements, we get a PKE scheme that is secure against Φ-CC-RKA for $\Phi = \Phi^{\text{affine}}$.

- The second scheme is presented by Hofheinz and Kiltz [15] based on the HR assumption. The scheme is an instantiation in the group QR_N^+ of "Diffie-Hellman integrated encryption scheme" (DHIES) [2], which is contained in several standard bodies, e.g. in IEEE P1363a, SECG and ISO 18033-2.

In the security proof, queries of the form (C, ϕ) are easy to answer since the simulator holds the secret key. Although there exists many $sk' \neq sk$ corresponding to which the challenge ciphertext C^* is valid, it is difficult for any PPT adversary $\mathcal{A}$ to submit a ϕ such that $\phi(sk) \neq sk$ and C^* is valid corresponding to $\phi(sk)$ under reasonable intractable assumptions.

Table 1 shows a comparison of known CC-RKA secure PKE schemes in the standard model. Take the second row for example: by combining [4] and [3], we can get Φ-CC-RKA secure schemes for $\Phi = \Phi^{\text{lin}}$ separately based on the DDH and DLIN assumption. From the table we can see that [4]+[3] and [19] can only achieve Φ-CC-RKA security for $\Phi = \Phi^{\text{lin}}$. Although [4]+[7] can achieve Φ-CC-RKA security for $\Phi = \Phi^{\text{poly}(d)}$, it is based on a q-type hardness assumption which is not so standard. Only [4]+[7] and our result can achieve Φ-CC-RKA security for $\Phi = \Phi^{\text{affine}}$ under widely accepted assumptions like BDDH, DDH and HR in the standard model.

Table 1. A comparison of known CC-RKA secure PKE schemes

Works	Φ	Assumptions
[4]+[3]	lin	DDH,DLIN
[4]+[7]	affine	BDDH
[4]+[7]	poly(d)	q-EBDDH
[19]	lin	factoring,BDDH,LWE
Ours	affine	DDH,HR

The rest of our paper is organized as follows: in section 2 we give definitions and preliminaries; in section 3 we give complexity assumptions; in section 4 we describe the PKE constructions and prove the security; section 5 is the conclusion of the whole paper.

2 Definitions and Preliminaries

2.1 Notation

We use PPT as the abbreviation of probabilistic polynomial time. Let $l(X)$ denote the length of X. Let X and Y be probability spaces on a finite set S, the statistical distance $SD(X,Y)$ between X and Y is defined as $SD(X,Y) := \frac{1}{2}\Sigma_{\alpha \in S}|\Pr_X[\alpha] - \Pr_Y[\alpha]|$, The min-entropy of a random variable X is defined as $H_\infty(X) = -\log_2(max_{x \in D}\Pr[X = x])$, wherein D is the domain of X.

2.2 Security Definition

Here we give the security definition of Φ-CC-RKA security. The security of a PKE scheme is defined using the following game between an adversary $\mathcal{A}$ and a challenger.

Setup: The challenger runs the key generation algorithm $Keygen(pp) \to (pk, sk)$, sends pk to the adversary $\mathcal{A}$, and keeps the secret key sk to itself.

Phase 1: $\mathcal{A}$ adaptively issues queries (ϕ, C) where $\phi \in \Phi$, the challenger responds with $Dec(\phi(sk), C)$.

Challenge: $\mathcal{A}$ submits two messages (m_0, m_1) to the challenger. The challenger picks a random bit b and responds with $Encrypt(pk, m_b)$.

Phase 2: $\mathcal{A}$ adaptively issues additional queries as in Phase 1, with the restriction that $(\phi(sk), C) \neq (sk, C^*)$.

Guess: $\mathcal{A}$ outputs a guess b' of b.

The advantage of $\mathcal{A}$ is defined as $Adv_{\mathcal{A},\Phi} = \left| \Pr[b' = b] - \frac{1}{2} \right|$.

Definition 1 (Φ-CC-RKA Security). *A PKE scheme is Φ-CC-RKA secure if for all PPT adversary $\mathcal{A}$, $Adv_{\mathcal{A},\Phi}$ is negligible in λ.*

Here our security definition follows the definition given by Bellare et al. [4]. However, in [4] it is required that the public key is completely determined by the secret key, while in our paper part of the elements in the public key can be randomly chosen and irrelevant to the secret key.

Symmetric Encryption. A symmetric encryption scheme consists of two polynomial time algorithms: $(\mathcal{E}, \mathcal{D})$. Let $\mathcal{K}_{SE}$ be the secret key space. The encryption algorithm $\mathcal{E}$ takes as input a message m and a secret key K and outputs a ciphertext χ, $\mathcal{E}(K, m) = \chi$; the decryption algorithm $\mathcal{D}$ takes as input the ciphertext χ and a secret key K and outputs a message m or $\bot$, $\mathcal{D}(K, \chi) = m$ or $\bot$. Here we require both algorithms are deterministic. For correctness we require that $\mathcal{D}(K, \mathcal{E}(K, m)) = m$.

Ciphertext Indistinguishability. Let $SE = (\mathcal{E}, \mathcal{D})$ be a symmetric key encryption scheme, the advantage of an adversary $\mathcal{A}$ in breaking the ciphertext indistinguishability (IND-OT) of SE is defined as:

$$Adv_{\mathcal{A}}^{IND-OT} = \left| \Pr \left[b = b' : \begin{array}{l} K^* \leftarrow_R \mathcal{K}_{SE}; (m_0, m_1) \leftarrow \mathcal{A}; b \leftarrow_R \{0, 1\}; \\ \chi^* \leftarrow \mathcal{E}(K^*, m_b); b' \leftarrow \mathcal{A}(\chi^*) \end{array} \right] - \frac{1}{2} \right|$$

We say that SE is one-time secure in the sense of indistinguishability (IND-OT) if for every PPT $\mathcal{A}$, $Adv_{\mathcal{A}}^{IND-OT}$ is negligible.

Ciphertext Integrity. Informally, ciphertext integrity requires that it is difficult to create a valid ciphertext corresponding to a random secret key for any PPT adversary $\mathcal{A}$, even $\mathcal{A}$ is given an encryption of a chosen message with the same key before. Let $SE = (\mathcal{E}, \mathcal{D})$ be a symmetric key encryption scheme, the advantage of an adversary $\mathcal{A}$ in breaking the ciphertext integrity (INT-OT) of SE is defined as:

$$Adv_{\mathcal{A}}^{INT-OT} = \left| \Pr \left[\chi \neq \chi^* \wedge \mathcal{D}(K^*, \chi) \neq \bot : \begin{array}{l} K^* \leftarrow_R \mathcal{K}_{SE}; m \leftarrow \mathcal{A}; \\ \chi^* \leftarrow \mathcal{E}(K^*, m); \chi \leftarrow \mathcal{A}(\chi^*) \end{array} \right] \right|$$

We say that SE is one-time secure in the sense of integrity (INT-OT) if for every PPT $\mathcal{A}$, $Adv_{\mathcal{A}}^{INT-OT}$ is negligible.

Authenticated Encryption. A symmetric encryption scheme SE is secure in the sense of one-time authenticated encryption (AE-OT) iff it is IND-OT and INT-OT secure. An AE-OT secure symmetric encryption can be easily constructed using a one-time symmetric encryption and an existentially unforgeable MAC [11,6].

2.3   Primitives

Here we introduce a primitive called 4-wise independent hash family [16] that can be used as a randomness extractor. A simple construction of 4-wise independent hash family is shown in [16].

Definition 2 (4-wise Independent Hash Family). *Let $\mathcal{HS}$ be a family of hash functions $\mathcal{H} : \mathcal{X} \to \mathcal{Y}$. We say that $\mathcal{HS}$ is 4-wise independent if for any distinct $x_1, x_2, x_3, x_4 \in \mathcal{X}$, the random variables $\mathcal{H}(x_1), ..., \mathcal{H}(x_4)$ are uniform and independently random, where $\mathcal{H} \leftarrow_R \mathcal{HS}$.*

The next two lemmata state that for a 4-wise independent hash function $\mathcal{H}$ and two random variables $X, \tilde{X}$ with $\Pr[X = \tilde{X}] = \delta$ negligible that even related, the random variable $(\mathcal{H}, \mathcal{H}(X))$ and $(\mathcal{H}, \mathcal{H}(X), \mathcal{H}(\tilde{X}))$ is close to uniformly random as long as the min-entropy of X and $\tilde{X}$ are large enough.

Lemma 1 (Leftover Hash Lemma [14]). *Let $X \in \mathcal{X}$ be a random variable where $H_\infty(X) \geq \kappa$. Let $\mathcal{HS}$ be a family of pairwise independent hash functions with domain $\mathcal{X}$ and range $\{0, 1\}^l$. Then for $\mathcal{H} \leftarrow_R \mathcal{HS}$ and $U_l \leftarrow_R \{0, 1\}^l$,*

$$SD((\mathcal{H}, \mathcal{H}(X)), (\mathcal{H}, U_l)) \leq 2^{(l-\kappa)/2}.$$

Lemma 2 (A Generalization of the Leftover Hash Lemma [16]). *Let $(X, \tilde{X}) \in \mathcal{X} \times \mathcal{X}$ be two random variables having joint distribution where $H_\infty(X) \geq \kappa, H_\infty(\tilde{X}) \geq \kappa$ and $\Pr[X = \tilde{X}] = \delta$. Let $\mathcal{HS}$ be a family of 4-wise independent hash functions with domain $\mathcal{X}$ and range $\{0, 1\}^l$. Then for $\mathcal{H} \leftarrow_R \mathcal{HS}$ and $U_{2l} \leftarrow_R \{0, 1\}^{2l}$,*

$$SD((\mathcal{H}, \mathcal{H}(X), \mathcal{H}(\tilde{X})), (\mathcal{H}, U_{2l})) \leq \sqrt{1 + \delta} \cdot 2^{l - \kappa/2} + \delta.$$

From the above lemmata we can get the following lemma that will be used in our security proof. Lemma 3 states that for a 4-wise independent hash function $\mathcal{H}$ and two random variables $X, \tilde{X}$ with $\Pr[X = \tilde{X}] = \delta$ negligible that even related, the output $\mathcal{H}(\tilde{X})$ is close to uniformly random even $\mathcal{H}(X)$ is fixed as long as the min-entropy of X and $\tilde{X}$ are large enough.

Lemma 3. *Let $\delta \leq \frac{1}{2}, l \leq 6$, $(X, \tilde{X}) \in \mathcal{X} \times \mathcal{X}$ be two random variables having joint distribution where $H_\infty(X) \geq \kappa, H_\infty(\tilde{X}) \geq \kappa$ and $\Pr[X = \tilde{X}] = \delta$. Let $\mathcal{HS}$ be a family of 4-wise independent hash functions with domain $\mathcal{X}$ and range $\{0, 1\}^l$. Then for $\mathcal{H} \leftarrow_R \mathcal{HS}$ and $U_l \leftarrow_R \{0, 1\}^l$,*

$$SD((\mathcal{H}, \mathcal{H}(X), \mathcal{H}(\tilde{X})), (\mathcal{H}, \mathcal{H}(X), U_l)) \leq 2^{l - \frac{\kappa - 1}{2}} + \delta.$$

Proof. Let Δ be the random variable $(\mathcal{H}, U_{2l})$, we can use the triangle inequality to get

$$\begin{aligned} SD((\mathcal{H}, \mathcal{H}(X), \mathcal{H}(\tilde{X})), (\mathcal{H}, \mathcal{H}(X), U_l)) \\ \leq SD((\mathcal{H}, \mathcal{H}(X), \mathcal{H}(\tilde{X})), \Delta) + SD(\Delta, (\mathcal{H}, \mathcal{H}(X), U_l)), \end{aligned} \tag{1}$$

Since we know that $H_\infty(X) \geq \kappa$, $\quad H_\infty(\tilde{X}) \geq \kappa$ and $X \neq \tilde{X}$. By using Lemma 2 we can upper bound the first term of (1) as

$$SD((\mathcal{H}, \mathcal{H}(X), \mathcal{H}(\tilde{X})), \Delta) \leq \sqrt{1 + \delta} \cdot 2^{\frac{2l - \kappa}{2}} + \delta \leq \sqrt{\frac{3}{2}} \cdot 2^{\frac{2l - \kappa}{2}} + \delta.$$

Similarly by using Lemma 1 we can upper bound the second term of (1) as

$$SD(\Delta, (\mathcal{H}, \mathcal{H}(X), U_l) \leq 2^{\frac{l - \kappa}{2}} \leq \frac{1}{8} \cdot 2^{\frac{2l - \kappa}{2}}.$$

$\square$

3   Complexity Assumptions

Decisional Diffie-Hellman Assumption (DDH). To formally define our assumption, we let $\mathcal{G}$ denote a group generation algorithm, which takes in a security parameter λ and outputs p and a group description G of order p.

Run $\mathcal{G}(1^\lambda)$ to get (p, G), and randomly choose $g_1, g_2 \in G, r \neq w \in \mathbb{Z}_p$. Set $T_0 = (g_1^r, g_2^r), T_1 = (g_1^r, g_2^w)$. The advantage of $\mathcal{A}$ is defined as

$$Adv_{\mathcal{A}}^{DDH} = \left| \Pr[\mathcal{A}(g_1, g_2, T_1) = 1] - \Pr[\mathcal{A}(g_1, g_2, T_0) = 1] \right|.$$

Definition 3 (DDH). *We say that $\mathcal{G}$ satisfies the DDH assumption if for all PPT algorithm $\mathcal{A}, Adv_{\mathcal{A}}^{DDH}$ is negligible in λ.*

Higher Residuosity Assumption (HR). Next we give the HR assumption as that in [15]. There are also similar assumptions in literatures [12,17,18]. We let RSA_{gen} denote a RSA generation algorithm, which takes in a security parameter λ and outputs (P, Q, N, S) such that $N = PQ, S|\varphi(N)/4$, let G_S denote the unique subgroup of order S of $\mathbb{Z}_N^*$. Generally speaking, HR assumption means that it is difficult to distinguish a random element in G_S from a random element in J_N, where $J_N = \{x \in \mathbb{Z}_N^* | (\frac{x}{N}) = 1\}$.

To formulate this notion precisely, run $RSA_{gen}(1^\lambda)$ to get (P, Q, N, S), and randomly choose $g, u_0 \in G_S$, $u_1 \in J_N$. The advantage of $\mathcal{A}$ is defined as

$$Adv_{\mathcal{A}}^{HR} = \left| \Pr[\mathcal{A}(g, u_1) = 1] - \Pr[\mathcal{A}(g, u_0) = 1] \right|.$$

Definition 4 (HR). *We say that $\mathcal{G}$ satisfies the HR assumption if for all PPT algorithm $\mathcal{A}, Adv_{\mathcal{A}}^{HR}$ is negligible in λ.*

For $\lambda = 80$ bits security one may choose $l(N) = 1024, l(S) = 256$. Then N may be chosen as follows: $P = 2P_S P_T + 1, Q = Q_S Q_T + 1, N = PQ, S = P_S Q_S$, where Q_S, Q_T, P_S, P_T are primes and $l(P_S), l(P_T) \approx 128$.

4 RKA Secure PKE Schemes

4.1 Construction Based on the DDH Assumption

In this section we describe a RKA secure PKE scheme based on the DDH assumption. The structure of our scheme inherits that in [16]. In the appendix we will show that the original PKE scheme in [16] is not RKA secure if Φ includes a function of the form $\phi_a^*(s) = as$. By applying a 4-wise independent hash function to more group elements, our scheme is Φ-RKA secure for Φ is a family of affine functions.

Run $\mathcal{G}(1^\lambda)$ to obtain (p, G), Let SE be an AE-OT secure symmetric encryption scheme with secret key space $\{0,1\}^l$. Let $\mathcal{HS}$ be a family of 4-wise independent hash functions with domain G^3 and image $\{0,1\}^l$. Public parameters are set as $pp = (p, G)$.

$Keygen(pp)$: The key generation algorithm chooses random $g_1, g_2 \in G$ and $\mathcal{H} \in \mathcal{HS}$. It picks random $x_1, x_2 \in \mathbb{Z}_p$ and computes $X = g_1^{x_1} g_2^{x_2}$. The public key is set as $pk = (g_1, g_2, X, \mathcal{H})$ and the secret key is set as $sk = (x_1, x_2)$.

$Enc(pk, m)$: The encryption algorithm chooses random $r \in \mathbb{Z}_p$ and computes the ciphertext $C = (C_1, C_2, C_3)$ as:

$$C_1 = g_1^r, C_2 = g_2^r, Y = X^r, K = \mathcal{H}(C_1, C_2, Y), C_3 = \mathcal{E}(K, m).$$

$Dec(C, sk)$: The decryption algorithm computes the message as:

$$Y = C_1^{x_1} C_2^{x_2}, K = \mathcal{H}(C_1, C_2, Y), m = \mathcal{D}(K, C_3).$$

Correctness can be easily verified for the correctness of the symmetric encryption scheme and $Y = C_1^{x_1} C_2^{x_2} = g_1^{r x_1} g_2^{r x_2} = X^r$. In terms of concrete security, it requires the image $\{0,1\}^l$ of $\mathcal{H}$ to be sufficiently small, i.e. $l \leq \frac{1}{4} \log_2 p$. Consequently for a symmetric cipher with $l = 80$ bits keys we should use groups of order $\log_2 p \geq 4l = 320$ bits.

Security Proof

Theorem 1. *If the DDH assumption holds, SE is an AE-OT secure symmetric encryption scheme with secret key space $\{0,1\}^l$, $\mathcal{HS}$ is a family of 4-wise independent hash functions with domain G^3 and image $\{0,1\}^l$, then our PKE scheme is Φ-CC-RKA secure for the class of affine functions Φ. In particular, for every advasary $\mathcal{A}$ on CC-RKA security of the above scheme, there exist adversaries $\mathcal{B}, \mathcal{C}, \mathcal{D}, \mathcal{E}$ with*

$$Adv_{\mathcal{A}}^{CC-RKA} \leq Adv_{\mathcal{B}}^{DDH} + q(2^{l-(\kappa-1)} + Adv_{\mathcal{C}}^{DL} + Adv_{SE,\mathcal{D}}^{INT-OT}) + Adv_{SE,\mathcal{E}}^{IND-OT}$$

where $\kappa = log_2(|G|)$.

First let us introduce two lemmata that will be used in our proof.

Lemma 4. *[11] Let S_1, S_2, F be events defined on some probability space that the events $S_1 \wedge \neg F$ occurs iff $S_2 \wedge \neg F$ occurs, then*

$$|\Pr[S_1] - \Pr[S_2]| \le \Pr[F].$$

Lemma 5. *[11] Let k, n be integers with $1 \le k \le n$, and let K be a finite field. Consider a probability space with random variables $\vec{\alpha} \in K^{n \times 1}$, $\vec{\beta} = (\beta_1, ..., \beta_k)^T \in K^{k \times 1}$, $\vec{\gamma} \in K^{k \times 1}$ and $M \in K^{k \times n}$ such that $\vec{\alpha}$ is uniformly distributed over $K^{n \times 1}$, $\vec{\beta} = M\vec{\alpha} + \vec{\gamma}$, and for $1 \le i \le k$, the i-th row of M and $\vec{\gamma}$ are determined by $\beta_1, ..., \beta_{i-1}$.*

Then conditioning on any fixed values of $\beta_1, ..., \beta_{k-1}$ such that the resulting matrix M has rank k, the value of β_k is uniformly distributed over K in the resulting conditional probability space.

Proof (of Theorem 1). Suppose that the public key is $(X, \mathcal{H})$ and the secret key is (x_1, x_2). The challenge ciphertext is denoted by $C^* = (C_1^*, C_2^*, C_3^*)$. We also denote by r^*, Y^*, K^* the values corresponding with r, Y, K related to C^*. We say that a ciphertext C is invalid if $C_1 = g_1^{r_1}, C_2 = g_2^{r_2}$ for some $r_1 \ne r_2$.

Let $\log(\cdot)$ denote $\log_{g_1}(\cdot)$ and $\omega = \log g_2$, then

$$logX = x_1 + \omega x_2 \tag{2}$$

To prove the security of our scheme, we define a sequence of games that any PPT adversary can not tell the difference between two adjacent games. Let q denote the number of decryption queries that the adversary makes during the whole game, here we denote an affine function as $\phi(sk) = (\phi_1(sk), \phi_2(sk)) = (a_1 x_1 + b_1, a_2 x_2 + b_2)$.

$Game_0$: the real security game.
$Game_1$: the same as $Game_0$ except that the challenge ciphertext is generated using the secret key. That is

$$Y^* = C_1^{*x_1} C_2^{*x_2}.$$

$Game_2$: the same as $Game_1$ except that the challenge ciphertext is invalid. That is (C_1^*, C_2^*) is replaced with a random pair $(g_1^{r_1^*}, g_2^{r_2^*})$ with $r_1^* \ne r_2^*$.
$Game_3$: the same as $Game_2$ except that the decryption oracle rejects all queries (ϕ, C) that satisfy $a_1 r_1 \ne a_2 r_2$, where $C_1 = g_1^{r_1}, C_2 = g_2^{r_2}$.
$Game_4$: the same as $Game_3$, except that SE encrypts m_b using a random key K^+ instead of K^*.

Let $Adv_{\mathcal{A}}^i$ denote $\mathcal{A}$'s advantage in $Game_i$ for $i = 0, 1, ..., 4$.
Clearly, $Adv_{\mathcal{A}}^0 = Adv_{\mathcal{A}}^1$.

Lemma 6. *Suppose that there exists a PPT adversary $\mathcal{A}$ such that $Adv_{\mathcal{A}}^1 - Adv_{\mathcal{A}}^2 = \epsilon$, then there exists a PPT adversary $\mathcal{B}$ with advantage ϵ in breaking the DDH assumption.*

Proof. $\mathcal{B}$ receives

$$D = (g_1, g_2, T := (u_1, u_2))$$

and its task is to decide whether D is a DDH tuple. $\mathcal{B}$ picks random $x_1, x_2 \in \mathbb{Z}_p$ and $\mathcal{H} \in \mathcal{HS}$. $\mathcal{B}$ computes $X = g_1^{x_1} g_2^{x_2}$ and sends $(pk = (g_1, g_2, X, \mathcal{H}))$ to $\mathcal{A}$.

Whenever $\mathcal{A}$ submits (ϕ, C), $\mathcal{B}$ simply runs the decryption oracle with the secret key $\phi(sk)$.

When $\mathcal{A}$ submits (m_0, m_1), $\mathcal{B}$ randomly chooses $b \leftarrow_R \{0,1\}$, it sets $C_1^* = u_1, C_2^* = u_2, Y^* = u_1^{x_1} u_2^{x_2}, K^* = \mathcal{H}(C_1^*, C_2^*, Y^*), C_3^* = \mathcal{E}(K^*, m_b)$ and responds with $C^* = (C_1^*, C_2^*, C_3^*)$.

When $\mathcal{A}$ outputs b', $\mathcal{B}$ outputs 1 if $b' = b$ and 0 otherwise.

Note that when D is a DDH tuple, then the above game perfectly simulates $Game_1$; when D is not a DDH tuple, the above game perfectly simulates $Game_2$. $\square$

Lemma 7. *Suppose that there exists a PPT adversary $\mathcal{A}$ in $Game_2$ and $Game_3$ such that it can submit a query (C, ϕ) satisfying $(C_1, C_2) = (C_1^*, C_2^*)$, $\phi(sk) \neq sk, Y = Y^*$ with probability δ, then there exists a PPT adversary $\mathcal{B}$ with advantage δ in breaking the DL assumption.*

Proof. $\mathcal{B}$ receives

$$D = (g, h)$$

and its task is to compute $\gamma \in \mathbb{Z}_p$ such that $h = g^\gamma$. $\mathcal{B}$ chooses random $s, t \in \mathbb{Z}_p$ with the constraint $h \neq g^t$ and computes $g_1 = g^s, g_2 = g^t$, so (g_1, g_2, g, h) is not a DDH tuple. Then it picks $x_1, x_2 \in \mathbb{Z}_p$, $\mathcal{H} \in \mathcal{HS}$. $\mathcal{B}$ computes $X = g_1^{x_1} g_2^{x_2}$ and sends $(pk = (g_1, g_2, X, \mathcal{H}))$ to $\mathcal{A}$.

Whenever $\mathcal{A}$ submits (ϕ, C), $\mathcal{B}$ simply runs the decryption oracle with the secret key $\phi(sk)$.

When $\mathcal{A}$ submits (m_0, m_1), $\mathcal{B}$ randomly chooses $b \leftarrow_R \{0,1\}, \gamma \in \mathbb{Z}_p$, it sets $C_1^* = g, C_2^* = h, Y^* = C_1^{*x_1} C_2^{*x_2}, K^* = \mathcal{H}(C_1^*, C_2^*, Y^*), C_3^* = \mathcal{E}(K^*, m_b)$ and responds with $C^* = (C_1^*, C_2^*, C_3^*)$.

Whenever $\mathcal{A}$ submits (ϕ, C) satisfying $(C_1, C_2) = (C_1^*, C_2^*), \phi(sk) \neq sk, Y = Y^*$, then we have $C_1^{*x_1} C_2^{*x_2} = C_1^{\phi_1(sk)} C_2^{\phi_2(sk)}$, and $h = g^\theta$, where $\theta = \frac{\phi_1(sk) - x_1}{x_2 - \phi_2(sk)}$, thus solve the DL problem. $\square$

Lemma 8. *Assume that the symmetric key encryption scheme is AE-OT secure, $\mathcal{HS}$ is a family of 4-wise independent hash functions, the DDH assumption holds, then $Adv_{\mathcal{A}}^2 - Adv_{\mathcal{A}}^3$ is negligible.*

Proof.

$$\log Y^* = r_1^* x_1 + w r_2^* x_2 \tag{3}$$

Let E be the event that a query (C, ϕ) is rejected in $Game_3$ but not rejected in $Game_2$. Then we have $|Adv_{\mathcal{A}}^2 - Adv_{\mathcal{A}}^3| \leq Pr[E]$.

Case 1: $(C_1, C_2) = (C_1^*, C_2^*)$.

– $\phi(sk) = sk$. We have

$$\begin{pmatrix} \log X \\ \log Y^* \end{pmatrix} = \underbrace{\begin{pmatrix} 1 & \omega \\ r_1^* & \omega r_2^* \end{pmatrix}}_{=:M^*} \cdot \begin{pmatrix} x_1 \\ x_2 \end{pmatrix}$$

Since $\det(M^*) = \omega(r_1^* - r_2^*) \neq 0$, as stated by Lemma 5, the distribution of Y^* is randomly distributed in G, so $H_\infty(Y^*) \geq \kappa$. From the leftover hash lemma, we know that K^* is randomly distributed. From the INT-OT property of the SE scheme, we can see that it is difficult to generate a $C_3 \neq C_3^*$ s.t. $\mathcal{D}(K^*, C_3) \neq \perp$.

– $\phi(sk) \neq sk$. Let Γ^* be the random variable (C_1^*, C_2^*, Y^*), Γ be the random variable (C_1, C_2, Y). From Lemma 7 it can be seen that $\Pr[Y = Y^*] = \delta$, hence $\Pr[\Gamma = \Gamma^*] = \delta$, where δ is negligible assuming DL problem is hard to solve.

$$\begin{pmatrix} \log X \\ \log Y \end{pmatrix} = \underbrace{\begin{pmatrix} 1 & \omega \\ a_1 r_1^* & \omega a_2 r_2^* \end{pmatrix}}_{:=M_1} \cdot \begin{pmatrix} x_1 \\ x_2 \end{pmatrix} + \begin{pmatrix} 0 \\ b_1 r_1^* + \omega b_2 r_2^* \end{pmatrix}$$

As analyzed above we have $H_\infty(\Gamma) \geq \kappa$. From Lemma 3 we know:

$$SD((pk, \mathcal{H}, \mathcal{H}(\Gamma^*), \mathcal{H}(\Gamma)), (pk, \mathcal{H}, \mathcal{H}(\Gamma^*), U_l)) \leq 2^{l-(\kappa-1)/2} + \delta.$$

Here U_l is uniformly random chosen from $\{0,1\}^l$. So the distribution of K looks random to the adversary $\mathcal{A}$, then from the INT-OT property of the SE scheme, with overwhelming probability $Dec(sk, C) = \perp$.

Case 2: $(C_1, C_2) \neq (C_1^*, C_2^*)$, and $a_1 r_1 \neq a_2 r_2$. In the following we let Γ^* be the random variable (C_1^*, C_2^*, Y^*), Γ be the random variable (C_1, C_2, Y), then $\Gamma \neq \Gamma^*$. Here we have

$$\begin{pmatrix} \log X \\ \log Y \end{pmatrix} = \underbrace{\begin{pmatrix} 1 & \omega \\ a_1 r_1 & \omega a_2 r_2 \end{pmatrix}}_{:=M_2} \cdot \begin{pmatrix} x_1 \\ x_2 \end{pmatrix} + \begin{pmatrix} 0 \\ b_1 r_1 + \omega b_2 r_2 \end{pmatrix}$$

Since $\det(M_2) \neq 0$, we have $H_\infty(Y) \geq \kappa$. Similar as Case 1, we have $H_\infty(\Gamma^*) \geq \kappa$, $H_\infty(\Gamma) \geq \kappa$ and $\Gamma^* \neq \Gamma$. From Lemma 3 we know:

$$SD((pk, \mathcal{H}, \mathcal{H}(\Gamma^*), \mathcal{H}(\Gamma)), (pk, \mathcal{H}, \mathcal{H}(\Gamma^*), U_l)) \leq 2^{l-(\kappa-1)/2}.$$

Here U_l is uniformly random chosen from $\{0,1\}^l$. So the distribution of K looks random to the adversary $\mathcal{A}$, then from the INT-OT property of the SE scheme, with overwhelming probability $Dec(sk, C) = \perp$.

From the above analysis, we can see that it is difficult to distinguish $Game_2$ and $Game_3$ for any PPT adversary. □

Lemma 9. *Assume that $\mathcal{HS}$ is a family of 4-wise independent hash functions, then $Adv_\mathcal{A}^3 - Adv_\mathcal{A}^4$ is negligible.*

Proof. Since in both $Game_3$ and $Game_4$, all decryption queries are rejected except those $((C_1, C_2, C_3), \phi)$ satisfying $Y = C_1^{a_1 x_1 + b_1} C_2^{a_2 x_2 + b_2}$ with $a_1 r_1 = a_2 r_2$, so for any information-theoretical adversary $\mathcal{A}$, all it can get from the decryption queries is :

$$\log Y - \theta = arx_1 + warx_2. \tag{4}$$

Here $\theta = b_1 r_1 + wb_2 r_2$ and $ar = a_1 r_1 = a_2 r_2$. Since eq. (4) is a linearly correlation of eq. (1). Conditioned on the the decryption answers, the distribution of Y^* is still randomly distributed in G, then $Game_3$ and $Game_4$ are indistinguishable. □

Lemma 10. *Suppose that there exists a PPT adversary $\mathcal{A}$ such that $Adv_{\mathcal{A}}^4 = \epsilon$, then there exists a PPT adversary $\mathcal{B}$ with the same advantage in breaking the IND-OT of the SE scheme.*

Proof. $\mathcal{B}$ chooses random $x_1, x_2 \in \mathbb{Z}_p$ and $\mathcal{H} \in \mathcal{HS}$. $\mathcal{B}$ computes $X = g_1^{x_1} g_2^{x_2}$ and sends $(pp = (G, p, g_1, g_2), pk = (X, \mathcal{H}))$ to $\mathcal{A}$.

Whenever $\mathcal{A}$ submits (ϕ, C), $\mathcal{B}$ simply runs the decryption oracle using the secret key $\phi(sk)$.

When $\mathcal{A}$ submits (m_0, m_1), $\mathcal{B}$ sends (m_0, m_1) to its challenger and receives C_3^*. Then $\mathcal{B}$ chooses random $r_1^* \neq r_2^*$ and sets $C_1^* = g_1^{r_1^*}, C_2^* = g_2^{r_2^*}$ and responds with $C^* = (C_1^*, C_2^*, C_3^*)$.

When $\mathcal{A}$ outputs b', $\mathcal{B}$ outputs b'. □

4.2 Construction Based on the HR Assumption

In this section we prove that the scheme proposed in [15] is Φ-CC-RKA secure for the class of affine functions Φ. This scheme is contained in several standard bodies, e.g., in IEEE P1363a, SECG and ISO 18033-2 as "Diffie-Hellman integrated encryption scheme" (DHIES) [2].

In the following we use $|u|$ to denote the absolute value of u, where u is represented as a signed integer in the set $\{-(N-1)/2, ..., (N-1)/2\}$. Let $QR_N^+ := \{|x| : x \in QR_N\}$ and $G_S^+ := \{|x| : x \in G_S\}$.

Let SE be an AE-OT secure symmetric encryption scheme with secret key space $\{0, 1\}^l$. Let $\mathcal{HS}$ be a family of 4-wise independent hash functions with domain $(QR_N^+)^2$ and range $\{0, 1\}^l$. In the following we let g^x denote $|g^x \bmod N|$.

Keygen(pp) : The key generation algorithm runs $RSA_{gen}(1^\lambda)$ to obtain (P, Q, N, S) and chooses random $g \in G_S^+$, it picks random $x \in [N/4]$ and $\mathcal{H} \in \mathcal{HS}$, it computes $X = g^x$. The public key is set as $pk = (N, g, X, \mathcal{H})$ and the secret key is set as $sk = x$.

Enc(pk, m) : The encryption algorithm chooses random $r \in [N/4]$ and computes the ciphertext $C = (C_1, C_2)$ as:

$$C_1 = g^r, Y = X^r, K = \mathcal{H}(C_1, Y), C_2 = \mathcal{E}(K, m).$$

$Dec(C, sk)$: The decryption algorithm first checks whether $C_1 \in QR_N^+$ and rejects if not. Then it computes the message as:

$$Y = C_1^x, K = \mathcal{H}(C_1, Y), m = \mathcal{D}(K, C_3).$$

Correctness can be easily verified from the correctness of the symmetric encryption scheme and $Y = C_1^x = g^{rx} = X^r$.

In the security proof we will use the following assumption HR$'$ directly.

Run $RSA_{gen}(1^\lambda)$ to get (P, Q, N, S), and randomly choose $g, u_0 \in G_S^+$, $u_1 \in QR_N^+$. The advantage of $\mathcal{A}$ is defined as

$$Adv_{\mathcal{A}}^{HR'} = \Big| \Pr[\mathcal{A}(g, u_1) = 1] - \Pr[\mathcal{A}(g, u_0) = 1] \Big|.$$

Definition 5 (HR$'$). *We say that $\mathcal{G}$ satisfies the HR$'$ assumption if for all PPT algorithm $\mathcal{A}$, $Adv_{\mathcal{A}}^{HR'}$ is negligible in λ.*

Clearly, the HR$'$ assumption is implied by the HR assumption.

Theorem 2. *If the HR$'$ assumption holds, SE is an AE-OT secure symmetric encryption scheme with secret key space $\{0, 1\}^l$, $\mathcal{HS}$ is a family of 4-wise independent hash functions with domain G^3 and image $\{0, 1\}^l$, then our PKE scheme is Φ-CC-RKA secure for the class of affine functions Φ. In particular, for every advasary $\mathcal{A}$ on CC-RKA security of the above scheme, there exist adversaries $\mathcal{B}, \mathcal{C}, \mathcal{D}$ with*

$$Adv_{\mathcal{A}}^{CC-RKA} \leq (q + 1)Adv_{\mathcal{B}}^{HR} + q(2^{l-(\kappa-1)} + Adv_{SE,\mathcal{C}}^{INT-OT}) + Adv_{SE,\mathcal{D}}^{IND-OT}.$$

where $\kappa = log_2(\lfloor N/4S \rfloor)$.

The proof methodology of Theorem 2 is similar to Theorem 1 and we put the concrete proof in Appendix B.

5   Conclusion

In this paper, we prove the security against related key attacks of two public key encryption schemes in the standard model. The first scheme is a variation of the KYPS09. While KYPS09 has been proved CCA secure under the DDH assumption, we show in the appendix that it is not secure against related key attacks when the key related function includes affine functions. We make a modification on KYPS09 and prove that the resulting scheme is Φ-CC-RKA secure for $\Phi = \Phi^{affine}$. We also prove the scheme in [15] is Φ-CC-RKA secure for $\Phi = \Phi^{affine}$ based on the HR assumption. The security relies heavily on a randomness extractor called 4-wise independent hash functions and we use game sequences in the proof. In the future we will study the CC-RKA security property for universal-1 hash proof systems.

Acknowledgments. We are very grateful to anonymous reviewers for their helpful comments. We also thank Yamin Liu for helpful discussions.

References

1. Abdalla, M., et al.: Searchable Encryption Revisited: Consistency Properties, Relation to Anonymous IBE, and Extensions. In: Shoup, V. (ed.) CRYPTO 2005. LNCS, vol. 3621, pp. 205–222. Springer, Heidelberg (2005)
2. Abdalla, M., Bellare, M., Rogaway, P.: The Oracle Diffie-Hellman Assumptions and an Analysis of DHIES. In: Naccache, D. (ed.) CT-RSA 2001. LNCS, vol. 2020, pp. 143–158. Springer, Heidelberg (2001)
3. Bellare, M., Cash, D.: Pseudorandom Functions and Permutations Provably Secure against Related-Key Attacks. In: Rabin, T. (ed.) CRYPTO 2010. LNCS, vol. 6223, pp. 666–684. Springer, Heidelberg (2010)
4. Bellare, M., Cash, D., Miller, R.: Cryptography Secure against Related-Key Attacks and Tampering. In: Lee, D.H., Wang, X. (eds.) ASIACRYPT 2011. LNCS, vol. 7073, pp. 486–503. Springer, Heidelberg (2011)
5. Bellare, M., Kohno, T.: A Theoretical Treatment of Related-Key Attacks: RKA-PRPs, RKA-PRFs, and Applications. In: Biham, E. (ed.) EUROCRYPT 2003. LNCS, vol. 2656, pp. 491–506. Springer, Heidelberg (2003)
6. Bellare, M., Namprempre, C.: Authenticated Encryption: Relations among Notions and Analysis of the Generic Composition Paradigm. In: Okamoto, T. (ed.) ASIACRYPT 2000. LNCS, vol. 1976, pp. 531–545. Springer, Heidelberg (2000)
7. Bellare, M., Paterson, K.G., Thomson, S.: RKA Security beyond the Linear Barrier: IBE, Encryption and Signatures. In: Wang, X., Sako, K. (eds.) ASIACRYPT 2012. LNCS, vol. 7658, pp. 331–348. Springer, Heidelberg (2012)
8. Biham, E., Shamir, A.: Differential Fault Analysis of Secret Key Cryptosystems. In: Kaliski Jr., B.S. (ed.) CRYPTO 1997. LNCS, vol. 1294, pp. 513–525. Springer, Heidelberg (1997)
9. Boneh, D.: Twenty Years of Attacks on the RSA Cryptosystem (1999)
10. Boneh, D., DeMillo, R.A., Lipton, R.J.: On the Importance of Checking Cryptographic Protocols for Faults. In: Fumy, W. (ed.) EUROCRYPT 1997. LNCS, vol. 1233, pp. 37–51. Springer, Heidelberg (1997)
11. Cramer, R., Shoup, V.: Design and Analysis of Practical Public-Key Encryption Schemes Secure against Adaptive Chosen Ciphertext Attack. SIAM J. Compt. 33(1), 167–226 (2003)
12. Groth, J.: Cryptography in subgroups of z_n. In: Kilian, J. (ed.) TCC 2005. LNCS, vol. 3378, pp. 50–65. Springer, Heidelberg (2005)
13. Halderman, J.A., Schoen, S.D., Heninger, N., Clarkson, W., Paul, W., Calandrino, J.A., Feldman, A.J., Appelbaum, J., Felten, E.W.: Lest We Remember: Cold-boot Attacks on Encryption Keys. Commun. ACM 52(5), 91–98 (2009)
14. Håstad, J., Impagliazzo, R., Levin, L.A., Luby, M.: A Pseudorandom Generator from any One-way Function. SIAM J. Comput 28(4), 1364–1396 (1999)
15. Hofheinz, D., Kiltz, E.: The Group of Signed Quadratic Residues and Applications. In: Halevi, S. (ed.) CRYPTO 2009. LNCS, vol. 5677, pp. 637–653. Springer, Heidelberg (2009)
16. Kiltz, E., Pietrzak, K., Stam, M., Yung, M.: A New Randomness Extraction Paradigm for Hybrid Encryption. In: Joux, A. (ed.) EUROCRYPT 2009. LNCS, vol. 5479, pp. 590–609. Springer, Heidelberg (2009); also Cryptology ePrint Archive, 2008/304

17. Kurosawa, K., Katayama, Y., Ogata, W., Tsujii, S.: General Public Key Residue Cryptosystems and Mental Poker Protocols. In: Damgård, I.B. (ed.) EUROCRYPT 1990. LNCS, vol. 473, pp. 374–388. Springer, Heidelberg (1991)
18. Naccache, D., Stern, J.: A new Public Key Cryptosystem based on Higher Residues. In: CCS 1998, pp. 59–66 (1998)
19. Wee, H.: Public Key Encryption against Related Key Attacks. In: Fischlin, M., Buchmann, J., Manulis, M. (eds.) PKC 2012. LNCS, vol. 7293, pp. 262–279. Springer, Heidelberg (2012)

Appendix A: A RKA attack on KPSY09

The PKE Scheme by KPSY09

The PKE scheme of [16] is given as follows:

$Keygen(1^\lambda)$: The key generation algorithm chooses random $x_1, x_2 \in \mathbb{Z}_p$ and $\mathcal{H} \in \mathcal{HS}$, it computes $X = g_1^{x_1} g_2^{x_2}$. The public key is set as $pk = (X, \mathcal{H})$ and the secret key is set as $sk = (x_1, x_2)$

$Enc(pk, m)$: The encryption algorithm chooses random $r \in \mathbb{Z}_p$ and computes the ciphertext $C = (C_1, C_2, C_3)$ as:

$$C_1 = g_1^r, C_2 = g_2^r, Y = X^r, K = \mathcal{H}(Y), C_3 = \mathcal{E}(K, m).$$

$Dec(C, sk)$: The decryption algorithm computes the message as:

$$Y = C_1^{x_1} C_2^{x_2}, K = \mathcal{H}(Y), m = \mathcal{D}(K, C_3).$$

The above scheme is not RKA secure if Φ includes a function $\phi_{a_1, a_2}^*(x_1, x_2) = (a_1 x_1, a_2 x_2)$. Once the adversary sees the challenge ciphertext C_1^*, C_2^*, C_3^*, it can create a query as $(C = (C_1^{*\frac{1}{a_1}}, C_2^{*\frac{1}{a_2}}, C_3^*), \phi^*)$, and it can get the decryption of the challenge ciphertext since $Y^* = C_1^{*x_1} C_2^{*x_2}$.

Appendix B: Proof of Theorem 2

Proof. Suppose that the public key is $(N, g, X, \mathcal{H})$ and the secret key is x. The challenge ciphertext is denoted by $C^* = (C_1^*, C_2^*)$. We also denote by r^*, Y^*, K^* the values corresponding with r, Y, K related to C^*. We say that a ciphertext C is invalid if $C_1 \in QR_N^+ \backslash G_S^+$. Let $\log(\cdot)$ denote $\log_g(\cdot)$. Then we have

$$x = logX + t \cdot S, \text{ where } t \in \{0, 1, ..., \lfloor N/4S \rfloor\} \tag{5}$$

To prove the security of our scheme, we define a sequence of games that any PPT adversary can not tell the difference between two adjacent games. Let q denote the number of decryption queries that the adversary makes during the whole game, here we write an affine function as $\phi(sk) = ax + b, a, b \in [N/4]$.

$Game_0$: the real security game.

$Game_1$: the same as $Game_0$ except that the challenge ciphertext is generated using the secret key. That is

$$Y^* = C_1^{*x}.$$

$Game_2$: the same as $Game_1$ except that the challenge ciphertext is invalid. That is $C_1^* \in QR_N^+ \backslash G_S^+$.

$Game_3$: the same as $Game_2$ except that the decryption oracle rejects all invalid queries.

$Game_4$: the same as $Game_3$, except that SE encrypts m_b using a random key K^+ instead of K^*.

Let $Adv_{\mathcal{A}}^i$ denote $\mathcal{A}$'s advantage in $Game_i$ for $i = 0, 1, ..., 4$.

Clearly, $Adv_{\mathcal{A}}^0 = Adv_{\mathcal{A}}^1$.

Lemma 11. *Suppose that there exists a PPT adversary $\mathcal{A}$ such that $Adv_{\mathcal{A}}^1 - Adv_{\mathcal{A}}^2 = \epsilon$, then there exists a PPT adversary $\mathcal{B}$ with advantage ϵ in breaking the HR' assumption.*

Proof. $\mathcal{B}$ receives

$$D = (g, T)$$

and its task is to decide whether $T \in G_S^+$. $\mathcal{B}$ picks random $x \in [N/4]$ and $\mathcal{H} \in \mathcal{HS}$. $\mathcal{B}$ computes $X = g^x$ and sends $pk = (N, g, X, \mathcal{H}))$ to $\mathcal{A}$.

Whenever $\mathcal{A}$ submits (ϕ, C), $\mathcal{B}$ simply runs the decryption oracle with the secret key $\phi(sk)$.

When $\mathcal{A}$ submits (m_0, m_1), $\mathcal{B}$ randomly chooses $b \leftarrow_R \{0, 1\}$, it sets $C_1^* = T, Y^* = T^x, K^* = \mathcal{H}(C_1^*, Y^*), C_2^* = \mathcal{E}(K^*, m_b)$ and responds with $C^* = (C_1^*, C_2^*)$.

When $\mathcal{A}$ outputs b', $\mathcal{B}$ outputs 1 if $b' = b$ and 0 otherwise.

Note that when $T \in G_S^+$, then the above game perfectly simulates $Game_1$; when $T \notin G_S^+$, the above game perfectly simulates $Game_2$. $\square$

Lemma 12. *Suppose that there exists a PPT adversary $\mathcal{A}$ in $Game_2$ and $Game_3$ such that it can submit a query (C, ϕ) satisfying $C_1 = C_1^*, \phi(sk) \neq sk, Y = Y^*$ with probability δ, then there exists a PPT adversary $\mathcal{B}$ with advantage δ in breaking the HR' assumption.*

Proof. $\mathcal{B}$ receives

$$D = (g, u)$$

and its task is to decide whether $u \in G_S^+$. Then $\mathcal{B}$ picks random $x \in [N/4]$, $\mathcal{H} \in \mathcal{HS}$. $\mathcal{B}$ computes $X = g^x$ and sends $pk = (N, g, X, \mathcal{H})$ to $\mathcal{A}$.

Whenever $\mathcal{A}$ submits (ϕ, C), $\mathcal{B}$ simply runs the decryption oracle with the secret key $\phi(sk)$.

When $\mathcal{A}$ submits (m_0, m_1), $\mathcal{B}$ randomly chooses $b \leftarrow_R \{0, 1\}, t \in QR_N^+$, then with overwhelming probability we have $ut \notin G_S^+$. It sets $C_1^* = ut, Y^* = C_1^{*x}, K^* = \mathcal{H}(C_1^*, Y^*), C_2^* = \mathcal{E}(K^*, m_b)$ and responds with $C^* = (C_1^*, C_2^*)$.

Whenever $\mathcal{A}$ submits (ϕ, C) satisfying $C_1 = C_1^*, \phi(sk) \neq sk, Y = Y^*$, then we have $C_1 = C_1^{\frac{\phi(x)}{x}}$. Since $C_1^* \in QR_N^+ \backslash G_S^+$, with overwhelming probability we have $\frac{\varphi(N)}{4} | ord(C_1^*)$, so $\frac{4\phi(x)}{x}$ is a multiple of $\varphi(N)$, then we can solve the factoring problem according to the method in [[9],Fact 1.]. $\qquad\square$

Lemma 13. *Assume that the symmetric encryption scheme is AE-OT secure, $\mathcal{HS}$ is a family of 4-wise independent hash functions, the HR' assumption holds, then $Adv_{\mathcal{A}}^2 - Adv_{\mathcal{A}}^3$ is negligible.*

Proof. Let F be the event that a query (C, ϕ) is rejected in $Game_3$ but not rejected in $Game_2$. Then we have $|Adv_{\mathcal{A}}^2 - Adv_{\mathcal{A}}^3| \leq \Pr[F]$. We consider the following cases:

Case 1: $C_1 = C_1^*$.
- $\phi(sk) = sk$. From eq. (5) we can see that t is information-theoretically hidden for any PPT adversary $\mathcal{A}$, so $H_\infty(Y^*) \geq \kappa$. As stated by the left-over hash lemma, K^* is randomly distributed. As a result, it is difficult to generate a $C_2 \neq C_2^*$ s.t. $\mathcal{D}(K^*, C_2) \neq \bot$ according to the INT-OT property of the SE scheme.
- $\phi(sk) \neq sk$. Let Γ^* be the random variable (C_1^*, Y^*), Γ be the random variable (C_1, Y). According to Lemma 12 we know that $\delta = \Pr[\Gamma = \Gamma^*] = \Pr[Y = Y^*]$ is negligible. From the choice of sk we know that $H_\infty(Y) \geq \kappa$, so $H_\infty(\Gamma^*) \geq \kappa$, $H_\infty(\Gamma) \geq \kappa$. From Lemma 3 we know:

$$SD((pk, \mathcal{H}, \mathcal{H}(\Gamma^*), \mathcal{H}(\Gamma)), (pk, \mathcal{H}, \mathcal{H}(\Gamma^*), U_l)) \leq 2^{l-(\kappa-1)/2} + \delta.$$

  Here U_l is uniformly random chosen from $\{0, 1\}^l$. So the distribution of K looks random to the adversary $\mathcal{A}$, then from the INT-OT property of the SE scheme, with overwhelming probability $Dec(sk, C) = \bot$.
Case 2: $C_1 \neq C_1^*$, and $C_1 \notin G_S^+$. Let Γ^* be the random variable (C_1^*, Y^*), Γ be the random variable (C_1, Y), then we have $\Gamma^* \neq \Gamma$. From the distribution of sk, we have $H_\infty(\Gamma^*) \geq \kappa$, $H_\infty(\Gamma) \geq \kappa$. Then according to Lemma 3 we have:

$$SD((pk, \mathcal{H}, \mathcal{H}(\Gamma^*), \mathcal{H}(\Gamma)), (pk, \mathcal{H}, \mathcal{H}(\Gamma^*), U_l)) \leq 2^{l-(\kappa-1)/2}.$$

Therefore, the distribution of K looks random to the adversary $\mathcal{A}$, then from the INT-OT property of the SE scheme, with overwhelming probability $Dec(sk, C) = \bot$.

From the above analysis, we can see that it is difficult to distinguish $Game_2$ and $Game_3$ for any PPT adversary. $\qquad\square$

Lemma 14. *Assume that $\mathcal{HS}$ is a family of 4-wise independent hash functions, then $Adv_{\mathcal{A}}^3 - Adv_{\mathcal{A}}^4$ is negligible.*

Proof. Since in both $Game_3$ and $Game_4$, all queries (C, ϕ) that are not rejected satisfy $C_1 \in G_S^+$, so for any information-theoretical adversary $\mathcal{A}$, all it can get from the decryption queries is :

$$\log Y = arx + b \bmod S$$
$$= ar \log X + b \bmod S$$

As a result, t is information-theoretically hidden, $H_\infty(Y^*) \geq \kappa$, then according to the leftover hash lemma we can see that K^* is randomly distributed, $Game_3$ and $Game_4$ are indistinguishable.

Lemma 15. *Suppose that there exists a PPT adversary $\mathcal{A}$ such that $Adv_{\mathcal{A}}^4 = \epsilon$, then there exists a PPT adversary $\mathcal{B}$ with the same advantage in breaking the IND-OT property of the SE scheme.*

Proof. $\mathcal{B}$ runs $RSA_{gen}(1^\lambda)$ to obtain (P, Q, N, S) and choose random $g \in G_S^+$. $\mathcal{B}$ computes $X = g^x$ and sends $pk = (N, g, X, \mathcal{H})$ to $\mathcal{A}$.

Whenever $\mathcal{A}$ submits (ϕ, C), $\mathcal{B}$ simply runs the decryption oracle with the secret key $\phi(sk)$.

When $\mathcal{A}$ submits (m_0, m_1), $\mathcal{B}$ sends (m_0, m_1) to its challenger and receives C_2^*. Then $\mathcal{B}$ chooses random $C_1^* \in QR_N^+ \backslash G_S^+$ and responds with $C^* = (C_1^*, C_2^*)$.

When $\mathcal{A}$ outputs b', $\mathcal{B}$ outputs b'. $\qquad \square$

Computationally Efficient Dual-Policy Attribute Based Encryption with Short Ciphertext

Y. Sreenivasa Rao and Ratna Dutta

Indian Institute of Technology Kharagpur
Kharagpur-721302, India
{ysrao,ratna}@maths.iitkgp.ernet.in

Abstract. We propose an efficient *dual-policy* Attribute Based Encryption (ABE), a logical combination of key-policy ABE and ciphertext-policy ABE, with *short* ciphertext for monotone access structures. We also present key-policy ABE schemes with *constant-size* ciphertexts for monotone as well as non-monotone access structures. While the secret key in all our schemes has quadratic size in the number of attributes, the number of bilinear pairing evaluations is reduced to *constant*. Compared with the available dual-policy and key-policy ABE schemes, our constructions provide better efficiency in terms of computation cost. All our schemes are provably secure under chosen plaintext attacks in selective-security model under the decisional n-Bilinear Diffie-Hellman Exponent assumption over prime order bilinear groups.

Keywords: key-policy, dual-policy, attribute-based encryption, monotone access structure, non-monotone access structure.

1 Introduction

Attribute Based Encryption (ABE) [4–6] is a generalization of Identity Based Encryption (IBE) [3]. Each user is ascribed a set of descriptive attributes where either (i) secret key is generated according to an access structure and ciphertext is associated with a set of attributes, yielding Key-Policy ABE (KP-ABE) [4, 5] or (ii) ciphertext is created according to an access structure and secret key is associated with a set of attributes, yielding Ciphertext-Policy ABE (CP-ABE) [6]. Decryption is successful in KP-ABE (or CP-ABE) only when the attribute set annotated to ciphertext (or secret key) satisfies the access structure ascribed to secret key (or ciphertext).

While the first ABE system proposed by Sahai and Waters [4] is considered as a KP-ABE with threshold access policy, the first CP-ABE system is devised by Bethencourt et al. [6] for more expressive Monotone Access Structures (MAS). Several improved CP-ABE schemes [7, 12, 2, 13] are suggested immediately after that having ciphertext size and bilinear pairing computations linear to the required attribute set size. The CP-ABE schemes [14, 11, 15, 16] exhibit constant-size ciphertext, but the access policies exploited in these schemes are less expressive and restricted to either AND-gate or threshold policy. The first

W. Susilo and R. Reyhanitabar (Eds.): ProvSec 2013, LNCS 8209, pp. 288–308, 2013.

KP-ABE system for MAS was designed by Goyal et al. [5]. There are quite a number of KP-ABE schemes [19, 17, 18] that allow Non-Monotone Access Structure (nonMAS). All the foregoing constructions except [2, 18] are proven to be *selectively* secure—the adversary commits to her target before the simulation is set up. The first *fully* secure KP-ABE and CP-ABE schemes were presented in [2] using Linear Secret-Sharing Scheme (LSSS)-realizable MAS in the standard model over composite order bilinear groups, whereas [18] proposed KP-ABE and CP-ABE schemes for nonMAS that are fully secure under the Decisional Linear (DLIN) assumption in the standard model over prime order groups. Attrapadung et al. [9] proposed the first constant-size ciphertext selectively-secure KP-ABE for MAS as well as nonMAS over prime order groups with constant number of bilinear pairings, but secret key size is quadratic in the number of attributes. Wang and Luo [10] proposed a KP-ABE scheme with constant-size ciphertext for MAS based on [11], but the security proof relies on random oracles.

Dual-Policy ABE. While the access structure annotated to user's secret key in KP-ABE enables what type of ciphertexts she can decrypt, the access structure associated with the ciphertext in CP-ABE decides what kind of recipients will be able to decrypt. As outlined in [1], some applications (e.g., Pay-TV system and body sensor networks), demand *simultaneous* access control where the message is encrypted under both a set of *objective* attributes that annotate the message itself and a *subjective* access structure that decides who can or cannot decrypt the ciphertext. A user obtains a secret key for both a set of *subjective* attributes that annotate user's credentials and an *objective* access structure that states which ciphertexts the user can decrypt. Such an ABE is called as *Dual-Policy ABE*, wherein the decryption will be successful only when the objective attribute set satisfies the objective access structure and the subjective attribute set satisfies the subjective access structure.

Attrapadung and Imai [1] proposed the first dual-policy ABE that is a conjunctively combined scheme between a KP-ABE [5] and a CP-ABE [7] where the KP-ABE component deals with objective attribute universe and the CP-ABE component deals with subjective attribute universe. If one ignores subjective (resp. objective) attributes, their dual-policy scheme becomes KP-ABE of [5] (resp. CP-ABE of [7]). Both subjective and objective access structures are monotone LSSS-realizable access structures. However, the size of ciphertext grows linearly with the number of subjective as well as objective attributes associated with the ciphertext and the number of bilinear pairing evaluations is linear to the number of objective attributes used in decryption. The scheme is proven to be selectively secure against chosen plaintext attacks (CPA) under the decisional n-Bilinear Diffie-Hellman Exponent (n-BDHE) assumption. Okamoto and Takashima [18] proposed fully secure dual-policy functional encryption for general relations using the concept of dual pairing vector spaces over prime order groups. Recently, Miyaji and Tran [8] introduced a dual-policy ABE scheme with constant number of pairings that exploits only AND-gate access policies. However, the decryption will not work in the way as described in [8]. The authors also stated that the size of ciphertext is constant as it contains only 3

Table 1. Computation Costs of LSSS-based dual-policy ABE schemes

Scheme	Encryption Cost		Decryption Cost		
	$\mathsf{Ex}_{\mathbb{G}}$	$\mathsf{Ex}_{\mathbb{G}_T}$	$\mathsf{Ex}_{\mathbb{G}}$	$\mathsf{Ex}_{\mathbb{G}_T}$	Pairings
[1]	$\mathcal{O}(\ell_s + |W_o|)$	1	$\mathcal{O}(|I_s| + |I_o|)$	$|I_o|$	$|I_o| + 2$
[18]	$\mathcal{O}(\ell_s + |W_o|)$	1	-	$|I_s| + |I_o|$	$|I_s| + |I_o| + 1$
Our	$\mathcal{O}(\ell_s)$	1	$\mathcal{O}(|I_s| + |I_o|)$	-	3

$B_{\mathbb{G}}$ (or $B_{\mathbb{G}_T}$) = bit size of an element in $\mathbb{G}$ (or $\mathbb{G}_T$, resp.), $\mathsf{Ex}_{\mathbb{G}}$ (or $\mathsf{Ex}_{\mathbb{G}_T}$) = number of exponentiations in a group $\mathbb{G}$ (or $\mathbb{G}_T$, resp.), L_s = set of subjective attributes in a user's secret key, ℓ_o (resp. ℓ_s) = number of rows in an objective (resp. subjective) LSSS access structure associated with secret key (resp. ciphertext), $\mathcal{V}_o$ = objective attribute space, W_o = set of objective attributes per ciphertext, I_o (resp. I_s) = minimum set of objective (resp. subjective) attributes used in decryption, n-dBDHE = decisional n-BDHE.

Table 2. Communication overheads of LSSS-based dual-policy ABE schemes

Scheme	Secret Key Size	Ciphertext Size	Assumption	Security
[1]	$\mathcal{O}(\ell_o + |L_s|) \cdot B_{\mathbb{G}}$	$(\ell_s + |W_o| + 1) \cdot B_{\mathbb{G}} + B_{\mathbb{G}_T}$	n-dBDHE	Selective
[18]	$\mathcal{O}(\ell_o + |L_s|) \cdot B_{\mathbb{G}}$	$(7 \cdot \ell_s + 7 \cdot |W_o| + 8) \cdot B_{\mathbb{G}} + B_{\mathbb{G}_T}$	DLIN	Full
Our	$\mathcal{O}(\ell_o|\mathcal{V}_o| + |L_s|) \cdot B_{\mathbb{G}}$	$(\ell_s + 2) \cdot B_{\mathbb{G}} + B_{\mathbb{G}_T}$	n-dBDHE	Selective

The meaning of all the symbols in Table 2 are found at the bottom of Table 1.

group elements, but the ciphertext consists of $|W_o| + 2$ group elements, where W_o is the set of objective attributes per ciphertext. Hence, ciphertext size is not constant. To the best of our knowledge, [1, 8, 18] are the only schemes in the dual-policy setting available in the literature.

Our Contribution. This paper is mainly aimed to construct efficient and secure dual-policy ABE. We use the CP-ABE framework of [7] to design the CP-ABE component of our dual-policy ABE and the KP-ABE component is designed by using the technique of threshold CP-ABE of [16].

Our proposed dual-policy ABE system realizes monotone LSSS access structures with shortened ciphertext consisting of $\ell_s + 2$ group elements regardless of the number of objective attributes annotated with the ciphertext, whereas the ciphertext in the dual-policy ABE schemes of [1, 18] consist of $\mathcal{O}(\ell_s + |W_o|)$ group elements, ℓ_s being the number of rows in a subjective LSSS access structure and $|W_o|$ being the number of attributes in an objective attribute set W_o. This comes at a cost of increasing the (objective attribute) secret key size by a factor of $|\mathcal{V}_o|$, where $\mathcal{V}_o$ is the set of objective attributes used in the system. However, decryption is much faster in contrast to [1, 18] as our scheme requires only 3 bilinear pairing computations and no pairing exponentiation during decryption, whereas [1] (resp. [18]) requires $|I_o|$ (resp. $|I_s| + |I_o|$) pairing exponentiations and $|I_o| + 2$ (resp. $|I_s| + |I_o| + 1$) pairing evaluations, I_o and I_s respectively being the minimum number of objective and subjective attributes required for decryption. Table 1 and 2 compare efficiency of our scheme with the only existing dual-policy schemes [1, 18] that support LSSS access structures.

Table 3. Comparison of constant-size ciphertext KP-ABE schemes for MAS

Scheme	Secret Key Size	Ciphertext Size	Enc. Cost		Dec. Cost		Assumption
			$\mathsf{Ex}_{\mathbb{G}}$	$\mathsf{Ex}_{\mathbb{G}_T}$	$\mathsf{Ex}_{\mathbb{G}}$	Pairings	
[9]	$\mathcal{O}(\ell \cdot \overline{n}) \cdot B_{\mathbb{G}}$	$2 \cdot B_{\mathbb{G}} + B_{\mathbb{G}_T}$	$\mathcal{O}(\phi)$	1	$\mathcal{O}(|I| \cdot \phi)$	2	n-dBDHE
[10]	$\mathcal{O}(\ell \cdot \overline{n}) \cdot B_{\mathbb{G}}$	$2 \cdot B_{\mathbb{G}} + B_{\mathbb{G}_T}$	$\mathcal{O}(\phi)$	1	$\mathcal{O}(|I| \cdot \phi)$	2	dGDHE
Our	$\mathcal{O}(\ell \cdot n) \cdot B_{\mathbb{G}}$	$2 \cdot B_{\mathbb{G}} + B_{\mathbb{G}_T}$	2	1	$\mathcal{O}(|I|)$	2	n-dBDHE

$B_{\mathbb{G}}, B_{\mathbb{G}_T}, \mathsf{Ex}_{\mathbb{G}}, \mathsf{Ex}_{\mathbb{G}_T}$ *are same as in Table 1 and 2, ℓ = number of rows in the user LSSS access structure matrix, n = number of attributes used in the system, ϕ = number of attributes in a ciphertext, $\overline{n}$ = maximum bound for ϕ (i.e., $\phi \leq \overline{n}$), $|I|$ = number of rows of LSSS matrix used in the decryption, dGDHE = General Decisional Diffie-Hellman Exponent. (The KP-ABE in [9, 10] supports large attribute universe with bound $\overline{n}$ on the number of attributes per ciphertext and $\overline{n} = n$ in the small attribute universe setting.)*

Table 4. Comparison of constant-size ciphertext KP-ABE schemes for nonMAS

Scheme	Secret Key Size	Ciphertext Size	Enc. Cost		Dec. Cost		Assumption
			$\mathsf{Ex}_{\mathbb{G}}$	$\mathsf{Ex}_{\mathbb{G}_T}$	$\mathsf{Ex}_{\mathbb{G}}$	Pairings	
[9]	$\mathcal{O}(\ell \cdot \overline{n}) \cdot B_{\mathbb{G}}$	$3 \cdot B_{\mathbb{G}} + B_{\mathbb{G}_T}$	$\mathcal{O}(\phi)$	1	$\mathcal{O}(|I| \cdot \phi)$	3	n-dBDHE
Our	$\mathcal{O}(\ell \cdot n) \cdot B_{\mathbb{G}}$	$3 \cdot B_{\mathbb{G}} + B_{\mathbb{G}_T}$	3	1	$\mathcal{O}(|I|)$	3	n-dBDHE

The meaning of all the symbols in Table 4 are same as the symbols in Table 3.

We separate the KP-ABE component of our dual-policy ABE scheme by neglecting subjective attributes, resulting a KP-ABE scheme for monotone LSSS-realizable access structure with constant-size ciphertext and constant number of bilinear pairing evaluations. The size of secret key is $\mathcal{O}(\ell \cdot n)$ group elements, where ℓ is the number of rows in the user LSSS matrix and n is the number of attributes in the attribute space. We emphasize that our KP-ABE needs $|I|$ exponentiations and 2 pairing computations, where $|I|$ is the number of rows of LSSS matrix used in the decryption. On the contrary, the first constant-size ciphertext KP-ABE scheme [9], which is derived from a particular identity based broadcast encryption scheme, performs $|I| \cdot \phi$ exponentiations followed by 2 pairing computations to decrypt a ciphertext, where ϕ denotes the number of attributes in a ciphertext. The KP-ABE scheme of [10] preserves the same functionality as that of [9]. Consequently, our scheme outperforms the KP-ABE schemes of [9, 10] in terms of exponentiations. In Table 3, we give a detailed comparison of our scheme with the previous constant-size ciphertext KP-ABE schemes for MAS.

We further extend our monotone KP-ABE approach to non-monotone KP-ABE by employing the technique of [19] for transforming a nonMAS over a set of attributes to a MAS over the same set of attributes and their negation. The resulting nonMAS KP-ABE construction features constant-size ciphertext, constant number of bilinear pairing evaluations, $|I|$ exponentiations in decryption while the secret key size is increased by a factor of n as in the monotone case. Table 4 compares efficiency of our nonMAS construction with the existing KP-ABE scheme [9] with constant-size ciphertext that supports nonMAS.

As the number of attributes in the attribute universe is a factor of the secret key size, our constructions deal with small attribute universe (the attributes are fixed at system setup phase as in [2, 4, 5, 7, 9, 11, 12, 14–16]). As the storage is becoming much cheaper nowadays, these new schemes are of independent interest for applications where the resources have limited computing power and bandwidth is the primary concern. Our approach is extendable to large universe setting (see Section 3.2), where the attribute parameters are dynamically computed after the system setup. All our schemes have been proven to be selectively CPA secure in the standard model under the decisional n-BDHE assumption over prime order bilinear groups.

2 Background

Notation. Let $x \in_R X$ denote the operation of picking an element x uniformly at random from the set X. We use the notation $[n]$ to represent the set $[n] = \{1, 2, \ldots, n\}$ of positive integers. *PPT* stands for probabilistic polynomial-time.

In this section, we recall necessary background from [1, 7].

Definition 1 (Access Structure). *Let U be the universe of attributes and $\mathcal{P}(U)$ be the collection of all subsets of U. Every subset $\mathbb{A}$ of $\mathcal{P}(U) \setminus \{\emptyset\}$ is called an access structure. An access structure $\mathbb{A}$ is said to be monotone access structure (MAS) if for any $C \in \mathcal{P}(U)$, with $C \supseteq B$ where $B \in \mathbb{A}$ implies $C \in \mathbb{A}$.*

2.1 Linear Secret-Sharing Schemes (LSSS)

Let U be the universe of attributes. A secret-sharing scheme $\Pi_{\mathbb{A}}$ for the access structure $\mathbb{A}$ over U is called *linear* (in $\mathbb{Z}_p$) if $\Pi_{\mathbb{A}}$ consists of the following two polynomial-time algorithms, where $\mathbb{M}$ is a matrix of size $\ell \times k$, called the *share-generating matrix* for $\Pi_{\mathbb{A}}$ and $\rho : [\ell] \to I_U$ is a row labeling function that maps each row of the matrix $\mathbb{M}$ to an attribute in $\mathbb{A}$, I_U being the index set of attribute universe U.

(i) Distribute($\mathbb{M}, \rho, \alpha$): This algorithm takes as input the share-generating matrix $\mathbb{M}$, row labeling function ρ and a secret $\alpha \in \mathbb{Z}_p$ which is to be shared. It randomly selects $z_2, z_3, \ldots, z_k \in_R \mathbb{Z}_p$ and sets $\boldsymbol{v} = (\alpha, z_2, z_3, \ldots, z_k) \in \mathbb{Z}_p^k$. It outputs a set $\{\boldsymbol{M_i} \cdot \boldsymbol{v} : i \in [\ell]\}$ of ℓ shares, where $\boldsymbol{M_i} \in \mathbb{Z}_p^k$ is the i-th row of the matrix $\mathbb{M}$. The share $\lambda_{\rho(i)} = \boldsymbol{M_i} \cdot \boldsymbol{v}$ belongs to an attribute $\rho(i)$.

(ii) Reconstruct($\mathbb{M}, \rho, W$): This algorithm will accept as input $\mathbb{M}, \rho$ and a set of attributes $W \in \mathbb{A}$. Let $I = \{i \in [\ell] : \rho(i) \in I_W\}$, where I_W is the index set of attribute set W. It returns a set $\{\omega_i : i \in I\}$ of secret reconstruction constants such that $\sum_{i \in I} \omega_i \lambda_{\rho(i)} = \alpha$ if $\{\lambda_{\rho(i)} : i \in I\}$ is a valid set of shares of the secret α according to $\Pi_{\mathbb{A}}$.

Lemma 1. *[1] Let $(\mathbb{M}, \rho)$ be a LSSS for an access structure $\mathbb{A}$ over the universe U of attributes, where $\mathbb{M}$ is share-generating matrix of size $\ell \times k$, and $W \subset U$. If $W \notin \mathbb{A}$ (in other words, W does not satisfy $\mathbb{M}$), there exists a polynomial time algorithm that outputs a vector $\boldsymbol{w} = (-1, w_2, \ldots, w_k) \in \mathbb{Z}_p^k$ such that $\boldsymbol{M_i} \cdot \boldsymbol{w} = 0$, for each row i of $\mathbb{M}$ for which $\rho(i) \in I_W$, I_W is the index set of attribute set W.*

2.2   Bilinear Maps and Hardness Assumption

We use multiplicative cyclic groups $(\mathbb{G}, \mathbb{G}_T)$ of prime order p with an efficiently computable mapping $e : \mathbb{G} \times \mathbb{G} \to \mathbb{G}_T$ such that $e(u^a, v^b) = e(u, v)^{ab}$, $\forall\, u, v \in \mathbb{G}$, $a, b \in \mathbb{Z}_p$ and $e(g, g) \neq 1_T$, where 1_T is the unit element in $\mathbb{G}_T$.

Decisional n-BDHE Assumption. An algorithm (or distinguisher) $\mathfrak{D}$ for solving the decisional n-BDHE (Bilinear Diffie-Hellman Exponent) problem in $(\mathbb{G}, \mathbb{G}_T)$ takes as input a tuple $(\overrightarrow{y}_{a,\theta}, Z) \in \mathbb{G}^{2n+1} \times \mathbb{G}_T$, where $a, \theta \in_R \mathbb{Z}_p, g \in_R \mathbb{G}, g_i = g^{a^i}, \forall i \in [2n], \overrightarrow{y}_{a,\theta} = (g, g^\theta, g_1, \ldots, g_n, g_{n+2}, \ldots, g_{2n})$ and determines whether $Z = e(g_{n+1}, g^\theta)$ or a random element in $\mathbb{G}_T$. The advantage of a $0/1$-valued algorithm $\mathfrak{D}$ in solving the decisional n-BDHE problem in $(\mathbb{G}, \mathbb{G}_T)$ is defined to be

$$
\begin{aligned}
\mathsf{Adv}_{\mathfrak{D}}^{n\text{-dBDHE}} = &\, |\Pr\left[\mathfrak{D}(\overrightarrow{y}_{a,\theta}, Z) = 1 | Z = e(g_{n+1}, g^\theta)\right] \\
&- \Pr\left[\mathfrak{D}(\overrightarrow{y}_{a,\theta}, Z) = 1 | Z \text{ is random}\right]|.
\end{aligned}
$$

Definition 2. *The decisional n-BDHE problem in $(\mathbb{G}, \mathbb{G}_T)$ is said to be $(\mathcal{T}, \epsilon)$-hard if the advantage $\mathsf{Adv}_{\mathfrak{D}}^{n\text{-dBDHE}} \leq \epsilon$, for any PPT distinguisher $\mathfrak{D}$ running in time at most $\mathcal{T}$.*

2.3   Dual-Policy ABE Template

The dual-policy ABE system [1] consists of the following four algorithms:

Setup$(\kappa, \mathcal{V}_s, \mathcal{V}_o)$. The Central Authority (CA) takes as input a security parameter κ, a subjective attribute universe $\mathcal{V}_s$ and an objective attribute universe $\mathcal{V}_o$, and returns public key PK and master secret key MK. The secret key MK is kept secret by CA and the public key PK is made public.

KeyGen$(\mathsf{PK}, \mathsf{MK}, L_s, \mathbb{A}_o)$. On input PK, MK, a set L_s of subjective attributes and an objective access structure $\mathbb{A}_o$, the CA outputs the secret key $\mathsf{SK}_{(L_s, \mathbb{A}_o)}$ associated with L_s and $\mathbb{A}_o$.

Encrypt$(\mathsf{PK}, M, \mathbb{A}_s, W_o)$. An encryptor executes a message M under a subjective access structure $\mathbb{A}_s$ and a set W_o of objective attributes by using PK, and returns a ciphertext $\mathsf{CT}_{(\mathbb{A}_s, W_o)}$ associated with $\mathbb{A}_s$ and W_o.

Decrypt$(\mathsf{PK}, \mathsf{SK}_{(L_s, \mathbb{A}_o)}, \mathsf{CT}_{(\mathbb{A}_s, W_o)})$. A decryptor takes as input $\mathsf{PK}, \mathsf{SK}_{(L_s, \mathbb{A}_o)}$ and $\mathsf{CT}_{(\mathbb{A}_s, W_o)}$, and outputs the message M encrypted under a subjective access structure $\mathbb{A}_s$ and a set W_o of objective attributes if $L_s \in \mathbb{A}_s$ and $W_o \in \mathbb{A}_o$; otherwise decryption will fail.

2.4   Selective-Security Model for Dual-Policy ABE

Following [1], we describe IND-CPA (ciphertext indistinguishability under chosen plaintext attacks) security model in terms of a game $\mathsf{Game}^{\mathsf{IND-CPA}}$ carried out between a challenger and an adversary. The challenger executes the relevant dual-policy ABE algorithms in order to answer the queries from the adversary. The game is as follows:

Init. The adversary announces the target subjective access structure $\mathbb{A}_s^*$ and the target objective attribute set W_o^* that he wishes to be challenged upon.

Setup. The challenger executes the **Setup** algorithm and gives public key PK to the adversary.

Query Phase 1. The adversary is allowed to make secret key queries for pairs of subjective attribute set and objective access structure $(L_s, \mathbb{A}_o)$ subject to the constraint that $L_s \notin \mathbb{A}_s^*$ or $W_o^* \notin \mathbb{A}_o$. The challenger then runs **KeyGen** algorithm and returns the corresponding secret key $\mathsf{SK}_{L_s, \mathbb{A}_o}$ to the adversary.

Challenge. The adversary submits two equal length messages M_0, M_1. The challenger flips a random coin $\mu \in \{0, 1\}$ and runs **Encrypt** algorithm in order to encrypt M_μ under the target pair $(\mathbb{A}_s^*, W_o^*)$ of subjective access structure and objective attribute set. The resulting challenge ciphertext $\mathsf{CT}^*_{(\mathbb{A}_s^*, W_o^*)}$ is given to the adversary.

Query Phase 2. Query Phase 1 is repeated.

Guess. The adversary outputs a guess bit $\mu' \in \{0, 1\}$ for the challenger's secret coin μ and wins if $\mu' = \mu$.

The advantage of an adversary $\mathcal{A}$ in the above IND-CPA game is defined to be $\mathsf{Adv}_{\mathcal{A}}^{\mathsf{IND-CPA}} = |\Pr[\mu' = \mu] - \frac{1}{2}|$, where the probability is taken over all random coin tosses of both adversary and challenger.

Definition 3. *A Dual-Policy ABE scheme is said to be selectively $(\mathcal{T}, q, \epsilon)$-IND-CPA secure if $\mathsf{Adv}_{\mathcal{A}}^{\mathsf{IND-CPA}} \leq \epsilon$, for any PPT adversary $\mathcal{A}$ running in time at most $\mathcal{T}$ that makes at most q secret key queries in the above game.*

3   Proposed Dual-Policy ABE

Let $\mathcal{V}_s$ and $\mathcal{V}_o$ be the universes of subjective and objective attributes, respectively. In our construction, both subjective and objective access structures are LSSS-realizable. We denote a LSSS subjective access structure by $(\mathbb{M}, \rho)$ and a LSSS objective access structure by $(\mathbb{N}, \phi)$. We assume that ρ is an injective function, i.e., each attribute is used only once in the row labeling of the subjective access matrix $\mathbb{M}$. However, we can remove such restriction by using a transformation from single-use to multi-use as described in [2]. We describe now our dual-policy ABE scheme as a set of the following four algorithms.

Setup$(\kappa, \mathcal{V}_s, \mathcal{V}_o)$. On receiving the implicit security parameter κ and the description of both subjective and objective attribute universes, generate a prime number p, a bilinear group $\mathbb{G}$, a generator $g \in_R \mathbb{G}$ and a bilinear map $e : \mathbb{G} \times \mathbb{G} \to \mathbb{G}_T$, where $\mathbb{G}$ and $\mathbb{G}_T$ are multiplicative groups of order p. Choose $\alpha, \beta \in_R \mathbb{Z}_p, K_0 \in_R \mathbb{G}$ and set $Y = e(g, g)^\alpha$, $T_0 = g^\beta$. For each attribute $att_x \in \mathcal{V}_s$ (resp., $att_y' \in \mathcal{V}_o$), select $T_x \in_R \mathbb{G}$ (resp., $K_y \in_R \mathbb{G}$). The public key and master secret key are $\mathsf{PK} = \langle p, g, T_0, K_0, Y, \{T_x : att_x \in \mathcal{V}_s\}, \{K_y : att_y' \in \mathcal{V}_o\}\rangle$ and $\mathsf{MK} = \langle \alpha, \beta \rangle$, respectively.

KeyGen$(\mathsf{PK}, \mathsf{MK}, L_s, \mathbb{A}_o)$. Here $L_s \subset \mathcal{V}_s$ and $\mathbb{A}_o$ is parsed as $(\mathbb{N}, \phi)$, where $\mathbb{N}$ is a share-generating matrix of size $\ell_o \times k_o$ and ϕ is a mapping from each row i of $\mathbb{N}$ to an attribute $att_{\phi(i)}'$.

- First execute $\mathsf{Distribute}(\mathbb{N}, \phi, \alpha + \beta r)$, where $r \in_R \mathbb{Z}_p$ and $\mathbf{1} = (1, 0, \ldots, 0)$ being a vector of length k_o and obtain a set $\{\lambda_{\phi(i)} = \boldsymbol{N_i} \cdot \boldsymbol{v_o} : i \in [\ell_o]\}$ of ℓ_o shares, where $\boldsymbol{v_o} \in_R \mathbb{Z}_p^{k_o}$ such that $\boldsymbol{v_o} \cdot \mathbf{1} = \alpha + \beta r$.
- For each row $i \in [\ell_o]$, choose $r_i \in_R \mathbb{Z}_p$ and compute

$$\mathsf{dO}_i = g^{\lambda_{\phi(i)}}(K_0 K_{\phi(i)})^{r_i}, \quad \mathsf{dO}_i' = g^{r_i},$$

$$\mathsf{dO}_i'' = \left\{ \mathsf{dO}_{i,y}'' : \mathsf{dO}_{i,y}'' = K_y^{r_i}, \forall\, att_y' \in V_o \setminus \{att_{\phi(i)}'\} \right\}.$$

Let $\mathsf{sk}_{(\mathbb{N},\phi)} = \langle (\mathbb{N}, \phi), \{\mathsf{dO}_i, \mathsf{dO}_i', \mathsf{dO}_i'' : i \in [\ell_o]\} \rangle$.
- Finally, calculate $\mathsf{dS} = g^r, \mathsf{dS}' = \{\mathsf{dS}_x : \mathsf{dS}_x = T_x^r, \forall\, att_x \in L_s\}$. Let $\mathsf{sk}_{L_s} = \langle L_s, \mathsf{dS}, \mathsf{dS}' \rangle$.
- Return the secret key associated with L_s and $(\mathbb{N}, \phi)$ as $\mathsf{SK}_{(L_s, \mathbb{A}_o)} = \langle \mathsf{sk}_{L_s}, \mathsf{sk}_{(\mathbb{N},\phi)} \rangle$.

Encrypt$(\mathsf{PK}, M, \mathbb{A}_s, W_o)$. $W_o \subset V_o$ and $\mathbb{A}_s$ is parsed as $(\mathbb{M}, \rho)$, $\mathbb{M}$ is a share-generating matrix of size $\ell_s \times k_s$ and ρ is a mapping from each row j of $\mathbb{M}$ to an attribute $att_{\rho(j)}$. Choose a secret $\theta \in_R \mathbb{Z}_p$. Run $\mathsf{Distribute}(\mathbb{M}, \rho, \theta)$ and obtain a set $\{\delta_{\rho(j)} = \boldsymbol{M_j} \cdot \boldsymbol{v_s} : j \in [\ell_s]\}$ of ℓ_s shares, where $\boldsymbol{v_s} \in_R \mathbb{Z}_p^{k_s}$ such that $\boldsymbol{v_s} \cdot \mathbf{1} = \theta$. The ciphertext is $\mathsf{CT}_{(\mathbb{A}_s, W_o)} = \langle (\mathbb{M}, \rho), W_o, C, C', \mathsf{ct}_{(\mathbb{M}, \rho)}, \mathsf{ct}_{W_o} \rangle$, where

$$C = M \cdot Y^\theta, \quad C' = g^\theta, \quad \mathsf{ct}_{W_o} = \left(K_0 \prod_{att_y' \in W_o} K_y \right)^\theta,$$

$$\mathsf{ct}_{(\mathbb{M}, \rho)} = \left\{ C_j : C_j = T_0^{\delta_{\rho(j)}} \cdot T_{\rho(j)}^\theta, \forall\, j \in [\ell_s] \right\}.$$

Decrypt$(\mathsf{PK}, \mathsf{SK}_{(L_s, \mathbb{A}_o)}, \mathsf{CT}_{(\mathbb{A}_s, W_o)})$. The secret key $\mathsf{SK}_{(L_s, \mathbb{A}_o)}$ and the ciphertext $\mathsf{CT}_{(\mathbb{A}_s, W_o)}$ are parsed as above. First obtain the corresponding secret reconstruction constants $\{\omega_i : i \in I_o\} = \mathsf{Reconstruct}(\mathbb{N}, \phi, W_o)$ and $\{\tau_j : j \in I_s\} = \mathsf{Reconstruct}(\mathbb{M}, \rho, L_s)$, where $I_o = \{i \in [\ell_o] : att_{\phi(i)}' \in W_o\}$ and $I_s = \{j \in [\ell_s] : att_{\rho(j)} \in L_s\}$. If L_s satisfies the subjective LSSS access structure $(\mathbb{M}, \rho)$ and W_o satisfies the objective LSSS access structure $(\mathbb{N}, \phi)$, then $\sum_{i \in I_o} \omega_i \lambda_{\phi(i)} = \alpha + \beta r$ and $\sum_{j \in I_s} \tau_j \delta_{\rho(j)} = \theta$. Note here that the shares $\{\lambda_{\phi(i)}\}_{i \in I_o}$ and $\{\delta_{\rho(j)}\}_{j \in I_s}$ are not explicitly known to the decryption process and hence so are $\alpha + \beta r$ and θ. However, these secrets $\alpha + \beta r$ and θ can correctly be recovered in the exponent if W_o satisfies $(\mathbb{N}, \phi)$ and L_s satisfies $(\mathbb{M}, \rho)$, respectively. Compute E_1, E_2, F_1 and F_2 as follows:

$$E_1 = \prod_{i \in I_o} \left(\mathsf{dO}_i \cdot \prod_{att_y' \in W_o, y \neq \phi(i)} \mathsf{dO}_{i,y}'' \right)^{\omega_i}, \quad E_2 = \prod_{i \in I_o} (\mathsf{dO}_i')^{\omega_i},$$

$$F_1 = \prod_{j \in I_s} C_j^{\tau_j}, \qquad\qquad F_2 = \prod_{j \in I_s} \mathsf{dS}_{\rho(j)}^{\tau_j}.$$

The message M is recovered by computing

$$C \cdot \frac{e(\mathsf{ct}_{W_o}, E_2) \cdot e(F_1, \mathsf{dS})}{e(C', E_1 F_2)} = M.$$

The correctness is included in Appendix A.

3.1   Proof of Security

Theorem 1. *If the objective attribute universe $\mathcal{V}_o$ has n attributes then our dual-policy ABE scheme is $(\mathcal{T}, q, \epsilon)$-IND-CPA secure in the selective IND-CPA security model (given in Section 2.4) with a challenge subjective access structure matrix of size $\ell_s^* \times k_s^*$, where $k_s^* \leq n$, assuming that the decisional n-BDHE problem in $(\mathbb{G}, \mathbb{G}_T)$ is $(\mathcal{T}', \epsilon')$-hard, where $\mathcal{T}' = \mathcal{O}(n^2 + |\mathcal{V}_s|) \cdot q \cdot \mathcal{T}_e$ and $\epsilon' = \epsilon/2$. Here, $\mathcal{T}_e$ denotes the running time of one exponentiation in $\mathbb{G}$.*

Proof. Suppose that an adversary $\mathcal{A}$ can $(\mathcal{T}, q, \epsilon)$-*break* our dual-policy ABE scheme in the selective IND-CPA security model, we will show that the decisional n-BDHE problem in $(\mathbb{G}, \mathbb{G}_T)$ is *not* $(\mathcal{T}', \epsilon')$-hard.

Suppose a distinguisher $\mathfrak{D}$ is given the decisional n-BDHE challenge $(\overrightarrow{y}_{a,\theta}, Z)$, where $\overrightarrow{y}_{a,\theta} = (g, g^\theta, g_1, \ldots, g_n, g_{n+2}, \ldots, g_{2n})$, $g_i = g^{a^i}$, and $Z = e(g_{n+1}, g^\theta)$ or Z is a random element of $\mathbb{G}_T$. Now, the distinguisher $\mathfrak{D}$ plays the role of a challenger in $\mathsf{Game}^{\mathsf{IND-CPA}}$ and interacts with $\mathcal{A}$ in order to solve the decisional n-BDHE problem (i.e., $\mathfrak{D}$ attempts to output 1 if $Z = e(g_{n+1}, g^\theta)$ and 0 otherwise) as follows. By our assumption $|\mathcal{V}_o| = n$. Let $\mathcal{V}_o = \{att_1', \ldots, att_n'\}$.

Init. The adversary $\mathcal{A}$ outputs a target subjective LSSS-realizable access structure $(\mathbb{M}^*, \rho^*)$ and a target objective attribute set W_o^*, where the size of LSSS matrix $\mathbb{M}^*$ is $\ell_s^* \times k_s^*$ with $k_s^* \leq n$. Let $\mathbb{M}^* = (M_{j,l}^*)_{j \in [\ell_s^*], l \in [k_s^*]}$.

Setup. The distinguisher $\mathfrak{D}$ selects a random value $\alpha' \in_R \mathbb{Z}_p$ and implicitly sets $\alpha = \alpha' + a^{n+1}$ by letting $Y = e(g, g)^\alpha = e(g, g)^{\alpha'} e(g^a, g^{a^n})$.

The distinguisher $\mathfrak{D}$ then programs the parameters $\{K_y : y \in [n]\}$ as follows. For $y \in [n]$, $\mathfrak{D}$ chooses a random value $\gamma_y \in_R \mathbb{Z}_p$ and computes $K_y = g^{\gamma_y} g_{n+1-y}$. Furthermore, to program K_0, the distinguisher selects a random $\gamma_0 \in_R \mathbb{Z}_p$ and computes $K_0 = g^{\gamma_0} \prod_{att_y' \in W_o^*} K_y^{-1}$. We note that the parameters $K_0, K_1, \ldots, K_n$ are distributed randomly due to the factor $g^{\gamma_0}, g^{\gamma_1}, \ldots, g^{\gamma_n}$, respectively.

The distinguisher $\mathfrak{D}$ programs the other parameters $T_0, \{T_x : att_x \in \mathcal{V}_s\}$ as follows. Set $T_0 = g_1 = g^a$. For each attribute $att_x \in \mathcal{V}_s$, $\mathfrak{D}$ randomly picks $t_x \in_R \mathbb{Z}_p$. For $att_x \in \mathcal{V}_s$, if there exists a $j \in [\ell_s^*]$ such that $\rho^*(j) = x$, then set $T_x = g^{t_x} \cdot \prod_{l \in [k_s^*]} g_l^{-M_{j,l}^*}$ (this is well defined since $k_s^* \leq n$). Otherwise, set $T_x = g^{t_x}, \forall att_x \in \mathcal{V}_s \setminus \{att_{\rho^*(j)} : j \in [\ell_s^*]\}$.

We point out that the parameters T_x are randomly distributed due to the g^{t_x} factor. By our restriction that ρ^* is an injective function, for any x there is at most one j such that $\rho^*(j) = x$, so that our assignment is unambiguous.

Query Phase 1. The adversary $\mathcal{A}$ queries for secret keys corresponding to objective access structure and subjective attribute set pairs $((\mathbb{N}, \phi), L_s)$ subject to the restriction that L_s does not satisfy $\mathbb{M}^*$ or W_o^* does not satisfy $\mathbb{N}$. The distinguisher then responds according to one of the following two cases.

Case 1: W_o^* does not satisfy $\mathbb{N}_{\ell_o \times k_o}$.

The distinguisher $\mathfrak{D}$ picks $r \in_R \mathbb{Z}_p$ and sets $\mathsf{dS} = g^r$ and $\mathsf{dS}' = \{\mathsf{dS}_x : \mathsf{dS}_x = T_x^r, \forall att_x \in L_s\}$.

Since W_o^* does not satisfy $\mathbb{N}_{\ell_o \times k_o}$, by Lemma 1, there exists a vector $\boldsymbol{w} = (-1, w_2, \ldots, w_{k_o}) \in \mathbb{Z}_p^{k_o}$ such that $\boldsymbol{N_i} \cdot \boldsymbol{w} = 0$, for all rows i where $att'_{\phi(i)} \in W_o^*$.

The distinguisher randomly selects $\sigma_2, \sigma_3, \ldots, \sigma_{k_o} \in_R \mathbb{Z}_p$ and implicitly sets $\boldsymbol{v_o} = (\alpha' + a^{n+1} + ar, -(\alpha' + a^{n+1} + ar)w_2 + \sigma_2, \ldots, -(\alpha' + a^{n+1} + ar)w_{k_o} + \sigma_{k_o}) \in \mathbb{Z}_p^{k_o}$, which will be used for generating shares of $\alpha + ar$ as in the original scheme. Note that $\boldsymbol{v_o}$ can be written as $\boldsymbol{v_o} = -(\alpha' + a^{n+1} + ar)\boldsymbol{w} + \boldsymbol{v'_o}$, where $\boldsymbol{v'_o} = (0, \sigma_2, \ldots, \sigma_{k_o})$. Observe that $\lambda_{\phi(i)} = \boldsymbol{N_i} \cdot \boldsymbol{v_o}$ contains the term a^{n+1} and hence $g^{\lambda_{\phi(i)}}$ contains terms of the form $g^{a^{n+1}} = g_{n+1}$ which is unknown to $\mathfrak{D}$. Therefore, $\mathfrak{D}$ must make sure that there are no terms of the form g_{n+1} involved in secret key components. To this end, the distinguisher implicitly creates suitable r_i values in such a way that the unknown terms will be canceled out automatically. Now, the secret key corresponding to each row $\boldsymbol{N_i}, i \in [\ell_o]$, of $\mathbb{N}$ is computed as follows:

Subcase 1(i): For i where $att'_{\phi(i)} \in W_o^*$.

In this case, the distinguisher randomly chooses $r'_i \in_R \mathbb{Z}_p$ and implicitly sets $r_i = r'_i - a^{\phi(i)}$. Since $att'_{\phi(i)} \in W_o^*$, $\boldsymbol{N_i} \cdot \boldsymbol{w} = 0$ and hence $\boldsymbol{N_i} \cdot \boldsymbol{v_o} = -(\alpha' + a^{n+1} + ar)\boldsymbol{N_i} \cdot \boldsymbol{w} + \boldsymbol{N_i} \cdot \boldsymbol{v'_o} = \boldsymbol{N_i} \cdot \boldsymbol{v'_o}$. Then the distinguisher computes

$$\mathsf{dO}_i = g^{\boldsymbol{N_i} \cdot \boldsymbol{v'_o}}(K_0 K_{\phi(i)})^{r'_i} g_{\phi(i)}^{-\gamma_o} \prod_{att'_y \in W_o^*,\ y \neq \phi(i)} \left(g_{\phi(i)}^{\gamma_y} \cdot g_{n+1-y+\phi(i)} \right),$$

$$\mathsf{dO}'_i = g^{r'_i} g_{\phi(i)}^{-1}, \quad \mathsf{dO}''_i = \left\{ \mathsf{dO}''_{i,y} : \mathsf{dO}''_{i,y} = K_y^{r'_i} g_{\phi(i)}^{-\gamma_y} g_{n+1-y+\phi(i)}^{-1}, \forall y \in [n] \setminus \{\phi(i)\} \right\}.$$

Subcase 1(ii): For i where $att'_{\phi(i)} \notin W_o^*$, i.e., $\phi(i) \neq y$, for all $att'_y \in W_o^*$.

Note that $\boldsymbol{N_i} \cdot \boldsymbol{v_o} = \boldsymbol{N_i} \cdot (\boldsymbol{v'_o} - \alpha' \boldsymbol{w}) - (\boldsymbol{N_i} \cdot \boldsymbol{w})a^{n+1} - a(r\boldsymbol{N_i} \cdot \boldsymbol{w})$. In this case the distinguisher selects a random $r'_i \in_R \mathbb{Z}_p$ and implicitly sets $r_i = r'_i + (\boldsymbol{N_i} \cdot \boldsymbol{w})a^{\phi(i)}$. Then the secret key components are computed as

$$\mathsf{dO}_i = g^{\boldsymbol{N_i} \cdot (\boldsymbol{v'_o} - \alpha' \boldsymbol{w})} g_1^{-(r\boldsymbol{N_i} \cdot \boldsymbol{w})} (K_0 K_{\phi(i)})^{r'_i} g_{\phi(i)}^{(\boldsymbol{N_i} \cdot \boldsymbol{w})\gamma_o}$$

$$\times \left(\prod_{att'_y \in W_o^*} \left(g_{\phi(i)}^{-(\boldsymbol{N_i} \cdot \boldsymbol{w})\gamma_y} \cdot g_{n+1-y+\phi(i)}^{-(\boldsymbol{N_i} \cdot \boldsymbol{w})} \right) \right) g_{\phi(i)}^{(\boldsymbol{N_i} \cdot \boldsymbol{w})\gamma_{\phi(i)}},$$

$$\mathsf{dO}'_i = g^{r'_i} g_{\phi(i)}^{\boldsymbol{N_i} \cdot \boldsymbol{w}},$$

$$\mathsf{dO}''_i = \left\{ \mathsf{dO}''_{i,y} : \mathsf{dO}''_{i,y} = K_y^{r'_i} g_{\phi(i)}^{(\boldsymbol{N_i} \cdot \boldsymbol{w})\gamma_y} g_{n+1-y+\phi(i)}^{\boldsymbol{N_i} \cdot \boldsymbol{w}}, \forall y \in [n] \setminus \{\phi(i)\} \right\}.$$

Since $1 \leq \phi(i) \leq n$ and $y \neq \phi(i)$, the secret key components $\mathsf{dO}_i, \mathsf{dO}'_i$ and dO''_i do not contain any term which implicitly contains g_{n+1} and hence the distinguisher can correctly distribute the secret key components. Therefore, the distribution of the secret key in this case is identical to that of the original scheme.

Case 2: W_o^* satisfies $\mathbb{N}_{\ell_o \times k_o}$.

In this case, L_s must not satisfy the subjective access structure matrix $\mathbb{M}^*$ of size $\ell_s^* \times k_s^*$. Then, by Lemma 1, there exists a vector $\boldsymbol{z} = (-1, z_2, \ldots, z_{k_s^*}) \in \mathbb{Z}_p^{k_s^*}$ such that $\boldsymbol{M_j^*} \cdot \boldsymbol{z} = 0$, for each row j for which $att_{\rho^*(j)} \in L_s$.

The distinguisher randomly picks $r' \in_R \mathbb{Z}_p$ and implicitly sets $r = r' + (-1)a^n + z_2 a^{n-1} + \cdots + z_{k_s^*} a^{n-k_s^*+1}$. Note that for $z_{k_s^*}$, $k_s^* \geq 2$. Now, the distinguisher calculates $\mathsf{dS} = g^{r'} \prod_{j \in [k_s^*]} g_{n-j+1}^{z_j} = g^r$. From the definition of r, we have

$$\alpha + ar = \alpha' + a^{n+1} + a(r' + (-1)a^n + z_2 a^{n-1} + \cdots + z_{k_s^*} a^{n-k_s^*+1})$$

$$= \alpha' + \boxed{a^{n+1}} + ar' + \boxed{(-1)a^{n+1}} + z_2 a^n + \cdots + z_{k_s^*} a^{n-k_s^*+2}$$

$$= \alpha' + ar' + z_2 a^n + \cdots + z_{k_s^*} a^{n-k_s^*+2}.$$

Now, $\alpha + ar$ does not contain the term a^{n+1}. It picks $\xi_2, \ldots, \xi_{k_o} \in_R \mathbb{Z}_p$ and implicitly sets $v_o = (\alpha + ar, \xi_2, \ldots, \xi_{k_o})$ similar to original scheme. It also picks $r_i \in_R \mathbb{Z}_p$, for each row $i \in [\ell_o]$ of the matrix $\mathbb{N}$. Now, the secret key components corresponding to each ith row N_i, parsed as $(N_{i,1}, N_{i,2}, \ldots, N_{i,k_o})$, of $\mathbb{N}$ are computed as follows:

$$\mathsf{dO}_i' = g^{r_i}, \ \mathsf{dO}_i'' = \{\mathsf{dO}_{i,y}'' : \mathsf{dO}_{i,y}'' = K_y^{r_i}, \forall y \in [n] \setminus \{\phi(i)\}\},$$

$$\mathsf{dO}_i = \left(g^{\alpha'} g^{r'} \prod_{l=2}^{k_s^*} g_{n-l+2}^{z_l} \right)^{N_{i,1}} \cdot \prod_{\nu=2}^{k_o} g^{\xi_\nu N_{i,\nu}} \cdot \left(K_0 K_{\phi(i)} \right)^{r_i}.$$

It can be seen that $\mathsf{dO}_i = g^{\lambda_{\phi(i)}} \left(K_0 K_{\phi(i)} \right)^{r_i}$ because of the fact that $\lambda_{\phi(i)} = N_i \cdot v_o = (\alpha' + ar' + z_2 a^n + \cdots + z_{k_s^*} a^{n-k_s^*+2}) N_{i,1} + \xi_2 N_{i,2} + \cdots + \xi_{k_o} N_{i,k_o}$.

Finally, the distinguisher computes dS_x for all $att_x \in L_s$ as follows. Any attribute $att_x \in L_s$ for which there is no j such that $\rho^*(j) = x$, set $\mathsf{dS}_x = \mathsf{dS}^{t_x} = g^{rt_x} = T_x^r$. Now, consider the case that an attribute $att_x \in L_s$ for which there is some j such that $\rho^*(j) = x$. Then $M_j^* \cdot z = 0$. In this case

$$\mathsf{dS}_x = \mathsf{dS}^{t_x} \cdot \prod_{l \in [k_s^*]} \left(g^{r'} \prod_{u \in [k_s^*], u \neq l} g_{n+1-u+l}^{z_u} \right)^{-M_{j,l}^*}, \text{ where } z_1 = -1.$$

Therefore, the distribution of the secret key in this case is identical to that of the original scheme as well.

Challenge. The adversary $\mathcal{A}$ submits two equal length messages M_0 and M_1 to the distinguisher $\mathfrak{D}$. Now, the distinguisher flips a random coin $\mu \in \{0,1\}$ and encrypts M_μ under the target subjective access structure $(\mathbb{M}^*, \rho^*)$ and the target objective attribute set W_o^*. The distinguisher first computes

$$C = M_\mu Z \cdot e(g^\theta, g^{\alpha'}), C' = g^\theta, \mathsf{ct}_{W_o^*} = (g^\theta)^{\gamma_0}.$$

It now picks $\eta_2, \ldots, \eta_{k_s^*} \in_R \mathbb{Z}_p$. Let $\eta = (0, \eta_2, \ldots, \eta_{k_s^*})$. It will then implicitly share the secret θ using the vector $v_s = (\theta, \theta a + \eta_2, \theta a^2 + \eta_3, \ldots, \theta a^{k_s^*-1} + \eta_{k_s^*})$, by setting

$$C_j = \left(\prod_{l=2}^{k_s^*} g_1^{M_{j,l}^* \cdot \eta_l} \right) \cdot (g^\theta)^{t_{\rho^*(j)}}, \text{ for each } j \in [\ell_s^*] \text{ such that } att_{\rho^*(j)} = att_x.$$

Let $\mathsf{ct}_{(\mathbb{M}^*,\rho^*)} = \{C_j : j \in [\ell_s]\}$. The challenge ciphertext

$$\mathsf{CT}_{((\mathbb{M}^*,\rho^*),W_o^*)} = \langle (\mathbb{M}^*,\rho^*), W_o^*, C, C', \mathsf{ct}_{(\mathbb{M}^*,\rho^*)}, \mathsf{ct}_{W_o^*} \rangle$$

is given to adversary.

We now show that if $Z = e(g_{n+1}, g^\theta)$, then the challenge ciphertext is a valid encryption of the message M_μ under the target subjective access structure $(\mathbb{M}^*, \rho^*)$ and the target objective attribute set W_o^*.
For,

$$C = M_\mu Z \cdot e(g^\theta, g^{\alpha'}) = M_\mu \cdot e(g_{n+1}, g^\theta) \cdot e(g^\theta, g^{\alpha'}) = M_\mu \cdot e(g,g)^{(\alpha'+a^{n+1})\theta},$$

$$\mathsf{ct}_{W_o^*} = (g^\theta)^{\gamma_0} = (g^{\gamma_0})^\theta = (K_0 \prod_{att'_y \in W_o^*} K_y)^\theta,$$

for each $j \in [\ell_s^*]$ such that $att_{\rho^*(j)} = att_x$,

$$C_j = T_0^{M_j^* \cdot v_s} \cdot T_{\rho^*(j)}^\theta = g^{aM_j^* \cdot v_s} \cdot \left(g^{t_{\rho^*(j)}} \cdot \prod_{l \in [k_s^*]} g_l^{-M_{j,l}^*} \right)^\theta$$

$$= g^{\theta \sum_{l \in [k_s^*]} a^l M_{j,l}^* + a \sum_{l=2}^{k_s^*} M_{j,l}^* \cdot n_l} \left(g^\theta \right)^{t_{\rho^*(j)}} g^{-\theta \sum_{l \in [k_s^*]} a^l M_{j,l}^*}$$

$$= g_1^{\sum_{l=2}^{k_s^*} M_{j,l}^* \cdot n_l} \left(g^\theta \right)^{t_{\rho^*(j)}} = \left(\prod_{l=2}^{k_s^*} g_1^{M_{j,l}^* \cdot n_l} \right) \cdot \left(g^\theta \right)^{t_{\rho^*(j)}}.$$

This concludes our claim.

If Z is a random element in $\mathbb{G}_T$, then the challenge ciphertext is independent of μ in the adversary's view.

Query Phase 2. $\mathfrak{D}$ proceeds exactly as it did in Query Phase 1.

Guess. The adversary $\mathcal{A}$ outputs his guess $\mu' \in \{0,1\}$ on μ. If $\mu' = \mu$, then $\mathfrak{D}$ outputs 1 in the decisional n-BDHE game to guess that $Z = e(g_{n+1}, g^\theta)$; otherwise it outputs 0 to indicate that Z is a random element in $\mathbb{G}_T$.

If $Z = e(g_{n+1}, g^\theta)$, then the adversary's view in the above game is identical to that in a real attack. In that case $|\Pr[\mu = \mu'] - 1/2| > \epsilon$. On the other hand, if Z is a random element in $\mathbb{G}_T$, then $\mathcal{A}$ cannot obtain any information about M_μ and hence $\Pr[\mu = \mu'] = 1/2$. Since the events $Z = e(g_{n+1}, g^\theta)$ and Z is random element in $\mathbb{G}_T$ are equiprobable, it is easy to see that $\mathsf{Adv}_{\mathfrak{D}}^{n\text{-dBDHE}} > \epsilon/2$. Thus, the decisional n-BDHE problem in $(\mathbb{G}, \mathbb{G}_T)$ is not $(\mathcal{T}', \epsilon')$-hard, where $\mathcal{T}' = \mathcal{O}(n^2 + |\mathcal{V}_s|) \cdot q \cdot \mathcal{T}_e$ and $\epsilon' = \epsilon/2$.   □

3.2   Large Universe Extension

With the symbols and notations used in Section 3, we sketch below the large universe realization of our dual-policy ABE construction. Similar to [7], the public parameters of subjective and objective attributes are generated dynamically by using algebraic functions $\mathcal{F}_s : \mathbb{Z}_p \to \mathbb{G}$ and $\mathcal{F}_o : \mathbb{Z}_p \to \mathbb{G}$, respectively. Let an attribute $att_x \in \mathcal{V}_s$ (resp. $att'_y \in \mathcal{V}_o$) be an element x (resp. y) of $\mathbb{Z}_p$. Define $T_x = \mathcal{F}_s(x) = \prod_{i=1}^{d_s} P_i^{x^i}$ and $K_y = \mathcal{F}_o(y) = \prod_{i=1}^{d_o} Q_i^{y^i}$, where $P_i, Q_i \in_R \mathbb{G}$ are fixed public parameters. Anyone can compute T_x and K_y using P_i, Q_i. We replace $K_0, \{T_x\}$ and $\{K_y\}$ by $\{P_i\}_{i=1}^{d_s}, \{Q_i\}_{i=1}^{d_o}$ in the public key PK. Consequently, the public key consists only of $\mathcal{O}(d_s + d_o)$ group elements (as opposed to $\mathcal{O}(|\mathcal{V}_s| + |\mathcal{V}_o|)$ group elements in the small universe setting), whereas d_s and d_o become bounds on the number of subjective and objective attributes that can associate with a secret key and ciphertext, respectively. However, one can remove these bounds, as in [7], by modeling $\mathcal{F}_s$ and $\mathcal{F}_o$ as random oracles.

Instead of including $|\mathcal{V}_o|$ group elements for each row of the objective LSSS matrix in the secret key, the key generation algorithm now includes only $|I_\mathbb{N}|$ (where $|I_\mathbb{N}| \leq \ell_o \leq |\mathcal{V}_o|$) group elements, $I_\mathbb{N}$ being the index set of distinct objective attributes in the objective LSSS matrix $\mathbb{N}$ of size $\ell_o \times k_o$. The secret key also includes one group element for each subjective attribute associated with it. Thus, the secret key contains maximum $\mathcal{O}(\ell_o^2 + |L_s|)$ group elements of the form

$$\mathsf{dO}_i = g^{\lambda_{\phi(i)}} \mathcal{F}_o(\phi(i))^{r_i}, \quad \mathsf{dO}''_i = \{\mathsf{dO}''_{i,y} : \mathsf{dO}''_{i,y} = \mathcal{F}_o(y)^{r_i}, \forall\, y \in I_\mathbb{N} \setminus \{\phi(i)\}\},$$

$$\mathsf{dO}'_i = g^{r_i}, \quad \mathsf{dS} = g^r, \quad \mathsf{dS}' = \{\mathsf{dS}_x : \mathsf{dS}_x = \mathcal{F}_s(x)^r, \forall\, att_x \in L_s\}.$$

On the other hand, the encryption algorithm replaces the single aggregate element for all the objective attributes associated with the ciphertext in small universe construction by a set of group elements one for each objective attribute. The subjective attribute ciphertext component is unchanged. Consequently, the ciphertext contains $\mathcal{O}(\ell_s + |W_o|)$ group elements, as in [1], which are of the form

$$C = M \cdot Y^\theta, \quad C' = g^\theta, \quad \mathsf{ct}_{W_o} = \{\mathsf{ct}_y : \mathsf{ct}_y = \mathcal{F}_o(y)^\theta, \forall\, att'_y \in W_o\},$$

$$\mathsf{ct}_{(\mathbb{M},\rho)} = \left\{ C_j : C_j = T_0^{\delta_{\rho(j)}} \cdot \mathcal{F}_s(\rho(j))^\theta, \forall\, j \in [\ell_s] \right\}.$$

Finally, the decryption algorithm aggregates the required objective attribute components of secret key and ciphertext, and computes $E_{\overline{W}_o}$ and $\mathsf{ct}_{\overline{W}_o}$ as follows:

$$E_{\overline{W}_o} = \prod_{i \in I_o} \left(\mathsf{dO}_i \cdot \prod_{att'_y \in \overline{W}_o, y \neq \phi(i)} \mathsf{dO}''_{i,y} \right)^{\omega_i}, \quad \mathsf{ct}_{\overline{W}_o} = \prod_{att'_y \in \overline{W}_o} \mathsf{ct}_y,$$

where E_2, F_1, F_2 are same as in the decryption algorithm of Section 3 and $\overline{W}_o = \{att'_y \in W_o : \exists\, i \in I_o \text{ such that } \phi(i) = y\}$. The message is recovered by computing $C \cdot e(\mathsf{ct}_{\overline{W}_o}, E_2) \cdot e(F_1, \mathsf{dS}) / e(C', E_{\overline{W}_o} F_2)$. The $\mathsf{ct}_{\overline{W}_o}$ component increases $|I_o|$ of modular multiplications over the decryption in Section 3. However, decryption requires $\mathcal{O}(|I_s| + |I_o|)$ exponentiations in $\mathbb{G}$ and 3 bilinear pairing evaluations, as opposed to $\mathcal{O}(|I_s| + |I_o|)$ exponentiations in $\mathbb{G}$, $|I_o|$ exponentiations in $\mathbb{G}_T$ and $|I_o| + 2$ pairing evaluations in [1], to decrypt any ciphertext in the system.

4 KP-ABE Variant for Monotone Access Structures

In this section, we present a KP-ABE system with constant-size ciphertext for monotone access structure by isolating the KP-ABE component of our dual-policy ABE system.

Let U be the attribute universe. The CA manages all the attributes and its keys, and is responsible for issuing secret keys to users according to access structure of user attributes. An encryptor encrypts a message under a set of attributes and returns the corresponding ciphertext so that only the user with access structure satisfied by the attribute set associated with the ciphertext can decrypt it. The access structure associated with secret key is any MAS which is LSSS-realizable. We describe our KP-ABE scheme for MAS as a set of the following four algorithms.

Setup(κ, U). The CA generates a tuple $(p, \mathbb{G}, g, \mathbb{G}_T, e)$ according to the implicit parameter κ. The description of these parameters is similar to previous scheme. It then chooses $\alpha \in_R \mathbb{Z}_p$, $K_0 \in_R \mathbb{G}$ and sets $Y = e(g, g)^\alpha$. For each attribute $att_y \in U$, it selects $K_y \in_R \mathbb{G}$. The public key and master secret key as $\mathsf{PK} = \langle p, g, K_0, Y, \{K_y : att_y \in U\}\rangle$ and $\mathsf{MK} = \alpha$, respectively. The master secret key MK is kept secret by CA and the public key PK is made public.

KeyGen($\mathsf{PK}, \mathsf{MK}, (\mathbb{N}, \phi)$). Each row i of the matrix $\mathbb{N}$, the share-generating matrix of size $\ell \times k$, is associated with an attribute $att_{\phi(i)}$. The CA first executes Distribute($\mathbb{N}, \phi, \alpha$) and obtains a set $\{\lambda_{\phi(i)} = \mathbf{N}_i \cdot \mathbf{v} : i \in [\ell]\}$ of ℓ shares, where $\mathbf{v} \in_R \mathbb{Z}_p^k$ such that $\mathbf{v} \cdot \mathbf{1} = \alpha$, $\mathbf{1} = (1, 0, \ldots, 0)$ being a vector of length k. For each row $i \in [\ell]$, it chooses $r_i \in_R \mathbb{Z}_p$ and computes

$$\mathsf{dO}_i = g^{\lambda_{\phi(i)}}(K_0 K_{\phi(i)})^{r_i}, \quad \mathsf{dO}'_i = g^{r_i},$$

$$\mathsf{dO}''_i = \left\{\mathsf{dO}''_{i,y} : \mathsf{dO}''_{i,y} = K_y^{r_i}, \forall\, att_y \in U \setminus \{att_{\phi(i)}\}\right\}.$$

It returns the secret key $\mathsf{SK}_{(\mathbb{N}, \phi)} = \langle(\mathbb{N}, \phi), \{\mathsf{dO}_i, \mathsf{dO}'_i, \mathsf{dO}''_i : i \in [\ell]\}\rangle$ associated with $(\mathbb{N}, \phi)$.

Encrypt(PK, M, W). To encrypt a message $M \in \mathbb{G}_T$ under a set W of attributes, the encryptor selects $\theta \in_R \mathbb{Z}_p$ and outputs the ciphertext $\mathsf{CT}_W = \langle W, C, C', \mathsf{ct}_W\rangle$, where $C = M \cdot Y^\theta$, $C' = g^\theta$ and $\mathsf{ct}_W = \left(K_0 \prod_{att_y \in W} K_y\right)^\theta$.

Decrypt($\mathsf{PK}, \mathsf{SK}_{(\mathbb{N}, \phi)}, \mathsf{CT}_W$). The decryptor first obtains a set $\{\omega_i : i \in I\} =$ Reconstruct($\mathbb{N}, \phi, W$) of secret reconstruction constants, where $I = \{i \in [\ell] : att_{\phi(i)} \in W\}$. Note that if W satisfies the LSSS matrix $\mathbb{N}$, then $\sum_{i \in I} \omega_i \lambda_{\phi(i)} = \alpha$. Finally, the decryptor computes

$$E_1 = \prod_{i \in I}\left(\mathsf{dO}_i \cdot \prod_{att_y \in W, y \neq \phi(i)} \mathsf{dO}''_{i,y}\right)^{\omega_i}, \quad E_2 = \prod_{i \in I}(\mathsf{dO}'_i)^{\omega_i}$$

and recovers the message M by computing $C \cdot e(\mathsf{ct}_W, E_2)/e(C', E_1)$.

Theorem 2 (Security Proof). *If the attribute universe U has n attributes then our KP-ABE scheme for MAS is $(\mathcal{T}, q, \epsilon)$-IND-CPA secure in the selective IND-CPA security model of KP-ABE (which can be derived by ignoring subjective attributes from the dual-policy selective-security model given in Section 2.4), assuming that the decisional n-BDHE problem in $(\mathbb{G}, \mathbb{G}_T)$ is $(\mathcal{T}', \epsilon')$-hard, where $\mathcal{T}' = \mathcal{T} + \mathcal{O}(n^2) \cdot q \cdot \mathcal{T}_e$ and $\epsilon' = \epsilon/2$. Here, $\mathcal{T}_e$ denotes the running time of one exponentiation in $\mathbb{G}$.*

The proof of Theorem 2 (given in Appendix B) can be derived from the proof of Theorem 1.

5   KP-ABE Variant for Non-Monotone Access Structure

To build a KP-ABE for Non-Monotone Access Structure (nonMAS) with constant-size ciphertext, we employ the *moving from MAS to nonMAS* technique [19] that represents non-monotone access structures in terms of monotone access structures with *negative* attributes (NOTabe is a negative attribute of the attribute abe). We discuss here the technique for completeness. For ease of reference, we call the attribute abe, a *positive* attribute and we denote its negation NOTabe by ¬abe. Let U be a positive attribute universe.

Given a family $\mathfrak{F} = \{\Pi_{\mathbb{A}} : \mathbb{A} \in \mathsf{MA}\}$ of linear secret-sharing schemes for a set of possible monotone access structures MA, and $\widetilde{U} = U \bigcup \{\neg att : att \in U\}$ is the underlying attribute universe for each monotone access structure $\mathbb{A} \in \mathsf{MA}$, a family NM of non-monotone access structures can be defined as follows. For each access structure $\mathbb{A} \in \mathsf{MA}$ over $\widetilde{U}$, one defines a possibly non-monotone access structure $N_{\mathbb{A}}$ over U in the following way.

- For every set $W \subset U$, form $N(W) = W \bigcup \{\neg att : att \in U \setminus W\} \subset \widetilde{U}$.
- Now, define $N_{\mathbb{A}}$ by saying that W is authorized in $N_{\mathbb{A}}$ if and only if $N(W)$ is authorized in $\mathbb{A}$, i.e., $W \in N_{\mathbb{A}}$ iff $N(W) \in \mathbb{A}$.

The family of non-monotone access structures is $\mathsf{NM} = \{N_{\mathbb{A}} : \Pi_{\mathbb{A}} \in \mathfrak{F}\}$. Note that the non-monotone access structure $N_{\mathbb{A}}$ will have only positive attributes in its access sets.

We combine the above methodology with our KP-ABE scheme for MAS in order to construct desired KP-ABE scheme for nonMAS. The scheme consists of the following four algorithms.

Setup(κ, U). The CA generates a tuple $(p, \mathbb{G}, g, \mathbb{G}_T, e)$ according to the implicit parameter κ. It then chooses $\alpha \in_R \mathbb{Z}_p, K_0, H_0 \in_R \mathbb{G}$ and sets $Y = e(g, g)^{\alpha}$. For each attribute $att_y \in U$, it selects $K_y, H_y \in_R \mathbb{G}$. The public key and master secret key are $\mathsf{PK} = \langle p, g, K_0, H_0, Y, \{K_y, H_y : att_y \in U\}\rangle$ and $\mathsf{MK} = \alpha$, respectively.

KeyGen$(\mathsf{PK}, \mathsf{MK}, \widetilde{\mathbb{A}})$. Given a non-monotone access structure $\widetilde{\mathbb{A}}$ such that we have $\widetilde{\mathbb{A}} = N_{\mathbb{A}}$ for some monotone access structure $\mathbb{A}$ over $\widetilde{U} = U \bigcup \{\neg att : att \in U\}$ and associated with a linear secret sharing scheme $\Pi_{\mathbb{A}} = (\mathbb{N}_{\ell \times k}, \phi)$, the CA first runs $\mathsf{Distribute}(\mathbb{N}, \phi, \alpha)$ and obtains a set $\{\lambda_{\phi(i)} = \boldsymbol{N_i} \cdot \boldsymbol{v} : i \in [\ell]\}$ of ℓ shares, where $\boldsymbol{v} \in_R \mathbb{Z}_p^k$ such that $\boldsymbol{v} \cdot \boldsymbol{1} = \alpha$. Note that each row $i \in [\ell]$ of $\mathbb{N}$ is associated with an attribute $\widetilde{att}_{\phi(i)} \in \{att_{\phi(i)}, \neg att_{\phi(i)}\}$. For each row $i \in [\ell]$, it chooses a random exponent $r_i \in_R \mathbb{Z}_p$ and computes

$$\mathsf{dO}_i = g^{\lambda_{\phi(i)}} (\widetilde{K}_0 \widetilde{K}_{\phi(i)})^{r_i}, \mathsf{dO}'_i = g^{r_i},$$

$$\mathsf{dO}''_i = \left\{ \mathsf{dO}''_{i,y} : \mathsf{dO}''_{i,y} = \widetilde{K}_y^{r_i}, \forall y \in I_U \setminus \{\phi(i)\} \right\},$$

where $\widetilde{K}_j = \begin{cases} K_j, \text{ if } \widetilde{att}_{\phi(i)} = att_{\phi(i)}, \\ H_j, \text{ if } \widetilde{att}_{\phi(i)} = \neg att_{\phi(i)}, \end{cases}$ for all $j \in \{0\} \cup I_U$ and I_U is the index set of attribute universe U. It returns the secret key $\mathsf{SK}_{\widetilde{\mathbb{A}}} = \langle \widetilde{\mathbb{A}}, \{\mathsf{dO}_i, \mathsf{dO}'_i, \mathsf{dO}''_i : i \in [\ell]\}\rangle$ associated with the non-monotone access structure $\widetilde{\mathbb{A}}$.

Encrypt(PK, M, W). To encrypt a message $M \in \mathbb{G}_T$ under a set W of attributes, the encryptor selects $\theta \in_R \mathbb{Z}_p$ and outputs the ciphertext $\mathsf{CT}_W = \langle W, C, C', \mathsf{ct}_W, \mathsf{ct}'_W \rangle$, where $C = M \cdot Y^\theta, C' = g^\theta, \mathsf{ct}_W = \left(K_0 \prod_{att_y \in W} K_y \right)^\theta$ and $\mathsf{ct}'_W = \left(H_0 \prod_{att_y \in W} H_y \right)^\theta$.

Decrypt(PK, $\mathsf{SK}_{\widetilde{\mathbb{A}}}$, CT_W). The decryptor first checks whether $W \in \widetilde{\mathbb{A}}$. If not, it outputs $\perp$. Otherwise, since $\widetilde{\mathbb{A}} = N_{\mathbb{A}}$ for some monotone access structure $\mathbb{A}$ over $\widetilde{U}$ associated with a linear secret sharing scheme $\Pi_{\mathbb{A}} = (\mathbb{N}_{\ell \times k}, \phi)$, we have $N(W) \in \mathbb{A}$. It runs $\mathsf{Reconstruct}(\mathbb{N}, \phi, N(W))$ and obtains a set $\{\omega_i : i \in I\}$ of reconstruction constants such that $\sum_{i \in I} \omega_i \lambda_{\phi(i)} = \alpha$, where $I = \{i \in [\ell] : \widetilde{att}_{\phi(i)} \in N(W)\}$. Let $I^+ = \{i \in [\ell] : \widetilde{att}_{\phi(i)} = att_{\phi(i)} \in N(W)\}$ and $I^- = \{i \in [\ell] : \widetilde{att}_{\phi(i)} = \neg att_{\phi(i)} \in N(W)\}$. Then $I = I^+ \bigcup I^-$. It now computes E_1, E_2 and E_3 as follows:

$$E_1 = \prod_{i \in I} \left(\mathsf{dO}_i \cdot \prod_{att_y \in W, y \neq \phi(i)} \mathsf{dO}''_{i,y} \right)^{\omega_i}, E_2 = \prod_{i \in I^+} (\mathsf{dO}'_i)^{\omega_i}, E_3 = \prod_{i \in I^-} (\mathsf{dO}'_i)^{\omega_i}.$$

The message is obtained by computing $C \cdot e(\mathsf{ct}_W, E_2) \cdot e(\mathsf{ct}'_W, E_3)/e(C', E_1)$.

Security Proof. The proof of the following theorem can be derived from the proof of Theorem 2 with the modification that in the simulation, the secret key generation uses K_j elements for positive attributes and H_j elements for negative attributes.

Theorem 3. *If the attribute universe U has n attributes then our KP-ABE for nonMAS is $(\mathcal{T}, q, \epsilon)$-IND-CPA secure in the selective IND-CPA security model of KP-ABE, assuming that the decisional n-BDHE problem in $(\mathbb{G}, \mathbb{G}_T)$ is $(\mathcal{T}', \epsilon')$-hard, where $\mathcal{T}' = \mathcal{T} + \mathcal{O}(n^2) \cdot q \cdot T_e$ and $\epsilon' = \epsilon/2$. Here, T_e denotes the running time of one exponentiation in $\mathbb{G}$.*

6 Conclusion

In this paper, we proposed an efficient dual-policy ABE system where the size of ciphertext is independent of objective attributes, thereby reduces ciphertext size. We also presented constant-size ciphertext KP-ABE schemes for both MAS and nonMAS. Security of all our schemes against selective adversary has been proven under the decisional n-BDHE assumption in the standard model. Our schemes outperform the existing schemes in terms of computation cost during encryption and decryption.

Acknowledgement. The authors would like to thank the anonymous reviewers of this paper for their valuable comments and suggestions.

References

1. Attrapadung, N., Imai, H.: Dual-Policy Attribute Based Encryption. In: Abdalla, M., Pointcheval, D., Fouque, P.-A., Vergnaud, D. (eds.) ACNS 2009. LNCS, vol. 5536, pp. 168–185. Springer, Heidelberg (2009)
2. Lewko, A., Okamoto, T., Sahai, A., Takashima, K., Waters, B.: Fully Secure Functional Encryption: Attribute-Based Encryption and (Hierarchical) Inner Product Encryption. Cryptology ePrint report 2010/110 (2010)
3. Shamir, A.: Identity-Based Cryptosystems and Signature Schemes. In: Blakely, G.R., Chaum, D. (eds.) CRYPTO 1984. LNCS, vol. 196, pp. 47–53. Springer, Heidelberg (1985)
4. Sahai, A., Waters, B.: Fuzzy Identity-Based Encryption. In: Cramer, R. (ed.) EUROCRYPT 2005. LNCS, vol. 3494, pp. 457–473. Springer, Heidelberg (2005)
5. Goyal, V., Pandey, O., Sahai, A., Waters, B.: Attribute Based Encryption for Fine-Grained Access Control of Encrypted Data. In: ACM Conference on Computer and Communications Security, pp. 89–98 (2006)
6. Bethencourt, J., Sahai, A., Waters, B.: Ciphertext-Policy Attribute-Based Encryption. In: IEEE Symposium on Security and Privacy, pp. 321–334 (2007)
7. Waters, B.: Ciphertext-Policy Attribute-Based Encryption: An Expressive, Efficient, and Provably Secure Realization. Cryptology ePrint report 2008/290 (2008)
8. Miyaji, A., Tran, P.V.X.: Constant-ciphertext-Size Dual Policy Attribute Based Encryption. In: Xiang, Y., Lopez, J., Kuo, C.-C.J., Zhou, W. (eds.) CSS 2012. LNCS, vol. 7672, pp. 400–413. Springer, Heidelberg (2012)
9. Attrapadung, N., Herranz, J., Laguillaumie, F., Libert, B., de Panafieu, E., Ràfols, C.: Attribute-Based Encryption Schemes with Constant-Size Ciphertexts. Theor. Comput. Sci. 422, 15–38 (2012)
10. Chang-Ji, W., Jian-Fa, L.: A Key-policy Attribute-based Encryption Scheme with Constant Size Ciphertext. In: CIS 2012, pp. 447–451. IEEE (2012)
11. Herranz, J., Laguillaumie, F., Ràfols, C.: Constant Size Ciphertexts in Threshold Attribute-Based Encryption. In: Nguyen, P.Q., Pointcheval, D. (eds.) PKC 2010. LNCS, vol. 6056, pp. 19–34. Springer, Heidelberg (2010)
12. Ibraimi, L., Tang, Q., Hartel, P., Jonker, W.: Efficient and Provable Secure Ciphertext-Policy Attribute-Based Encryption Schemes. In: Bao, F., Li, H., Wang, G. (eds.) ISPEC 2009. LNCS, vol. 5451, pp. 1–12. Springer, Heidelberg (2009)

13. Rouselakis, Y., Waters, B.: New Constructions and Proof Methods for Large Universe Attribute-Based Encryption. Cryptology ePrint report 2012/583 (2012)
14. Emura, K., Miyaji, A., Nomura, A., Omote, K., Soshi, M.: A Ciphertext-Policy Attribute-Based Encryption Scheme with Constant Ciphertext Length. IJACT 2(1), 46–59 (2010)
15. Chen, C., Zhang, Z., Feng, D.: Efficient ciphertext policy attribute-based encryption with constant-size ciphertext and constant computation-cost. In: Boyen, X., Chen, X. (eds.) ProvSec 2011. LNCS, vol. 6980, pp. 84–101. Springer, Heidelberg (2011)
16. Ge, A., Zhang, R., Chen, C., Ma, C., Zhang, Z.: Threshold ciphertext policy attribute-based encryption with constant size ciphertexts. In: Susilo, W., Mu, Y., Seberry, J. (eds.) ACISP 2012. LNCS, vol. 7372, pp. 336–349. Springer, Heidelberg (2012)
17. Lewko, A., Sahai, A., Waters, B.: Revocation Systems with Very Small Private Keys. In: IEEE Symposium on Security and Privacy, pp. 273–285 (2010)
18. Okamoto, T., Takashima, K.: Fully Secure Functional Encryption with General Relations from the Decisional Linear Assumption. Cryptology ePrint report 2010/563 (2010)
19. Ostrovksy, R., Sahai, A., Waters, B.: Attribute Based Encryption with Non-Monotonic Access Structures. In: ACM Conference on Computer and Communications Security, pp. 195–203 (2007)

A   Correctness of Decryption in Dual-Policy ABE

$$E_1 = \prod_{i \in I_o} \left(g^{\lambda_{\phi(i)}} (K_0 K_{\phi(i)})^{r_i} \cdot \prod_{att'_y \in W_o, y \neq \phi(i)} K_y^{r_i} \right)^{\omega_i}$$

$$= g^{\sum_{i \in I_o} \omega_i \lambda_{\phi(i)}} \prod_{i \in I_o} \left(K_0^{r_i} \prod_{att'_y \in W_o} K_y^{r_i} \right)^{\omega_i} = g^{\alpha + \beta r} \left(K_0 \prod_{att'_y \in W_o} K_y \right)^{\sum_{i \in I_o} r_i \omega_i}$$

$$E_2 = \prod_{i \in I_o} (dO'_i)^{\omega_i} = \prod_{i \in I_o} g^{r_i \omega_i} = g^{\sum_{i \in I_o} r_i \omega_i}$$

$$F_1 = \prod_{j \in I_s} C_j^{\tau_j} = \prod_{j \in I_s} \left(T_0^{\tau_j \delta_{\rho(j)}} T_{\rho(j)}^{\theta \tau_j} \right) = g^{\beta \sum_{j \in I_s} \tau_j \delta_{\rho(j)}} \prod_{j \in I_s} T_{\rho(j)}^{\theta \tau_j} = g^{\beta \theta} \prod_{j \in I_s} T_{\rho(j)}^{\theta \tau_j}$$

$$F_2 = \prod_{j \in I_s} dS_{\rho(j)}^{\tau_j} = \prod_{j \in I_s} T_{\rho(j)}^{r \tau_j}.$$

The message can then be obtained by computing

$$\frac{e(\mathsf{ct}_{W_o}, E_2) \cdot e(F_1, \mathsf{dS})}{e(C', E_1 F_2)} = \frac{e((K_0 \prod_{att'_y \in W_o} K_y)^{\theta}, g^{\sum_{i \in I_o} r_i \omega_i}) e(g^{\beta \theta} \prod_{j \in I_s} T_{\rho(j)}^{\theta \tau_j}, g^r)}{e(g^{\theta}, g^{\alpha + \beta r}) \left(K_0 \prod_{att'_y \in W_o} K_y \right)^{\sum_{i \in I_o} r_i \omega_i} \prod_{j \in I_s} T_{\rho(j)}^{r \tau_j})}$$

$$= \frac{e(g^{\beta \theta}, g^r)}{e(g^{\theta}, g^{\alpha + \beta r})} = \frac{1}{e(g^{\theta}, g^{\alpha})} = \frac{1}{Y^{\theta}}.$$

Now, $C \cdot \frac{1}{Y^{\theta}} = M \cdot Y^{\theta} \cdot \frac{1}{Y^{\theta}} = M$.

B   Security Proof of KP-ABE for MAS

Suppose that an adversary $\mathcal{A}$ can $(\mathcal{T}, q, \epsilon)$-*break* our KP-ABE scheme for MAS in the selective IND-CPA security model, which is derived by ignoring subjective attributes from the dual-policy selective-security model given in Section 2.4 and is same as the one in [5]. We will show that the decisional n-BDHE problem in $(\mathbb{G}, \mathbb{G}_T)$ is *not* $(\mathcal{T}', \epsilon')$-hard.

Suppose a distinguisher $\mathfrak{D}$ is given the decisional n-BDHE challenge $(\overrightarrow{y}_{a,\theta}, Z)$, where $\overrightarrow{y}_{a,\theta} = (g, g^{\theta}, g_1, \ldots, g_n, g_{n+2}, \ldots, g_{2n})$, $g_i = g^{a^i}$, and $Z = e(g_{n+1}, g^{\theta})$ or Z is a random element of $\mathbb{G}_T$. Now, the distinguisher $\mathfrak{D}$ plays the role of a challenger in $\mathsf{Game}^{\mathsf{IND-CPA}}$ and interacts with $\mathcal{A}$ in order to solve the decisional n-BDHE problem (i.e., $\mathfrak{D}$ attempts to output 1 if $Z = e(g_{n+1}, g^{\theta})$ and 0 otherwise) as follows. By our assumption $|U| = n$. Let $U = \{att_1, \ldots, att_n\}$.

Init. The adversary $\mathcal{A}$ outputs the target attribute set W^*.

Setup. The distinguisher $\mathfrak{D}$ selects a random value $\alpha' \in_R \mathbb{Z}_p$ and implicitly sets $\alpha = \alpha' + a^{n+1}$ by letting $Y = e(g, g)^{\alpha} = e(g, g)^{\alpha'} e(g^a, g^{a^n})$.

The distinguisher $\mathfrak{D}$ then programs the parameters $\{K_y : y \in [n]\}$ as follows. For $y \in [n]$, $\mathfrak{D}$ chooses a random value $\gamma_y \in_R \mathbb{Z}_p$ and computes $K_y = g^{\gamma_y} g_{n+1-y}$. Furthermore, to program K_0, the distinguisher selects at random $\gamma_0 \in_R \mathbb{Z}_p$ and computes $K_0 = g^{\gamma_0} \prod_{att_y \in W^*} K_y^{-1}$. We note that the parameters $K_0, K_1, \ldots, K_n$ are distributed randomly due to the factor $g^{\gamma_0}, g^{\gamma_1}, \ldots, g^{\gamma_n}$, respectively. The public key $\mathsf{PK} = \langle p, g, K_0, Y, K_1, K_2, \ldots, K_n \rangle$ will be given to the adversary $\mathcal{A}$.

Query Phase 1. In this phase, the adversary $\mathcal{A}$ requests for secret keys corresponding to the LSSS access structures $(\mathbb{N}, \phi)$ subject to the condition that W^* does not satisfy $\mathbb{N}$ and then the distinguisher responds as follows.

Let the size of a share-generating matrix $\mathbb{N}$ be $\ell \times k$. Since W^* does not satisfy $\mathbb{N}$, by Lemma 1, there exists a vector $\boldsymbol{w} = (-1, w_2, \ldots, w_k) \in \mathbb{Z}_p^k$ such that $\boldsymbol{N_i} \cdot \boldsymbol{w} = 0$, for all rows i where $att_{\phi(i)} \in W^*$.

The distinguisher randomly selects $\sigma_2, \sigma_3, \ldots, \sigma_k \in_R \mathbb{Z}_p$ and implicitly sets

$$\boldsymbol{v} = (\alpha' + a^{n+1}, -(\alpha' + a^{n+1})w_2 + \sigma_2, \ldots, -(\alpha' + a^{n+1})w_k + \sigma_k) \in \mathbb{Z}_p^k,$$

which will be used for generating shares of α as in the original scheme. Note that $\boldsymbol{v}$ can be written as $\boldsymbol{v} = -(\alpha' + a^{n+1})\boldsymbol{w} + \boldsymbol{v}'$, where $\boldsymbol{v}' = (0, \sigma_2, \ldots, \sigma_k)$. Observe that $\lambda_{\phi(i)} = \boldsymbol{N_i} \cdot \boldsymbol{v}$ contains the term a^{n+1} and hence $g^{\lambda_{\phi(i)}}$ contains terms of the form $g^{a^{n+1}} = g_{n+1}$ which is unknown to $\mathfrak{D}$. Therefore, $\mathfrak{D}$ must make sure that there are no terms of the form g_{n+1} involved in secret key components. To this end, the distinguisher implicitly creates suitable r_i values in such a way that the unknown terms will be canceled out automatically. Now, the secret key corresponding to each row $\boldsymbol{N_i}, i \in [\ell]$, of $\mathbb{N}$ is computed as follows:

Case 1: For i where $att_{\phi(i)} \in W^*$.

In this case, the distinguisher randomly chooses $r_i' \in_R \mathbb{Z}_p$ and implicitly sets $r_i = r_i' - a^{\phi(i)}$. Since $att_{\phi(i)} \in W^*$, $\boldsymbol{N_i} \cdot \boldsymbol{w} = 0$ and hence $\boldsymbol{N_i} \cdot \boldsymbol{v} = -(\alpha' + a^{n+1})\boldsymbol{N_i} \cdot \boldsymbol{w} + \boldsymbol{N_i} \cdot \boldsymbol{v}' = \boldsymbol{N_i} \cdot \boldsymbol{v}'$. Then the distinguisher computes

$$\mathsf{dO}_i = g^{N_i \cdot v'}(K_0 K_{\phi(i)})^{r'_i} g^{-\gamma_0}_{\phi(i)} \prod_{att_y \in W^*,\ y \neq \phi(i)} \left(g^{\gamma_y}_{\phi(i)} \cdot g_{n+1-y+\phi(i)}\right),$$

$$\mathsf{dO}'_i = g^{r'_i} g^{-1}_{\phi(i)}, \ \mathsf{dO}''_i = \left\{\mathsf{dO}''_{i,y} : \mathsf{dO}''_{i,y} = K_y^{r'_i} g^{-\gamma_y}_{\phi(i)} g^{-1}_{n+1-y+\phi(i)}, \forall y \in [n] \setminus \{\phi(i)\}\right\}.$$

Case 2: For i where $att_{\phi(i)} \notin W^*$, i.e., $\phi(i) \neq y$, for all $att_y \in W^*$.

Note that $N_i \cdot v = N_i \cdot (v' - \alpha' w) - (N_i \cdot w)a^{n+1}$. In this case the distinguisher selects a random $r'_i \in_R \mathbb{Z}_p$ and implicitly sets $r_i = r'_i + (N_i \cdot w)a^{\phi(i)}$. Then the secret key components are computed as

$$\mathsf{dO}_i = g^{N_i \cdot (v' - \alpha' w)}(K_0 K_{\phi(i)})^{r'_i} g^{(N_i \cdot w)\gamma_0}_{\phi(i)}$$

$$\times \left(\prod_{att_y \in W^*} \left(g^{-(N_i \cdot w)\gamma_y}_{\phi(i)} \cdot g^{-(N_i \cdot w)}_{n+1-y+\phi(i)}\right)\right)^{(N_i \cdot w)\gamma_{\phi(i)}} g^{(N_i \cdot w)\gamma_{\phi(i)}}_{\phi(i)},$$

$$\mathsf{dO}'_i = g^{r'_i} g^{N_i \cdot w}_{\phi(i)}, \mathsf{dO}''_i = \left\{\mathsf{dO}''_{i,y} = K_y^{r'_i} g^{(N_i \cdot w)\gamma_y}_{\phi(i)} g^{N_i \cdot w}_{n+1-y+\phi(i)}, \forall y \in [n] \setminus \{\phi(i)\}\right\}.$$

Since $1 \leq \phi(i) \leq n$ and $y \neq \phi(i)$, the secret key components $\mathsf{dO}_i, \mathsf{dO}'_i$ and dO''_i do not contain any term which implicitly contains g_{n+1} and hence the distinguisher can correctly distribute the secret key components. Therefore, the distribution of the secret key in this case is identical to that of the original scheme. Finally, the distinguisher sends the secret key $\mathsf{SK}_{(N,\phi)} = \langle(N, \phi), \{\mathsf{dO}_i, \mathsf{dO}'_i, \mathsf{dO}''_i : i \in [\ell]\}\rangle$ associated with (N, ϕ).

Challenge. The adversary $\mathcal{A}$ submits two equal length messages M_0 and M_1 to the distinguisher $\mathfrak{D}$. Now, the distinguisher flips a random coin $\mu \in \{0,1\}$ and encrypts M_μ under the challenge attribute set W^*. The components of challenge ciphertext CT_{W^*} are computed as follows:

$$C = M_\mu Z \cdot e(g^\theta, g^{\alpha'}), C' = g^\theta, \mathsf{ct}_{W^*} = (g^\theta)^{\gamma_0}.$$

The challenge ciphertext $\mathsf{CT}_{W^*} = \langle W^*, C, C', \mathsf{ct}_{W^*}\rangle$ is returned to $\mathcal{A}$.

If $Z = e(g_{n+1}, g^\theta)$, then the challenge ciphertext CT_{W^*} is a valid encryption of the message M_μ under the attribute set W^* as

$$C = M_\mu Z \cdot e(g^\theta, g^{\alpha'}) = M_\mu \cdot e(g_{n+1}, g^\theta) \cdot e(g^\theta, g^{\alpha'}) = M_\mu \cdot e(g, g)^{(\alpha' + a^{n+1})\theta},$$

$$\mathsf{ct}_{W^*} = (g^\theta)^{\gamma_0} = (g^{\gamma_0})^\theta = (K_0 \prod_{att_y \in W^*} K_y)^\theta.$$

On the contrary, if Z is a random element in $\mathbb{G}_T$, then the challenge ciphertext CT_{W^*} is independent of μ in the adversary's view.

Query Phase 2. $\mathfrak{D}$ proceeds exactly as it did in Query Phase 1.

Guess. The adversary $\mathcal{A}$ outputs his guess $\mu' \in \{0,1\}$ on μ. If $\mu' = \mu$, then $\mathfrak{D}$ outputs 1 in the decisional n-BDHE game to guess that $Z = e(g_{n+1}, g^\theta)$; otherwise it outputs 0 to indicate that Z is a random element in $\mathbb{G}_T$.

If $Z = e(g_{n+1}, g^\theta)$, then the adversary's view in the above game is identical to that in a real attack. In that case $|\Pr[\mu = \mu'] - 1/2| > \epsilon$. On the other hand, if Z is a random element in $\mathbb{G}_T$, then $\mathcal{A}$ cannot obtain any information about M_μ and hence $\Pr[\mu = \mu'] = 1/2$. Since the events $Z = e(g_{n+1}, g^\theta)$ and Z is random element in $\mathbb{G}_T$ are equiprobable, it is easy to see that $\mathsf{Adv}_{\mathfrak{D}}^{n\text{-dBDHE}} > \epsilon/2$. Thus, the decisional n-BDHE problem in $(\mathbb{G}, \mathbb{G}_T)$ is not $(\mathcal{T}', \epsilon')$-hard, where $\mathcal{T}' = \mathcal{O}(n^2) \cdot q \cdot \mathcal{T}_e$ and $\epsilon' = \epsilon/2$. $\qquad\square$

Factoring-Based Proxy Re-Encryption Schemes

Toshiyuki Isshiki[1], Manh Ha Nguyen[2,*], and Keisuke Tanaka[2,*]

[1] NEC Corporation, Japan
t-issiki@bx.jp.nec.com
[2] Tokyo Institute of Technology, Japan
{nguyen9,keisuke}@is.titech.ac.jp

Abstract. Proxy re-encryption (PRE) realizes delegation of decryption rights, enabling a proxy holding a re-encryption key to convert a ciphertext originally intended for Alice into an encryption of the same message for Bob, and cannot learn anything about the encrypted plaintext. To the best of our knowledge, all of the existing PRE schemes are based on the Diffie-Hellman assumption and its variants. In this paper, we present the first factoring-based PRE schemes. In particular, we first propose a bidirectional multi-hop PRE scheme which is secure against chosen-plaintext attack in the standard model (i.e., without the random oracle idealization). We then propose a bidirectional single-hop PRE scheme which is secure against chosen-ciphertext attack (CCA) in the random oracle model. Finally, we extend the bidirectional single-hop PRE scheme to obtain a CCA-secure unidirectional single-hop PRE scheme.

Keywords: proxy re-encryption, factoring, chosen-ciphertext attack.

1 Introduction

1.1 Background

Proxy re-encryption (PRE) introduced by Blaze, Bleumer, and Strauss [4] in EURO-CRYPT'98, allows a semi-trust proxy to translate a ciphertext intended for Alice into another ciphertext intended for Bob. The proxy, however, cannot learn anything about the underlying messages. According to the direction of transformation, PRE can be categorized to *bidirectional* PRE, in which the proxy can transform from Alice to Bob and vice versa, and *unidirectional* PRE, in which the proxy cannot transform ciphertexts in the opposite direction. PRE can also be categorized to *multi-hop* PRE, in which the ciphertexts can be transformed from Alice to Bob and then to Charlie and so on, and *single-hop* PRE, in which the ciphertexts can only be transformed once.

In [4], Blaze et al. proposed the first bidirectional PRE scheme. Ateniese, Fu, Green, and Hohenberger [1,2] presented unidirectional PRE schemes from bilinear maps in 2005. All of these schemes are only secure against chosen-plaintext attack (CPA). Canetti and Hohenberger [7] presented the first bidirectional multi-hop PRE scheme that is secure against replayable chosen-ciphertext attack (RCCA) in the standard model. Libert and Vergnaud [15] proposed a unidirectional single-hop PRE scheme, which is

---

* Supported by Ministry of Education, Culture, Sports, Science and Technology.

W. Susilo and R. Reyhanitabar (Eds.): ProvSec 2013, LNCS 8209, pp. 309–329, 2013.

also RCCA-secure in the standard model. Recently, Isshiki, Nguyen, and Tanaka [14] presented a CCA-secure unidirectional single-hop PRE scheme. The above schemes all rely on bilinear maps. In 2012, Hanaoka, Kawai, Kunihiro, Matsuda, Weng, Zhang, and Zhao [11] proposed the first generic construction of CCA-secure unidirectional single-hop PRE. However, since they only gave a concrete example which also uses bilinear maps, it is unknown whether there is an instantiation without bilinear maps.

All of the above PRE schemes inherently rely on decisional assumptions, e.g., the decisional Diffie-Hellman (DDH) or the DBDH assumption. In general, decisional assumptions are a much stronger class of assumptions than computational assumptions based on search problems, such as factoring, finding shortest vectors in lattices, or even the CDH problem. Indeed, there are groups, such as certain elliptic curve groups with bilinear pairing map, where the DDH assumption does not hold, but the CDH problem appears to be hard. As such, schemes based on search problems are generally preferred to those based on decisional assumptions. However, such schemes seem to be very hard to obtain.

In 2010, Deng, Weng, Liu, and Chen [9] proposed the first PRE scheme based on a computational assumption, namely the CDH assumption (in the random oracle model). Since then, there are several works show how to base CCA-secure PRE on the same assumption [8,6]. However, there are not any PRE scheme constructed based on the hardness of the factoring problem, or finding shortest vectors in lattices.

1.2 Our Contributions

In this paper, we propose the first PRE schemes based on the hardness of the factoring problem. We make the following contributions:

1. We present a CPA-secure bidirectional and multi-hop PRE scheme, under the factoring assumption, in the standard model (i.e., without the random oracle idealization). Our scheme based on the public key encryption (PKE) scheme proposed by Wee [19] which is indistinguishable against chosen-plaintext attack (IND-CPA). (See Section 5.1).

2. We present a bidirectional and single-hop PRE scheme which is secure against the chosen-ciphertext attack, under the factoring assumption in the random oracle model. In order to construct the scheme, we modify the IND-CPA-secure PKE [19] such that it achieves the IND-CCA security by using Fujisaki-Okamoto transformation. We also propose a new factoring-based strongly unforgeable signature scheme which is a variant of the Schnorr scheme [17]. By combining these two primitives, we obtain a CCA-secure PRE scheme. Our scheme achieves the CCA security on both second-level and first-level (i.e., the original and transformed, respectively) ciphertext in the random oracle model. (See Section 5.2).

3. We present a CCA-secure unidirectional and single-hop PRE scheme by using "token-controlled encryption" technique to extend the above bidirectional and single-hop PRE scheme. Hence, the security of this scheme is also proven in the random oracle model, assuming the hardness of factoring. This scheme also achieves the CCA security on both second-level and first-level ciphertext. (See Section 5.3).

See Table 1 for details of the comparison on our results with related previous works. ROM stands for the random oracle model. "1st-CCA" means that the CCA security of the first-level ciphertext. "↔" and "→" mean "bidirectional" and "unidirectional", respectively.

Table 1. Comparison of our results with previous works

Authors	Assumption	Security of 2nd-level CT	1st-CCA	Bilinear Map	ROM	Direction	Hop
BBS98 [4]	DDH	CPA	no	no	no	↔	multi
AFGH05 [1]	eDBDH	CPA	no	yes	no	→	single
CH07 [7]	DBDH	RCCA	no	yes	no	↔	multi
LV08 [15]	3-wDBDHI	RCCA	no	yes	no	→	single
DWLC08 [9]	CDH	CCA	no	no	yes	↔	single
CWYD10 [8]	CDH	CCA	no	no	yes	→	single
CDL11 [6]	CDH	CCA	yes	no	yes	→	single
HMY+11 [12]	3-wDBDHI	RCCA	no	yes	no	→	single
HKK+12 [11]	DBDH	CCA	no	yes	no	→	single
INT13 [14]	6-AmDBDH & 2-AmCDH	CCA	yes	yes	no	→	single
Ours-1	**Factoring**	**CPA**	**no**	**no**	**no**	↔	**multi**
Ours-2	**Factoring**	**CCA**	**yes**	**no**	**yes**	↔	**single**
Ours-3	**Factoring**	**CCA**	**yes**	**no**	**yes**	→	**single**

1.3 Roadmap

The paper is organized as follows: we give the preliminaries to describe our scheme in Section 2. In Section 3, we introduce a new factoring-based strongly unforgeable signature scheme which will be used to construct our schemes. We recall the concept of bidirectional proxy re-encryption and its security models in Section 4. In Section 5, we propose the factoring-based PRE schemes. Finally, we conclude this paper in Section 6.

2 Preliminaries

2.1 Notation

We denote by $\mathbb{N}$ the set of all integers, and for an integer $k \in \mathbb{N}$ we denote by $[k]$ the set $\{1, \ldots, k\}$. If $\mathbf{S}$ is a set then $s \leftarrow_R \mathbf{S}$ denotes the operation of picking an element s of $\mathbf{S}$ uniformly at random. For a probabilistic algorithm A, we denote $y = A(x; R)$ the process of running A on input x and with randomness R, and assigning y the result. We write $y = A(x; \cdot)$ if the randomness R is unknown. We write $y \leftarrow A(x)$ for $y = A(x; R)$ with uniformly chosen R from the randomness space of A. We use $negl(n)$ to denote a negligible function in n, i.e., it always holds that $negl(n) < 1/n^c$ for any $0 < c \in \mathbb{Z}$ for sufficiently large n.

2.2 Factoring

Let $N = PQ$ be a Blum integer for safe primes P, Q, i.e., $P, Q \equiv 3 \pmod 4$ where $p = (P-1)/2$ and $q = (Q-1)/2$ are both primes. Let $\mathbb{J}_N$ denote the subgroup of $\mathbb{Z}_N^*$ with Jacobi symbol $+1$, and let $\mathbb{QR}_N$ denote the subgroup of quadratic residues (i.e. $\mathbb{QR}_N := \{x \in \mathbb{Z}_N^* : \exists y \in \mathbb{Z}_N^* \text{ with } y^2 = x \bmod N\}$). Following [13], we work over the cyclic group of signed quadratic residues, given by the quotient group $\mathbb{QR}_N^+ := \mathbb{QR}_N/ \pm 1$. $\mathbb{QR}_N^+$ is a cyclic group of order pq and is efficiently recognizable (by verifying that the Jacobi symbol is $+1$). In addition, the map $x \mapsto x^2$ is a permutation over $\mathbb{QR}_N^+$. Furthermore, assuming that factoring Blum integers are hard on average and that safe primes are dense, the family of permutations $\mathsf{SQ} : x \mapsto x^2$ (indexed by N) acting on the groups $\mathbb{QR}_N^+$ is one-way.

Factoring Assumption. We assume a probabilistic polynomial time (PPT) algorithm **BlumGen** that, on input a security parameter 1^k, generates two random safe λ-bit primes $P = 2p + 1$ and $Q = 2q + 1$, then outputs a Blum integer $N = PQ$.

Definition 1 (Factoring Assumption [13]). *For an algorithm $\mathcal{A}$, we define its* factoring advantage *as*

$$\mathrm{Adv}^{\mathrm{Fac}}_{\mathbf{BlumGen}, \mathcal{A}}(k) := \Pr\left[N = PQ : N \leftarrow \mathbf{BlumGen}(1^k), \mathcal{A}(N) = (P, Q)\right].$$

We say that the (t, ϵ)-Factoring assumption for **BlumGen** *holds if no t-time algorithm $\mathcal{A}$ has factoring advantage at least ϵ.*

Iterated Squaring. Following [19], in our constructions, we make use of (N, g) as a part of the public parameter, where N is a random 2λ-bit Blum integer and g is chosen uniformly from $\mathbb{QR}_N^+$. We will henceforth assume g is a generator for $\mathbb{QR}_N^+$, which happens with probability $1 - O(1/\sqrt{N})$. Assuming that factoring Blum integers are hard on average and that safe primes are dense, the family of permutations $\mathsf{ISQ} : x \mapsto x^{2^\lambda}$ (indexed by N) acting on the groups $\mathbb{QR}_N^+$ is one-way. Using the Blum-Blum-Shub (BBS) pseudorandom generator [5], we may extract λ hard-core bits from $x \in \mathbb{QR}_N^+$ that are pseudorandom even given x^{2^λ}, that is:

$$BBS_N(x) := \left(\mathsf{lsb}_N(x), \mathsf{lsb}_N(x^2), \ldots, \mathsf{lsb}_N(x^{2^{\lambda-1}})\right).$$

The pseudorandomness of BBS is defined as follows.

Definition 2 (Pseudorandomness of BBS Generator [13]). *For an algorithm $\mathcal{A}$, define*

$$\mathrm{Adv}^{\mathrm{BBS}}_{\mathcal{A}}(\lambda) = \left|\Pr[\mathcal{A}(N, z, BBS_N(u)) = 1] - \Pr\left[\mathcal{A}(N, z, U_{\{0,1\}^\lambda}) = 1\right]\right|,$$

where $N \leftarrow \mathbf{BlumGen}(1^\lambda), u \leftarrow_R \mathbb{QR}_N, z = u^{2^\lambda}$, and $U_{\{0,1\}^\lambda} \in \{0,1\}^\lambda$ is independently and uniformly chosen. We say that $\mathcal{A}$ (t, ϵ)-breaks BBS if $\mathcal{A}$'s running time is at most $t = t(\lambda)$ and $\mathrm{Adv}^{\mathrm{BBS}}_{\mathcal{A}}(\lambda) \geq \epsilon = \epsilon(\lambda)$.

The following theorem says that any BBS-distinguisher can be used to factor Blum integers. See [13] for the detail proof.

Theorem 1 (*BBS*-**distinguisher** $\Rightarrow$ **Factoring Algorithm [5,13]**). *For every algorithm $\mathcal{A}$ that $(t_{BBS}, \epsilon_{BBS})$-breaks BBS, there is an algorithm $\mathcal{B}$ the $(t_{fac}, \epsilon_{fac})$-factors Blum integers, where $t_{fac} \approx k^4 t_{BBS}/\epsilon_{BBS}^2$ and $\epsilon_{fac} = \epsilon_{BBC}/\lambda$.*

Therefore, since the factoring assumption implies the one-wayness of ISQ, we have the following trivial theorem.

Theorem 2 ([13]). *ISQ is a one way function $\Longleftrightarrow$ the factoring problem is hard.*

3 Strongly Unforgeable Signature Scheme from Factoring

In this section, we first review the models of strongly unforgeable signature scheme which is an important primitive in the construction of our PRE schemes. We then present a new factoring-based strongly unforgeable signature scheme.

3.1 Models

The following definitions describe the functionality of a signature scheme, and the security notion of strong unforgeability that is used in this paper.

Definition 3 (Signature Scheme). *A signature scheme is a triplet* (**SigGen, Sig, Vrf**) *of probabilistic polynomial-time algorithms such that:*

1. *The key generation algorithm* **SigGen** *receives as input a security parameter 1^n and outputs a verification key vk and a signing key sk.*
2. *The signing algorithm* **Sig** *receives as input a signing key sk and a message m (in some implicit message space), and outputs a signature σ.*
3. *The verification algorithm* **Vrf** *receives as input a verification key vk, a message m, and a signature σ, and outputs a bit $b \in \{0, 1\}$.*
4. *For any message m it holds that* **Vrf**$(vk, m, \textbf{Sig}(sk, m)) = 1$ *with overwhelming probability over the internal coin tosses of* **SigGen**, **Sig**, *and* **Vrf**.

Definition 4 (Strong Unforgeability). *A signature scheme* (**SigGen, Sig, Vrf**) *is said to be strongly unforgeable if the success probability of any probabilistic polynomial-time adversary $\mathcal{A}$ in the following interaction is negligible in the security parameter:*

1. **SigGen**(1^n) *outputs (vk, sk), and $\mathcal{A}$ is given vk.*
2. *$\mathcal{A}$ can make signing queries by outputting messages m_i and is then given in return $\sigma_i = \textbf{Sig}(sk, m_i)$. If $\mathcal{A}$ chooses not to output any message, we set $(m, \sigma) = (\perp, \perp)$.*
3. *$\mathcal{A}$ outputs a pair (m^*, σ^*).*

We say that $\mathcal{A}$ succeeds if **Vrf**$(vk, m^*, \sigma^*) = 1$ *and $(m^*, \sigma^*) \neq (m_i, \sigma_i)$ for any i.*

3.2   The Scheme

The proposed signature scheme is a variant of the Schnorr signature [17]. Its strong unforgeability is based on the hardness of the factoring problem. We call the scheme factoring-based Schnorr signature (FB-Schnorr, for short) scheme.

Let param $= (1^\lambda, N, \mathbb{QR}_N^+, g, H)$ be the public parameter, where $N \leftarrow$ **BlumGen**(1^λ), $g \leftarrow_R \mathbb{QR}_N^+$, and $H : \{0,1\}^* \to \mathbb{Z}_{2^\lambda}^*$ is a hash function.

The FB-Schnorr scheme is as follows:

SigGen(param): Choose $x \leftarrow_R [(N-1)/4]$. Set $sk := g^x$, $vk := g^{2^\lambda x}$.
   Output (vk, sk).
Sign(sk, m): Choose $r \leftarrow_R [(N-1)/4]$. Compute $c = g^{2^\lambda r}, t = H(m, c)$, and $s = g^r \cdot sk^t$. Output $\sigma = (c, s)$.
Vrf(vk, σ, m): Parse $\sigma = (c, s)$. Compute $t = H(m, c)$.
   If $s^{2^\lambda} = c \cdot vk^t$ holds, then return 1, else return 0.

Correctness of the scheme is straight-forward.

The strong unforgeability of the above scheme is guaranteed by the following theorem.

Theorem 3. *The FB-Schnorr signature scheme is strongly unforgeable in the random oracle model, if the factoring assumption holds.*

Proof (Sketch). We will prove that, if there exists an algorithm $\mathcal{A}$ that breaks the strong unforgeability of the scheme with non-negligible probability ϵ, then there is an algorithm $\mathcal{B}$ that breaks the one-wayness of the permutation ISQ (i.e., the permutation: $x \mapsto x^{2^\lambda}$ acting on the groups $\mathbb{QR}_N^+$) with non-negligible probability.

To construct $\mathcal{B}$, we make use of $\mathcal{A}$ as an internal algorithm we are using, in which we are able to dive into the code of the algorithm and take snapshots of its state after every step. This way, we can backtrack to any state that the attacker was in at any point during its execution.

Without the loss of generality we assume that:

– $\mathcal{A}$ makes at most q_H random oracle queries.
– $\mathcal{A}$ never makes the same random oracle query twice.
– If $\mathcal{A}$ outputs (m, c, s) then it had previously queried $H(m, c)$.

We build an algorithm $\mathcal{B}$ which is, given an instance (N, h), computing an iterated square root of h (i.e. computing $h^{2^{-\lambda}}$), using the adversary $\mathcal{A}$. Algorithm $\mathcal{B}$ is defined as:

1. Pick $i^* \leftarrow_R \{1, 2, \ldots, q_H\}$.
2. Choose a generator $g \leftarrow_R \mathbb{QR}_N^+$, and set $vk := h$. $\mathcal{B}$ provides $\mathcal{A}$ the public parameter $PP := (N, g, H)$ and the verify key vk, where H is a random oracle simulated by $\mathcal{B}$ as follows.
   Random Oracle Simulation. $\mathcal{B}$ maintains a hash list H^{list} which is initially empty, and simulates H as follow:
   – $H(m, c)$: If there is a tuple (m, c, t) in H^{list} then return t, otherwise choose $t \leftarrow_R \mathbb{Z}_{2^\lambda}$, add the tuple (m, c, t) to H^{list} and return t.

3. Simulate $\mathcal{A}$:
   - When $\mathcal{A}$ makes its ith oracle query then response by using the above simulation of H. In addition, if $i = i^*$, then $\mathcal{B}$ records this state as $st_1 = (m_{i^*}, c_{i^*}, t_1)$.
   - When $\mathcal{A}$ requests to sign a message m, choose $s \leftarrow_R \mathbb{QR}_N^+, t \leftarrow_R \mathbb{Z}_{2^\lambda}$, compute $c = s \cdot vk^{-t}$, add the tuple (m, c, t) to H^{list} and return a signature (c, s).
4. After $\mathcal{A}$ finishes, it outputs (m^*, c^*, s_1). If $(m^*, c^*) \neq (m_{i^*}, c_{i^*})$, then $\mathcal{B}$ outputs $\perp$ and halts. Otherwise, it rewinds $\mathcal{A}$ from the point that $\mathcal{A}$ queries the i^*th oracle query. $\mathcal{B}$ now chooses $t_2 \leftarrow_R \mathbb{Z}_{2^\lambda}$, add the tuple (m, c, t_2) to H^{list} and returns t_2. Then $\mathcal{B}$ records this state as $st_2 = (m_{i^*}, c_{i^*}, t_2)$. $\mathcal{B}$ proceeds exactly the same as above to simulate $\mathcal{A}$. Finally, $\mathcal{A}$ finishes, it outputs (m^*, c^*, s_2). Now, since $s_1^{2^\lambda} \cdot vk^{-t_1} = c^* = s_2^{2^\lambda} \cdot vk^{-t_2}$ and $vk = h$, $\mathcal{B}$ obtains

$$\left(h^{t_2-t_1}\right)^{2^{-\lambda}} = s_1 \cdot s_2^{-1}.$$

Using Shamir's GCD in the exponent algorithm [18], $\mathcal{B}$ recovers $z = h^{2^{-\lambda}}$ as follows:
(a) Let $\delta = t_2 - t_1$. Since $|t_2 - t_1| < 2^\lambda$ we have that $\text{GCD}(\delta, 2^\lambda) = 1$. By Euclid's algorithm, $\mathcal{B}$ computes integers a, b such that $a\delta + b2^\lambda = 1$.
(b) $\mathcal{B}$ obtains

$$z = h^{2^{-\lambda}} = \left(h^{a\delta+b2^\lambda}\right)^{2^{-\lambda}} = h^{a\delta2^{-\lambda}} \cdot h^b = (s_1 \cdot s_2^{-1})^a \cdot h^b$$

Finally, $\mathcal{B}$ outputs z as the answer.

This completes the description of the simulation.

Analysis. The index i^* chosen by $\mathcal{B}$ in the first step represents a guess that $\mathcal{A}$ will forge on its i^*th oracle query (i.e. (m_{i^*}, c_{i^*})). Since, $\mathcal{A}$ queries at most q_H random oracle queries, the probability that $\mathcal{B}$ success in breaking the one-time strong unforgeability of the scheme is at least ϵ/q_H. This is non-negligible if ϵ is non-negligible. The theorem follows.

4   Models

In this section, we will review the concept of bidirectional multi-hop PRE and bidirectional single-hop PRE and their security models. Due to the lack of space, we do not describe here the models of unidirectional single-hop PRE. The details can be found in [14].

4.1   Bidirectional and Multi-Hop Proxy Re-Encryption

In this section, we first review the definition of bidirectional and multi-hop PRE proposed in [7], and then present its security model.

Definition 5. (Bidirectional and Multi-Hop PRE). *A bidirectional and single-hop PRE scheme is a tuple of algorithms $\Pi = (\textbf{Setup}, \textbf{KGen}, \textbf{RKGen}, \textbf{Enc}, \textbf{ReEnc}, \textbf{Dec})$ for message space $\mathcal{M}$:*

- **Setup**$(1^\lambda) \to PP$. *Given a security parameter* 1^λ, *the setup algorithm outputs a public parameter PP.*
- **KGen**$(PP) \to (pk, sk)$. *Given a public parameters PP, the key generation algorithm outputs a public key pk and a secret key sk.*
- **RKGen**$(PP, sk_i, sk_j) \to rk_{ij}$. *Given two secret keys* sk_i *and* sk_j, *the re-encryption key generation algorithm outputs a bidirectional re-encryption key* rk_{ij}.
- **Enc**$(PP, pk, m) \to CT$. *On input a public key pk and a message* $m \in \mathcal{M}$, *the encryption algorithm outputs a ciphertext CT.*
- **ReEnc**$(PP, rk_{ij}, CT_i) \to CT_j$. *Given a re-encryption key* rk_{ij} *and a ciphertext* CT_i *for i, the re-encryption algorithm outputs a ciphertext* CT_j *for j or the error symbol* $\perp$.
- **Dec**$(PP, sk, CT) \to m$. *Given a secret key sk and a second-level ciphertext CT, the decryption algorithm* **Dec** *outputs a message* $m \in \mathcal{M}$ *or the symbol* $\perp$.

To lighten notations, from now, we will omit the public parameters PP from the inputs of the algorithms.

For all $m \in \mathcal{M}$ and all pair $(pk_i, sk_i), (pk_j, sk_j)$, these algorithms should satisfy the following conditions of correctness:

$$\mathbf{Dec}(sk_i, \mathbf{Enc}(pk_i, m)) = m;$$
$$\mathbf{Dec}(sk_j, \mathbf{ReEnc}(\mathbf{RKGen}(sk_i, sk_j), \mathbf{Enc}(pk_i, m))) = m.$$

BM-CPA SECURITY. We present the formal definition of CPA security of bidirectional and multi-hop PRE, denoted by BM-CPA. The game framework for BM-CPA security is as follows.

Definition 6 (Game Framework of BM-CPA Security).

Setup. *The challenger* $\mathcal{C}$ *takes a security parameter* λ *and executes the setup algorithm to get the system parameter* PP. $\mathcal{C}$ *initializes two empty lists* L_{un} *and* L_{corr}, *then maintains it to record all uncorrupted users and corrupted users, respectively, in the game.*

Phase 1. $\mathcal{A}$ *can adaptively query to the following oracles* $\mathcal{O}_{unKGen}$, $\mathcal{O}_{corrKGen}$, $\mathcal{O}_{RKGen}$, *and* $\mathcal{O}_{ReEnc}$:
  - $\mathcal{O}_{unKGen}$ *takes i and returns the error symbol* $\perp$ *if* $i \in L_{un} \cup L_{corr}$; *otherwise returns* $(pk_i, sk_i) \leftarrow \mathbf{KGen}(PP)$ *and adds i in* L_{un}.
  - $\mathcal{O}_{corrKGen}$ *takes i and returns the error symbol* $\perp$ *if* $i \in L_{un} \cup L_{corr}$, *otherwise returns* $(pk_i, sk_i) \leftarrow \mathbf{KGen}(PP)$ *and adds i in* L_{corr}.
  - $\mathcal{O}_{RKGen}$ *takes* i, j *and returns* $rk_{ij} \leftarrow \mathbf{RKGen}(sk_i, sk_j)$ *if* $i \neq j \in L_{un}$ *or* $i \neq j \in L_{corr}$; *otherwise returns the error symbol* $\perp$.
  - $\mathcal{O}_{ReEnc}$ *takes* i, j *and a ciphertext* CT_i. *If* $i \neq j \in L_{un}$ *or* $i \neq j \in L_{corr}$, *then it computes* $rk_{ij} \leftarrow \mathbf{RKGen}(sk_i, sk_j)$, *and returns* $CT_j \leftarrow \mathbf{ReEnc}(rk_{ij}, CT_i)$; *otherwise returns the error symbol* $\perp$.

Challenge. *When* $\mathcal{A}$ *decides that Phase 1 is over, it outputs a target public key* pk_{i^*} *(we require* $i^* \in L_{un}$ *for* $\mathcal{A}$ *to win) and two equal-length plaintexts* $m_0, m_1 \in \mathcal{M}$. *The challenger* $\mathcal{C}$ *flips a random coin* $\sigma \in \{0, 1\}$, *and sends to* $\mathcal{A}$ *a challenge ciphertext* $CT^* \leftarrow \mathbf{Enc}(pk_{i^*}, m_\sigma)$.

Phase 2. $\mathcal{A}$ *issues queries as in Phase 1.*
Guess. *Finally, $\mathcal{A}$ outputs a guess $\sigma' \in \{0, 1\}$.*

We define $\mathcal{A}$'s advantage in attacking the PRE scheme as $\mathrm{Adv}_{\mathbf{PRE},\mathcal{A}}^{\mathrm{BM\text{-}CPA}}(\lambda) = \big|\Pr[\sigma' = \sigma] - 1/2\big|$, *where the probability is taken over the random coins consumed by the challenger and the adversary. A bidirectional and multi-hop PRE scheme is defined to be* $(q_{rk}, q_{re}, q_{dec})$-*BM-CPA secure, if for any PPT adversary $\mathcal{A}$ who makes at most q_{rk} re-encryption key generation queries, at most q_{re} re-encryption queries and at most q_{dec} decryption queries, we have* $\mathrm{Adv}_{\mathbf{PRE},\mathcal{A}}^{\mathrm{BM\text{-}CPA}}(\lambda) \leq negl(\lambda)$.

4.2 Bidirectional and Single-Hop Proxy Re-Encryption

In this section, we first review the concept of bidirectional single-hop PRE, and then present its security model.

Definition 7. (Bidirectional and Single-Hop PRE [15]). *A bidirectional single-hop PRE scheme is a tuple of algorithms* $\Pi = (\mathbf{Setup}, \mathbf{KGen}, \mathbf{RKGen}, \mathbf{Enc}, \mathbf{ReEnc}, \mathbf{Dec}_1, \mathbf{Dec}_2)$ *for message space $\mathcal{M}$:*

- **Setup**$(1^\lambda) \to PP$. *On input a security parameter 1^λ, the setup algorithm outputs a public parameters PP.*
- **KGen**$(PP) \to (pk, sk)$. *On input parameters, the key generation algorithm outputs a public key pk and a secret key sk.*
- **RKGen**$(PP, sk_i, sk_j) \to rk_{ij}$. *Given two secret keys sk_i and sk_j, the re-encryption key generation algorithm outputs a bidirectional re-encryption key rk_{ij}.*
- **Enc**$(PP, pk, m) \to CT$. *On input a public key pk and a message $m \in \mathcal{M}$, the encryption algorithm outputs a second-level ciphertext CT that can be re-encrypted into a first-level one (intended for a possibly different receiver) using the suitable re-encryption key.*
- **ReEnc**$(PP, rk_{ij}, CT_i) \to CT_j$. *Given a re-encryption key rk_{ij} and an original ciphertext CT_i for i, the re-encryption algorithm outputs a first-level ciphertext CT_j for j or the symbol $\perp$.*
- **Dec**$_1(PP, sk, CT) \to m$. *Given a secret key sk and a first-level ciphertext CT, the decryption algorithm outputs a message $m \in \mathcal{M}$ or the symbol $\perp$.*
- **Dec**$_2(PP, sk, CT) \to m$. *Given a secret key sk and a second-level ciphertext CT, the decryption algorithm outputs a message $m \in \mathcal{M}$ or the symbol $\perp$.*

To lighten notations, from now, we will omit the public parameters PP as the input of the algorithms.

For all $m \in \mathcal{M}$ and all pair $(pk_i, sk_i), (pk_j, sk_j)$ these algorithms should satisfy the following conditions of correctness:

$$\mathbf{Dec}_2(sk_i, \mathbf{Enc}(pk_i, m)) = m;$$
$$\mathbf{Dec}_1(sk_j, \mathbf{ReEnc}(\mathbf{RKGen}(sk_i, pk_j), \mathbf{Enc}(pk_i, m))) = m.$$

BS-CCA SECURITY. We present a CCA security (BS-CCA, for short) definition for bidirectional single-hop PRE, which extends that of [9] by proposing a CCA security for the first-level ciphertext. In particular, we allow the adversary to make both first and second-level decryption queries. In the challenge phase, the adversary will challenge with either second-level ciphertex or first-level (re-encrypted) ciphertext. This corresponds to the game framework for unidirectional and single-hop PRE which is defined in [6,14].

Definition 8. (Game Framework of BS-CCA Security).

Setup. *The challenger C takes a security parameter λ and executes the setup algorithm to get the system parameter PP. C initializes two empty lists L_{un} and L_{corr}, then maintains it to record all uncorrupted users and corrupted users, respectively, in the game.*

Phase 1. *A can adaptively query to the following oracles $\mathcal{O}_{unKGen}$, $\mathcal{O}_{corrKGen}$, $\mathcal{O}_{RKGen}$, $\mathcal{O}_{ReEnc}$, $\mathcal{O}_{Dec_1}$, and $\mathcal{O}_{Dec_2}$:*

- *$\mathcal{O}_{unKGen}$ takes i and returns $\perp$ if $i \in L_{un} \cup L_{corr}$; otherwise returns $(pk_i, sk_i) \leftarrow \mathbf{KGen}(PP)$ and adds i in L_{un}.*
- *$\mathcal{O}_{corrKGen}$ takes i and returns $\perp$ if $i \in L_{un} \cup L_{corr}$, otherwise returns $(pk_i, sk_i) \leftarrow \mathbf{KGen}(PP)$ and adds i in L_{corr}.*
- *$\mathcal{O}_{RKGen}$ takes i, j and returns $rk_{ij} \leftarrow \mathbf{RKGen}(sk_i, pk_j)$ if $i \neq j$; otherwise returns the error symbol $\perp$.*
- *$\mathcal{O}_{ReEnc}$ takes i, j and a ciphertext CT_i. If $i \neq j$, then it computes $rk_{ij} \leftarrow \mathbf{RKGen}(sk_i, pk_j)$, and returns $CT_j \leftarrow \mathbf{ReEnc}(rk_{i \to j}, CT_i)$; otherwise returns the error symbol $\perp$.*
- *$\mathcal{O}_{Dec_1}$ takes a public key pk and a ciphertext CT, then returns $m \leftarrow \mathbf{Dec}_1(sk, CT)$.*
- *$\mathcal{O}_{Dec_2}$ takes a public key pk and a ciphertext CT, then returns $m \leftarrow \mathbf{Dec}_2(sk, CT)$.*

Challenge. *When A decides that Phase 1 is over, it also decides which type of ciphertext for the challenge is first-level (re-encrypted) or second-level. In the case that challenge ciphertext is second-level, A outputs a target public key pk_{i^*} (we require $i^* \in L_{un}$ for A to win) and two equal-length plaintexs $m_0, m_1 \in \mathcal{M}$. Challenger C flips a random coin $\sigma \in \{0, 1\}$, and sends to A a challenge ciphertext $CT^* \leftarrow \mathbf{Enc}(pk_{i^*}, m_\sigma)$. In the case that challenge ciphertext is first-level, A outputs a (corrupted or not) public key $pk_{i'}$, a target public key pk_{i^*}, and two "good messages" CT_0, CT_1 (i.e. the messages which can be re-encrypted from $pk_{i'}$ to pk_{i^*}). Challenger C flips a random coin $\sigma \in \{0, 1\}$, computes $rk_{i' \to i^*} \leftarrow \mathbf{RKGen}(sk_{i'}, pk_{i^*})$, and sends to A a challenge ciphertext $CT^* \leftarrow \mathbf{ReEnc}(rk_{i' \to i^*}, CT_\sigma)$.*

Phase 2. *A issues queries as in Phase 1.*

Guess. *Finally, A outputs a guess $\sigma' \in \{0, 1\}$.*

The precise conditions of the attacks to second and first-level ciphertexts are described separately as follows.

The Security of Second-Level Ciphertexts. Intuitively speaking, in this model the adversary A challengs with an untransformed ciphertext encrypted by **Enc** for a target user i^*. In a PRE scheme, however, A can ask for the re-encryption of many ciphertexts or even a set of re-encryption keys. These queries are allowed as long as they would not allow $\mathcal{A}$ to decrypt trivially. For examples, $\mathcal{A}$ should not get the re-encryption key from user i^* to user j if the secret key of user j has been compromised; however, $\mathcal{A}$ can certainly get a re-encryption of the challenge ciphertext from user i^* to user j as long as j is an honest user and the decryption oracle of user j has not been queried with the resulting transformed ciphertext. This explains the intuition behind the notion of derivative and the associated restrictions.

Definition 9 (2nd-BS-CCA Security). *For the 2nd-BS-CCA security, the adversary $\mathcal{A}$ plays the CCA game with the challenger $\mathcal{C}$ as in Definition 8, where the challenge ciphertext is formed by $CT^* \leftarrow \mathbf{Enc}(pk_{i^*}, m_\sigma)$, and $\mathcal{A}$ has the following additional constraints:*

1. *$\mathcal{O}_{RKGen}(i, j)$ is only allowed if if $i \neq j \in L_{un}$ or $i \neq j \in L_{corr}$.*
2. *If $\mathcal{A}$ issues $\mathcal{O}_{ReEnc}(i, j, CT_i)$ where $j \in L_{corr}$, (pk_i, CT_i) cannot be (pk_{i^*}, CT^*).*
3. *$\mathcal{O}_{Dec_1}$ is only allowed if (pk, CT) is not a derivative of (pk_{i^*}, CT^*) (to be defined later).*

We define $\mathcal{A}$'s advantage in attacking the PRE scheme at level 2 as $\mathrm{Adv}_{PRE,\mathcal{A}}^{2nd\text{-}CCA}(\lambda) = |\Pr[\sigma' = \sigma] - 1/2|$, where the probability is taken over the random coins consumed by the challenger and the adversary. A unidirectional PRE scheme is defined to be 2nd-BS-CCA secure, if for any PPT adversary $\mathcal{A}$, the advantage $\mathrm{Adv}_{PRE,\mathcal{A}}^{2nd\text{-}CCA}(\lambda)$ is negligible.

Definition 10 (Derivative for Chosen-Ciphertext Security [8]). *Derivatives of (pk_{i^*}, CT^*) in the CCA setting is defined as below:*

1. *Reflexivity: (pk_{i^*}, CT^*) is a derivative of itself.*
2. *Derivative by re-encryption: If $\mathcal{A}$ has issued a re-encryption query (i^*, j, CT^*) and obtained the resulting re-encryption ciphertext CT_j, then (pk_j, CT_j) is a derivative of (pk_{i^*}, CT^*).*
3. *Derivative by re-encryption key: If $\mathcal{A}$ directly obtains the re-encryption key rk_{ij} by issuing a re-encryption key generation query (i^*, j), or indirectly obtains the re-encryption key rk_{i^*j} from two directly obtained re-keys rk_{i^*k}, rk_{jk} in the case that the scheme meets the transitivity between re-encryption keys, and computes $CT_j \leftarrow \mathbf{ReEnc}(rk_{i^*j}, CT^*)$, then (pk_j, CT_j) is a derivative of (pk_{i^*}, CT^*).*

The Security of First-Level Ciphertexts. The above definition provides adversaries with a second-level ciphertext in the challenge phase. A complementary definition of security captures their inability to distinguish first-level ciphertexts as well. The definition is as follows.

Definition 11 (1st-BS-CCA Security). *For the 1st-BS-CCA security, the adversary $\mathcal{A}$ plays the CCA game with the challenger $\mathcal{C}$ as in Definition 8, where the challenge ciphertext is formed by $CT^* = \mathbf{ReEnc}(rk_{i'i^*}, CT_\sigma)$, and $\mathcal{A}$ has the following additional constraints:*

1. *$\mathcal{O}_{RKGen}(i, j)$ is only allowed if $i \neq j \in L_{un}$ or $i \neq j \in L_{corr}$.*
2. *$\mathcal{O}_{Dec_1}(pk_{i^*}, CT^*)$ is not allowed.*

We define $\mathcal{A}$'s advantage in attacking the PRE scheme at level 1 as $\mathrm{Adv}_{PRE,\mathcal{A}}^{1st\text{-}CCA}(\lambda) = |\Pr[\sigma' = \sigma] - 1/2|$, where the probability is taken over the random coins consumed by *the challenger and the adversary. A unidirectional PRE scheme is defined to be 1st-BS-CCA secure, if for any PPT adversary $\mathcal{A}$, the advantage $\mathrm{Adv}_{\mathrm{PRE},\mathcal{A}}^{\mathrm{1st\text{-}CCA}}(\lambda)$ is negligible.*

Definition 12 (BS-CCA Security). *We say a PRE scheme is BS-CCA secure if the scheme is 1st-BS-CCA and 2nd-BS-CCA secure.*

5   The Proposed Schemes

In this section, we first propose a bidirectional multi-hop PRE scheme and show that it meets the BM-CPA security under the factoring assumption, in the standard model (i.e., without using random oracles). We then present our main scheme which is BS-CCA secure (in the random oracle model) under the factoring assumption. Finally, we show how to extend our main scheme to achieve a unidirectional and single-hop PRE scheme which is secure in the sense of chosen-ciphertext attack.

5.1   BM-CPA Secure PRE

In this section, we first review the IND-CPA secure PKE scheme proposed by Wee [19]. We then show the construction of our BM-CPA secure PRE scheme.

Wee Encryption Scheme [19]. We make use of a public parameter $PP = (N, g)$ for the scheme, where N is a random 2λ-bit Blum integer and g is chosen uniformly from $\mathbb{QR}_N^+$. The Wee encryption scheme for λ-bit message is as follows.

KGen(PP): Choose $x \leftarrow_R [(N-1)/4]$. Set $sk := x$, $pk := g^{2^\lambda x}$. Output (pk, sk).
Enc(PP, pk, m): Choose $r \leftarrow_R [(N-1)/4]$. Output $(g^{2^\lambda r}, (pk \cdot g)^r, BBS_N(g^r) \oplus m)$.
Dec(PP, sk, CT): Parse $CT = (c_1, c_2, c_3)$. Output $BBS_N(c_2 \cdot c_1^{-sk}) \oplus c_3$.

As shown in [19], the above scheme is IND-CPA secure under the factoring assumption in the standard model.

Construction. Our PRE scheme is an extension of the Wee encryption, in which the algorithms **KGen**, **Enc**, and **Dec** are exactly the same as that of the Wee encryption, the other are as follows:

Setup(1^λ): Output a public parameter $PP = (N, g, h)$, where $N \leftarrow \mathbf{BlumGen}(1^\lambda)$, $g \leftarrow_R \mathbb{QR}_N^+$, and $h := g^{2^\lambda}$.
RKGen(PP, sk_i, sk_j): Output $rk_{ij} := sk_i - sk_j$.
ReEnc(PP, rk_{ij}, CT_i): Parse $CT_i = (c_1, c_2, c_3)$. Set $c_2' := c_2 \cdot c_1^{rk_{ij}}$. Output (c_1, c_2', c_3).

Security Analysis. The security of the scheme is guaranteed by the following theorem.

Theorem 4. *The above PRE scheme is BM-CPA secure under the factoring assumption.*

The proof is straight-forward, and follows that of the IND-CPA security of the underlying encryption (i.e., the Wee encryption).

5.2 BS-CCA Secure PRE

Idea of the Construction. We first observe that the Wee encryption scheme can be made IND-CCA secure, in the random oracle, thanks to Fujisaki-Okamoto's technique [10] (we call it here the modified Wee encryption scheme). We then follow the idea of constructing bidirectional single-hop PRE proposed by Deng et al. [9]. In particular, we propose a new (and the first) CCA-secure factoring-based PRE scheme by using the FB-Schnorr scheme as an one-time strong signature and integrating it with the modified Wee encryption scheme. Since both the underlying signature and encryption schemes are secure under the factoring assumption (See Section 3), our scheme achieves the highest security level (i.e. the BS-CCA security) under the same assumption in the random oracle model.

Description of the Construction. The proposed scheme $\mathbf{PRE} = (\mathbf{Setup}, \mathbf{KGen},$ $\mathbf{RKGen}, \mathbf{Enc}, \mathbf{ReEnc}, \mathbf{Dec_1}, \mathbf{Dec_2})$ is as follows:

Setup(1^λ): Generate $N \leftarrow \mathbf{BlumGen}(1^\lambda), g \leftarrow_R \mathbb{QR}_N^+$, and set $h := g^{2^\lambda}$. Choose four hash function $H_1 : \{0,1\}^* \times \{0,1\}^{\ell_1} \rightarrow [(N-1)/4], H_2 : \mathbb{QR}_N^+ \rightarrow \{0,1\}^{\ell_0+\ell_1}, H_3 : \{0,1\}^* \rightarrow \mathbb{Z}_{2^\lambda}^*, H_4 : \{0,1\}^* \rightarrow \mathbb{QR}_N^+ \times \mathbb{QR}_N^+ \times \{0,1\}^{\ell_0+2\ell_1}$. Output a public parameter $PP = (N, g, h, H_1, H_2, H_3, H_4)$.

KGen(PP): Choose $x \leftarrow_R [(N-1)/4]$. Set $sk := x, pk := h^x$. Output (pk, sk).

RKGen(PP, sk_i, sk_j): Output the re-encryption key $rk_{ij} = sk_j - sk_i$.

Enc(PP, pk, m): this algorithm works as follows:
1. Pick $v \leftarrow_R [(N-1)/4], \omega \leftarrow_R \{0,1\}^{\ell_1}$, and compute $u = H_1(m, \omega)$.
2. Compute $c_0 = h^v, c_1 = h^u, c_2 = (pk \cdot g)^u, c_3 = H_2(g^u) \oplus (m\|\omega)$, and $s = g^{v+ut}$, where $t = H_3(c_0, c_1, c_2, c_3)$.
3. Output the ciphertext $CT = (c_0, c_1, c_2, c_3, s)$.

ReEnc(PP, rk_{ij}, CT_i): this algorithm works as follows:
1. Parse CT_i as $CT_i = (c_0, c_1, c_2, c_3, s)$.
2. Compute $t = H_3(c_0, c_1, c_2, c_3)$ and check whether $s^{2^\lambda} = c_0 \cdot c_1^t$ holds. If not, output $\perp$.
3. Otherwise, compute $c_2' = c_2 \cdot c_1^{rk_{ij}}$. Let $\bar{m} := (c_1, c_2', c_3)$.
4. Pick $\omega_2 \leftarrow_R \{0,1\}^{\ell_1}$, and compute $r = H_1(\bar{m}, \omega_2)$.
5. Compute $A = h^r, B = (pk_j \cdot g)^r$, and $C = H_4(g^r) \oplus (\bar{m}\|\omega_2)$, and output the first-level ciphertext $CT_j = (A, B, C)$.

Dec$_2$(PP, sk, CT): this algorithm works as follows:
1. Parse CT as $CT = (c_0, c_1, c_2, c_3, s)$.
2. Compute $t = H_3(c_0, c_1, c_2, c_3)$ and check whether $s^{2^\lambda} = c_0 \cdot c_1^t$ holds. If not, output $\perp$.
3. Compute $m\|\omega = c_3 \oplus H_2(c_2 \cdot c_1^{-sk})$, and return m if $c_1 = h^{H_1(m,\omega)}$ holds, and $\perp$ otherwise.

Dec$_1$(PP, sk, CT): this algorithm works as follows:
1. Parse CT as $CT = (A, B, C)$, and compute $\bar{m}\|\omega_2 = C \oplus H_4(B \cdot A^{-sk})$. Check whether $A = h^{H_1(\bar{m}, \omega_2)}$ holds. If not, output $\perp$. Otherwise, parse $\bar{m}$ as $\bar{m} := (c_1, c_2', c_3)$.
2. Compute $m\|\omega = c_3 \oplus H_2(c_2' \cdot c_1^{sk})$, and return m if $c_1 = h^{H_1(m,\omega)}$ holds, and $\perp$ otherwise.

Security Analysis. The intuition of CCA security of the proposed scheme can be seen from the following properties.

1. The validity of the original ciphertexts can be publicly verifiable by everyone including the proxy; otherwise, it will suffer from an attack as illustrated in [9,16]. For our scheme, we integrate the FB-Schnorr signature scheme with the CCA-secure PKE, that is how we get public verifiability. More precisely, the ciphertext component c_1, s in the original ciphertext $CT = (c_0, c_1, c_2, c_3, s)$ can be viewed as a signature signing the message (c_0, c_2, c_3).

2. It should be impossible for the adversary to transform the second-level ciphertext to the first-level one without knowledge of delegator's secret key or re-encryption key; otherwise, it only yields the RCCA security. In our scheme, the component $c'_2 = c_2 \cdot c_1^{rk_{ij}}$ is computed using re-encryption key and completely hidden in C, so the adversary cannot transform the second-level ciphertext to ciphertext re-encrypted by **ReEnc** if he has no knowledge of re-encryption key.

3. It should be impossible for the adversary to compute the re-encryption key from the target user i^* to itself (i.e., $rk_{i^* \to i^*}$), otherwise it will suffer from an attack as illustrated in [14]. In our scheme, it is clear since the re-encryption key $rk_{i \to i} = sk_i - sk_i = 0$ for all i.

4. For a first-level ciphertext CT_j re-encrypted from a second-level ciphertext CT_i, CT_j should not exhibit any component of CT_i; otherwise, it will fail in achieving CCA-security of **ReEnc** (i.e., 1st-level-CCA security). In our scheme, all of the components from the original ciphertext are hidden in C. Furthermore, we use a CCA-secure PKE in the re-encryption algorithm to guarantee the CCA security of re-encrypted ciphertext.

5. In our scheme, **ReEnc** and **Dec₂** use the same algorithm of checking the validity of the second-level ciphertext CT_i. So in the security game, providing the adversary with a second-level decryption oracle is useless. Indeed, ciphertexts encrypted under public keys from L_{un} can be re-encrypted for corrupted users by using re-encryption oracle. Besides, second-level ciphertext under pk_{i^*} can be translated for other honest users by using $rk_{i^* j}$ (where $j \in L_{un}$) and the resulting ciphertext can be queried for decryption at the first-level by using $\mathcal{O}_{Dec_1}$. This does not contradict the observation of Hanaoka et al. [11].

Theorem 5. *The above PRE scheme is BS-CCA secure in the random oracle model, if the factoring assumption holds.*

The proof of the above theorem is given in Appendix B.

5.3   Extension to Unidirectional and Single-Hop PRE Scheme

In this section, we show that our BS-CCA-secure PRE scheme can be extended to achieve a unidirectional and single-hop PRE (US-PRE, for short) scheme which is secure in the sense of chosen-ciphertext attack. Following [8], by using the "token-controlled encryption" technique, we obtain the first factoring-based unidirectional and single-hop PRE scheme. In particular, the US-PRE scheme inherits the algorithms **KGen**, **Enc**, and **Dec₂** from the original PRE scheme. The other algorithms are as follows:

Setup(1^λ): This algorithm is almost the same at that of the original PRE scheme, except that the domain of the hash function H_4 is modified to agree with the new re-encryption algorithm. Concretely, the hash function now becomes $H_4 : \{0,1\}^* \to \mathbb{QR}_N^+ \times \{0,1\}^{\ell_0+\ell_1} \times \mathbb{QR}_N^+ \times \mathbb{QR}_N^+ \times \{0,1\}^{\ell_1}$.

RKGen(PP, sk_i, pk_j): Output the re-encryption key $rk_{i \to j} = (R_1, R_2, R_3, R_4)$, where R_1, R_2, R_3, and R_4 are computed as follows:

1. Pick $\alpha \leftarrow_R [(N-1)/4], \omega_1 \leftarrow_R \{0,1\}^{\ell_1}$, and compute $r_1 = H_1(\alpha, \omega_1)$.
2. Compute $R_1 = sk_i - \alpha$.
3. Compute $R_2 = h^{r_1}, R_3 = (pk_j \cdot g)^{r_1}$, and $R_4 = H_2(g^{r_1}) \oplus (\alpha || \omega_1)$.

ReEnc$(PP, rk_{i \to j}, CT_i)$: this algorithm works as follows:

1. Parse CT_i as $CT_i = (c_0, c_1, c_2, c_3, s)$ and $rk_{i \to j}$ as $rk_{i \to j} = (R_1, R_2, R_3, R_4)$.
2. Compute $t = H_3(c_0, c_1, c_2, c_3)$ and check whether $s^{2^\lambda} = c_0 \cdot c_1^t$ holds. If not, output $\perp$.
3. Otherwise, compute $c_2' = c_2 \cdot c_1^{R_1}$. Let $\bar{m} := (c_2', c_3, R_2, R_3, R_4)$.
4. Pick $\omega_2 \leftarrow_R \{0,1\}^{\ell_1}$, and compute $r = H_1(\bar{m}, \omega_2)$.
5. Compute $A = h^r, B = (pk_j \cdot g)^r$, and $C = H_4(g^r) \oplus (\bar{m} || \omega_2)$, and output the first-level ciphertext $CT_j = (A, B, C)$.

Dec$_1$ (PP, sk, CT): this algorithm works as follows:

1. Parse CT as $CT_= (A, B, C)$, and compute $\bar{m} || \omega_2 = C \oplus H_4(B \cdot A^{-sk})$. Check whether $A = h^{H_1(\bar{m}, \omega_2)}$ holds. If not, output $\perp$. Otherwise, parse $\bar{m}$ as $\bar{m} := (c_2', c_3, R_2, R_3, R_4)$.
2. Compute $\alpha || \omega_1 = R_4 \oplus H_2(R_3 \cdot R_2^{-sk})$. Check whether $R_2 = h^{H_1(\alpha, \omega_1)}$ If not, output $\perp$.
3. Compute $m || \omega = c_3 \oplus H_2(c_2' \cdot g^{-\alpha})$, and return m if $c_1 = h^{H_1(m, \omega)}$ holds, and $\perp$ otherwise.

The CCA security (US-CCA, for short) model of the above scheme is considered in the framework of that proposed in [14]. We have the following theorem.

Theorem 6. *The above PRE scheme is US-CCA secure in the random oracle model, if the factoring assumption holds.*

The proof of the above theorem is similar to that of the original PRE scheme (i.e. the BS-CCA secure PRE scheme) which is given in Appendix B.

6 Concluding Remarks

In this paper, we have proposed the first factoring-based PRE schemes. In particular, we have presented three PRE schemes. The first is a CPA-secure bidirectional and multi-hop PRE scheme. The second is a CCA-secure bidirectional and single-hop PRE scheme. The last is a CCA-secure unidirectional and single-hop PRE scheme. The former is in the standard model, and the others are in the random oracle model. In order to construct the second and the third schemes, we have proposed a new factoring-based strong signature scheme which is a variant of the Schnorr signature scheme.

It would be interesting to construct a CCA-secure factoring-based PRE scheme without random oracles.

Acknowledgements. We thank the anonymous reviewers for their helpful comments.

References

1. Ateniese, G., Fu, K., Green, M., Hohenberger, S.: Improved proxy re-encryption schemes with applications to secure distributed storage. In: NDSS (2005)
2. Ateniese, G., Fu, K., Green, M., Hohenberger, S.: Improved proxy re-encryption schemes with applications to secure distributed storage. ACM Trans. Inf. Syst. Secur. 9(1), 1–30 (2006)
3. Baek, J., Safavi-Naini, R., Susilo, W.: Certificateless public key encryption without pairing. In: Zhou, J., López, J., Deng, R.H., Bao, F. (eds.) ISC 2005. LNCS, vol. 3650, pp. 134–148. Springer, Heidelberg (2005)
4. Blaze, M., Bleumer, G., Strauss, M.: Divertible protocols and atomic proxy cryptography. In: Nyberg, K. (ed.) EUROCRYPT 1998. LNCS, vol. 1403, pp. 127–144. Springer, Heidelberg (1998)
5. Blum, L., Blum, M., Shub, M.: A simple unpredictable pseudo- random number generator. SIAM Journal on Computing 15(2), 364–383 (1986)
6. Canard, S., Devigne, J., Laguillaumie, F.: Improving the security of an efficient unidirectional proxy re-encryption scheme. Journal of Internet Services and Information Security 1(2), 140–160 (2011)
7. Canetti, R., Hohenberger, S.: Chosen-ciphertext secure proxy re-encryption. In: ACM Conference on Computer and Communications Security, pp. 185–194. ACM Press (2007)
8. Chow, S.S.M., Weng, J., Yang, Y., Deng, R.H.: Efficient unidirectional proxy re-encryption. In: Bernstein, D.J., Lange, T. (eds.) AFRICACRYPT 2010. LNCS, vol. 6055, pp. 316–332. Springer, Heidelberg (2010)
9. Deng, R.H., Weng, J., Liu, S., Chen, K.: Chosen-ciphertext secure proxy re-encryption without pairings. In: Franklin, M.K., Hui, L.C.K., Wong, D.S. (eds.) CANS 2008. LNCS, vol. 5339, pp. 1–17. Springer, Heidelberg (2008)
10. Fujisaki, E., Okamoto, T.: Secure integration of asymmetric and symmetric encryption schemes. In: Wiener, M. (ed.) CRYPTO 1999. LNCS, vol. 1666, pp. 537–554. Springer, Heidelberg (1999)
11. Hanaoka, G., Kawai, Y., Kunihiro, N., Matsuda, T., Weng, J., Zhang, R., Zhao, Y.: Generic construction of chosen ciphertext secure proxy re-encryption. In: Dunkelman, O. (ed.) CT-RSA 2012. LNCS, vol. 7178, pp. 349–364. Springer, Heidelberg (2012)
12. Hayashi, R., Matsushita, T., Yoshida, T., Fujii, Y., Okada, K.: Unforgeability of re-encryption keys against collusion attack in proxy re-encryption. In: Iwata, T., Nishigaki, M. (eds.) IWSEC 2011. LNCS, vol. 7038, pp. 210–229. Springer, Heidelberg (2011)
13. Hofheinz, D., Kiltz, E.: Practical chosen ciphertext secure encryption from factoring. In: Joux, A. (ed.) EUROCRYPT 2009. LNCS, vol. 5479, pp. 313–332. Springer, Heidelberg (2009)
14. Isshiki, T., Nguyen, M.H., Tanaka, K.: Proxy re-encryption in a stronger security model extended from CT-RSA2012. In: Dawson, E. (ed.) CT-RSA 2013. LNCS, vol. 7779, pp. 277–292. Springer, Heidelberg (2013)
15. Libert, B., Vergnaud, D.: Unidirectional chosen-ciphertext secure proxy re-encryption. In: Cramer, R. (ed.) PKC 2008. LNCS, vol. 4939, pp. 360–379. Springer, Heidelberg (2008)
16. Matsuda, T., Nishimaki, R., Tanaka, K.: CCA proxy re-encryption without bilinear maps in the standard model. In: Nguyen, P.Q., Pointcheval, D. (eds.) PKC 2010. LNCS, vol. 6056, pp. 261–278. Springer, Heidelberg (2010)
17. Schnorr, C.P.: Efficient signature generation by smart cards. J. Cryptology 4(3), 161–174 (1991)

18. Shamir, A.: On the generation of cryptographically strong pseudorandom sequences. ACM Trans. Comput. Syst. 1(1) (1983)
19. Wee, H.: Efficient chosen-ciphertext security via extractable hash proofs. In: Rabin, T. (ed.) CRYPTO 2010. LNCS, vol. 6223, pp. 314–332. Springer, Heidelberg (2010)

A   Definitions of Primitives

A.1   Public-Key Encryption

The following definition describes the functionality of a public-key encryption scheme:

Definition 13 (Public-Key Encryption). *A public-key encryption scheme is a triplet* $(\mathbf{KGen}, \mathbf{Enc}, \mathbf{Dec})$ *of probabilistic polynomial-time algorithms such that:*

- $\mathbf{KGen}(1^n) \to (pk, sk)$. *On input 1^n, the key generation algorithm outputs a public key pk and a secret key sk.*
- $\mathbf{Enc}(pk, m) \to c$. *On input a public key pk and a message m (in some implicit message space), the encryption algorithm outputs a ciphertext c.*
- $\mathbf{Dec}(sk, c) \to m$. *Given a secret key sk and a ciphertext for c, the decryption algorithm outputs a message m or the symbol $\bot$.*

For any message m it holds that $\mathbf{Dec}(sk, \mathbf{Enc}(pk, m)) = m$ *with overwhelming probability over the internal coin tosses of* $(\mathbf{KGen}, \mathbf{Enc}, \mathbf{Dec})$.

In this paper we make use of public-key encryption schemes that are secure against adaptive chosen-ciphertext attacks, defined as follows.

Definition 14 (Chosen-Ciphertext Security). *A public-key encryption scheme* $(\mathbf{KGen}, \mathbf{Enc}, \mathbf{Dec})$ *is said to be CCA-secure if the advantage of any PPT adversary $\mathcal{A}$ in the following interaction is negligible in the security parameter:*

1. $\mathbf{KGen}$ *outputs (pk, sk), and $\mathcal{A}$ is given pk.*
2. *$\mathcal{A}$ may adaptively query a decryption oracle $\mathcal{O}_{dec}$.*
3. *At some point $\mathcal{A}$ outputs two messages m_0 and m_1 with $|m_0| = |m_1|$, and receives a challenge ciphertext $c = \mathbf{Enc}(pk, m_b)$ for a uniformly chosen bit $b \in \{0, 1\}$.*
4. *$\mathcal{A}$ may continue to adaptively query the decryption oracle $\mathcal{O}_{dec}$ on any ciphertext other than the challenge ciphertext.*
5. *Finally, $\mathcal{A}$ outputs a bit b'.*

We say that $\mathcal{A}$ succeeds if $b' = b$, and denote the advantage of $\mathcal{A}$ by $\mathrm{Adv}_{\mathbf{PKE},\mathcal{A}}^{\mathrm{IND\text{-}CCA}}(1^n)$.

B   Proof of Theorem 5

We split up the proof of Theorem 5 into two parts: we prove that our scheme is 2nd-BS-CCA secure and 1st-BS-CCA secure. Combining both parts yields Theorem 5.

Due to the lack of spaces, we leave the latter (i.e. the proof of the 1st-BS-CCA security) in the full version of this papers. The proof sketch of the 2nd-BS-CCA security is as follows.

Proof of the 2nd-BS-CCA Security. Since the permutation ISQ (i.e., the permutation : $x \mapsto x^{2^\lambda}$ acting on the groups $\mathbb{QR}_N^+$) is one-way function if only if the factoring problem is hard (Theorem 2), it is sufficient to prove that if there exists an adversary $\mathcal{A}$ that breaks the 2nd-BS-CCA security of the scheme with a non-negligible probability, then there exists an adversary $\mathcal{B}$ that breaks the one-wayness of ISQ with an overwhelming probability. Let $\mathrm{Adv}_\mathcal{B}^{\mathsf{ISQ}}(\lambda)$ denote the advantage of $\mathcal{B}$ in breaking the one-wayness of ISQ.

Since the fact that the FB-Schnorr scheme is one-time strongly unforgeable under the factoring assumption, we can assume that the signature scheme used to sign the challenge ciphertext CT_i^* (i.e. the scheme with the verify/sign keys pair are (c_1^*, h^{u^*})) is one-time strongly unforgeable.

We build an algorithm $\mathcal{B}$ which is, given a factoring instance $(N, g, g^{2^\lambda a})$, computing (g^a), using the 2nd-BS-CCA adversary $\mathcal{A}$. $\mathcal{B}$ runs the adversary $\mathcal{A}$ simulating its view as in the 2nd-BS-CCA security game as follows:

Setup. $\mathcal{B}$ initializes two empty lists L_{un} and L_{corr}, then maintains it to record all un-corrupted users and corrupted users, respectively, in the game. $\mathcal{B}$ sets $h := g^{2^\lambda}$, then provides $\mathcal{A}$ the public parameter $PP := (N, g, h, H_1, H_2, H_3, H_4)$, where H_1, H_2, H_3, and H_4 are the random oracles simulated by $\mathcal{B}$ as follows.

Hash Oracles Simulation. At any time $\mathcal{A}$ can issue the random oracle queries H_1, H_2, H_3, and H_4. $\mathcal{B}$ maintains four hash lists $H_1^{\mathrm{list}}, H_2^{\mathrm{list}}, H_3^{\mathrm{list}}$, and H_4^{list} which are initially empty, and respond as follow:

- $H_1(m, \omega)$: If there is a tuple (m, ω, r) in H_1^{list} then return r, otherwise choose $r \leftarrow_R [(N-1)/4]$, add the tuple (m, ω, r) to H_1^{list} and return r.
- $H_2(X)$: If there is a tuple (X, β) in H_2^{list} then return β, otherwise choose $\beta \leftarrow_R \{0, 1\}^{\ell_0 + \ell_1}$, add the tuple (X, β) to H_2^{list} and return β.
- $H_3(c_0, c_1, c_2, c_3)$: If there is a tuple (c_0, c_1, c_2, c_3, t) in H_3^{list} then return t, otherwise choose $t \leftarrow_R \mathbb{Z}_{2^\lambda}^*$, add (c_0, c_1, c_2, c_3, t) to H_3^{list}, and return t.
- $H_4(f)$: If there is a tuple (f, γ) in H_4^{list} then return γ, otherwise choose $\gamma \leftarrow_R \mathbb{QR}_N^+ \times \mathbb{QR}_N^+ \times \{0, 1\}^{\ell_0 + 2\ell_1}$, add the tuple (f, γ) to H_4^{list} and return γ.

Find stage (i.e. Phases 1 and 2). $\mathcal{B}$ simulates the oracles $\mathcal{O}_{unKGen}, \mathcal{O}_{corrKGen}, \mathcal{O}_{RKGen}, \mathcal{O}_{ReEnc}$, and $\mathcal{O}_{Dec_1}$ to answer the questions issued by $\mathcal{A}$ as follows:

- $\mathcal{O}_{unKGen}(i)$: $\mathcal{B}$ returns $\perp$ if $i \in L_{un} \cup L_{corr}$; otherwise $\mathcal{B}$ chooses randomly $x_i \leftarrow_R [(N-1)/4]$, sets and returns $pk_i := h^{x_i} \cdot g^{-1}$ (meaning that $sk_i = x_i - \frac{1}{2^\lambda} \bmod |\mathbb{QR}_N^+|$). $\mathcal{B}$ adds i to L_{un}. Note that, $\mathcal{B}$ no need to know sk_i.
- $\mathcal{O}_{corrKGen}(i)$: $\mathcal{B}$ returns $\perp$ if $i \in L_{un} \cup L_{corr}$; otherwise $\mathcal{B}$ chooses randomly $x_i \leftarrow_R [(N-1)/4]$, and returns (pk_i, sk_i), where $pk_i := h^{x_i}, sk_i := x_i$. $\mathcal{B}$ adds i to L_{corr}.
- $\mathcal{O}_{RKGen}(i, j)$: if $i \neq j \in L_{un}$ or $i \neq j \in L_{corr}$ $\mathcal{B}$ returns $rk_{ij} := x_j - x_i$; otherwise returns the symbol $\perp$.
- $\mathcal{O}_{ReEnc}(i, j, CT_i)$: $\mathcal{B}$ parses $CT_i = (c_0, c_1, c_2, c_3, s)$, and does as follows:
  1. If $i = j$, then return $\perp$.

2. if $i \neq j \in L_{un}$ or $i \neq j \in L_{corr}$ $\mathcal{B}$ computes the re-encryption key $rk_{ij} := x_j - x_i$. Next, $\mathcal{B}$ follows the algorithm **ReEnc** to compute the ciphertext CT_j by using rk_{ij} and simulating the hash oracles H_1, H_3, H_4 as follows:

   (a) Search in the lists H_3^{list} to see whether there exist $(a_0, a_1, a_2, a_3, t) \in H_3^{\text{list}}$ such that $(a_0 = c_0) \wedge (a_1 = c_1) \wedge (a_2 = c_2) \wedge (a_3 = c_3)$. If there exists no such tuple, then return $\perp$. (This corresponds to the event ReEncErr$_1$ to be explained).

   (b) Check whether $s^{2^\lambda} = c_0 \cdot c_1^t$ holds. If not, then return $\perp$.

   (c) Search in the lists H_1^{list} to see whether there exist $(m, \omega, r) \in H_1^{\text{list}}$ such that $h^r = c_1, (pk_i \cdot g)^r = c_2$. If there exists no such tuple, then return $\perp$. (This corresponds to the event ReEncErr$_2$ to be explained).

   (d) Compute $c_2' = c_2 \cdot c_1^{rk_{ij}}$. Let $\bar{m} := (c_1, c_2', c_3)$.

   (e) Pick $\omega_2 \leftarrow_R \{0,1\}^{\ell_1}, r_1 \leftarrow_R [(N-1)/4]$, and add $(\bar{m}, \omega_2, r_1)$ to the H_1^{list}.

   (f) Compute $A = h^{r_1}, B = (pk_j \cdot g)^{r_1}$,

   (g) Search in the lists H_4^{list} to see whether there exist (f, γ) such that $f = g^{r_1}$. If there exists no such tuple, then pick $\gamma \leftarrow_R \mathbb{QR}_N^+ \times \mathbb{QR}_N^+ \times \{0,1\}^{\ell_0 + 2\ell_1}$, add the tuple (f, γ) to H_4^{list}.

   (h) Compute $C = \gamma \oplus (\bar{m}\|\omega_2)$, and output the first-level ciphertext $CT_j = (A, B, C)$.

3. If $(i = i^*) \wedge (j \in L_{corr}) \wedge (c_1 = c_1^*)$, then return $\perp$. Since c_1^* is the verify key of the one-time strong signature scheme **SIG** used to sign the challenge ciphertext CT^*, CT_i is indeed the challenge ciphertext CT^*. Therefore, $\mathcal{B}$ should return $\perp$.

4. If $i \in L_{corr}, j \in L_{un}$ or $i \in L_{un}, j \in L_{corr}$, then $\mathcal{B}$ does as follows:

   (a) Search in the lists H_3^{list} to see whether there exist $(a_0, a_1, a_2, a_3, t) \in H_3^{\text{list}}$ such that $(a_0 = c_0) \wedge (a_1 = c_1) \wedge (a_2 = c_2) \wedge (a_3 = c_3)$. If there exists no such tuple, then return $\perp$.

   (b) Check whether $s^{2^\lambda} = c_0 \cdot c_1^t$ holds. If not, then return $\perp$.

   (c) Search whether there exists a tuple $(m, \omega, r) \in H_1^{\text{list}}$ such that $h^r = c_1, (pk_i \cdot g)^r$. If there no such tuple, then return $\perp$.

   (d) Compute $c_2' = (pk_j \cdot g)^r)$. Let $\bar{m} := (c_1, c_2', c_3)$.

   (e) Pick $\omega_2 \leftarrow_R \{0,1\}^{\ell_1}, r_1 \leftarrow_R [(N-1)/4]$, and add $(\bar{m}, \omega_2, r_1)$ to the H_1^{list}.

   (f) Compute $A = h^{r_1}, B = (pk_j \cdot g)^{r_1}$,

   (g) Search in the lists H_4^{list} to see whether there exist (f, γ) such that $f = g^{r_1}$. If there exists no such tuple, then pick $\gamma \leftarrow_R \mathbb{QR}_N^+ \times \mathbb{QR}_N^+ \times \{0,1\}^{\ell_0 + 2\ell_1}$, add the tuple (f, γ) to H_4^{list}.

   (h) Compute $C = \gamma \oplus (\bar{m}\|\omega_2)$, and output the first-level ciphertext $CT_j = (A, B, C)$.

- $\mathcal{O}_{Dec_1}(i, CT_i)$: If $i \in L_{corr}$, then $\mathcal{B}$ does as the algorithm **Dec$_1$** to decrypt the ciphertext CT_i by using $sk_i = x_i$ and hash lists $H_1^{\text{list}}, H_2^{\text{list}}, H_3^{\text{list}}$, and H_4^{list}. Otherwise $\mathcal{B}$ parses CT_i as $CT_i = (A, B, C)$, and does as follows:

1. Search in the lists H_1^{list} and H_4^{list} to see whether there exist $(m, \omega, r) \in H_1^{\text{list}}$ and $(f, \gamma) \in H_4^{\text{list}}$ such that

$$h^r = A, (pk_i \cdot g)^r = B, \gamma \oplus (m\|\omega) = C, \text{ and } f = g^r. \qquad (1)$$

   If there exists no such tuple, then return $\bot$. (This corresponds to the event DErr_1 to be explained).
2. Parse $\bar{m}$ as $\bar{m} := (c_1, c_2', c_3)$.
3. Search in the lists H_1^{list} to see whether there exist $(m, \omega, r) \in H_1^{\text{list}}$ such that $h^r = c_1, (pk_j \cdot g)^r = c_2'$. If there exists no such tuple, then return $\bot$.(This corresponds to the event DErr_2 to be explained).
4. Compute $m\|\omega = c_3 \oplus H_2(g^r)$, and returns m if $c_1 = h^{H_1(m,\omega)}$ holds, and $\bot$ otherwise.

Challenge. When $\mathcal{A}$ decides that Phase 1 is over, it outputs a target public key pk_{i^*} and two equal-length plaintexts $m_0, m_1 \in \{0,1\}^\lambda$. If $i^* \in L_{corr}$, then $\mathcal{B}$ outputs $\bot$ and holds, since we require $i^* \in L_{un}$ for $\mathcal{A}$ to win the game. Otherwise, $\mathcal{B}$ flips a random coin $\sigma \in \{0,1\}$ and does as follows:

1. Pick $s^* \leftarrow_R \mathbb{QR}_N^+, t^* \leftarrow_R \mathbb{Z}_{2^\lambda}$, and compute $c_0^* = (s^*)^{2^\lambda} \cdot (g^{2^\lambda a})^{-t^*}$.
2. Define $c_1^* = g^{2^\lambda a}$ (meaning that $u^* = a$).
3. Compute $c_2^* = (g^{2^\lambda a})^{x_{i^*}}$.
4. Pick $c_3^* \leftarrow_R \{0,1\}^{\ell_0 + \ell_1}$ and define $H_3(c_0^*, c_1^*, c_2^*, c_3^*) = t^*$.
5. Pick $\omega^* \leftarrow_R \{0,1\}^{\ell_1}$, and implicitly define $H_2(g^a) = c_3^* \oplus (m_\sigma\|\omega^*)$ and $H_1(m_\sigma\|\omega^*) = a$ (note that $\mathcal{B}$ does not know a and g^a).
6. Return $CT^* = (c_0^*, c_1^*, c_2^*, c_3^*, s^*)$ as the challenge ciphertext to $\mathcal{A}$.

Observe the following to see that, CT^* is identically distributed as the real one from the construction. Let $g^{v^*} := s^* \cdot g^{-at^*}$ and $u^* := a$. We have

1. $c_0^* = (s^*)^{2^\lambda} \cdot (g^{2^\lambda a})^{-t^*} = (s^* \cdot g^{-at^*})^{2^\lambda} = g^{2^\lambda v^*} = h^{v^*}$.
2. $c_1^* = g^{2^\lambda a} = g^{2^\lambda u^*} = h^{u^*}$.
3. $c_2^* = (g^{2^\lambda a})^{x_{i^*}} = (g^{2^\lambda x_{i^*}})^a = (g^{2^\lambda sk_{i^*}+1})^{u^*} = (pk_{i^*} \cdot g)^{u^*}$. (Note that $sk_{i^*} = x_{i^*} - \frac{1}{2^\lambda} \bmod |\mathbb{QR}_N^+|$ since $i^* \in L_{un}$).
4. $c_3^* = H_2(g^a) \oplus (m_\sigma\|\omega^*) = H_2(g^{u^*}) \oplus (m_\sigma\|\omega^*)$.
5. $s^* = s^* \cdot g^{-at^*} \cdot g^{at^*} = g^{v^*+u^*t^*} = g^{v^*+u^*H_3(c_0^*, c_1^*, c_2^*, c_3^*)}$.

Guess. Finally, $\mathcal{A}$ outputs a guess $\sigma' \in \{0,1\}$.

Output. If $\sigma' = \sigma$, then $\mathcal{B}$ searches (X, β) from the list H_2^{list} such that $X^{2^\lambda} = g^{2^\lambda a}$, and output X as the solution; otherwise $\mathcal{B}$ outputs $\bot$ and halts.

This completes the description of the simulation. It remains to related the probability for success and the execution time, which will be shown in the following lemma (Lemma 1).

Before describing the lemma we set $q := |\mathbb{QR}_N^+|$, and assume that $\mathcal{A}$ issues at most $q_{H_1}, q_{H_2}, q_{H_3}, q_{H_4}, q_u, q_c, q_{rk}, q_{re}$, and q_d queries to $H_1, H_2, H_3, H_4, \mathcal{O}_{unKGen}, \mathcal{O}_{corrKGen}, \mathcal{O}_{RKGen}, \mathcal{O}_{ReEnc}$, and $\mathcal{O}_{Dec_1}$, respectively.

The lemma is as follows.

Lemma 1. *If $\mathcal{A}$ can break the 2nd-BS-CCA security of the scheme with advantage ϵ within time t, then $\mathcal{B}$ can break the one-wayness of ISQ with advantage ϵ' within time t' where*

$$t' \leq t + (q_{H_1} + q_{H_2} + q_{H_3} + q_u + q_c + q_{rk} + q_{re} + q_d)\mathcal{O}(1)$$
$$+ (q_u + q_c + (2q_{H_1} + q_{H_4})q_{re} + 5q_{H_1}q_d)t_{exp},$$
$$\epsilon' \geq 2\epsilon - \frac{q_{re} + q_d(q_{H_1} + 2)}{q} - \frac{q_{H_1}}{2^{\ell_1}} - \frac{q_{H_3}}{2^{\ell_0 + \ell_1}} - \frac{q_d(q_{H_4} + 1)}{q^2 \cdot 2^{\ell_0 + 2\ell_1}},$$

t_{exp} *denotes the running time of an exponentiation in group* $\mathbb{QR}_N^+$.

The main idea of the proof of the above lemma is borrowed from [9,3]. Due to the lack of space, we leave the detail proof in the full version of this paper.

Towards a Secure Certificateless Proxy Re-Encryption Scheme*

Hui Guo, Zhenfeng Zhang, Jiang Zhang, and Cheng Chen

Trusted Computing and Information Assurance Laboratory, Institute of Software,
Chinese Academy of Sciences, Beijing, China.
{guohui,zfzhang,zhangjiang,chencheng}@tca.iscas.ac.cn

Abstract. Proxy re-encryption (PRE) is an attractive paradigm, which gives good solutions to the problem of delegation of decryption rights. In proxy re-encryption, a semi-trusted proxy translates a ciphertext for Alice into a ciphertext of the same plaintext for Bob, without learning any information of the underlying message. As far as we know, previous PRE schemes are mainly in traditional public key infrastructure or identity-based cryptography, thus they suffer from certificate management problem or key escrow problem in practice. In order to solve these practical problems, we aim at constructing certificateless proxy re-encryption (CL-PRE) schemes.

In this paper, we first introduce a security definition against (replayable) chosen ciphertext attack (CCA) for certificateless proxy re-encryption. In our security model, the adversary is allowed to adaptively corrupt users (in a specific pattern). Then, we give some evidence that it is not easy to construct a secure CL-PRE. Actually, we present an attack to the chosen plaintext secure CL-PRE scheme proposed by Xu et al. [1]. We also show a novel generic construction for certificateless public key encryption (CL-PKE) can not be trivially adapted to CL-PRE by giving an attack to this generic construction. Finally, we present an efficient CL-PRE scheme and prove its security in the random oracle model based on well-known assumptions.

1 Introduction

Proxy re-encryption (PRE) was first proposed by Blaze, Bleumer and Strauss [2] in 1998, which allows the proxy to transform a ciphertext for Alice into a ciphertext of the same message for Bob. During the transformation, the proxy learns nothing about the underlying message. Having the proxy transform ciphertext and simultaneously keeping the message private from the proxy is the main goal for proxy re-encryption.

According to the direction of transformation, PRE schemes can be classified into two types: unidirectional and bidirectional schemes. In a unidirectional PRE scheme, the proxy can only transform the ciphertext from Alice to Bob; while in a bidirectional one, the proxy can transform in both directions. Essentially, we can construct a bidirectional

* The work is supported by the National Basic Research Program of China (No. 2013CB338003), and the National Natural Science Foundation of China (No.61170278, 91118006).

W. Susilo and R. Reyhanitabar (Eds.): ProvSec 2013, LNCS 8209, pp. 330–346, 2013.

PRE scheme by simply combining two unidirectional PRE schemes. In this paper, we only restrict our attention to unidirectional PRE schemes.

Proxy re-encryption has many applications, such as email forwarding [3], distributed files systems [4] and revocation systems [5]. Below we take Personal Health Record (PHR) sharing [6] as an example and explain the importance of constructing CL-PRE schemes.

A telemedical system involves patients, doctors and electronic medical records servers. Patients outsource their personal health records, which include various medical data, such as surgery, family history, laboratory test results, to be stored at the electronic medical server. Since patients do not hope to expose the records to those electronic medical records servers or unauthorized parties, they usually choose to encrypt their personal health records before outsourcing. When a telemedical consultation occurs, the electronic medical records server re-encrypts related personal health records to the involved doctors. During the process, the patient would not like to expose his secret key to either the server or any doctor. Proxy re-encryption provides a good solution to this problem.

When we examine the existing schemes, we find the schemes are inappropriate in the telemedical system. Schemes in [4,3,7] are all of traditional PKI-supported PRE. Since the amount of patients and doctors are huge, public key management will be the most costly and cumbersome part that reduces the efficiency of the system. Schemes in [8,9] are of identity-based proxy re-encryption (IB-PRE) and schemes in [10,11] are of attribute-based proxy re-encryption (AB-PRE). In IB-PRE or AB-PRE schemes, a trusted third party computes all private keys and is able to read all messages in the system, which is contrary to the *Health Insurance Portability and Accountability Act (HIPPA)* privacy rules. To avoid the expensive certificates in PKI and the key escrow problem inherited from IBE or ABE, we resort to certificateless public key cryptography (CL-PKC).

CL-PKC was introduced by Al-Riyami and Paterson [12] in 2003. The concept is to enjoy the advantage of identity-based public key cryptography without suffering from the key escrow problem. In CL-PKC, a sender needs both the receiver's identity and public key to encrypt a message. However, the public key here needs no certificate, which is different from the public key used in traditional PKI-supported cryptography. When decrypting, the receiver needs two parts to recover the message: one is called the partial private key corresponding to his identity which is generated by the key generation center (KGC); the other is the secret value related to the public key produced by himself. Therefore, the KGC cannot recover ciphertexts in the system in that the KGC has no information about the secret values chosen by users. We construct CL-PRE schemes for the telemedical system to enjoy both the efficiency and security provided by CL-PKC.

1.1 Related Work

Certificateless Public Key Cryptography. Since the notion CL-PKC was introduced in 2003, a variety of certificateless public key encryption (CL-PKE) schemes have been proposed. In 2005, Baek et al. [13] proposed the first CL-PKE scheme without pairing in the random oracle model. The formulation for the certificateless encryption is different from Al-Riyami and Paterson [12]: a user has to receive the partial private key before producing their public key. In 2006, Libert et al. [14] and Chow et al's [15] proposed the generic construction of certificateless encryption respectively. Libert et al. presented the generic composition idea : given a CPA IBE scheme and a CPA public key encryption (PKE) scheme, a CCA CL-PKE scheme can be obtained in the random oracle model. Chow et al. presented a generic construction for security-mediated certificateless encryption which provides instant revocation. In 2007, Lai et al. [16] proposed two variants of Baek et al. scheme [13]. CL-PKE schemes to strengthen the scheme of Baek et al. [13], respectively. Sun et al. modified the scheme and enabled the Type I adversary to replace the public key associated with the target identity, but still disallowed the adversary to extract the partial private key of the target identity. While in Lai et al.'s scheme, the user engages in a protocol with the KGC when computing their full public and private keys, to allow the Type I adversary to extract the partial private key of the target identity. Both of the two schemes are secure against chosen ciphertext attacks in the random oracle model.

Proxy Re-Encryption. In 1998, Blaze et al. [2] proposed the concept of proxy re-encryption and constructed a bidirectional scheme, which is semantically secure in the random oracle model. In 2007, Canetti and Hohenberger [3] presented the first bidirectional scheme which is replayable chosen ciphertext secure in the standard model. In 2008, Libert and Vergnaud [7] proposed the first unidirectional single-hop PRE scheme, which is replayable CCA-secure in the standard model. In 2010, Chow et al. [17] proposed an efficient unidirectional PRE scheme without pairings.

The above schemes are in traditional public key infrastructure, which cannot avoid the certificate management problem. In 2007, Green and Ateniese [9] introduced the concept of identity based proxy re-encryption (IB-PRE) and proposed the first IB-PRE scheme in the random oracle model. In the same year, Chu and Tzeng [8] presented the first CCA secure IB-PRE scheme in the standard model. In 2010, Luo et al. [11] proposed an AB-PRE scheme.

IB-PRE and AB-PRE solve the certificate management problem, but bring in the key escrow problem. In order to solve this problem, we focus on realizing a secure CL-PRE scheme.

1.2 Our Contribution

In this paper, we introduce the syntax of CL-PRE and formulate a replayable CCA (RCCA) security model for CL-PRE. Firstly, our model considers both the Type I adversary and the Type II adversary. The Type I adversary represents attacks from outsiders with the ability to replace user's public key on his will. The Type II adversary stands for the honest but curious PKG who has access to the master secret key. Secondly, in our security model of CL-PRE, the Type I adversary has the ability to set up the dishonest user's public key or replace honest user's public key. Thirdly, our model allows the Type I adversary to adaptively corrupt honest users in a specific way. For example, it can replace the public key and query the partial private key of the honest user.

Then, we give some discussions on constructing RCCA secure CL-PRE schemes. First we present an attack to Xu et al.'s scheme [1], which was claimed to be secure against chosen plaintext attack (CPA) in the random oracle model. Unfortunately, we show their scheme is insecure by giving a CPA attack. Secondly, we show a novel generic construction of CL-PRE which is adapted from the generic construction of CL-PKE in [14] is vulnerable to the Type I adversary under adaptively chosen ciphertext attacks. Both evidences show that it is difficult to construct a secure (especially RCCA secure) CL-PRE scheme.

Next, we present a RCCA secure CL-PRE scheme. The idea is to construct a CL-PRE scheme based on Sun et al.'s CL-PKE scheme [18] (which is the modification of Baek et al.'s CL-PKE scheme [13]). Firstly, we extend Sun et al.'s scheme into the pairing based setting. Secondly, in order to allow the adversary to extract challenger's partial private key (which is not allowed in Sun et al's sheme) and reach the RCCA security, we generate each entity's public key and private key by engaging a protocol with the KGC, similar to Lai et al.'s scheme in [16]. In the re-encryption key generation process, the delegator computes re-encryption keys on input his own private key and the public key of the delegatee. Finally, we present the security proof of the scheme in the random oracle model. As far as we know, the proposed scheme is the first CL-PRE scheme that is RCCA secure against both Type I and Type II adversaries.

2 Preliminaries

In this section, we recall the complexity assumption required in our scheme. In our paper, we use λ to denote the security parameter.

2.1 Bilinear Maps and Assumptions

In this section, we recall the definitions of the bilinear groups [19,20] and q-wDBDHI assumption based on the bilinear groups. We write $\mathbb{G} = \langle g \rangle$ to denote that g generates the group $\mathbb{G}$. Let $\mathbb{G}$ and $\mathbb{G}_T$ be two cyclic groups of prime order p, a map $e\colon \mathbb{G} \times \mathbb{G} \to \mathbb{G}_T$ is said to be a bilinear map if it satisfies the following conditions:

1. for all $u, v \in \mathbb{G}$ and $a, b \in \mathbb{Z}_p$, we have $e(u^a, v^b) = e(u, v)^{ab}$.
2. e is non-degenerate (i.e. if $\mathbb{G} = \langle g \rangle$, then $\mathbb{G}_T = \langle e(g, g) \rangle$).
3. e is efficiently computable.

Let $\mathbb{G}$, $\mathbb{G}_T$ and e be bilinear groups defined as above, we recall the following hardness assumptions over the groups.

CDH Assumption. For an algorithm $\mathcal{B}$, define its advantage as

$$\mathrm{Adv}_{\mathcal{B}}^{\mathrm{CDH}}(\lambda) = |\Pr[\mathcal{B}(g, g^a, g^b) = g^{ab}]|$$

where $a, b \leftarrow \mathbb{Z}_p^*$ are randomly chosen. We say that the CDH (Computational Diffie-Hellman) assumption holds, if for any probabilistic polynomial time (PPT) algorithm $\mathcal{B}$, its advantage $\mathrm{Adv}_{\mathcal{B}}^{\mathrm{CDH}}(\lambda)$ is negligible in λ.

q-wDBDHI Assumption. For an algorithm $\mathcal{B}$, define its advantage as

$$\mathrm{Adv}_{\mathcal{B}}^{q\text{-wDBDHI}}(\lambda) = |\Pr[\mathcal{B}(g, g^a, \ldots, g^{a^q}, g^b, e(g, g)^{b/a}) = 1]|$$

$$- \Pr[\mathcal{B}(g, g^a, \ldots, g^{a^q}, g^b, e(g, g)^z) = 1]|$$

where $a, b, z \leftarrow \mathbb{Z}_p^*$ are randomly chosen. We say that the q-wDBDHI (q-weak Decision Bilinear Diffie-Hellman Inversion) assumption holds, if for any PPT algorithm $\mathcal{B}$, its advantage $\mathrm{Adv}_{\mathcal{B}}^{q\text{-wDBDHI}}(\lambda)$ is negligible in λ.

In our scheme, we use the 1-wDBDHI assumption (i.e., $q = 1$), which is slightly stronger than the DBDH assumption. We note that 1-wDBDHI assumption is also used in several other interesting cryptographic constructions [7,21].

2.2 Target-Collision Resistant Hash Function

Let $\mathcal{F} = (\mathrm{TCR}_s)_{s \in S}$ be a family of hash functions for security parameter λ and with seed $s \in S$. For an algorithm $\mathcal{A}$, define its advantage as

$$\mathrm{Adv}_{\mathcal{A}}^{\mathrm{TCR}}(\lambda) = \Pr[\mathrm{TCR}_s(x) = \mathrm{TCR}_s(x') \wedge x \neq x' | s \leftarrow S,$$

$$x \leftarrow X, x' \leftarrow \mathcal{A}(\mathrm{TCR}_s, x)].$$

We define hash function family TCR is target collision resistant if for any PPT algorithm $\mathcal{A}$, its advantage $\mathrm{Adv}_{\mathcal{A}}^{\mathrm{TCR}}(\lambda)$ is negligible in λ.

3   Certificateless Proxy Re-Encryption

In this section, we present the syntax of CL-PRE. A certificateless proxy re-encryption scheme consists of the following algorithms:

Setup(λ) : This is a PPT algorithm run by the KGC, which takes a security parameter λ as input, outputs a list of public parameter $param$ and a randomly chosen master secret key msk.

UserKeyGen($param, ID$) : This is a PPT algorithm run by the user, which takes a list of public parameters $param$ as inputs, outputs a secret key sk and a public key pk.

PKeyExt($param, msk, ID, pk$) : This is a PPT algorithm run by the KGC, which takes a list of public parameters $param, msk$, a user's identity ID and pk as inputs, outputs a partial private key psk and a partial public key ppk.

KeyGen($param, ID, psk, ppk, sk, pk$) : This is a PPT algorithm run by the user, which takes a list of public parameters $param, ID, psk, ppk, sk$ and pk as inputs, outputs the user's public key and private key (PK, SK).

ReKeyGen($param, ID_i, SK_i, PK_i, ID_j, PK_j$) : This is a PPT algorithm run by the user, which takes a list of public parameters $param$, a user's ID_i, SK_i, PK_i and another user's ID_j, PK_j as inputs, outputs the re-encryption key $rk_{i \to j}$ or an error symbol $\perp$.

Enc$_1$($param, m, ID, PK$) : This is a PPT algorithm run by the sender, which takes a list of parameters $param$, a message m, a receiver's ID and PK as inputs, outputs a 1st level ciphertext C which can not be re-encrypted.

Enc$_2$($param, m, ID, PK$) : This is a PPT algorithm run by the sender, which takes a list of parameters $param$, a message m, a receiver's ID and PK as inputs, outputs a 2nd level ciphertext C which can be re-encrypted.

ReEnc($param, C, ID_i, ID_j, rk_{i \to j}$) : This is a PPT algorithm run by the proxy, which takes a list of public parameters $param$, users' identity ID_i and ID_j and a 2nd level ciphertext C under ID_i as inputs, outputs a 1st level ciphertext C' of ID_j or an error symbol $\perp$.

Dec_1($param, C, SK$) : This is a deterministic algorithm run by the recipient, which takes a list of public parameters $param$, a 1st level ciphertext C and SK as inputs, outputs the plaintext m or an error symbol $\perp$.

Dec_2($param, C, SK$) : This is a deterministic algorithm run by the recipient which takes a list of public parameters $param$, a 2nd level ciphertext C and SK as inputs, outputs the plaintext m or an error symbol $\perp$.

Correctness. For any public parameters $param$ generated by Setup(λ), for any message $m \in \{0, 1\}^{l_0}$, in which l_0 denotes the length of the message, if SK_i and SK_j are corresponding with PK_i and PK_j, the above algorithms should satisfy the following requirements:

- $Dec_2(param, Enc_2(param, m, ID_i, PK_i), SK_i) = m$.
- $Dec_1(param, Enc_1(param, m, ID_i, PK_i), SK_i) = m$.
- If $rk_{i \to j} = ReKeyGen(param, ID_i, SK_i, ID_j, PK_j)$,
  $C'_j = ReEnc(param, Enc_2(param, m, ID_i, PK_i), ID_i, ID_j, rk_{i \to j})$, then
  $Dec_1(param, SK_j, C'_j) = m$.

3.1 Security Model

In CL-PKC, adversaries are divided into two types: the Type I adversary, who can replace user's public key on his choice; and the Type II adversary, holding the master secret key of the KGC. The Type I adversary describes the outsider's attack, while the Type II adversary stands for the curious but honest KGC, who can generate all the partial keys with the master secret key. To protect data privacy, we require that the adversary cannot gain any protected information unless holding both the partial private key and the secret value at the same time. When we take the two types of adversaries into consideration in the security models of CL-PRE, the circumstances seem to become more complex.

Unlike previous model in [7], we consider the model where the adversary can adaptively choose public keys for malicious users. In addition, we allow the Type I adversary to (partially) adaptively corrupt users, different from the previous model [7].

To capture the RCCA security notion for single-hop unidirectional CL-PRE schemes, we consider the security of ciphertexts at both levels against the Type I adversary and the Type II adversary separately. $\mathcal{A}$ denotes a Type I adversary or a Type II adversary. We associate to a CL-PRE adversary $\mathcal{A}$ the following CL-PRE RCCA experiment with parameters $(\mathcal{O}', \delta)$, where $\mathcal{O}'$ is a set of oracles provided to $\mathcal{A}$, and $\delta \in \{1, 2\}$ specifies which level ciphertext that $\mathcal{A}$ attacks. Both parameters will be instantiated in Definition 1, 2, 3 and 4.

Experiment Exp$_{\Pi_s,\mathcal{A}}^{\text{clpre,rcca}}(\lambda)$

$\quad param \leftarrow \text{Setup}(\lambda),$

$\quad (m_0, m_1, ID^*) \leftarrow \mathcal{A}^{\mathcal{O}'}(param),$

$\quad d^* \leftarrow \{0, 1\},$

$\quad C^* = \text{Enc}_\delta(m_{d^*}, ID^*),$

$\quad d' \leftarrow \mathcal{A}^{\mathcal{O}'}(param, C^*)$

$\quad$If $d' = d^*$ return 1, else return 0

The advantage of $\mathcal{A}$ is defined as $\text{Adv}_{\Pi_s,\mathcal{A}}^{\text{clpre,rcca}}(\lambda) = |\Pr[\text{Exp}_{\Pi_s,\mathcal{A}}^{\text{clpre,rcca}}(\lambda) = 1] - \frac{1}{2}|$.

Security against the Type I Adversary. First, we consider the RCCA security notion against the Type I adversary at the 2nd level ciphertext. Before setting up the oracles, the challenger creates two lists: the HU list and the L list. The HU list is a list of honest users' identities. When a user is corrupted, the challenger removes the user's identity from the HU list. The L list is a list of $\langle ID, PK, \widehat{PK}\rangle$, where $ID \in HU, PK$ and $\widehat{PK}$ denote the original public key and the current public key of ID. The list is to record whether the public key of a specific identity has been replaced. The challenger sets $\widehat{PK} = PK$ initially. In Definition 1 and Definition 2, the Type I adversary is provided with the following oracles:

- Honest key generation $\mathcal{O}_{\text{hkg}}$: on input ID, compute $(sk, pk) \leftarrow \text{UserKeyGen}(ID)$, $(psk, ppk) \leftarrow \text{PKeyExt}(ID, pk)$ and $(PK, SK) \leftarrow \text{KeyGen}(ID, ppk, psk)$. Return PK.
- Delegation $\mathcal{O}_{\text{deleg}}$: on input $(ID_i, ID_j, \widehat{PK_j})$, where $\widehat{PK_j}$ may be an arbitrary public key supplied by $\mathcal{A}$, compute the re-encryption key $rk_{i\to j} = \text{ReKeyGen}(ID_i, SK_i, PK_i, ID_j, \widehat{PK_j})$. Return $rk_{i\to j}$.
- Re-encryption $\mathcal{O}_{\text{renc}}$: on input $(ID_i, ID_j, \widehat{PK_j}; C)$, where $\widehat{PK_j}$ may be an arbitrary public key supplied by $\mathcal{A}$, compute the re-encrypted ciphertext $C' = \text{ReEnc}(\text{ReKeygen}(ID_i, ID_j, \widehat{PK_j}); C)$. Return C'.
- First level decryption $\mathcal{O}_{\text{1-dec}}$: on input a pair $(ID; C)$, compute the plaintext $m = \text{Dec}_1(ID; C)$. Return m.
- Second level decryption $\mathcal{O}_{\text{2-dec}}$: on input a pair $(ID; C)$, compute the plaintext $m = \text{Dec}_2(ID; C)$. Return m.
- Partial key extract oracle $\mathcal{O}_{\text{pex}}$: on input a pair (ID, PK), compute $(ppk, psk) = \text{PKeyExt}(ID_i, pk)$ (pk can be extracted from PK). If $ID \in HU$ and $\widehat{PK} \neq PK$, the challenger updates $HU = HU \backslash ID$. Return (ppk, psk).
- Public key replace oracle $\mathcal{O}_{\text{pkr}}$: on input a pair $(ID, \widehat{PK})$, replace the user's public key with $\widehat{PK}$ and set $\langle ID, PK, \widehat{PK}\rangle$ on the L list.

Now, let's consider the RCCA security against the Type I adversary at the 2nd level.

Definition 1 (RCCA Security against the Type I Adversary at the 2nd Level Ciphertext). *For any single-hop unidirectional CL-PRE scheme Π_s, we instantiate the CL-PRE RCCA experiment with the Type I adversary $\mathcal{A}_I$, $\mathcal{O}' =$*

$\{\mathcal{O}_{hkg}, \mathcal{O}_{deleg}, \mathcal{O}_{renc}, \mathcal{O}_{1\text{-dec}}, \mathcal{O}_{2\text{-dec}}, \mathcal{O}_{pex}, \mathcal{O}_{pkr}\}$ *and* $\delta = 2$. *Suppose the challenger ciphertext* C^* *is generated under* ID^* *and* $\widehat{PK^*}$, *where* $\widehat{PK^*}$ *denotes the current public key of* ID^*. *We require that* $ID^* \in HU$ *and* $|m_0| = |m_1|$. *If* C^* *denotes the challenge ciphertext,* $\mathcal{A}_I$ *can never make following queries:*

- *Delegation query* $\mathcal{O}_{deleg}(ID^*, ID_x)$, *if* $ID_x \notin HU$.
- *Decryption query* $\mathcal{O}_{2\text{-dec}}(ID^*, C^*)$, *if* $\widehat{PK^*} = PK^*$.
- *Re-encryption query* $\mathcal{O}_{renc}(ID^*, ID_x, C^*)$, *if* $ID_x \notin HU$ *and* $\widehat{PK^*} = PK^*$.
- *Decryption query* $\mathcal{O}_{1\text{-dec}}(ID', C')$, *if* $\mathrm{Dec}_1(ID', C') \in \{m_0, m_1\}$.

We say Π_s *is secure against (replayable) chosen ciphertext attacks at the 2nd level if for any polynomial time adversary* $\mathcal{A}_I$, *the advantage function* $\mathrm{Adv}_{\Pi_s, \mathcal{A}_I}^{clpre, 2\text{-rcca}}(\lambda)$ *is negligible in* λ.

When we consider the security notion at the 1st level ciphertext, we remove the restriction of re-encryption key queries. There is no reason to keep any re-encryption keys from the adversary, even those from the target entity to corrupted entities. Since $\mathcal{A}$ can do arbitrary re-encryption with re-encryption keys, $\mathcal{O}_{renc}$ is unnecessary. Then, we formulate the security definition as follows:

Definition 2 (RCCA Security against the Type I adversary at the 1st Level Ciphertext). *For any single-hop unidirectional CL-PRE scheme* Π_s, *we instantiate the CL-PRE RCCA experiment with the Type I adversary* $\mathcal{A}_I$, $\mathcal{O}' = \{\mathcal{O}_{hkg}, \mathcal{O}_{deleg}, \mathcal{O}_{1\text{-dec}}, \mathcal{O}_{2\text{-dec}}, \mathcal{O}_{pex}, \mathcal{O}_{pkr}\}$ *and* $\delta = 1$. *Suppose the challenger ciphertext* C^* *is generated under* ID^* *and* $\widehat{PK^*}$, *where* $\widehat{PK^*}$ *denotes the current public key of* ID^*. *We require that* $ID^* \in HU$ *and* $|m_0| = |m_1|$. *If* $\widehat{PK^*} = PK^*$ *where* PK^* *denotes the original public key of* ID^*, $\mathcal{A}$ *is not allowed to make decryption query* $\mathcal{O}_{1\text{-dec}}(ID^*, C^*)$ *after seeing the challenge ciphertext* C^*. *We say* Π_s *is secure against (replayable) chosen ciphertext attacks at the 1st level if for any polynomial time adversary* $\mathcal{A}$, *the advantage function* $\mathrm{Adv}_{\Pi_s, \mathcal{A}_I}^{clpre, 1\text{-rcca}}(\lambda)$ *is negligible in* λ.

Remark 1. In our model, when an honest entity's public key has been replaced, the challenger will still use his original secret key to decrypt and generate re-encryption keys. Since the honest entity would not possess the secret key corresponding with the replaced public key, we cannot force the honest entity to run algorithms with an unknown value in reality. Therefore, it is a reasonable assumption that the challenger manages oracles $\mathcal{O}_{deleg}$, $\mathcal{O}_{1\text{-dec}}$ and $\mathcal{O}_{2\text{-dec}}$ with the secret key related to the original public key.

Remark 2. Adversary $\mathcal{A}_I$ could corrupt honest entity in a specific way: first $\mathcal{A}_I$ replaces the honest user's public key; then queries the oracle $\mathcal{O}_{pex}$ to gain the partial private key. Since we do not allow the adversary to directly query the secret key of an honest user, our model is partially adaptive. With the oracle $\mathcal{O}_{pex}$, the adversary can also generate secret keys of corrupted users.

Remark 3. In [22], Hanaoka et al. illustrated the adversary with both the 2nd level decryption oracle and the 1st level decryption oracle is strictly stronger than the adversary who can only access to the 1st level decryption oracle. Therefore, in our model we provide the adversary with the oracle $\mathcal{O}_{2\text{-dec}}$ as well as the oracle $\mathcal{O}_{1\text{-dec}}$ to achieve a higher level security.

Security Against the Type II Adversary. Let's consider the security definition against the Type II adversary. Since the Type II adversary stands for the curious KGC, we provide $\mathcal{A}_{II}$ with an oracle $\mathcal{O}_{\text{msk}}$ to obtain the master secret key. $\mathcal{A}_{II}$ could produce arbitrary partial private key with the master secret key, therefore the oracle $\mathcal{O}_{\text{pex}}$ is unnecessary in the security experiment. In Definition 3 and Definition 4, the oracles work as follows:

- Master secret key $\mathcal{O}_{\text{msk}}$: on input the security parameter λ, return the master secret key msk.
- Honest key generation $\mathcal{O}_{\text{hkg}}$: on input ID, compute $(sk, pk) \leftarrow$ UserKeyGen (ID), $(psk, ppk) \leftarrow$ PKeyExt(ID) and $(PK, SK) \leftarrow$ KeyGen$(param, ID, ppk, psk)$. Return PK.
- Delegation $\mathcal{O}_{\text{deleg}}$: on input (ID_i, ID_j, PK_j), compute the re-encryption key $rk_{i \to j} = \text{ReKeyGen}(ID_i, SK_i, PK_i, ID_j, PK_j)$. Return $rk_{i \to j}$.
- Re-encryption $\mathcal{O}_{\text{renc}}$: on input $(ID_i, ID_j, PK_j; C)$, compute the re-encrypted ciphertext $C' = \text{ReEnc}(\text{ReKeyGen}(ID_i, ID_j, PK_j); C)$. Return C'.
- First level decryption $\mathcal{O}_{\text{1-dec}}$: on input $(ID; C)$, compute the plaintext $m = \text{Dec}_1(ID; C)$. Return m.
- Second level decryption $\mathcal{O}_{\text{2-dec}}$: on input $(ID; C)$, compute plaintext $m = \text{Dec}_2(ID; C)$. Return m.

We define the RCCA security against Type II adversary at the 2nd level ciphertext as follows:

Definition 3 (RCCA Security against the Type II Adversary at the 2nd Level Ciphertext). *For any single-hop unidirectional CL-PRE scheme Π_s, we instantiate the CL-PRE RCCA experiment with the Type II adversary $\mathcal{A}_{II}$, the $\mathcal{O}' = \{\mathcal{O}_{\text{msk}}, \mathcal{O}_{\text{deleg}}, \mathcal{O}_{\text{renc}}, \mathcal{O}_{\text{1-dec}}, \mathcal{O}_{\text{2-dec}}\}$ and $\delta = 2$. We require that $ID^* \in HU$ and $|m_0| = |m_1|$. If C^* denotes the challenge ciphertext, $\mathcal{A}_{II}$ can never make following queries:*

- *Delegation query $\mathcal{O}_{\text{deleg}}(ID^*, ID_x)$, if $ID_x \notin HU$.*
- *Decryption query $\mathcal{O}_{\text{2-dec}}(ID^*, C^*)$.*
- *Re-encryption query $\mathcal{O}_{\text{renc}}(ID^*, ID_x, C^*)$, if $ID_x \notin HU$.*
- *Decryption query $\mathcal{O}_{\text{1-dec}}(ID', C')$, if $\text{Dec}_1(ID', C') \in \{m_0, m_1\}$.*

We say Π_s is secure against (replayable) chosen ciphertext attacks at the 2nd level if for any polynomial time adversary $\mathcal{A}$, the advantage function $\text{Adv}_{\Pi_s, \mathcal{A}_{II}}^{\text{clpre,2-rcca}}(\lambda)$ is negligible in λ.

Then, we consider the security notion at the 1st level ciphertext. As Definition 2, the oracle $\mathcal{O}_{\text{renc}}$ is unnecessary. We define the RCCA security against the Type II adversary at the 1st level ciphertext as follows:

Definition 4 (RCCA Security against the Type II Adversary at the 1st Level Ciphertext). *For any single-hop unidirectional CL-PRE scheme Π_s, we instantiate the CL-PRE RCCA experiment with the Type II adversary $\mathcal{A}_{II}$, $\mathcal{O}' = \{\mathcal{O}_{\text{msk}}, \mathcal{O}_{\text{deleg}}, \mathcal{O}_{\text{1-dec}}, \mathcal{O}_{\text{2-dec}}\}$ and $\delta = 1$. We require that $ID^* \in HU$, $|m_0| = |m_1|$ and $\mathcal{A}_{II}$ is not allowed to make decryption query $\mathcal{O}_{\text{1-dec}}(ID^*, C^*)$ after seeing the* challenge ciphertext C^*. We say Π_s is secure against (replayable) chosen ciphertext attacks at the 1st level if for any polynomial time adversary A_{II}, the advantage function $\mathrm{Adv}^{clpre,1\text{-}rcca}_{\Pi_s,A_{II}}(\lambda)$ is negligible in λ.

4 Discussion on CL-PRE Scheme

In this section, we first observe and give attack to Xu et al.'s [1] scheme. Then, we show an insecure generic construction of CL-PRE, to illustrate the key point to present a RCCA secure CL-PRE scheme.

4.1 Security Analysis of Xu et al.'s Scheme

In order to leverage cloud for encryption based access control and key management, Xu et al. [1] proposed a certificateless proxy re-encryption scheme in 2012. Their scheme was claimed to be chosen plaintext secure in the random oracle model. However, the scheme is vulnerable when facing the Type I adversary.

In their scheme, the public key of user ID is $pk = (H(ID), g^{s \cdot x})$, where $H(\cdot)$ is a hash function, s is the master secret key and x is chosen by the user. The encryption algorithm is $C = (g^r, m \cdot e(H(ID)^r, g^{s \cdot x}))$. If the Type I adversary replaces $pk = (H(ID), g^{s \cdot x})$ with $pk = (H(ID), g^t)$, where t is selected on the adversary's choice, the ciphertext would be $C = (C_1, C_2) = (g^r, m \cdot e(H(ID)^r, g^t))$. Consequently, the adversary can successfully decrypt the ciphertext with t by computing $m = m \cdot e(H(ID)^r, g^t)/e(H(ID), g^r)^t = C_2/e(H(ID), C_1)^t$. The Type I adversary breaks the CPA security of Xu et al.'s scheme.

4.2 An Extension of a Generic Construction Is Vulnerable

Libert et al. [14] proposed a generic construction from a CPA secure PKE scheme and a CPA secure IBE sheme to a CCA CL-PKE scheme. Intuitively, can we directly combine a CCA PRE scheme and a CCA IB-PRE scheme to obtain a RCCA secure CL-PRE scheme by using their technique? Unfortunately, we find the resulting scheme is vulnerable to the Type I adversary. We will present a Type I attack after the description of the generic scheme.

Let Π^I be a CCA secure IB-PRE scheme and Π^P denote a CCA secure PRE scheme. Using a CCA secure Π^P and a CCA secure Π^I as building blocks, we construct a CL-PRE scheme Π by Libert et al.'s generic construction technique [14] as follows:

- The key generation algorithm for Π is to run the key generation algorithms Π^P.KeyGen of Π^P and Π^I.KeyExtract of Π^I. Return $SK = (SK^P, SK^I)$ and $PK = PK^P$.
- The re-encryption key generation algorithm for Π is to run both the re-encryption key generation algorithms of Π^P and Π^I. Return $(rk_1, rk_2) = (rk^P, rk^I)$.
- The second level encryption algorithm for Π first split a plaintext m into $m = m_1 \oplus m_2$. Run the second level encryption of Π^I and Π^P to generate ciphertexts $C_1 = \mathcal{E}^P_{PK}(m_1||\sigma, H(m||\sigma||pk||ID))$ and $C_2 = \mathcal{E}^I_{ID}(m_2||\sigma, H(m||\sigma||pk||ID))$. Return $C = (C_1, C_2)$.

- The second level decryption algorithm Π with input $C = (C_1, C_2)$ runs $\Pi^P.\text{Dec}_2$ with C_1 and runs $\Pi^I.\text{Dec}_2$ with C_2. If the result is m_1 and m_2, compute $m = m_1 \oplus m_2$ and return m.
- The re-encryption algorithm for Π with $C = (C_1, C_2)$ runs $\Pi^P.\text{ReEnc}$ with C_1 to obtain re-encrypted ciphertext C_1' and runs $\Pi^I.\text{ReEnc}$ with C_2 to obtain re-encrypted ciphertext C_2'. Return $C' = (C_1', C_2')$.
- The first level decryption algorithm for Π with $C' = (C_1', C_2')$ as input runs $\Pi^P.\text{Dec}_1$ with C_1' to obtain the plaintext m_1 and runs $\Pi^I.\text{Dec}_1$ with C_2' to obtain the plaintext m_2. Compute $m = m_1 \oplus m_2$ and return m.

If we just consider the key generation algorithm, the encryption algorithm and the decryption algorithm of Π, the resulting scheme $\Pi' = (\Pi.\text{KeyGen}, \Pi.\text{Enc}_2, \Pi.\text{DEC}_2)$ is a CCA CL-PKE according to Libert et al.'s result [14]. However, Π is an insecure CL-PRE scheme against the Type I adversary. We show that the Type I adversary can break the 2nd level RCCA security of Π as follows:

1. After receiving the challenge ciphertext $C^* = (C_1^*, C_2^*)$, the adversary first queries the partial private key of ID^*, namely $SK_{ID^*}^I$ of ID^*. $\mathcal{A}$ decrypts C_2^* with $SK_{ID^*}^I$ and obtains m_2.
2. The adversary replaces an honest user ID's public key with $\widehat{PK}$ on his choice. Note that he knows the corresponding secret value, i.e. $\widehat{SK}^P$.
3. The adversary queries the re-encryption of C^* from ID^* to ID, and obtains $C' = (C_1', C_2')$, where $C_1' = \Pi^P.\text{ReEnc}(C_1^*)$. With the secret value $\widehat{SK}^P$, he can easily decrypt C_1' and obtain m_1.
4. The adversary computes $m = m_1 \oplus m_2$ and breaks the RCCA security of Π.

A CCA IB-PRE plus a CCA PRE can not trivially make a RCCA CL-PRE using Libert et al.'s generic construction technique [14]. Why not? Let us have a look at the re-encryption keys first. A delegator's private key has two parts, one part is his partial private key, and the other part is the secret value. When the delegator generates a re-encryption key, he should insert his private key into the re-encryption key. Unfortunately, we find that rk_2 is only relevant to his partial private key, and it has no relation with the secret value, while rk_1 is just the reverse. This kind of construction destroys the bindings of delegator's identity and public key. Such weakness in the re-encryption key generation directly results in vulnerability of the scheme.

Informally speaking, the re-encryption key of CL-PRE should integrate the receiver's public key and identity tightly to achieve the RCCA security notion. We will present an efficient solution to this problem in the next section.

5   Replayable CCA Secure CL-PRE Scheme

In this section, we extend Sun et al's scheme [13] to the pairing based setting and construct the first RCCA secure CL-PRE. In order to achieve the RCCA security notion, we derive the re-encryption key in a manner somewhat like that in [23].

5.1 Construction

Setup(λ) : Let λ be the security parameter, $\mathbb{G}$ and $\mathbb{G}_T$ be groups of prime order p, and $e: \mathbb{G} \times \mathbb{G} \to \mathbb{G}_T$ be a bilinear map . It then performs as follows:

1. Choose a group generator $g \in \mathbb{G}$.
2. Select $x, \alpha \in \mathbb{Z}_p$ at random and set $y = g^x$.
3. Choose target collision resistant hash functions $H_0 : \{0,1\}^* \to \mathbb{G}$, $H_1 : \{0,1\}^* \times \mathbb{G} \times \mathbb{G} \to \mathbb{Z}_p$, $H_2 : \{0,1\}^{l_0} \times \{0,1\}^{l_1} \to \mathbb{Z}_p$, $H_3 : \mathbb{G} \times \mathbb{G} \times \mathbb{G} \to \mathbb{G}$, $H_4 : \mathbb{G}_T \to \{0,1\}^l$ and $H_5 : \{0,1\}^* \times \mathbb{G} \times \mathbb{G} \to \mathbb{G}$, where $l = l_0 + l_1 \in \mathbb{N}$. Here, l_0 and l_1 denote the bit-length of a plaintext and a random bit string.

The public parameters are $param = (p, g, y, e(g,g)^\alpha, H_0, H_1, H_2, H_3, H_4, H_5)$. The master secret key is (x, g^α). The plaintext space is $\{0,1\}^{l_0}$.

UserKeyGen($param, ID$) : Pick $z \in \mathbb{Z}_p$ at random and compute $\mu = g^z$. Return user's key $(sk, pk) = (z, \mu)$.

PKeyExt($param, msk, ID, pk$) : Pick $s, s' \in \mathbb{Z}_p$ at random and compute $\omega = g^s$, $t = s + x H_1(ID, pk, \omega)$, $K = g^\alpha H_5(ID, pk, \omega)^{s'}$ and $L = g^{s'}$. Return the partial public key $ppk = (\omega, K, L)$ and the partial private key $psk = t$.

KeyGen($param, ID, psk, ppk, sk, pk$) : Set public key $PK = (\mu, \omega, K, L)$ and private key $SK = sk + psk = z + t$. Return (PK, SK).

ReKeyGen($param, ID_i, SK_i, PK_i, ID_j, PK_j$) : On input ID_i, SK_i, PK_i and ID_j, PK_j, this algorithm generates the re-encryption key $rk_{i \to j}$ as follows:

1. Parse PK_j as $(\mu_j, \omega_j, K_j, L_j)$.
2. Check whether $e(K_j, g) = e(g,g)^\alpha e(H_5(ID_j, \mu_j, \omega_j), L_j)$. If not, return "$\perp$".
3. Select $\theta \in \mathbb{Z}_p$ at random.
4. Compute $A_{ij} = (\mu_j \omega_j y^{H_1(ID_j, \mu_j, \omega_j)})^{SK_i^{-1}} H_0(ID_i)^\theta$ and $B_{ij} = (\mu_i \omega_i y^{H_1(ID_i, \mu_i, \omega_i)})^\theta$.
5. Return $rk_{i \to j} = (A_{ij}, B_{ij}, PK_i)$.

Note that PK_i here is corresponding with the private key SK_i.

Enc$_1$($param, m, ID, PK$) : On input ID, PK and a message $m \in \{0,1\}^{l_0}$, this algorithm encrypts m to a 2nd level ciphertext as follows:

1. Parse PK as (μ, ω, K, L).
2. Check whether $e(K, g) = e(g,g)^\alpha e(H_5(ID, \mu, \omega), L)$. If not, return "$\perp$".
3. Pick $\sigma \in \{0,1\}^{l_1}$ at random and compute $r = H_2(m, \sigma)$.
4. Compute $c_0 = H_4(e(g,g)^r) \oplus (m || \sigma)$, $c_1' = e(\mu \omega y^{H_1(ID, \mu, \omega)}, g)^r$.
5. Return the 2nd level ciphertext $C' = (c_0, c_1')$.

Enc$_2$($param, m, ID, PK$) : On input ID, PK and a message $m \in \{0,1\}^{l_0}$, this algorithm encrypts m to a 1st level ciphertext as follows:

1. Parse PK as (μ, ω, K, L).
2. Check whether $e(K, g) = e(g,g)^\alpha e(H_5(ID, \mu, \omega), L)$. If not, return "$\perp$".
3. Pick $\sigma \in \{0,1\}^{l_1}$ at random, and compute $r = H_2(m, \sigma)$.
4. Compute $c_0 = H_4(e(g,g)^r) \oplus (m || \sigma)$, $c_1 = (\mu \omega y^{H_1(ID, \mu, \omega)})^r$, $c_2 = H_0(ID)^r$, $c_3 = H_3(c_0, c_1, c_2)^r$.
5. Return the 1st level ciphertext $C = (c_0, c_1, c_2, c_3)$.

ReEnc($param, C, ID_i, ID_j, rk_{i \to j}$) : On input re-encryption key $rk_{i \to j}$ and the ciphertext C of ID_i, re-encrypt the ciphertext C to ID_j as following:

1. Parse C as (c_0, c_1, c_2, c_3), and $rk_{i \to j}$ as (A_{ij}, B_{ij}, PK_i) and PK_i as $(\mu_i, \omega_i, K_i, L_i)$.
2. Check whether $e(c_3, \mu_i \omega_i y^{H_1(ID_i, \mu_i, \omega_i)}) = e(c_1, H_3(c_0, c_1, c_2))$ and $e(H_0(ID_i), c_3) = e(c_2, H_3(c_0, c_1, c_2))$. If not, return "$\perp$".
3. Compute $c_1' = e(c_1, A_{ij})/e(c_2, B_{ij})$.
4. Return the re-encrypted ciphertext $C' = (c_0, c_1')$.

$Dec_1(param, C', SK)$: On input the ciphertext C', user ID's private key SK and public key PK, recover the plaintext m as follows:

1. Parse C' as (c_1', c_2), and PK as (μ, ω, K, L).
2. Compute $m||\sigma = H_4(c_1'^{SK^{-1}}) \oplus c_0$ and $r = H_2(m||\sigma)$.
3. Check whether $c_1' = e(\mu \omega y^{H_1(ID, \mu, \omega)}, g)^r$. If not, return "$\perp$".
4. Return plaintext m

$Dec_2(param, C, SK)$: On input the ciphertext C, user ID's private key SK and public key PK, recover the plaintext m as:

1. Parse C as (c_0, c_1, c_2, c_3), and PK as (μ, ω, K, L).
2. Compute $m||\sigma = c_0 \oplus H_4(e(g, c_1^{SK^{-1}}))$ and $r = H_2(m||\sigma)$.
3. Check whether $c_1 = (\mu \omega y^{H_1(ID, w, \mu)})^r$, $c_2 = H_0(ID)^r$, $c_3 = H_3(c_0, c_1, c_2)^r$. If not, return "$\perp$".
4. Return plaintext m.

Correctness. To simplify the computation, we denote $\mu \omega y^{H_1(ID, \mu, \omega)}$ as $\mathcal{Y}$. Then we have $\mathcal{Y} = \mu \omega y^{H_1(ID, \mu, \omega)} = g^{SK}$. The CL-PRE scheme satisfies the correctness property at each level:

- Decryption of a 2nd level ciphertext is correct. If $C = (c_0, c_1, c_2, c_3)$ is a 2nd level ciphertext, we obtain

$$c_0 \oplus H_4(e(g, C_1^{SK^{-1}})) = H_4(e(g, g)^r) \oplus (m||\sigma) \oplus H_4(e(g, \mathcal{Y}^{r \cdot SK^{-1}})) = m||\sigma.$$

- Decryption of a 1st level ciphertext is correct. If $C' = (c_0, c_1')$ is a 1st level ciphertext, we obtain

$$H_4(c_1'^{(SK)^{-1}}) \oplus c_0 = H_4(e(\mathcal{Y}, g)^{r \cdot SK^{-1}}) \oplus H_4(e(g, g)^r) \oplus (m||\sigma) = m||\sigma.$$

- Decryption of a re-encrypted ciphertext is correct. If $C' = (c_0, c_1')$ is a re-encrypted ciphertext of $C = (c_0, c_1, c_2, c_3)$ and $rk_{i \to j} = (A_{ij}, B_{ij}, PK_i)$ is the re-encryption key, first we obtain

$$c_1' = e(c_1, A_{ij})/e(c_2, B_{ij}) = \frac{e(\mathcal{Y}_i^r, \mathcal{Y}_j^{SK_i^{-1}} \cdot H_0(ID_i)^\theta)}{e(H_0(ID_i)^r, \mathcal{Y}_i^\theta)} = e(g, \mathcal{Y}_j)^r$$

Then, as the decryption of original ciphertext at level 1, we have $H_4(c_1'^{SK^{-1}}) \oplus c_0 = m||\sigma$.

Remark 4. The scheme is replayable CCA secure at the second level ciphertext which is arguably sufficient for most practical applications [24]. Since a re-encryption key $rk_{* \to *} = (H_0(ID^*)^\theta, PK^{*\theta}, PK^*)$ can always be generated by picking θ at random, the adversary can re-encrypt the challenge ciphertext to ID^* itself [25], resulting in the replayable CCA security.

5.2 Discussions

In our scheme, each user has to generate a secret key using UserKeyGen before querying the partial public key and partial private key. This method enables us to reach a security proof. Though readers might consider that the partial keys would be independently generated from the choice of users in a certificateless scheme, we note that it is not always the case. Actually, in a survey of certificateless encryption [26,27], the authors classified certificateless schemes into three different infrastructures, namely, the AP formulation [12], the BSS formulation [13] and the LK formulation [16]. In the AP formulation, the receiver can generate the public key at anytime. While in the BSS formulation, the receiver can only generate the public key after receiving the partial private key from the KGC. In this paper, we have adopted the LK formulation for the CL-PRE scheme, namely, when generating the public key the receiver should complete a protocol with the KGC.[1] The BSS or LK formulations are the minimum requirements to achieve denial of decryption security [28] in CL-PKE.

Interestingly, Dent [27] also instantiated the LK formulation of certificateless encryption by the traditional notion of PKI-based encryption as follows: first the receiver generates encryption key pair and send it to the KGC; then the KGC creates a digital signature to bind the encryption key to his identity. The receiver's full public key contains the public key and the digital certificate. If a sender wishes to encrypt a message, he should first checks the certificate. The difference between such a certificateless scheme and a traditional public-key scheme in the PKI system is the security consideration. Interested readers may refer to [29] for a discussion on self-generated-certificate encryption versus public-key encryption.

In this paper, we adopted the Dent's instantiation to the PRE setting. But there are two main differences in our scheme 1) the full private key of a user is generated from two resources to protect the users privacy: one part is generated by the user himself and the other part related to his identity is from the KGC, and 2) the KGC creates a proof on not only the public key (generated by the user) but also an additional group element (picked up by KGC itself). The differences let us achieve a strong security without harming the efficiency, which seems optimal for a PRE scheme to the best of our knowledge. However, we also left the problem of designing a PRE in other formulation (e.g., the AP formulation) in our future work.

5.3 Security and Efficiency Comparisons

Now, we give some intuitions for the security of the scheme.

1. Public verification. Since the 2nd level ciphertext includes two short signatures, i.e. (c_1, c_3) and (c_2, c_3), everyone in the system can verify its validity. Therefore, the re-encryption algorithm will not reveal sensitive information to the adversary.

---

[1] The LK formulation is a reasonable relaxed formulation, since "*The Lai-Kou formulation can be viewed as a generalisation of the BSS formulation. Instead of a single message (the partial private key) being passed between the receiver and the KGC prior to public key publication, the receiver and the KGC must undertake a protocol before the receiver can publish its public key*" [27].

Table 1. Comparisons between the IB-PRE scheme in [9] and our CL-PRE scheme. $n(\cdot)$ denotes a polynomial function of the security parameter λ. $|\mathbb{G}|, |\mathbb{G}_T|, |m|$ and $|ID|$ denote the bit-length of an element in $\mathbb{G}$, an element in $\mathbb{G}_T$, a plaintext and an identifier of the user. (*: The scheme is unfortunately vulnerable to a collusion attack [30].)

Shemes	IB-PRE scheme in [9]	Our CL-PRE scheme
ReKeyGen	$1t_p$	$3t_e$
Enc$_2$	$3t_e$	$4t_e$
Dec$_1$	$1t_e + 2t_p$	$2t_e + 1t_p$
Dec$_2$	$4t_e + 2t_p$	$4t_e + 1t_p$
$|C'|$	$|\mathbb{G}| + |\mathbb{G}_T| + |m| + |n(\lambda)| + |ID|$	$|\mathbb{G}_T| + l$
$|C|$	$2|\mathbb{G}| + |\mathbb{G}_T| + |m|$	$3|\mathbb{G}| + l$
Secrutiy	CCA? *	RCCA
Assumption	DBDH	1-wDBDHI&CDH
Random oracle	Yes	Yes
Other property	Dec$_1(\cdot)$ requires the identifier of the delegator.	Dec$_1(\cdot)$ does not requires the identifier of the delegator.

2. RCCA security at level 2 & level 1. Fujisaki and Okamoto [31] transformation ensures its RCCA security.

Theorem 1. *Our CL-PRE scheme is RCCA secure in the random oracle model, assuming that the CDH problem and 1-wDBDHI problem are intractable.*

The above theorem is obtained by combining of Lemma 1-4. Due to the space limit, proofs of Lemma 1- 4 will appear in the full version of this paper.

Lemma 1. *Assume $H_0, H_1, H_2, H_3, H_4, H_5$ are random oracles and the CDH problem and 1-wDBDHI problem are intractable. The CL-PRE scheme is RCCA secure at the 2nd level ciphertext against the Type I adversary.*

Lemma 2. *Assume $H_0, H_1, H_2, H_3, H_4, H_5$ are random oracles and the CDH problem and 1-wDBDHI problem are intractable. The CL-PRE scheme is RCCA secure at the 1st level ciphertext against the Type I adversary.*

Lemma 3. *Assume $H_0, H_1, H_2, H_3, H_4, H_5$ are random oracles and the CDH problem and 1-wDBDHI problem are intractable. The CL-PRE scheme is RCCA secure at the 2nd level ciphertext against the Type II adversary.*

Lemma 4. *Assume $H_0, H_1, H_2, H_3, H_4, H_5$ are random oracles and the CDH problem and 1-wDBDHI problem are intractable. The CL-PRE scheme is RCCA secure at the 1st level ciphertext against the Type II adversary.*

Efficiency. In Table 1, we compare our CL-PRE scheme with the IB-PRE scheme in [9]. t_e and t_p denote the the computation time for an exponentiation and a bilinear pairing. In our scheme, we assume $\mu\omega y^{H_1(ID,\mu,\omega)}$ is pre-computed and $e(K, g) = e(g, g)^{\alpha} e(H_5(ID, \mu, \omega), L)$ is pre-checked. The comparison indicates that the efficiency of our scheme is comparable with the IB-PRE scheme.

6 Conclusion

We introduced the RCCA security model for CL-PRE. We showed a vulnerable generic construction to illustrate constructing a RCCA secure scheme is nontrivially and meaningful. Finally, we presented a CL-PRE scheme and proved it to be RCCA secure in the random oracle model.

References

1. Xu, L., Wu, X., Zhang, X.: Cl-pre: a certificateless proxy re-encryption scheme for secure data sharing with public cloud. In: Proceedings of the 7th ACM Symposium on Information, Computer and Communications Security. ASIACCS 2012, pp. 87–88. ACM (2012)
2. Blaze, M., Bleumer, G., Strauss, M.J.: Divertible protocols and atomic proxy cryptography. In: Nyberg, K. (ed.) EUROCRYPT 1998. LNCS, vol. 1403, pp. 127–144. Springer, Heidelberg (1998)
3. Canetti, R., Hohenberger, S.: Chosen-ciphertext secure proxy re-encryption. In: Proceedings of the 14th ACM Conference on Computer and Communications Security, pp. 185–194. ACM (2007)
4. Ateniese, G., Fu, K., Green, M., Hohenberger, S.: Improved proxy re-encryption schemes with applications to secure distributed storage. ACM Transactions on Information and System Security (TISSEC) 9, 1–30 (2006)
5. Yu, S., Wang, C., Ren, K., Lou, W.: Attribute based data sharing with attribute revocation. In: Proceedings of the 5th ACM Symposium on Information, Computer and Communications Security, ASIACCS 2010, pp. 261–270. ACM (2010)
6. Li, M., Yu, S., Zheng, Y., Ren, K., Lou, W.: Scalable and secure sharing of personal health records in cloud computing using attribute-based encryption. IEEE Transactions on Parallel and Distributed Systems, 131–143 (2013)
7. Libert, B., Vergnaud, D.: Unidirectional chosen-ciphertext secure proxy re-encryption. In: Cramer, R. (ed.) PKC 2008. LNCS, vol. 4939, pp. 360–379. Springer, Heidelberg (2008)
8. Chu, C.-K., Tzeng, W.-G.: Identity-based proxy re-encryption without random oracles. In: Garay, J.A., Lenstra, A.K., Mambo, M., Peralta, R. (eds.) ISC 2007. LNCS, vol. 4779, pp. 189–202. Springer, Heidelberg (2007)
9. Green, M., Ateniese, G.: Identity-based proxy re-encryption. In: Katz, J., Yung, M. (eds.) ACNS 2007. LNCS, vol. 4521, pp. 288–306. Springer, Heidelberg (2007)
10. Liang, X., Cao, Z., Lin, H., Shao, J.: Attribute based proxy re-encryption with delegating capabilities. In: Proceedings of the 4th International Symposium on Information, Computer, and Communications Security, pp. 276–286. ACM (2009)
11. Luo, S., Hu, J., Chen, Z.: Ciphertext policy attribute-based proxy re-encryption. In: Soriano, M., Qing, S., López, J. (eds.) ICICS 2010. LNCS, vol. 6476, pp. 401–415. Springer, Heidelberg (2010)
12. Al-Riyami, S.S., Paterson, K.G.: Certificateless public key cryptography. In: Laih, C.-S. (ed.) ASIACRYPT 2003. LNCS, vol. 2894, pp. 452–473. Springer, Heidelberg (2003)
13. Baek, J., Safavi-Naini, R., Susilo, W.: Certificateless public key encryption without pairing. In: Zhou, J., López, J., Deng, R.H., Bao, F. (eds.) ISC 2005. LNCS, vol. 3650, pp. 134–148. Springer, Heidelberg (2005)
14. Libert, B., Quisquater, J.-J.: On constructing certificateless cryptosystems from identity based encryption. In: Yung, M., Dodis, Y., Kiayias, A., Malkin, T. (eds.) PKC 2006. LNCS, vol. 3958, pp. 474–490. Springer, Heidelberg (2006)

15. Chow, S.S.M., Boyd, C., González Nieto, J.M.: Security-mediated certificateless cryptography. In: Yung, M., Dodis, Y., Kiayias, A., Malkin, T. (eds.) PKC 2006. LNCS, vol. 3958, pp. 508–524. Springer, Heidelberg (2006)
16. Lai, J., Kou, W.: Self-generated-certificate public key encryption without pairing. In: Okamoto, T., Wang, X. (eds.) PKC 2007. LNCS, vol. 4450, pp. 476–489. Springer, Heidelberg (2007)
17. Chow, S.S.M., Weng, J., Yang, Y., Deng, R.H.: Efficient unidirectional proxy re-encryption. In: Bernstein, D.J., Lange, T. (eds.) AFRICACRYPT 2010. LNCS, vol. 6055, pp. 316–332. Springer, Heidelberg (2010)
18. Sun, Y., Zhang, F.T., Baek, J.: Strongly secure certificateless public key encryption without pairing. In: Bao, F., Ling, S., Okamoto, T., Wang, H., Xing, C. (eds.) CANS 2007. LNCS, vol. 4856, pp. 194–208. Springer, Heidelberg (2007)
19. Boneh, D., Boyen, X.: Efficient selective-ID secure identity-based encryption without random oracles. In: Cachin, C., Camenisch, J.L. (eds.) EUROCRYPT 2004. LNCS, vol. 3027, pp. 223–238. Springer, Heidelberg (2004)
20. Boneh, D., Franklin, M.: Identity-based encryption from the weil pairing. In: Kilian, J. (ed.) CRYPTO 2001. LNCS, vol. 2139, pp. 213–229. Springer, Heidelberg (2001)
21. Libert, B., Vergnaud, D.: Unidirectional chosen-ciphertext secure proxy re-encryption. IEEE Transactions on Information Theory 57, 1786–1802 (2011)
22. Hanaoka, G., Kawai, Y., Kunihiro, N., Matsuda, T., Weng, J., Zhang, R., Zhao, Y.: Generic construction of chosen ciphertext secure proxy re-encryption. In: Dunkelman, O. (ed.) CT-RSA 2012. LNCS, vol. 7178, pp. 349–364. Springer, Heidelberg (2012)
23. Chu, C.-K., Weng, J., Chow, S.S.M., Zhou, J., Deng, R.H.: Conditional proxy broadcast re-encryption. In: Boyd, C., González Nieto, J. (eds.) ACISP 2009. LNCS, vol. 5594, pp. 327–342. Springer, Heidelberg (2009)
24. Canetti, R., Krawczyk, H., Nielsen, J.B.: Relaxing chosen-ciphertext security. In: Boneh, D. (ed.) CRYPTO 2003. LNCS, vol. 2729, pp. 565–582. Springer, Heidelberg (2003)
25. Isshiki, T., Nguyen, M.H., Tanaka, K.: Proxy re-encryption in a stronger security model extended from CT-RSA2012. In: Dawson, E. (ed.) CT-RSA 2013. LNCS, vol. 7779, pp. 277–292. Springer, Heidelberg (2013)
26. Dent, A.W.: A survey of certificateless encryption schemes and security models. International Journal of Information Security 7, 349–377 (2008)
27. Dent, A.W.: A brief introduction to certificateless encryption schemes and their infrastructures. In: Martinelli, F., Preneel, B. (eds.) EuroPKI 2009. LNCS, vol. 6391, pp. 1–16. Springer, Heidelberg (2010)
28. Liu, J.K., Au, M.H., Susilo, W.: Self-generated-certificate public key cryptography and certificateless signature/encryption scheme in the standard model. In: Proceedings of the 2nd ACM Symposium on Information, Computer and Communications Security, pp. 273–283. ACM (2007)
29. Chow, S.S.M.: Certificateless Encryption. In: Identity-Based Cryptography. IOS, pp. 135–155 (2008)
30. Koo, W.K., Hwang, J.Y., Lee, D.H.: Security vulnerability in a non-interactive id-based proxy re-encryption scheme. Information Processing Letters 109, 1260–1262 (2009)
31. Fujisaki, E., Okamoto, T.: Secure integration of asymmetric and symmetric encryption schemes. In: Wiener, M. (ed.) CRYPTO 1999. LNCS, vol. 1666, pp. 537–554. Springer, Heidelberg (1999)

Author Index